EUROPEAN CITIES IN COMPETITION

EUROPEAN SCIENCE FOUNDATION

The European Science Foundation is an association of its 59 member research councils and academies in 21 countries. The ESF brings European scientists together to work on topics of common concern, to coordinate the use of expensive facilities and to discover and define new endeavours that will benefit from a cooperative approach.

The scientific work sponsored by ESF includes basic research in the natural sciences, the medical and biosciences, the humanities and the social sciences.

The ESF links scholarship and research supported by its members and adds value through cooperation across national frontiers. Through its function as a coordinator, and also by holding workshops and conferences and by enabling researchers to visit and study in laboratories throughout Europe, the ESF works for the advancement of European science.

Further information on ESF activities can be obtained from:

European Science Foundation
1 quai Lezay-Marnesia
67000 Strasbourg
France

European Cities in Competition

Edited by
Chris Jensen-Butler
Arie Shachar
Jan van Weesep

Avebury

Aldershot • Brookfield USA • Hong Kong • Singapore • Sydney

Published by
Avebury
Ashgate Publishing Company
Gower House
Croft Road
Aldershot
Hants GU11 3HR
England

Ashgate Publishing Company
Old Post Road
Brookfield
Vermont 05036
USA

British Library Cataloguing in Publication Data
European cities in competition. – (ESF series)
   1. Cities and towns – Europe   2. Urban economics – Europe
   3. Cities and towns – Social aspects – Europe   4. Cities and
   towns – Government policy – Europe
   I. Jensen Butler, Chris   II. Shachar, Arie   III. Weesep, J. van
   (Jan)   IV. European Science Foundation
   307.7'6'094

ISBN 1 85628 610 X

Library of Congress Catalog Card Number: 96–79513

Printed and bound by Athenaeum Press, Ltd.,
Gateshead, Tyne & Wear.

Typeset by Manton Typesetters, 5–7 Eastfield Road, Louth, Lincolnshire
LN11 7AJ, UK.

Contents

List of tables

List of figures

List of contributors

Antoine S. Bailly is Professor of Geography in the Faculty of Economic and Social Sciences at the University of Geneva.

Guy Burgel is Professor of Geography and Director of the Urban Geography Research Centre at the University of Paris (X) in Nanterre.

Gert de Roo is a lecturer in environmental studies in the Faculty of Spatial Sciences at the University of Groningen.

Sten Engelstoft is a senior lecturer in the Institute of Geography at the University of Copenhagen.

György Enyedi is Professor of Geography and member of the Joint Committee of the Hungarian Academy of Sciences in Budapest.

Jorge Gaspar is Professor of Geography and Planning at the University of Lisbon.

Loïc Grasland is Research Associate of RECLUS in the Institute of Geography of the University of Montpellier, and a lecturer at the University of Avignon.

Chris Jensen-Butler is Professor of Urban and Regional Economics in the Department of Economics at the University of St Andrews, Scotland.

John Jørgensen is a lecturer in the Institute of Geography at the University of Copenhagen.

Michael Krantz is a lecturer in the Institute of Economic Geography at the University of Hanover.

Lila Leontidou is a senior lecturer in geography at King's College, University of London.

William F. Lever is Professor of Urban Economics in the Department of Social and Economic Research at the University of Glasgow.

Tomaso Pompili is a senior lecturer in the Department of Economics at the University of Pavia.

Joan-Eugeni Sánchez is Professor of Geography in the Department of Geography at the University of Barcelona.

Ludwig Schätzl is Professor of Economic Geography at the University of Hanover.

Arie Shachar is Professor of Geography in the Faculty of Social Sciences at the Hebrew University of Jerusalem.

Jan van Weesep is Professor of Urban Geography and Urban Policy in the Faculty of Geographical Sciences at Utrecht University.

Bo Wijkmark is the former director of planning of Stockholm County.

Preface

Urban Europe is in the throes of change as the new global economy calls for a thorough restructuring. Manufacturing industries – not so long ago the economic base of the cities – have lost their competitive edge and have been eclipsed by new activities in the service sector. The transition has posed a challenge to the cities. They have to adjust their economy to safeguard the welfare of their population. But promoting new activities has caused severe social inequalities to emerge. Entire categories of people are experiencing the hardship of exclusion from the new economy. In fact, the cities face a dilemma: the more vigorously they pursue economic efficiency, the greater their potential for loss of equity. In the long run, this may endanger their very ability to complete the transition. Moreover, the cities need to limit the negative side-effects of their continuing development if they are to retain their attractiveness for the new economy and for the people that make it work.

What is also new is that the local authorities need to rely largely on themselves to devise and implement the new policies. Within the new political reality of European unification, the relations between the nation-states and the local authorities have been altered fundamentally. The cities can rely less and less on their respective national governments to help them adjust to the new realities. Some cities have sought to carry out the needed reforms by cutting expenses and balancing their budgets. Others have devised creative new strategies and formed new coalitions to see these through to implementation. Urban government itself has changed in the process, and this is reflected in a city's choice of strategies for redevelopment. These strategies may accentuate various means to boost economic development. Alternatively, they may be focused on control of emerging social conflicts, or on abatement of severe environmental problems. Urban marketing is widely practised to draw the attention of potential investors. Whatever mix of strategies is selected, one thing is clear: to be successful, a city needs to have its house in order and bring as many of the relevant actors into the fold as possible. In many cases, this implies the need to foster conditions for cooperation between the city and its suburban communities. Those conditions have to be carefully wrought in the realm of urban policy. In the process, the urban policy maker must evolve from a physical planner and administrator into an entrepreneur.

Against the backdrop of the fundamental economic and societal changes – the topic of the research programme *Regional and Urban Restructuring in Europe* (RURE) completed under the auspices of the European Science Foundation – this book focuses on the diverse policy responses from major cities and in particular on the competition among them. The book emanates from the discussions in Working Group 4 of the RURE programme. The members of this working group devoted their scientific efforts to considering the societal responses to the new conditions. The discussions dealt with the nature of the changes in urban Europe, with the various forms of marginalization that resulted, and with the way in which the new conditions pitted individual cities against one another in the pursuit of economic growth and social well-being. Each of these topics has resulted in a separate publication, and this book is one of them.

This volume is in three parts. The first part introduces the concept of competition, the purpose of this game, the strategies used to play it, and the cities that are involved. This introductory part is followed by ten vignettes on individual cities. While they all deal with the way in which local policy reacts to broad societal changes, the working group decided to leave the emphasis up to the individual authors. Together the studies run the gamut of societal responses to the current restructuring in Europe. In the third part, the remaining chapters cut across these case studies. Each takes one of the policy formats introduced in Chapter 1 as a starting point to discuss the policy initiatives encountered throughout Europe. Functioning as the warp and the weft of this volume, the chapters of Parts II and III thus reveal the intricate fabric of the competition between European cities.

Most of the chapters of this book were written by members of the working group. For some policy fields and for some vignettes of cities, contributions were solicited from experts outside the group. The discussions at the regular meetings of the group, under the able chairmanship of Jorge Gaspar, proved to be immensely stimulating. In keeping with the purpose and the tradition of the European Science Foundation, all members have benefited greatly from the open exchange of views and the generous sharing of experience by participants from all over Europe. The book can only partially represent this scientific learning process, but we hope that it transmits to the reader a sense of the enthusiasm and the solid scholarship which the ESF brought together. As editors, we feel that the book could stimulate the general debate on the effects of regional and urban restructuring in Europe and the responses these have generated.

The working group as a whole, and the editors in particular, have chalked up some debts in the process of completing their task. In the first place, we express our thanks to the European Science Foundation for providing an organizational setting for our work and the means to meet and exchange our views. We also acknowledge the seminal work of the designers of the RURE programme, who mapped the terrain to be covered. All the contributors cooperated admirably when asked to make changes in their texts and showed patience when its completion – a long project owing to an incremental workplan – proved to take longer than anticipated. Anders Malmberg was an able programme coordinator, inquiring of progress at the right times, but never showing loss of faith in its completion. The presence of John Smith of the ESF at many of the meetings was a demonstration of interest in the work from beyond the circle of insiders. Numerous other people at universities, service agencies and the publishing house have contributed generously to make this book an attractive product. However, the usual disclaimers about taking the blame for any mistakes apply.

One last observation is pertinent. Much fuss is made in the recent geographic literature about the vast benefits to international communication brought about by travelling the Information Highway. Undoubtedly, the production of this book has benefited from our ease of access to faraway colleagues and remote sources of data. But the frightful mix of technologies, rules of the road and driving habits encountered on our trip down this virtual highway led to as many bottlenecks, backed-up traffic, accidents and delays as in real travel. Understandably, we give a sigh of relief that the journey has been completed.

C.N. J.-B., A.S. and J.v.W.
St Andrews, Jerusalem and Utrecht

PART I
CONCEPTS

1 Competition between cities, urban performance and the role of urban policy: a theoretical framework

Chris Jensen-Butler

As an introduction to this volume, we examine the concepts of interurban competition and urban success, with special reference to the European urban system. These concepts are related to urban policy and a framework for the analysis of urban policy in the context of competition and success is developed.

Competition between European cities: an introduction

There is general agreement that competition between European cities is growing (van den Berg *et al.*, 1990; CEC, 1991), but the concepts of interurban competition and urban success remain diffuse. Interurban competition basically is rivalry between cities in the European urban system for the creation or attraction of economic activity which produces income. The capacity to create income is in turn related to other aspects of urban economy and society such as levels of service, size of the tax base, infrastructure, quality of life, and educational and cultural facilities.

There are a number of reasons why competition between European cities is at present increasing. Technological change in transport and telecommunications has, for many types of economic activity, almost removed locational constraints and barriers; many types of economic activity have become footloose. Production is also becoming increasingly more global in scale and transnational enterprises are not constrained by national, regional and local economic, social, political or ideological bonds. Changes in production technology and related changes in industrial organization have created new opportunities for flexibility in location: in large firms different parts of the same process of production can be located independently of each other, taking advantage of the specific qualities of different locations, while the tendency towards increased externalization of functions in the production process

(Williamson, 1985; Scott, 1988) has also contributed to greater free-dom from locational constraint for parts of the production pro-cess. Mergers and rapid growth of transnational corporations (TNCs) have simultaneously contributed to the development of an international arena for investment decisions. Amin (1992) pro-vides evidence of the increasing internationalization of invest-ment, on both global and European scales.

This globalization of production has created the paradox that, whilst economic activity now has wide margins of locational al-ternatives, small differences in the characteristics and qualities of places can have decisive influence upon locational choice which constitutes the new tension between globality and locality (Stöhr, 1990). Cities are the most differentiated and complex localities of all, hence the growth of competition between them. Internation-alization also means that cities having similar roles in their own national urban hierarchies are now facing competition from each other across national boundaries, while changes in the production system also mean that competition for growth and investment can increasingly occur between quite dissimilar cities. Internationa-lization also affects professional services, hitherto strongly protected by national legislation. This increased competition is essentially interurban and the consequent reorganization of this market will probably lead to concentration of this type of activity in urban areas. At the same time, one can expect an increasing decoupling of the city from the economy of its region or even nation. This suggests that the city will, over time, trade more with distant cities as well as with itself, at the expense of trade with its own region. What scant evidence exists, American admittedly, seems to indicate that this may well be happening already. This question is discussed in more detail in the next chapter.

An important factor related to the local effects of globalization is the partial breakdown of the international monetary order and increasing monetary instability after 1980. This has been associ-ated with rapid increases of *spatial switching*, as noted by Swyngedouw (1992), where threat of sudden devaluation pro-vokes development of business strategies designed to minimize production and consumption times. This global factor strengthens the importance of place-specific and currency-specific capital ac-cumulation: short-term investments and rapid spatial switching highlight the importance of urban differences and different urban development trajectories; the effect of spatial inertia on invest-ment is drastically reduced. This factor has also furthered the development of the entrepreneurial city. Swyngedouw suggests that 'this unbridled competition [between cities] ... intensifies the threat of devaluation, which, if it occurred, would turn today's growth areas into tomorrow's social and economic wastelands' (p.58). While monetary instability reinforces urban economic instability and competition between cities, it seems perhaps not entirely correct to relate the threat of economic and currency devaluation and its consequences to entrepreneurial activity by the city.

Institutional factors also play a role in the increasing competition between cities, especially inside the European Union. The underlying logic of the *single market* is that of comparative advantage – involving a high level of mobility of commodities and lower levels of factor mobility. Cities try to exploit their comparative advantage in the competition for investment. As European *economic union* develops out of the single market, with a common currency and higher levels of factor mobility, the principle of comparative advantage will gradually be replaced by that of absolute advantage (CEC, 1990a; De Grauwe, 1992). However, this idealized version of the future must be tempered by a more realistic vision: labour mobility will continue to be substantially less than perfect where labour accepts low wage levels or high unemployment without responding through migration. There are two limits to this type of labour stickiness: one is migration and the other is local social conflict, which provokes policy intervention. Thus the shift from comparative to absolute advantage will not be as clear-cut as discussed here. In theory, everything else being equal, high levels of factor mobility will tend to eliminate the comparative advantages of different localities. However, everything else is not equal, as there are elements constituting localities, particularly urban localities, which are not very mobile. The built environment and urban infrastructure remain for a very long period place-specific. More important, there are place-specific factors such as information-rich environments, networks of information and material flows, knowledge-based innovatory industrial milieux, termed by Andersson (1985) *creative regions*, and these milieux are very immobile. They are institutionally, socially and locationally specific, they often develop because of unique sets of interactions, not least interpersonal, and they are highly immobile (De Castro and Jensen-Butler, 1991). Thus conditions for the development of creative behaviour, innovation and technological change will continue to vary between cities. In this sense, comparative advantage continues to exist, even in an economic union, in the fields of creativity, information availability and transfer, innovation, disembodied technological change and network structure, and here the urban dimension is critically important. This place fixity can be counterbalanced, in part at least, by a strategy of innovation and technological change building on technology embodied in purchased and imported capital equipment. However, at the regional level such embodied technological change is associated with lower levels of labour productivity than the disembodied variety (De Castro and Jensen-Butler, 1991).

The local social, cultural, ideological and political environment can affect the development of industrial structure and the innovatory potential of localities. These factors are also relatively immobile as it is the simultaneous occurrence of certain types of social and political relations, in specific cultural and ideological contexts, which seems to have a positive – or negative – effect on economic development. The main reason why these factors exhibit place fixity is the necessity of their simultaneous occurrence in space and time in order to create a positive effect; this is a synergy effect, which cannot easily be recreated elsewhere. Asheim (1990) has developed this approach, relating socioeconomic, sociocultural and political and institutional factors to technological and innovative capacity. He presents a theoretical framework based upon Gidden's structuration theory, which can be used to analyse the interrelationships, and applies the framework to the analysis of industrial districts. However, it seems equally applicable to cities, perhaps even more so than in the case of industrial districts.

The benefits of an economic union depend strongly upon the degree of factor mobility, especially labour mobility, inside the union (De Grauwe, 1992). However, increased factor mobility will create a more volatile economic environment, changing rapidly the economic fortunes of cities. Greater volatility will encourage entrepreneurial behaviour by cities: they will compete more directly. This also helps to explain the growth of new coalitions of actors, public and private, seeking a common response to an uncertain environment.

A further institutional factor is the relative weakening of the national state in relation to the region and the city. Competence is gradually being transferred from states to regions and cities, which has in itself increased differentiation in the spheres of public service provision and regulation of economic activity (Swyngedouw, 1992) and has thus intensified interurban competition. The local state becomes more differentiated and these differences are important for investors. Swyngedouw identifies five differentiated local regulatory mechanisms: capital–labour bargaining; shop floor organization; regulations on health, safety, job security and pay; pensions and insurance systems; and degree of financial autonomy of the local authorities. The growth of privatization in the provision of services formerly provided by the public sector on a more uniform basis also contributes to the creation of spatial differentiation.

As European integration develops, some cities take on a *gateway* role, linking the national urban and regional systems to the international level. This is a form of comparative advantage for the gateway city. The largest cities, usually the capital cities, are multifunctional gateways (Gaspar and Jensen-Butler, 1992), while smaller cities can become gateways for specific national sectors or networks. As networks become more international, gateway functions will be modified and this comparative advantage will disappear.

Competition between European cities is thus multilayered and complex. The world cities of London and Paris compete on one level; other smaller cities compete in certain sectors, defined increasingly by their intangible endowments. Camagni (1991a) argues that urban competitive success is linked to the development of specific filières related to the sector having comparative advantage. This will enhance urban competitive advantage but it will also create a fixity and inflexibility which has negative aspects in a rapidly changing production system. It should be remembered that, despite great interest in such questions as innovation and creativity, income and employment multipliers related to inter- and intra-urban linkages continue to play an important role in income generation in cities.

Competition means that there are winners and losers, but what is a winner, a successful city? The line of argument here would suggest that success is first and foremost enhanced income-generating capacity. But this concept of competition is not without problems. First, is the city an entity which actually competes, or is it groups of urban actors, perhaps with conflicting interests, which are driving the competition forward; to what extent can the city as a unit influence its own chances of success? Secondly, success in income generation assumes a certain stability in income generation over a longer period. Thirdly, it seems clear that we are not dealing with a zero-sum game; all cities in a given city set have the potential to benefit from competition, which implies that cities in fact compete with respect to relative rankings rather than absolute income levels. Fourthly, a factor related both to income-generating capacity and to stability is of course power – primarily power of decision and capacity to determine the behaviour of other actors. Successful cities are powerful cities, but city power is very difficult to measure. Fifthly, cities are located within a city system and indirect and induced effects of income generation can spread unevenly within the system. Sixthly, income generation

usually implies employment generation, but this is not necessarily the case, as process innovation increasingly seems to be
labour-saving. If the city's total product grows faster than city
productivity, then employment will grow, otherwise it will decline.
The parameters of the Verdoorn equation for the individual city
will determine the employment outcome of urban economic
growth:

$$\dot{P}_c = a + b\dot{Y}_c$$

where:

$\dot{P}_c$ = growth rate of city productivity,
$\dot{Y}_c$ = growth rate of city product,
a, b = parameters.

If $b>1$, then employment stagnation or decline is likely, though at
low levels of growth the value of a (the rate of growth of productivity when the rate of growth of the product is zero) can affect the
outcome.

Finally, it is not certain that success, in the form of greater income-generating capacity, necessarily improves the well-being of
the city dweller. There are other dimensions to success, involving
questions of income distribution, negative externalities created by
increased income generation and success for the local authority as
an economic unit. Improved income-generating capacity is a necessary but not sufficient condition for competitive success.

Long-term and stable income generation is at the heart of competitive success in the city system. This implies that the city is an
actor in the system of production: it can influence the development of the productive system and it is itself influenced by the
development of the system (Gaspar, 1992). Evaluation of city success also involves, in addition to a set of theoretical and practical
measurement problems, examination of the city's capacity to forecast future development trajectories of the production system and
its ability to interact with these. There is little agreement about
future trajectories, for a number of reasons, most important of
which is the fact that the trajectory of the system depends upon
the interactions between knowledge, technology and organizational forms. We know little – in the nature of things – of the
future development of these factors and even less of their future
interactions.

A brief example illustrates the point. There is considerable disagreement in the meta-theoretical literature about the overall devel-

opment trajectory of the productive system. Following upon the work of Piore and Sabel (1984), there is a division of agreement concerning the relative performance of mass-production Fordist-type industrial organization in recent decades and its future (Dunford and Benko, 1991). Fordism and neo-Fordism are contrasted with production systems based upon flexible specialization, involving small and medium-sized firms in new industrial districts, enjoying external scale and scope economies in local innovative milieux, which operate in specific social and political contexts. These milieux, it is argued, promote cooperation, mutual trust, business alliances and inter-firm solidarity (Scott, 1988). Some authors argue that a major paradigm shift towards flexible production is occurring (Schoenberger, 1988; Cooke, 1988), while others reject the idea of such a shift (Sayer, 1989; Gertler, 1988; Amin and Robins, 1992). The technologies involved in these two paradigms, as well as the organizational forms, are substantially different, as are the locational outcomes. The debate seems rather long on theory and short on empirical analysis (Feldman, 1991). A third point of view has been put convincingly by Amin and Robins (1991), who argue that the real forces shaping national, regional and local economies are the global corporations, following a variety of strategies, and here other models of industrial development are hypothesized. Clearly, the potential long-term success of urban policy strategy should be seen in relation to a paradigmatic model of industrial development, but this as yet remains difficult.

In this volume the focus is on the relationship between urban policy and urban success in a competitive environment. Identifying the components of success is difficult and measuring the contribution of urban policy to this success even more so. This chapter presents the outline of a framework for the analysis, which the following case studies, in part at least, fill out.

The city as an actor in the spatial–economic system

A clear shift of focus in analysis of spatial development questions is appearing: towards the urban and away from the regional. European spatial and regional policy is increasingly addressed to urban problems (CEC, 1991; Engelstoft, 1990). There are a number of reasons for this shift. First, as argued above, there is an increasing interaction between global processes and locality. Local socio-economic structures can promote or retard the operation of these processes and even transform the processes themselves; the city is the locality which commands greatest interest because of its importance, size, diversity and complexity. Secondly, knowledge-rich and innovative environments have a strong urban component (Drewett *et al.*, 1992) and innovation and technical change will be key growth factors in the future. Thirdly, social conflict is most clearly revealed in the urban environment (Keith, 1989). This has been the case for a very long time, but the development of media and communications enables the projection of these local processes into the global sphere, as the Los Angeles or Brixton riots illustrate: a case of the local becoming global. Fourthly, the urban component of the growing environmental problem is of central importance (Nijkamp and Perrels, 1990; Engelstoft and Jensen-Butler, 1993). Cities create more pollution per square kilometre than any other type of human occupation. Finally, some cities are facing severe financial crisis. Bankruptcy on a large scale is potentially an urban phenomenon (Badcock, 1984).

At the same time, interest in developing specifically urban policies to tackle spatial problems is growing (Van den Berg *et al.*, 1982; OECD, 1983; Cheshire *et al.*, 1988). The reasons for this are to address problems of urban decline, to create better conditions for rapid growth and to solve environmental problems. The EC Green Paper on the Urban Environment (CEC, 1990b) is an indicator of the growing concern about environmental problems having their origins in cities.

The successful city: correlates of success

While the causal mechanisms creating urban success are more difficult to identify, there is wider agreement about the correlates of urban success. Successful cities are cities which exhibit some or all of the following characteristics.

Sectoral composition

The sectoral shift in western society of both production and employment from industry to services is most marked in urban areas (Bailly and Maillat, 1991). There are various views on the causes of the shift (Rowthorn, 1986), but successful cities seem to be in the forefront of this change (Daniels, 1991b).

Types of tertiary activity

Inside the service sector, the growth of specific high value-added sub-sectors, such as R&D, financial services and business services, usually appears as an indicator of success. The growth of producer services is related to the development of flexible production systems (Coffey and Bailly, 1992) and new technologies, especially information and communications technology. They have a clear urban orientation (Daniels, 1991b).

Innovation and technological change

Innovation, and particularly product innovation, exhibits strong regional differentiation (Goddard *et al.*, 1986). It has also a strong urban component, not least because of the role of positive externalities and the importance of transaction costs for small and medium-sized innovative firm (Scott, 1988). Amin and Goddard (1986) point out the key role of provincial cities in innovation-led development, while expressing greater reservation about London, a world city, as an innovatory centre. Innovation is closely related to technological change and the growth of high-tech firms in urban areas. Fundamental innovations depend highly upon the existence of well developed information-rich and knowledge-rich environments, which are basically urban. Industrial districts can be well suited to diffusion of innovations, while their role in creating fundamental innovations is more doubtful. Krätke (1991) takes issue with the flexible production theorists who argue that new territorial production complexes are not specifically urban (Moulaert and Swyngedouw, 1989, for example), pointing out that this development is highly urban in Germany. Successful cities are more innovative and have higher growth rates in high-tech industries than unsuccessful cities, and high-tech firms have above-average rates of job creation and turnover increase than other types of firm (Oakey and Rothwell, 1986). This implies that for these types of city the Verdoorn coefficient is less than unity.

Decision-making power

Changes in the organization of production have frequently resulted in the functional and spatial division of the process of production. Massey (1984) argues that decision, strategic management, R&D and similar functions tend to be located in major urban areas, while routine production functions are located in peripheral areas, and more specialized production in traditional industrial areas. Concentration of decision-making power in urban areas seems to be an indicator of success (Daniels, 1991a). This is of course related to the fact that, for large or multinational firms, the part of value-added going to profits is often attributed to the headquarters location.

Knowledge-based production

Closely related to the question of innovation is the fact that knowledge-intensive localities will play a more important role in income generation in the future (Andersson, 1985; Van den Berg *et al.*, 1990). Pugel (1992) documents both the importance of human capital endowments in explaining differences in national growth rates and interactions between this variable and R&D expenditures. Highly qualified labour has considerable market power and generally has specific demands with respect to amenities, environment and services. Successful cities are those which are able to respond to these demands.

Class structure

The changes in the productive system noted above relate to changes in the structure of social class in urban areas. There seems to be a long-term trend in western societies towards changes in the qualification structure of the labour force, as shown in Figure 1.1. An increasing social polarization is emerging, based upon qualification and job function between people with technical and administrative qualifications and unskilled labour. The group of skilled workers is declining in both relative and absolute terms, not least because many of their skills are being built into the software used in computer-based technology. These changes have a number of consequences. One is that the urban middle class grows quickly, so that successful cities tend to have a large and rapidly growing urban middle class with rising levels of qualification. Another consequence is that the numbers of unskilled and marginalized people increase; this is related to changes in qualification structure, loss of industrial jobs in the city, changes in the housing market and the urban location of specific marginalized groups, such as immigrants. Thus, paradoxically, the successful city may also face increasing problems of social polarization (Badcock, 1984, pp.166–7).

Conflict management

Following on from the previous point is that one outcome of these social and economic changes is growing social tensions and conflict in the city, manifesting themselves in crime, drug and alcohol abuse, and riots (Herbert and Smith, 1989). The successful management of these conflicts, involving alternatives which range from policing to large-scale income redistribution, is also a criterion of

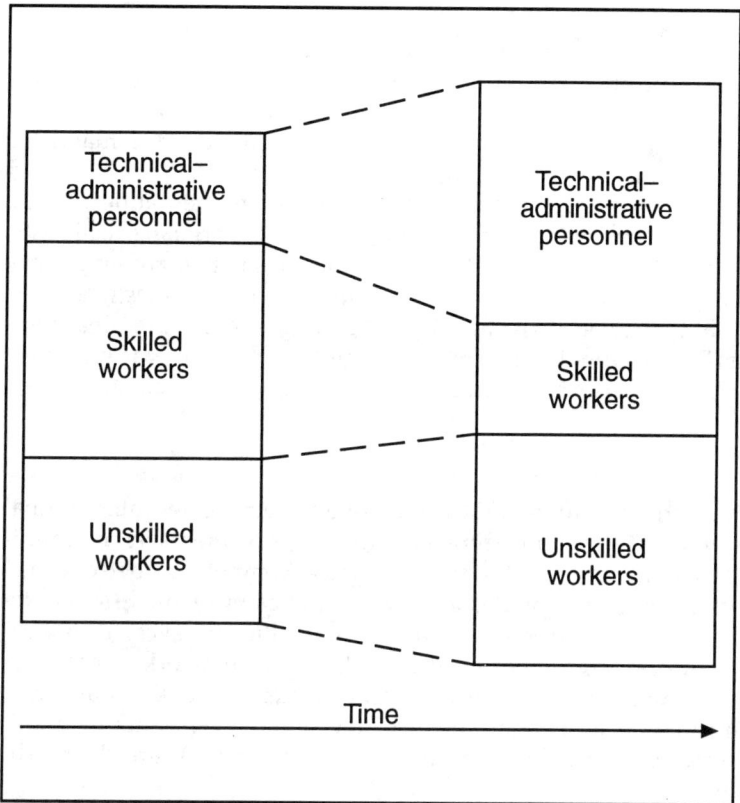

Figure 1.1   Changes in qualification structure of the urban labour force

success. Clearly, housing provision plays an important role in urban success.

Amenity, environment and non-material values

Related to growth of the urban middle class and relative wealth is the increasing importance of non-material values in western European society (Inglehart, 1990). In the urban context, this is reflected in rising demands from the qualified and growing urban middle class for amenities, pleasant environments, high-quality service and cultural and recreational facilities. This is one reason why arts and culture provision have become an indicator of urban success, related in turn to the growth of a competitive culture industry (Shapiro *et al.*, 1992).

Negative externalities

Rising incomes are based upon increased production and they create increased consumption, involving rising levels of car ownership, greater travel activity and also increases in demand for heating and other forms of energy consumption. This increased production and consumption creates negative externalities, where marginal private costs are no longer equal to marginal social costs. In the urban case, congestion and pollution are two growing types of negative externality. Successful cities tend to be cities where the equality between private marginal costs, and social marginal costs has been restored; they are less congested and cleaner (Lundqvist, 1991), as well as being, in economic terms, more efficient.

External links

Internationalization of the productive system creates international as well as intranational travel, while improvements in communications and transport systems increase competition between urban areas. This provides an obvious indicator of success: the degree of external orientation of the city, which is revealed in various indicators, such as location in transport networks, passenger flows, numbers of connections and frequencies, both air and rail, information exchange, network development and strategic alliances. Level and development of external relations are clear indicators of success.

Income and employment

One result of the processes described above is that successful cities will, in general, have a high and/or rapidly growing gross domestic product (GDP) per inhabitant. Disposable income is a less adequate indicator as, in some countries, considerable interregional redistribution of income occurs. As noted above, this usually implies employment growth, though this need not always be the case. For example, parts of the tertiary sector are facing major productivity increases, with labour shedding as a consequence. Clearly this will have an effect on urban employment. Rising income also implies an expanding tax base and developing infrastructure and public service.

Urban policy and urban success

Increasingly, the question is being raised to what extent cities themselves can, through their own policies, affect their performance and success. Analysis of the role and effects of policy on urban competitivity and success is difficult, for a variety of reasons. First, there is the statistical problem of defining the city. Change in urban performance can be disguised by lack of correspondence between the city as a functional unit and the city as an administrative–statistical unit.

Secondly, different countries have different frameworks of both a formal and informal nature with respect to the hierarchical level at which policy formulation and execution takes place. There are different areas of conflict between the different administrative levels in different countries. Pickvance (1990) has illustrated the conflicts between central and local government with respect to executive power in Britain in the 1970s and 1980s. Traditionally, executive power is more centralized in southern Europe, where public administration is still based upon Napoleonic traditions. This question is of course related to differences in taxation systems and local authority finance and power of decision.

Thirdly, three different types of policy can have marked local and urban effects: national-level economic policy – having (unintended) different effects in different localities – an example of which is the redistributive effect of public expenditure and taxation, which can have regional economic effects of a greater dimension than regional policy itself (Hansen and Jensen-Butler, 1996); national-level policy specifically directed towards the cities, and here the individual city can have a greater or lesser degree of influence on policy when it is applied at the city level (an example of this type of policy is British inner cities policy); and true local policy, developed at the city level, designed specifically for the city in question. Where all three policy types are present, the actual outcome will be the result of all three and of their interactions.

Fourthly, there are considerable problems involved with identifying what is the city as a unit: who develops and determines urban policy at the city level. Here we have to consider the question of actors in the city development game. Different authors have identified different sets of actors. Van den Berg *et al.* (1982) identify *households*, the *industrial (and service) sector* and the (city) *government*; Solesbury (1974), adopting a more local economy-based approach, identifies *operators*, both public and private, providing goods and services, *developers*, who create capital assets, *consumers*, the foundation of the system, *local government*, which in principle is responsive to local demands and *central government*, whose activities can have specific local impacts. A similar definition is adopted by McKay and Cox (1979), who also include *protest movements* and *organized professional interests* as actors. It is now clear that these rigid definitions of actors are inadequate. Urban policy is increasingly being developed by more corporative bodies, representing different interests and actors, often private–public partnerships, one example being development associations and companies. Harvey (1989) argues that this is a qualitatively new development in urban policy formation, where the local government element is used by the partnership to attract external sources of funding, whilst the public sector assumes the risk and the private sector takes the benefits. In Europe, it is true that much new urban policy is being developed in partnership structures, though this is perhaps older than generally believed (Fosler and Berger, 1982)

Fifthly, policy success or failure is strongly related to city, region and nation-specific factors. As Urry (1990) points out: 'emergence, implementation and effectiveness of local policies depends upon the complex of economic, social and political conditions found within and beyond a given locality' (p.187). This is even more true when making international comparisons. Policy must therefore be related to specific national, regional, local and historical contexts. As Harloe *et al.* (1990) illustrate, of particular importance for the success of urban policy is the configuration of class power and relations in the city, seen in relation to policy.

A number of studies of urban performance in Europe have directly or indirectly incorporated an analysis of the role of urban policy in urban performance. These studies are reviewed in the following chapter.

Metatheoretical positions on urban policy

Much has been written on the role of the state in advanced capitalist societies (see, for example, Jessop, 1982). There are a number of Marxist-inspired theories of the state and policy formulation, in which a central theoretical question is the degree of relative autonomy of the state, particularly the local state, in capitalist society in relation to the overall process of capital accumulation. One interesting distinction in Marxist-inspired theory is the notion that the central state looks after production-related functions whilst the local state takes care of consumption-related functions, a thesis proposed by Cawson and Saunders (1983). This in turn is related to the idea that collective consumption is *the* specifically urban social activity, suggested by Castells (1978). The distinction is interesting in that its clear outdatedness illustrates the change in the content of urban policy which has occurred in many European countries in the last ten years. Pickvance (1990) correctly concludes that much of the Marxist theorizing seems misdirected, and that the more tenable explanations of local government policies are far more prosaic.

This more prosaic approach includes functionalist, institutionalist and sociological explanations of the role of the local state, focusing on such problems as relations between central and local government and the relative freedom of action of local authorities in policy implementation. Alternatively, local government policy can be seen as the outcome of relations of power in a local institutional environment, where conflict resolution and consensus theory play important roles. The approach here differs from the two metatheoretical approaches mentioned above, but incorporates elements of both. Many of the Marxist-inspired theories tend to be structuralist, in the sense that they conclude that policy is, in the final analysis, determined by requirements imposed by capital accumulation. A structural concept, that of the production system, is retained here. A voluntarist tendency can be discerned in some non-Marxist approaches, where city policy making is seen from the point of view of the actor, where this actor, the city, has considerable freedom of policy choice and also potential for creating fundamental economic and social change in the city itself. Here the city is an actor and the structure is the production system.

The structuration approach of Giddens (1979, 1984; see also Thrift, 1983; Cloke *et al.*, 1990) offers an alternative metatheoretical position. The basic principle is that structures *enable* and *constrain* behaviour, but behaviour can influence and transform the structure. At the same time the agent is transformed. Thus there is a duality of structure and agency. The city is one (but only one) of the agents acting to transform the structure of the productive system, while simultaneously being transformed by the system. The development of the productive system creates change in the urban system, provoking policy response. This response is dual: in part it accommodates the city to change in the system and in part it attempts to change one or more aspects of that system (location or technology, for example). As the city both adapts to economic change and strives to transform the productive system (to the transformation of which it contributes), the city is itself transformed, along with other actors.

Economic structures determine who survives and who does not in the competitive process. In this sense ex-post worlds exist objectively. But agents do not react rationally to structural conditions. Agents have ex-ante bounded rationality and often act on the basis of routine behaviour. However, a non-rational world, incorporating routine behaviour, can produce an ordered world via the structures generated by the behaviour. Economic structure determines, in this sense, objective reality and, in turn, objective reality determines structure, but the way in which this happens is indeterminate, as the effect of agents on structure depends on not only the agents' behaviour, including the agents' bounded rationality and routine behaviour, but also the contingent relations in which the behaviour takes place. The mixture of ex-ante bounded rationality on the part of actors and ex-post selection determined by structural conditions would seem to offer promise of developing a non-dogmatic and non-mechanical structuralist approach.

Social rules determine appropriate behaviour for the agent and they themselves can be modified and changed during interactions between structures and agents. Clearly, some major role reformulation is occurring in the field of urban policy. Furthermore, relations of power and domination can only be understood in specific spatial and historical contexts, which is also true for urban policy. Moos and Dear (1986) have attempted to develop a model for structuration of urban space. It involves politicians, bureaucrats, interest groups, influential individuals and ordinary citizens as actors and communicative, political, economic and sanction structures as the structures with which they interact, producing both intended and unintended outcomes. These in turn enable and constrain new action. This approach is interesting, but illustrates one weakness of Giddens' theoretical ideas: that it is difficult to establish causal priority amongst the structures which condition behaviour. Here we treat economic structures as a prime determinant of urban development.

Thus the general approach to understanding urban policy adopted here is that urban policy is a response to structural change, resulting from change in the productive system. It is simultaneously adaptive and innovative with respect to the system. At the same time, it enables some and constrains other developments in the system itself. Both, system and city, are transformed.

The nature of urban policy

Viewed from the perspective of the individual city, urban policy is a cyclical process involving a number of stages, as illustrated in Figure 1.2. It includes analysis (of problems and strategies), design of measures, implementation and evaluation (leading to urban change in the city in question), changes in other cities and changes in the production system. The production system is also transformed by exogenous economic change. Different actors are involved in the process of goal formulation and the effects of policy are different for the different actors. Significant changes in the city and in the entire urban system arise through exogenous changes, of which changes in the production system are the most important. Thus political processes involved with goal formulation and evaluation, and planning processes, involving design and implementation incorporating both public investment and consumption, are included in the definition of urban policy.

Urban policy is here understood both as the operation of national policy designed to operate in specific localities – over which the city has some influence – and specific urban policies developed by the individual city. In order to analyse the effects of policy in the urban system, a meaningful categorization of policy and policy effects must be established. Traditionally, variations in urban policy and its effects have been examined in a number of different ways.

One approach is to examine policy in terms of sector and problem: housing, social services, transport, the inner city, unemployment and the elderly, for example. This type of approach is adopted in many studies of policy, for example Herbert and Smith (1989). Another approach to policy analysis is provided by Urry (1990) who proposes three dimensions: *'conditions'*, relating to the enabling or constraining economic, social and political circumstances; *'resources'*, relating to the institutional resources available to the decision makers, including financial, organizational and environmental resources, as well as questions of legitimacy; and *'strategies'*, which include private/public mix, type of involvement, area of policy (economic, social and so on) and aims of policy (growth, stability). The problem with this type of approach is that it confounds type of policy, policy environment and policy effects. Badcock (1984) suggests a more limited approach to policy analysis, being the (re)distributional effect of area-based policies in cities. This approach involves a restricted view of policy, as being fundamentally a redistributive mechanism.

In this volume we are interested in the effects of policy in creating successful metropolitan areas. The framework of analysis pro-

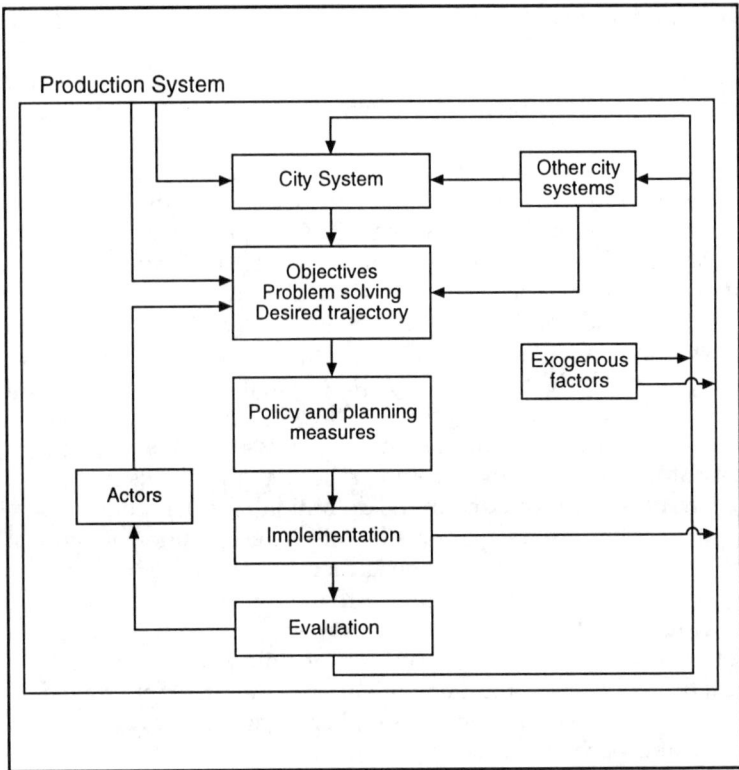

Figure 1.2   Urban policy and planning

posed uses the classical dimensions of policy analysis derived from economic theory and applies these in the urban context. The rationale of policy intervention rests upon the normative assumption that, in certain circumstances, public intervention in the economy can improve the aggregate performance of the economy, as compared with leaving economic development to the market (Cullis and Jones, 1992). These circumstances are discussed elsewhere in more detail by Jensen-Butler (1996). In brief, taking as our point of departure the case for policy intervention at the national level, the classical reasons and policy objectives are usually subsumed under three headings: efficiency, stability and equity (CEC, 1990a). Urban policy analysis is here based upon similar but not identical objectives, discussed below.

Four underlying dimensions of urban policy are identified as:

- efficiency,
- equity,
- control of negative externalities, and
- budgetary goals.

These dimensions are increasingly to be found in cities' own policy statements, which often encompass such objectives as competitive ability, equality of opportunity and improved housing provision, environmental sustainability and amenity, and manageability as an economic unit. These (and similar) urban policy objectives are clear reflections of the four principal dimensions. Numerous city policy statements illustrate the fundamental nature of these dimensions: for example, New York (Regional Plan Association, 1990), Copenhagen (Lord Mayor's Office, 1991), Stockholm (City of Stockholm, 1991), Birmingham (Davies, 1989), Milan (Cappellin, 1989), Liverpool (Parkinson, 1990), Rotterdam (Van den Berg *et al.*, 1990) and Dublin (Drudy, 1989).

Three essential points must be remembered when using these dimensions for policy analysis. First, they all are interrelated: for example, policy motivated by efficiency considerations will usually have consequences for equity and can also have negative external effects (Jensen-Butler, 1991). Secondly, they may in many circumstances represent conflicting goals, implying decisions concerning trade-offs (Jensen-Butler, 1996). Thirdly, they apply in all spatial contexts, but their importance is especially strong in cities (Bish and Nourse, 1975).

Dimensions of urban policy analysis

The efficiency dimension

This classical policy dimension has central and growing importance in urban policy. The theoretical rationale of policy in relation to this dimension is that intervention by the city in allocation of resources in certain circumstances can improve the aggregate performance of the urban economy, which means that greater income can be produced for the same inputs. There are a number of different urban policy types related to the efficiency dimension, which can be examined using the no-policy option as a background.

No intervention policy   This type of urban policy is based upon the laissez-faire principle that only the operation of the market will produce Pareto-optimal outcomes (Cullis and Jones, 1992). Thus policy, to the extent one can speak of policy at all, is directed towards ensuring an improved operation of the market mechanism. Pareto optimality rests upon a number of assumptions, including that income distribution does not influence optimality, that inputs are mobile and malleable and, perhaps most problematic, that outputs and outcomes are qualitatively similar to what is known already. In the urban context, examples of this type of policy include privatization policies, enterprise zones and freeports.

Indicators which can be used for measuring success of this type of policy include growth rate of city GDP, changes in GDP per employee (productivity) and changes in GDP per capita. Increase in employment may be a success criterion, if it is simultaneously related to productivity and GDP growth.

Policies oriented to situations involving market breakdown   The classic case for policy intervention in the market economy is that of market breakdown, where market solutions no longer result in equivalence between a private and a social optimum (Bish and Nourse, 1975). Market breakdown covers a number of different situations. First, the existence of externalities, both positive and negative, implies that private marginal benefits and costs diverge from social marginal net benefits and costs. Cities are especially susceptible to such distortions because of concentrations of people and activities in confined areas. In the analytical framework developed here, control of negative externalities has been defined as a specific policy dimension, even though it really belongs to efficiency considerations, and is treated more fully later. Secondly, the provision of public goods – characterized by joint consumption and non-exclusion – cannot be provided at an optimal level without cooperative action, as the market mechanism breaks down. Public goods (for example, street lighting, parks and policing) are important in cities. Thirdly, common pool resources are a type of public good, where consumption by one consumer reduces the value of the resource for others, as for example with water resources. Fourthly, natural monopolies are types of economic activity which usually have high entry costs and continuously declining L-shaped long-run average cost curves. Rail services, district heating, electricity and telephone provision are typical examples. Here provision by one central authority will usually be more efficient than competitive provision – again a typically urban situation. Finally, policy will tend to be stronger in areas (usually urban) where the number of people involved prevents recognition of interdependencies and inhibits capacity to organize for negotiation in the market with the creators of externalities or the potential providers of public goods.

Success of policy designed to improve efficiency in cases of market breakdown is difficult to measure. Policy with respect to externalities and common pool resources is discussed below. In relation to natural monopolies and public goods, urban success can be measured using cost-effectiveness indicators for public services, including costs of service provision per inhabitant or per user and changes in these relations, and costs per passenger kilometre on public transport and changes in these. A key problem facing international studies in this field is determination of comparative criteria for quality of public service. A particular area of interest is transport infrastructure investment, as this type of investment, often a public good, has three main effects: it increases accessibility, it strengthens positive externalities (agglomeration advantages) and it creates economic activity via investment. Market breakdown can also be related to the question of transaction costs (Williamson, 1985). Transaction costs are high, according to Williamson, where transactions occur under conditions of great uncertainty, with low frequency and where the specificity of the assets involved (in terms of alternative uses) is high. Urban infrastructure investment and, to a lesser degree, housing investment involve all of these problems. Speculative gains can perhaps be regarded as a reward for high transaction costs. Public intervention is justified to counteract the effects of speculation and to undertake investment which is not suitable for private decision, because of high transaction costs.

The city as entrepreneur   There are clear signs that cities are becoming more entrepreneurial in their actions and policies (Harvey, 1989; Keating, 1991; Parkinson, 1991). They are entering directly as actors in markets rather than simply intervening in cases of market breakdown. Parkinson (1991) identifies a number of reasons for the emergence of the entrepreneurial city, including the impact of economic restructuring, administrative decentralization, failure of regional policy, renewed interest in urban living and, not least, increased competition between cities. The list is very broad and contains other policy dimensions than efficiency. If we examine the changing role of the city as entrepreneur, that is, an actor in the market, there seem to be two basic and rather different philosophies underlying the growth of this entrepreneurial role.

First, the deepening economic crisis facing western Europe is also an employment crisis having major social and economic effects in the cities. As both the market and national-level economic policies for employment generation are seen to fail, more local responsibility is assumed for employment creation, resulting in urban policies operating basically in the form of cost subsidies for private investment (see, for example, Lever, 1992). While it is not clear that these policies contribute to long-term efficiency, in the short and medium term their success is measurable in terms of job creation and cost efficiency. Employment creation policies are considered in the next section.

The second entrepreneurial role for cities has a more long-term and dynamic perspective, related to increasing competition between cities. Cities are no longer content to leave the long-run development of the urban economy to market forces. This is for a number of reasons. First, transformation of urban structure is a very long-term project involving considerable inflexibilities. Absence of certain types of investment can have long-run negative consequences for the city. Some types of investment (in education and R&D, for example) have very long pay-back periods and can be very uncertain in terms of returns on invested capital. Net benefits accruing at the end of a very long period will have a present value close to zero, using usual discounting rates. Thus the incentive for private enterprise to invest in this and other important urban development activities can be limited. Furthermore, the relative fixity of much urban investment increases risk. For these reasons, innovation centres and technology and science parks almost always involve some level of public funding (Rothwell and Dodgson, 1991).

Secondly, achievement of Pareto optimality through the market process assumes a constant adjustment of resource allocation. This in turn assumes that inputs, outputs and economic outcomes are qualitatively similar to those already known, and that they are relatively stable. This means that routine behaviour amongst entrepreneurs will also be optimizing behaviour. However, in periods of rapid innovation and technological change these assumptions no longer hold. Cities are clearly entering the arena of innovation and technological change, asserting that their capacity to make non-routine decisions concerning radical investments is as good as that of the private sector. In some respects it is perhaps even better. The city can create the necessary confidence to promote investment and it can have a very important risk-bearing function. Again the theory of transaction costs leads us to the conclusion that there are some areas of economic activity (for example, research) which are better performed by the public sector, because of uncertainty, frequency and asset specificity.

Thirdly, the notion of synergy implies the conscious bringing together of a number of elements so that their combined effect becomes more than the sum of their individual parts. In a sense, the concept of synergy is the reverse of that underlying the market, which involves a large number of atomistic and competing actors where total utility is the simple sum of individual utilities. Synergies are created in a local industrial milieu (Ratti, 1991; Maillat, 1991; Bramanti and Senn, 1991) which is also an innovative environment. In addition, such environments contribute to the reduction of uncertainty, especially important for small firms (Camagni, 1991b). The public sector can play a key role in creating innovative milieux and is itself an actor in them; they are frequently urban (Drewett *et al.*, 1992).

Fourthly, technology policy must relate directly to specific local conditions if it is to succeed. These conditions include local innovative capacity and tradition, the local institutional framework, supply of labour, labour qualifications, degree of flexibility in the labour force, experience with technological change, labour mobility, age of capital stock, flexibility of capital stock and existence of upstream and downstream linkages. Such policy must therefore be differentiated locally and regionally and here the city plays a key role as mediator between the local environment and technological change. National or international-level technology policy applied indiscriminately at the local level will be less effective than a policy which is specifically local in its orientation, a point made by Shachar and Felsenstein (1992) in the case of technology policy in Israel.

These conditions are an important reason for growth of policy-based entrepreneurial intervention by cities. In the light of developments in the production system, a number of key policy areas would seem to be important for long-term urban success. First, the importance of development of human capital endowments – the knowledge base of the city – for urban success is clear, as illustrated by Pompili (1992) and by Drewett *et al.* (1992), where labour qualifications were identified by firms in 20 European cities as the crucial factor related to innovation. The public sector has a clear stake in this area through the educational system. Secondly, information-rich environments are conducive to innovation and here public policy also plays a clear role. Expenditure on R&D is clearly related to information production, to innovation and technological change, and to growth in GDP (Steinle, 1992). There is a basic conflict between the private appropriation of benefits of R&D investment and the social benefits which arise if diffusion of results occurs. Andersson (1985) demonstrates that a private profitability calculation always underestimates the total efficiency of R&D investment, as R&D-based discoveries are usu-

ally of great value to others. This will result in sub-optimal investment in R&D, which means that there is a very strong argument
for public cost sharing. As transmission systems for this type of
discovery are strongly related to interpersonal contacts (Drewett
et al., 1992), the importance of the city in this type of policy is
obvious. Furthermore, a well-developed network of interpersonal
contacts is intrinsically immobile, even in an age of advanced
telecommunications. Thirdly, an important element of urban policy
today is promotion of innovation and technology transfer (Rothwell
and Dodgson, 1991). Fourthly, successful industrial milieux are
also rich in entrepreneurial ability (Oakey and Rothwell, 1986;
Pompili, 1992) the development of which is a question increasingly being addressed by urban policy. Finally, networks and information exchange play an important role in dynamic industrial
milieux (Perrin, 1991). The integration of information technology
and telecommunications is important in this respect. Provision of
telematics infrastructure has become an important urban development factor as the information city develops (Newton, 1991). However, as Hepworth (1990) has pointed out, development of the
information city raises several different policy options and different cities have had varying degrees of success with these. In the
interesting case of the proposed Øresund bridge linking Copenhagen with Malmö in Sweden, a number of authors consider that
infrastructural investment in the form of the bridge will contribute to the development of new innovative knowledge-based networks (Matthiessen, 1992).

This type of long-term urban entrepreneurial strategy involves
various indicators of urban policy success:

- changes in levels of professional skills,
- changes in R&D expenditures,
- changes in numbers of patent applications,
- new firm creation rates and employment generation,
- new firm creation in high-tech branches, and
- coverage with fibre-optic cable in the city, degree of digitali-
  zation and telefax coverage.

Job-creation policy: cost subsidies   In some countries, cities are involved actively in job-creation policy. This has been the case in
both the UK and the USA. It is not immediately obvious that job-
creation policy is efficiency-oriented. In many cases there are clear
equity considerations behind the policy. However, it is possible to
argue a case for job-creation policy on efficiency grounds (Cameron,
1990). The basic argument is that cities facing economic decline

cannot adjust their economies smoothly as there are considerable rigidities present in the urban economy: labour does not migrate, new firm creation is affected negatively, the land market does not adjust smoothly and housing disinvestment occurs. These are also forms of market breakdown. Job-creation policy can thus increase urban incomes and employment, accepting the existence of such rigidities. Viewed in the context of the urban system as a whole, the results of such policy may not result in efficiency increases, but from the point of view of the individual city it can represent a local increase in efficiency. A wide range of policies and measures are used to create jobs. The more usual ones include measures to lower factor costs for firms in the city, for example through the provision of cheap land, infrastructure, capital subsidies and labour training. These are standard regional economic policy measures applied in urban situations. Sometimes more entrepreneurial approaches enter job creation programmes, such as technology transfer centres or business innovation centres. There are many problems involved with assessing the effects of such programmes (Storey, 1990), particularly the attribution problem, which is iden-tification of the specific policy contribution to job creation. In addition, identification of job displacement from other locations presents a problem. Storey demonstrates that the efficiency of the mix of urban policies is maximized when the marginal cost of producing any constant number of jobs is equal for each policy measure applied. This measure of policy efficiency is too demand-ing in terms of both data and concepts to be applied to the Euro-pean urban system, so a more simple approach must be used. Employment increase in the city can be used as a very crude indicator of policy success, though additional employment cre-ated would be a better indicator. Ideally, the cost of new jobs created should be used as an indicator of policy success. A further problem is when job creation policy is directed to specific areas inside the city (for example, inner cities): the policy applied to one part of the city may produce success in another area of the city, rendering definition of success problematic. However, from the point of view of the city as a unit, suitable indicators are city employment growth, net job creation related to policy, and cost-effectiveness of employment creation policy.

The city as actor in an international arena   The effects of all of the types of efficiency-related policies discussed above will be re-flected in a number of general indicators showing the changing relation of the individual city with the outside world. These in-clude changes in passenger flows, changes in frequencies of links

with other cities and changes in numbers of corporate headquarters.

A global criterion   A potential criterion for city success on the
efficiency dimension is real increases in land values in the centre
of the city, though this involves making assumptions concerning
industrial structure, development controls and speculation. In principle, urban success implies increasing economic activity and increasing demand for land (Hochman, 1990). In Chapter 13 of this
volume Lever discusses efficiency-oriented policies for the city.

The equity dimension

Equity is a difficult concept to use in policy analysis (Richardson,
1979) because of its ambiguity. It is also important to differentiate between distributional equity in social terms and spatial
equity. The former refers to the distribution of income in a population, measured typically by share of total income earned by the
richest or the poorest decile. Spatial equity refers to the distribution of per capita disposable income by area or other income-
related variables. The two types of equity are interlinked. Changes
in social equity almost always imply changes in spatial equity
and vice versa. Sometimes equity is treated as accessibility to
public service, but this can, in principle, be expressed in monetary terms. Improvement of equity is usually tackled by income
transfers, but the distribution (social and spatial) of tax incidence must also be considered. Just as a taxation system can be
built up on progressive, proportional or regressive principles, so
too can a city be developed. For example, Lever (1992) has shown
that housing schemes in Glasgow are inequitable in terms of
accessibility to places of employment. Changes in a fare structure for public transport will also have a distributional effect
(Jensen-Butler, 1991).

Housing provision is especially interesting, as it provides a link
between social and spatial equity, giving this link a physical expression. Differentiated housing provision for different social and
income groups in a city is usually a major policy option open to
cities to promote redistribution of income (Keating, 1991). The
tensions involved when using housing policy to promote equity,
and the interrelation of this type of policy with efficiency-oriented
policy, are illustrated in the Dutch case by Van Weesep and Van
Kempen (1992). The relationship between housing, housing policy
and equity issues in the city is discussed by Van Weesep in Chapter 14 of this volume.

City success is related to income distribution. Extremely inequitable income distributions create urban social problems, in the form of poverty, ill-health, crime, drug and alcohol abuse, which sometimes assume dramatic forms of social conflict, as in Los Angeles, Brixton and Bristol. Urban conflicts of this dimension are a major source of urban policy initiatives (Keith, 1989). These types of problem impinge upon more general policy areas, such as policy towards ethnic minorities, the elderly, single parents and drug abusers. Social problems arising from social and spatial inequity can directly affect economic efficiency: cities with major equity problems become less attractive for investment and residence. Furthermore, entrepreneurial activity by the city may increase rather than decrease equity problems, as may be the case in Barcelona and Seville (Parkinson, 1991). It should also be remembered that decentralization of governmental responsibility implies corresponding decentralization of taxation systems and that local taxation systems, unlike national systems, are rarely progressive: they are usually proportional or regressive. This implies that, everything else being equal, locally financed economic initiatives will increase disparities in disposable income in cities.

There are, broadly speaking, two extreme approaches to the problem of spatial and social equity in cities. In the USA, the problem is usually tackled by increased policing and territorial demarcation between safe and dangerous areas of the city. The result is marked spatial segregation within the city, so that the relation between social and spatial equity becomes more clear. At the other extreme, we find the Scandinavian cities where large-scale income redistribution between social groups creates the image of the homogeneous middle-class city. On any major social indicator relating to equity, these cities are more successful than their American counterparts. However, inside Scandinavian cities spatial patterns of social and economic segregation are to be found (Andersen, 1991); social inequality has a spatial expression even here.

It is often difficult to distinguish between the effects of national-level policy on income redistribution and city-based policy. For example, in Denmark much of the extensive social security system is financed nationally but administered locally. Housing provision usually has a more clear local base, as does provision of educational opportunity and public transport. A number of indicators can be used to identify success of urban policy on the equity dimension. These include:

- changes in the percentage of total disposable income going to the top or bottom decile of the urban population,

- changes in the percentage of unemployed,
- changes in the percentage of sub-standard housing, and
- changes in rates of serious crime.

A recurrent theme in discussion of policy is the question of whether or not efficiency and equity are conflicting goals, implying a trade-off (Richardson, 1979; Jensen-Butler, 1996), or whether urban and regional policy can simultaneously improve both. In any circumstances, the choices made with respect to the relative importance placed on each, in a given city, reflect the preference function of the decision makers. Until recent years, these two dimensions have, explicitly or implicitly, been the two principal objectives of urban policy. This has now changed radically with the emergence of the environmental question.

The negative externalities dimension

Whilst the existence of externalities was treated earlier as a relatively minor policy question in connection with market failure, the question of negative externalities now occupies a major position in urban policy formulation and modifies in important ways other policy choices, particularly with respect to efficiency objectives. The related problems of pollution and traffic congestion are becoming serious threats both to efficiency and to health in cities. Control of negative externalities has become a fundamental dimension of urban policy.

The nature and seriousness of the environmental problem of cities depends basically upon the technologies involved. In a study of 20 European cities, Drewett *et al.* (1992) identify a rank order of environmental problems:

- air pollution,
- noise,
- ground water,
- solid waste,
- surface water pollution.

Here it is clear that the transport sector is the most important source of pollution, while heating and electricity generation also play important roles, not only in northern Europe, but also in some southern European countries. For example, emissions from heating plants constitute a serious atmospheric problem in Madrid in winter.

Traffic congestion is a major urban problem and many European cities are experiencing increasing paralysis caused by the motor car. Coordination and punctuality of deliveries and meeting times are vitally important questions in flexible production systems (Sayer, 1986). The congested city becomes an inefficient city and the problem is one of a classical negative externality. In terms of policy, negative externalities can be tackled in two ways, either by environmental taxes or by control, or a mixture of both. Public transport improvements usually involve creation of positive externalities (where marginal social costs are lower than marginal private costs) which is one of the two main economic justifications for subsidization of public transport in cities, the other being equity considerations. Subsidies can be defended on economic grounds when positive externalities are created. Another classic case involving positive external effects is cleaning buildings and improving the physical environment of cities, as in the case of Glasgow or Antwerp.

As indicators of policy success in cities a number of variables can be used:

- changes in levels of air pollution for the major emissions: CO_2, NOx, CO, SO_2, lead, and particles;
- changes in levels of untreated sewage;
- changes in percentage of solid waste recycling;
- changes in average travel speeds in the city;
- changes in average and relative use of public transport;
- changes in quality of surface water in the city.

In Chapter 15, De Roo discusses environmental problems and urban policy.

Budgetary goals

Finally, all cities face budgetary constraints to policy. Unlike national public budgets, city budgets usually have to balance. In the urban case this means either raising tax incomes or other receipts, or reducing public expenditure. The option of borrowing for capital expenditure (or, in the case of some American cities, even to finance current expenditure, contributing to a number of major urban fiscal crises) is used less in Europe.

Two types of city potentially face fiscal crisis: cities in a situation of economic and social crisis, with rising unemployment, incomes and rapidly rising expenditures, often related to growing social problems (Badcock, 1984, pp.247–53) and the interventionist, rapidly expanding city, facing rapidly rising policy-related expenditures and tax incomes. The issue of relative levels of fiscal stress is, however, obscured by the degree of central finance of local authority expenditure. Thus no easy measure of fiscal stress can be identified, though perhaps growth in total city expenditure per inhabitant is a possible indicator.

Combining the dimensions

Most urban policy measures have consequences for all four dimensions. For example, public transport provision has clear consequences for efficiency, equity, negative externalities and for city budgets. Furthermore, if we assume that the three first dimensions represent conflicting goals, then we have a three-dimensional trade-off, resolved by the city's explicit or implicit three-dimensional preference function. Getting the balance right on these three dimensions, within the constraint of the city budget, is the key to identifying successful policy and the successful city. However, the policy combination giving success may differ from one regional and national context to another. It is to the problem of measurement of policy success that we now turn.

Measuring policy success

The basic problem of measuring policy success is that of determining what would have happened without policy. For all indicators, assessment can be based upon a comparison of extrapolated trends in a weak or no-policy period with the same measure after a period of policy application. But this method rests upon a number of problematic assumptions, the most important of which is that policy alone has created the measurable difference.

For the composite measures of success, such as GDP or employment growth, solutions adopted in connection with analysis of the effects of regional policy, pioneered by Moore and Rhodes (1973) and used by many others, can be applied. The essence of these methods, in brief, is as follows: a longer time period is divided up into different periods, some with weak policy intervention and some with strong. The principles of shift-share analysis are then applied to employment or income data. First, city shift (of employment or income, for example) is calculated for each year:

$$S = C - N$$

where:

S = city shift (here measured in employment terms),
C = city employment change,
N = growth in employment in the city if the growth rate was identical with the national rate;

then differential shift, D, is calculated:

$$D = S - P$$

where:

P = growth in city employment if each sector in the city grew at the national sectoral growth rate, that is:

$$P = \Sigma_i \left(E_{it0} \cdot g_i \right)$$

where:

E_{it0} = employment in sector i at time t_0 in the city
g_i = National growth rate in sector i in the year after t_0.

D represents the city-specific contribution to growth, including policy. The effect of sectoral mix in the city has been removed. Linear extrapolation of the values of D is made from a period of weak policy into and through the period of strong policy. The difference between the actual value of D and the extrapolated value of D (D_e) at any time, t, can be taken to be an expression of policy effects, as shown in Figure 1.3 at t_3.

Moore and Rhodes have proposed some improvements of this basic method (see Department of Trade and Industry, 1983). In one of the few quantitative studies of the effects of urban policy yet published, Bradbury *et al.* (1982) use this technique to assess policy effects in Cleveland, Ohio, on a range of variables, including employment, population, income and taxes.

This procedure is, however, with the present state of data on cities, only an ideal. A more simple and qualitative way forward is as follows. Urban development trends for the city set in question can be determined for each of the first three dimensions: efficiency, equity and control of negative externalities. This involves establishment of standard qualitative procedures for combining disparate data, a difficult but not impossible task. Cities are then classified into two groups on each dimension: strong/weak movements towards efficiency; strong/weak movements towards greater equity, and strong/weak movements towards reduction of nega-

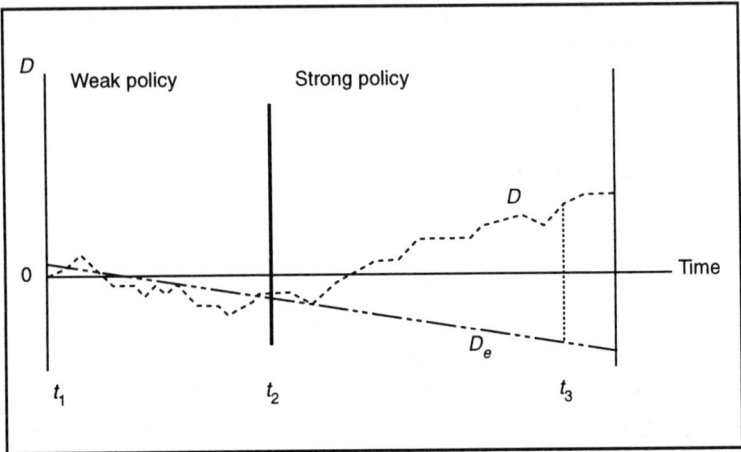

Figure 1.3   Measuring policy effects

tive externalities. Cities can then be placed in one of eight classes
in three-dimensional space, and discrimination can be made between cities facing fiscal pressure and those not. This conceptual
framework is shown in Figure 1.4(a).

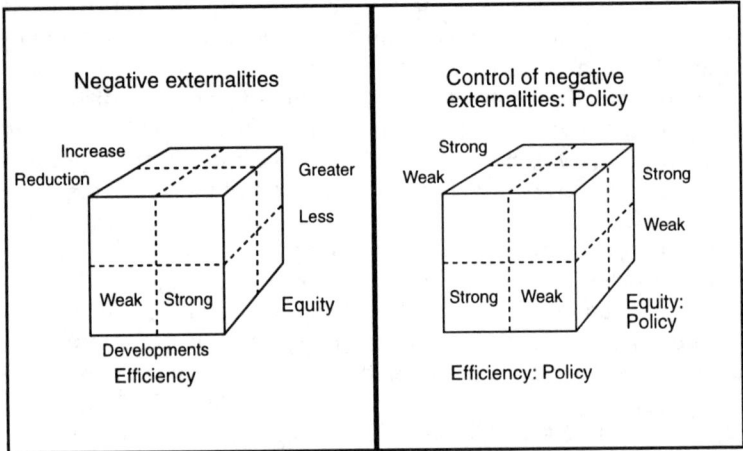

*Figure 1.4(a)   City locations on   Figure 1.4(b)   Policy dimensions
each major policy   and policy strength:
dimension   city locations*

Then, and more difficult, cities can be classified according to policy strength on each of the three basic dimensions. This involves in most cases subjective methods of assessment, and various research techniques can be employed to this end. Cities are then placed again in a three-dimensional classification, as shown in Figure 1.4(b). This enables some initial comparison of policy and effects, intended and unintended. Finally, an 8×8 matrix with policy on one dimension and effects on the other can be created, in which cities are placed, and this matrix can be searched for patterns, including problems of fiscal stress. The analysis can be undertaken for a complete set of cities or, as in the case of the present book, for individual case studies; the framework is quite general.

The subjective dimension

Selling the city, city marketing, which is an example of place marketing, has become an important element in urban entrepreneurial policy. A significant element in urban competition has become that of selling the image: the successful, dynamic, peaceful, clean city. As Harvey (1989) points out, the interests of the city as an economic unit here frequently coincide with the city population's sense of social solidarity, civic pride and sense of place, in an increasingly 'placeless' world. Examples of radical image restructuring are numerous, as with Glasgow, the London Docklands, Antwerp, Barcelona and Stockholm.

The theoretical origins of city marketing are twofold. One is in the theory of environmental perception, translated to a sociological and social–psychological framework, where the meaning of place is socially constructed (Shields, 1990). Ashworth and Voogd (1990) represent another source. They regard the place as a product and the users as its customers. The customer purchases a set of values and attributes by acquiring the physical product. The image arises from the interaction between the physical product and its cultural interpretation, which can change over time (for example, through conversion of degraded warehouses to luxury apartments). Thus place marketing proceeds by both physical development and promotion of place image, based upon a selection of place characteristics projected through cultural norms. Selecting the key characteristics and getting the future cultural norms right is a key to success. There is often a trigger to such promotion, for example in the form of a fair (Hanover), the Olympic Games (Barcelona, Berlin) or a world exhibition (Seville). Both of these approaches tend to ignore the fact that economic interests also lie behind place marketing. The success of both city marketing and trigger events depends considerably upon the ability of the city to generate and exploit rising demand for space and buildings. Urban multiplier and input–output studies continue to be of relevance in this respect.

Van den Berg *et al.* (1990) relate city marketing more closely to the urban economy. The thrust of their argument is that the aim of city marketing is to improve the city's own competitive position, and as such should become one aspect of municipal policy along with employment policy and spatial planning. This policy should be based upon a SWOT (strengths, weaknesses, opportunities, threats) analysis, strategy selection and definition of market objectives. Their theoretical framework builds explicitly upon marketing science, identifying special features of the urban product, such as its lack of flexibility in basic urban characteristics, its special price-formation logic – based upon costs and political choice – and the spatial permanence of city and region. They argue that successful city marketing will depend upon the ability to sell an image related to quality of living and environmental quality as well as questions of access to the rest of the European urban system. This can best be achieved, they argue, by marketing cities which satisfy the demands of the affluent well-educated labour force, having considerable market power, which will form the basis of the coming knowledge-based economy. Various proposals are made for future city structures which perform this function. This sort of approach also explains why provision of cultural facilities and amenities, preservation of the urban heritage and improvement of the quality of the urban environment are strategies entering both urban analysis and urban policy. However, the idea that the economic and the symbolic are intimately connected is not new (Adorno and Horkheimer, 1979). It is being rediscovered in new forms.

This thesis, while interesting, rests upon a restrictive view of the future development of the production system, and tends to ignore distributional questions and the creation of new types of negative externality. Some 15 years ago 'The good city' according to Donnison and Soto (1980) was the city which cared for the needs of its deprived sub-populations. The current version of the good city cares for the needs of the young, well-educated urban professional. He or she may well be instrumental in generating more indirect and induced employment, and a wider tax base, but this policy orientation in itself does not necessarily solve distributional questions. Indeed, new seeds of conflict may be being sown.

An important point made by Van den Berg *et al.* (1990) is that lack of correspondence between the city as a functional unit and urban product on the one hand, and as an administrative unit on the other, will create serious problems for the new urban entrepreneur engaged in city marketing, as control over product development – and the development of the product – is weaker. The Greater London Council, the English metropolitan counties and the Copenhagen Metropolitan Area, all authorities set up to create functional and administrative coherence, were abolished, curiously enough, principally because of city marketing. The image being sold was politically unacceptable to the national government. These questions are discussed later in this volume by Sánchez in Chapter 16.

There is some relation between the approach of Van den Berg *et al.* and the interesting observations made by Inglehart (1988) on the growth of the new type of urban leader in the USA, the 'New Fiscal Populists', representing the new affluent urban middle class. Inglehart identifies five main traits which characterize this group: fiscal conservatism, progressive policies and views on social issues, populism in political approach, distrust of organized groups and a stress on public goods which appeal to all citizens. Inglehart explains the growth of this new type of urban politician on the basis of a fundamental shift in western and European social values from material to post-material values and a greater participation by individuals in political life, based in turn on higher educational levels and greater subjective political competence. However, the approach of Inglehart is not sufficient to explain the variety of change in urban policy orientation and approaches to place marketing observable in Europe. Changes in fundamental values are a consequence rather than a cause of deeper structural change in the economy.

What is fascinating about city marketing is its integration of economic, social, cultural and ideological questions in one place. It also builds upon the idea that fundamental economic choices depend upon social and cultural values. However, in the last analysis city image cannot run too far ahead of the economic and social realities. Somewhere along the line, a buoyant image depends upon a buoyant economy, which depends in turn on such factors as place productivity, linkages in the urban economy and innovation, and place creativity.

Acknowledgements

The author wishes to thank Eduardo Anselmo de Castro, Bjørn Asheim, Carme Vila, Christian Wichmann Mathiessen, Eric Clark and Joaquina Soares for helpful comments on an earlier draft of the manuscript. The usual disclaimer applies.

References

Adorno, T.W. and M. Horkheimer (1979) *The Dialectic of Enlightenment*, London: Verso.
Amin, A. (1992) 'Big firms versus the regions in the single European market', in M. Dunford and G. Kafkalas (eds), *Cities and Regions in the New Europe: The Global–Local Interplay and Spatial Development Strategies*, London: Belhaven, pp.127–49.
Amin, A. and J. Goddard (eds) (1986) *Technological Change, Industrial Restructuring and Regional Development*, London: Allen & Unwin.
Amin, A. and K. Robins (1991) 'These are not Marshallian times', in R. Camagni (ed.), *Innovation Networks. Spatial Perspectives*, London: Belhaven, pp.105-118.
Amin, A. and K. Robins (1992) 'The re-emergence of regional economies? The mythical geography of flexible accumulation', *Environment and Planning D: Society and Space*, **8**, pp.7–34.
Andersen, H.T. (1991) 'The political urbanization. Fringe development in Copenhagen', *Espace, Populations, Sociétés*, **2**, pp.367–79.
Andersson, Å. (1985) 'Creativity and regional development', *Papers of the Regional Science Association*, **56**, pp.5–20.
Asheim, B.T. (1990) 'Innovation diffusion and small firms: between the agency of lifeworld and the structure of systems', in E. Cicotti, N. Alderman and A. Thwaites (eds), *Technological Change in a Spatial Context*, Berlin: Springer, pp.37–55.
Ashworth, G.J. and H. Voogd (1990) *Selling the City*, London: Belhaven.
Badcock, B. (1984) *Unfairly Structured Cities*, Oxford: Blackwell.
Bailly, A. and D. Maillat (1991) 'Service activities and regional metropolitan development: a comparative study', in P.W. Daniels (ed.), *Services and Metropolitan Development*, London: Routledge, pp.129–45.
Bish, R.L. and H.O. Nourse (1975) *Urban Economics and Policy Analysis*, New York: McGraw-Hill.
Bradbury, K.L., A. Downs and K.A. Small (1982) *Urban Decline and the Future of American Cities*, Washington, DC: Brookings.
Bramanti, A. and L. Senn (1991) 'Innovation, firm and milieu: a dynamic and cyclic approach', in R. Camagni (ed.), *Innovation Networks. Spatial Perspectives*, London: Belhaven, pp.89–104.
Camagni, R. (1991a) 'Metropolitan areas and the effects of 1992', in M. Quevit (ed.), *Regional Development Trajectories and the Attainment of the European Internal Market*, Louvain-la-Neuve: Gremi, pp.187–204.
Camagni, R. (1991b) 'Local "milieu", uncertainty and innovation networks: towards a new dynamic theory of economic space', in R. Camagni (ed.), *Innovation Networks. Spatial Perspectives*, London: Belhaven, pp.121–44.
Cameron, G. (1990) 'First steps in urban policy evaluation in the United Kingdom', *Urban Studies*, **27**, pp.475–95.
Camhis, M. and S. Fox (1991) 'The European Community as a catalyst for European urban networks', *Ekistics*, **59**, (352/353), pp.4–6.
Cappellin, R. (1989) 'Milan', in L.H. Klaasen, L. Van den Berg and J. Van der Meer (eds), *The City: Engine behind Economic Recovery*, Aldershot: Avebury, pp.151–67.

Castells, M. (1978) *City, Class and Power*, London: Macmillan.

Cawson, A. and P. Saunders (1983) 'Corporatism, competitive policies and class struggle', in R. King (ed.), *Capital and Politics*, London: Routledge and Kegan Paul, pp.102–25.

CEC (1990a) 'One market, one money', *European Economy*, **44**, Brussels: Commission of the European Communities.

CEC (1990b) *Green Paper on the Urban Environment*, Brussels: Commission of the European Communities.

CEC (1991) *Europe 2000. Outlook for the Development of the Community Territory*, Brussels: Commission of the European Communities.

Cheshire, P., D. Hay, G. Carbonaro and N. Bevan (1988) *Urban Problems and Regional Policy in the European Community*, Brussels: Commission of the European Communities.

City of Stockholm (1991) *The Development of Stockholm*, Stockholm: City of Stockholm.

Cloke, P., C. Philo and D. Sadler (1990) *Approaching Human Geography*, London: Paul Chapman.

Coffey, W.J. and A.S. Bailly (1992) 'Producer services and systems of flexible production', *Urban Studies*, **29**, pp.857–68.

Cooke, P. (1988) 'Flexible integration, scope economies and strategic alliances: social and spatial mediations', *Environment and Planning D: Society and Space*, **6**, pp.281–300.

Cullis, J. and P. Jones (1992) *Public Finance and Public Choice*, London: McGraw-Hill.

Daniels, P.W. (1991a) 'Service sector restructuring and metropolitan development: processes and prospects', in P.W. Daniels (ed.), *Services and Metropolitan Development*, London: Routledge, pp.1–25.

Daniels, P.W. (1991b) 'Services and urban economic development', in J. Fox-Przeworski, J. Goddard and M. De Jong (eds), *Urban Regeneration in a Changing Economy*, Oxford: Clarendon, pp.75–95.

Davies, H.W.E. (1989) 'Birmingham', in L.H. Klaasen, L. van den Berg and J. van der Meer (eds), *The City: Engine behind Economic Recovery*, Aldershot: Avebury, pp.80–99.

De Castro, E. Anselmo and C.N. Jensen-Butler (1991) *Putting the Social into the Economic*, Aarhus: University of Aarhus, Institute of Political Science.

De Grauwe, P. (1992) *The Economics of Monetary Integration*, Oxford: Oxford University Press.

Department of Trade and Industry (1983) *Regional Industrial Policy: Some Economic Issues*, London: HMSO.

Donnison, D. and P. Soto (1980) *The Good City. A Study of Urban Development and Policy in Britain*, London: Heinemann.

Drewett, R., R. Knight and U. Schubert (1992) *The Future of European Cities: The Role of Science and Technology*, Prospective Dossier No. 4, Part 1: Synthesis. DGXII FAST-MONITOR PROGRAMME, Brussels: Commission of the European Communities.

Drudy, P.J. (1989) 'Dublin', in L.H. Klaasen, L. van den Berg and J. van der Meer (eds), *The City: Engine behind Economic Recovery*, Aldershot: Avebury, pp.112–27.

Dunford, M. and G. Benko (1991) 'Neo-Fordism or post-Fordism? Some conclusions and further remarks', in G. Benko and M. Dunford (eds), *Industrial Change and Regional Development: The Transformation of New Industrial Spaces*, London: Belhaven, pp.286–305.

Engelstoft, S. (1990) 'Technology, cities and planning for the 21st. century', *Cities and the global environment*, Proceedings of a European Workshop, The Hague, 5–7 December 1990, Dublin: European Foundation for the Improvement of Living and Working Conditions, pp.211–24.

Engelstoft, S. and C.N. Jensen-Butler (1993) 'Copenhagen's overall project', *Sistema Terra*, **II**, (1), pp.73–9.

Feldman, M. (1991) 'Technological change, industrial organisation and the restructuring of United States manufacturing', in J. Brotchie, M. Batty, P. Hall and P. Newton (eds), *Cities of the 21st Century. New Technologies and Spatial Systems*, Harlow: Longman, pp.307–22.

Fosler, R.S. and R.A. Berger (1982) *Public–private partnership in American cities*, Lexington Mass: Lexington Books.

Gaspar, J. (1992) 'Societal response to changes in the production system', *Urban Studies*, **29**, pp.827–37.

Gaspar, J. and C.N. Jensen-Butler (1992) 'Social, economic and cultural transformations in the Portuguese urban system', *International Journal of Urban and Regional Research*, **16**, pp.442–61.

Gertler, M. (1988) 'The limits to flexibility: comments on the post-Fordist version of production and its geography', *Transactions of the Institute of British Geographers*, **13**, pp.419–32.

Giddens, A. (1979) *Central Problems in Modern Social Theory*, London: Macmillan.

Giddens, A. (1984) *The Constitution of Society*, Berkeley: University of California Press.

Goddard, J., A. Thwaites and D. Gibbs (1986) 'The regional dimension to technological change in Great Britain', in A. Amin and J. Goddard (eds), *Technological Change, Industrial Restructuring and Regional Development*, London: Allen & Unwin, pp.140–56.

Hansen, F. and C.N. Jensen-Butler (1996) 'Economic crisis and the regional and local effects of the welfare state: The case of Denmark', *Regional Studies*, **30**, (2), pp.167–87.

Harloe, M., C. Pickvance and J. Urry (eds) (1990) *Place, Policy and Politics. Do Localities Matter?*, London: Unwin Hyman.

Harvey, D. (1989) 'From managerialism to entrepreneurialism: The transformation in urban governance in late capitalism', *Geografiska Annaler*, **71B**, pp.3–17.

Hepworth, M. (1990) 'Planning for the informational city: the challenge and response', *Urban Studies*, **27**, pp.537–58.

Herbert, D. and D.M. Smith (1989) *Social Problems and the City*, Oxford: Oxford University Press.

Hochman, O. (1990) 'Cities, scale economies, local goods and local governments', *Urban Studies*, **27**, pp.45–66.

Inglehart, R. (1988) 'The rise of a new political style', in *Urban Challenges – Report to the Commission on Metropolitan Problems*, Stockholm: Allmäna Forlaget, pp.209–35.

Inglehart, R. (1990) *Culture Shift in Advanced Industrial Societies*, Princeton, NJ: Princeton University Press.

Jensen-Butler, C.N. (1991) 'Transport policy and social integration in cities', *Social integration in cities*, Proceedings of a European Workshop, Berlin, 27–29 September 1991, Dublin: European Foundation for the Improvement of Living and Working Conditions, pp.73–90.

Jensen-Butler, C.N. (1996) 'Urban economic policy', in W.F. Lever and A. Bailly (eds), *The Spatial Impacts of Economic Changes in Europe*, Aldershot: Avebury, pp.251–93.

Jessop, B. (1982) *The Capitalist State*, Oxford: Martin Robertson.

Keating, M. (1991) *Comparative Urban Politics*, Aldershot: Edward Elgar.

Keith, M. (1989) 'Riots as a social problem in British cities', in D. Herbert and D.M. Smith (eds), *Social Problems and the City*, Oxford: Oxford University Press, pp.289–306.

Krätke, S. (1991) 'Cities in transformation: the case of West Germany', in G. Benko and M. Dunford (eds), *Industrial Change and Regional Development: The Transformation of New Industrial Spaces*, London: Belhaven, pp.250–72.

Lever, W.F. (1992) 'Local authority responses to economic change in West Central Scotland', *Urban Studies*, **29**, pp.935–48.

Lord Mayor's Office (1991) *Municipal Plan for Copenhagen. Proposal for revision 1991*, Copenhagen: Municipality.

Lundqvist, L. (1991) *Traffic and environment in Nordic capitals*, ERU, S-103 33 Stockholm, Sweden, paper presented to the Nordic RSA conference, November, Sandbjerg, Denmark.

Maillat, D. (1991) 'Local dynamism, milieu and innovative enterprises', in J. Brotchie, M. Batty, P. Hall and P. Newton (eds), *Cities of the 21st Century. New Technologies and Spatial Systems*, Harlow: Longman, pp.265–74.

Marlow, D. (1991) 'Eurocities: from urban networks to a European urban policy', *Ekistics*, **59**, pp.28–32.

Massey, D. (1984) *Spatial Divisions of Labour: Social Structures and the Geography of Production*, London: Macmillan.

Matthiessen, C.W. (1992) 'Metropoles and capitals. Copenhagen and the changing south Scandinavian scene', *Geografisk Tidskrift*, Copenhagen, Occasional Papers 9, pp.39–47.

MacKay, D.H. and A.W. Cox (1979) *The Politics of Urban Change*, London: Croom Helm.

Moore, B. and J. Rhodes (1973) 'Evaluating the effects of Britain's regional economic policy', *Economic Journal*, **83**, pp.87–110.

Moos, A.I. and M.J. Dear (1986) 'Structuration theory in urban analysis: 1 theoretical exegesis', *Environment and Planning A*, **18**, pp.231–52.

Moulaert, F. and E. Swyngedouw (1989) 'A regulation approach to the geography of the flexible production system', *Environment and Planning D: Society and space*, **7**, pp.327–45.

Newton, P.W. (1991) 'Telematic underpinnings on the information economy', in J. Brotchie, M. Batty, P. Hall and P. Newton (eds), *Cities of the 21st Century. New Technologies and Spatial Systems*, Harlow: Longman, pp.95–126.

Nijkamp, P. and A. Perrels (1990) 'The potential of European cities for sustainable environmental/energy policy', *Cities and the global environment*, Proceedings of a European Workshop, The Hague, 5–7 December 1990, Dublin: European Foundation for the Improvement of Living and Working Conditions, pp.107–24.

Oakey, R.P. and R. Rothwell (1986) 'High technology small firms and regional industrial growth', in A. Amin and J. Goddard (eds), *Technological Change, Industrial Restructuring and Regional Development*, London: Allen and Unwin, pp.258–83.

OECD (1983) *Urban Policies for the 1980s*, Paris: OECD.

Parkinson, M. (1990) 'Leadership and regeneration in Liverpool: confusion, confrontation or coalition?', in D. Judd and M. Parkinson (eds), *Leadership and Urban Regeneration. Cities in North America and Europe*, London: Sage, pp.241–57.

Parkinson, M. (1991) 'The rise of the entrepreneurial European city: Strategic responses to economic changes in the 1980s', *Ekistics*, **58**, pp.299–307.

Perrin, J-C. (1991) 'Technological innovation and territorial development: an approach in terms of networks and milieux', in R. Camagni (ed.), *Innovation Networks. Spatial Perspectives*, London: Belhaven, pp.35–54.

Pickvance, C. (1990) 'Introduction: the institutional context of local economic development: central controls, spatial policies and local economic policies', in M. Harloe, C. Pickvance and J. Urry (eds), *Place, Policy and Politics. Do Localities Matter?*, London: Unwin Hyman, pp.1–41.

Piore, M.J. and C.F. Sabel (1984) *The Second Industrial Divide: Possibilities for Prosperity*, New York: Basic Books.

Pompili, T. (1992) 'The role of human capital in urban system structure and development: The case of Italy', *Urban Studies*, **29**, pp.905–34.

Pugel, T.A. (1992) 'A comparative analysis of industrial restructuring in Europe, the US and Japan', in K. Cool, D.J. Neven and I. Walter (eds), *European Industrial Restructuring in the 1990s*, London: Macmillan, pp.57–76.

Ratti, R. (1991) 'Small and medium-size enterprises, local synergies and spatial cycles of innovation', in R. Camagni (ed.), *Innovation Networks. Spatial Perspectives*, London: Belhaven, pp.71–88.

Regional Plan Association (1990) *Visions for the Region Tomorrow. Towards a New Regional Plan*, New York: Regional Plan Association.

Richardson, H.W. (1979) 'Aggregate efficiency and interregional equity', in H. Folmer and J. Oosterhaven (eds), *Spatial Inequalities and Regional Development*, Boston: Martinus Nijhoff, pp.161–84.

Rothwell, R. and M. Dodgson (1991) 'Regional technology policies: The development of regional technology transfer infrastructures', in J. Brotchie, M. Batty, P. Hall and P. Newton (eds), *Cities of the 21st Century. New Technologies and Spatial Systems*, Harlow: Longman, pp.323–38.

Rowthorn, B. (1986) 'De-industrialisation in Britain', in R. Martin and B. Rowthorn (eds), *The Geography of De-industrialisation*, London: Macmillan, pp.1–30.

Sayer, A. (1986) 'New developments in manufacturing: the just-in-time system', *Capital and Class*, **30**, pp.43–72.

Sayer, A. (1989) 'Post-Fordism in question', *International Journal of Urban and Regional Research*, **13**, pp.666–95.

Schoenberger, E. (1988) 'From Fordism to flexible accumulation: technology, competitive strategies and international location', *Environment and Planning D: Society and Space*, **6**, pp.245–62.

Scott, A.J. (1988) 'Flexible production systems and regional development: the rise of new industrial space in North America and Western Europe', *International Journal of Urban and Regional Research*, **12**, pp.171–86.

Shachar, A. and D. Felsenstein (1992) 'Urban economic development and high technology industry', *Urban Studies*, **29**, pp.839–56.

Shapiro, D., N. Abercrombie, S. Lash and C. Lury (1992) 'Flexible specialisation in the culture industries', in H. Ernste and V. Meier (eds), *Regional Development and Contemporary Industrial Response*, London: Belhaven, pp.179–94.

Shields, R. (1990) *Places on the Margin*, London: Routledge.

Solesbury, W. (1974) *Policy in Urban Planning*, Oxford: Pergamon.

Steinle, W. (1992) 'Regional competitiveness and the single market', *Regional Studies*, **26**, pp.307–18.

Stöhr, W.B. (1990) *Global Challenge and Local Response*, New York: United Nations University, Mansell.

Storey, D. (1990) 'Evaluation of policies and measures to create local employment', *Urban Studies*, **27**, pp.669–84.

Swyngedouw, E. (1992) 'The Mammon quest. "Glocalisation", interspatial competition and the monetary order: the construction of new scales', in M. Dunford and G. Kafkalas (eds), *Cities and Regions in the New Europe: the Global–Local Interplay and Spatial Development Strategies*, London: Belhaven, pp.39–67.

Thrift, N. (1983) 'On the determination of social action in space and time', *Environment and Planning D: Society and Space*, **1**, pp.23–57.

Urry, J. (1990) 'Conclusion: places and policies', in M. Harloe, C. Pickvance and J. Urry (eds.), *Place, Policy and Politics. Do Localities Matter?*, London: Unwin Hyman, pp.187–204.

Van Weesep, J. and R. van Kempen (1992) 'Economic change, income differentiation and housing: Urban response in the Netherlands', *Urban Studies* **29**, pp.979–90.

Van den Berg, L., L.H. Klaasen and J. van der Meer (1990) *Marketing metropolitan regions*, Rotterdam: Erasmus University, EURICUR.

Van den Berg, L., R. Drewett, L.H. Klaasen, A. Rossi and C.H.T. Vijverberg (1982) *Urban Europe. A Study of Growth and Decline*, Oxford: Pergamon.

Williamson, O.E. (1985) *The Economic Institutions of Capitalism*, New York: Free Press.

2 The set of cities

Loïc Grasland and Chris Jensen-Butler

Competition between European cities

At first glance, it seems paradoxical that, in the context of globalization of the economy, the European countries are engaged in the creation of a regional–continental bloc, the European Union. The first major phase of creation of this bloc was the establishment of a customs union. This was followed by the single market, where the remaining institutional and technical barriers to trade are, in theory at least, removed. In addition, a market for factors of production exists – again at least in theory – though in practice the barriers to labour mobility in Europe, institutional, cultural and linguistic, remain considerable. The final stage, that of monetary and economic union, is at present a subject of intense discussion. It is with the development of such a union that conventional economic theory argues that the greatest positive effects will occur. These arise primarily from dynamic effects on the economy (cost reduction through continuous competition, dynamic scale economies, external economies, as well as a number of advantages arising from a monetary union).

Conventional economic theory also shows that the welfare gains from the creation of a customs union need not necessarily be positive (Vickerman, 1992). The results are dependent upon the patterns of trade diversion and creation which emerge. Thus there are arguments based upon trade theory which would suggest that creation of new supernational blocs in an age of globalization of the economy might involve fewer benefits than free trade. Why then the creation of this European phenomenon? A number of explanations seem possible.

First, it seems certain that the efficiency gains from the dynamic effects of economic union far outweigh any potential loss from trade diversion. However, these efficiency gains are not distributed evenly in time and space. Localities and regions which are best able to reap the benefits of such gains are those best suited to respond to increasing competition, to benefit from positive externalities and to gain from dynamic economies of scale. The regions best able to gain are in general the more advanced and central regions of Europe (Camagni, 1992). Perhaps more important, however, are the *localities* which stand to gain. These are primarily the cities.

Secondly, one major step towards globalization lies in the continentalization of economies, that is the opening of the market on a continental scale. Europe as well as North America are good examples. Gradual enlargement of markets towards continental and then global markets could be a rationale lying behind the European Union. Different types of markets are involved: commodities, finance, capital and labour. There are efficiency gains to be reaped by opening both factor and commodity markets in Europe.

Thirdly, the leap from national to global economy would, for many national economies, be too violent and destabilize social and economic development. Thus there do seem to be gains from cooperation, competition and alliances with other organizations and firms having some geographical and cultural proximity. Such positive externalities are traditionally dependent upon the distance involved.

Fourthly, it is also clear that Europe is facing a situation of triad power: the three blocs of the USA, Japan and Europe are emerging as the principal global competitors. Deregulation is proceeding fastest within each of the blocs of the triad, hence the gains are greatest at present within a continental bloc.

In the field of European competition and cooperation the city is, for similar reasons to those in the global case, emerging as the key type of locality (Brunet, 1989). Positive externalities (untraded benefits related to interdependencies) tend to be greater in cities, as here potential interdependencies are greater in number. Moreover, the scope for the creation of positive externalities is greater. This is making the cities the prime locus for growth-creating economic activity. In addition, the symbolism of the city and the relationship of this symbolism with the notion of the quality of life are gaining ascendancy, a further positive externality.

Urban development strategies have come to the fore in terms of both political and scientific interest. Various elements typically enter such strategies. Promotion of high-tech activities figures prominently, offering as it does the prospect of restructuring traditional industrial areas. There are numerous success stories in western Europe and the USA, but these are often associated with unique sets of economic and social conditions, not easily reproducible elsewhere. It does, however, seem to hold out some potential prospects for some European cities, particularly 'sunbelt' cities (Grasland, 1988). Another element is the promotion of positive multiplier effects locally and also the deliberate creation of synergy effects in the urban environment. In such areas, infrastructural, cultural and natural aspects compensate for the rather weak initial impact of high-tech activity in terms of employment (Bruhat, 1989, 1993). Such valorization of the urban environment is usually understood to improve the position of the city in global competition (Grasland, 1988, 1994). Another common element in urban development strategies is the promotion of high-level transport and telecommunications networks, which reinforce urban competition and also reinforce competitive position (Kunzmann and Wegener, 1991). A further common aspect of urban development policy is related to quality of life, which means that smaller cities are not always at a disadvantage. The notion of quality of life includes services, the physical environment and low social costs. All of these elements enter into the notion of the image of the city.

This concept of the image of the city and the preoccupation with the idea of quality of life is closely linked with urbanism. In spite of major philosophical shifts since the 1970s (such as post-modernism) urbanism has to assume the heavy heritage of the functional architecture of the 1930s, the era of the *Trente Glorieuses*, the reconversion of large industrial sites and, in relation to this, of intense spatial segregation. A great part of the megalopolis is again characterized by these signs of wealth of an age that has gone. Today's urban development shows the tension between two contradictory trends. On the one hand, the return to regional architecture and on the other the search for international architecutral signs. This dualism shows the urbanists' double constraint of having to use the symbols of the local identity and culture and their involvement in the search for international recognition through prestigious signs.

This management of urban space also has to integrate new modernist elements such as the reconciliation of economic specialization – or some activities which could justify it – and an image or expressions in keeping with the dominant discourse of the moment. This is what modernity is all about. In France, it brings new concepts with the suffix *-pole*: innopole, technopole, agropole, europole, atlanpole. Even if it is associated with *great* or replaced by *metropole*, the term 'city' is insufficient. This means a qualitative evolution of the concept of city, and explains why cities have recourse to advertising: the city should be quite different from another territory, it needs to appear as an economic, social and cultural single product – in short, to be a marketed object.

In spite of the growing importance of the city as a productive locality and as an independent economic actor, it must be remembered that the national state remains a key actor in economic development. The national state in a sense sets the scene for the city to act in international competition through, for example, international agreements and internationally oriented infrastructure investment. In addition, the national state negotiates at the European Union level in many areas which affect the city and defines its possibilities for action. There is, at the same time, an increasing tension between regions in Europe, usually dominated by a major city, and the national states with respect to which level has the right to partial self-determination. This is the problem area known as the 'Europe of Regions' (Gaspar and Jensen-Butler, 1995).

Conceptual and theoretical problems

Defining the city

Establishing a satisfactory definition of the city is not easy (Equipe P.A.R.I.S., 1993b). Cities were initially defined on the basis of population size and density. However, as it became increasingly appreciated that the city constitutes an economic system with a certain level of independence and self-determination, more functional definitions began to appear. Flows of goods and services, for both intermediate and private consumption, determine patterns of linkages. Consequently, relative concentration of flows and high levels of linkage can be used to identify the city. The other principal market, the factor market, also defines the city in functional terms, such as commuting zones or types of labour qualification. Finally, cities are centres of information exchange and the extent and depth of information fields can define a city functionally.

Alternatively, the city can be defined administratively, which is important for a number of reasons. First, available statistics often necessitate such a definition. Secondly, as the city is increasingly becoming an actor in the economic arena in its own right, the importance of the political and professional leadership of the city and its ability to enter into alliances with other groups of actors in the urban economy grows. Finally, a number of positive externalities and public goods are limited in their effects by jurisdictions, which further emphasizes the importance of the city being defined in political and administrative terms. A major problem arises when there is a fundamental lack of correspondence between the city defined functionally and the city defined in administrative terms. This problem is exacerbated when the city acts as entrepreneur and embarks upon place marketing. Sánchez discusses these problems in Chapter 16 of the present volume.

In general, the studies of this volume have adopted an approach based upon a definition of the city as an administrative unit, partly because of data difficulties involved with defining the city as a functional unit. This is of course problematic, as much of the discussion of the changing role of the city is, in fact, related to function.

The paucity of theoretical models

The theoretical foundations for analysis of competition between cities is weakly developed. Some city-based growth areas – typically arcs – seem to be appearing in Europe (Brunet, 1989). These include the well-known banana-shaped growth arc from London through the Rhine–Ruhr area to northern Italy. A Mediterranean growth arc ranging from northern Italy along the French Mediterranean coast to Barcelona may also be emerging. East European growth arcs are also being hypothesized. The existence of these growth zones has largely been established empirically. However, any attempt to deal with them systematically must rest upon a classification which has its roots in theoretical understanding.

From hierarchies to networks

Much of our understanding of city systems rests upon concepts related to central place theory (Berry, 1968). This type of theoretical model assumes that the city is a central place in relation to a complementary region: it serves as the prime locus of market activity for producers located in the complementary region. Proceeding up the urban hierarchy, the complementary region of any city includes more and more urban areas of lower hierarchical orders. Thus complementarity has both a regional and an urban component. In the ideal model, cities have marginal hierarchical functions of the highest threshold values, which distinguish them from cities at lower levels. Lower-order goods are also provided by large cities but to spatially more limited complementary regions than the regions to which the city supplies the marginal hierarchical good. Central place theory enables us to identify idealized patterns of urban places, where the concept of pattern includes size, spacing, functional composition and size of complementary region. The model is ideal in the sense that it rests upon unreal assumptions and operates with idealized concepts, such as economic rationality. This type of model rests upon a very specific notion of market competition. The behaviour of the individual consumer lies at the base of the system which determines the nature of the urban hierarchy which emerges.

The hierarchical city system model assumes a relationship between city performance and the region or nation of which it is the centre. As Lever (1993) points out, there was an increasing tendency for cities through the 1980s to break away from their national identities and indeed to perform economically and socially in a different pattern as compared with the nation to which they belong. Lever also argues that this tendency has been accompanied by the growth of regionalism in Europe, often led by a dominant city.

This type of approach to urban systems is no longer adequate for understanding the modern urban systems. The central place type of model viewed the city as a market-place for commodities produced in the complementary region and in the city itself. In the resulting pattern of cities, competition between the cities themselves was virtually absent, as city performance and function were functionally determined inside the central place system. Each city had its economic role in a national or regional city system. Specialization occurred at the level of the marginal hierarchical function and cities were related hierarchically to each other through their functions and in their market areas.

The modern city is a prime location for the production of goods and services which may be marketed elsewhere, including other cities. Furthermore, information has become a factor of production and in cities the market is of vital importance to the urban economy. Also the city is better able to ensure economic efficiency in this market than most other types of location. A larger share of national income is now produced in the service sector than in the manufacturing sector, where transport costs and mobility for marketable services are radically different from the agricultural and industrial societies, out of which central place models grew. The actors competing are now firms and organizations and even cities themselves. In many cases they are not actors based solely on one location, as in the case of multinational enterprises.

One of the contributions which has promoted a change in theoretical perspective was the work of Pred (1976) on the distribution of innovation in city systems. For the first time, the interaction between cities across different central place systems appeared as a determinant of economic success. The globalization and continentalization of economic systems has transformed the earlier basis for development of systems of cities. As all markets –

commodity, factor, and financial – become continental or global, and as cities become centres of production rather than distribution, in a global economy where transport constraints are minimal the notion of complementary region and national market disappears. Instead, each locality and each city competes with other localities and cities for promotion of inward investment and for the creation of economic, social and physical environments which can promote endogenous investment. One important aspect of this investment concerns innovation. The capacity of the city to generate innovation and to absorb innovations coming from outside is a key element in competitive success. The quality of human capital in a city is a vital ingredient in this competition (Pompili, 1992). The essential spatial feature of high modern city systems is the nature of connectivity and interaction between cities. The cities have become nodes in networks, and space has become topological space. Remoteness and proximity have become network-related concepts, symbolized by degree of connectivity and level of flow: information, people, goods and finance.

These new spatial qualities have been superimposed upon the old. Patterns of earlier urban functional specialization underlie new roles and patterns of competition and cooperation. The deindustrialization of major cities is a case in point. Major cities were earlier national manufacturing centres but now their role has been transformed to that of high-level service provision in an international context. The capacity to adapt old structures to the new demands of urban competition is the cornerstone of urban economic policy. Clearly, in this new arena of competition cities have some comparative advantages based upon their earlier specializations, but these forms of comparative advantage are rapidly being eroded. Cities themselves can contribute to the development of new forms of comparative advantage which will enable them to survive and even succeed in the new arena of competition.

Camagni (1992) has presented three city network 'logics': (1) a territorial network logic, based upon control of a limited market area; (2) a competitive logic, based upon attempts to maximize share of the global market; and (3) the true network logic, based upon maximization of innovation potential. To these three logics correspond three kinds of city network: (1) hierarchical networks, based on control of regional or national markets; (2) complementarity networks, based upon an interurban division of labour; and (3) synergy networks, based upon network externalities, with high levels of interconnection and information exchange. Thus a network economy is not only a competitive economy, it is also an economy where positive externalities arising through network-based cooperation can arise. All parties cooperating in a network can experience benefits of cooperation. Thus there is a duality of cooperation and competition in the growing network economy. This is symbolized in the growth of city networks, often based upon the application of advanced telecommunications. One response to increased competition between cities has indeed been the growth of networking between European cities. There are a number of reasons for entering such a network, including raising city status to acquire credibility, specialization in relation to problem solving, development of common projects and transfer of technology and knowledge. These are the same sorts of principles upon which strategic alliances between firms are based. *Eurocities* is an example of such a network, involving over 40 cities in the EU, developing cooperation in such fields as economic development, environment, technology, urban regeneration and culture (Marlow, 1991). Other networks in Europe include *The Union of Capital Cities*, the *Commission des Villes* and the *Eurometropolis Club* (Camhis and Fox, 1991).

Recent studies of the European urban system

A number of studies have attempted to examine the mechanisms lying behind urban success. Most of these studies equate success with urban economic performance, such as income and employment growth. Typical indicator variables chosen are population and demographic structure; GDP and employment/unemployment; headquarters of multinationals; financial transactions; human capital and innovation capacity, that is, levels of education, numbers of research institutions and expenditure; and the image of the city, identifying attractive cities with a high quality of life and cultural facilities. Some studies incorporate external relations and connections: passenger flows, financial flows, position in transport networks.

What is perhaps notable is that other types of variables, related to equity considerations, are frequently ignored. These could include distribution of income, levels of unemployment, diversity of employment opportunity, housing quality and availability, access to education, cultural diversity and local democracy. There is a certain danger involved in choosing only efficiency-related variables as success indicators, as indicated in the previous chapter. Failure to solve equity-related social problems and the existence of major negative externalities can seriously impinge upon efficiency. In many studies, the discussion of the causes of success or failure of the cities' urban policy is dealt with in a very peripheral manner. In the following, more specific examination is made of the way in which urban policy has been treated in these studies: how far can urban policy explain urban performance?

One of the first studies with European coverage was made by Hall and Hay (1980), using only population and employment data as success criteria. This study laid the foundation of the concept of a functional urban region (FUR). The analysis of causes of success remained inconclusive, partly because employment and population are poor indicators of success. Likewise, an evaluation of the effects of urban policy also produced inconclusive results. For American cities, Bradbury *et al.* (1982) defined urban decline in terms of changes in population, employment and income. They found that population growth is related to the local economy, to climate and to the ethnic composition of the city, while employment growth is related to the strength of the local market. It was more difficult to explain income growth and, furthermore, while population and employment growth were clearly related, they had little relation to income growth. An examination of patterns of population change in American cities in four five-year periods between 1970 and 1990 revealed markedly different patterns in the different periods. Their policy recommendations are strongly based upon income support for the poorer sections of urban populations, rather than policies aimed at attracting firms or households to the city. Their work serves to demonstrate that population change is not a satisfactory indicator of success, which can be confirmed by examining the fluctuating population growth pattern for European cities for five-year periods from 1970 to 1990 (CEC, 1991, p.137). This American study is one of the very few which explicitly consider the question of the link between equity and urban success.

The well-known DATAR (also termed RECLUS) study (Brunet, 1989) classified 165 European cities on the basis of 16 indicators, ranging from population to numbers of headquarters of multinational corporations, through universities to culture and research expenditure. While many interesting data are provided, there are a number of methodological problems involved in the study, particularly concerning weighting and multicollinearity. Size appears as the main criterion of success, which is not really a policy-related variable. Cities with positive residuals are identified in relation to three factors: cities with an international role (Amsterdam), cities with a gateway role in the transport network (Basle) and cities with a strong profile in research and culture (Grenoble).

Unsuccessful cities seem to be related to one of a number of factors: 'incomplete' cities (Berlin), specialized industrial cities (Liverpool), cities with larger population concentrations than their economic activity would suggest (Oporto) and cities located close to a metropolis (Saragossa). The variables associated with the positive residuals are variables where, in principle, policy can play an important role.

This study has been followed by similar French studies (Sallez and Vérot, 1991; Equipe P.A.R.I.S., 1993a) which also place principal weight upon the population variable and its relation to the functional composition of the cities. Thus the question of success tends to be overshadowed by the size effect. In the Equipe P.A.R.I.S. study, successful cities have more and more diverse functions than less successful cities, when controlling for population size.

Bruinsma *et al.* (1991) refer to a Dutch study of attractiveness of European cities from the viewpoint of multinational firms, identifying five success criteria: presence of corporate headquarters, level of R&D activity, presence of high-tech producers, distribution firms and the existence of producer services. These factors can only be influenced indirectly by policy.

Lever (1992a) refers to a study of 16 non-capital cities in Europe undertaken for the city of Glasgow, where GDP per person employed, income per head, the rate of new firm formation and the presence of corporate head offices are success criteria. These variables are linked with infrastructure variables, such as housing, facilities, air links, universities and advisory help on EU matters, to indicate policy variables available to the city of Glasgow.

Cheshire *et al.* (1986) and Cheshire (1990) use four key variables to represent urban health: GDP per capita, unemployment rate, net migration and travel demand (hotel beds per capita). Discriminant analysis is used for each variable, minimizing variance between cities in health groups and maximizing variance between the groups. The coefficients of the discriminant function are then used to rank cities according to health. These rankings are subsequently related to potential explanatory variables. The causes of urban success are identified as city size, centrality in Europe and skill-based urban industrial economies (rather than resource based); in addition, port cities fare badly. Again it is clear that most of these variables are not policy variables (except perhaps to a limited extent sectoral composition of the economy). The residual unexplained variation (20 per cent) is of interest. The presence of autocorrelation indicates the omission of one or more significant variables. The prime suspect variable omitted is suggested by Cheshire (1990) to be urban policy. He presents a qualitative analysis of distinctive urban policy which can possibly explain some of the residual variance.

Lever (1993) has also reworked Cheshire's data to examine patterns of convergence and divergence amongst European cities and he uses data available in another study (Cambridge Econometrics, 1991) to test a number of hypotheses concerning urban success in Europe. As a measure of success, seven variables – all related to GDP and its growth – are used and the following hypotheses are confirmed: capital cities are generally more successful than other cities, the cities of northern Europe are more successful than those of the south, and the cities of the centre are substantially more successful than those of the periphery. None of these variables is a policy variable.

These studies seem to indicate that urban success is primarily determined by structural factors not amenable to change under the influence of policy. Thus policy becomes a residual, a modifying factor, which follows the general trends of development in the productive sector, rather being an initiator of fundamental change. Jensen-Butler (1992) concluded in a similar vein in a recent analysis of regional and urban industrial policy in Denmark. However, recent years have witnessed remarkable success stories in some European cities, stories which seem to be related to urban policy decisions. Lever (1992b) provides an example in the case of Glasgow and Sánchez (1992) with Barcelona. Lyons has also had considerable success with its technopolis policy (Drewett *et al.*, 1992) and Stockholm appears to have had major successes with environmental policies (City of Stockholm, 1989).

Urban policy is an expression of local economic, political and social interests. The origin of urban policy is essentially political: the growth of municipal socialism in industrial cities in the west at the turn of the century. This turned into urban managerialism (Pahl, 1969), whereby the city essentially administered the local state. It partly solved equity-related problems at the local and real-world level, which the national governments were unable to solve. In more recent decades it seems that urban policy has become more entrepreneurial and cities are behaving increasingly as actors in the market, moving away from interests in equity-related questions to interest in economic efficiency (Jensen-Butler, 1996). This raises interesting questions of how far equity can be ignored in the pursuit of efficiency, when city administrations are highly and locally accountable. Therefore it is time to reassess the role of policy in creating urban success and in competition between cities (see Klaasen *et al.*, 1989). It is to this question we now turn.

The conceptualization of competition and success: methodological considerations

In Chapter 1 three basic dimensions of success were identified: economic performance, levels of social equity and control of negative externalities. These three basic dimensions will be carried forward into our consideration of typologies of European cities. The key element in city success or failure treated in the present book is the relation of city performance to urban policy.

Definitions

Defining competing cities is not an easy task. A prime element is population. Population is related to weight of local production, levels of diversification of activities, specialization of infrastructure and activity, and to transport and communication networks. Generally, a common threshold is accepted in the studies considered above. Most of the researchers seem to agree to define the cities as agglomerations with at least 200 000 inhabitants. This demographic threshold is arbitrary and the effects of the choice of threshold on the results is rather unclear.

According to performance and importance, some cities should be in the list of cities considered to be in competition, but their population is lower than the threshold. This is the case of very specialized cities in some fields, for example with scientific, financial, governmental or international activities: Cambridge, Heidelberg, Monaco, Lugano, Berne, Luxemburg. Some cities are not treated as individual cities as they belong to multi-city agglomerations, especially in most urbanized regions: Randstad Holland, the British Midlands, the Ruhr agglomeration in Germany and the *départements* Nord–Pas de Calais in northern France.

There are other cities with a population above the threshold that rank poorly in these studies, or have even been overlooked. This concerns particularly cities with poor accessibility, a negative image or with traditional activities. These include port cities (Livorno, Trieste, Aberdeen); large agglomerations in southern Europe without a marked specialization and a large share of young people in their population: Parma, Oviedo, Tarragona, Vitoria, Cadiz, Jerez; tourist cities of southern Europe: Las Palmas, Palma de Majorca, Santa Cruz, Cannes; old or transforming industrial cities: Valenciennes, Lens, Béthune; cities at some distance from a major cluster of agglomerations such as the Randstad: Enschede, Arnhem, Tilburg; peripheral or isolated cities, particularly those (at the time) outside the EU: Graz, Lausanne, Linz, but also Århus,

Odense, Groningen and cities of western France such as Brest, Angers, Caen, Tours and Le Mans. These cities have few decision-making functions or even supervisory functions and have borne the brunt of the negative consequences of internationalization and globalization. In many ways, the fate of cities is now more determined by their image – the negative or weak image of an old industrial city or cities with a poor mix of activities – than by the characteristics of their labour supply.

The problem of threshold is also one of the spatial criteria. What are the appropriate urban units and are they statistically comparable between countries? Equipe P.A.R.I.S. (1993b) shows that these statistical definitions can be reduced to four main types: central city, multi-district urban area, urban region and multicentred urban region. Municipal administrative limits correspond poorly to functional entities and, therefore, the urban region seems to be the more useful unit of comparison. But this unit can be defined in a variety of ways: urban unit, agglomeration, metropolitan area (standard metropolitan area (SMA), metropolitan economic labour area (MELA), functional urban region (FUR)) and researchers use these different definitions in their studies. Sometimes statistical definitions relevant to different problems are used. The problem of data availability must not of course be underestimated. Cheshire *et al.* (1988) base their analysis on the FUR; RECLUS (Brunet, 1989) on the agglomeration; Equipe P.A.R.I.S. (1993a) and Bonneville *et al.* (1991) on the metropolitan area. The aim is to find a spatial unit which contains the functions which are relevant to analysis of competition between cities. However, these functions must also be analysable using quantitative or qualitative data.

The methodology of the French studies

We now look more closely at the results and methodology of the recent French studies as a background for the choice of cities studied in the present volume. These studies will be used to help identify the international city: the cities in competition. The studies which classify European cities usually reveal about seven to nine classes of cities (Brunet, 1988; Sallez and Vérot, 1991; Equipe P.A.R.I.S., 1993a). Generally, these classes group all cities over 200 000 inhabitants on the world scale, but the European countries do not have cities in all the classes at the top of the urban hierarchy, and also, in some countries, some intermediate classes are empty. These studies are widely known, and some general characteristic emerge from them.

First, there seems to be a regularity in decrease in urban size and more cities appear in the lower-size classes. The rank size rule applies to the cities of western Europe, as can be seen in Figure 2.1 (Moriconi-Ebrard, 1993). Furthermore, the different classes seem to have no great gaps between, implying a continuum. This suggests stability in the network of cities. Secondly, the demographic weight of cities remains an essential criterion of discrimination. The relation between the importance of population size and the diversity of urban functions is basic. Where differences can be observed, the successful cities tend to have a larger range of functions than the less successful cities (Robert and Bertrand, 1993). Thirdly, the cities which perform best are in two rather different groups. 'Complete cities' (Conti and Spriano, 1990) with global functions dominate in the upper class. In the following classes, specialized larger cities are often ranked higher than more diversified cities. Generally, Class 1 groups together the larger cities in terms of population number. They offer a flexibility of policy ('all-

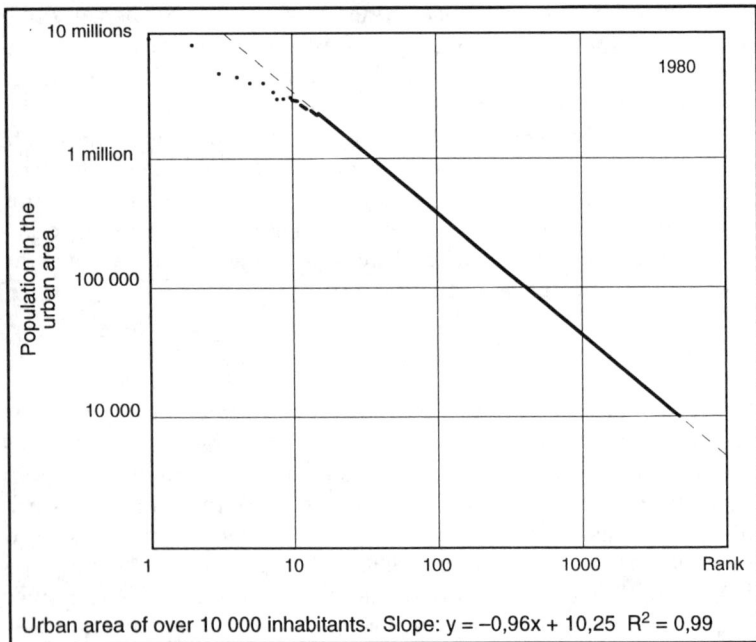

Urban area of over 10 000 inhabitants. Slope: $y = -0,96x + 10,25$ $R^2 = 0,99$

Source: F. Moriconi-Ebrard (1993).

Figure 2.1   Rank and size of cities in western Europe

risks policy cities': Veltz, 1993), both from the point of view of enterprises, which find a broad diversity of services and for people who can more easily find employment in a context of economic uncertainty. This class includes the great economic national and international metropolises: London, Paris, Milan, Madrid, Barcelona.

The other group includes more specialized cities which are able to gain considerable power from their specialization even if they include larger cities with numerous functions. This group of cities appears in classes which also contain less successful cities, such as those which specialize in sectors such as mining and textiles. Some of the successful cities in these classes (Frankfurt, Zurich, Munich) have several high-level economic functions, or thrive on a single specialized function (Geneva, Rotterdam or, at a lower level, Florence, Eindhoven, Antwerp and Montpellier). In the same classes, we also find capital cities which may be more or less successful, such as Athens, Vienna, Lisbon and large cities of southern Europe such as Oporto, Malaga and Palermo. They are interspersed with specialized industrial centres – often in crisis – such as Liverpool, Sheffield, Bilbao, Newcastle, Wuppertal, Duisburg and Liège.

As noted above, the RECLUS study (Brunet, 1989) incorporates 16 variables to measure competitive position, but the results are heavily influenced by population size. The basic eightfold classification of 165 European cities is shown in Table 2.1.

The Equipe P.A.R.I.S. (1993a) study has eliminated the effect of population size from their classification and thus modified the classes used in the Brunet study. The Equipe P.A.R.I.S. study defines eight types of metropolitan area:

A. dominant international metropolis,
B. international metropolis with specialized functions,
C. international metropolis with incomplete range of functions,
D. regional metropolis with strong international orientation,
E. national metropolis moving towards internationalization,
F. isolated national metropolis,
G. regional peripheral metropolis with weak international orientation,
H. regional metropolis with weak international orientation and highly specialized.

Furthermore, this division of the European cities has been crossed with categories representing the basis of urban attraction, to result in the following classification (see also Table 2.2 below):

Table 2.1   Classification of European cities by class

Class 1	
London	83
Paris	81
Class 2	
Milan	70
Class 3	
Madrid	66
Munich/Frankfurt	65
Rome, Brussels, Barcelona	64
Amsterdam	63
Class 4	
Manchester	58
Berlin, Hamburg	57
Stuttgart, Copenhagen, Athens	56
Rotterdam, Zurich	55
Turin	54
Lyons	53
Geneva	52
Class 5	
Birmingham, Cologne, Lisbon	51
Glasgow	50
Vienna, Edinburgh	49
Marseilles	48
Naples	47
Seville, Strasbourg	46
Basle, Venice, Utrecht	45
Düsseldorf, Florence, Bologna, The Hague, Antwerp, Toulouse	44
Valencia, Genoa	43
Class 6	
Bonn	42
Lille, Nice	41
Bristol, Bordeaux, Hanover, Grenoble	40
Montpellier, Nantes, Dublin, Oporto	39
Nuremberg, Eindhoven, Bilbao	38
Palermo, Bari, Mannheim	37
Liège, Leeds, Rennes	36
Trieste, Essen	35
Class 7	
Saragossa, Mainz–Wiesbaden, Wiesbaden	34
Liverpool, Southampton, Newcastle, Salonika, Tarento, Berne, Nancy, Lausanne	33

Table 2.1   continued

Karlsruhe, Bremen, Gant, Rouen	32
Malaga, Padua, Calghari, Arnhem	31
Cardiff, Münster, Brunswick, Metz, Palma	30
Augsburg	29
Angers, Verona, Dortmund, Aix-en-Provence, Nijmegen, Orléans, Clermont	28
Cadiz, Catania, Parma, Groningen, Reims	27
Las Palmas, Valladolid, Granada, Bochum, Tours	26
Class 8	
Saarbrücken, Belfast, Vigo, Tarragone, Saint-Etienne	25
Cordoba, Murcia, Coventry, Alicante, Messina, Odense, Modena, Kiel, Aarhus, Kassel, Duisburg	24
Haarlem, Le Havre, Santa Cruz Plymouth, Nottingham, Linz, Graz, Friburg-Br., Wuppertal, Tilburg	23
Aberdeen, San Sebastian, Caen, Reggio, Brescia, Bielefeld, Enschede, Dijon, Sheffield	22
Brest, Santander, Teesside, Hull, Pamplona, Leghorn, Cannes, Amiens, Dordrecht	21
La Corunya, Oviedo, Leicester, Lübeck, Valenciennes	20
Le Mans, Lens, Gijon, Vitoria, Toulon	19
Stoke-on-Trent, Charleroi, Mönchen Gladbach	18

Source: Brunet (1989).

1.   concentration of decision making,
2.   concentration of multinational corporate headquarters,
3.   importance of international institutions,
4.   diversified economic base,
5.   specialized economic base,
6.   weak tertiary sector and poor quality of life,
7.   poor accessibility by air,
8.   growth trends.

Although the studies carried out by RECLUS and Equipe P.A.R.I.S. used different methodologies, the resulting classifications are broadly comparable; the outcomes have been summarized in Figure 2.2. In Figure 2.2(b), the rank order of the Equipe P.A.R.I.S. study has been changed, enhancing the position of the 'national metropolis moving towards internationalization'. In gen-

Table 2.2 Position of European cities

Type of metropolitan area	Concentration of decision making	Concentration of multinational corporate headquarters	Importance of international institutions	Diversified economic base	Specialized economic base	Weak tertiary sector and poor quality of life	Poor accessibility by air
Dominant international metropolis	London Paris						
International metropolis with specialized functions		Amsterdam Düsseldorf Frankfurt Hamburg Munich Zurich					
International metropolis with incomplete range of functions		Brussels	Geneva Strasbourg	Berlin Copenhagen Vienna			
Regional metropolis with strong international orientation		Basle	Luxembourg	Antwerp Bremen Hanover Cologne–Bonn Lyons Marseilles Nuremberg Rotterdam Stuttgart	Berne Bologna Bristol Nice Salzburg	Florence Manchester Naples Rome The Midlands	
National metropolis moving towards internationalization						Barcelona Madrid Milan	

Isolated national metropolis				Dublin Belfast	
Regional peripheral metropolis with weak international orientation	Eindhoven Clemont-Ferrand	Bordeaux Nantes Toulouse	Edinburgh Innsbruck Münster Southampton	Athens Bilbao Graz Lille Lisbon Palermo Oporto Seville Salonika Genoa Glasgow Linz Malaga Turin Tyneside Valenciennes Venice	Montpellier Plymouth Granada Grenoble
Regional metropolis with weak international orientation and highly specialized			Cardiff	Alicante Bari Catania Liège West Yorkshire Saragossa	Murcia Pamplona Rennes Saint-Etienne Valladolid Toulon Kiel Corunna Le Havre San Sebastian Santander Vigo

Source: Equipe P.A.R.I.S. (1993a).

Classification 'Equipe P.A.R.I.S.'

Classes	A	B	C	D	E	F	G	H
1	2							
2					1			
3	3	1	1	2				
4	2	3	4			2		
5	1	2	8			8		
6			4		1		9	4
7			2				5	3
8					1	2		13

Classes	A	E	B	C	D	G	F	H
1	2							
2		1						
3		2	3	1	1			
4		2	3	4	2			
5		1	2	8	8			
6				4		9	1	4
7				2		5		3
8						2	1	13

Classification 'Villes Euopéennes' (RECLUS)

(a) Gross table   (b) Table after finding equivalent classes

Figure 2.2   Contigency tables of two classifications of cities (RECLUS (Brunet, 1989), Equipe P.A.R.I.S.)

eral, Figure 2.2(b) indicates good correspondence between the two studies; the deviations from the principal diagonal are greatest for the middle groups 4, 5, and 6 and for the classes D and G.

The two great metropolises fall into the same group in each classification. The strong metropolises that formed one class in the RECLUS study (Class 3) have distributed amongst four levels of the Equipe P.A.R.I.S. study. This outcome is related to differences in the level of internationalization of the metropolis:

- international metropolis with specialized functions,
- international metropolis with incomplete range of functions,
- regional metropolis with strong international orientation,
- national metropolis moving towards internationalization.

In the RECLUS Class 4, the level of internationalization is again high, except for two cities which are more peripheral: Turin and Athens. But the cities in Class 4 are clearly less endowed with powerful functions than the higher categories in the classification. This is well reflected in the inclusion of capital cities of lesser importance (Berlin, Copenhagen) and of less complete cities in functional terms: Rotterdam, Lyons, Stuttgart, Manchester. In relation to their economic and financial power, two cities should be in Class 3 according to Equipe P.A.R.I.S.: Zurich and Hamburg. A third RECLUS category, Class 5, combines ten cities with notable international functions, but at a lower level; these cities are also less diversified in functional terms. Nine other cities in this class are weaker on the international scene: Edinburgh, Lisbon, Glasgow, Toulouse, Strasbourg, Valencia, Geneva, Seville and Venice.

Another way of examining the level of international orientation of European cities is to compare the set of 30 international cities defined in the N.I.C.E. study (Bonneville *et al.*, 1992) with the international cities identified in the RECLUS and Equipe de P.A.R.I.S. studies. The N.I.C.E. study excludes capital cities (Soldatos, 1989a). The outcome of the comparison is presented in Table 2.3. The first group includes the international cities defined in the two RECLUS–Equipe P.A.R.I.S. studies and compares them with the N.I.C.E. study. There is a fair, but imperfect, correspondence. The second group appears also to present a reasonable correspondence; these cities have more specialized functions, but their international influence is weak. The differences between the classes show up less in their economic performance than in their demographic strength. The third group shows major deviations: three French cities are defined as international in the N.I.C.E. study, but not in the RECLUS/Equipe P.A.R.I.S. studies.

Next, we can compare these classifications with the outcome of the study by Cheshire *et al.* (1988), in which functional urban regions were classified by population change and problem score using aggregate data for a ten-year period (1971–81). The results are found in Figure 2.3, where the international cities of RECLUS, Equipe P.A.R.I.S. and N.I.C.E.–Europe are underlined. The figure shows a typology of the main national groups of international cities on the two dimensions. It is interesting to note that several international cities have a high problem score and a negative population change: Manchester, Birmingham, Turin and Rotterdam. Others have both low problem scores and positive population change: Paris, Lyons, Strasbourg, Brussels and Rome. Generally, Figure 2.3 suggests that there is no clear relationship between demographic change and economic performance. Successful cities such as Madrid, Munich and Lyons have rapidly growing populations, while Düsseldorf, Frankfurt and Amsterdam experience decreases.

The majority of international or internationalizing cities are found in northern and central Europe, more precisely in the megalopolis (Figure 2.4 below) though even some of these have problems of

Table 2.3   Cross-classification of cities (on the basis of the RECLUS, P.A.R.I.S., and N.I.C.E. studies)

	Class in contingency tables (Figure 2.2)	Cities in survey N.I.C.E.–Europe
1. International cities (5 first classes of RECLUS–P.A.R.I.S.)		
London	1A	(capital)
Paris	1A	(capital)
Milan	2E	X
Madrid	3E	(capital)
Barcelona	3E	X
Munich	3B	X
Frankfurt	3B	X
Amsterdam	3B	(capital)
Brussels	3C	(capital)
Rome	3D	(capital)
Hamburg	4B	X
Zurich	4B	X
Copenhagen	4C	(capital)
Berlin	4C	(capital)
Geneva	4C	X
Manchester	4D	X
Stuttgart	4D	X
Rotterdam	4D	X
Lyons	4D	X
Düsseldorf	5B	—
Vienna	5C	(capital)
Strasbourg	5C	X
Birmingham	5D	X
Cologne	5D	X
Marseilles	5D	—
Naples	5D	—
Basle	5D	—
Florence	5D	—
Bologna	5D	—
Antwerp	5D	X

Table 2.3   continued

	Class in contingency tables (Figure 2.2)	Cities in survey N.I.C.E.–Europe
2. Less international cities for RECLUS–P.A.R.I.S. and N.I.C.E.–Europe		
• generally with a good specialization		
Bristol	6D	—
Nuremberg	6D	—
Hanover	6D	—
Nice	6D	—
Bremen	7D	—
Berne	7D	(capital)
• generally with a good demographic weight		
Turin	4G	X
Athens	4G	(capital)
Valencia	5G	—
Genoa	5G	—
Lisbon	5G	(capital)
Glasgow	5G	X
Edinburgh	5G	—
Seville	5G	—
Toulouse	5G	X
Venice	5G	—
3. International cities for N.I.C.E.–Europe, less international for RECLUS–P.A.R.I.S.		
Grenoble	6G	X
Lille	6G	X
Liège	6H	X

Notes: X: the city is included by Soldatos; —: the city is not included by Soldatos; (capital): in N.I.C.E., the capitals are excluded.

Source: Soldatos (1989a).

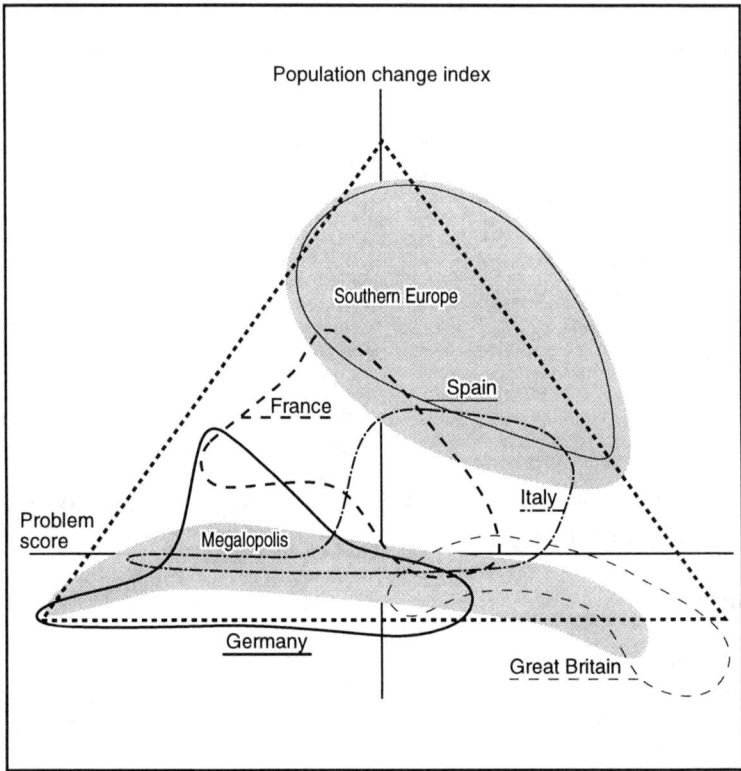

Source: Cheshire and Hay (1989).

Figure 2.3   Position of main national groups of cities with respect to problem score and population change index, 1971–84

restructuring. Southern Europe, and particularly Spain, appear peripheral and have only a few international cities, mainly capitals and ports; only Barcelona stands out as a case apart. Together with part of Italy, France is in an intermediate position.

City promotion: from classical approaches to new concepts

Competition between cities involves a diversity of tools of urban promotion. The advantages of different strategies are also clear in different policy approaches to development and these can be identified through the analysis of the variables used. Four distinct policy formats prove to be ideally suited to the purpose of development in the sense that they can be combined in concrete applications.

The functional approach

This approach is defined by an emphasis on economic factors. The comparative advantages of a place or its economic specializations are brought to bear. The policy emphasizes the availability of local resources and especially the locally found mix of production sectors, local know-how and human capital, the availability of capital, and the place and capacity of the local production system in the context of the international division of labour. This is the classical promotional approach, backed up by subsidies for entrepreneurship. This type of policy is frequently encountered in cities in crisis, with major problems of industrial restructuring and short-term and long-term unemployment.

This approach is also used by central governments (for example, in France by DATAR) or regional governments and their agencies (such as regional development agencies) which intervene in different ways to maintain, strengthen or even eliminate some sectors. Some cities succeed in setting up policies of employment substitution with the help of these political agencies, but one result is progressive disappearance of their specializations and their comparative advantages.

Cities with an economy based on mining, textiles, shipbuilding and metal working often opt for this approach, because of the major social and economic problems they have to resolve. Usually, they have not yet developed alternative broader or long-term strategies. However, in terms of competition, they know how to create a skilled labour force, to find subsidies for the enterprises which want to be involved in restructuring, and to draw in local actors to valorize any new resource (other firms, chambers of commerce, unions, local governments and so on).

The environmental approach

For various reasons, cities now emphasize elements beyond the realm of their economic structure in their self-promotion. This shift is related to the persistent economic crisis, the freedom of movement experienced by footloose industries, the expansion of tertiary activities, the general increase of labour qualifications, the prevalence of environmental concerns and the labour force's growing preference for high amenity value. The city is nowadays 'sold'

on the basis of positive externalities and its environmental qualities, and these elements are increasingly encountered in their promotional materials.

The image of the city lies at the root of this new concern. Alongside its economic dimension, it incorporates elements which touch
everyday life, the needs of identity, of recognition and of satisfac-
tion with a space. This concern may be very broad, including
quality of life, symbolic meanings of physical and cultural environments, absence of problems of labour management and good
accessibility based upon well-developed communications infrastructure. In fact, this strategy fits well with the expectations of
enterprises and workers, but the target is perhaps more specific
than in the former strategy. The typical enterprise is a SME (small
and medium-sized enterprise) in the high-tech field or in the field
of business services, and the typical worker an engineer, technician or member of the managerial staff of such an enterprise. Such
workers are well remunerated, they demand a pleasant lifestyle
with an elitist image, in a distinct physical and cultural environment. If this strategy succeeds, these firms and workers in turn
contribute to development of the image and the socioeconomic
and cultural environment of these cities.

Some cities of southern Europe played this card during the
1980s. This followed upon the events occurring in eastern Europe
which increased the overall competition, and was also a reaction
to failures of some cities with a weaker industrial tradition. Thus,
since the early 1990s, some cities have been obliged to rethink
their promotional strategy.

The geostrategic approach

This strategy is based on the idea of belonging to a specific class of
cities. It is the syndrome of the club: that is, the fear of being
excluded from groups of cities with the same characteristics and
the same pretensions. In this approach, local government takes
over from the market actors and elaborates new strategies, often
outside institutional frameworks in order to assert membership of
the club (para-diplomacy, identified by Soldatos, 1989b). Cities
also base their strategies on the urban research studies which they
themselves often sponsor. Opening the city to the outside world is
the key here. The strategy is not only to present the advantages of
a city, but to develop real exchanges with equivalent cities and to
join the same club, the same functional network of cities. The
criteria defining membership of these clubs are not always the
same and are often not clearly identified. Membership is often

based on pseudo-objective criteria such as population size, the use of similar strategies for development and existing partnerships, on local governments belonging to the same political 'families' or on similar feelings of kinship, or on the need to lobby jointly in the context of EU programmes.

Cities choosing this strategy also base their policies on new concepts, such as the international city, eurocity or technopole. By using such terms, the cities try to profit from a new contextual image and they also try, through these networks, to gain elitist features they could not obtain by themselves.

The integrated approach

This approach is less clear-cut than the ones discussed above, but it groups together, perhaps somewhat artificially, the initiatives of cities which use a wide range of measures to redefine, both globally and for the long term, their place on the regional, national and international scale. It is based on the intervention of many political and economic actors. The strategy can be seen in the elaboration of comprehensive urban projects that may take up to 25–30 years to develop.

The cities objectives tend to be broadly defined and are typically related to the economic, social or cultural fields. But local governments also take into account relations with other jurisdictions, with the region or higher-level territories. Cities are not only places of development, connected to international networks of cities, they are also places of regional polarization and nodes which articulate regions and international environments.

In this approach, all political and economic initiatives are meant to converge towards common objectives, those of the comprehensive project. Cities try to gain the support of higher authorities. The projects are elaborated in the expectation that they will be subsidized or that they will be supported by the decentralization of activities. The main constraint to this strategy is that local, regional or national governments are often politically opposed to each other. The approach is most frequent in the strategies of medium-sized cities as apparently it is easier to control development at this size.

The set of cities

In this volume, the promotional strategies and policies of a number of European cities are described and analysed. The case-study approach is adopted in Part II, with in-depth studies of representative cities. The choice of cities was not easy. First, they had to illustrate urban policy with respect to the three main policy dimensions used here: efficiency, equity and control of negative externalities. Secondly, they should present examples of the four main types of promotional strategies identified in the previous section. Thirdly, they should provide a reasonable coverage of the classes of international city which can be identified, for example using the classifications of RECLUS and Equipe P.A.R.I.S. Finally, they should bear some relation to the interests of the researchers involved. Certain boundary conditions applied: at the beginning of the RURE project it was only the cities of western Europe which were to be the objects of study and, furthermore, the main emphasis was on cities inside the European Union.

The final choice comprised the following cities: Athens, Barcelona, Budapest, Copenhagen, Geneva, Glasgow, Lisbon, Milan, Paris and Stockholm (Figure 2.4). Paris was chosen as an example of a truly global city, with clear policies designed to improve urban economic efficiency. Milan, which falls in Class 2 of the RECLUS study, seemed to be an example of success with minimal policy intervention. Barcelona also provided an example of apparent economic success, with aggressive city marketing and efficiency-oriented policies. Copenhagen, in RECLUS Class 4, was known to be a city where distributional considerations are important, which could be contrasted with Athens, also in Class 4, where major urban problems are present, and where urban policy appears weak. Geneva, also in Class 4, provided a special example of a city with strong international orientation, good economic performance and high environmental standards. Lisbon and Glasgow are both in Class 5. Lisbon, a peripheral capital with some strong international connections and weak urban policy, faces many problems of urban development and peripherality, while Glasgow is known for its strong urban policy and economic restructuring, having some degree of success. Distributional considerations have always been an important element in urban policy in Glasgow. Thus these cities provide a coverage of Classes 1–5, the international cities, in the RECLUS typology.

Stockholm was included partly as an example of a non-EC city (before 1995) and as a city which has placed environmental quality at the forefront of its promotional efforts. Finally, the group decided to include one east European city, Budapest, in order to illustrate, albeit in a brief manner, some of the urban policy problems involved in the transition to a market economy. Budapest serves as a point of comparison between west and east European cities.

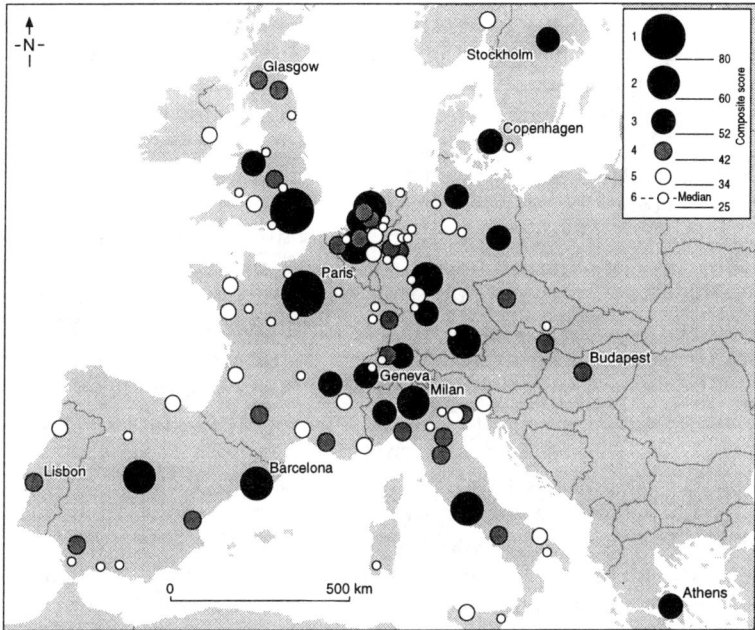

Figure 2.4   The set of cities and their relative importance

Conclusions

This presentation has neglected a growing element of competition between cities in Europe, namely the fact that cities increasingly are cooperating in order to improve their competitive position. There are two basic forms of cooperation. One involves cooperation between adjacent cities within conurbations, while the other involves the establishment of networks on a Europe-wide basis. The advantages arising from these forms of cooperation are widely undervalued in the studies referred to earlier. For many cities, networks of cooperation are becoming an essential element in their development strategies.

This presents many problems in the analysis of competition of cities. Paradoxically, it also shows that a result of this competition is decrease in competition and more cooperation. The notion of competition between cities could, therefore, be translated into competition between city networks, which raises a number of unanswered questions. We may conclude that the city is no longer only a locus of central and diversified functions, but is also a 'milieu' of symbolic identity and territorial roots entering into larger schemes of cooperation and competition. The analysis of locality in a global economy is primarily an analysis of the city, even if this creates many methodological and theoretical problems.

The nature of the relationship between cities and regions remains unclear. The future of links between regions and cities, whether casual or contractual, is unknown; it also remains unclear how the positive effects of cooperation agreements with other cities may be maximized. There is a clear risk of economic marginalization, and regions will become even more dependent because of their geographical and topological distance from the cities which amass complementary urban functions with the centre of the particular region. One future lies in their function as a territorial reserve for the deconcentration of population and activities from the large, successful cities.

As argued above, the key to understanding the development of the European city system lies in the network concept. Camagni (1993) argues that, with the networks, the classical hierarchy of cities could be reduced to three levels of network:

- a network of world cities which assume all the functions of cities and, even in competition, have privileged and high-level relations through elaborate communication networks;
- a network of specialized national cities which have input–output relations, trade relations and exchange technology;
- a network of specialized regional cities which have the same relations as the former network, but at a lower level.

Participation in these networks is becoming the object of competition between some cities. But partnership can also concern different levels of cities and the cities' networks can become interlinked. Perhaps networks of cities is one of the best results of competition between cities. Another form of place differentiation, in terms of functions in networks, is developing, and global competition in the sense of eliminating place may well be a transient phenomenon. A new European spatial structure is emerging.

References

Berry, B.J.L. (1967) *A Geography of Market Centers and Retail Distribution*, Englewood Cliffs, NJ: Prentice-Hall.

Bonneville, M., M.-A. Buisson, N. Commerçon and N. Rousier (1992) *Villes Européennes et Internationalisation* [European cities and internationalization], Lyons: Programme Rhône–Alpes de recherches en sciences humaines.

Bradbury, K.L., A. Downs and K.A. Small (1982) *Urban Decline and the Future of American Cities*, Washington, DC: Brookings.

Bruhat, T. (1989) *Vingt Technopoles: Un Premier Bilan* [Twenty Technopoles: a first assessment], Paris: DATAR/La Documentation Française.

Bruhat, T. (1993) *Technopoles et Développement Régional. Eléments d'Evaluation de la Valeur Ajoutée des Technopoles* [Technopoles and regional development. Elements of the evaluation of the added value of Technopoles], Paris: DATAR/La Documentation Française.

Bruinsma, F., P. Nijkamp and P. Rietveld (1991) 'Infrastructure and metropolitan development in an international perspective: Survey and methodological exploration', in R.W. Vickerman (ed.), *Infrastructure and Regional Development*, European Research in Regional Science 1, London: Pion, pp.189–206.

Brunet, R. (ed.) (1989) *Les Villes Européennes* [The cities of Europe], Montpellier–Paris: RECLUS-DATAR, la Documentation Française.

Camagni, R. (1992) 'Development scenarios and policy guidelines for the lagging regions in the 1990s', *Regional Studies*, **26**, pp.361–74.

Camagni, R. (1993) 'Organisation économique et réseaux de villes' [Economic organization and urban networks], in A. Sallez (ed.), *Les Villes, Lieux d'Europe*, Paris: DATAR/Editions de l'Aube, pp.107–28.

Cambridge Econometrics (1991) *European Regional Prospects: Analysis and Forecasts to the Year 1995 for European Cities and Regions*, Cambridge: Cambridge Econometrics.

Camhis, M. and S. Fox (1991) 'The European Community as a catalyst for European urban networks', *Ekistics* **59**, (352/353), pp.4–6.

CEC (1991) *Europe 2000. Outlook for the Development of the Community Territory*, Brussels: Commission of the European Communities.

Cheshire, P. and D. Hay (1989) *Urban Problems in Europe, an Economic Analysis*, London: Unwin Hyman.

Cheshire, P., D. Hay, G. Carbonaro and N. Bevan (1988) *Urban Problems and Regional Policy in the European Community*, Luxembourg: Office for Official Publications of the European Communities.

Cheshire, P.C. (1990) 'Explaining the recent performance of the European Community's major urban regions', *Urban Studies*, **27**, pp.311–33.

Cheshire, P.C., G. Carbonaro and D.G. Hay (1986) 'Problems of urban decline and growth in EEC countries: or measuring degrees of elephantness', *Urban Studies*, **23**, pp.131–49.

City of Stockholm (1989) *The Development of Stockholm*, Stockholm: City of Stockholm.

Conti, S. and G. Spriano (1990) *Efetto Città* [Urban influences], Turin: Agnelli.

Drewett, R., R. Knight and U. Schubert (1992) *The Future of European Cities: The Role of Science and Technology*, Prospective Dossier No. 4, Part 1: Synthesis, DGXII FAST-MONITOR PROGRAMME, Brussels: Commission of the European Communities.

Equipe P.A.R.I.S. (1993a) 'Le poids économique des villes dans le système urbain européen' [The economic significance of cities in the European urban system], in A. Sallez (ed.), *Les Villes, Lieux d'Europe*, Paris: DATAR/Editions de l'Aube.

Equipe P.A.R.I.S. (1993b) *The Statistical Concept of the Town in Europe*, Luxembourg: Commission of the European Communities.

Grasland, L. (1988) 'Technopolisation et développement régional' [The proliferation of Technopoles and regional development], in R. Brunet, L. Grasland, J-P. Garnier, R. Ferras and J-P. Volle, *Montpellier Europole*, Montpellier: G.I.P., RECLUS, pp.53–140.

Grasland, L. (1994) *Des Projets Technopolitains Intégrés à l'Intégration des Territoires par les Technopoles* [From the development of Technopoles to integration of regions through Technopoles], Actes du Symposium Européen de Recherche sur les Technopoles; Outils d'Evaluation Dynamique des Technopoles et Réseaux, Rennes, 5–7 April, Rennes-Atalante: DATAR/Programme SPRINT.

Hall, P. and D. Hay (1980) *Growth Centres in the European Urban System*, London: Heinemann.

Jensen-Butler, C.N. (1992) 'Rural industrialisation in Denmark and the role of public policy', *Urban Studies*, 29, pp.881–904.

Jensen-Butler, C.N. (1995) 'A Europe of regions: Myth or reality?', paper presented to the Regional Studies Association Conference, Gothenburg, May.

Jensen-Butler, C.N. (1996) 'A theoretical analysis of urban economic policy', in W.F. Lever and A. Bailly (eds), *The Spatial Impacts of Economic Changes in Europe*, Aldershot: Avebury, pp.251–93.

Klaasen, L.H., L. van den Berg and J. van der Meer (eds) (1989) *The City: Engine behind Economic Recovery*, Aldershot: Avebury.

Kunzmann, K. and M. Wegener (1991) *The Pattern of Urbanization in Western Europe 1960–1990*, Report for DG-XVI of the European Communities, Brussels: European Commission.

Lever, W.F. (1992a) 'Competition Between European Cities', unpublished manuscript, Department of Social and Economic Research, University of Glasgow.

Lever, W.F. (1992b) 'Local authority responses to economic change in West Central Scotland', *Urban Studies*, 29, pp.935–48.

Lever, W.F. (1993) 'Competition within the European urban system', *Urban Studies*, 30, pp.935–48.

Marlow, D. (1991) 'Eurocities: from urban networks to a European urban policy', *Ekistics*, 59, (352/353), pp.28–32.

Moriconi-Ebrard, F. (1992) *L'Urbanisation du Monde depuis 1950* [The urbanization of the world since 1950], Paris: Anthropos.

Pahl, R.E. (1969) 'Urban social theory and research', *Environment and Planning A*, 1, pp.145–53.

Pompili, T. (1992) 'The role of human capital in urban system structure and development: the case of Italy', *Urban Studies*, 29, pp.905–34.

Pred, A. (1976) 'The inter-urban transmission of growth in advanced economies: Empirical findings versus regional planning assumptions', *Regional Studies*, 10, pp.151–71.

Robert, B. and I. Bertrand (1993) *En France, des Réseaux de Villes* [Urban networks in France], Paris: DATAR.

Sallez, P. and P. Vérot (1991) 'Strategies for cities to face competition in the framework of European integration', *Ekistics*, 58, (350–351), pp.292–8.

Sallez, P. and P. Vérot (1993) 'Les villes en question' [The cities in question], in A. Sallez (ed.), *Les villes, lieux d'Europe*, Paris: DATAR/Editions de l'Aube, pp.147–78.

Sánchez, J-E. (1992) 'Societal responses to changes in the production system: The case of Barcelona metropolitan region', *Urban Studies*, 29, pp.949–64.

Soldatos, P. (1989a) 'The N.I.C.E. project', unpublished manuscript, University of Montreal.

Soldatos, P. (1989b) *Lyon, Ville Internationale à Géométrie Variable* [Lyon, international city of changing configuration], Lyon: Institut d'Etudes des Villes Internationales, IEVI.

Veltz, P. (1993) 'Logiques d'enterprises et territoires: les nouvelles règles du jeu' [The logic of businesses and territories: the new rules of the game], in M. Savy and P. Veltz (eds), *Les Nouveaux Espaces de l'Entreprise*, Paris: DATAR/Editions de l'Aube, pp.47–79.

Vickerman, R.W. (1992) *The Single European Market*, London: Harvester Wheatsheaf.

PART II
CITY VIGNETTES

3 Glasgow: the post-industrial city

William F. Lever

Introduction

The process of economic restructuring, involving shifts between sectors, new forms of capital and production processes, and new labour relationships is thought to be a relatively recent process related to the 'crisis of capitalism' and the emergence of post-Fordism and post-industrial society, yet the history of Glasgow shows several phases of restructuring and crises in the capitalist system. What is different about the current phase is, firstly, the speed of the change and, secondly, the nature of public-sector involvement in it, both as a facilitator and as an unwitting instigator.

Glasgow's current economic identity can be regarded as the city's fifth in a long historic succession. The city was a mediaeval foundation in the fifteenth century with a cathedral, a university and burghal status, with power shared between the church and the burghers. The opening up of the transatlantic trade to the West Indian and North American colonies offered Glasgow a second economic character, based upon merchant houses trading in cotton, sugar and tobacco, in the seventeenth century. Trade developed more rapidly after 1707, with the union of Scotland and England, giving the Scottish city freer access to the formerly English colonies. Capital for these merchant ventures came from landed Scottish families and venture trusts. The loss of the American colonies and the Napoleonic wars seriously damaged Glasgow's mercantile trade.

By the mid-nineteenth century, another major economic transformation of the city was occurring. The transatlantic trade had created a need for a shipbuilding industry. The discovery of coal and iron ore around Glasgow led to the development of an iron, and subsequently steel, shipbuilding industry. By 1903, 39 shipyards within the city, with a workforce in excess of 100 000, were launching over 400 vessels a year, representing a total of one-third of all British and one-fifth of total world production. It has been estimated that in 1900 almost one-half of the iron-built seagoing ships in the world had been built on Clydeside.

This industrial concentration was supported by a local steel-producing industry which also serviced the heavy-engineering sectors such as the manufacture of railway locomotives, mining equipment and armaments. The industrial workforce for this rapid growth was supplied by Ireland and the Highlands of Scotland. The rural crofting population of the Highlands was driven from the land by changes in landownership and agricultural practices. In Ireland, famine caused by the failure of the potato harvest drove rural populations abroad to seek work. The great industrialization of Glasgow and the surrounding towns was funded both by Scottish capital and by capital from southern England. English shipyards, for example, moved from the Thames to the Clyde.

Clydeside's rapid expansion in the last decades of the nineteenth century and its heavy-industrial base were the first problematic legacy for the twentieth-century process of deindustrialization. Demand for heavy capital products declined with the loss of colonial markets, with new competition in product markets such as ships and engineering plant, and with greater emphasis on consumer rather than capital goods. Thus Glasgow's manufacturing base was forced into deep recession in 1930, a depression only alleviated by war and postwar recovery, but one which was resumed in the 1960s. There followed an attempt, government policy-led, to attract industries producing consumer goods – especially those with assembly line plants – to Clydeside to produce cars, electrical domestic goods, office equipment and electronic equipment.

There were two concerns about this 'fourth wave' of production in the city. First, overdependence on a 'branch plant' economy, reliant on large segments of employment in assembly work for multinational companies, left the Glasgow manufacturing base vulnerable to remotely taken decisions to close marginal capacity. A classic example of such concerns is the car manufacturing plant, employing at its maximum some 12 000 workers west of Glasgow. It was brought initially by government incentives from the English Midlands, but became successively owned by US and Belgian companies before closure. The second concern was that an industrial labour force whose production techniques were craft-oriented and whose products were bespoke, one-off and without scale economies (for example, shipbuilding, power station production, coal mining equipment) was unlikely to adapt easily to assembly-line Fordist production techniques. By the 1970s, a number of these large assembly plants had closed, and Glasgow was in search of a fifth new economic paradigm.

Post-industrialism and deindustrialization can be seen in three contexts: positive, neutral and negative. At the national level, deindustrialization can be attributed to the trade specialization thesis, the maturity thesis and the failure thesis (Rowthorn, 1986). The same three theses can be applied in the case of the Glasgow conurbation.

Under the positive, trade specialization, thesis, the city has chosen to concentrate upon its strengths – business services, health care, personal services, education and property development – none of which are in the manufacturing sector. The belief is that tradable services have become the city's economic base, in a classic basic–non-basic theoretical way. Accordingly, policy has been framed to help these sectors. Under the neutral, maturity thesis, the city's economy has evolved away from resource-based (coal, iron ore, glass sands) production as resources were exhausted, turning towards manufacturing and subsequently services in a non-problematic way. The third, negative, failure thesis argues that the city's economy would have wished to retain a strong manufacturing base but has failed to do so because of its inability to compete in local and world markets. Its diversion into the service sector is thus seen as a compromise and policy is directed at minimizing the unfortunate consequences of this shift, such as labour-skills mismatches.

Throughout these processes, macro trends can be discerned. First, there has been a growing spatial scale in the context of the city's economy: from local to national to global in terms of its markets, sources and competition. Secondly, the sourcing of capital, and thus the locus of power, has become increasingly remote from the city, often with severe problems. Lastly, the relative public and private shares of investment in, and control of, the city have changed. From an intensely private-sector city in the nineteenth century, the city became dominated by the public sector during the twentieth century. The public sector could take hold through the nationalization of staple industries (coal, steel, ships and so on), through the continued high level of state intervention in private industry, through the growth of public-sector services (administration, health care, education) and through increasing state ownership of housing in a city where, by the end of the 1970s, 70 per cent of all housing was in municipal or state ownership. The reduction in funding for the state sector after 1979 has inevitably meant a further crisis of adaptation for the city. The problem is that the private sector has had to be induced to reinvest in the city after decades of neglect.

Functional and structural shifts

In terms of labour demand, three quite clear trends can be discerned in the Clydeside conurbation since 1950. First, there was a substantial decline in total employment between 1950 and 1987, followed by a slight rise. Secondly, there has been a major shift out of manufacturing and into services. Thirdly, there has been considerable suburbanization of employment; until recently, this left Glasgow with a decreasing share of the conurbation's total stock of jobs.

The data presented in Table 3.1 spell out the pattern of deindustrialization during the period 1952–89 for the conurbation as a whole. Total employment fell from 844 000 in 1952 to 615 000 in 1987, before rising to 629 000 in 1989; the largest absolute falls occurred in the periods 1978–81 and 1981–4. The development of manufacturing employment has been much more dramatic, declining from 424 000 jobs in 1952 to 135 000 jobs in 1989. Thus manufacturing employment fell from just over one-half of all employment in 1952 (50.2 per cent) to just over one-fifth of all employment (21.4 per cent) in 1989. Employment in services grew from 289 000 in 1952 to 431 000 in 1981, fell back to 414 000 by 1984 and then rose again to 438 000 in 1989. Services thus comprise a continuously rising share of total employment, increasing from 34.2 per cent in 1952 to 69.6 per cent in 1989. The balance of employment is made up of sectors such as primary industries, construction and public utilities.

The data in Table 3.1 show a classic case of deindustrialization, but, as Table 3.2 shows, the process falls into three distinct phases. Between 1952 and 1978, there was a slow loss of jobs overall, but, whilst manufacturing employment was declining, service sector employment was rising. There is, therefore, some possibility that workers who lost their jobs in manufacturing could find employment in the service sector. Or, if this is unlikely because of the

Table 3.1   Employment change, 1952–89: totals (thousands)

	1952	1961	1971	1981	1984	1987	1989
Total employment	844.2	840.2	789.5	685.5	630.3	615.2	629.3
Manufact employment	423.8	387.1	306.3	187.5	160.2	142.4	134.8
%	50.2	46.0	38.8	27.4	25.4	23.1	21.4
Service employment	288.7	315.3	406.7	431.2	413.6	417.7	437.9
%	34.2	37.5	51.5	62.9	65.6	67.9	69.6

skills mismatch, household incomes might have been sustained by other household members finding work in the expanding service sector. After 1978, however, the rate of total job loss accelerated to about five times what it was in 1961–78. The rate of job loss in manufacturing accelerated rapidly and the service sector also lost employment at a slow but increasing rate. There was much less potential, therefore, for households hit by the loss of employment in manufacturing to find alternative sources of income in other sectors. After 1984, the third phase began to resemble the first stage of the 1960s. The rate of job loss in manufacturing declined from the terrible levels of the late 1970s and early 1980s, and the service sector once again began to create net additional jobs.

Table 3.2   Annualized rates of employment change

	1952–61	1961–71	1971–78	1978–81	1981–84	1984–87	1987–89
Manufacturing	−1.01	−2.09	−2.29	−9.04	−4.85	−3.70	−2.67
Services	+1.02	+2.89	+0.87	−0.02	−0.13	+0.33	+2.42
Total	−0.11	−0.61	−0.50	−2.50	−2.68	−0.80	+1.20

These aggregate figures conceal a further set of changes, specifically changes in employment location within the conurbation. Table 3.3 shows how the inner city's (here defined as Glasgow) share of total employment in the conurbation declined from 66.8 per cent in 1952 to 55.1 per cent in 1984, before experiencing a slight but sustained rise thereafter. This shift has occurred as the result of a number of processes. The physical relocation of manufacturing plants from Glasgow to the periphery has been of only relatively minor importance. New and incoming plants have shown a marked preference for greenfield sites, especially in the two New Towns of East Kilbride and Cumbernauld. New businesses in both manufacturing and services preferred the outer ring locations to the inner city, in a ratio of 2:1. Not only have new businesses preferred to set up in the suburbs, but they have been bigger at their inception and have grown more quickly than those in the inner city. The (very modest) resurgence of the inner city since 1984 reflects several trends. These include the collapse of much outer-city manufacturing in the late 1980s and the emergence of new service sectors in the inner city from the mid-1980s onwards. These new sectors are for the most part business services and some personal services, such as health, education and

Table 3.3　Decentralization of employment

	1952	1961	1971	1978	1981	1984	1987	1989
Inner city*	66.8	64.3	58.6	57.2	58.2	55.1	55.7	55.7
Outer city	33.2	35.7	41.4	42.8	41.8	44.9	44.3	44.3

Note:　*Here defined as Glasgow.

leisure. At the same time, some services, such as retailing, showed strong decentralization tendencies.

These major shifts in the patterns of labour demand have created major problems in the form of unemployment. The idealized picture of a post-industrial city presented by writers (for example, Bell, 1973) in reality has profound redistributive effects which more often than not lead to increased social and economic polarization (Gappert, 1979; Lever, 1991). While the physical environment of Glasgow has undoubtedly improved with deindustrialization and the reduction of carbon emissions, some segments of the job market have suffered. Significant numbers of manufacturing workers made redundant by plant closures have had great difficulty in finding re-employment. Table 3.4 focuses on the worst periods for job losses, 1978–81 and 1981–84. During those periods, only a few sectors (out of a total of 45 sectors) were expanding, and these growth sectors failed to provide sufficient replacement jobs. Furthermore,

Table 3.4　Growth sectors, 1978–84 (absolute numbers)

1978–81		1981–84	
Sector	Empl. change	Sector	Empl. change
Oil and gas extraction	+525	Solid fuels	+13
Gas supply	+60	Mineral extraction	+288
Water supply	+271	Chemicals,plastics	+1 001
Aerospace equipment	+826	Office equipment	+490
Telecommunication	+278	Electronics	+2 267
Business services	+1 825	Instrument eng.	+115
Education	+2 672	Hotels & catering	+818
Medical	+7 678	Business services	+6 934
Other misc. services	+14 587	Other misc. services	+6 508
Total gains	+28 137	Total gains	+18 434
Total losses	−122 962	Total losses	−71 185
Balance	−94 825	Balance	−52 751

those additional jobs were in sectors unlikely to recruit from the male, manual unemployed labour pool. Job creation totalled about 46 000 jobs to offset about 200 000 jobs lost, or only about 20–25 per cent. The job gains were in sectors typical of sunrise industries – energy, synthetics, electronics, business services – which are unlikely to take redundant manual workers. Or the gains were in particular sectors – education, health care, and leisure and personal services – which took new workers such as school-leavers and housewives, who were not registered as unemployed.

More recent data, at a less sectorally disaggregated level in Table 3.5, confirm that this trend has continued. Data for 1987–9 show that job growth has remained concentrated in services. The data for 1989–93 are based on estimates for 1993 and are probably pessimistic. If one looks at relative change rather than predicted absolute change, once again services undoubtedly do better than manufacturing in employment terms.

Table 3.5   Employment change, 1987–9 and 1989–93

Sector	1987–89[a]	1989–93[b]
Agriculture, forestry, fish	+6.7	–11.7
Energy, water	–15.9	–21.4
Chemicals, metal mfr.	–8.8	–29.8
Engineering, vehicles	–0.3	–17.1
Food, clothing, misc. mfr.	–5.3	–17.0
Construction	+4.2	–7.4
Distribution, hotels	+10.9	–6.5
Transport, communications	+4.5	–4.4
Banking, business services	+11.1	–8.6
Health, education, administration	+8.5	+0.6
Total	+5.3	–7.1

Notes:
[a] Strathclyde Region.
[b] Estimates from Cambridge Econometrics for 1993.

As redundant workers from the shrinking manufacturing sector fail to find re-employment, the unemployment rate rises. Table 3.6 compares male unemployment within the conurbation with that of Great Britain as a whole. Scotland has always been (until very recently) one of Britain's most depressed regions, and Clydeside

Table 3.6   Male unemployment, 1971–93 (per cent)

Area	1971	1981	1984	1988	1990	1993
Glasgow	12.9	23.5	26.7	25.9	20.5	22.0
Suburbs	3.6	7.3	8.9	8.1	5.5	8.0
New towns	6.1	12.6	13.9	12.2	7.9	10.0
Old industrial towns	8.9	18.0	19.5	17.3	12.8	16.6
Total conurbation	10.3	18.8	20.9	19.4	14.8	17.3
UK	4.6	9.6	12.7	11.4	8.9	14.4
Conurbation total, 000s	224	195	165	170	166	120

is one of the most depressed areas within Scotland. Thus, through-out the 1970s and early 1980s, Clydeside's male unemployment rate was about twice the national average. From the mid-1980s onwards, Clydeside's rate was about 70 per cent above the na-tional rate. The recession of the 1990s, however, has adversely affected the south and Midlands of Britain more severely than Scotland and the north. Thus, in early 1993, Scotland's unemploy-ment rate was below the British average, and the male unemploy-ment rate in the Clydeside conurbation was only 20 per cent above the British average.

Relating unemployment to deindustrialization creates a picture of the typical unemployed Clydeside worker as a male, middle-aged semi- or unskilled manual worker released by an old heavy industry. Analysis of data on the last occupation held by the un-employed indicates that this stereotype is not always accurate. Of the 140 000 registered unemployed males and females in the con-urbation when unemployment reached its peak in 1982, the 'un-classified' were the largest single group (32 000) primarily because they were school-leavers and had never had a job. After these, in descending order, were former workers in construction (21 000), distributive trades (15 000), personal services (13 000) and public administration (8000) and only then mechanical engineering (6000), food and drink (5000) and vehicles (4000); metal workers contributed 5400 to the total of the unemployed. This surprising finding reflects the length of the period of deindustrialization. Heavy industrial workers had either been retired or been laid off over a long period, with perhaps one or more intervening periods of work outside manufacturing before the 1982 count. And this finding also reflects the volatility of employment in many of the new sectors. More recent data for 1992 (Table 3.7) indicate that in the relatively more prosperous period of the early 1990s, with the accompanying growth of service-sector employment, a more normal distribution of occupation by previous employment has been restored. Unskilled manual workers made up 34.5 per cent of the unemployed, while skilled (craft) manual and machine operators make up a further 28.8 per cent. The growth of post-school training and work experience programmes has reduced quite significantly the proportion of the unemployed who lack any work experience. Table 3.7 also indicates that the long-term unemployed (defined as those out of work for more than one year) are even more concentrated amongst unskilled manual workers. The conurbation's unemployed were also, by comparison with national figures, concentrated in the younger age groups (31.4 per cent below 25, and 30.2 per cent between 25 and 34) and in the unqualified group.

Table 3.7   Last occupation of unemployed, 1992

	All unemp. (%)	Long-term
Managers/administrators	3.0	1.9
Professions	2.3	1.3
Technical	3.6	2.3
Clerical/secretarial	9.3	6.8
Crafts, related jobs	18.4	17.2
Personal and protective services	8.1	6.9
Sales	6.8	5.4
Plant and machine operators	10.4	10.8
Unskilled	34.5	43.4
No work experience	3.7	4.0

The structure of the city

Like most conurbations, the west of Scotland conurbation can be defined as having a core, namely the city of Glasgow, and a periphery. This latter divides into a rather heterogeneous outer ring of contiguous settlements comprising two new towns, East Kilbride and Cumbernauld; several old industrial towns, including Clydebank (shipbuilding), Motherwell (steel), Airdrie and Coatbridge (metal working), Paisley (textiles) and Hamilton (light engineering); and a number of largely residential middle-class suburbs.

Beyond this are the exurbs, freestanding towns and villages and rural areas linked to the conurbation proper by commuting and income flows.

The population of the region as a whole has declined from 2.58 million in 1961 to 2.22 million in 1991. Within this total, however, there have been major changes, as Table 3.8 shows. The most fundamental of these changes is the decline of the central core city of Glasgow, from 1.14m inhabitants in 1961 to 654 500 in 1991, with particularly sharp falls in the 1970s. About 40 per cent of this loss has been accommodated in the outer ring – a classic case of suburbanization – and only a very small proportion in the exurban zone. The balance (about 53 per cent) left the region either for other parts of Scotland or, much more commonly, for England and abroad.

Table 3.8   Population distribution within the conurbation (thousands and per cent)

Area	1961	1971	1981	1991
Glasgow	1 140.0	982.3	765.9	654.5
%	(44.1)	(38.1)	(31.5)	(29.5)
Outer ring	792.2	920.3	952.5	906.8
%	(30.6)	(35.7)	(39.6)	(40.9)
Exurban	651.7	672.9	686.1	656.9
%	(25.2)	(26.1)	(28.5)	(29.6)
Region	2 583.9	2 575.5	2 404.5	2 218.2

The substantial growth of the outer ring prior to the mid-1980s can be explained in several ways. By the 1950s, Glasgow had the worst housing stock of any major city in western Europe. A number of slum-clearance programmes began in the 1950s. But with the very high residential densities encountered in the core city, these were possible only with the massive outward movement of population. Much of the mobility was through formal 'overspill' agreements and the inception of a New Towns programme (Smith and Farmer, 1985). This somewhat ad hoc approach was replaced in 1960 by an integrated programme of renewal for the city of Glasgow. According to this plan, 40 per cent of the core city's population would be rehoused but not all of it within the city's administrative limits, despite the adoption of a major programme of high-rise residential building in the public sector. Table 3.9 shows how the two new towns grew by 85 000 people between 1961 and 1981, while other families moved from Glasgow to more distant Scottish new towns at Livingston, Irvine and Glenrothes. Thus suburbanization and even exurbanization in the west of Scotland were in large part municipal, public sector-driven processes.

Table 3.9   Composition of the outer ring population (thousands)

Type of area	1961	1971	1981	1991
Suburban residential	128.8	163.2	180.2	181.5
New town	59.5	117.8	144.9	142.4
Old industrial town	603.8	637.3	627.4	582.9

This suburbanization could not have happened without some accompanying movement of employment opportunities (Champion, 1989, pp.99–100). The White Paper on Central Scotland (Scottish Development Department, 1963) announced a regional development strategy based upon 'growth poles' which were very largely suburb-, exurb- or new town-based (Wannop and Smith, 1985). At the same time, the new towns were proving to be the major magnets for new employment within the west of Scotland. They captured some 35 000 jobs which might otherwise have been attracted to Glasgow's inner areas (Henderson, 1974, 1980) and attracted some jobs directly from Glasgow.

The scale of the redevelopment programme in Glasgow, together with the implementation of a major urban motorway programme, caused many jobs to leave the city. In the early years of this process, displaced industry often found alternative locations within the city core. But as the stock of old, cheap, industrial premises was systematically eroded by redevelopment, more and more firms were driven to find safe locations in the new towns and in exurban locations away from Glasgow (Cameron and Clark, 1966; McKean, 1975).

Thus the public sector was pursuing policies which had the effect of driving investment in residential and industrial development out of the city. Meanwhile, the market in private housing was also strongly directed towards the suburbs and beyond. So acute were Glasgow's housing problems in the 1960s that all vacant land, both greenfield and cleared, which was zoned for housing was allocated to public-sector housing. Before 1980, fewer than 100 dwellings per year were being created by the private sector (mostly through the subdivision of older houses) throughout the whole city. Since 1980, the figure has never fallen below 1000 and it is now substantially above that. The private sector was therefore driven to find sites outside the city of Glasgow throughout the 1960s and 1970s. Most of the land for new private-sector house building was provided by three suburban areas: Bearsden and Milngavie, Eastwood and Strathkelvin – which, as planning authorities, were separate from Glasgow.

Glasgow and the west of Scotland have historically been areas of high levels of public-sector house ownership. The regional level is about 65 per cent; in some towns, such as Clydebank, it has been as much as 80 per cent. The period of the 1970s was one of rising real incomes. Accordingly, an increasing proportion of households in west-central Scotland were aspiring to home ownership, particularly of modern detached and semi-detached houses. Rising car ownership, admittedly from levels which were low relative to UK averages, permitted these households to look to more distant locations. The environment of Glasgow remained poor. The extensive renewal programmes were a disincentive to the owner-occupied sector (both builders and buyers) for a considerable period. At the same time, the withdrawal of subsidies to private schools in the city centre and the improvement of comprehensive schools in the areas of better housing on the periphery fuelled further residential decentralization (Wannop, 1986, p.96). The consequence was that there was substantial suburban owner–occupier growth northwest, north and south of Glasgow. The 'old town' section of the outer ring attracted some of this new suburban owner-occupied growth but this was offset by declines in the central areas of these older towns.

The most recent period, since the mid-1980s, has seen a change in some of these patterns. Despite the overall decline of the population of the core city of Glasgow, the true city centre has seen a substantial revival of its population. Young childless couples and single adults have been moving back to the city centre, into high-value, prestigious developments. This trend has led to some reurbanization. A succession of deals and major land-reclamation exercises have brought private-sector developers back to the inner areas of Glasgow (Lever, 1993). Much of Glasgow's population loss, therefore, is now attributable to the four very large public-sector housing estates at the four corners of Glasgow city. Table 3.9 also indicates a slight fall in the population of the two new towns in 1981–91. This reflects the government's changed attitudes to the British New Towns programme, as well as the removal of financial assistance and special status from the new towns after 1987.

These population and housing changes within the conurbation are clearly reflected in labour market conditions. Thus, in 1993, the male unemployment rate for the conurbation as a whole was 17.3 per cent (UK 14.4 per cent). The separate figures for Glasgow (22.0 per cent), the old industrial towns (16.6 per cent), the new towns (10.0 per cent) and the middle-class suburbs (8.0 per cent) show these four areas to be quite separate and different labour inlets. The data in Table 3.6 show that this ratio of 130:90:60:40 (conurbation rate = 100) is a phenomenon of long standing.

These spatial differences are partly explained by the suburban shift in employment, particularly the preference of new enterprises for the new towns, the suburbs and the exurban areas. At the same time, they are explained partly by changes in commuting patterns. In an analysis of the distribution of male unemployment within the city, McGregor and Mather (1986) point to the remarkable shifts which occurred during the 1970s and early 1980s. The map of unemployment in 1971 shows the anticipated peaks in the inner city in the city's East End, in Maryhill and in Govan, where two-thirds of the zones of highest unemployment were to be found. By the mid-1980s, this inner-city concentration was much reduced. Over half the worst zones were concentrated in the city's peripheral social housing estates. It is unclear whether these residents became unemployed first and were transferred to social housing through housing allocation policies which reflected their deteriorating incomes. Alternatively, they may have been relocated first as a consequence of slum clearance in the inner city and then were consequently more likely to lose their employment. More recently, employment in the city centre has increased in association with office development, leisure activities and producer services, which has helped inner-city residents to find work. Although many of these activities are low-skill, poorly paid and at antisocial hours, they have provided employment which often only inner-city residents can fill because of the structure and pricing of public transport within the city (Lever, 1993).

Table 3.10 indicates how labour market conditions are linked to housing market processes. Of the eight worst areas for male unemployment, five (Easterhouse, Queenslie, Drumry, Milton and Nitshill) are large areas of social housing on the outskirts of Glasgow, while three (Cowlairs, Carntyne and Calton) are more typical inner-city problem areas. The list of the best areas, with rates below 10 per cent in early 1993, mainly comprises areas of

Table 3.10   *Local male unemployment rates, 1993*

Worst area	Rate	Best area	Rate
Cowlairs	39.0	Bearsden	5.8
Carntyne	34.9	Eastwood North	6.5
Calton-Centre	32.6	Eastwood South	6.7
Easterhouse	32.4	Milngavie	7.9
Queenslie	30.0	Bishopbriggs	9.4
Drumry	29.9	Kelvinside	9.8
Milton	26.3		
Nitshill	25.8		

speculatively built owner-occupied housing on the conurbation periphery. The exception is Kelvinside, which is a unique older middle-class enclave close to the centre of Glasgow.

The conurbation as a whole is an example of acute social polarization. Those with secure incomes have been able to buy themselves pleasant environments and good local services. They have access to a political locale within small towns and local authorities where there is considerable scope for individuals to exercise significant political power and choice. These are places with low taxes and good employment opportunities. The poorer households, however, are trapped either in the inner city of Glasgow or in the inner areas of the older industrial towns. When these households are assigned homes outside these areas through the process of urban renewal, these are typically the equally unpopular high-rise flats or peripheral housing estates which are poorly serviced, highly taxed and in areas with few employment opportunities.

The industrial development of Glasgow in the nineteenth century had been very dense, with middle-class and working-class communities living in close proximity. This offered considerable scope for 'trickle down', by which the income of the middle classes might provide employment for the working class. Thus geographically and socially middle-class Kelvinside and Hyndland were close to working-class Partick and Maryhill (Lever, 1989). At the same time, individual communities such as Parkhead, Whiteinch or Govan had evolved around a single industry or a single employer in steel or shipbuilding. Such a context generated a single destiny for the middle class and working class alike. With the processes of deindustrialization and disurbanization, these links have been broken. Much greater social polarization has developed, while restructuring in the labour market has exacerbated the divisions between the classes.

Urban policy

The history of recent urban policy in Glasgow can be seen as having three strands. First, there is urban economic policy, concerned with reducing unemployment and increasing employment, income and investment. Secondly, there is urban environmental policy, which in Glasgow's case is overwhelmingly concerned with housing and urban transport. Thirdly, there is urban social policy, which deals with low income, with community failure and with health and welfare.

Urban economic policy over time has moved from being the preserve solely of central government departments, mainly the Department of Trade and Industry, to the preserve of local government, regional development agencies and public–private partnerships. Environmental policies have largely been implemented by local government, whose programmes have in some cases worked against programmes of economic growth. This has occurred where deliberations over the routes of urban motorways have created corridors of uncertainty through the urban structure in which investment in new or expanding industry has been problematic in consequence. Lastly, social policy has largely been a mixture of national social welfare payment systems and area-based programmes of selective or enhanced assistance in education, community capacity building or health care.

The early phase of deindustrialization was characterized by the failure of the old stock of indigenously owned companies producing capital goods such as ships (Lever, 1988). The first policy response in the 1960s and 1970s was to use regional development grants to attract replacement manufacturing industry to the conurbation. Such policies were likely only to be successful when the national economy was expanding and there was mobile investment and employment available for transfer. Some 65 000 jobs were brought to the conurbation by the use of regional assistance between 1945 and 1970 (Henderson, 1980), but it was quickly apparent that these inward-investing companies were rarely interested in the inner city of Glasgow, where the unemployment was worst. They much preferred greenfield sites, and particularly the new towns. A study in the late 1970s and early 1980s confirmed this tendency. Of the £30m of Regional Development Grant allocated in 1979–83, almost 70 per cent was awarded to the outer ring of the conurbation. That area had only 43 per cent of the manufacturing labour force and less than 40 per cent of the registered unemployed. The paradox was easily explained: development grants were tied to growth, and growth was occurring in the outer areas of the conurbation, and these were the areas of least (relative) need.

By the 1980s, the programme to attract inward investment was passed to the Scottish Development Agency (SDA): the 'Locate in Scotland' arm. The SDA had been set up in 1976 with the objective (amongst others) of revitalizing the Scottish economy. Locate in Scotland, however, had no specific remit to help Glasgow. It was clear that, in competing for foreign investment against other western European countries, especially where European Union legislation limits the amount of financial assistance which may be given, environmental and labour market factors are likely to be of greatest importance. In this context, the agency found some difficulty in advancing the claims of Glasgow and the older parts of the outer ring. Table 3.11 shows the distribution of manufacturing employment in 1987 attributable to foreign investment. The region of Strathclyde as a whole, with about half of Scotland's population and employment, has attracted 43 per cent of the foreign-owned employment. However, within the Strathclyde total, the core city of Glasgow, with 33 per cent of Strathclyde's population and 40 per cent of its employment, has drawn only 5.5 per cent of the foreign-owned jobs. In comparison, the new towns in the region and the exurban areas have drawn a disproportionately large share of foreign-owned employment. Environmental quality has played a part in these locational choices, but incoming companies have also been suspicious of Scottish industrial relations. They have tended to choose locations with no long history of disputes and strikes (MacInnes, 1987) or to find locations such as freestanding towns, where there are few alternative sources of employment, thus assuring themselves of a relatively compliant workforce (Lever, 1984).

Even where agencies such as Locate in Scotland have been successful in attracting inward investment in manufacturing, this strategy is not without problems. Many branch plants were marginal elements of capacity. They were prone to closure in downturns in the economy or when global corporate restructuring relocated capacity to new locations in southern Europe or in the Newly Industrializing Countries (Hood and Young, 1982). There was a clear point of transition in the role of exogenously owned firms in the conurbation's economy at the end of the 1970s. In 1975–8, their

Table 3.11   Foreign-owned companies, 1987

Area	North American No.	North American Employment	European and other No.	European and other Employment	Totals No.	Totals Employment
Strathclyde	76	22 698	51	4 902	127	27 600
Rest of Scotland	123	26 793	61	9 533	184	36 326
Glasgow	9	1 279	8	242	17	1 521
New Towns	23	4 263	18	779	41	5 042
Old towns	21	6 857	18	2 963	39	9 793
Exurban	23	10 299	7	945	30	11 244

aggregate employment was still rising and doing better than local capital, but in 1978–81 their employment fell sharply and did much worse than local capital. Townsend and Peck (1987) have drawn attention to the extent to which foreign-owned job losses in Great Britain have been concentrated in west-central Scotland. In the period 1976–81, they identified 19 foreign corporations whose British operations had contracted by more than 1400 jobs. Of these, eight were in west-central Scotland. Those eight covered a wide range of sectors, including cars, tractors, sewing machines, tyres, domestic appliances, synthetic fibres and oil rigs.

While the economy of Glasgow has been buoyed up by a flow of jobs from inward-investing manufacturing firms, the associated problems have led to economic policies moving in other directions. First amongst these has been the realization that the rate of locally owned firm formation should be enhanced. In that sector, at least, the city's economic destiny would not be so remotely controlled. Glasgow is notorious for its low rate of new firm formation. Mason (1987) indicated that new firm formation rates in 1980–83 were 16 per cent below the British average. Cross (1981) showed that, during the 1970s, Scottish rates were 30 per cent below the best British regional rates and Glasgow's rates were less than 40 per cent of those of Scotland. It has been suggested (Checkland, 1976; Gould and Keeble, 1984) that, in a regional economy dominated by very large steel, shipbuilding, metalworking and engineering plants, the gap between capital and labour is so great that it hampers entrepreneurialism. Few workers are able to envisage themselves as owner–managers. As most new entrepreneurs create businesses in sectors with which they are familiar, and the industrial staples of the west of Scotland have high entry costs, fewer new firms will result.

In consequence, assistance towards new firm formation has had to be multifaceted: advice, finance, premises and labour-training

have all played a part. Assistance to small firms offers an interesting perspective on the role of government in the west of Scotland.
The area, at both levels of local government (district and region),
is overwhelmingly in the control of Labour (socialist) administrations. Such councils have, historically, had difficulty in working
with the private sector and specifically in offering financial help
to what it has regarded as speculative capitalist enterprises. It was
not the role of local authorities, they felt, to use tax revenues to
underwrite or enhance private profit. It was also true that local
authorities whose membership was drawn from workers rather
than managers and white-collar employees felt that they were not
well qualified to offer advice to private enterprise. Thus a study of
support for small businesses in the 1980s (Moore and Booth, 1986)
by the local authorities indicated that about 75 per cent of expenditure was allocated to 'hardware' in the form of premises,
land assembly, site preparation and engineering works. Only 25
per cent was allocated to 'software' in the form of advice, financial
assistance and labour training. The logic behind this distribution
is that, if the assisted enterprise fails, monies devoted to software
are lost with it. In contrast, investment in physical infrastructure
is retrievable and is available to replacement enterprises.

The bulk of assistance to small firms and new firms in Glasgow
has therefore come from the private sector or public–private ventures. The most wide-ranging system of financial assistance and
advice has come from the Small Business Division of the former
Scottish Development Agency. Assistance now supports some 3000
jobs in the west of Scotland conurbation at relatively low cost per
job. There are no geographical restrictions on the location of new
enterprises, but they may gain more help if located in the district
of one of the area-based programmes such as the eastern inner
area of Glasgow, the shipbuilding town of Clydebank, the steel
town of Motherwell, and the metal working town of Coatbridge.
Similarly, there are no specific targets for new firm formation in
the Small Business Division programme. However, it is recognized that certain types of new small business have particular
problems and these may have specific programmes of assistance.
Thus particularly risky ventures unlikely to attract other, more
conservative forms of investment may attract help from venture
capital funds such as Clydebank VCF, which is geographically
limited to the depressed shipbuilding town. The youth unemployed are specific targets of an Enterprise Fund for Youth, which
makes unsecured loans to people under 25 years of age who would
otherwise not attract loan finance. Unemployed former steelwork-
ers are assisted in setting up in business in the Clyde workshops.

Because each of these programmes aims at specifically difficult segments of the new firm creation process, their costs per job provided are significantly above the non-specific assistance of the Small Business Division.

The decline of the manufacturing sector generally has led to a switch in policy. The focus has turned to assistance to the service sector, particularly to business services and mobile service investment. In some cases, previous policies were equally applicable to manufacturing and services – help with new firm formation, for example. The Enterprise Fund for Youth provided assistance to 75 businesses created in 1984–7. Of these start-up firms, 37 per cent were in business services, 30 per cent were in personal services, 25 per cent were in retailing and only 8 per cent were in manufacturing. The figure for businesses helped by the SDA's Small Business Division (40 per cent in services) was somewhat lower.

A more radical approach to the service sector within the conurbation was taken by Glasgow Action, a public–private partnership set up by the Scottish Development Agency. By actively marketing the city, it was hoped to attract headquarter offices and public-sector agencies, to boost visitor revenue and to develop specialist exportable services. Between its inception in 1985 and 1992, some 20 000 jobs were created in connection with this initiative. It has not proved easy to attract corporate, private-sector office jobs to the city, and major successes such as the location of BP's European oil exploration offices have been undermined by subsequent corporate restructuring. As ever, Glasgow remains a city of the public sector. There has been a great deal more success in attracting public-sector bodies to the city (Ministry of Defence, Passport Office, Student Loans, Census of Population Office and so on).

Within Scotland, Edinburgh appears to have an inbuilt advantage, as the seat of government and the location of the headquarters of the Scottish banks. Yet Glasgow has achieved modest success in attracting the financial services sector. These services include insurance, commodity and stockbroking, and mortgaging. Most of these enterprises offer white-collar managerial or clerical jobs, yet there has been a concomitant rise in the demand for low-skilled manual workers such as cleaners, security guards, messengers and so on, which has had a beneficial impact on the inner-city labour market. The personal leisure sector has boomed within the city, partly as a consequence of the change in the city's image and partly as a result of one-off entertainment events such as the International Garden Festival (1988) and the European City of Culture designation (1990). In consequence, there has been a major increase in the number of hotels in the city. These, plus the net increase in related facilities (restaurants, theatres and so on), have created some 15 000 additional jobs, although many are part-time and poorly paid. Again, the major impact of these additional jobs has been on the inner-city labour market.

Much of the explanation of this growth in high-level services is to be found in the city's decision to market the city. An effort was made to change its image, which hitherto had been one of urban dereliction, crime and poor living standards. The use of public relations consultants, the role of Glasgow Action and more recently Glasgow Development Agency, and competitions for 'hallmark' events have effectively raised the profile of the city within the competition of European cities (Paddison, 1993). Environmental improvement and the designation of areas such as 'the Merchant City' and the trend towards reurbanization have brought a great deal of private capital back to the city. By 1991, major construction projects to the value of £3.5bn were under way in the city, revitalizing the retail, office and hotel sectors. The major boosts to the city's economy from the International Garden Festival and its designation as European City of Culture created a large number of short-term jobs. But these events created major permanent physical assets for the city's subsequent use, such as an international concert hall, several hotels and a major land-reclamation site on old docklands close to the city centre. There was some argument that events such as Glasgow's period as European City of Culture in 1990 were elitist and merely represented the use of working-class taxpayers' money to subsidize the preferences of affluent middle-class suburbanites (Boyle and Hughes, 1991). These statements have generally been countered by studies of the direct employment effects and the longer-term effects of upgrading the city's image and enhancing the Glasgow Development Agency's claim that Glasgow is 'A Great European City' (GDA, 1992; Myerscough, 1988, 1991).

Urban policy in Glasgow has thus moved from central government, manufacturing-led incentives for employment to more partnership-led initiatives attracting services and raising the image of the city. Were the mechanics of filtering and 'trickle down' perfect, this alone might be sufficient. There would then be an explicit assumption that any income or investment brought to the city would – through the direct, indirect and induced multipliers and through redistributive fiscal effects – generate, in turn, income and employment for the least advantaged in the labour market. Experience suggests, however, that there are considerable numbers of people of working age who are unlikely to be drawn into the labour force in this formal way. In consequence, a number of programmes have been developed, at the individual or community level, to provide employment for which no market-led process would have generated a demand. In many cases, these jobs are engaged in the provision of non-market services. They may thus not only provide employment but enhance the quality of life for many of the city's more deprived population. If the market-led programmes were difficult for local authorities to comprehend or assist, these social programmes lie very firmly in the bailiwick of the local authorities.

There are a number of programmes aimed at individuals, to train them or to give them work experience after lengthy periods of unemployment. For instance, Workwise and Heatwise have taken some 3000 workers into programmes as diverse as insulating houses, retailing and personal leisure services, drawing them from multiply deprived areas of social housing and focusing on the young. On leaving the programme, between a half and two-thirds find employment, but the cost per job procured is very high. The regional council uses its own resources and those of the EU's Social Fund to subsidize unemployed workers into employment. They provide wage subsidies which cover between 40 and 60 per cent of wage costs for up to one year. Some 15 000 workers were thus subsidized between 1982 and 1987. At the same time, the Training and Employment Grants Scheme, also with Social Fund financing, provided recruitment and training subsidies covering up to 66 per cent of costs to employers of unemployed youth and the long-term unemployed, of whom some 4000 benefited.

In all these cases, the deliberate provision of assistance to the most difficult cases raises the cost of these programmes. The cost per job, after allowing for deadweight (that is, counting only net effects and excluding what would have happened even in the absence of such a policy) and displacement, is around £15 000 per head. This contrasts sharply with the creation of jobs in the formal economy, where costs are perhaps one-third of this amount. It is obviously a clear political choice to meet the much higher costs of these programmes on the grounds that they are aimed at the most disadvantaged individuals who would be extremely unlikely to be drawn into the formal workforce otherwise.

A similar choice is encountered at the community level, where local authorities focus additional expenditure on areas of multiple deprivation. In some cases, these provisions are part of national programmes, such as additional finance for Educational Priority Areas. In other cases, however, local authorities have designated areas to receive additional help to enhance community capacity.

Initially, many of these were focused in the inner city but, as the map of the geography of multiple deprivation has been redrawn, the focus of such interventions has been drawn to the peripheral estates of social housing. Local authorities have supported Community Businesses, of which there are about 25 in the conurbation with about 1200 jobs. These are community-owned enterprises, the majority of which provide non-market services (for example house improvement had environmental projects). Interestingly, their social and economic objectives may come into conflict. On the one hand, they seek to maximize employment, while, on the other, they must retain some budgetary control. On the social housing estates, a wide range of community enterprise activity exists. But retailing, the provision of industrial property in the form of managed workspaces and miscellaneous services (painting, security, cleaning, banking, and housing management) make up the greater part (McArthur and McGregor 1989). Within the conurbation, it is difficult to estimate the number of jobs thus provided, as many are part-time and in many cases there is a substantial voluntarist element. The concern here is more about community capacity enhancement than jobs and cost per job.

Conclusion

In some respects, Glasgow and the west-central Scotland conurbation may be regarded as a laboratory for urban policy. On the European scale, the city has more problems, environmental and economic, than most. The level of public-sector intervention is amongst the highest in western Europe. By the late 1980s, the 'success' of Glasgow was frequently quoted in the fora where urban development programmes were debated and assessed. It is true that, without such massive intervention, unemployment rates would be higher and the environment poorer. But can a city be considered a success when its male unemployment rate was over 17 per cent (in early 1993), even over 30 per cent in some districts? Is it fair to speak of a success story when these rates have been reduced mainly by major outmigration? The problem lies in establishing the counterfactual: what would the city have been like without such intervention? The answer is that it would have been significantly worse. Policy since the late 1970s has probably brought to the city some 50–60 000 jobs, or 10 per cent of the current total. In addition, the environment is immeasurably improved. The city's image, a nightmare some 20 years ago, has been completely turned around. It is true that this improvement has not touched everyone equally: by the early 1990s, an underclass had emerged which appears unlikely to be eradicated by the end of the millennium. Like much of Thatcherite and post-Thatcherite Britain, Glasgow is a city of growing social and economic polarities. The mechanisms for the transmission of income and quality of life from the 'haves' to the 'have-nots' are as yet inadequately developed.

References

Bell, D. (1973) *The Coming of Post-industrial Society*, New York: Basic Books.

Boyle, M. and G. Hughes (1991) 'The politics of representation of "the real": discourses from the Left on Glasgow's role as European City of Culture, 1990', *Area* 23, pp.217–28.

Cameron, G.C. and B.D. Clark (1966) *Industrial Movement and the Regional Problem*, Social and Economic Studies, Occasional Papers 5, Edinburgh: Oliver and Boyd.

Champion, A.G. (1989) 'United Kingdom: population deconcentration as a cyclic phenomenon', in A.G. Champion (ed.), *Counterurbanisation: the Changing Pace and Nature of Population Deconcentration*, London: Arnold, pp.83–102.

Checkland, S. (1976) *The Upas Tree: Glasgow 1875-1975*, Glasgow: University of Glasgow Press.

Cross, M. (1981) *New Firm Formation and Regional Development*, Aldershot: Gower.

Gappert, G. (1979) *Post Affluent America*, New York: Franklin Watts.

Glasgow Development Agency (1992) *Glasgow: a Great European City*, Glasgow: GDA.

Gould, A. and D. Keeble (1984) 'New firms and rural industrialisation in East Anglia', *Regional Studies*, **18**, pp.189–201.

Henderson, R.I. (1974) 'Industrial Overspill from Glasgow, 1958–65', *Urban Studies*, **11**, pp.61–79.

Henderson, R.I. (1980) 'The location of immigrant industry within a UK Assisted Area: the Scottish experience', *Progress in Planning*, **14**, pp.137–50.

Hood, N. and S. Young (1982) *Multinationals in Retreat: the Scottish Experience*, Edinburgh: Edinburgh Press.

Lever, W.F. (1984) 'Industrial change and urban size: a risk theory approach', in B.M. Barr and N.M. Waters (eds), *Regional Diversification and Structural Change*, Vancouver: Tantalus, pp.153–67.

Lever, W.F. (1988) 'Stagnation and decline: the postwar shipbuilding industry in Clydebank', in J. Hood (ed.), *The History of Clydebank*, Carnforth: Parthenon.

Lever, W.F. (1989) 'Topographic constraints on the industrial development of the west central Scotland conurbation', paper presented to the International Conference on Hillside Cities, UNCRD; Nagasaki.

Lever, W.F. (1991) 'Deindustrialisation and the reality of the post-industrial city', *Urban Studies*, **28**, pp.983–99.

Lever, W.F. (1993) 'Reurbanisation – the policy implications', *Urban Studies*, **30**, pp.267–84.

McArthur, A. and A. McGregor (1989) 'Community economic initiatives in public sector housing estates', in A. McArthur (ed.), *Community Economic Initiatives*, Glasgow: University of Glasgow.

McGregor, A. and F. Mather (1986) 'Developments in Glasgow's labour market', in W.F. Lever and C. Moore (eds), *The City in Transition: Policies and Agencies for the Economic Regeneration of Clydeside*, Oxford: Oxford University Press, pp.22–43.

MacInnes, J. (1987) *Economic Restructuring relevant to Industrial Relations in Scotland*,

Centre for Urban and Regional Research, Discussion Paper 26, Glasgow: University of Glasgow.

McKean, R. (1975) *The Impact of Comprehensive Area Development Policies on Industry in Glasgow*, Urban and Regional Discussion Papers 15, Glasgow: University of Glasgow.

Mason, C.M. (1987) 'The small firm sector', in W.F. Lever (ed.), *Industrial Change in the United Kingdom*, Harlow: Longman, pp.125–48.

Moore, C. and S. Booth (1986) 'The pragmatic approach: local political models of regeneration', in W.F. Lever and C. Moore (eds), *The City in Transition: Policies and Agencies for the Economic Regeneration of Clydeside*, Oxford: Oxford University Press, pp.92–106.

Myerscough, J. (1988) *Economic Importance of the Arts in Glasgow*, London: Policy Study Institute.

Myerscough, J. (1991) *Monitoring Glasgow 1990*, report for Glasgow City Council, Strathclyde Regional Council and Scottish Enterprise, Glasgow: City Council.

Paddison, R. (1993) 'City marketing, image reconstruction and urban regeneration', *Urban Studies*, **30**, pp.339–50.

Rowthorn, B. (1986) 'De-industrialisation in Britain', in R. Martin and B. Rowthorn (eds), *The Geography of De-industrialisation*, London: Macmillan, pp.1–30.

Scottish Development Department (1963) *Central Scotland: A Programme for Development and Growth*, Cmnd 2188, Edinburgh: HMSO.

Smith, R. and E. Farmer (1985) 'Housing, Population and Decentralisation', in R. Smith and U. Wannop (eds), *Strategic Planning in Action: the Impact of the Clyde Valley Regional Plan, 1946–82*, Aldershot: Gower, pp.41–72.

Townsend, A. and F. Peck (1987) 'Spatial redeployment through plant closure and redundancy by foreign countries in the United Kingdom', in H. Muegge and W.B. Stohr (eds), *International Economic Restructuring and the Regional Community*, Aldershot: Avebury, pp.202–17.

Wannop, U. (1986) 'Glasgow/Clydeside: a century of metropolitan evolution', in G. Gordon (ed.), *Regional Cities in the U.K., 1890–1980*, London: Harper & Row, pp.83–98.

Wannop, U. and R. Smith (1985) 'Robustness in regional planning', in R. Smith and U. Wannop (eds), *Strategic Planning in Action: the Impact of the Clyde Valley Regional Plan, 1946–82*, Aldershot: Gower, pp.210–41.

4 Paris: city of opposites

Guy Burgel

The economic and social evolution of the Ile-de-France (the Seine river basin around Paris – Figure 4.1) can only be understood against the background of the deep-seated thrust of urban development in the world's greatest metropolitan areas. At the same time, the policies that propel it, accompany it or mitigate its effects must be taken into account. The policy intentions are described in public urban planning documents and are reflected in public interventions, yet it would be illusory to deny the autonomy, and thus the influence, of economic and demographic actors – local businesses and households. It would be equally naive to abandon ourselves to a laissez-faire attitude. To do so might, in the long run, upset the social and political balance of the region. That, in turn, could jeopardize the region's credibility and efficiency in international competition. Public plans and regulations on the one hand, and private-sector initiatives, on the other, are the – often contradictory – mechanisms of constraint. They illustrate the forces in action in their continuity and their breaks. At the same time, they shed light on the regional and national stakes which underlie the interventions in the French capital.

Continuity and breaks: four fundamental tendencies

Our present time is one of intense economic turbulence, which is more than a series of passing adjustments. The severity of the urban crisis forces us to question the validity of present geographical systems. These were born at the juncture of two trends: continuous growth of individual income and increasing collective wealth. Established urban theories have been unable to withstand the test of economic and demographic reversals. Even the facts themselves, attested to by decades of continuity, seem to become ambiguous and are being called into question. This is the case with regard to the geography of economic activity and the evolution of the relationship between the French capital and the rest of the country. The whole postwar generation had lived according to

103

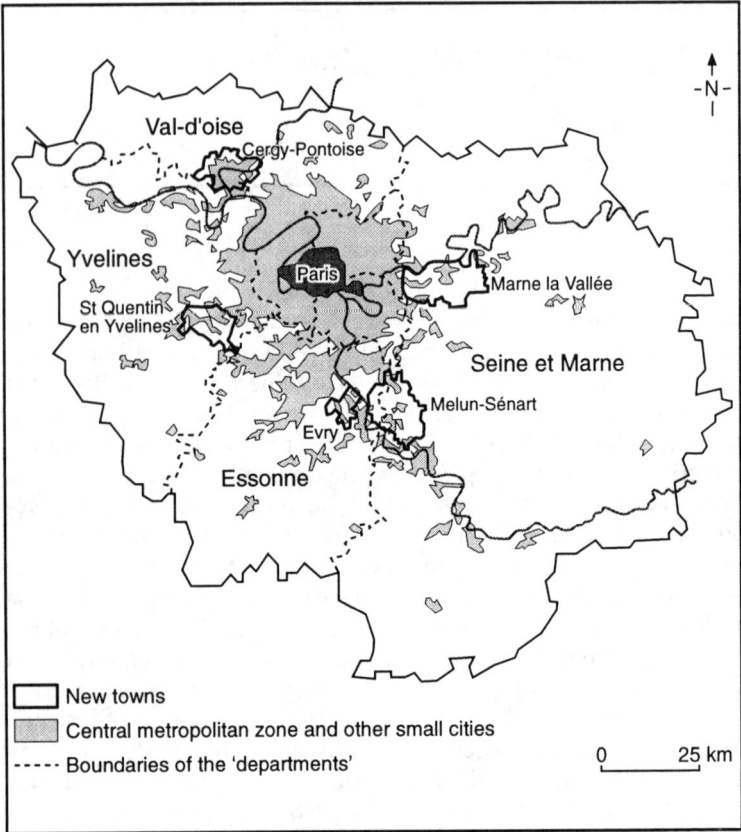

Figure 4.1   The urban region of Paris (Ile-de-France)

the image – and the reality – of Paris surrounded by the French desert. That generation was able to bring about the triumph of its decentralization policies in the 1950s and 1960s, when the gradual development of technologies and change of mentality was leading to a spread of growth. Nowadays, we still think and live in terms of the dispersion and diffusion of initiatives, consumption and lifestyles, at a time when new principles of centrality are being observed. This contradiction between temporalities and periodicities leads us to look beyond the facts, which are widely known, to an analysis of tendencies in terms of continuity and breaks. The contradiction leads us to search the mass of statistics for deviant data. The aim is to discover that which only reorients the system in place or which portends a new order of things.

Demographic slowdown or acceleration?

A few salient characteristics will be reiterated here to enable us to depict the French capital and its surrounding area. Though a caricature, this picture does resemble Paris. The first of these characteristics is the unquestionable demographic slowdown (Table 4.1). However, the results of the 1990 census show a renewed acceleration of the capital's demographic growth, with a net gain of almost 600 000 inhabitants between 1982 and 1990. In the course of the intercensal period (1975–82), the annual rate of growth was 0.3 per cent, less than the average for the whole of France (0.4 per cent). But these figures were respectively 0.7 per cent and 0.5 per cent in the last intercensal period (1982–90). Yet this continued positive growth rate is only due to a natural surplus. Since 1975, at least, the internal migratory balance has been negative: 40 000 fewer people per year from 1975 to 1982; 6000 fewer in the period 1982–90. Thus the ever-increasing massing of people in the largest urban area in the country is over and will not recur for some time to come. In this respect, Paris is only following the rhythm of a decrease in the hierarchical organization of urban growth, a trend that is perceptible in all the developed countries. In the same way, over a relatively long period of time, there has been a noticeable stabilization, if not a slight decrease, of total employment figures in the Ile-de-France. Particularly since the end of the 1960s, there has been a clear shift in favour of the provinces. That shift is away from a nationwide development of salaried employment and towards job creation in Paris. In spite of activity rates higher than the French average, except for young people under 25 (who have enjoyed better and longer schooling) and more women in the professions, the advantages for Paris are largely due to the inertia of certain phenomena; the most rapid gains have been made elsewhere.

The lesson of the last two decades is that a century and a half of unique economic and demographic concentration has resulted in a multifaceted polarization of French geographical space. The possible reorientation due to structural reversals is not to be found in simple statistical shifts (increase in population or in the number of economically active persons). More likely, it is to be found in the increasing flexibility of the relationship that an area's inhabitants have with their place of residence or their jobs. Localized enumeration is no longer the best indicator of urban space.

Table 4.1 Ile-de-France: population development in major sectors, 1962–90

	Total population (thousands)		Annual change (thousands)			
	1962	1990	1962–68	1968–75	1975–82	1982–90
Central metropolitan zone (including the city of Paris)	7 261 (2 790)	7 725 (2 152)	80 (–33)	13 (–42)	–28 (–18)	11 (–3)
Peripheral zone (including the new towns)	1 209 (112)	2 935 (617)	50 (6)	77 (13)	55 (24)	62 (26)
Total Ile-de-France	8 470	10 660	130	90	27	73

Source: Atlas des Franciliens, Vol. I (IAURIF, INSEE, 1991).

Geographical outward movement

The population of the Paris area accounts permanently for about one-sixth of the national population but, in spite of this stable ratio, we are witnessing a slow but continuous internal adjustment in the localization of people and their activities. Geographical outward movement (from centre to suburbs) is the crux of the matter (Figures 4.2 and 4.3; Table 4.2). Between 1975 and 1982, the city of Paris and two out of three of the bordering *départements* (Hauts-de-Seine and Val-de-Marne) saw a decline in their population. On average, the annual rate of decline ranged between –0.3 per cent and –0.8 per cent. But it ran far behind the four peripheral départements (+2.5 per cent between 1975 and 1982, +2.4 per cent between 1982 and 1990). And the rest of the demographic development reflects these classical contrasts between the city centre and the suburbs: those aged under 20 account for 18.5 per cent of the Paris population, while the figure is 32.1 per cent in Seine-et-Marne (and 27.1 per cent in the whole of the Ile-de-France). The unadjusted birth rate for Paris (1982–90) was 14.7 per thousand and 16.5 per thousand in the Val-d'Oise, even though one of the inner départements, namely Seine–Saint-Denis, was the front runner in regional fertility (17.5 per thousand). These differences were due to social and economic characteristics of the respective populations.

The built-up area of Paris is still spreading to greenfield sites in outlying areas, in spite of the major urban renewal projects in city centres. In 1982, the flats and houses built before 1968 accounted for more than 42 per cent of the total in the greater Paris area, as against only 27 per cent in the inner suburbs and 16 per cent in the city of Paris (an average of 29 per cent in the whole of the Ile-de-France). As far as the spatial pattern of economic activity is concerned, some simple statistics suffice to show both the inertia of most of the businesses and the dynamics of their location pattern. In the 1980s, the service sector alone, which represents more than 70 per cent of salaried employment in the area, was heavily concentrated in the city of Paris (44 per cent). The three inner départements contained 31 per cent, and no more than 25 per cent was found in the four outlying départements of the greater Paris area.

Similar patterns may be discerned with respect to the closure and the creation of business establishments in the private sector. Structural phenomena, which are linked to the spatial distribution of existing establishments, are predominant in both cases. Economic activity, both vibrant and defunct, still shows strong tendencies of centrality. The vast majority of new firms and of the

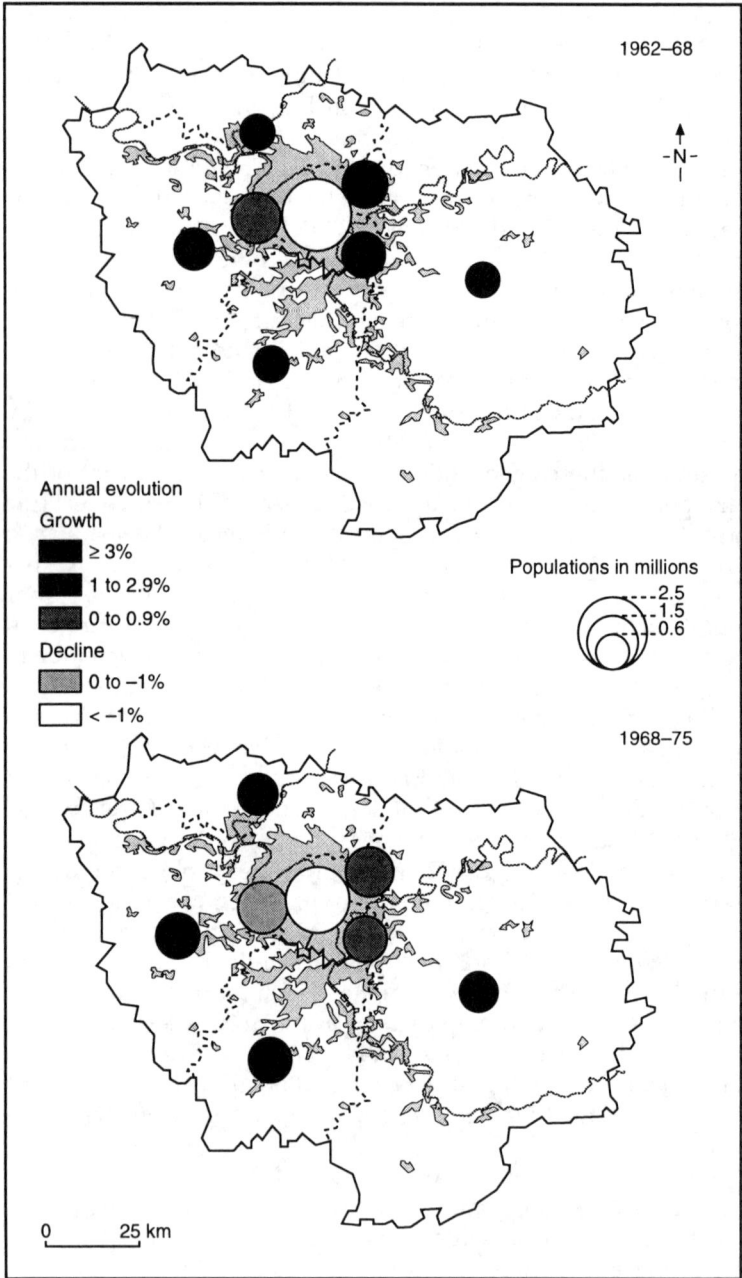

Figure 4.2   Population change, 1962–75

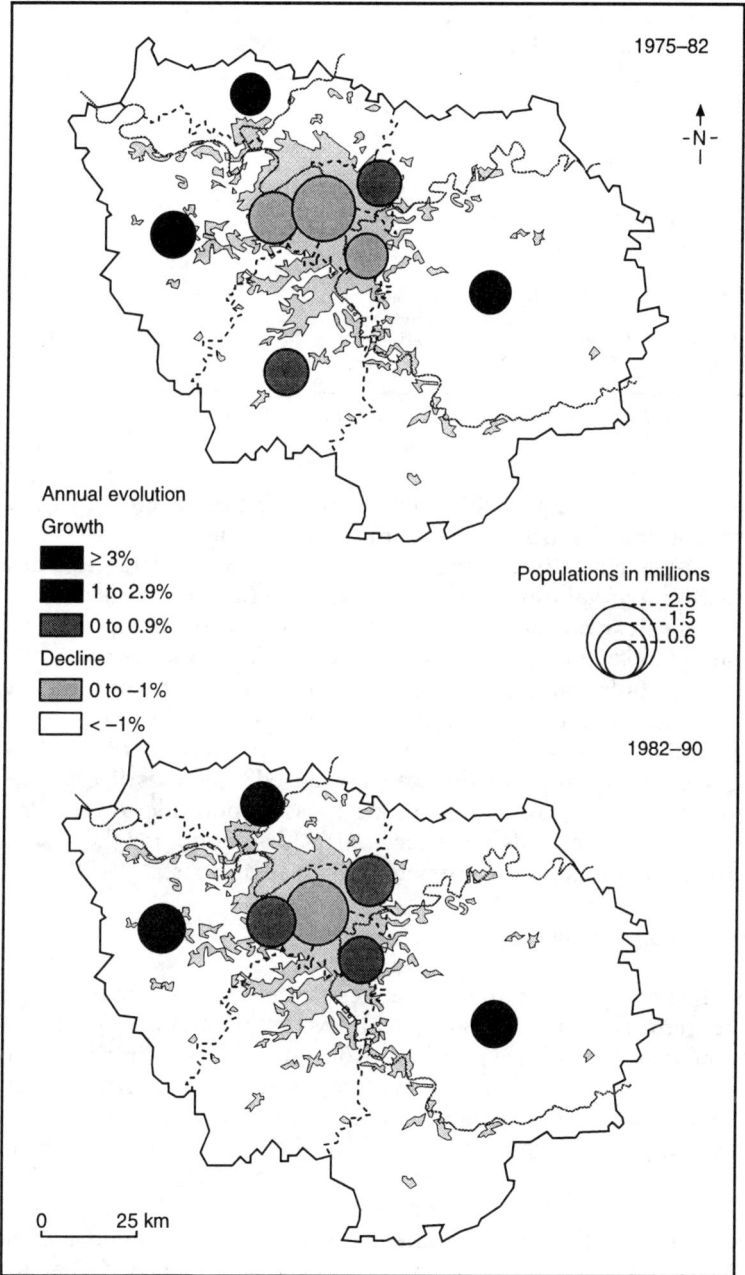

Figure 4.3   Population change, 1975–90

Table 4.2   Ile-de-France: development of the average annual rate of population change in major sectors, 1962–90 (per cent)

	1962–68	1968–75	1975–82	1982–90
Central metropolitan zone	1.07	0.17	−0.36	0.14
including the city of Paris	−1.23	−1.69	−0.78	−0.14
including the inner suburbs	1.18	0.07	−0.46	0.06
including the outer suburbs	4.26	2.30	−0.15	0.48
Peripheral zone	3.79	4.47	2.50	2.35
including the new towns	5.07	6.87	7.93	5.26
Total Ile-de-France	1.48	0.95	0.28	0.71
Total metropolitan France	1.14	0.81	0.45	0.51

Source: *Atlas des Franciliens*, Vol. I (IAURIF, INSEE, 1991).

closures of existing establishments are found in the Paris districts and the interior fringe of the inner départements (the whole of Hauts-de-Seine, the western part of Seine–Saint-Denis and the northwest of Val-de-Marne). This pattern reflects both the population density and the economic importance of the areas. The creation of jobs remains proportionate to the size of the economically active population and in line with the historical role of the area. Does this volatile performance reflect the efficiency of urban concentration? Does this pattern presuppose the existence of a supply of real estate property that can be reused? Or does it emanate from a lack of imagination among those responsible for creating jobs? In any case, this dynamic is food for thought for those who periodically predict the impending demise of cities.

The development of the service sector

At the same time, profound changes in the economy have become apparent. These may be summed up as deindustrialization, development of the service sector and decline of labour-intensive industries. In just one intercensal period – from 1975 to 1982, which by no means covers the time of most rapid transformation – manufacturing lost more than 200 000 workers in the Ile-de-France. Manufacturing employment dropped from 36.2 per cent to 30.6 per cent of the total active population (the national average is 34 per cent). In the same period, the service sector gained almost 300 000 jobs. In 1982, the share of the sector exceeded that for France as a whole by more than 10 per cent (68 per cent of the total active population in the Ile-de-France, as opposed to 57.7 per

Table 4.3 Economic trends in three départements around the city of Paris, 1983–91 (development of the number of salaried workers)

	Hauts-de-Seine (new CBD with La Défense)		Seine–Saint-Denis (old industrial location)		Val-d'Oise (new urban periphery with the new town of Cergy-Pontoise)	
	Development (%)	Number in 1991 (thousands)	Development (%)	Number in 1991 (thousands)	Development (%)	Number in 1991 (thousands)
Total workers	+10	800	+20	400	+40	300
Industry	–30	249	–21	114	+2	66
Management	+78	340	+49	147	+64	109
Social welfare (local and state administration)	+85	54	+257	57	+168	29

cent in the country as a whole). This means that, here too, the long-range trend is away from basic industries in favour of administrative and control functions, to the detriment of production. Obviously, this long economic trend exerts a major impact on the social structure of both the capital city and the region. In 1982, executives and professionals represented 15 per cent of the active population in Ile-de-France; that is, nearly 5 per cent above the national average. The share of blue-collar workers in France as a whole (44 per cent) was almost twice the rate in the Paris area (24 per cent). In spite of the underlying trend of homogenization of lifestyles, and diminishing social cleavages, the gap between Paris and the rest of France still exists.

Since 1982, the divergent trend was further accentuated by the economic revival, notably between 1986 and 1990. The growth of the tertiary sector accelerated. This, in turn, produced ever more striking divisions within the Paris region: zones of rapid business expansion, zones of transformations and zones of growth without change. The two-speed city is both a social and an economic phenomenon in Paris (Table 4.3).

Innovation

The apparent complexity of economic development stems from the fact that the French capital has always played an innovative role. And innovation is the fourth tendency to be distinguished. Its effect is both social and economic, visible in the development of lifestyles and in the economic structure. Of course, it is always difficult to collate exact figures on the economic effects of innovation. It is easier to show its role as a precursor and the part it plays as a harbinger of the mechanisms at work behind the events of civilization. We know that the 1982 census put 'single-parent families' in the spotlight of public opinion. In fact, they represent nearly one-tenth of the total number of households in the city of Paris (9.6 per cent), while they represent 7.9 per cent of the households in the Ile-de-France, and only 6.3 per cent in the country as a whole. These statistical facts signal more than a simple demographic anomaly in the evolution of morals. They are a sign that Paris remains different from the rest of French society. Every day, the information and transport revolution is making societies and spaces more standardized and interdependent. Nevertheless, a few central places continue to stand out by launching something entirely new.

Success and failure in Parisian urban policies

How do the contradictory tendencies discussed above show up in the spatial policies of the various tiers of government and in private-sector development? This question pertains to all contemporary cities of some importance, but it merits special attention in the case of Paris, owing to the traditions of French interventionism and the particular concern that all levels of government have about the national capital (Carmona, 1979; Roncayolo, 1985; Merlin and Choay, 1988). In this respect, for the last three decades, the centrepiece of planning has been the *Schéma Directeur d'Aménagement et d'Urbanisme* (SDAU) – the master plan – of the Paris region. It was formulated in 1965 and finally approved and implemented after revision in 1976.

The big undertaking: the new towns

The guidelines were very simple: devise a plan to lead and control the spatial growth of the agglomeration. Its heritage of a century of heavy industrialization and increasingly rapid population growth was deemed to be anarchic and threatening. The *banlieue* (suburbs), with their legacy of castoffs ejected from the city (factories, cemeteries, large transport infrastructure), their confusing road network, their mediocre architecture, their concentration of the 'working classes and its dangerous classes', appear to embody the worst type of evil (Bastié, 1961; Burgel, 1990).

Faced with this negative diagnosis, the cure prescribed to create order from chaos was relatively straightforward: follow the capital's 'natural' directions of geographic development, along two axes oriented south-east/north-west encompassing the Seine valley to the north and the south; flank this compact urban fabric with five advanced strongholds, the new towns, which were destined at the same time to stem the migratory provincial influx to Paris; provide a functional organization for the available space; and create modern architectural and social forms (Figure 4.4). The result has been that, for the last 30 years, Cergy-Pontoise and Saint-Quentin-en-Yvelines in the west, Marne-la-Vallée, Evry and Melun–Senart in the east have constituted the jewels of Parisian urban politics. There all governments have invested, with remarkable continuity, a wealth of funds, creativity and authority.

The new towns of Paris were developed under the strong and affluent Gaullist regime. At that time, central power and local authority were united in the well-known figure of Prefect Delouvrier. These new towns have stood up remarkably well,

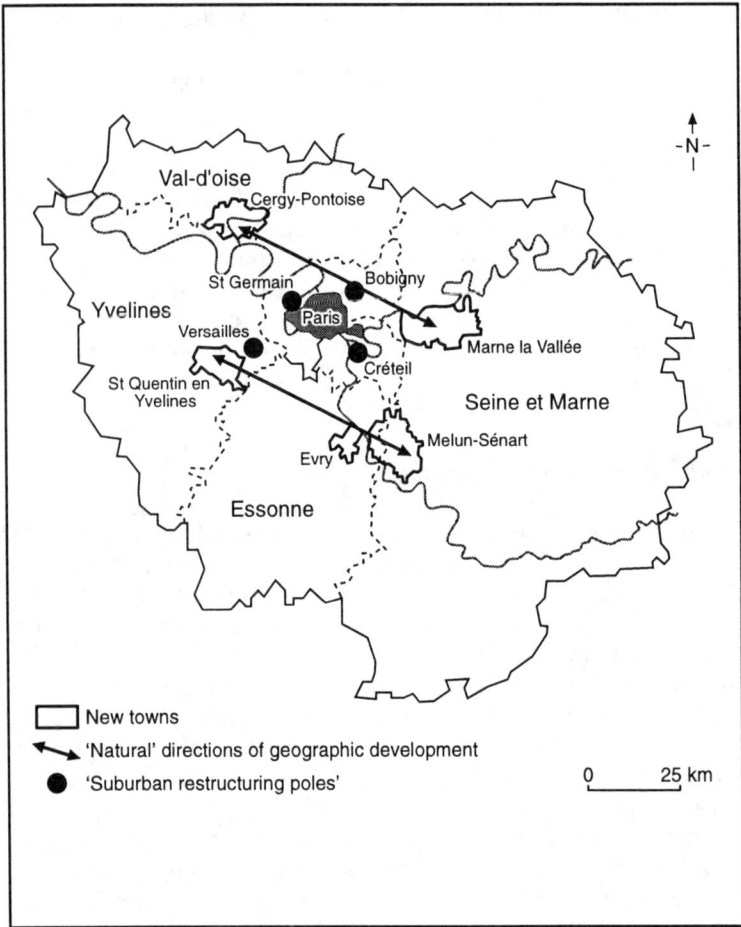

Figure 4.4   The 1965 master plan of the Paris region: main outlines

through economic recession, to a succession of more or less inspired decision makers, changes in urban fashion and, since 1981,
to socialist rule, but, above all, they have resisted decentralization,
which is generally unfavourable to grand urban initiatives, as
well as to spontaneous development. The new town movement is
living proof of the continuity of the state. At the same time, it
demonstrates that wide-ranging policies necessitate long-term planning.

Compared to the massive and constant effort represented by the
new towns, the other Parisian urban policies may seem to be

merely cosmetic in scope. They merely touch up the space inherited from the nineteenth century (the Haussmannian renovation projects) or the first half of the twentieth century. The traditional suburb is almost devoid of policy. This area has seen only a few important accomplishments. One is the development of a limited number of 'suburban restructuring poles', new urban centres introduced in the 1965 master plan (Créteil, Bobigny). Another milestone was reached after 1981. This was the kindling of a revolutionary spirit by the architects animating the *'Banlieues 89'* (the suburbs of 1989), such as Roland Castro and Michel Cantal-Dupart. In hindsight, their contribution was more important for stirring up ideas than for giving birth to a new reality. But the main change was accomplished by the unseen work of dozens of mayors carrying out incidental urban renovation work in their town centres. Of course, we must mention one exception to this rather gloomy picture of suburban intervention. From 1958 onwards, an immense business centre was developed around the district of La Défense at the western gates of Paris. The area is bristling with tower blocks erected on a huge concrete platform. The buildings were designed to host the head offices of national corporations, which had become cramped in their traditional setting along the Boulevard Haussmann or the Champs-Élysées. Only three decades later – and continuous government effort has helped here as well – La Défense is now effectively the central business district of Paris. This business area has become the main weapon waged by the French capital in international competition. It forms an integral part of the city's image. Indeed, the Spreckelsen Arch – a 'must' for the Paris tourist – ranks along with the Pompidou Centre and the Orsay Museum.

It is clear that the suburbs formed an area ignored by the governmental urban policies. In stark contrast, the city of Paris has been subject to constant governance. Encircled by its ring road, shut in by immutable administrative frontiers since the middle of the nineteenth century, but under a single jurisdiction and with an elected mayor only since 1977, Paris has remained essentially a personal battlefield for private investment, prestigious improvements and presidential enrichment (Chaslin, 1985). We should not forget the so-called 'major renovation operations', which are of public origin. Located in the peripheral districts of Paris (Italie in the south, Belleville in the east) their high silhouette and Corbusian design were landmarks of Paris during the 1960s. The Parisian landscape was violated even more in time and space by the construction of the Fronts-de-Seine, a project which crosses the city from Bercy to Javel. But such abrupt and intentional transformations of the urban fabric are limited, compared to the spontaneous changes brought about by the private sector, affecting both urban forms and social content, or compared to the monumental and symbolic projects of the central government. Each president of the French Republic has sought to leave his imprint on the capital. In some cases, this is simply to commemorate his time by having his name embedded in concrete. In another case, this has served to mark the bicentenary of the French Revolution. And each president has effectively realized this aim. The importance of each project goes beyond the construction of the edifice itself. The Georges Pompidou Centre stimulated the renovation of the district of Les Halles. The Orsay Museum and the Grand Louvre have both had a significant impact upon the cultural revival of the city centre. Further to the east, the Finance Ministry at Bercy and the Opéra–Bastille were needed in order to rebalance the development of the city, which had been pulled westward by La Défense.

Superimposed on these forces in Parisian urban policies, there are other factors at play. Clearly, we detect currents of thought and the emergence of new problems of national or even international importance. During the 1960s, urban renewal, with the havoc it wrought to the built environment and its new road infrastructure, gradually gave way to urban renovation. The new tactic was to preserve the facades and existing streets. This was deemed a softer approach, more in conformity with the aims of the social and cultural heritage. But, since then, winds of change have been felt everywhere in Europe. The functionalism inherited from Le Corbusier and the CIAM movement's Charter of Athens seems to have been broken down. In its place we see post-modernism, which is supposedly more concerned with aesthetic form and the human presence (Burgel and Genestier, 1988). In the same way, the social consequences of a lasting economic crisis reverberate in urban policies for the Paris region. Here the most underprivileged suburban areas were rehabilitated again in the 1980s. In the process, the neighbourhood policies (addressed by the programme 'Habitat et Vie Sociale' – 'Habitat and Social Life') were applied to places most strongly affected by underemployment and delinquency. These, however, were national programmes. They were policies to assuage the social impact of unemployment or to improve living conditions. They were not formulated specifically for the capital, where the lines of force had been drawn since the mid-1960s.

An achievement: the spatial configuration of the agglomeration

It is without doubt the strength and perseverance of the planning department that ultimately provide the trademark of planning in Paris. Its signature remains the large spatial programmes (Burgel, 1993a). Of these, most notable is the design of the major traffic infrastructure, providing the backbone of the agglomeration (Figure 4.5). If we compare the 1965 master plan with current satellite imaging of the capital, we see the resemblance between reality and the formal designs of the agglomeration. These include the peripheral extensions formed by the new towns, development of residential areas and industrial estates focused on the circular and main radial expressways and concentration around public transport corridors, especially the regional express train, *Réseau Express Régional* (RER).

Although we see a resemblance, the perspectives were wrong and the realities have changed. The discrepancies are greatest with respect to the volume and direction of demographic growth, the pace and nature of economic shifts, the goals and content of the social transformations, and the forces and relations of political power. But the physical space of the city of 1993 and the visionary space of 1965 are surprisingly superimposable. Is this a sign of strength and weakness at the same time?

This apparent success of planning may be explained as the joint effect of objective constraints and private-sector initiatives. The limits were imposed by the planning policies, while the impetus for change came from the economic and social players. Government was responsible for the layout and financing of major transport infrastructure (roads and expressways, extensions of rail networks). And public authorities prompted massive housing construction and the development of industrial estates in the five new towns, mainly via a generous supply of building sites. Accordingly, public bodies are responsible for the way spatial growth takes place in the agglomeration. In other words, its compactness as well as its peripheral offshoots are the result of public policy. Of course, the choice for a relatively concentrated agglomeration was made collectively by the economic decision makers and French households. Therefore they reflect the conceptual models of a city rather than its functional necessities. This decision-making process explains the success of the Parisian blueprint for spatial development. The 'suburbanization' phenomenon – American-style or even Dutch – remains a reality largely foreign to France, and particularly its capital, in spite of peripheral urban sprawl (Beaucire and Burgel, 1992). We should keep in mind that, even though the city of Paris houses less than one-fifth of the region's population, 40 per cent of the jobs of the capital region are concentrated in the city itself.

The infringement of urban functions on rural areas is a less serious problem in the Ile-de-France than in other metropolitan areas of the same importance (Table 4.4). Yet here, as elsewhere, ecological interest groups and some experts keep calling attention to the impending catastrophe and irreversible damage supposedly caused by metropolitan expansion. The alarm is particularly justified with regard to water pollution (the Seine is very dirty, including the stretch across Paris) and the groundwater is being contaminated. But nibbling away of rural space is limited in the Ile-de-France, which in fact, remains one of the prime agricultural regions in the country. The region has areas of very low population density (nature areas represent 81 per cent of the total area of the region, compared to 14 per cent built-up area). The very early designation of nature reserves and the satisfactory degree of compliance with land-use rules – in conjunction with the prevalence of an urban mentality – currently provide Paris with the best guarantees for preserving the natural environment. These factors together bear more weight than all the pressure exerted by the Green movement elsewhere.

Table 4.4   *Demographic and spatial growth of the Parisian agglomeration, 1982–90*

	Total population growth (thousands)	Use of natural space (in km²)
Central metropolitan zone	89	22
(including the city of Paris)	(24)	0.1
Peripheral zone within	418	111
the agglomeration	(209)	48
(including the new towns)		
Rural areas	81	16
Total Ile-de-France	588	149

Source: *Atlas des Franciliens*, Vol. I (IAURIF, INSEE, 1991).

A relative failure: social and demographic mobility

The pattern of the Paris agglomeration may seem to conform to the planning policies, but the demographic and social mechanisms underlying those policies have been poorly assessed, underestimated or misunderstood by institutional decision makers. The first major mistake lies in the projections of the size and location of the regional population. The 1965 master plan forecast about 15 million inhabitants for the year 2000. However, the Ile-de-France accounted for 11 million inhabitants at the last census in 1990. The drop in the French birth rate since the middle of the 1960s, and above all the reversal of the migration between Paris and the provinces, explain this large discrepancy. These demographic developments should have given the 'catastrophists' and other 'retro-ruralists' something to think about. They had sounded the alarm because the capital region increased by 600 000 inhabitants between 1982 and 1990, instead of by 300 000, as expected. At the same time, the outward mobility of the population of the city and the first suburban belt was underestimated – happily for the new towns! Instead of preventing migration to the province, they welcomed the emigrants from Paris *en masse*. Of course, the one trend fully compensated the other. (There are 150 000 inhabitants, on average, in each of the new towns, whereas 500 000 were projected.) Fortunately, it had been decided to locate these new towns 30 kilometres from Paris, instead of 100 kilometres away. Taking into account the economic and social dynamism, placing new towns farther away would have condemned them to absolute stagnation. Nevertheless, peopled mainly by Parisians, the new towns are perceived as new, more comfortable, better-equipped suburbs, rather than new, autonomous cities.

Similarly, the social composition of Paris and its development may seem to be a relative failure. This is not because social segregation, the dread of the 1960s and 1970s, increased there significantly, but because it made an unexpected advance. The main expectation was that the combination of building programmes and their financing in the new towns would create a mixed social profile. That, in turn, would have brought a mixture of rented housing, owner-occupied flats (helped greatly by low-interest loans) and detached houses or better-quality dwellings. Thereby it was hoped to prevent the massive scale and the concentration of working-class groups in the *grands ensembles* (these are the social housing areas that had invaded the Parisian suburbs in the 1950s and 1960s, at the height of the housing crisis and the country's urban growth). The result tends to maintain the rifts of the agglomeration. These trends are matched by a statistically – which does not mean to say relationally – marked mixture of social categories. Seemingly contradictory is the concomitant appearance of a few pockets of poverty. These ghettos are a particularly worrying development (*Données Sociales Ile-de-France*, 1989).

On the one hand, the contrast between a gentrified Paris and a more working-class or median-income periphery has been largely sustained. In fact, it has even expanded, in so far as gentrification has reached the *arrondissements* (boroughs) in the east of the capital. Hitherto, these areas had been inhabited typically by working-class and craftsmen groups, but, at the same time, the near suburbs, with their working-class and industrial populations – the famous 'red belt' of Paris – became more middle class. The newcomers profited from the closure of the factories and the proximity to the centre of the agglomeration. In general, the entire western periphery (Versailles, Saint-Germain) accentuated its attraction to the better-off, in some cases coming to resemble the American urban periphery. The new towns themselves had an 'average' profile: there is not the wide range of groups characteristic of Parisian society (the very rich and the very poor); rather, there is a plethora of white-collar workers, technicians and management (more middle management than higher management). While remaining faithful to their cultural heritage, the towns have in a sense become 'mediocre'. On the other hand, as in all western metropolises, the two-track society has become accentuated. This is mainly visible in some large peripheral social housing areas. In those districts, signs of social exclusion have accumulated: concentrations of foreigners, a low level of educational attainment, drug abuse, unemployment and delinquency. These trends show that the reality of residential mobility and the transformation of French society clearly win over policies.

Finally, the issues of urban transport and geographic mobility of the populations illustrate the difficulty of bringing together urban programming, technical progress and social change. The 1965 master plan was based upon two simple aims: to bring place of work and residence closer together, and to improve the regional transport network, both road and rail. These aims have been achieved beyond all expectations. Although not perfect, particularly with respect to the ring roads, a programme of major work on the infrastructure (rail regional express network, expressway interchanges, several hundred kilometres of expressway) has effectively given the Ile-de-France a tool for internal relations, which it badly needed (Figure 4.5). Yet we may ask whether it is sufficient to make transport more efficient. Good access to all

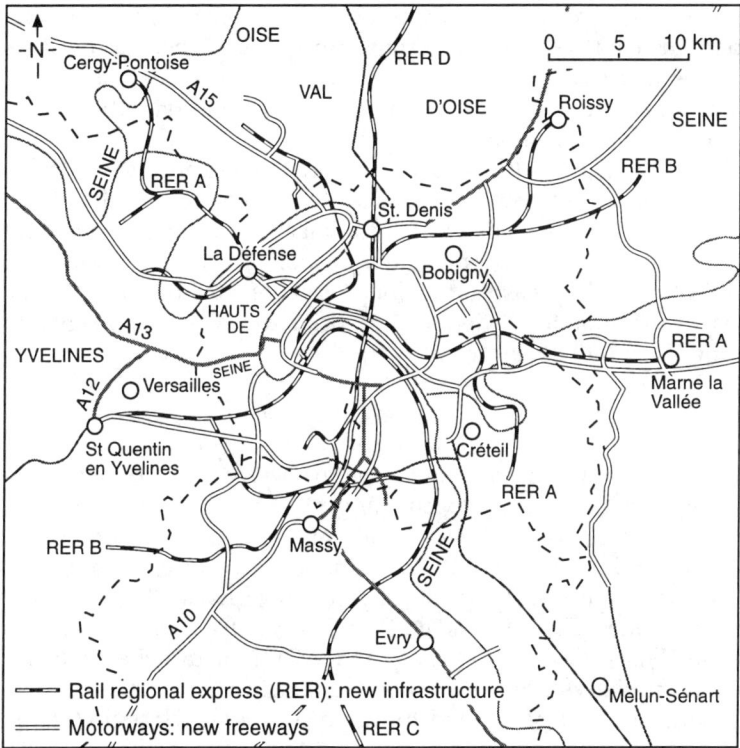

Figure 4.5   Improvement of the regional transport networks since 1965

inhabitants must also be assured. Today's planners recognize a number of weaknesses in the improvements (*Ile-de-France, Projet de Schéma Directeur*, 1992).

The first problem is the underestimation of the need for mobility. With less than 11 million inhabitants, the network is already saturated (inner periphery, east–west RER line) although it was initially planned for a population of 15 million. The second difficulty stems from the geographic changes in traffic patterns. Improvements to the networks have been essentially radial, based upon the classic exchange between the centre and the periphery. The greatest movement of traffic has been tangential: from suburb to suburb. Transport improvement projects are pertinent when they are based on the qualitative and quantitative needs and set out to meet them. They are less so when they set out to reduce mobility by bringing work and home closer together. In a complex urban society, where structural mobility is constantly increasing, such an objective is a dangerous and old-fashioned decoy if its main effect is to draw more and more women into the labour force. In the same way, the accent placed today upon public transport may seem desirable and productive, but it leaves the two million Franciliens (those who live in the region of the Ile-de-France) in 'low-density towns' – which included the inhabitants of the new towns – condemned to make part of their journey by car because of the pattern of urbanization. They are not the most well-off, nor the least active in production. In this respect, the goals of economic efficiency and social equity seem for once to coincide, and to be wrong.

The economy: lack of initiative or misinterpretation of development

As usual in an open economy, it is in the economic domain that urban policies are least specific and most fragmented. It was assumed that most initiatives would emanate from the private sector. This did not prevent the institutional voices from formulating a general critique of the nation's global objectives and of the spatial inequities (*Commissariat du Plan, Délégation à l'Aménagement du Territoire et à l'Action Régionale*: DATAR). Nor did the room for private initiative keep authorities from trying to determine where activities should be created by imposing fiscal regulation or by creating industrial and tertiary zones. After 1982 and the triumph of administrative decentralization, local communities (local councils, departments and regions) took the initiative to create or preserve jobs in their respective areas, in response to the persisting crisis. In the Paris region, these structural contradictions and fluctuations in regulation were expressed in the misinterpretation of the spontaneous development mechanisms (Burgel, 1987, 1988, 1989; Anastassiadis and Burgel, 1992).

Since the 1950s and up to the early 1980s, the key to French economic planning was decentralization. At that time, the aim was to disperse industry geographically and thereby reduce congestion in the Paris region (Gravier, 1947). There are well-known measures to implement this policy goal, aimed first at industry and subsequently at the tertiary sector. We cannot describe all of these policies here. Some were restrictive measures. For instance, from 1955 onward, procedures were in place to discourage the establishment and expansion of firms in the capital zone. Every request was submitted for approval to the *Comité de Décentralisation* – the Decentralization Committee. Other measures took a stimulating approach. For instance, zones of economic activity were to be set up in the provinces. Alternatively, the eight largest regional agglomerations were promoted as 'métropoles d'équilibre', regional centres to balance the national urban development (1963). In 1982, and again in 1985, it became easier for small and middle-sized companies (those with less than 100 employees) to set up in the Paris region. The permit procedure was even completely abolished in the new towns (Merlin and Choay, 1988). Recently, policy makers have gone back to stricter controls on the growth of employment in the Ile-de-France (*Ile-de-France Projet de Schéma Directeur*, 1992).

What should we think about these apparent continuities, their reversals and, above all, about their effects? First, there is a remarkable timelessness in interpretations of the French urbanization trends. There are still those who think that Paris constitutes a drain on the French economy. They believe that the concentration of activities there should be diminished, but this way of thinking seems to be fading. The later policies tend to bolster the spontaneous trends of the French economy rather than redirect them. The obvious success attributed to the economic decentralization measures in the 1960s and 1970s came mainly from costly efforts to deconcentrate production and consumption. The ensuing distribution of activities throughout France resulted more from private-sector decision making than from forced relocations. The easing of the pressure to decentralize in the 1980s follows, in fact, the revival of urban centrality which fits the overall trend of economic restructuring. This provided clear benefits to the largest cities (Burgel, 1993a). In this perspective, the current wavering over which policies should be applied produces as much economic uncertainty as the debate on the efficiency and the equity of preceding policies.

Development initiatives in the capital region were often direct responses to local economic crises. This was the case with the policy to redevelop industrial wastelands. In the 1970s and 1980s, a number of industrial strongholds, particularly in the western and northern suburbs of Paris, were to be given a new use. The economic downturn was acutely felt in the chemicals, metal working and automotive sectors. Over the decades, a class-based coalition grew, bringing together firms, working-class housing interests, proletarian grass-roots organizations and the essentially communist municipal power structure. In such a context, any factory closure was perceived as a financial, social and ideological injustice.

However, resisting the trends was generally as futile as it was tragic. The inevitable changes resulted in long periods of impo-

tence or series of lost battles. Some communes (the smallest French
territorial division) in the Paris suburbs could have been amalga-
mated to give them more clout. This could have had beneficial
effects in the département of Seine–Saint-Denis in particular, in
the old industrial regions in the north of the country, or in the
Lorraine, all of which have had their economies devastated. In
other geographic areas, in contrast, the sudden switch from left-
majority councils to conservative teams (Levallois, Suresnes)
triggered major shifts in the 1980s. This resulted in overbuilding
of offices, extreme tertiarization of activity patterns and accelerated
gentrification. The Paris economy, dedicated neither to heavy industry nor to the total abandonment of its productive activities
(Beckouche *et al.*, 1990), surely deserved better than rearguard
battles. It could have done without this *laissez-faire* attitude to
which urban policies seemed to have been condemned.

Options for action

When the definitive report has been made and the issues have
been outlined, the debate will take place on political grounds.
This aspect must be clarified before a choice can be made among
spatial options or opposing master plans. The playing-field is
political on two counts. First of all, the key issues pose a social
problem: once wealth has been accumulated, what can we do to
share it as equitably as possible among all social strata? The question is also political because the decisions imply an interaction
between the institutional actors – from the cities to the state – with
its own rules. But it would be useful to recall the terms of the
debate and the possible means of action.

*A national debate: the contribution made by Paris to the wealth of
France*

A key question preoccupies the political parties and the public
throughout the country: does the Paris region generate money for
France, or is the region a drain on the national economy? Indecisiveness about the answer to this question, rather than the rifts
between left and right, explains that for nearly five years now the
capital's master plan remains unfinished. As often happens, the
opinions of the experts are contradictory (*Ile-de-France: pouvons-
nous éviter le scénario catastrophe?* 1990). Some maintain that the
Paris region is the trump card of the national economy (Burgel,
1991; Prudhomme, 1993). This is especially clear in periods of

increasing international competition. They base their assessment on the sheer magnitude of economic investment in the region and the productivity of the workforce. Others espouse the view that, far from ensuring profitability, overinvestment in the region costs the country too much. Specifically, it lowers the productive capacity and creates social and spatial imbalances (Voisard and Lavallard, 1993).

Part of the disagreement is due to the fact that the same effects have not been measured. There are discrepancies in the length of observation time, the relative importance given to production of goods or services, the social costs, the agglomeration diseconomies and, above all, the real capacity for initiative and innovation. The short-term study (1990–92) held recently by the *Centrale des Bilans* of the Bank of France seems to be biased. It casts doubt on the profitability of capital invested in the Ile-de-France compared to other regions in France. The regional accumulation and the capacity of one place to produce wealth is measured over decades or even centuries. And that capacity seems to be poorly linked to the record of annual stocktaking. Similarly, the well-known assertion that the hours spent by Parisians stuck in traffic jams would be equivalent to the gross domestic product of the country's second urban agglomeration, Lyons, is facetious. It has no significance if one does not take into account the profits generated by the capital, for itself and for the national economy. The optimum urban size demonstrated historically by Alonso on the cost curves and profits remains unreal as long as the decision makers do not put it into practice. A study by the *Institut National de Statistiques et d'Études Économiques* (INSEE) has shown that the survival rate of new businesses is higher in Limoges (in the Massif Central) than in Paris. But it should be kept in mind that there are very few new businesses in Limoges and lots of initiatives in the capital city. As in human demography, a greater economic vitality gives rise to a higher mortality.

All the same, contrasting Paris with the provinces may rekindle an old set of problems. Recent research carried out on the period of rapid change in the 1980s (Burgel, 1993b) shows that the main economic and social rifts actually occur in the interior of the Paris region (see Table 4.3 above). Three suburban départements may reflect three situations typical of the whole of contemporary France. One is the Hauts-de-Seine. Within it, La Défense and a conglomerate of high-performance small and medium-sized companies are characteristic of the places of innovation and decision. This characteristic does not apply to all of Paris, as is often erroneously assumed. Another example is the Val d'Oise. More peripheral, it is still quite close. This département has modern industrial and tertiary sector activities as well as a middle class, all characteristic of a dynamic provincial town. The third is the Seine–Saint-Denis, an old industrial suburb. With its economic transformation, social problems and public social assistance activities, it is similar to some of the départements in the north or east of France, steeped in a deep crisis.

A regional debate: Paris versus the suburbs, east versus west

This national debate is also a regional debate. Even when applied to another geographic scale, the issues are not really very different. Paris hosts more decision-making activities and more decision makers than its periphery. But does Paris have to be penalized by planning policies for that reason? Such policies are detrimental to Paris and beneficial to its suburbs. Why not pass on the benefits to the 'towns an hour away from Paris'? For a long time now, the west of Paris has been characterized as the 'best districts'. That is where head offices tend to cluster. Recently, that area has attracted high-tech activities and more employment. But is that a reason to favour the east with the creation of infrastructure and all the investment in physical plant that follows? These questions have been asked emphatically at least twice over the last three years. In 1990, it was decided to double the size of the business district of La Défense in order to enhance the international competitive position of the capital. That decision sparked a general outcry, even though the government assured the population that two square metres of housing would be built for every square metre of office space. Since then, the parties have been wavering between two alternatives: to promote intraregional balance or to preserve the international advantage of Paris. In 1992 and 1993, the site on which to build the big stadium to host the 1998 soccer World Cup was changed several times. Such indecisiveness has triggered a politics, media and pseudo-planner soap opera. The stadium was initially designated for the new town of Melun–Sénart, 50 kilometres east of Paris. That location beat Nanterre–La Défense, which was deemed too central and already too well-off. But at the end of 1993, the projected site for the stadium was brought back to a northern inner suburb. Owing to its urban centrality, the efficiency of the location – in this case, the ability to fill the stadium – seemed assured. At the same time, the east–west equilibrium has hardly been changed by choosing a location halfway between the two main contenders. Still, some people would have preferred to see the stadium built in the provinces, or in Lyons or Marseilles!

Actually, it might be necessary to rephrase the question. Is it still necessary to balance the territory by striving to attain spatial egalitarianism for activities and the built-up environment? Is it necessary to ensure the equity of services and opportunities provided for the inhabitants (Burgel, 1993a)? The fiscal inequality among local communities appears to have more serious political and financial consequences than all the material inequalities of localization. The reason lies in the relation between financial position and the collective conscience. In short, this relation is associated with equality between citizens. A recent report on fiscal wealth in the Ile-de-France (Jean, 1990) shows that 'the working-class communes overtax their businesses through employment taxes (*taxe professionnelle*) and their owners through real-property taxes (*taxe sur le foncier bâti*) and also, albeit to a lesser degree, their inhabitants. At the same time, hardly anyone is overtaxed in middle-class municipalities. The result is paradoxical and contradicts the accumulation of territorial inequity. In working-class communes, people pay much more tax in proportion to their income. But this higher tax rate does not yield enough revenue to cover the community's social needs, which are relatively great. At the same time, this higher tax rate might discourage business and overburden the inhabitants, creating a vicious circle of decline and deprivation.

It should come as no surprise that of all the measures recently applied in the Ile-de-France, the one that provoked the most hostility was introduced to redistribute money only slightly. To maintain efficiency, local solidarity was called for. For the first time, people no longer talked about space but about democracy.

A political debate: local authority against the state

The appeal for solidarity remains fashionable in France – and fashion is not always wrong. That appeal came at a time when the edifice of political power was crumbling. The disintegration was brought about by the administrative decentralization of 1982–3. This led to a big difference from the 1960s and the 1965 master plan. Although a caricature, we might say that, during a period of growth, a strong planning power had recourse to outdated or inaccurate means (like the theory of urban networks) to solve relatively simple problems. Today we are in a period of public and private regulation of investments. In the meantime, the democratic urban society has become more complex, while people's knowledge is certainly better founded. But the real power to intervene remains limited (Burgel, 1993c).

This is the case of Paris. Today the state apparatus, which makes its presence felt throughout the region on account of the national importance of the capital, must share its prerogatives. The power sharing involves a region, eight départements and 850 municipalities in the built-up area of the agglomeration – nearly 1300 if the dispersed periphery is included. Each of these tiers consists of elected authorities and therefore has a representative in the public domain. Each tier has the power to make spatial and economic decisions, powers that are juxtaposed by law, rather than ranked hierarchically. Therefore, in each municipality, it is the mayor who issues building permits and develops zoning, the *Plan d'Occupation des Sols*. Of course, different interpretations have emerged through ten years of administrative decentralization following centuries of political centralism. Taking into account these interpretations and the entrenched rifts between the left and the right, the task of administration seems daunting. How is it possible to manage and plan a city encompassing 12 million people when power is dispersed and self-interest remains rampant?

This impasse in the Paris region could eventually reduce the levels of efficiency and the equity previously attained in the French capital. This realization leads us to question the contemporary concepts of 'autonomy' of the state or the 'city actor' (see Chapter 1). The problem is not so much to evaluate the dependence of the policy with respect to the constraints of the dominant social and economic players; that was the approach commonly used in the French Marxist urban sociology of the 1970s. Rather, it is now advisable to define its capacity to identify the general interest and to arbitrate between individual and local interests. It is the very nature and scale of local democracy which is being questioned. Should the effectiveness of the democratic system be measured in the French capital on the scale of the borough (in the city of Paris) or the commune (in the suburbs), of the region or of the nation? Similarly, the capacity of a mayor to take charge of the development of the municipality – the Parisian suburbs provide many examples – should be critically appraised. Such an evaluation could shed light on the possibility of extending the system to the whole of the agglomeration. Obviously, the biggest obstacle to intermunicipal cooperation is often the presence of feared and envied dynamic personalities.

A methodological debate: what is democratic urban policy?

Beyond the choice of methods for achieving the best economic and social results possible for Paris, there is another way to look at the situation. We can elaborate the two disaster scenarios that must be avoided at all cost. Neither one is spatial. When it comes down to it, geographers do not really trust an explanation based on space, whether it be positive or negative.

The first of these is a punitive scenario. It would be a mistake to penalize Paris in favour of the provinces on the pretext that there are more people in the provinces than in Paris. Penalizing the capital would be to the detriment of the nation. The second disaster scenario would be to give free rein to the natural consequences of a liberal system of growth. This would allow the development of a dual urban society and spatial inequities in the distribution of wealth, of consumer goods and services, and mentalities. To do so would be the surest way to produce a divided society. It would generate passive or violent clashes (which already define the acute crisis in many suburbs). And its consequences on the whole of French society, its political destiny and even its economic efficiency would be unpredictable, considering the importance of Paris to the country as a whole.

Between these two disaster scenarios there is a narrow but crucial path. It is of no use to pave this way with old-fashioned voluntarism. All the experiments with incentives – in the east as well as in the west of the metropolitan area, during periods of growth, crisis or recovery – failed when they ignored underlying social trends. It would be much better, in the name of a political objective, be it social equity or perhaps democratic control over the exercise of power, to act with determination, imagination and realism.

From this point on, the paired attributes of interdependence and a mixed economy should be brought to bear. The key elements in this process should be not to penalize accumulation or to redistribute it, which will only foster interdependence. At first glance, this may seem to be wishful thinking. Even though there is very little likelihood of Paris becoming another Beirut, or even another New York, it is possible that social and ethnic tensions, and the difficulty of making a decent living, might intensify and become intolerable. First of all, this would apply to the most impoverished, but, in time, it would also affect the great majority of the population. Here again, the cure might prove to be worse than the disease. Serious thinking about the relationship between spaces and societies should not be based on rigid interventionism or incrementalism. It should focus on the mechanisms which determine spatial inequality.

The solutions must deal with all the consequences of a mixed society and economy, in the spirit of imagination and experimentation which is a tradition in French society. On that basis, the contributions from private initiative and public decision making should be reconciled. Where are they compatible; what are the benefits to the nation as a whole and to each individual citizen; how can flexibility be maintained? This pits the private sector, with its record of performance and transparent responsibilities, against the public sector, characterized by its inability to define the general interest. The wager on the outcome of this confrontation must be won at the end of this century. This does not so much concern spatial issues, as political ones. To illustrate this point, let us consider the university. The location of new universities in the Paris area is of less importance – on the condition that there be a close collaboration with the area as a whole – than endowing them with innovating structures. These would make it possible to combine the public university's traditions of humanism and raising fundamental questions with the flexibility of management and adaptation of private universities.

We must have the courage in these uncertain times to take daring steps. Voluntarism and authoritarian spatial planning, in the guise of forceful intervention, would take us back half a century. If we want to win the fight against political, social and economic egocentrism, the time has come for creative imagination. The future will not be determined by rigid technocratic master plans!

References

Anastassiadis, A. and G. Burgel (1992) *Concentration et dispersion du peuplement: étude comparative en France et en Grèce* [Concentration and dispersal of population: a comparative study of France and Greece], paper presented to the International Symposium of IAPS, Marmara (Greece).

Atlas des Franciliens (1991–2). Paris: IAURIF, INSEE.

Bastié, J. (1961) *La croissance de la banlieue parisienne* [The growth of the Parisian suburbs], Paris: PUF.

Beaucire, F. and G. Burgel (eds) (1992) 'Les périurbains de Paris' [The exurbs of Paris], *Villes en parallèle*, **19**, Paris: Laboratoire de Géographie Urbaine.

Beckouche, P., J. Cohen, F. Damette and J. Scheibling (1990) *Métropolisation et aires métropolitaines, internationalisation et enjeux urbains* [Metropolization and metropolitan zones, internationalization and the urban debate], Paris: Strates, Université de Paris I.

Burgel, G. (1987) 'Structure et tendance: trois ans (1981–1984) de vie et de mort de l'initiative privée en Ile-de-France' [Structure and development: three years of life and death of private initiative in the Parisian region], *Emplois, entreprises et équipements en Ile-de-France*, Paris: GIP-Reclus, pp.29–41.

Burgel, G. (1988) 'Tendances de l'évolution de l'emploi et des actifs en Ile-de-France' [Development of employment and labour force in the Parisian region], *Espace, Populations, Sociétés*, 1988–3, pp.447–53.

Burgel, G. (1989) 'Mythes en question? Les dynamismes de l'emploi privé en Ile-de-France (1981-1985)' [Myths in question? The development of private employment in the Parisian region], *Ile-de-France, un nouveau territoire*, Paris: GIP-Reclus, Documentation française, pp.105–23.

Burgel, G. (ed.) (1990) 'Peuplements en banlieue' [Population development in the suburbs], *Villes en parallèle*, **15–16**, Paris: Laboratoire de Géographie Urbaine.

Burgel, G. (1991) 'Intervilles 80: la centralité urbaine, entre le local et le mondial' [Interville 80: urban centrality between the local and the global], *Géographie Sociale*, **11**, pp.341–50.

Burgel, G. (1993a) *La ville aujourd'hui* [Today's city], Paris: Hachette.

Burgel, G. (1993b) *Atlas économique et social du Nord-Ouest parisien* [Economic and social atlas of northwestern Paris], Paris: Laboratoire de Géographie Urbaine.

Burgel, G. (1993c) 'Politiques urbaines: doutes sur l'efficacité ou incertitudes sur la méthode', [Urban politics: doubts on the efficiency or the uncertainty of method], *Mutations économiques et urbanisation*, Paris: La Documentation française, pp.199–210.

Burgel, G. and Ph. Genestier (eds) (1988) 'Formes urbaines' [Urban forms], *Villes en parallèle*, **12–13**, Paris: Laboratoire de Géographie Urbaine.

Carmona, M. (1979) *Le Grand Paris, l'évolution de l'idée d'aménagement de la Région parisienne* [Greater Paris, the evolution of the idea of the planning of the Paris region], Paris.

Chaslin, F. (1985) *Les Paris de François Mitterrand* [The many Parises of François Mitterand], Paris: Gallimard.

Données Sociales Ile-de-France (1989) Paris: Direction Régionale Ile-de-France de l'INSEE.

Gravier, F. (1947) *Paris et le désert français* [Paris and the French desert], Paris: Flammarion.

Ile-de-France: pouvons-nous éviter le scénario catastrophe? [Can we avoid the catastrophe scenario?] (1990) Paris: Économica.

Ile-de-France, Projet de Schéma Directeur [The master plan project] (1992), Paris: Préfecture de Région d'Ile-de-France.

Jean, O. (1990) 'Richesse et pauvreté fiscales des communes d'Ile-de-France' [Fiscal wealth and poverty of the municipalities in the Parisian region], *Regards sur l'Ile-de-France*, **10**, Paris: INSEE.

Merlin, P. and F. Choay (eds) (1988) *Dictionnaire de l'urbanisme et de l'aménagement* [Dictionary of urbanism and planning], Paris: PUF.

Prudhomme, R. (1993) *Les bénéfices de la concentration parisienne* [The advantages of the Parisian concentration], Paris: L'œil, Université de Créteil.

Roncayolo, M. (ed.) (1985) *Histoire de la France urbaine* [The history of urban France], Tome V, Paris: Seuil.

Voisard, J. and F. Lavallard (1993) *Population et migrations intérieures* [Population and domestic migration], Paris: La Documentation française.

5 Geneva: urban policy in its infancy

Antoine S. Bailly[1]

One of the major phenomena that have marked Europe in the latter half of the twentieth century is the growth of metropolitan areas. Europe is currently engaged in a massive functional and spatial restructuring of its systems of production and consequently of its urban systems. In this process, European countries and cities have varying capacities for adjustment. On the one hand, organizational imperatives are favouring vertical disintegration and the search for increasing flexibility in peripheral regions (Scott, 1988; Coffey and Bailly, 1992). On the other hand, owing to the increasing internationalization of economic activity, some metropolitan areas are becoming centres of production networks. Thus it is desirable to place the evolution of metropolitan areas in Europe in a broad context in order to identify particular strengths and weaknesses, and to see how its components fit into the newly emerging world economic order.

In this chapter we examine the economic and social structures of metropolitan Geneva. This research, originally undertaken as part of a planning exercise for the government of the canton of Geneva, focuses primarily on its economic evolution. To better understand the specific contribution of these activities, it is necessary to examine the economy as a whole. This approach is particularly important, given that it is becoming increasingly difficult to separate the production of goods from the production of services (Coffey and Bailly, 1990). In addition, the economic structure and socioeconomic evolution of metropolitan Geneva can be better understood by placing it in a wider comparative context.

In the following sections we examine the economic structure of Geneva: its structural configuration in 1985, its evolution over the period 1975–85, its recent development and its (lack of) urban policies. A set of general comments on the economic and social structures of metropolitan areas then concludes the chapter.

The Geneva metropolitan area

The 'Regio Genevensis' cannot be limited to Geneva Canton; often considered as a pioneer in transnational cooperation, the Franco-Geneva region includes Geneva Canton (380 000 inhabitants in 1990), some neighbouring districts of the Vaud Canton (Nyon, Rolle and Aubonne, with 66 000 inhabitants) and some parts of French *départements* (Ain and Haute Savoie) (Figure 5.1). The total population is about 600 000 people. Even if this figure is small compared with other metropolitan areas in Europe,

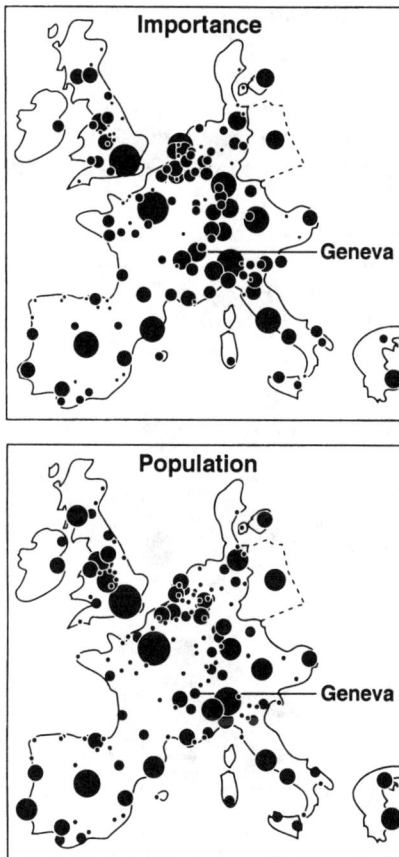

Source: Brunet, R. (ed.), (1989, pp.21 and 55).

Figure 5.1   Geneva: importance and size in Europe

Geneva is classified by many studies (Brunet, 1989; Soldatos, 1989; Bonneville *et al.*, 1992; Messerli, 1991) as one of the major international cities in Europe. Using the evaluation system developed by N.I.C.E. – *Villes Européennes et Internationalisation* (Bonneville *et al.*, 1992), Geneva ranks on 13 criteria with Amsterdam, Barcelona and Frankfurt; the three cities 'present, despite their differences in size, many similarities ... due to their internationalism:

- importance of airport flows, with international flights
- importance of foreign population, from developed countries
- importance of foreign firms in the financial sectors
- number of high quality hotels for foreign customers'[2]

Geneva is one of Europe's most specialized cities in international relations at the world level (Bonneville *et al.*, 1992, p.175). The findings of N.I.C.E. are in line with other recent studies. The DATAR report (Brunet, 1989) ranks Geneva behind Paris, London

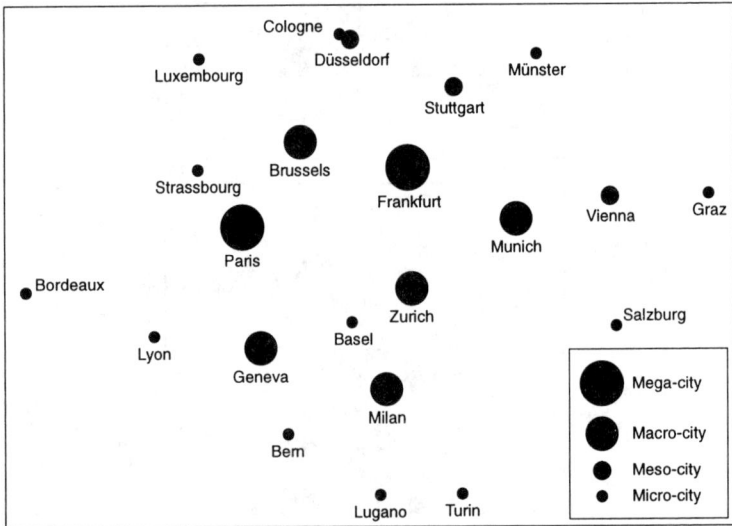

Source: Messerli (1991, p.500). Messerli uses a typology of four classes to differentiate the world cities (mega-cities), from the European cities (macro-cities), the national cities (meso-cities) and the regional cities (micro-cities). He selected travel time as the most relevant measure of distance for business contacts.

Figure 5.2   Cities in central Europe

and Milan, but at the same level as Amsterdam, Brussels, Frankfurt and Barcelona. And in a study of cities in Central Europe (Messerli, 1991), Geneva is considered to be one of the 'macrocities' after Paris and Frankfurt, but with Brussels, Zurich, Munich and Milan (Figure 5.2).

With 208 712 full-time jobs in 1985 and more than 220 000 in 1990,[3] metropolitan Geneva possesses the highest employment/population ratio in Switzerland – 53 per cent. If we include part-time work, the total rises to 243 772 jobs in 1985, and the employment/population ratio to 61.8 per cent. By way of comparison, for full-time employment, metropolitan Basle has a ratio of 50.5 per cent, metropolitan Zurich a ratio of 49.8 per cent, and for all of Switzerland the ratio is 45.6 per cent. Evidently, Geneva has a strong concentration of employment.

Metropolitan Geneva in evolution

The term 'deindustrialization' is often employed to describe the changes that are occurring in the economic structure of metropolitan Geneva. It is true that, using Clark's typology, the secondary sector (manufacturing and construction) represented only 22.8 per cent of total employment in 1985 (down from 27.5 per cent in 1975) and that the tertiary sector (services) represented 75.9 per cent (up from 71 per cent in 1975). With the inclusion of part-time employment, the gap appears even wider, with 77.7 per cent of total employment in the tertiary sector in 1985 (72.5 per cent in 1975) and only 20.5 per cent in the secondary sector. Such a picture is overly simplistic; because this typology ignores service jobs in the manufacturing sector (as well as manufacturing jobs in the service sector), it provides only a partial view of the nature of the metropolitan production system.

Employing an alternative typology based upon the role played by an establishment, we obtain the following portrait of full-time employment in metropolitan Geneva's economy in 1985 (Figure 5.3 and Table 5.1). Three roles (distribution, circulation and fabrication) represent major shares of total employment (between 25 per cent and 31 per cent); these are complemented by employment in the regulation role, which represents an important aspect of Geneva's production system. In the case of each of these roles, certain activity networks are dominant. The portrait that emerges is that of a highly diversified, but relatively balanced, economy.

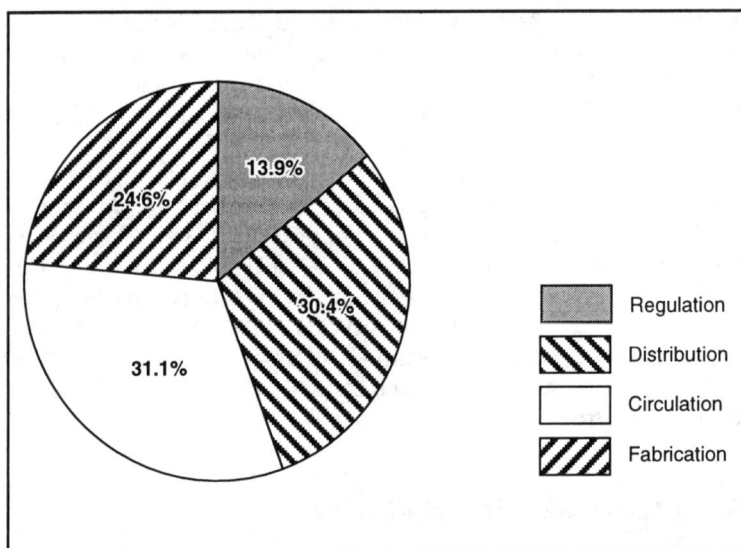

Source: Bailly and Boulianne (1992).

Figure 5.3   Economic roles, metropolitan Geneva, 1985

Table 5.1   Selected major activity networks, metropolitan Geneva, 1985

Role and activity network	Percentage of total employment
Fabrication	
Manufactured goods	12.8
Construction and civil engineering	9.1
Circulation	
Information flows	9.1
Financial flows	9.2
Distribution	
Retailing	8.7
Restaurants and hotels	6.4
Health-related	6.4
Regulation	
International regulation	8.1

Source: Bailly and Boulianne (1992).

Table 5.2 Economic structure by occupational function, metropolitan Geneva, 1985

Function	Fabrication	Circulation	Distribution	Regulation	All
Research & development	2.9	4.3	2.4	2.3	3.1
Logistics	4.7	8.3	6.2	4.7	6.5
Management	12.3	40.3	16.2	61.8	26.5
Production & operations	73.4	7.2	11.3	2.2	24.8
Sales & marketing	6.2	37.0	58.2	24.8	35.7
Unidentified	0.5	2.9	5.7	4.2	3.4
Total	100.0	100.0	100.0	100.0	100.0

Source: Bailly and Boulianne (1992).

As noted above, an alternative manner of analysing economic structure is through the use of occupation, producing a portrait of economic function (Table 5.2). This table holds few surprises, indicating, for example, that the highest concentration of occupation type in fabrication activities is in production and operations; in circulation activities, it is in management, and sales and marketing; in distribution, it is in sales and marketing; and in regulation activities, it is in management. For the metropolitan economy as a whole, sales and marketing functions have the highest percentage, followed by management, and production and operations.

An examination of the evolution of the Geneva economy raises issues concerning the most efficient structural configuration of the production system, one that will ensure the long-term growth of the metropolitan economy. Figure 5.4 indicates the changes in economic structure that occurred over the period 1975–85. There is clearly a reorientation of activities towards the circulation role (a gain of 4.2 percentage points). In particular, it is information

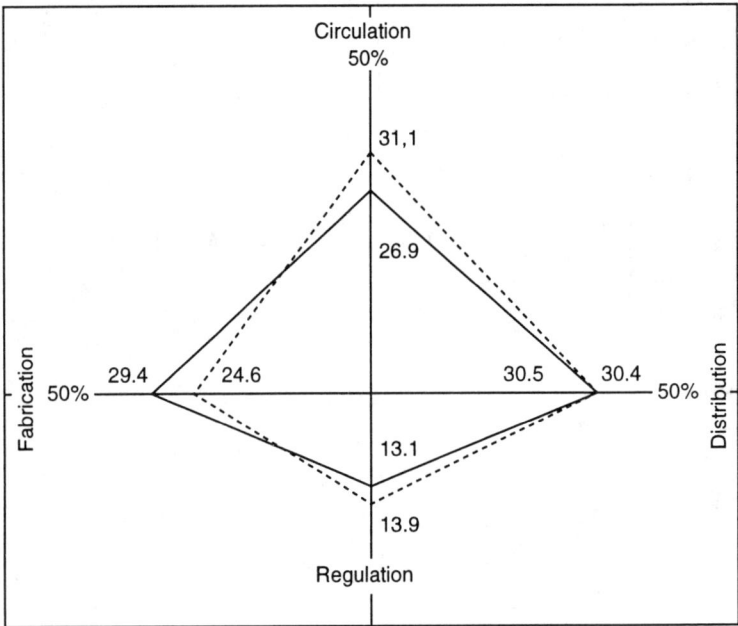

Source: Bailly and Boulianne (1992).

Figure 5.4   Evolution of roles, metropolitan Geneva, 1975–85

flows (+1.7 per cent) and financial flows that are the most developed, reflecting the ability of a large metropolitan area such as Geneva to minimize the transaction costs of firms. Information processing for firms is growing at the most rapid pace, illustrating the necessity of these services for all firms, whether they be classified in the primary, secondary or tertiary sectors. Banking and wholesaling have also witnessed significant employment increases.

Distribution activities have remained stable over the period (–0.1 percentage points). Contrary to the often-held image of Geneva as primarily a commercial centre, retailing employment declined over the period by 2.1 per cent, while the restaurant–hotel sector and the health sectors increased by 0.7 per cent and 0.8 per cent, respectively. It appears that the upper limit for some of these activities has been reached in several functional areas.

Regulation activities have similarly been very stable, contrary to the image projected of a proliferation of private and public regulation in Geneva. With the exception of international regulation which, as we have seen, accounted for 8.1 per cent of total employment in 1985, Geneva remains relatively poorly endowed with both public-sector (+0.6 per cent increase) and private-sector regulation. The latter, for example, represents only 2 per cent of total employment, clearly inferior to the circulation activities in both Zurich and Basle.

Finally, the increase in the circulation category is compensated for by a significant decrease (–4.8 percentage points) in fabrication activity, jobs related to the transformation of material or the production of goods. This tendency is not unique to Geneva, but reflects a general trend in which new production techniques require fewer less-skilled workers. While the goods-producing sector is the most affected (–4.5 per cent), the construction and civil engineering sector remained relatively stable. In part, the reduction of fabrication employment reflects the greater utilization of both internalized and externalized service inputs in the goods production process.

Table 5.3 indicates the evolution of both full-time and part-time employment by economic roles, and their major sub-sets in metropolitan Geneva over the study period. In sum, metropolitan Geneva has been able to take advantage of both the general expansion of circulation activities in the economy and certain specific activity networks within the distribution and regulation roles. In spite of a certain logical contraction of specific roles due to changes in the way in which both goods and services are produced, the metropolitan economy remains both dynamic and diversified. Finally, the two major sub-systems (fabrication and circulation) went from

Table 5.3   Evolution of economic roles, metropolitan Geneva, 1975–85:
             full-time and part-time employment

	Full-time		Part-time	
	1975	1985	1975	1985
Fabrication	29.5	24.6	28.1	22.8
Resource Exploit.	3.1	2.7	3.2	2.9
Construction & Eng.	9.0	9.1	8.2	8.0
Manufactured goods	17.4	12.8	16.7	11.9
Circulation	26.9	31.1	25.6	29.0
Material & persons	11.7	12.8	11.2	12.0
Information	7.4	9.1	7.0	8.5
Financial	7.8	9.2	7.4	8.5
Distribution	30.5	30.4	33.7	34.8
Consumer	19.9	18.9	20.4	20.0
Social	10.6	11.5	13.3	14.8
Regulation	13.1	13.9	12.6	13.4
Public	3.2	3.8	3.5	4.0
Private	1.9	2.0	1.5	1.8
International	8.0	8.1	7.6	7.6
Total	100.0	100.0	100.0	100.0

Source: Bailly and Boulianne (1992).

56.3 per cent to 55.7 per cent of total employment (–0.6 per cent), while the 'social' sub-system (distribution and regulation) increased from 43.7 per cent to 44.3 per cent. This remarkable stability of the two major sub-systems indicates that rearrangements of the economic structure are occurring at the level of individual activity networks.

Economic and social restructuring towards a decline?

With the rise of flexible forms of production, the role of Geneva changed in the 1980s. The result for the metropolitan area is both an internal restructuring and the departure of firms looking towards a location in the EU. The region is becoming more specialized: some strategic financial and commercial activities stay close to the centre to benefit from face-to-face contact. Other service activities are located in peripheral areas to get cheaper land; the choice of peripheral location is linked to communication networks (airport and express ways). This deconcentration of activities reaches neighbouring France and Vaud Canton, and even places located one hour from Geneva.

This specialization of activities generates social and spatial divisions of labour. Many skilled and international workers are moving to France and Vaud, where the cost of living is lower. The result of this recent trend is the departure of firms and people from Geneva city, with major consequences for the income taxes of the canton and the city. Other consequences can be felt in the housing market and office rental. Geneva is entering a difficult economic period that has to be analysed in detail in this chapter.

The principal reasons for firms choosing a large urban centre are the following (Marshall, 1988):

- need for skilled labour;
- need to be close to complementary activities (offices functions, financial institutions, other services);
- need to be located close to the market; and
- environmental, cultural and social amenities.

Another factor explaining the centralization of new activities is linked to the locational dependence between them and the head offices of major corporations. Headquarters purchase their services in their direct proximity and, since they are highly concentrated in a few large metropolitan areas, the demand for services is also concentrated.

Urban centres, well endowed with head office establishments, are in a favourable position, as is shown in Paris, Zurich and Frankfurt, for example. Considerations of head office location and of corporate control are of vital importance for understanding the evolution of European cities (Illeris, 1989). In the case of Geneva, the following points apply:

- skilled labour is expensive and limited, owing to Swiss laws regarding immigration;
- if complementary activities can be found for international regulation (UN) and financial institutions, as a result of its specialization Geneva does not possess a variety of high-level service activities (as Zurich does);
- Geneva, small in size, is not a market, and the political situation of Switzerland in Europe (outside the European Union) does not favour an expansion of its size;

- with regard to Geneva's environmental, social and cultural amenities, the city enjoys a good image, thanks to its lake, the Alps, and its theatres and cultural activities;
- many Swiss head offices and major corporations have moved over the last ten years from Geneva to Zurich; and questions concerning the location of European headquarters of many US firms are raised by the political and economic isolation of Switzerland.

Most of these factors do not favour Geneva as a location for new economic activities in the 1990s. The city lacks forces of agglomeration which tend to produce what may be termed 'a complex of corporate activities': the spatial clustering and mutual symbiosis of (1) the head or divisional offices of primary, secondary and tertiary-sector firms; (2) high-order financial establishments; and (3) the producer-services firms that provide inputs to the first two types, as well as to each other. This complex of corporate activities is analogous to the complex of manufacturing activities that characterizes a 'new industrial space', in terms of its tightly woven network of input–output linkages. Further, with increasing vertical disintegration in the producer-services sector, the external economies of such corporate complexes are becoming more pronounced, and are increasingly found in the biggest metropolitan areas of Europe.

Urban policy

As shown in the preceding sections, in Geneva the economic structures guide the development of the metropolitan area. By chance, more than by deliberate marketing policies, Geneva is one of the most successful cities in Europe in terms of income, standard of living and quality of environment. Benefiting from a pleasant natural environment, a good level of arts and culture, and a high quality of services, Geneva became a functional urban region (FUR) in a context of liberalism and 'laissez-faire'. It is through federal policies of immigration and land use that the canton develops its urban policy, long oriented towards stability; controls over labour permits and urban growth, especially on agricultural land, have been widely used. Simple zoning laws, allowed by the 'Loi sur l'Aménagement du Territoire' (LAT[4]) could prevent the development of new offices and manufacturing plants around the built-up areas. And in the case of new projects (such as freeways, parking lots, airports and residential or industrial developments) the democratic control, through local referendum, could delay them by five to ten years, and even reject them. The result is a strict control of urban sprawl and an extension into France of some of its activities. The low social housing provision in Geneva and the 'frontaliers' policy mean that many blue-collar workers commute from France, illuminating a clearly spatial division of labour.

Geneva is a clear example of a city which evolved on the basis of free market forces, with a form of regulation derived from social control. In many cities, such an approach to urban policy generates major equity problems, such as poor housing provision for some social groups, poor access to services (medical and social services) and often high crime rates and serious social problems. In Geneva, where the unemployment rate was very low during the 1980s (under 2 per cent) and where the average wages were higher than in most other European countries (for example, a typical French service worker doubles his wages when he takes a job in Geneva), these equity problems did not emerge. There are no ghettos in Geneva, and dilapidation of neighbourhoods (used sometimes by 'legal' squatters) is as a rule a sign of impending rehabilitation. Geneva appears to be an island of wealth, with good services and a high standard of living, where few social problems can be discerned.

The consequences of the high standard of living are mainly felt in high housing prices and in a high rate of traffic congestion, due to the widespread use of the motor car. The latter problem is confronted by indirect policies only. The question of environmental pollution has led to the adoption of lead-free petrol laws (the first of their kind in Europe) and the construction of a new freeway network. Other recent measures include the improvement of the public transport system, which makes extensive use of electric tramways, and the construction of a regional network to reduce congestion. With respect to the housing problems, the situation benefited from a recent decrease in demand, linked to the economic crisis. This led to an average reduction in rent prices. The economic trend suggests that Geneva can be affected – like any city – by the growing unemployment rate, which could result in serious social problems. To avert such a danger and to prolong its success, Geneva will now need to make a more deliberate attempt to attract international agencies and private-sector headquarters. To this end, some changes are appearing in the city's policies. In 1993, a marketing campaign, 'Genève Gagne', was started at the behest of the Chamber of Commerce. The campaign aimed to develop a new image of a dynamic city, but based on its history, its culture and its environment. Influential individuals and interest groups (private banks) are the leaders of the project. The federal government has been asked to help, by providing improvements in infrastructure (public transport, projects linked to the headquarters of the United Nations). The cantonal government is expected to provide support by not being as strict as usual where permits for development and for foreign employees are concerned.

Geneva's urban policy can only be understood in the context of transnational cooperation and the new European flexible economy. Its future depends on the answer to one major question: will Switzerland eventually join the EU, in spite of the rejection of its candidacy by the electorate? The Geneva region remains divided into two states, two *départements*, two cantons. These administrative units are the source of urban policies, but they are not always in agreement when the time comes to set goals. Many measures are now being taken to innovate in the functioning of the region; these measures recognize that metropolitan problems do not always stop at jurisdictional boundaries. Although progress is being made, much remains to be done if metropolitan Geneva is to maintain its standing as an important international city.

Geneva's international administrative centre is just as fragile as its standing as an economic centre. The attempts of Kurt Waldheim to move the United Nations' offices from Geneva to Vienna when he served as its General Secretary were an obvious sign of Geneva's vulnerability to political decisions beyond its control. There are also some recent examples that demonstrate that major airlines do not consider Geneva to be a major hub in Europe; this is one of the reasons for the departure of American Airlines. Negative urban externalities – such as high wages, high land prices, shortage of housing and traffic congestion – played a role in the decision of some organizations either to move away from the Geneva metropolitan area altogether or to select another location within or outside the city. Battelle Institute moved to Frankfurt, the First City Bank of Boston moved to Luxembourg and, after a systematic search for a location, Euronews landed in Lyons.

Even at the intrametropolitan level, there is a movement towards neighbouring cantons and to France. Non-strategic activities (back office function in producer services for example) show a tendency to move to the Vaud and Neuchatel cantons. In Archamps, in France, just across the Swiss border, a new technology park is trying to attract high-tech activities and offices geared towards the European Union as a market. Even if Geneva manages to hold on to its 'golden triangle', its still favourably situated airport, its new European headquarters (Dupont) and its reputation as a well-known place for exhibitions (Palexpo), many enterprises are already settling partly or entirely in France because of their need to expand.

These movements reflect the difficulties of a small metropolitan area, located in a 'closed' country. As a result of the 6 December 1992 referendum rejecting the proposed integration of Switzerland in the European Union, these trends will grow stronger in the near future. Some firms, looking towards the European Union, are searching for more attractive locations in the French regions around Geneva. And in Switzerland regulation activities are moving to the main economic city, Zurich. In sum, the picture is one of specialization in international political activities, where Geneva has comparative advantages, and a loss of economic activities, owing to the massive restructuring of European production systems.

Conclusion

A new metropolitan network is appearing in Europe; the result of these changes is a functional redistribution of activities among cities. On the one hand, we see the increasing importance of international political activities in the Geneva economy, with its multiplier effect on tourism and retail trade. On the other hand, new forms of inter-firm organization are pushing firms towards Zurich or the EU countries. Consequently, Geneva is losing its industrial base and some offices that play key roles in the evolution of the Swiss production system. The city also stands to lose firms supplying business services to producers who are shifting location to take advantage of the new integrated Europe.

These structural changes occurring in Geneva are not unique; what is unique is its specialization in world international activities. Is this specialization a chance for the future? If Geneva can play, at this level, the role of a 'new service space', it will retain its attraction. But many cities are now competing for these activities and, since Switzerland is not a member of the UN, Geneva is going to have more and more difficulties attracting additional UN agencies and offices; the most recent example being the UN environment office, where New York was preferred to Geneva. In the new world networks, Geneva will play a role in the future only if it keeps its comparative advantages in international and financial affairs.

Notes

1   The author acknowledges the useful comments on this paper from Professor L.J. Gibson.
2   In 1990: 144 hotels and 13 350 beds, with 1 959 717 nights spent by foreigners and 361 000 by Swiss.
3   The term 'metropolitan Geneva' is equated with its canton where statistical data are concerned.
4   The LAT was passed by the federal government after the Swiss electorate turned down the C.K. 75 project, which would have given the federal government planning controls (*aménagement du Territoire*). The LAT requires all the cantons to prepare a master plan, but, 15 years after it was passed, some cantons still have not complied.

References

Bailly, A. (1992) 'Genève: maillage spatial et relations transfrontalières' [Geneva: spatial texture and cross-border relations], *Revue Géographique de l'Est*, 3, pp.217–31.

Bailly, A. and L. Boulianne (1992) *L'évolution des activités économiques du Canton de Genève* [Economic development in the Canton of Geneva], Genève: Département de l'Economie Publique.

Bonneville, M., M.-A. Buisson, N. Commerçon and N. Rousier (1992) *Villes européennes et internationalisation* [European cities and internationalization], Recherches en Sciences Humaines 9, Université de Lyon.

Brunet, R. (ed.) (1989) *Les villes européennes* [The cities of Europe], Paris: La Documentation Française.

Coffey, W. and A. Bailly (1990) 'Service Activities and the Evolution of Production Systems: An International Comparison', *Environment and Planning A*, 22, pp.1607–20.

Coffey, W. and A. Bailly (1992) 'Producer Services and Systems of Flexible Production: An exploratory analysis', *Urban Studies*, 29, pp.857–68.

Illeris, S. (1989) *Services and Regions in Europe*, Aldershot: Gower.

Marshall, J.N. (1988) *Services and Uneven Development*, Oxford : Oxford University Press.

Messerli, P. (1991) 'Die Schweiz und Europa' [Switzerland and Europe], *Geographische Rundschau*, 9, pp.494–502.

Scott, Allen (1988) *New Industrial Spaces*, London: Pion.

Soldatos, P. (1989) *The N.I.C.E. Project*, unpublished manuscript, University of Montreal.

6   Lisbon: metropolis between centre and periphery

Jorge Gaspar

Introduction

The Lisbon metropolitan area (LMA) had 2.5 million inhabitants in 1991, amounting to approximately a quarter of the population of Portugal. It is the country's main urban centre. Its closest competitor is the Oporto metropolitan area, 300 kilometres to the north, with 1.2 million inhabitants. These two are followed at some distance by a number of cities and small conurbations, each with about 100 000 inhabitants: Coimbra, Braga, Funchal (Madeira), Faro and Aveiro (Figure 6.1). Thus the outstanding characteristic of the Portuguese urban system is that it revolves around two main centres. Some other important aspects are the proliferation of small urban centres of 5000 to 50 000 inhabitants and the existence of dispersed urbanization, chiefly in the coastal strip to the north of the Lisbon metropolitan area. This is a narrow strip that accounts for a fifth of the country's land area and includes Lisbon and Oporto and three-quarters of the population (Gaspar and Jensen-Butler, 1992). With the recent improvement in the means of communication and the speeding up of the urbanization process in this coastal strip, a potential 'Portuguese Metropolitan Region' is beginning to take shape. With its 7.5 million inhabitants, it will be a remarkable urban area in the context of both the Iberian Peninsula and the Atlantic seaboard of Europe (see DGDR, 1993).

Lisbon became an urban community at the time of the Roman Empire, when the fishing port in the Tagus estuary acquired a municipal statute that gave it the same rights as the imperial capital. During the Muslim domination between 791 and 1146, the port was an important link between the Mediterranean and the Atlantic seaboard. However, it was only with the formation of the state of Portugal in the middle of the thirteenth century that Lisbon began to increase in importance. It became the country's political and economic capital, a sea and river port, a crucial link between the Mediterranean and the Atlantic, and a point of de-

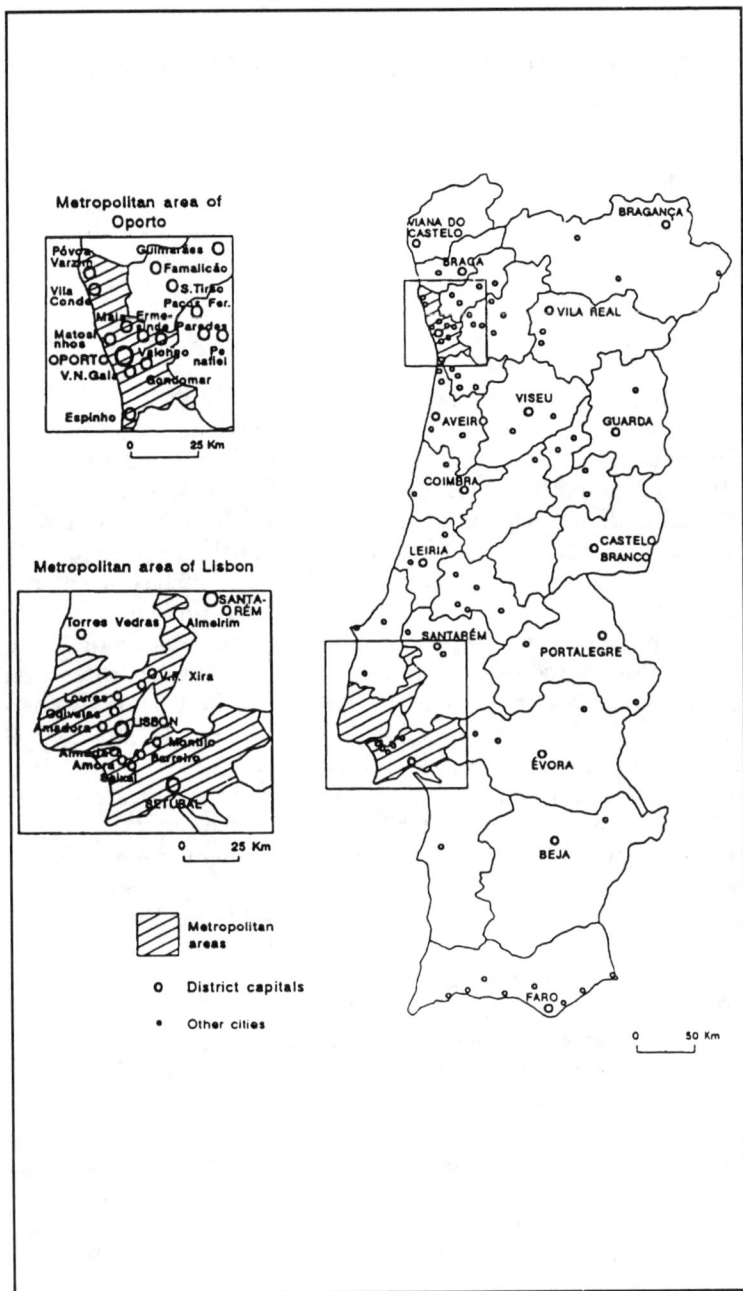

Figure 6.1   The Portuguese urban system

parture for ocean navigation started by the Portuguese in the fifteenth century.

Lisbon was one of the most important cities in Europe in the sixteenth century and was the pivot of a very unbalanced urban system. The capital had about 100 000 inhabitants, while no other city in the country could boast more than 15 000. Until the city of Oporto began to grow at a faster rate in the middle of the nineteenth century, Portugal revolved around Lisbon.

The concentration of political and economic power at one central point that was endowed with exceptionally favourable natural conditions gave Lisbon competitive advantage in relation to other European cities between the thirteenth and the seventeenth centuries, and this helped to strengthen national unity (Gaspar, 1993). The fact that Portugal built up a solid economy based on overseas trade and, later, on its colonial empire, enabled it to retain its independence from Spain.

Lisbon was the leader of urban systems that first stretched throughout North Africa and India and later included the cities founded by the Portuguese in Brazil and, in the nineteenth and twentieth centuries, in Angola and Mozambique. In 1974, Lisbon headed an urban system with Luanda, Oporto and Lourenço Marques (today Maputo) as its secondary centres. Lisbon was cut off from the African territories when these gained their independence, which in turn led to a loss of its functional and political importance. Most of the important firms in the manufacturing and energy sectors, as well as banks and insurance companies with head offices in Lisbon, were nationalized in 1974–5. This undercut Lisbon's economic control function. At the same time, Oporto, the centre of an area of labour-intensive manufacturing – especially textiles and footwear – that mainly produced for the export market, saw its power increase.

Decolonization in 1975 caused upheaval of another type as well. It led to the repatriation of about 600 000 Portuguese citizens from the former colonies, around a half of whom settled in the Lisbon metropolitan area. This sudden inflow accentuated the problems of unemployment and urban chaos, and led to a certain degradation of the capital. Portugal's integration into the European Community on 1 January 1986 gave Lisbon a new lease of life. It benefited greatly from the process of denationalization, which began in the 1980s and strengthened the city's economic, financial and political importance at the national and the international level (Gaspar, 1992).

Throughout history, Lisbon's primacy and importance as the country's capital have been strongest in periods when Portugal played an important role internationally and enjoyed internal prosperity. Portugal's peripheral situation in the Iberian Peninsula and in Europe determined this phenomenon. In other words, primacy goes hand-in-hand with competitiveness, which is one of the costs of being peripheral.

The city and the metropolitan area: structure and functions

The city of Lisbon stands on the northern bank of a small inland sea in the Tagus estuary, being linked to the ocean by a narrow channel. A riverside city closely associated with both ocean and river navigation, Lisbon spread along its river until the nineteenth century. It was with the advent of mechanized transport, first the railway, then the tramway, that the city began to expand inland. River shipping has linked the two banks of the river from the beginning, the southern bank always being subordinate to its northern counterpart. Development on the southern bank gave rise to a multicentred urban system rather than the total domination of the centre on the northern bank.

Population dynamics

Covering an area of 84 square kilometres, the municipality of Lisbon reached its population peak of 807 937 inhabitants in 1981. The 1980s saw a sharp demographic decline as a result of the growth of the service sector and a rise in living space per capita. The census of 1991 showed that Lisbon had 663 404 inhabitants.

The metropolitan area covers 3122 square kilometres, having 18 municipalities and 2 535 679 inhabitants, a density of 812 inhabitants per square kilometre. The settlement pattern, however, is very unbalanced. The northern bank, with its 1185 inhabitants per square kilometre, is more densely populated than the southern bank, which has 421 inhabitants per square kilometre. But the contrasts are even greater when examined at the municipal level, ranging from a high density of 7913 inhabitants per square kilometre in Lisbon to a low of 75 inhabitants per square kilometre in Azambuja (Table 6.1).

Suburban development occurred rather late. Although it began to appear at the end of the nineteenth century, it was only during the Second World War that the growth of the city's population speeded up. Growth was fuelled by the exodus from the provinces. The population increase was much more pronounced in the municipalities on the northern bank that were served by the rail-

Table 6.1   The Lisbon metropolitan area: extent and population, 1991

	Resident population	Area (km^2)	Population density (Inhabs/km^2)
Amadora	177 167	23.76	7 457
Azambuja	19 568	261.65	75
Cascais	153 294	97.06	1 579
Loures	322 158	186.49	1 727
Mafra	43 731	291.42	150
Oeiras	151 342	45.75	3 308
Sintra	260 951	316.05	826
V.F. Xira	103 571	293.88	352
Alcochete	10 169	94.49	108
Almada	151 783	69.98	2 169
Barreiro	85 768	33.81	2 537
Moita	65 086	55.08	1 182
Montijo	36 038	347.36	104
Palmela	43 857	461.82	95
Seixal	116 912	93.58	1 249
Sesimbra	27 246	194.98	140
Setúbal	103 634	170.58	608
Lisbon	663 404	83.84	7 913
Northern bank excl. Lisbon	1 231 782	1 516.06	812
Southern bank	640 493	1 521.68	421
Lisbon MA	2 535 679	3 121.58	812

way. The Tagus was a barrier to the development of the southern bank and it was only from the beginning of the 1960s, following the construction of the bridge (opened in 1966) that the population growth rate increased, especially in the municipalities that were nearest Lisbon and were served by river transport. The bridge also had the psychological effect of overcoming the barrier, as there was also a pronounced rise in the number of passengers using the ferry-boats that ply between the two banks in the first years after its opening (Gaspar, 1972a).

The population of the city of Lisbon remained stable while the suburban population in municipalities on the northern and the southern banks grew rapidly in the 1960s and 1970s. The 1980s saw a distinct about turn in this development. Despite the above-mentioned decline in the population of the city-metropolis, the

Table 6.2 Population trends in the Lisbon metropolitan area, 1960–91

	Resident population				Change (%)		
	1960	1970	1981	1991	60/70	70/81	81/91
Lisbon	801 155	769 044	807 937	663 404	-4.01	5.06	-17.89
Northern bank excl. Lisbon	412 293	669 821	1 109 459	1 231 782	58.20	65.64	11.03
Southern bank	201 459	400 876	584 648	640 493	37.54	45.84	9.55
Lisbon MA	1 504 907	1 839 741	2 502 044	2 535 679	21.08	36.00	1.34

Table 6.3 The changing population structure of the Lisbon metropolitan area, 1981–91

	Young dependants		Elderly dependants		Total dependants		Ageing index	
	1981	1991	1981	1991	1981	1991	1981	1991
Lisbon	28.4	21.4	21.4	27.7	49.8	49.2	75.5	129.3
N. bank excl. Lisbon	38.8	24.3	10.7	16.6	49.4	40.8	27.5	68.3
Southern bank	37.8	28.0	12.3	13.5	50.1	43.5	32.7	55.2
Lisbon MA	35.2	24.2	14.5	17.5	49.7	41.7	41.2	72.5

overall population of the metropolitan area changed very little, showing an increase of 1.3 per cent between 1981 and 1991 (Table 6.2). At the same time, there was a clear inversion in the development of the two banks. While the northern bank lost population, chiefly owing to the decline in Lisbon, there was a sharp increase, of 9.55 per cent, on the southern bank. Overall, the metropolitan area lost 43 558 people during the 1980s.

Some special points must be stressed concerning this overall trend. The main influx in the 1960s was of rural workers, while in the 1970s it was of Portuguese citizens returning from the former colonies; in the 1980s, the migrants came predominantly from Portuguese-speaking African countries, mainly Cape Verde, Guinea-Bissau and Angola. In the interior of the metropolitan area, the main movement was from the city of Lisbon to the suburban municipalities and from the northern to the southern bank. The pattern of outflow is not so clear, but in addition to emigration abroad – mainly to other European countries and North America – migration to the provinces has assumed distinct importance. This flow is composed both of the younger generation and of retired people who return to their birthplace where, usually, significant improvements in basic infrastructure have been achieved (Tables 6.3 and 6.4).

Table 6.4   Households and household size in the Lisbon metropolitan area, 1981–91

	Families		Average Family Size	
	1981	1991	1981	1991
Lisbon	285 960	247 020	2.83	2.69
Northern bank excl. Lisbon	346 192	414 596	3.20	2.97
Southern bank	185 013	212 849	3.16	3.01
Lisbon MA	817 165	874 465	3.06	2.90

Changes in the economy

Owing to its size, the Lisbon metropolitan area contains an important agricultural zone, especially in terms of production. Fishing still has an important place in the national economy, although

Table 6.5   Employment structure by sector in the Lisbon metropolitan area, 1981–91

	Industry			Tertiary			Total		
	1982	1986	1991	1982	1986	1991	1982	1986	1991
Northern bank	19.5	17.5	14.8	47.1	45.2	44.1	31.1	29.5	27.4
Southern bank	8.3	6.5	5.4	4.1	4.4	5.0	6.3	5.5	5.3
Lisbon MA	27.8	24.0	20.2	51.2	49.6	49.1	37.4	35.0	32.7
Mainland Portugal	100.0	100.0	100.0	100.0	100.0	100.0	100.0	100.0	100.0

154

both the number of persons employed in the sector and the total catch have been declining. The economy of the metropolitan area is based on the secondary and tertiary sectors. Employment in the manufacturing industries accounted for 20 per cent of the national total of this sector, while tertiary activities accounted for 49 per cent (Tables 6.5 and 6.6).

Table 6.6   Share of technical and administrative personnel in total employment, 1981–91

	1981	1986	1991
Northern bank	3.2	4.4	4.5
Southern bank	1.5	1.8	1.8
Mainland Portugal	1.8	2.3	2.3

The Lisbon metropolitan area is traditionally the leading innovator of manufacturing industry and tends to maintain a greater concentration of technologically advanced industries and capital-intensive units. In the past, production was mainly geared to the home market, in contrast to the central and north coast areas, where more traditional and labour-intensive industries are to be found, sometimes relocated from the Lisbon area, with production geared to foreign markets. (Signs for the 1990s point to a sharp rise in production for export.)

As industrialization took off in the 1950s, basic industries were chiefly set up in the Lisbon area. Soon afterwards, traditional industries such as textiles, cork and fish canning gradually lost their importance. This process became more pronounced up to the beginning of the 1970s, as specialized centres of an international dimension were developed, such as shipbuilding and ship repair and petrochemical industries. An effort was made to expand production for the home market in the motor car sector, first through setting up assembly lines and the production of components and later through the reinforcement of the 'filière' (Ferrão and Vale, 1995; CCRLVT, 1987).

Urban growth, resulting in the expansion of the potential market and a rapid rise in the supply of labour, especially female, attracted both national and foreign investments in other sectors such as food, clothing and electronic materials (Baptista, 1989). The crisis of early 1973, which continued until the mid-1980s, had a serious effect on manufacturing in the Lisbon metropolitan area, and many obsolete and non-competitive units closed down. The state intervened in the basic sectors, either by nationalizing or in other ways, which maintained high levels of employment but also caused low profitability. Contrary to normal developments, the crisis led to a temporary strengthening of the labour-intensive sectors, and also those geared to export markets. Despite the recurring crises, civil construction and public works maintained high levels of employment during the period, with the overall effect of strengthening secondary activities in the Lisbon area and stabilizing its share of national employment throughout the 1970s. Then, from the mid-1980s, and as a result of Portugal's entry into the European Community, the Lisbon area's industrial base was restructured, developing a distinct international dimension.

The economic crisis and the political and social upheavals which the country suffered after 1974 did not allow a restructuring of the economy in the same way as in other industrialized nations. The service sector underwent a very slow process of modernization, which becomes clear if it is analysed in qualitative terms; nevertheless, services tend to play an ever-increasing part in the economy. In a national context, the services sector of the Lisbon metropolitan area basically maintained their importance during the 1970s, which in practice was expressed in a slight increase in their importance in the area itself and a rise in quality at national level.

The functional structure corresponds to a complex spatial pattern, despite the fact that a fairly simple model can be seen in its general outlines. Lisbon city has increased its importance in the service sector in both quality and quantity. Decentralization that began towards the end of the 1980s and the beginning of the 1990s has not yet proceeded far enough to change the dominance of the city of Lisbon as the heart of the service, business and related activities sectors; in addition, Lisbon still has industrial activity, accounting for 7 per cent of national industrial employment in 1991. The municipalities on the northern bank have a diversified economic and social composition. Yet there are regional differences, with the services sector and middle-class strata being more important in the west, while industry is still important to the north and east along the River Tagus. As a result of the industrial policy of the 1950s and 1960s, the southern bank retains its importance with regard to manufacturing industries, despite the fact that various sectors are declining and have not yet been replaced by new industries. The tertiary sector became the largest employer in the nine municipalities of the southern bank by the end of the 1970s, at the same time as they became more dependent on the labour market of the northern bank. But the southern bank continues to be one of the major areas of concentration of Portugal's industrial proletariat (Baptista, 1989). As a result of the crisis and the economic and social structures that it created, it is also the area with the highest rate of unemployment, which reached 20.1 per cent in the first half of the 1980s. It is over 14 per cent at present, compared to 6.5 per cent for the country as a whole (Table 6.7).

Table 6.7   Lisbon's share of unemployment, 1981–91 (per cent)

	1981	*1986*	*1991*
Northern bank	18.8	21.0	14.6
Southern bank	7.2	11.6	13.2
Lisbon MA	26.0	32.6	27.8
Mainland Portugal	100.0	100.0	100.0

Administrative structure

The main building-block of the administrative unit of the Lisbon metropolitan area is the municipality. The Lisbon metropolitan area was instituted in 1991 in the form of a special type of two-tier municipal association – the Metropolitan Assembly and the Metropolitan Board – both mainly made up of elected councillors. As the main party in 11 of the 18 municipal mayorships, the Communist Party chairs both organs. The power of the two organs is very limited, but can be widened by extra powers being delegated either by the municipalities or by central government.

The 305 Portuguese municipalities are among the biggest in Europe, with an average population of 32 337 inhabitants. Those of the Lisbon metropolitan area average 140 871 people. The powers of each municipality, however, are the same and, in relation to their size, their functions and financial resources are extremely limited in comparison to their European counterparts: the share of the municipalities in the total public spending of Portugal does not exceed 8 per cent.

Thus, despite the size of the LMA's municipalities, their powers and financial resources are limited and the main policy decisions regarding the chief sectors of the area – transport, education, health, energy, culture and so on – are made by the central government.

Urban policies: agents and plans

The recent political measures in Lisbon and its metropolitan area can be divided into three groups: national, metropolitan and municipal. As a result of the fragility and short life of the metropolitan area, it is the other two levels that basically influence the development of the urban area.

The positive integration of several sectoral policies, expressed in development and land management planning, is manifest at the national level in the Regional Development Plan (RDP), at the intermediary level in the Regional Land Management Plan for the Lisbon Metropolitan Area (PROTAML) and at the municipal level in the Municipal Land Management Plans (PDM). The main aim of the RDP is to negotiate a Community Support Framework (CSF) with the European Union. As part of a global development strategy for the country, the RDP only includes programmes, sub-programmes and measures that may be financed by the European Union. Besides including medium-term interrelated projects, it determines a great part of the public spending for the same period and an appreciable part of private investment. The first RDP of this type was the basis of the CSF that was in force between 1989 and 1993 (CCE, 1989). In 1993, Portugal presented a new RDP in Brussels, which forms the basis of the second CSF that will be in force between 1994 and 1999. The effects on urban development are remarkable in both cases, the RDP being one of the most effective support instruments for the process of urbanization.

The strategic options (DGDR, 1993) which underlie the present RDP set out the general guidelines for the country's urban policy, laying particular emphasis on the metropolitan areas of Lisbon and Oporto because of their strong international competitive potential. This strategic aim was spelled out explicitly: 'To strengthen the competitiveness of the metropolitan areas of Lisbon and Oporto' (DGDR, 1993, II). It is to be achieved through the RDP, which for the Lisbon metropolitan area means heavy investment in communications, education, professional training, scientific research, modernization of the economic base, urban renewal and environmental improvement. It also supports the preparations for Expo 98, which will lead to the renovation of the eastern part of the city and the relocation of its industries. Although not contemplated by the CSF, the strategic options place great emphasis on housing, especially in the Lisbon metropolitan area, including a plan to eliminate shanty towns, to recover and expand council housing, to improve rent support schemes, to revise the leasehold system as well as the development contracts in a joint public–private venture for the construction of houses with controlled rents, and to renovate the urban fabric.

Most of the investments proposed in the RDP and assigned to the CSF, with EU participation, are made by the central administration (including public enterprises), although there is also a significant contribution on the part of local authorities in the field of housing, transport and the environment (DGDR, 1993, III).

The Regional Land Management Plan (PROTAML) specifies guidelines for a 10-year development plan and coordinates the actions of the different bodies involved in the metropolitan area: municipalities, the central administration, and private and public operators of public services (CCRLVT, 1992). The PROTAML was launched as an initiative of the government through the Lisbon and Tagus Valley Region Planning Commission, and builds on the collaboration of the municipalities of the metropolitan area and the relevant sectoral government bodies. All these agents are represented in the Monitoring Committee. The plan was published in 1992, and has been scrutinized by the government, but has not yet been subjected to a final review by the Monitoring Committee.

The proposal for the PROTAML was well received on the part of the municipalities, despite the wide range of political parties. Rather, it was at ministerial level that most of the objections were raised, especially with regard to transport, health and education. Many important decisions were taken in the meantime concerning transport infrastructure that went against the PROTAML proposals, the most important being the one that restricts the expansion of the underground railway to the city of Lisbon. Measures have also been taken by the relevant ministries in the field of urban renewal and, above all, in council housing, that may have violated the guidelines of the PROTAML. Since they will lower the environmental quality of certain areas, they also contravene the strategic options.

The PDMs are land management plans at the municipal level that either cover the entire territory of a municipality (municipal master plans – MCP) or deal with specific areas in detail. MCPs are the most important land management instruments in Portugal today. Although they are basically limited to physical planning, MCPs necessarily have a strategic framework. In some cases, they may take the form of a strategic plan, articulating national and regional economic and social development policies. Municipal development guidelines and medium- and long-term policies are also defined (CML, 1992, 1993). In the absence of a PDM, the coordination of proposals and actions of the different municipalities is a delicate problem, with respect both to planning guidelines and to physical planning and implementation of measures accepted.

It would seem to make sense to confer powers upon the metropolitan authority and its two organs – assembly and board – so that it can assume responsibility for the coordination and viability of the actions promoted by central and local authorities. The PROTAML is a support instrument that responds to these demands. The realization of such an initiative, which would apparently gain a consensus of opinion, has run up against political difficulties at various levels. The party in power (PSD) is at present in a minority in the municipalities of the metropolitan area. As most of the mayors belong to the Communist Party, which is not even the main opposition party in Parliament, this party holds a majority on both the assembly and the board. Unlike the other 17 municipalities of the metropolitan area, the majority of the city of Lisbon council is made up of a coalition of the Socialist and Communist Parties, the mayor belonging to the former.

Policy areas

Economic policy

At the end of the 1960s and in the early 1970s, national economic development policy had an important urban component in proposals for creation of growth poles as instruments to promote territorial equilibrium, assisting the development of a network of medium-sized cities. The creation of a public corporation to promote industrial estates was the most significant instrument supporting this policy, even though the infrastructure created in some cities of the interior was not successful in its aims.

The first Community Support Framework for Portugal, working through a system of industrial incentives, can be regarded as a policy designed to develop and consolidate urban areas. Meanwhile, two complementary systems existed in terms of territorial restructuring. This meant that other tendencies continued or developed, influenced by other policies, such as transport policy, education, training and other types of infrastructure provision. The exception to this was the peninsula of Setúbal (in the southern part of the LMA). It enjoyed excellent labour market conditions and boosted high-quality infrastructure, especially in the field of transport. By virtue of an integrated development operation, it experienced convergence of public and private investments, both in productive sectors and in infrastructure (CCE, 1989; CCRLVT, 1987; Williams and Gaspar, 1992).

It is curious to note that the effects of this operation accelerated the transformation of some parts of the productive system, while in other parts they resulted in maintaining more or less obsolete conditions. For example, new investment and restructuring were attracted to engineering and transport, while in sectors such as clothing or cork, restructuring involving modernization and infrastructure development failed because the measures applied were insufficient.

At the level of the LMA, suitable conditions for the creation of economic policy exist currently, even though the metropolitan authority does not have the means, materials or logistic systems to undertake activities directed at the productive system. However, a project for the creation of an urban development agency is being launched, the principal object of which will be urban marketing and image creation. The municipalities of the LMA are also developing their own economic policies, which vary considerably from case to case. The most usual type of initiative is the provision of sites with suitable infrastructure, sometimes at below-market prices, and with due regard to urban marketing and image creation.

Data concerning the results of recent industrial restructuring are not yet available. Some specific analyses suggest that, as in the past, the Lisbon region is leading the process of innovation and modernization. The gains in productivity appear to be above the national average. A newly emerging reality concerns the Lisbon area's position in terms of exports; until the 1980s, manufacturing was more oriented towards the internal market, while in recent years the new industries have become more export-oriented. This tendency will be underscored by the new Ford–Volkswagen project, which produces for export.

Transport policy

The main vectors of transport policy in the LMA have been defined by central government and in particular, though not exclusively, by the Ministry of Transport (as an integrated part of public works projects). The absence of a metropolitan authority means that there is no coordination unit for the different transport operators. In addition, the most important operators are from the public sector, being under the complete or partial control of the Ministry of Transport.

The two major policy fields are accessibility, both internal and external, and the different means of transport. With respect to accessibility, the metropolitan area of Lisbon has benefited from important investments, both in infrastructure and in services. In the context of Portuguese geography, it has a clear advantage with respect to expressways and roads, which favours the use not only of the private car but also of trucks and buses, at the expense of rail transport. Investments in rail have been very limited and very selective. They have been directed almost exclusively at improvements in the Lisbon–Oporto corridor and in suburban lines, all lines with high levels of demand (Figure 6.2).

These policy options with respect to accessibility to the LMA from the rest of the country have, in general, been unrelated to a more comprehensive policy of territorial development. They have led to serious negative consequences, including environmental pollution, traffic congestion, loss of competitiveness in certain locations and, not least, anarchy in urban growth. However, it is

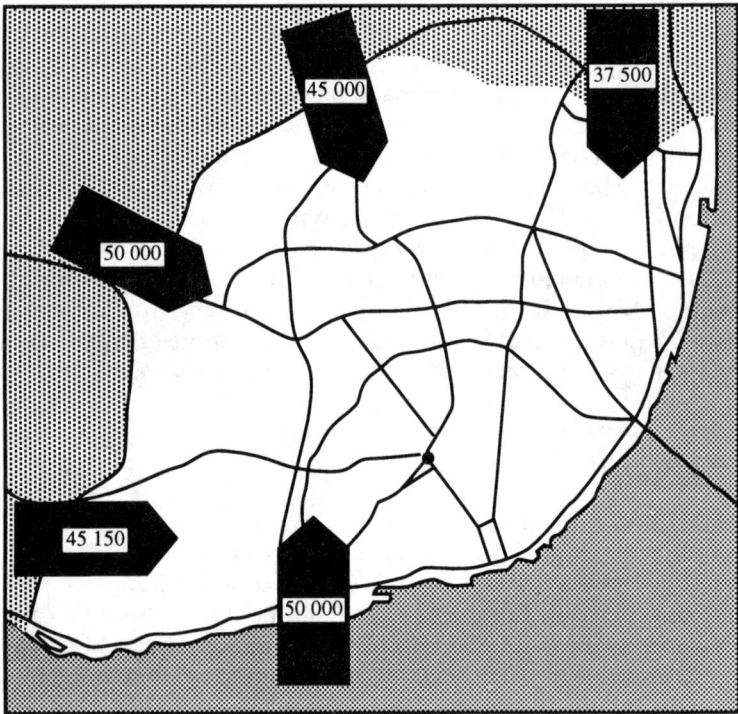

Figure 6.2   Inflow of traffic to Lisbon, 1990 (number of vehicles/day)

difficult to assess whether or not the economic system has become more competitive on the whole, as may have resulted from the increased accessibility of the main cities, both at the national and the regional level.

In general, changes in external accessibility with respect to road and rail traffic have provoked changes in the location of economic activity, in manufacturing and in services. This is clearly reflected in the decentralization, especially of industry, but also of those types of services not requiring high levels of demand. At the same time, the LMA has been strengthened in such fields as producer services of the type which require a location at a high level in the urban hierarchy and which also are affected profoundly by internationalization.

The transport system which links the LMA with the centre of the city involves five principal types of transport: private cars, buses, rail, metro, trams and ships (linking the two sides of the river Tagus). The metro, the tram, the ships and an important component of bus transport are provided by public enterprises, which are heavily subsidized by the state (CCRLVT, 1992). Investments in improvement of internal accessibility in the metropolitan area, including current investments, have favoured the private car and some segments of public transport (the metro and the train). There has been a qualitative and quantitative decline in the supply of river and bus transport, and trams have almost been abandoned, even though they have existed since the beginning of the century.

General deficiencies in the supply of transport have created severe pressure on suburban trains and on the metro in the city of Lisbon. Analysis and forecasts are unanimous in their conclusions that decentralization is necessary, and they recommend the improvement of accessibility to new central areas outside the city of Lisbon. Nevertheless, employment is still concentrated in the central area of Lisbon, especially tertiary employment. Its growth extends outwards from the centre and is supported by the limited metro network and penetration of suburban rail. In addition, this growth has been supported by transport improvements geared towards the private car. The recent privatization of bus services will not lead to an improved coordination of the public transport system. Futhermore, it will result in lower levels of service at locations where demand does not justify the operation of services which must run at a profit.

The only tendencies counter to the monocentric pattern of transport are related to the suburban expressway from Lisbon to Cascais, where business centres with considerable office employment are

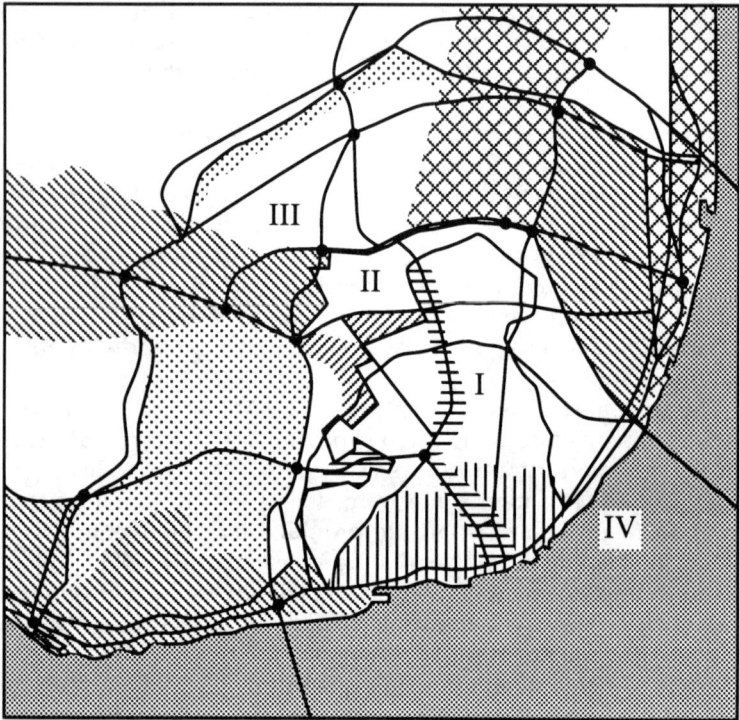

Urban Model – Zoning

I	Lisbon central area: city and metropolitan centre	▦	Historical centre
II	Urban fringe: tertiary belt	▤	Existing tertiary strip
III	Transitional ring: metropolitan-articulation	▨	Areas of expansion of tertiary activity
IV	Waterfront: linkage between the city and the river	▩	Inter-municipal urban continuous
		▧	Area for special uses

Figure 6.3   Zoning in the agglomeration of Lisbon

developing, and access to which is exclusively by private car. At the same time, the traditional industrial suburbs have expanded their dormitory role, which has attracted some services, but not enough to compensate for the loss of industrial employment. This problem is felt especially in the most important of these areas on the southern bank of the Tagus, the city of Barreiro. This city was the foremost industrial concentration of Portugal, connected to Lisbon by a ferry service, but after the completion of the new Tagus bridge it will experience a loss of relative centrality. This will boost its unemployment, its demographic decline and the aging of its population as a result of the outmigration of younger and more qualified people to other municipalities in the LMA.

The most important trends related to location of economic activity and residential development are as follows (Figure 6.3):

- the strengthening of the city of Lisbon, as the principal nucleus of tertiary activity;
- the emergence of tertiary centres, related to the use of the private car and oriented towards expressways, having an important land speculation component;
- a growing concentration of population on the axis served by railways;
- the spread of residential areas of low density, based upon transport by private car.

The construction of the new Tagus bridge and a rail link using the existing bridge will not necessarily reduce the level of congestion on the existing bridge, as current plans aim at increasing the interaction between the two major territorial units, the northern and southern banks of the Tagus. The new bridge will enter the city of Lisbon, but its southern end is located in areas of agriculture and forest. Therefore its completion will not contribute to reducing traffic pressure on the existing bridge. At the same time, new possibilities for land and property speculation will be opened up (CCRLVT, 1992; Silva, 1989; Silva, 1990a and 1990b).

Housing policy

Housing is one of the principal problems confronting the municipalities of the Lisbon metropolitan area and in particular the metropolis itself. It has not succeeded in responding to the needs accumulated over decades and to the demands generated by new influx of population, for example those arising from the return wave of migrants from Africa. The answers to these problems have been provided, following legislation, by the municipalities and by the central administration. The municipalities undertake planning and infrastructure provision, while the state, through INH (the National Housing Institute) and IGAPHE (the National Institute for the Administration and Transfer of National Heritage Properties of the State) provides finance. This takes place through contracts within programmes established by municipalities or co-operatives, offering reduced interest rates or loans to these bodies and even to private persons and institutions (Tables 6.8 and 6.9).

The supply of subsidized housing during the last 20 years has not kept pace with demand, which has been largely satisfied by the market, either in the formal or the informal sectors, including construction of one's own house. In the 1970s, the level of informal sector housing provision was very high indeed. In that decade, the number of shanties and other non-legal housing units grew very rapidly, accompanied by rapid increases in housing density. At the same time, serious deficiencies in provision of water, electricity and sewage disposal developed (Gaspar, 1984). In the 1980s, no marked changes occurred, except for improvements in provision of water and electricity. The municipalities, using the support of the European Regional Development Fund, have contributed to significant reductions in the number of houses with these deficiencies, though not in areas of illegal housing or shanties. During this decade, the number of housing units in the LMA grew by 10.3 per cent, principally in the municipalities of Lisbon, Sintra, Almada and Seixal.

The pressure of demand arising from immigration and from demand for secondary housing has resulted in the development of vast areas of illegal housing. These are found principally in the municipalities of Loures, Vila Franca de Xira and Cascais, north of the Tagus, and Seixal, Almada, Palmela and Setúbal, south of the river. At the same time as the development of illegal occupation, the progressive degradation of illegal housing already constructed also emerged.

In summary, the housing sector has been severely influenced by (1) the long-term lack of a rental market, because of inadequate flexibility of existing legislation, notably through the fixing of rents; (2) high levels of house prices and very high interest rates; and (3) profound distortions in rent levels of older property, resulting in disinvestment, loss of property value and lack of maintenance of buildings. For the immediate future, the principal policy objective for this sector was proposed in 1993, when the government approved a package of instruments designed to remove the shanties of the LMA by the turn of the century – the 'Special

Table 6.8 Occupied dwellings by type in the Lisbon metropolitan area, 1981–91

	Family dwellings									Persons/ dwelling	Families/ dwelling
	Normal		Shanties		Others		Total				
	No.	%	No.	%	No.	%	No.	%			
1981											
Lisbon	252 991	95.99	8 744	3.32	1 817	0.69	263 552	100.00		3.07	1.09
N. bank excl.											
Lisbon	363 982	97.43	7 146	1.91	2 458	0.66	373 586	100.00		2.97	0.93
Southern bank	208 989	98.11	1 934	0.91	2 093	0.98	213 016	100.00		2.74	0.87
Lisbon MA	825 962	97.15	17 824	2.10	6 368	0.75	850 154	100.00		2.94	0.96
1991											
Lisbon	268 930	96.71	6 741	2.42	2 410	0.87	278 081	100.00		2.39	0.89
N. bank excl.											
Lisbon	511 408	98.44	5 522	1.06	2 597	0.50	519 527	100.00		2.37	0.80
Southern bank	282 863	98.96	1 104	0.39	1 882	0.66	285 849	100.00		2.24	0.74
Lisbon MA	1 063 201	98.13	13 367	1.23	6 889	0.64	1 083 457	100.00		2.34	0.81

Table 6.9 Tenure structure of the housing stock in the Lisbon metropolitan area, 1981–91

	1981			1991			
	Ownership	Others	Total	Ownership	Rented	Others	Total
Lisbon	43 910	195 873	239 783	79 782	139 015	7 683	226 480
N. bank excl. Lisbon	140 936	179 916	320 852	250 350	129 622	13 996	393 968
Southern bank	77 102	98 953	176 055	132 349	69 183	6 600	208 132
Lisbon MA	261 948	474 742	736 690	462 481	337 820	28 279	828 580
Percentage							
Lisbon	18.3	81.7	100.0	35.2	61.4	3.4	100.0
N. bank excl. Lisbon	43.9	56.1	100.0	63.5	32.9	3.6	100.0
Southern bank	43.8	56.2	100.0	63.6	33.2	3.2	100.0
Lisbon MA	35.6	64.4	100.0	55.8	40.8	3.4	100.0

Rehousing Programme'. In fact, the degradation of large segments of territory in the LMA and in the Oporto MA was reaching disastrous proportions, with severe negative consequences for social cohesion and for economic development in the two most dynamic agglomerations of Portugal. Degradation of some suburban zones has led to the outward movement of parts of the middle class, principally the lower middle class, and a concentration of the most disadvantaged population groups, with an important ethnic component. The increasing degradation of these zones will create ghetto-like situations, with social unrest and ethnic and social confrontations, which are already beginning to appear.

The lack of housing and of access to basic services has increased the marginalization of considerable numbers of people. The resolution of these housing and infrastructure problems in areas of shanties and other degraded areas of the metropolitan areas will certainly have significant positive effects on social cohesion and on integration in the educational system and the labour market. The approach used to resolve the problems consists of a partnership between the central and local administrations on the basis of 50 per cent financial contribution from each, with responsibility for planning and construction being placed at the level of the municipality. In addition, other measures have been proposed:

- Provision of national heritage housing by IGAPHE in the Lisbon and Oporto MAs, donated to the municipalities, involving 15 000 dwellings with a total value of about 40 billion escudos.
- Creation of a programme of construction of low-cost housing in the two metropolitan areas. IGAPHE makes land available at reduced prices and there is a public competition for contracts to build low-cost housing, while housing quality is controlled by the National Civil Engineering Laboratory (LNEC).
- The opportunity for municipalities to acquire immediately on the market dwellings needed badly for rehousing.
- Inclusion of charitable institutions on equal terms in the programme of rehousing. These institutions obtain identical conditions concerning finance and writing off of debts.
- In addition, revision of rental agreements and of rental assistance in urban areas will be made, to correct the distortions created by earlier policies, and to adjust rent contracts and conditions of ownership.

In this context, as a part of the regional development plan for 1994–9 adopted by the national government, policies and activities have been proposed to renew the zones occupied by shanties in the metropolitan areas of Lisbon and Oporto (DGDR, 1993, III).

Taking into account that revitalization and urban renewal in these areas requires rehousing the local population in more humane living conditions, the objective of this line of action is to support site acquisition and the provision of these sites with infrastructure and facilities, commercial services and green spaces for recreation, in addition to housing.

The financial programme was developed on the basis of European Union support covering 50 per cent of the costs of site acquisition and the provision of necessary infrastructure. An area of 700 hectares is involved, which will provide accommodation for 25 000 families. In this context, IGAPHE has made general agreements of cooperation with municipalities in the two metropolitan areas involved in promotion of these activities. These agreements involve IGAPHE writing off 50 per cent of the cost of rehousing, and the municipalities have the option of obtaining long-term INH loans at low interest to cover the rest of the costs.

Green area policies and policies for environmental conservation

The green area policy of the Lisbon metropolitan area can be defined at two levels, the municipal and the central. This field is yet another in which it is clearly necessary to have an intermediate level of administration for the metropolitan area, at least for definition of strategies and the coordination of implementation and management. The above-named plan for the LMA (PROTAML) proposes a policy for green areas, but lack of approval and implementation threatens its viability in the future.

At the metropolitan level, the Department of Environment, working through the Institute of Environmental Protection, is the principal actor. Under its jurisdiction are such important areas as the Arrabida nature reserve, the protected area of Sintra-Cascais (at present being converted to a nature reserve), the nature reserves of the Tagus and Sado estuaries, and other protected zones and botanical reserves. At the local level, the municipalities limit their activities to intra-urban green spaces of varying dimensions, which usually are fairly small. The principal exception is to be found in Lisbon, where the forest park of Monsanto, developed in the 1940s, covers more than half a million hectares. Through the municipal plans, the municipalities have the capability of defining land use in their own areas. But the problem of implementation persists which, in many cases, after designation for non-urban use, can result in perverse effects. This situation can deteriorate in zones

designated as ecological or even agricultural areas by the legislation relating to competence over defining land use available to
departments of the environment and agriculture. Nevertheless,
the use of the environmental reserve was made for the first time
by municipalities in their local plans, which created a number of
problems, including the lack of uniform criteria for demarcation,
and difficulties of intermunicipal compatibility.

Thus we can observe the need for an intermediate level of planning and administration. The LMA retains a considerable potential for development of green areas, woods and agricultural zones,
which should be integrated in the urban and metropolitan structures. The importance of these options is underlined in a period of
major infrastructure and transport investment and new types of
industrial and urban development.

Cultural policy

Cultural activities and the development of relevant infrastructure
are an important policy issue for Lisbon. They fall under the jurisdiction of both the central and local administrations. In addition
to affirming the role of Lisbon at local, regional and national levels,
this policy has important consequences at the international level,
contributing to the international competitiveness of the city. The
availability of a large number of instruments and activities,
including many private organizations, does not in itself constitute
cultural policy. Duplication and lack of integration mean that,
despite many initiatives and the expenditure of much energy, the
opportunity for generating synergies is lost. However, it is clear
that, through the multiplicity of activities, reinforced by the development of infrastructure, the area of culture is one in which Lisbon and the municipalities of the LMA have made considerable
progress.

Cooperation occurs between the central administration and the
municipalities in the promotion of cultural activities with an international orientation. However, more recently a new form of partnership between state and municipality has resulted in the creation of an organization which had responsibility for coordination
and implementation of the programme for Lisbon 94 – the cultural capital of Europe. For the municipality of Lisbon, this is a
case of city marketing.

The International Exhibition of 1998 can be viewed in the same
perspective of cultural policy. The same year marks the centenary
of the arrival of Vasco de Gama in India and, in relation to this, the
theme of the exhibition is 'The Oceans as the Permanent Frontier

of Discovery'. The planning of EXPO 98 is being undertaken by the government and the municipality of Lisbon, supported by all of the municipalities of the LMA. A limited liability company has been created (Parque EXPO 1998 SA), involving public capital, including financial contributions from Lisbon and the neighbouring municipality of Loures, on whose territory initiatives of an urban character related to EXPO 98 will also take place.

From the beginning, this initiative has had two major objectives: the promotion of Lisbon and Portugal outside the country and the regeneration of the eastern part of Lisbon, which was heavily afflicted by the process of industrialization between 1870 and 1970. This area of about 300 hectares along the bank of the Tagus is dominated by a number of obsolete industrial enterprises, including a refinery and a petrochemical plant and a large number of inadequate units of logistical support for the port of Lisbon, often using infrastructure developed for industry (CML, 1992; 1993).

Thus EXPO 98 is a pretext for renovating an urban zone in Lisbon and its immediate periphery. This zone has much potential for new urban functions, but the process of regeneration can only with great difficulty be completed by using the normal mechanisms of municipal administration. In addition to being situated in two municipalities, the land belongs to oil companies and other small and medium-size enterprises, and a part of the land is under the jurisdiction of the administration of the port of Lisbon, a public organization with long tradition of conflict with Lisbon and other municipalities on both banks of the Tagus.

In spite of the exceptional legislation passed, difficulties dominate the negotiations between Parque EXPO 98 SA and the firms in the area, which raises the question of whether or not it would have been more efficient to develop a broader partnership, involving the state, municipalities and private interests.

Evaluation of urban policies in Lisbon

Until now, no scientific evaluation has been undertaken of the result of territorial and sectoral policies affecting the city and metropolitan area of Lisbon. In the light of this, the following points of evaluation are necessarily general and imprecise. It is also the intention to raise questions in relation to two of the principal dimensions which we can use to evaluate urban policy: efficiency and equity.

Efficiency

With respect to efficiency, we can examine a number of indicators: political–electoral, economic and infrastructural. The electoral test is perhaps the easiest to evaluate, as the results of elections can be regarded as a general evaluation undertaken by the electorate. The initial conclusion is that, in general, the lines of policy followed by the elected politicians at the level of the municipality have satisfied the electorate; the large majority of mayors and dominant parties have maintained their majorities, either relative or absolute. Apart from some shifts between socialist and communist majorities on the southern bank of the Tagus, it is possible to discern some recent movements from right to left in Lisbon, Cascais and Sintra, three of the largest municipalities of the LMA. In each of these places, the majority votes centre–right in parliamentary elections. Considering that the electorate in the LMA is among the best informed of the national electorate, we can perhaps draw some conclusions from the fact that, since the mid-1980s, the majority has voted for the PSD in the national elections, while in the municipal elections they have preferred the left opposition. A majority of the municipalities in the LMA (11, both in 1990 and in 1993) are communist. The socialist party had the majority in two municipalities in 1990 and four in 1993. In the city of Lisbon a clear, absolute majority supports a socialist–communist alliance. Thus we can say that the electorate allows the improvement of political control, creating different powers at the national and local levels. Moreover, the population is largely satisfied with the policies of the elected representatives, even when they are not in agreement with their ideological orientation.

With respect to economic performance, we may conclude that the implemented policies have produced positive results, to the extent that the economic growth in the LMA has resulted in a per capita income approaching the average value of GDP in the European Union, even though the rate of growth in the last decade has been slightly lower than the average for Portugal. Simultaneously, we are witnessing a convergence at the European level and the reduction of regional economic differences between the capital and the rest of the country.

The question of competitiveness is more difficult to answer. There are no clear results visible yet from the process of economic restructuring, which was embarked upon in the 1980s and which continues to follow the lines to which we referred above. With respect to production, an improvement in Lisbon's capacity to export is not yet evident. However, Lisbon – thanks to its well-developed infrastructure, its role in the European Union and its role as the national capital – appears more frequently in lists of possible locations for service activities, giving it an intermediate position in the ranking of the principal European cities. Yet these considerations and classifications do not necessarily reflect concrete options on the part of the economic agents. Lisbon may reveal itself as more competitive, creating higher levels of economic growth at the national level and a better integration of Portugal; this may also intensify the links between Portugal and Spain. Also there is no general study of the major investments which have been made in infrastructure in terms of their contribution to efficiency. Without doubt the supply of infrastructure has, in general, improved markedly, but it has not always increased at the same rate as demand and the deficiencies remain obvious in such areas as public transport, education and health.

The essential question is to decide whether or not it is possible to do more or better with the same instruments. That means that it is not sufficient to analyse changes in the level of overall efficiency of the system; it is also necessary to analyse the efficiency of the individual policy decisions involving investments. In the cases of education and health, where the infrastructure options chosen have not always been the best, the larger problem is in the quantitative and qualitative deficiencies of human capital and in the persistence of significant deficiencies in infrastructure.

As said before, it is clear that the options chosen for transport improvements are founded on dubious arguments. The long-term effects and budgetary implications are that individual transport is privileged at the expense of public transport. Major investments are being made in the metro, which is limited to the city of Lisbon, with obvious effects. The location of the new bridge over the Tagus is compounding the errors by opting for road transport, when there is no rail link between the two sides of the metropolitan area. The proposal for a rail link using the existing bridge – constructed in the 1960s – is a partial solution at best as it involves severe constraints on operations (especially for freight).

More effective have been the policies of development of infrastructure for water, sewage and refuse, involving improvement of access and improvement of environmental quality. In some cases, they have also led to increased profitability for enterprises (through improved water supply). With respect to the infrastructure component of social housing, we may consider efficiency to have been reduced, translated into higher costs and incapacity to respond to demand.

A part of the lack of efficiency described could be removed through a better collaboration between the different levels of administration. Lack of coordination and cooperation has been translated into serious inefficiency, with major economic and social costs.

Equity

The dimension of equity can be examined in two ways, territorial and social. For some time it appeared to be less relevant to speak of territorial inequality, as the question of equity seemed to be set fundamentally in the context of relations between people (social groups). But now, once again, geographic questions are gaining the upper hand, and the question of territorial equity is being raised more forcefully.

If we consider these two dimensions, territorial and social, we observe that, in the interior part of the LMA, inequality has increased. There are clear signs of increased social polarization and also of increased segregation between different areas. These two dimensions are closely linked and the one accentuates the other. Thus social polarization increases spatial segregation and, on the other hand, territorial marginalization (for example, through the development of differential access to or unequal provision of public service) furthers social polarization.

Public policies, of either central or local powers, have not furthered social and territorial equity. Education, especially higher education, has become increasingly inaccessible to low-income groups. In the sector of health, the private component is large and growing. In the transport sector, investment has favoured individual transport and public transport has a very uneven territorial coverage. The provision of social housing is insufficient and, although the quality of construction is good in general, in the context of urban development its urban location is very poor. Social housing continues to promote the creation of true social ghettos, which in turn generate greater social inequality.

It is clear that this lack of equity, which originates in specific urban policies, provokes, not only an increase in inequality of opportunity and income, but also increases in inefficiency throughout the metropolitan area. To varying degrees, this pattern is repeated in the different territorial units of which it consists.

Externalities

The different policies to which we have referred have led to the creation of externalities, arising from the activities of competent authorities, both local and central. On the positive side, there have been significant improvements in the environment, resulting from the process of deindustrialization or industrial restructuring. At the same time, improvements in infrastructure and better environmental control have contributed positively to the quality of the environment.

However, there has also been an increase in negative externalities. Traffic congestion, resulting from the policy option of individual transport, has enormous consequences, not only for the general efficiency of the urban economy, but also for the quality of life of the population. The increasing importance of private and public road transport of passengers and freight is one of the main causes of increases in atmospheric pollution and noise in Lisbon.

Such political options in the fields of transport, and the lack of coordination in infrastructure planning, contribute to chaos in the organization of the territory. This not only translates into the destruction of resources (financial and natural) but also decreases general efficiency in the metropolitan area.

Financial deficits and budgetary options

As capital city and main economic and demographic centre, Lisbon has benefited from considerable investment in central administration. This is, according to local politicians, the cost of being the capital city, the suggestion being that the payment for this role remains insufficient. On the other hand, the rest of the country feels left behind, in relation to certain options, and discontent is not uncommon. This is clear in the case of the second city, Oporto, and the northern region, which is the most populous.

In reality, Lisbon and its metropolitan area have suffered chronic deficits, and permanent budget deficits affect most of the municipalities. Yet it is the LMA which, because of its relative income level, makes budgetary transfers to more needy areas, especially in the interior and the islands. In order to maintain and develop its competitive level internationally, Lisbon and its metropolitan area must overcome deficiencies in infrastructure provision, housing, and quality of life. This implies an understanding of the implications of their policy at various levels of political decision making, from the national to local, yet it is clear that it is necessary to operationalize the authority of the metropolitan area through coordination of efforts between its 18 municipalities with the central administration.

It is precisely in the Lisbon metropolitan area that, in the context of Portugal, it should be possible to attain, through adequate policies, a convergence between efficiency objectives, both local and national, and equity objectives, both social and territorial.

References

Baptista, A.J. Mendes (1989) 'Perspectivas de desenvolvimento económico da Área Metropolitana de Lisboa' [Perspectives on the development of the Lisbon metropolitan area], *Sociedade e Território*, **10/11**, Lisbon, pp.43–8.

CCE – Commission des Communautées Européennes (1989) *Cadre Communautaire d'Appui pour Portugal 1989–1993* [Community framework for Portugal 1989–1993], Brussels: Commission of the European Communities.

CCRLVT – Comissão de Coordenação da Região de Lisboa e Vale do Tejo/Centro de Estudos e Desenvolvimento Regional e Urbano (1987) *Estudo Preparatório para a Operação Integrada de Desenvolvimento para a Península de Setúbal* [Preparatory study for the Setubal Peninsula, integrated development operation] Lisbon.

CCRLVT – Comissão de Coordenação da Região de Lisboa e Vale do Tejo (1992), 'Plano Regional de Ordenamento do Território da Área Metropolitana de Lisboa' [Regional physical plan for the Lisbon metropolitan area] (2ª phase – Estratégia; unpublished), Lisbon.

CML – Câmara Municipal de Lisboa (1992) *Plano Estratégico de Lisboa* [Lisbon Strategic plan], Lisbon.

CML – Câmara Municipal de Lisboa (1993) *Plano Director Municipal de Lisboa* [Lisbon Municipality physical plan], Lisbon.

DGDR – Diracção-general do Desenvolvimento Regional (1993) *Preparar Portugal para o Século XXI* [Portugal towards the 21st century], (I vol.: Análise Económica e Social; II vol.: Opções Estratégicas; III vol.: Plano de Desenvolvimento Regional) Lisbon.

Ferrão, J. and M. Vale (1995) 'Multi-purpose vehicles, a new opportunity for the periphery? Lessons from the Ford VW project (Portugal)', in R. Hudson and E. Schamp (eds) *Towards a New Map of Automobile Manufacturing in Europe*, London: Springer, pp.195–217.

Gaspar, J. (1972a) *A Ponte Salazar e o Tráfego entre Lisboa e a Outra Banda* [The Salazar bridge and traffic between the two river banks], Lisbon: CEG.

Gaspar, J. (1972b) *Aspectos da Dinâmica Funcional do Centro de Lisboa* [On the functional dynamics of the Lisbon CBD], Lisbon: CEG.

Gaspar, J. (1984) 'Urbanization: growth, problems and policies', in Allan Williams (ed.), *Southern Europe Transformed*, London: Harper & Row, pp.208–35.

Gaspar, J. (1992) 'The new map of Portugal', in Michael Hebbert and J. Christian Hansen (ed.), *Unfamiliar Territory. The Reshaping of European Geography*, Aldershot: Avebury, pp.101–16.

Gaspar, J. (1993) *The Regions of Portugal*, Lisbon: DGDR.

Gaspar, J. and C. Jensen-Butler (1992) 'Social, economic and cultural transformations in the Portuguese urban system', *International Journal of Urban and Regional Research*, **16**, pp.442–61.

Silva, Fernando Nunes da (1989) 'Travessia do Tejo e a cidade de duas margens' [The new bridge and the city on the two banks], *Sociedade e Território*, **10/11**, Lisbon.

Silva, Fernando Nunes da (1990a) 'Estratégia Europeia, Modelo de Desenvolvimento e Sistema de Transportes para a Área Metropolitana de Lisboa' [European strategy, development model and the transportation system in the Lisbon metropolitan area], *Cadernos Urbe*, **1**, Lisbon.

Silva, Fernando Nunes da (1990b) 'Lisbonne: Ville de Deux Rives et Métropole. Les Défis à Relever' [Lisbon, city on two banks and metropolis. Disadvantages to be remedied], special issue, 'Portugal: Enjeux Sociaux et Transformations du Territoire', *Sociedade e Território*.

Williams, A. and J. Gaspar (1992) *Southern Portugal in the 1990s. A European Investment Region*, London: Economist Intelligence Unit.

7 Barcelona: the olympic city

Joan-Eugeni Sánchez

The foundations of Barcelona's current status

Barcelona is an old city with a rich cultural and economic past. During the Middle Ages, it was the capital of the Kingdom of Aragón. When it lost this status at the end of the fifteenth century, the city entered a long period of economic crisis. Its recovery dates from the eighteenth century. The recovery was based on manufacturing and trade, which provided it with a sound foundation for a significant role in the Spanish industrial revolution of the nineteenth century. Since then, its economy and population have grown steadily, based on vigorous industrial development.

By the end of the 1960s, Barcelona and its region were the most important industrial area in Spain, but once more the city entered a phase of decline. The new international division of labour plunged its dominant textile sector into a deep crisis. Political change at the national level heralded the end of the 'pro-development' economic model of the Franco regime of the 1960s and 1970s, and local political leadership and democratic initiative remained scarce, having been pre-empted by the strong political centralization of the Franco era. These problems were exacerbated by the effects of the international economic recession of the late 1970s.

The restoration of democracy at the end of the 1970s brought a new, younger generation of politicians to power. They took up the challenge to renew the city's economic base, and a similar political impulse was felt throughout the metropolitan region of Barcelona (Borja, 1991). Their first priority became the physical restructuring and the social revitalization of city and region after decades of speculation and chaotic town planning. A major project was to serve as a catalyst for the restructuring and for the mobilization of the local population. In 1982, the mayor of Barcelona rekindled an old but previously frustrated desire of Barcelona: to be the city of the Olympic Games. During the ten years between the relaunching of the idea and its successful implementation, the preparations for the Games dominated the urban policy of Barcelona and transformed the very nature of the city.

The extent of the metropolitan region of Barcelona

The city of Barcelona has 1.7 million inhabitants and covers an area of 99 square kilometres. The agglomeration is populated by 2.7 million people and extends over 223 square kilometres, divided into 13 municipalities. It forms the core of a wider metropolitan region of 838 square kilometres with 3.3 million people (55 municipalities). Barcelona's economic hinterland is even larger. The Greater Metropolitan Economic Region extends approximately 30 kilometres from the centre and includes more than 4.1 million people, living in 116 municipalities. The statistical Barcelona region (NUTS 3) covers an area of well over 7000 square kilometres with 4.6 million inhabitants.

Catalonia, the administrative region over which Barcelona presides as the capital city, enjoys the status of an Autonomous Community (*Comunidad Autónoma*) in the present political and administrative organization of Spain. It contains no less than six million inhabitants (Parellada, 1990; Conjuntura, 1991; Area d'Economia i Empreses, 1992; Lleonart, 1992). Topography and hydrology are as important for the current pattern of settlement of the region as the transport and communication networks. Barcelona is boxed in between the Mediterranean Sea and Collserola Mountain, flanked by the unhealthy delta of the Llobregat river. The urban core of the region consists of the central city, the contiguous municipalities in the coastal plain and the piedmont, and the territory surrounding Collserola Mountain.

Beyond this territory, the metropolitan region forms a first ring with a radius of 20–30 kilometres, which is well integrated by means of ground transport (expressways and railways) and a telecommunications network. It must be underlined that the metropolitan area of Barcelona incorporates several important medium-sized cities, with old traditions. Around this wider area, a second ring of consolidated development is now gradually taking shape.

The territorial extent of the labour market marks the limits of these zones. The city of Barcelona exerts a remarkable attraction on its hinterland, which results in a strong diurnal population movement. Delineated on the basis of commuting, the core of the region includes the labour market territory of Barcelona residents with jobs in the surrounding area, and the residential areas of the people working in Barcelona. This area covers 52 municipalities within a radius of approximately 15 kilometres of the centre. The first ring, defined by the journey to work in Barcelona of between 5 and 15 per cent of the active municipal labour force, covers a radius of more than 30 kilometres. This ring includes the labour markets of the towns of Sabadell, Terrassa, Granollers, Martorell and Mataró (Esteban Quintana, 1990; Clusa 1992).

Overall, commuters filled 13 per cent of the jobs in Barcelona in 1986; that is, more than 160 000 people make the daily journey to the central city. The reverse flow is much smaller, but it still numbers more than 60 000: 43 000 people commute from Barcelona to jobs in the other municipalities of the core region and 20 000 more travel to destinations in the first ring. The resulting traffic flows are augmented by the trips of people moving between municipalities within this ring. At present, these figures are even higher than those of the radial flows.

Approximately 30 per cent of the total labour force of Catalonia live in the city of Barcelona. More than half of the Catalan working population resides in Barcelona and its adjacent municipalities. If the workforce of the first ring is added to Barcelona's, only one-third of the Catalan working population is found in the rest of the territory. Consequently, there are three points to emphasize: economic activity is largely concentrated in the Barcelona economic region (1.2 million jobs in 1986); there is a massive diurnal mobility; and Barcelona dominates the metropolitan territory.

Economic activity, housing problems and social welfare

Economic activity

The industrial revolution provided Barcelona and the towns in its surrounding area with a strong base in textiles and metal working (Parellada, 1990). The industrialization through the first half of the twentieth century led to a rapid increase in the city's population. The most rapid growth occurred between the mid-1940s and the mid-1970s. It was borne by major migration movements within Spain, especially from the east and south of the Iberian peninsula. Initially, this process was based on the expulsion of inhabitants of rural areas, but when Spain began its development in the 1960s, the pull of the urban industrial areas on labour increased the migration flows.

At first, migrants to old industrial cities like Barcelona located in the suburbs. This set off a classic process of urban transformation. Land in these suburban municipalities remained fully occupied, while industrial sites became obsolete. It was impossible to expand the plants, and environmental conditions turned progressively worse. The pressure on land forced its price up. This led to windfall profits wherever industrial land could be converted to residential or service functions. From the 1960s onwards, the expansion of existing industries and the siting of new plants took place in the new suburbs. These locations were better suited for such activities, and the land prices were lower there. The prevailing urban planning model in Spain during this period boosted this process. The General Urban Plans (*Planes Generales de Urbanismo*) prevented industrial renovation inside the city and forced firms to relocate to new industrial zones in the periphery.

Does this mean that Barcelona is now in the process of deindustrialization and deconcentration, as some authors would have it (Trullen *et al.*, 1989)? Before this question can be answered, it is necessary to recall the significance of territorial change. This change occurred with the transition from the municipal to the metropolitan scale as the new functional entity. This is clearly manifested as population growth in the older big cities. It also appears as contraction of the territory in terms of time–space relations because of changes in transport and communication networks. These processes were alluded to above in the outline of the new labour market relationships. But the pre-existing administrative divisions have not changed. This has led to a major contradiction between the current functional–territorial changes and the permanence of the municipality as a locus of territorial decision making. At the level of the municipality, a tendency towards deindustrialization may be seen. This is not discernible at the metropolitan level, however.

In fact, many plants have relocated to the metropolitan hinterland, while old industrial sites within the city (especially Poble Nou and Poble Sec) have effectively died. Nonetheless, Barcelona remains the premier industrial municipality of Catalonia. Its position shows up in terms both of production volume and of the extent of the area used by manufacturing. Barcelona has 10.7 per cent of its surface devoted to industrial use. This represents 6 per cent of all industrial land in Catalonia and 10.2 per cent of the industrially zoned area in the Metropolitan Region of Barcelona (15.2 per cent of the land actually used by manufacturing plants). The Metropolitan Region of Barcelona contains 58.5 per cent of all industrial land in Catalonia. Barcelona's industrial acreage is still proportionally larger than that of those municipalities which are seen as the region's new industrial locations, such as Terrassa (6.4 per cent) or Sabadell (7.8 per cent; cf. Sanz Barcena, 1992). Moreover, there are major differences in the proportions of industrially zoned land actually used as such among the metropolitan rings. In the Barcelona agglomeration, this applies to nearly 95 per cent of the land designated as industrial by the planners. In the remainder of the metropolitan region, the use is as low as 60 per cent, while the balance is still available for industry. These ratios are larger still in the rest of Catalonia. The conclusion that the city of Barcelona has been deindustrialized is obviously too hasty.

Housing demand has been steadily rising, largely as a result of the high volume of immigration during the past few years. The strong demand for residential space has led to the proliferation of building. There is now little vacant space within the city limits, while the progressive incursion of Barcelona into suburbia has created a vast metropolis. Under these circumstances, it was unavoidable that expanding firms would move out of the city. This was even more compelling for newly established plants, above all for foreign companies, and for such space-extensive enterprises as distribution centres. In addition to lack of space, the price differential between urban and suburban sites promotes decentralization. This process has helped accelerate the classic steps toward tertiarization of the central city. At the same time, it has hastened the restructuring of rural areas in the urban hinterland by spreading industrial and service activities throughout a large area (Clusa, 1992).

Even though manufacturing is expanding in the surroundings of the city and disappearing from its central areas, we cannot conclude that Barcelona is undergoing deindustrialization. Nor can we infer that deconcentration is a signal that the urban economy has entered a neo-Fordist and post-modern phase of development. Rather, the functional space limits have been modified by several factors: a lack of space, increasing locational obsolescence, the nature of the applied urban planning model, road building and the installation of advanced traffic control and communication. But on the scale of the metropolis, the conditions of concentration and centralization still exist. This shows up clearly in the pattern of new industrial investment, as we will explain below (see also Serra Batiste, 1991).

This course of development was further stimulated by major infrastructure projects. They permitted the incorporation of the surroundings of Barcelona into the metropolitan region. In the 1960s, the modernization of the national transport network was started, which also affected Barcelona. Expressways were planned from Barcelona to France, to the rest of Spain, and to the large cities in the region. In addition, three ring roads around Barcelona were projected: two urban and a peri-urban one. Since 1969, more than 600 kilometres of expressways have been built in and around Barcelona. These new roads have created a potential corridor for the location of industries and services inside the metropolitan region. They also permitted the development of other industrial focal points in Catalonia, though these remain oriented towards Barcelona.

The construction of the network of expressways in Barcelona gave the city a greater significance. As soon as Spain was linked to the European expressway network, Barcelona became the gateway through which the rest of the peninsula could be integrated into Europe. This locational advantage was reinforced from the moment Spain joined the European Community.

Housing problems and housing policy

In the 1980s, the shortage of housing was no longer a serious problem. This situation was markedly different from that of the 1940s and 1950s. The severity of the housing problem in that period was remedied by means of massive social housing construction during the 1960s and 1970s. This meant that, by the beginning of the 1980s, *'barraquismo'* (shanty towns) had been all but eradicated. But, at the same time, another problem was created: low-quality construction and poor urban planning. In response, the recent housing policy of all the political institutions, from central to local government, has emphasized urban renewal rather than new construction (Busquets, 1987; Política, 1992).

Conditioned by this legacy of poor planning and low-quality construction, municipal urban policy has concentrated on the huge task of reurbanization. Its aim has been to lower the density of the urban spaces and at the same time to refurbish and embellish them (Esteban, 1992). But the refurbishing of the existing built environment prevented the creation of public land ownership. Therefore upgrading did not prevent speculative price increases. Also the financial policy was geared towards the needs of the construction sector rather than promoting access to housing for low-income groups (Herce, 1992). Leaving the provision of housing to the market led to a significant increase in house prices, above all in the central area of Barcelona. This was aggravated by the scarcity of land and the competition for space from the tertiary sector. The supply of housing remains out of step with demand, with severe repercussions for starters on the housing market (Problemàtica, 1992).

In the period 1981–9, the housing stock increased more rapidly in the metropolitan region than in the city. The increase was only 4.76 per cent (46 961 units) with respect to the 1980 stock in the Barcelona agglomeration, as against 12.92 per cent (31 262 units) in the remainder of the metropolitan area and 14.13 per cent (43 545 units) in the remainder of the functional region (Conjuntura, 1991). The scarcity of affordable housing encouraged emigration from Barcelona to other places in the metropolitan area. This squeeze affected not only younger couples with low incomes but also the new middle-class households looking for more attractive residential environments and single-family dwellings. In fact, younger people make up the bulk of this outward flow: 64 per cent of the emigrants are 35 years of age or under. This will have a strong effect on the aging of the population in the central area, eventually resulting in a decline in population. Homeowners, on the contrary, tend to be immobile, which is emphasized by the increase in prices (Jover, 1992).

Outmigration has stimulated the rate of commuting, which was facilitated by improvements in transport. Moving usually does not bring people closer to their place of work (only around 2 per cent of the migrants attributed their move to this motive). This implies that the number of commuters kept increasing. Research has shown that 67 per cent of the migrants work outside the municipality they live in (Jane and García Almirall, 1992).

The two motives underlying this migration flow – the search for lower prices and the best quality housing – reproduce the classic socioterritorial division inside the cities in the greater metropolitan area, but now on a municipal scale. Some municipalities attract the emerging middle class by offering the best residential environments. Others are the destination for the working class; they are the ones that lie close to industrial areas. Among the first set of places, one finds towns near the sea, such as Sant Cugat and the area of the Maresme, where single-family houses and high-quality construction predominate. The second category comprises municipalities such as Barberà, Santa Coloma de Gramanet and Hospitalet.

In Barcelona, these tendencies still have not led to the depopulation of the centre of the city. Even the incipient development of a business centre – starting in Plaça Catalunya and expanding along the Passeig de Gràcia and Avinguda Diagonal – has allowed the retention of residential and commercial activities. Local policy aims to avoid the creation of monofunctional business centres. Even the emergence of new business areas and the expansion of such centres in several parts of the metropolitan region (for example, in older cities such as Sabadell or Terrassa, or in new business centres near the airport or in Sant Cugat) will not lead to increased segregation.

In order to revitalize the centre of the city, the current urban policy utilizes several strategies. One of these is to permit the subdivision of older apartments in the Eixample into smaller units, adapted to the decreasing size of households. This keeps afford-able dwellings on the real estate market. Another strategy is to limit the development of office buildings in the city centre and to promote the retail function. The goal is to maintain an equilibrium of the residential function and economic activity, which will keep the streets lively.

One final aspect to note is related to the social housing stock built during the 1960s and 1970s. The poor quality of construction has accelerated its decline. This has fuelled the need to renew or even to rebuild a large part of the housing stock. A major renewal effort is already being made, especially by the autonomous gov-ernment, and will continue to be a priority of housing policy in the future.

Obviously, the housing problem also relates to wider issues of the quality of life. Therefore improvement of the residential envi-ronment has been emphasized in municipal policy in recent years. That policy has scored some successes (Institut d'Estudis Metropolitans de Barcelona, 1986; 1992; Subirats, 1991; Riera, 1993). The quality of life has improved in all the municipalities of the metropolitan region. This has had the effect of increasing the ex-pectations of the population (Subirats, 1991). It is interesting to note that, on some occasions, neighbourhood pressure has led to improved public proposals.

In spite of this general improvement, Barcelona and its region still suffer from environmental problems. Local policy has achieved notable successes with respect to decongestion, the development of new green space and the revitalization of the most dilapidated areas (such as the Old Centre (Ciutat Vella) of Barcelona and Poble Nou). But further improvements require a change of attitude, ac-cording to the noted ecologist Terrades (Ciudad, 1987). A new attitude must be cultivated, not only among the population of Barcelona itself, since the environmental problems in the city have an important external component. There are signs that, also out-side the city, people's sensitivity to environmental problems has increased. One of these signs is the creation of a Department of the Environment by the autonomous government.

Social welfare

All analysts seem to agree that, to understand the central city, it is necessary to relate it to the rest of the metropolitan area. This becomes abundantly clear when we consider the socioterritorial distribution of the inhabitants from the point of view of the labour force or from a commercial, symbolic or leisure perspective. Barcelona itself serves as the centre for a population of a wider geographical area. The city is where the upper class and the middle class are concentrated and where many of the indigenous Catalan population and the elderly live.

The central city seems to be becoming more socially homogeneous, but comparison of the 1985 metropolitan public opinion poll with the results of 1990 suggests that the lower class is diminishing. This results from the migration of the youngest members of the lower class to surrounding municipalities in numbers as large as among the new middle class. Nevertheless, there remains an important core of poverty in the city. Urban policy aims to displace the poor: rather than resolving the problem, it shifts it to areas outside the city. This does, however, reduce intra-urban social differences. The classic socio-spatial division of the city now also shows up on the metropolitan scale. That division is evident in the new labour-market area in the first metropolitan ring. Housing allocation is a concrete reflection of social inequalities. In general, the socio-spatial division creates disparity of access to a variety of social resources according to place of residence and results in differing degrees of access to services and cultural facilities (Subirats, 1991).

Increased homogeneity inside the city must be understood in relative terms. It is quite different in various parts of the city. This is shown by the variation in economic potential of households, the '*Index de capacitat econòmica familiar a Barcelona*' (Carcel Ferrer and Canals Ramon, 1991). It ranged from a minimum of 32 to a maximum of 292, the average being 93.4. The distribution reflects the classic asymmetric distribution of wealth. It shows up clearly on the ground: the highest incomes are concentrated in the central segment of the Eixample, advancing along the Avinguda Diagonal, and covering the area of Bonanova-Sarria-Pedralbes. The lowest income groups are concentrated in the old industrialized areas – Poble Sec, Poble Nou, Bon Pastor – and the areas where the migrants who arrived in the middle of this century are concentrated. The lowest income level is found in the oldest part of the city, the Ciutat Vella. Therefore, in spite of its renewal, we cannot speak of a gentrification process in Ciutat Vella.

A comparison of metropolitan surveys underscores those differences, which show up as contrasts between the central city and remainder of the core area, as well as contrasts within the central city. During the period of increasing economic prosperity, well-being also increased in general. This was reflected in the higher quality of facilities and public services. It is interesting to observe the consolidation of the central city as a residential area (Subirats, 1991).

We must not forget that these overall figures mask individual situations that reveal a tendency toward a bipolar society. The increase in general welfare coincided with a social polarization and the emergence of marginal places, located in the most dilapidated parts of the city. The increase in temporary employment, the persistent economic crisis, rising unemployment and the expansion of the underground economy affect those with little or no formal education, often the latest illegal immigrants. At the same time, these developments have a strong impact upon the young, plunging them into disillusionment. They live in the most depressed parts of the metropolitan area, such as Ciutat Vella or suburbs like Sant Adrià. In light of the diminishing social solidarity, public life should be revitalized and collective activities should be stimulated. As Soledad García says, 'If we accept the premise that a lack of solidarity is related to the social fragmentation in the labour market and of the real estate market, those just might be the areas where we should look for ways to rebuild community identity in order to recuperate a public performance capable of supporting balanced policies' (García, 1990).

Changes in the metropolitan region

The reindustrialization of Barcelona

During the past 25 years, Barcelona's industries have undergone a deep crisis because of the changes in the international division of labour. If Catalonia was to remain an important industrial region, it had to change its industrial composition. In the ensuing restructuring, the textile sector lost its primacy. Chemicals, pharmaceuticals, rubber, publishing and printing, wood products and furniture, and food and beverages made substantial gains, while metal working came to be the most important activity in the metropolitan region (Parellada, 1990). Between the late 1960s and 1985, the city of Barcelona lost 42 per cent of its manufacturing jobs and 69 per cent of its construction jobs. During that period, employment in services increased by 12 per cent. This growth meant that Barcelona increasingly became a service centre. At present, Barcelona accounts for three-quarters of the jobs in the tertiary sector in the entire metropolitan region.

In the early 1980s, the central government in Madrid chose to implement a reindustrialization policy to combat the high levels of unemployment in the industrial zones. By building on the existing physical and social infrastructure, the policy could take advantage of local conditions to revitalize the industrial base. Areas in desperate need of reindustrialization (*Zonas de Urgente Reindustrialización*: ZUR) were identified. The area around Barcelona was designated as one of these areas. An analysis of the effects of this reindustrialization process allows us to forecast the future development of the new industrial structure. Investments were directed towards electronics, computers, motor vehicles and auxiliary industries, plastics, rubber and printing. In general, these are sectors that demand a high level of technical know-how. Reindustrialization therefore required, not only a major industrial realignment, but also the creation of a large number of new firms. New companies accounted for approximately 40 per cent of all industrial establishments during this time. Many of them were set up with foreign capital.

The policy secured the industrial capacity of the metropolitan region. From 1989 to 1992, 62 per cent of the new firms and 54 per cent of all investments in Catalonia were found in the metropolitan region. No less than 18 per cent of the firms and 12 per cent of the investments were located within the Barcelona agglomeration. This reinforced the industrial role of the city, even when the surrounding area also underwent rapid industrialization. Foreign investors determined to a large extent the sectoral composition and the locations of new investment. They provided existing Spanish companies with a fresh source of capitalization. Foreign capital also resulted in a multitude of new firms. Nevertheless, this has not led to a dramatic change in the spatial pattern of manufacturing. Rather, it has replicated the present structure at a metropolitan level. The process of economic expansion required room for new industrial activities in the saturated central area. The concentration of manufacturing in urban areas was maintained, despite political efforts to change it. This pattern has actually been reinforced by the development of the new axes of transport and infrastructure throughout the region. Technological innovation has only changed the time–space relationship (Sánchez, 1992b).

The remainder of the metropolitan region absorbed a large share of the new industrial space. Peripheral areas accommodate a major portion of the new service activities, which need extensive sites. Thus emerged such centres as the Vallès Technology Park, large new retail and commercial areas, hospitals, TV studios, the campus of the Autonomous University, a race track and extensive new business centres. As Barcelona expands, it superimposes its functions on the existing settlement system. At the same time, the old industrial centres in the metropolitan region are showing signs of healthy revitalization. Many succeed in attracting and developing major industrial activities, producer services, commercial areas and management centres. Barcelona's urban and economic policy constitutes the model that other centres try to emulate but, in the process, they have to adapt the scale of action (Conurbació, 1993). Within the built-up area, in the older cities of the metropolitan region, and above all in the city of Barcelona, obsolete industrial sites have become available for redevelopment. These sites provide room for new public spaces within the city, for new residential areas for services, and for corporate headquarters. Thus infill development furthers the goal of consolidating the city of Barcelona as a management centre.

Spain's entry into what was then the European Community triggered an influx of foreign investment. In 1991, 42.9 per cent of total foreign investment in Spain was concentrated in Catalonia, most of it in the metropolitan area. Barcelona became the point of entry into a rapidly expanding market of nearly 50 million increasingly affluent Iberian consumers (39 million in Spain, plus 9.9 million in Portugal). At the same time, Barcelona became a gateway to the rest of Europe because of its expressways, railway, maritime routes and its airport (8 million passengers in 1991, 5.7 on domestic flights and 3.3 on international flights, and 61 700 metric tons of cargo, more than half of it international). The port grew in importance, making Barcelona one of the foremost Mediterranean seaports (cargo traffic in 1991 amounted to 5 254 000 metric tons loaded and 13 059 000 off-loaded). Especially with respect to its container traffic, the port has surpassed the volume of Marseilles, Genoa and Valencia, not least because of its competitive pricing strategy. For instance, fees were reduced by some 5 per cent in 1993 to attract more international traffic (de Forn and Pascual, 1991).

In short, the influx of industrial investment in the early 1990s helped the recovery of profits. At the same time, industrial restructuring led to the growth and diffusion of R&D activities. But it also stimulated the emergence of oligopolistic markets. This development benefited from various incentives to promote manufacturing and to attract foreign investment (Bosch i Jou, 1990).

Changes in the labour force and in the industrial structure

During the period spanning economic crisis and recovery, Barcelona's labour market in the city itself declined, from 796 800 jobs in 1975 to 626 800 in 1986, only to increase again to 780 300 jobs in

1990 (Table 7.1). The trend for the metropolitan area was similar, but there were more jobs in 1990 than in 1975 (dropping from 1 469 700 to 1 221 800 and then rising to 1 490 100, respectively in the three key years). Throughout this period, more than 50 per cent of all jobs were concentrated in the city and about 65 per cent in the agglomeration. Thus the agglomeration and the ring still have a long way to go before their territory is fully utilized. In other words, they have great potential for growth.

The breakdown of the totals by types of activity is shown in Table 7.2. In 1990, Barcelona provided 202 700 jobs in manufacturing, 43 000 in construction and 533 100 in services. The city accounted for almost 61 800 jobs in the advanced services sector (Table 7.3). In the entire metropolitan region, one finds 419 000 manufacturing jobs, 46 000 jobs in construction and 566 000 in services, of which 85 000 jobs are in the advanced services sector. This means that the city still accounts for over 25 per cent of the jobs in manufacturing, while the agglomeration accounts for a third. The loss of manufacturing jobs is compensated by a proportionate rise in employment in the services. The tertiary sector now represents 68.3 per cent of all employment in the city and 63.7 per cent in the metropolitan region. The importance of the older cities in the first ring is reflected by the share of the service sector in their employment structure. Sabadell and Terrassa occupy second and third place in the hierarchy of service centres, but are far behind Barcelona (Llarch *et al.*, 1987; Roses, 1989; Anguera and Casas, 1990; Roa, 1992).

Finally, it should be noted that small and medium-sized firms are dominant in the region of Barcelona (Table 7.4). There are 48 194 small firms, each employing fewer than 25 people (94.5 per cent). But jointly they account for 35.8 per cent of the active labour force. At the other end of the scale, the 114 big firms (with more than 500 employees each) represent 26 per cent of the wage earners. Overall, the quality of management is good, benefiting from accumulated experience and a long industrial tradition. The firms can draw upon a growing services sector for all their specific business needs. Furthermore, they are supported by an improved university system, particularly with respect to its research centres in sciences, technology, philosophy, social science and business administration.

To sum up, economic crisis and reindustrialization have wrought major changes in the industrial structure. Traditional sectors have been replaced by innovative products and processes. This shift in investment targets led to a change in industrial concentration through the obsolescence of old manufacturing centres, the satu-

Table 7.1 Evolution of the spatial distribution of some basic variables in the Metropolitan Region of Barcelona, 1986–9

Area	Population (000s)				Jobs (000s)			Jobs in FIRE*	Industrial investment	Housing completions
	1960	1975	1986	1991	1975	1986	1990	1986	1988–90	1981–9
Barcelona	1 557.9	1 751.1	1 701.8	1 623.5	796.8	626.8	780.3	73.8	18.6	24.8
Rest of the agglomeration	338.5	919.0	956.3	922.5	215.7	169.5	193.7	7.2	19.0	9.9
First ring	178.3	492.4	626.9	670.9	156.9	147.2	184.7	4.4	29.1	23.1
Second ring	494.9	857.2	944.6	975.9	300.3	278.3	331.4	14.6	33.3	42.2
Total Metro Region	2 569.6	4 019.7	4 229.6	4 192.8	1 469.7	1 221.8	1 490.1	100	100	100
Percentage										
Barcelona	60.6	43.6	40.3	38.7	54.2	51.3	52.4			
Rest of the agglomeration	13.2	22.9	22.6	22.0	14.7	13.9	13.0			
First ring	6.9	12.2	14.8	16.0	10.7	12.0	12.4			
Second ring	19.3	21.3	22.3	23.3	20.4	22.8	22.2			
Total Metro Region	100	100	100	100	100	100	100			

Note: *Quaternary sector: finance, insurance, real estate.

Table 7.2 Evolution of the sectoral structure of jobs in Catalonia, 1986–90

	Agriculture		Industry		Construction		Services		Total jobs	
	1986	1990	1986	1990	1986	1990	1986	1990	1986	1990
Jobs (x 1000 workers)										
Barcelona	1.8	1.5	195.8	202.7	24.0	43.0	405.2	533.1	626.8	780.3
Rest of the urban agglomeration	1.3	1.1	82.0	89.1	5.8	10.4	80.4	93.1	169.5	193.7
First ring	3.2	2.7	80.6	91.0	7.9	14.2	55.5	77.1	147.2	184.9
Second ring	10.1	8.4	137.6	150.9	16.9	30.3	113.7	142.0	278.3	331.6
Total Metro Region	16.4	13.7	496.0	533.7	54.6	97.9	654.8	845.3	1 221.8	1 490.6
Sectoral structure (%)										
Barcelona	0.3	0.2	31.2	26.0	3.8	5.5	64.6	68.3	100	100
Rest of the urban agglomeration	0.8	0.6	48.4	46.0	3.4	5.4	47.4	48.1	100	100
First ring	2.2	1.4	54.8	49.2	5.4	7.7	37.7	41.7	100	100
Second ring	3.6	2.5	49.4	45.5	6.1	9.1	40.9	42.8	100	100
Total Metro Region	1.3	0.9	40.6	35.8	4.5	6.6	53.6	56.7	100	100
Spatial structure (%)										
Barcelona	11.0	10.9	39.5	38.0	44.0	43.9	61.9	63.1	51.3	52.3
Rest of the urban agglomeration	7.9	8.0	16.5	16.7	10.6	10.6	12.3	11.0	13.9	13.0
First ring	19.5	19.7	16.3	17.1	14.5	14.5	8.5	9.1	12.0	12.4
Second ring	61.6	61.3	27.7	28.3	31.0	30.9	17.4	16.8	22.8	22.2
Total Metro Region	100	100	100	100	100	100	100	100	100	100

Table 7.3 Jobs in the quaternary sector, 1986

Municipality	Jobs in FIRE* (a)	Rank	Total jobs (b)	Rank	% a/b	Rank	Total population	Rank
Barcelona	61 778	1	626 830	1	9.9	1	1 701 812	1
Sabadell	2 871	2	49 797	2	5.7	6	186 115	4
Terrassa	2 206	3	41 094	4	5.4	7	160 105	5
L'Hospitalet	1 909	4	44 583	3	4.3	14	279 779	2
Badalona	1 485	5	37 531	5	4.0	19	225 016	3
Mataró	1 308	6	30 634	6	4.9	15	100 021	7
Granollers	1 081	7	18 722	7	5.8	4	47 967	12
Vilafranca	673	8	8 591	19	7.8	2	26 433	24
Rubí	574	9	13 107	10	4.4	12	46 360	14
Sant Cugat	526	10	9 154	16	5.8	5	35 302	19
Cornellà	514	11	14 697	9	3.5	30	86 928	8
Sta Coloma	457	12	12 484	13	3.7	28	135 258	6
Vilanova i G.	321	17	12 308	14	2.6	50	44 977	16
Martorell	223	22	9 333	15	2.4	61	16 170	31

Notes: *Quaternary sector: finance, insurance, real estate.
Rank refers to position among 162 municipalities in the metropolitan region.

Table 7.4   Evolution of the Barcelona labour force (number of wage earners) and number of firms, 1985–8

Size of firm	Workers			Firms		
	1985	*1988*	*% 88/85*	*1985*	*1988*	*% 88/85*
1–5	79 252	94 826	+19.70	41 754	48 194	+15.40
6–25	116 059	150 131	+29.40	10 262	13 360	+30.20
26–100	106 918	129 935	+21.50	2 328	2 864	+23.00
101–500	112 767	130 727	+15.90	553	632	+14.30
>500	184 029	177 353	–3.60	113	114	+0.90
Total	599 025	682 972	+14.00	55 010	65 164	+18.50
(%)						
1–5	13.23	13.88		75.90	73.96	
6–25	19.37	21.98		18.65	20.50	
26–100	17.85	19.02		4.23	4.40	
101–500	18.83	19.14		1.01	0.97	
>500	30.72	25.97		0.21	0.17	
Total	100	100		100	100	

ration of central locations and the provision of new sites for the expansion needs of new plants.

Some general features of Barcelona's urban policy

The development of Barcelona in recent years is closely tied to the Olympic Games, which the city hosted in 1992. Obtaining the nomination and organizing the event formed the centrepiece of its urban policy for an entire decade. This city is therefore a model for other ones that seek to take advantage of a particular event to promote themselves in the current framework of competition among cities. Barcelona's recent history demonstrates how policy can have a major impact on urban restructuring. The policy was intended to move the city to centre stage on a continental and global scale (Borja and de Forn, 1990). In the particular case of Barcelona, however, it is necessary to consider another ingredient, namely the restoration of local democratic institutions in 1980. From a political perspective, it is significant that, in Barcelona and its metropolitan region, local power shifted to the political parties of the left. This emanated from Barcelona's traditionally strong industrial base.

Barcelona exemplifies a city where intense urban renewal was used as an urban policy tool. During the past 100 years, the organization of three successive events permitted the city to implement far-reaching urban renovations. On each of these occasions, the economic cycles of growth and decline have been truncated by a massive thrust of policy-induced urban development. Barcelona was the venue for the World Exposition of 1888. Organizing that event helped the city to remodel the old military citadel and to develop the space occupied by defensive installations outside the old city walls, which had been demolished in 1854. In 1860, the Cerdà Plan was approved for the development of this area, now known as the Eixample. In 1929, a second World Exposition was held in Barcelona. For this occasion, the steep terrain of Montjuic was developed. At the same time, the underground railway system was constructed. Thereafter, the civil war and the postwar period had strong negative effects on the city. Finally, the 1992 Olympic Games offered an opportunity to complete the important infrastructure of the city and, in certain respects, that of the metropolitan region. A key element was the installation of the telecommunications network (Vegara *et al.*, 1991). That network also made it possible to redevelop obsolete industrial areas (for example, Poble Nou, where the Olympic village was built) and to provide an urban technological infrastructure of international standards (Sánchez, 1992a; Güell i Ferrer, 1993).

Each of these three events can be clearly identified in the morphology of the city. The impact of the two exhibitions was limited to the fabric of the central city. The recent intervention went much deeper, within the city and beyond it. The city was no longer only a stage for economic activity but a commodity, traded in a global market-place. The challenge for urban policy is to reconcile three potentially conflicting goals: to make the city a suitable place for production; to offer it for consumption by outsiders; and to make it a good place to live.

To attain the first goal, Barcelona built an up-to-date telecommunications infrastructure as well as an international network of transport. These improvements prompted the remodelling of the airport and the port. There is a continuing local power struggle to integrate the city in the European TGV network. The second goal required the improvement and completion of the transport network and the creation of space for economic activities. The third goal was approached by taking advantage of the obsolete industrial areas in its central area, especially in Poble Nou and the extensive Vall d'Hebrò.

All the frantic activity going on since the early 1980s has accelerated the expansion of Barcelona. The outlines of the process were already clear (Serra Batiste, 1991), but as the process picked up speed it allowed the rapid construction of projects that would otherwise have needed many years to complete. Still, the recent transformation of Barcelona only reinforced the current tendencies of metropolitan development.

Analysis of the urban policies in the Barcelona metropolitan region

Competing agencies

The competition between political parties in control at different levels in Spain has strongly influenced the metropolitan area of Barcelona. The central government was controlled by the socialists, the regional government by the centre-right nationalists, and nearly all the local governments in the metropolitan area of Barcelona by the socialists and communists. This created much tension.

At the regional level, there have been many struggles for power. Barcelona acted as a counterweight to the regional government (Generalitat), which was in the process of consolidation. The dispute first came to a head over the decision to dissolve the CMB (Corporació Metropolitana de Barcelona). The CMB had been created in 1974 as a 'specific tool to stimulate, coordinate, manage, protect and implement the urban plan, and to provide services with relevance to the entire metropolitan area'. It included 27 municipalities, which made up a large part of the central area. Its size was a mere 470 square kilometres (1.5 per cent of Catalonia), but the area housed nearly half its population (3.1 million inhabitants).

The CMB was abolished in 1985 and replaced by a range of joint commissions. Each consisted of representatives of a variable number of municipalities, and each dealt with a specific problem, such as water supply, sanitation, public transport and waste disposal. To maintain some coherence, a new institution without executive responsibilities was created, to conduct studies and to coordinate policies: the Metropolitan Area of Barcelona. Yet the abolition of a government for the whole metropolitan area seems to have been too hasty. The Catalonia Territorial Plan, currently under public discussion, proposes to re-establish a metropolitan government (Vallès and Nel.lo, 1993).

Considering the recent history of the region, we may well question the effects of the fierce rivalry between the Generalitat and the Barcelona City Council, personified in their leaders. Has the competition caused delays in projects and initiatives? Or did it create an incentive to produce more and better, in order to prevail over the opponent? For instance, each of the two institutions developed its own strategy to gain influence in Europe. The two leaders reached similar levels of visibility at the Community level simultaneously. Jordi Pujol, president of the Government of Catalonia, became president of the Assembly of European Regions, whereas Pascual Maragall, mayor of Barcelona, became president of the European Council of Municipalities and Regions. The peripheral municipalities may have been the real losers in this dispute. They were affected by the problems exported by the big city. But they could not share in the benefits of its growth, as municipal resources cannot be transferred.

The other municipalities are also players in this competition between the major city and the region. Competing with Barcelona and among themselves, their first objective is to maintain their autonomy. As independent territorial units, these municipalities combine the advantages of proximity to the central city with the ability to devise their own strategies. But at the same time their size increases the risk of poor coordination, especially with respect to the creation of infrastructure. Small units also lack the room to separate incompatible forms of land use.

External conditions affecting Barcelona's economic development

Barcelona's recent development has largely been determined by the city's capacity to mobilize its own resources as well as to attract resources from outside. The policies of outside agencies have been responses to the city's needs and its ability to press them into cooperation. In the new democratic framework, accumulated historical problems, competition among municipalities themselves and their competition with Barcelona, have favoured a set of actions with positive effects on the area. But the local actions have not been entirely independent of external processes or forces, such as the strategies of multinational companies.

There is, in fact, a whole complex of external policies affecting Barcelona and its metropolitan region. The economic policies of the central government, of the Generalitat and of the adjacent municipalities have all helped to attract foreign investment. The success of these efforts calls attention to the lack of a policy to attract investment by large Spanish companies. The regional government has tried to promote Catalonia on the world scene. Seeking cooperation with other European regions, the Generalitat projected an image of the Barcelona region as a powerful economic area with great potential. During the expansion years, Catalonia, Baden–Württemberg, Rhône–Alpes and Lombardy were depicted as the 'four powerhouses of Europe'. Barcelona and its metropolitan region were cast as an essential component.

In the early 1980s, intervention in the industrial fabric was needed to head off a deeper crisis. The central government planned a reindustrialization policy for the industrial sector. Meanwhile, the regional government opted to support small and medium-sized firms, though without formulating a true industrial policy. Its efforts centred upon attracting foreign firms. Those firms demanded various comparative advantages, including industrial sites. In an attempt to bring about a more balanced territorial development within Catalonia, the regional government made such industrial sites available. Its actions were supported by the aims of decentralization and technological modernization, two prime objectives of the national government. This thrust reinforced R&D investments. New establishments located in the metropolitan area include the National Microelectronics Centre, the Analysis and Test Laboratory and the Advanced Studies Centre.

Lately, liberal winds have affected spatial development policy. Strong redistributive policies have been abandoned, leaving only an infrastructure policy in place. Although the basic expressway network had already been constructed, the Generalitat made plans for a regional traffic network to boost the metropolitan area. One of these expressways will link Barcelona with Toulouse in the future, in the hope of developing a European macro region centred on Barcelona.

Cities are invariably affected by the general image projected by their countries. The reputation of a nation as a whole and its role in the world can add prestige to a city's efforts to promote specific projects. On the other hand, that image may form a liability for its development. Within the European Union (EU), this potential tension between a state and a city can have severe effects. At this level, the role of central governments is dominant, while the cities appear to be mere pawns. Many examples have shown how cities were cast as competitors, while in fact the countries of the EU squabbled among themselves. The decision on where to locate the headquarters of new European agencies is a case in point. Cities loudly advertised themselves as the most suitable locations for certain agencies, but the final allocation reflected the ambition and the relative power of the member states. The determining factor was not whether Frankfurt, London, Copenhagen or Barcelona offered the best locational advantages. Rather, the decision was made on the basis of conflicting opinions among Germany, the UK, Denmark and Spain. Barcelona had become deeply involved in advertising its attractions but, in the end, two agencies were allocated to Spain, without being assigned to specific cities. Barcelona's struggle to obtain the European medicine evaluation agency proved to be mere shadow-boxing.

Municipal policies

Current urban policy has been very successful in its attempts to amass resources. It has managed to create a critical mass of investment that could have taken many years to accumulate, or might never have been invested at all. This has allowed Barcelona to benefit from multiplier effects. Since the early 1980s, Barcelona's urban planning strategy has been a three-pronged approach: the city attempted a spatial reorganization through widespread intervention in its neighbourhoods; at the same time, it identified options for spot development, which could improve the quality of daily life for many inhabitants; and finally, it embarked on the large project of organizing the Olympic Games. This effort was intended to help restructure the metropolitan area as a whole (Arees, 1987; Pla, 1987; Projectar, 1987; Urbanisme, 1987).

The implementation of these strategies brought about wholesale change. The administration of the city was overhauled. Responsibilities were reallocated among city agencies and decentralized. A new model for internal cohesion was applied. This led to further diversification of the city's central areas. It also prompted specific interventions in neighbourhoods to rectify major deficiencies. An important tool, but one that was difficult to wield, was known as PERI (Interior Urban Reform Plan). This plan was devised to stimulate public debate in every field of intervention. Thus democratic principles were introduced to urban management. The ambitious urban renewal programme and the economic and social revitalization of the Ciutat Vella (Old City) offer a good example of how PERI has changed urban policy (Ciutat Vella, 1991; Revitalització, 1991). The programme aimed to revitalize the most run-down neighbourhood in the historic town centre. Furthermore, it sought to transform the adjacent port through careful urban restoration (Barcelona, 1992a, 1992b; Busquets, 1987).

Another field of action opened up with the selection of areas for service centres and business facilities. The objective was to avoid the classic pattern of concentration in the city centre, which typically leads to the displacement of the residential function. Instead, a much wider distribution of business centres was aimed for. Each was to be big enough to generate economies of agglomeration and to offer suitable locations for foreign companies. But they should not be so big that they would transform a large area into a sterile business environment without a lively mixture of urban activities. Only industrial areas are meant to be monofunctional, to prevent causing nuisance for their neighbours.

The second type of policy concerns site redevelopment, which takes advantage of every opportunity to remove derelict buildings in order to create public space in the crowded parts of the city. The policy has resulted in street remodelling, the creation of public squares and mini-parks – which have attracted international attention – and the conversion of many older industrial buildings into facilities for social and cultural activities. The careful redevelopment of urban spaces has enhanced the existing image of Barcelona as a city of architectural renown. Controversies over projects actually helped to focus public attention on many of them, providing the city's promotion campaign with a great deal of publicity. The Olympic project has been particularly helpful in this respect, since it required so many new structures. The projects designed by famous Barcelona architects and renowned international ones such as Foster, Calatrava, Isozaki, Meier and Aulenti have renewed Barcelona's image as a cosmopolitan city.

The desired economic revitalization formed the backdrop to all this activity. But investment was especially promoted by the Olympic project. Organizing the 1992 games was seen as a way to provide a great economic impulse for the entire region. The preparations for this event brought a high volume of investment. The official data indicate a direct investment of no less than 9264 million US dollars. Of this total, 60 per cent was spent on infrastructure and 40 per cent on buildings and facilities. Data on the geographical distribution show that 40 per cent benefited projects in the city of Barcelona, 30 per cent was spent in the remainder of the metropolitan area and 12 per cent ended up elsewhere in Catalonia (18 per cent was spent on general expenses without a specific geographical component). Two-thirds of the budget was provided by the public sector, and one-third was accounted for by private-sector investments (Barcelona, 1992b; Vegara *et al.*, 1991).

After these investments in infrastructure had been made, the challenge was to attract economic activities. The city is billing itself as an attractive site for manufacturing and services as well as for real-estate investment in general. To facilitate this development, it maintains institutions such as the Economic Promotion Agency of the City Council, the Free Port (*Zona Franca*) Consortium and the Technology Park of the Vallès. It also promotes itself as a commodity, banking on its history, architecture and culture. The city has also demonstrated its capacity to organize events as well as to accommodate conventions and international trade fairs.

There are clearly two types of policy. Some aim at the comprehensive transformation of the region, while others reflect specific assets of the individual cities in the area. Each municipality fiercely defends its independence and competes with all others for development opportunities, above all with Barcelona. This has had a positive effect on the public and private sector, sparking a flurry of building activity. Sabadell is a case in point. This city has launched an ambitious urban programme of commercial development in Macia Ax, comparable to the intervention in Barcelona. Sant Cugat also stands out, having planned projects to convert itself into a major telematics centre as an alternative to Barcelona. It is trying to attract firms involved in this kind of technology. A third example is Cornellà, which set up a programme of local development. The local authority assumes a leading role in providing specialized business parks, managing industrial land and promoting new firms. Its Enterprises Creation Centre provides a concentration of business services and shopping centres. And the municipality organizes trade fairs to stimulate its own economic and spatial development. In each of these cases, the local city council has seized the initiative. But the downside of all these local initiatives is the threat of poor coordination, the watering down of visions and the inability to tackle large projects.

Private actors

Barcelona lacks large companies of local origin that are capable of implementing an international strategy. The multitude of small and medium-sized firms are only capable of exerting localized effects through physical development of a specific site or by cashing in on speculative value increases following change of land use. Business associations have not assumed a leadership role either; they continue to subordinate their common interest to the interests of their individual members. Nevertheless, an institution such as the Chamber of Commerce (*Càmara Oficial de Comerç, Industria y Navegació de Barcelona*) has actively participated in major projects for the economic revitalization of Barcelona. It has been part of all the important mixed (public and private) organizations, such as the Trade Fair and the Technology Park. Furthermore, the Chamber of Commerce has also assisted in the development of the Strategic Plan (Barcelona, 1990a, 1990b) and other activities.

International capital plays a dual role. Recent years have been a good time for making profits from speculative investment, given the overvaluation of the Spanish peseta and the size of the urban revitalization projects. By implementing supranational strategies, transnational corporations have been able to profit from Spain's membership of the European Union. On the one hand, it offers them access to the Spanish domestic market and the Spanish productive structure. On the other hand, firms such as Sony, Nissan, and Deutsche Bank have profited from the opportunities offered by Barcelona to open plants with good access to Southern Europe (Ludevid, 1989).

Much of the private-sector involvement in the preparation for the Olympic Games in Barcelona is made up of international capital. But it remains to be seen whether local commercial forces will be able to take full advantage of all this potential by accelerating autonomous development. The development can still backfire, creating a much greater economic and managerial dependency and a concomitant loss of control over the local economic system.

Conclusion: Barcelona still on the map

Over the next few years, an increase in international economic activities may be expected as the new infrastructure begins to be integrated in the productive system. This process will offer new economies of scale and economies of agglomeration. The physical plant is up-to-date and well located and will help to make Barcelona competitive within the European Union. Yet, given the current depressed state of the economy, and the impact of the recession on the manufacturing and the real-estate sector, it is difficult to forecast the city's prospects. But the renewal has given Barcelona new courage to enter the twenty-first century. Indeed, the city looks with confidence to the recovery of the European and world economy, providing a field in which to take advantage of its renewed potentials.

Barcelona has clearly not exhausted its capacity for renewal. The Olympic period was the first step, not the last one. As the mayor of Barcelona has put it,

The renewal of the city of Barcelona did not end with the 1992 Olympic Games. They have made Barcelona much more competitive internationally, and made the city a far more attractive site for business, for professionals, and for public and private institutions. But we did not stop there. On the contrary, the Games spurred us on to continue, and today 1000 hectares of city property are being developed and renewed in what is one of Europe's most sweeping projects of urban change. That programme will be carried out in the next four to five years. (Barcelona, 1993)

Transport, communications, retailing, offices, leisure services, housing, manufacturing, urban parks, a convention area, cultural institutions, a biomedical park, advanced business services, research centres and the enlargement of the seaport are some of these renewal projects. In this direction, the promotion of Barcelona remains one of the most important goals of municipal policy. At the current stage of implementation, major sums of local and international capital have already been committed. And the profitability of this investment must be ensured by the economic promotion of the city.

At the level of international relations, the traditional role in the nation-state of restricting cities' activities is called into question. Europe is evolving as a fabric of cities pursuing their own objectives. Where the urban network is most dense, the most concentrated development can be observed. This is aided by the development of dense networks of transport, including air transport, and telecommunications. The classic perception of cities is that they increasingly dominate their surroundings, as traditional city-states did. The first scenario for the renewal of Barcelona, developed in the early-1980s, was grounded in this perception. However, recent activities suggest a change of model. The new scenario appears to be focused on international relations rather than on territorial control. The change stems from political and administrative difficulties in exerting effective control over the region, mostly because of the fierce competition between the city and the autonomous government.

The new strategy allows greater freedom of action. The city is thought of as a link in the international information network, having bilateral relations with other cities and territories. Essentially, these relationships are functional, but physical connections remain important; hence the emphasis on developing road and rail links, including the high-speed trains. The network of contacts and connections is not limited to complementary nodes in the contiguous areas. Connections are also established with cities farther away that have similar functions and objectives. In the present technological context, distance is hardly a barrier. Financial, technological, research and cultural networks, as well as business and trade relationships, need to be tapped into. As a result of the change in perception, the strategy of local actors is increasingly focused on cooperation with other cities on a global scale, rather than on developing links with nearby cities. This accounts for current attempts to strengthen the relationships with South American cities, and for the strategic alliance with the city of Atlanta in the USA, based on the transfer of experience concerning the organization of the Olympic Games.

These strategies underlie the second phase of the Strategic Plan of Barcelona, which is to be completed by the year 2000. The goal is to achieve the full integration of Barcelona in the world economy by that year. To this end, it is proposed to complete the tertiarization of Barcelona's economy, but, at the same time, the city's industrial power is to be revitalized, on the basis of its historical assets. These are not seen as conflicting goals. Manufacturing still performs important functions of its own but, over and above this, the manufacturing sector is intimately related to the services sector, high-technology development and R&D activities (Vallès and Nel.lo, 1993).

Other municipalities in the metropolitan area, such as Terrassa, Sabadell, Sant Cugat, Cornellà, L'Hospitalet, Badalona, Rubí and Cerdanyola are pursuing similar aims. Together with Barcelona, they shape the dynamic landscape of the region (Esteban, 1991; Conurbació, 1993).

The perspective outlined up to this point has emphasized the successful transformations of recent years, yet many grave problems persist in the city and its metropolitan region. These problems include unemployment, especially of the former manufacturing workforce. There are also problems of poor social integration, lack of solidarity and even blatant discrimination. Housing remains a thorny issue, especially for younger couples, trying to make a start. The perspective on the future remains blurred. The global economic recession does not seem to let up. Industrial production continues to decline, especially in the motor car sector, which is so important in Barcelona because of the presence of Seat, Nissan and many auxiliary plants. The competition from elsewhere is ever-growing and shifting. Most recently, the transitions in Eastern Europe have added an entirely new element of uncertainty. It is therefore difficult to be blindly optimistic about Barcelona's future, in spite of the city's great potential in human resources and the rich endowment of its built environment.

Irrespective of the economic and social problems, the inhabitants of the Barcelona region were in general satisfied with the city as it had taken shape by 1992. Let us consider the words of the columnist of Barcelona's right-centrist newspaper, *La Vanguardia*, one year after the Games: 'In spite of the deep economic crisis, the newly shaped city of Barcelona is widely approved by its citizens. The lesson to be drawn from this is that the restructuring must indeed go beyond the resolution of immediate problems, and prepare the city for its tasks in the future' (*La Vanguardia*, 18 July 1993).

The current situation of the Barcelona region is far from rosy, but without the efforts made to restructure the city in preparation for the Olympic Games the situation would have been much worse. The preparations renewed the city. They also created the confidence that remaining problems will also be resolved. The crisis has not discouraged local actors from staying the course of renewal. Indeed, they continue to improve the physical structure in order to increase the well-being of its inhabitants.

References

Anguera, J. and J.B. Casas (eds) (1990) *L'economia del Vallès Occidental. De la industria al serveis* [The economy of Vallès Occidental: from manufacturing to services], Barcelona: Caixa d'Estalvis de Catalunya.

Area d'Economia i Empreses (1992) *Barcelona economy*, Barcelona: COCINB/Ajuntament de Barcelona.

Arees (1987) *Arees de nova centralitat* [New central areas], Barcelona: Ajuntament de Barcelona.

Barcelona (1990a) *Barcelona 2000 Economic and Social Strategic Plan*, Barcelona: Ajuntament de Barcelona.

Barcelona (1990b) *Barcelona centre financer europeu* [Barcelona, European financial centre], Barcelona: Ajuntament de Barcelona.

Barcelona (1992a) *Barcelona, la ciutat i el 92* [Barcelona, the city and 92], Barcelona: Barcelona Holding Olímpic.

Barcelona (1992b) *Barcelona olímpica. La ciutat renovada* [Olympic Barcelona: the renewed city], Barcelona: Holsa/Ambit Serveis Editorials.

Barcelona (1993) *Barcelona. New Projects*, Barcelona: Ajuntament de Barcelona.

Borja, J. (1991) 'Les institucions locals i el planejament territorial a la Regió Metropolitana de Barcelona' [Local institutions and physical planning in the Barcelona region], *Papers, Regió Metropolitana de Barcelona*, 1, pp.9–14.

Borja, J. and M. de Forn (1990) *Barcelona y el sistema de ciudades europeo* [Barcelona and the European system of cities], Barcelona: Ajuntament de Barcelona.

Bosch i Jou, J. (1990) 'El sector industrial a Catalunya' [The industrial sector in Catalonia], *Monografies d'Industria*, 7.

Busquets, J. (1987) 'Del creixement a la requalificació', *Urbanisme*, pp.ix–xx.

Carcel Ferrer, C. and R.M. Canals Ramon (1991) 'Index de capacitat econòmica familiar a Barcelona', *Barcelona economia* [Index of economic potential in Barcelona], 13, pp.93–100.

Ciudad (1987) 'Ciudad y medio ambiente' [The city and its nearby region], *Barcelona Metròpolis Mediterrànea*, 5, pp.65–127.

Ciutat Vella (1991) 'Ciutat Vella: La hora decisiva' [Ciutat Vella (Old Town): the decisive hour], *Barcelona Metròpolis Mediterrànea*, 18, pp.65–128.

Clusa, J. (1992) 'La distribució territorial de la indústria i els serveis a la regió' [The spatial pattern of manufacturing and services in the region], papers, *Regió Metropolitana de Barcelona*, 12, pp.9–39.

Conjuntura (1991) *Conjuntura demogràfica i sòcio-econòmica a la Regió metropolitana de Barcelona, 1981–1990* [Demographic and socio-economic trends in the Barcelona metropolitan region, 1981–1990], Barcelona: Area Metropolitana de Barcelona.

Conurbació (1993) 'La conurbació barcelonina: realitzacions i projectes' [The Barcelona conurbation: completed and planned projects], *papers, Regió Metropolitana de Barcelona*, **13**, pp.7–91.

De Forn, M. and J.M. Pascual (1991) 'Aproximació a l'impacte de l'Acta Unica Europea en el sistema productiu. El paper de Barcelona i la competitivitat de Catalunya' [On the possible impact of an integrated Europe on the economy of Barcelona and the competitiveness of Catalonia], *Papers, Regió Metropolitana de Barcelona*, **3**, pp.45–72.

Esteban, J. (1991) 'Els objectius territorials per a la regió metropolitana' [The territorial objectives for the metropolitan region], *Papers, Regió Metropolitana de Barcelona*, **2**, pp.9–20.

Esteban, J. (1992) 'Avanç de propostes per al planejament territorial de la regió metropolitana de Barcelona' [Preliminary proposals for planning in the Barcelona metropolitan region], *Papers, Regió Metropolitana de Barcelona*, **12**, pp.55–77.

Esteban Quintana, M. (1990) *Distribució de la mobilitat per treball a la Regió metropolitana de Barcelona. Anàlisi dels mercats de treball* [Differences in labour mobility in the Barcelona metropolitan region. Analysis of the labour market], Barcelona: Area Metropolitana de Barcelona.

Garcia, S. (1990) 'Desigualtats social metropolitanes. El centre ric enfront de la periferia pobra' [Social imbalances in the metropolis. Wealthy centre, poor periphery], *Barcelona Metròpolis Mediterrània*, **15**, pp.86–9.

Güell i Ferrer, X. (1993) 'Una reflexió sobre la Barcelona postolímpica' [Post-Olympic Barcelona, a reflection], *Nota d'Economia*, **46**, pp.105–17.

Herce, M. (1992) 'Algunas medidas urbanísticas coadyuvantes a las políticas de vivienda', *Papers, Regió Metropolitana de Barcelona*, **9**, pp.27–35.

Institut d'Estudis Metropolitans de Barcelona (1986) *Enquesta Metropolitana 1985–1986. Activitts i formes de vida de la població* [1985–1986 metropolitan survey: activities and lifestyles of the population], Barcelona: UAB/CMB.

Institut d'Estudis Metropolitans de Barcelona (1992) *Enquesta de la regió metropolitana de Barcelona 1990: condicions de vida i hàbits de la població* [1990 survey of the Barcelona metropolitan region: living and housing conditions], Barcelona: Institut d'Estudis Metropolitans de Barcelona.

Jane, A. and P. García Almirall (1992) 'El mercía de l'habitatge com a factor incentivador de l'emigració. El cas de Barcelona' [The housing market as an incentive for emigration. The case of Barcelona], *Barcelona economia*, **16**, pp.85–93.

Jover, A. (1992) 'Breu incursió en els problemes de l'habitatge' [Concise overview of housing problems], *Papers, Regió Metropolitana de Barcelona*, **9**, pp.9–14.

Llarch, E., X. Saez, X. Güell and M.R. Rodriguea (1987) *Dimensió económica i territorial del Barcelonès* [Economic and territorial aspects of Barcelona], Barcelona: Caixa d'Estalvis de Catalunya.

Lleonart, P. (1992) *Catalonia: a land, an economy*, Barcelona: COCINB/CCCT.

Ludevid, M. (1989) 'Barcelona en el mercat europeu. Punts forts i punts febles de l'Area Econòmica de Barcelona' [Barcelona in the European market. Strong and weak aspects of the Barcelona economy], *Revista Econòmica de Catalunya*, **10**, pp.91–7.

Parellada, M. (ed.) (1990) *Estructura económica de Cataluña* [The economic structure of Catalonia], Madrid: Espasa-Calpe.

Pla (1987) *Pla de costes. Proposta d'ordenació dela zona costanera metropolitana de Barcelona* [Proposed regulation in the coastal zone of the Barcelona metropolitan area], Barcelona: Corporació Metropolitana de Barcelona.

Política (1992) 'Política de sòl i habitatge' [Land policy and housing], *Papers, Regió Metropolitana de Barcelona*, **9**, pp.7–72.

Problemàtica (1992) 'La problemàtica de l'habitatge a Barcelona' [Housing problems in Barcelona], *Barcelona economia*, **15**, pp.89–94.

Projectar (1987) *Projectar la ciutat metropolitana. Obres, plans i projectes 1981–1986* [The future of the metropolitan area. Work, plans and projects], Barcelona: Corporación Metropolitana de Barcelona.

Revitalització (1991) *Revitalització urbana, economica i social. Primeres Jornades Ciutat Vella* [Urban, economic and social revitalization. First meeting Ciutat Vella], Barcelona: Ajuntament de Barcelona.

Riera, P. (1993) 'Rendibilitat social de les rondes de Barcelona', *Barcelona economia*, **18**, pp.21–5.

Roa, M. (1992) 'La construcció urbana de les activitats a la primera corona metropolitana. El cas del Baix Llobregat i l'Hospitalet' [The spatial structure of activities in the first metropolitan ring. The case of Baix Llobregat and Hospitalet], *Papers, Regió Metropolitana de Barcelona*, **12**, pp.41–5.

Roses, J. (ed.) (1989) *L'economia del Baix Llobregat. Creixement i desequilibris* [The economy of Baix Llobregat. Growth and disequilibrium], Barcelona: Caixa d'Estalvis de Catalunya.

Sánchez, J.-E. (1992a) 'Transformation dans l'espace productive en Barcelone, 1975-1990' [The transformation of work areas in Barcelona, 1975–1990], *Villes et Territoires*, **4**, pp.87–116.

Sánchez, J.-E. (1992b) 'Societal responses to changes in the production system: The case of metropolitan region of Barcelona', *Urban Studies*, **29**, pp.949–64.

Sanz Barcena, J. (1992) *El sòl industrial* [Industrial space], Barcelona: Direcció General d'Indústria.

Serra Batiste, J. (1991) 'La ciutat metropolitana. Delimitacions, desconcentracions, desequilibris' [The metropolis: delimitation, deconcentration, disequilibrium], *Papers, Regió Metropolitana de Barcelona*, **6**, pp.31–51.

Subirats, M. (1991) 'Enquesta metropolitana de Barcelona (1990): Primers resultats' [The 1990 metropolitan survey of Barcelona: first results], *Papers, Regió Metropolitana de Barcelona*, **7**, pp.9–103.

Trullen, J., A. Matas, J.L. Roig, L. Farran, E. Puig and A. Santigosa (1989) 'Canvi econòmic durant la crisi a l'area metropolitana de Barcelona: una aproximació territorial', *Revista Econòmica de Catalunya*, **10**, pp.68–79.

Urbanisme (1987) *Urbanisme a Barcelona. Plans cap al 92*, Barcelona: Ajuntament de Barcelona.

Valles, J.M. and O. Nel.lo (1993) 'De Ciutat a Metrópolis. Notes per a una lectura del Pla Estratègic Barcelona-2000 des d'una perspectiva metropolitana' [From city to metropolis. Notes for a lecture on the strategic plan Barcelona-2000 from a metropolitan perspective], *Barcelona economia*, **18**, pp.7–20.

Vegara, J.M., D. Cotrina and M. Sauri (1991) 'L'impacte econòmic dels Jocs Olímpics de 1992' [The economic impact of the 1992 Olympic Games], *Revista Econòmica de Catalunya*, **18**, pp.32–6.

8 Copenhagen: a redistributive city?

Sten Engelstoft and John Jørgensen

Introduction

During the late 1980s and early 1990s Copenhagen, like numerous
European cities, has been engaged in a territorial competition.
Eventually, this competition could lead to a redistribution of the
economic and political relations between city regions in Europe. A
whole range of factors – including the globalization of the economy,
the integration process within the European Union and the break-
up of Eastern Europe – have prompted these developments. The
changes came in the wake of a couple of decades of transition, as
most West European cities were profoundly restructured, both
economically and socially. Furthermore, in the political climate of
the 1980s, the postwar planning machine came under severe attack. Because of these changes, urban policies are partly formulated – and partly implemented – outside the official planning
system. Public–private partnerships and interest groups are manifestations of such trends. Another consequence is that equity-
oriented policies may have to give way to efficiency-oriented
policies.

Based on the Copenhagen case, this chapter discusses the shift
in urban policy from welfare planning to entrepreneurialism in a
'redistributive city'. Copenhagen is the largest Scandinavian city.
Consistent with the trend in Scandinavia, a wide range of welfare
functions have been built up over the years. Some of these programmes have been encouraged by national policies, while others
were initiated locally. At the same time, politicians and decision
makers have become more and more involved in efforts to create a
new industrial base for the city. Therefore the redistribution mechanisms may change dramatically, both socially and spatially. The
key question is whether (or to what degree) the redistributive city
is still recognizable. If so, is the image of the redistributive city a
marketable asset in the continuing competition with other European cities?

This shift towards entrepreneurialism has affected the outcome
of decisions on huge investments in infrastructure in the Copen-

hagen area, for example. The decision-making process has been marked by heated discussion between two groups. On the one side is an emerging pro-growth coalition, which consists of the major parties in the Danish Parliament and local government as well as industrialists and contractors in Denmark (and Sweden, for that matter). On the other side is a more critical group (left-wing political parties, environmentalists and urban social movements) opposing the idea of a comercialized booming Copenhagen. In some ways, the participants in this debate rely heavily on the classic concept of an efficiency/equity trade-off. Most members of the Danish Parliament (*Folketinget*) argue that efficiency (in terms of infrastructure and facilities directed towards foreign business people) will lead to a more prosperous and 'just' city. The proponents of this view are found in the Labour Party (*Socialdemokratiet*), the business community and, to a certain degree, among local politicians, including Labour. Other people refute these arguments. For instance, citizens of Copenhagen, supported by the political left, have argued that the single most important objective is to create a livable city. Its amenities should primarily serve the inhabitants themselves, but a livable city also attracts tourists, thus stimulating economic activity. It would, however, be simplistic to infer that arguments put forward by the main actors participating in the discussion can be explained solely in terms of the analytical continuum spanning the political left and right. In order to grasp the issues in the debate, one also has to consider another dimension of great importance. That is, people, groups or organizations advocating economic growth present arguments that revolve around the theme of ecological balance. There appears to be a range of parties across the middle of the political spectrum, in particular Labour and the Conservative Party, that are the main 'political' constituents of the pro-growth movement – both locally and nationally. Furthermore, the no-growth movement seems to consist of a variety of organizations and parties, such as the Socialist People's Party (*Socialistisk Folkeparti*) and parties 'playing on the mid-field'. The latter in particular are represented by the Liberal Left Party (*Det radikale Venstre*), which has attracted a lot of 'green' votes over the last decades.

Within the setting of a redistributive city in a Scandinavian welfare state, equity should not only be seen as a question of allocation of assets and economic activities. Public authorities have tried to promote equity for decades. In their discourse, the equity argument follows a certain train of thought related to urban planning. From this point of view, equity also implies equal access to public transport. It also implies equal access to green space for people living in the densely populated parts of the city. Thus public investment in public transport or green space may be seen as redistribution.

At this point, we will not go on to present a wide (and more complete) range of cases. Instead, we will concentrate on four sectoral policies and three major development plans/projects. These have been selected to demonstrate how the shift towards entrepreneurialism has been easily perceptible within some areas related to urban policy in the Greater Copenhagen Region, whereas it has affected other areas less. We use the analytical distinction between four dimensions of urban policy: economic efficiency, social and spatial equity, control of negative externalities and budgetary constraints (see Chapter 1 in this volume). The analysis will proceed as follows:

- a presentation of the Danish administrative structure, the block grants and inter-municipal economic equalization systems, and the major changes in the planning system;
- a discussion of a number of important sectors relating to urban policy, namely urban renewal, transport, energy and, finally, culture and tourism;
- a summary and an evaluation of some larger projects designed to strengthen the overall profile and competitiveness of the region, namely the harbour front development, the decision to develop 'Ørestad' (a new urban development area to the southeast of Copenhagen) and, in connection with this, to develop the Sound Link, a fixed rail and road link to southern Sweden;
- an evaluation of the attempts that have been made to promote the city as a serious contender on the European urban scene.

In the analysis of sectoral policies, the emphasis lies on the four dimensions of urban policy. In contrast, the discussion of the 'Grand Projects' focuses on whether the developments in the 1980s are producing, as Harding (1991) puts it, a 'comfortable capital or growing Eurocity'.

Administrative framework

In order to fully understand the selected cases on sectoral and spatial development policies, their context should be taken into account. Therefore some basic knowledge on the three-tiered administrative structure and the financial conditions under which counties and municipalities have created and operated the local welfare state in the last couple of decades has to be provided. This is necessary in order to understand the specific conditions and problems of the Copenhagen metropolitan region. Particular attention will be given to the abolition of the Greater Copenhagen Council (*Hovedstadsrådet*) in 1989. Finally, the Danish planning system and the relation between sectoral and spatial planning will be described in brief.

Denmark has a three-tiered administrative and governmental structure of state, counties and municipalities. The highest level consists of the state and the sector ministries. The next level down is that of the county (*amt*), also termed the region; there are 14 counties in Denmark. In the early 1970s, administrative reform was carried out. Accordingly, each county now has a directly elected council that is responsible for a small number of sectors, of which health is by far the most important. Furthermore, upper secondary schools, some infrastructure (road planning, building and maintenance), specific areas of environmental planning (especially water resources) and regional planning are the responsibility of the county. The third level is that of the municipality (*kommune*), of which there are 275. According to the administrative reform of the early 1970s, municipalities and counties are subject to the same law prescribing the same administrative structure and procedures, including the system of direct election and the right of independent (income) taxation. Duties and rights are different, though. Consequently, whether it is an urban or a rural community, the municipality is led by an elected council and has gained (or retained) responsibility for a distinct set of functions. These include primary education, social security, child care and care of the elderly, culture, some road works and municipal land use planning.

This general administrative structure has been modified in the Copenhagen metropolitan region. The Copenhagen metropolitan region – or the metropolitan area – comprises the three counties of Frederiksborg, Copenhagen and Roskilde (a total of 48 municipalities), together with the two municipalities of Copenhagen and Frederiksberg, which fall geographically and administratively outside the county structure. These two municipalities are different from all others. They have the same status and responsibilities as both a municipality and a county, a fact that has caused discussion for many years (Kommissionen om hovedstadsrådet, 1983). Figures 8.1 and 8.2 show the location of the local authorities and their populations. Until 1989, a body existed that was indirectly

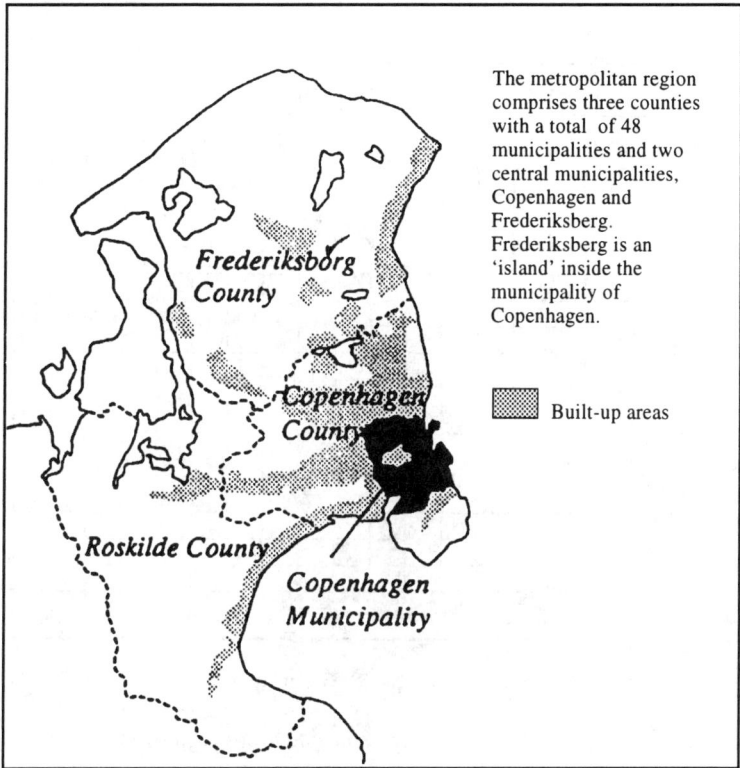

The metropolitan region comprises three counties with a total of 48 municipalities and two central municipalities, Copenhagen and Frederiksberg. Frederiksberg is an 'island' inside the municipality of Copenhagen.

Built-up areas

Source: Lord Mayor's Office (1992, p.4).

Figure 8.1   Copenhagen metropolitan region

elected by municipalities, the Greater Copenhagen Council (*Hovedstadsrådet*). This body had overall responsibility for certain areas, including public transport and regional planning. In many ways, it was a similar construction to the Greater London Council (GLC). Moreover, for political reasons, it met the same fate as the GLC, being abolished on 1 January 1990 (Bruun, 1991). Today there is no overall administrative body covering the functional region of Greater Copenhagen. The absence of such an umbrella creates serious problems of coordination. On the eve of its demise, the Greater Copenhagen Council produced a regional plan, a document which synthesized many of the planning initiatives undertaken previously and which proposed new lines of development, including many environment-related improvements. New regional

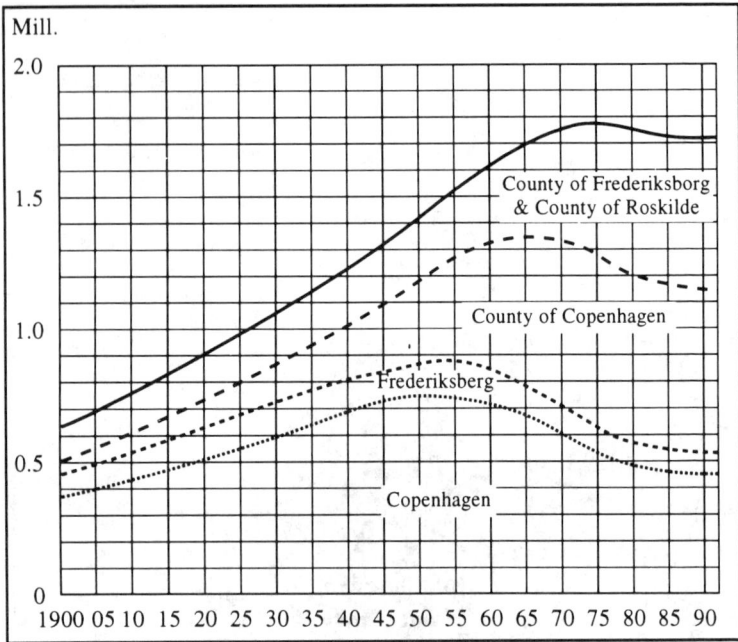

Source: *Statistical Yearbook of Copenhagen*, 1993, Part B, p.23.

Figure 8.2   Population, Copenhagen metropolitan region, 1901–93

plans have been prepared in the different parts of the area formerly covered by the Council. As a result, the two municipal
plans (of the municipalities of Copenhagen and Frederiksberg)
now have the status of regional plans. Thus what was formerly
covered by one overall regional plan is now to be found in five
different plans. These plans, of course, exhibit a much lower level
of coherence and coordination than the 1989 plan.

The administrative reform has facilitated the decentralization of
the welfare state. In principle, the *Folketinget* passes laws containing general guidelines and rules for planning and administration
at the three administrative levels. In accordance with certain
legally defined norms and/or financial criteria, the build-up of the
local welfare state has been the responsibility of the counties and
municipalities. This, of course, is only possible because (income)
tax is levied at each of these administrative levels, thus giving
each county and municipality a relatively high degree of financial
latitude. However, the economic situation of the 1980s has nar-

rowed their radius of action. Along with the implementation of the administrative reform, changes were made in local government finance. The main principle was that 'burden' should follow 'responsibility'. This has been stressed by gradually changing the former system of state reimbursements to a system of block grants distributed to the local governments according to 'objective criteria of need'. The principle on which the grants are allocated forces municipalities to set political priorities. They have to scrutinize the relative importance of locally identified needs. They can no longer saddle the community with expenses for unnecessary facilities, with the rationale that they would eventually be reimbursed by the state. Furthermore, a system of economic equalization between the municipalities has been worked out. That system is supposed to level out the differences in the so-called 'taxation/service relationship'. Without equalization, a municipality with a high income base or low outlays would have low taxation. The purpose of equalization, therefore, is to ensure a certain level of services. At the same time, it promotes a more equal taxation independent of income, that is the tax base, and expenditure needs of the population (cf. Figure 8.3).

As shown in Figure 8.3, it is fairly obvious that the difference between municipalities diminishes as a consequence of equalization. Equalization has two elements: equalization of the tax base and equalization of the per capita expenditure. But the redistributive effect is less than complete, especially regarding the equalization of per capita expenditure needs. The levels of equalization have been set as follows (Ministry of the Interior, 1993, p.30):

- 35 per cent in the countrywide equalization for municipalities;
- 25 per cent additionally in the metropolitan area (equalization measures for the municipalities within the metropolitan area, where segregation is most pronounced, are added to the former);
- 85 per cent in the county equalization.

The equalization of the tax base is a very elaborate measure, financed by a joint grant pool provided by the state (cf. Figure 8.3). The level of equalization of the tax base within the metropolitan area is nearly 90 per cent. This again means that the 'rich' municipalities in the metropolitan area are not given any great incentive to make tax assessment (which is done locally in Denmark) efficient. The problem is that the lion's share of the possible extra revenue would have to be transferred to the 'poorer' municipal-

216   European Cities in Competition

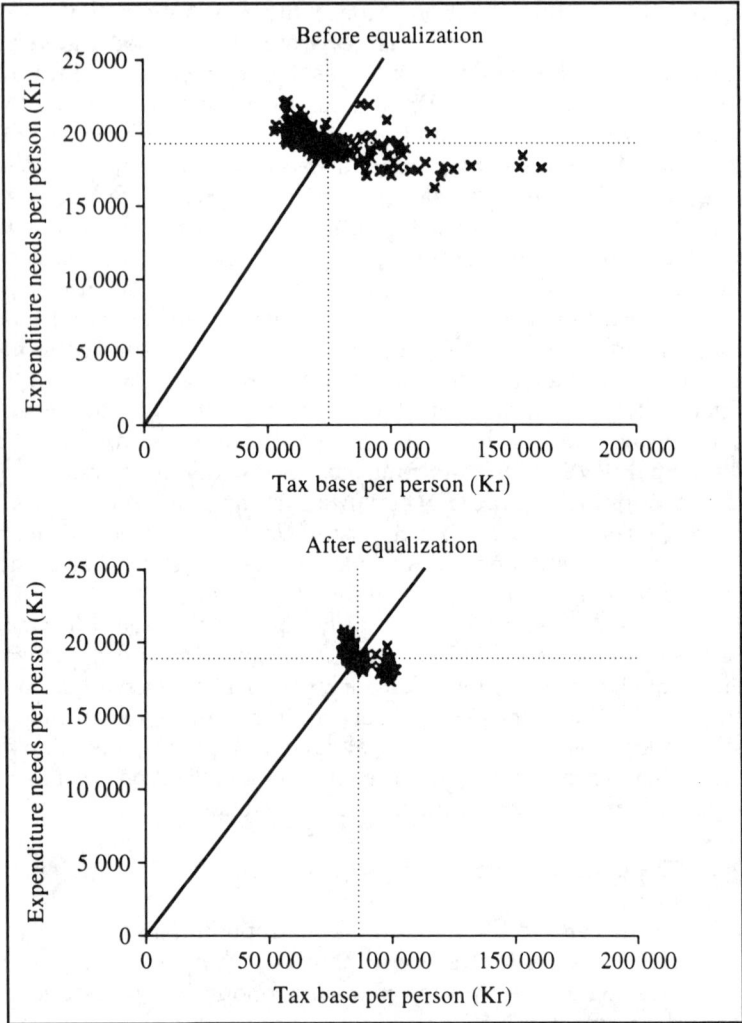

Source: Ministry of the Interior (1993, pp.25–6).

Figure 8.3   Economic equalization between Danish municipalities

ities in the region. Paradoxically, the very measures that should ensure economic equalization within the metropolitan area are in fact preserving the segregated structure. Meanwhile, those measures indirectly protect high-income taxpayers in certain municipalities from tax audits.

From the late 1970s onward, the state has applied long-term budget control strategies to local governments. Central regulation based on financial targets, including 'rate capping', as opposed to service standards and norms, were thereby intensified. This has meant a decrease in the municipal budgets, while rises in local government expenditures were suspended (Tonboe, 1991). Despite these reductions, Danish municipalities still hold a unique position, from a European point of view. They are special because of the pronounced decentralization of taxation and tasks. Consequently, local government expenses, as a percentage of total public expenditure, exceed 50 per cent. In an international comparison, this puts Denmark in a league of its own.

Whereas the 1970s were characterized by heavy public investments, the 1980s were characterized by scarce economic resources and a high degree of public–private ambiguity. This circumstance can be recognized in the privatization of several public functions, such as public transport.

Urban renewal

Danish society is usually considered to be fairly homogeneous and egalitarian, with large public involvement and a high degree of transfer payments. Still, the metropolitan region is characterized by rather large economic and social differences. Andersen (1991) describes the origin of these differences in terms of political urbanization. The distinct social segregation is particularly due to two factors:

- the local self-government (including individual taxation) in the 50 municipalities that comprise the region (see the previous section);
- the existing housing structure, developed through the last 100 years or more.

One particularly important factor is housing structure: the composition of housing stock with respect to age, size, quality and tenure. In the same vein, the housing policies of the municipalities are also important factors. In this connection, the municipality of Copenhagen has some special problems. Table 8.1 demonstrates one of these, namely the age of the housing stock.

Whereas only 40 per cent of the housing stock in the metropolitan region as a whole was built before 1940, the corresponding figure for the central municipality exceeds 70 per cent. Further-

Table 8.1   *Number of dwellings according to year of completion*

Area	Built before 1940	Built 1940–59	Built 1960–69	Built after 1969	Total
Municipality of Copenhagen	197 436 (70.9%)	40 901 (14.7%)	15 652 (5.6%)	24 217 (8.7%)	278 206 (100%)
Metropolitan region	331 506 (39.6%)	159 158 (19.2%)	21 257 (2.5%)	324 826 (38.8%)	836 747 (100%)

Source: Statistical Yearbook of Copenhagen (1992).

more, less than 10 per cent of the dwellings in the central municipality were built from 1970 and onwards, compared to a figure of
almost 40 per cent in the region as a whole.

From a general point of view, the table demonstrates one of the
most striking character traits of the city: its dynamism. Its physical structure changes as it grows. New functions, plants and buildings are added by new generations. As new neighbourhoods grow,
old ones are not automatically replaced. Often they start to decline. This process of decay is both physical and social. As buildings deteriorate, the increasing concentration of economic and
socially weak population groups adds to the problem. An almost
inexorable spiral of decline sets in unless public authorities take
measures against it.

Improvement of bad housing has been on the political agenda
for a long time. Ever since the effects of unplanned late nineteenth-century housing became clear, urban renewal has been an
important factor of urban policy in Denmark. From the turn of the
century, it has been generally accepted that, if the degradation
caused by poor housing conditions is to be overcome, public authorities have to commit themselves to the task of urban renewal.
Ideas have changed on how to solve the problems and which
methods should be used, and the legislative framework has evolved
too. The present Urban Renewal Act was adopted in 1983 (*Lov om
Byfornyelse 1983*), though its origins date back to 1939. Typically,
attempts to promote the renewal process have been plagued by
insufficient capital.

The core of the problem is economic. Whereas development of
new and vacant plots can be profitable, a relative economic loss
will inevitably ensue from an alternative renewal process on previously developed urban land. Any private developer will thus
prefer vacant land unless this loss is covered. The extra cost arises

from demolishing old buildings and preparing the site, as well as from the extra red tape. In order to sustain the necessary renewal, these extra costs, called 'urban renewal loss' (*saneringstab*), are shouldered jointly by state and municipality, each of them normally paying half of the amount.

The larger the stock of old and outdated buildings, the more serious the financial problems. Under such conditions, the local authority is faced by severe budgetary constraints. In 1992, the municipality of Copenhagen had a budget for urban renewal amounting to D.Kr. 1.1bn and similar amounts were expected for the following years (Københavns Kommunes Plandirektorat, no date). Public capital invested in urban renewal is a classic example of a redistributive measure. Without public initiative and investment, very little or no renewal of housing would take place at all. In principle, public money spent on urban renewal is supposed to benefit the less privileged. Even if there are still severe problems, great improvements have been made since the 1970s (see Table 8.2).

Table 8.2   Number of dwellings in the municipality of Copenhagen, 1950–92

Number of dwellings	1950	1960	1970	1980	1986	1992
Total	269 460	278 860	285 214	283 242	278 320	277 420
With 2 rooms or smaller	151 886	151 400	155 969	150 626	141 235	137 936
Without private bath	155 846	140 420	133 240	122 365	90 090	23 215
Without private toilet	–	36 910	31 780	15 527	13 513	9 924

Source: Statistical Yearbook of Copenhagen, various years.

The table summarizes some key figures illustrating the quality and development of the Copenhagen housing stock. The total number of dwellings grew from 270 000 in 1950 to a peak of 285 000 in 1970. Since then, the number has declined slightly; according to the latest figures (1992), the total now amounts to 277 000. The increase in total number of dwellings during the first half of the period is a sign of postwar housing shortage and the attempts to overcome it. In the late 1960s, however, more or less all vacant land within the boundaries of the municipality was developed. At the same time, the rising affluence made it possible for still more people to afford owner-occupied detached housing in the suburban municipalities. Since 1970, the total number of dwellings has been reduced by almost 8000 (3 per cent). The figures for various types of dwellings reveal striking shifts in the composition of the total stock, indicating that large gross changes have taken place. From 1970 to 1992, more than 18 000 (12 per cent) small flats (that is, with two rooms or fewer) have been either demolished or expanded. Almost 120 000 (83 per cent) dwellings without a bath have been removed from the stock or have been fitted with one. And more than 21 000 dwellings (69 per cent) that previously had no toilet of their own have been fitted with one. All these changes can be related to various urban renewal programmes.

Urban renewal follows a typical sequence of events. A semi-public urban renewal association (*saneringsselskab*) is in charge of the process. It buys the properties involved, prepares a plan for the renewal process and manages the process of rehousing. The association may improve the buildings or demolish them and then prepares the site before selling it to a developer. At this stage, public funding of the urban renewal loss can be calculated and paid out. The renewal of buildings, together with the general redistribution of population in the region, has led to a continuously decreasing size of population. This is occurring, not only in the areas involved in urban renewal, but also in the municipality as a whole. Since 1950, when the population of the municipality reached its peak of more than 750 000 inhabitants, Copenhagen has lost almost 300 000 people. Since 1970, the population has declined by more than 150 000 (see Figure 8.2).

The combination of a decreasing population and increasing quality of individual dwellings has brought Copenhagen closer to the ultimate goal of improving the overall quality of the building stock. Today there are fewer flats that lack basic sanitary facilities such as a toilet, bath or central heating. At the same time, the number of available flats has decreased, while the average family size on the housing market has decreased as well. Together, these developments result in a decreasing population density.

The process and result of renewal as described in the preceding paragraphs seems to be a fairly simple and straightforward example of redistribution. Public funds are invested in order to solve an actual problem that cannot be solved by the market itself. The extra costs incurred have been an enormous burden on the municipality, even if the central government pays half of the costs involved. There are, however, several 'negative externalities' (in the sense of unwanted side-effects) associated with the process. These are discussed below.

The political power structure of bodies dominated by the Labour Party and their explicit wish to favour the underprivileged have been compelling factors in the urban renewal process. For political reasons, virtually all the renewed buildings have ended up as tenement houses owned by semi-public housing associations. Consequently, the municipality has ended up with a new set of unsolved problems. First, the local authority paid its share of the direct costs of the renewal process. Then it had to solve problems primarily associated with the fact that the renewed areas have a one-sided population composition, adding to the segregation in the region.

- The new dwellings are mostly state-supported housing association tenement buildings. Therefore they primarily attract a low-income segment of the population. Not only are these groups 'bad' taxpayers, but they often represent segments of the population likely to require extra housing support and public (municipal) aid. Extra costs are thus incurred on top of the ones associated with the renewal process itself.
- Even if the physical conditions of the housing stock have been improved, the resulting dwellings do not constitute a real alternative for the high-income groups that are so desperately needed to improve the tax base of the city.
- As mentioned earlier, the cost of urban renewal and other social benefits – outlays that are often associated with each other – induces still higher taxes. Tax hikes encourage people (who have the choice) to move to suburban environments where taxes are lower (see the previous section).

By pursuing the primary political goal of urban renewal, that is, to create a higher degree of equity on the housing market, the municipality of Copenhagen has got itself into even deeper trouble. The age structure of the housing stock, combined with the relative economic independence, made problems difficult enough as they were. Thus urban renewal, as carried out in Copenhagen, in several cases has aggravated the socially one-sided composition of the population and the problems associated herewith.

The active policy on urban renewal, combined with a generally high housing standard, tight rent control and the relatively low rate of crime and delinquency of the city, could truly be marketed

as an asset. It must be realized, though, that the particular circumstances of a municipality present special problems of equalization
within the region. Such problems arise where the housing stock is
largely composed of worn-out buildings and has to act as a low-
income housing reserve for the region as a whole.

Transport

Most inhabitants of the central parts of Copenhagen tend to regard the environment and congestion problems arising from traffic as severe. These problems do not, however, reach the level of
nuisance found in many other European cities. Many factors contribute to this.

- Compared to most other West European countries, car-own-
  ership is less prevalent in Denmark (only Ireland, Greece,
  Portugal and Spain have fewer cars per 1000 inhabitants).
  This is largely because cars are heavily taxed. Especially in
  the municipality of Copenhagen, where only 22 per cent
  possess a car, ownership is less common. This, of course, is
  connected with the pronounced concentration of low-income
  households, including many students, and a densely built-
  up environment well served by a public transport network.
  This means that the intra-urban traffic flows involving cars
  are comparatively light.
- A plan – typical of the prevailing planning ideas of the late-
  1960s – to build a semicircular motorway (*Søringen*) around
  the western part of the city was never implemented. It is
  widely recognized that Copenhagen thereby prevented a
  'planning disaster', in the sense that some distinctive urban
  milieus were preserved. Furthermore, the absence of an effective transport corridor in the vicinity of the city has most
  likely contributed to the relative decentralization of industrial activities within the metropolitan area over the last
  couple of decades.
- The fact that Copenhagen has grown along the railway lines
  in the postwar period (according to the ideas that were
  sketched in the *Fingerplan* in 1947) has meant that many
  people have had (and still have) a realistic possibility of
  commuting by means of public transport.

Although the problems of congestion are comparatively moderate, traffic and environmental issues are high on the local political

agenda. This has to do with the overall emphasis on environmental considerations, but recent developments in travel patterns are also important. In this respect, transport is a good example of a sector forcing a deliberate choice between the policy dimensions mentioned above: efficiency, equity, control of negative externalities and budgetary constraints.

Figure 8.4 demonstrates the development of passenger travel, by car and by public transport, in the Greater Copenhagen Area. From 1975 to 1978, total travel increased, falling in the period 1978–81, and increasing again quite significantly. It is evident that this trend is due to an increase in car travel. One principal explanation for this is the relative change in prices between travel by car and by public transport (see Figure 8.5).

It is interesting to note that, throughout the period 1975–87, the number of trips made in central areas of Copenhagen remained more or less constant. Car trips declined a little, while train trips increased. The modal split in the inner areas is thus significantly different from that in the outer areas. Measured at a distance of about 1.5 km from the centre, only about 45 per cent of all trips crossing an arbitrary boundary were made by car. About 8 per cent were by bicycle. The reasons for the relatively low number of

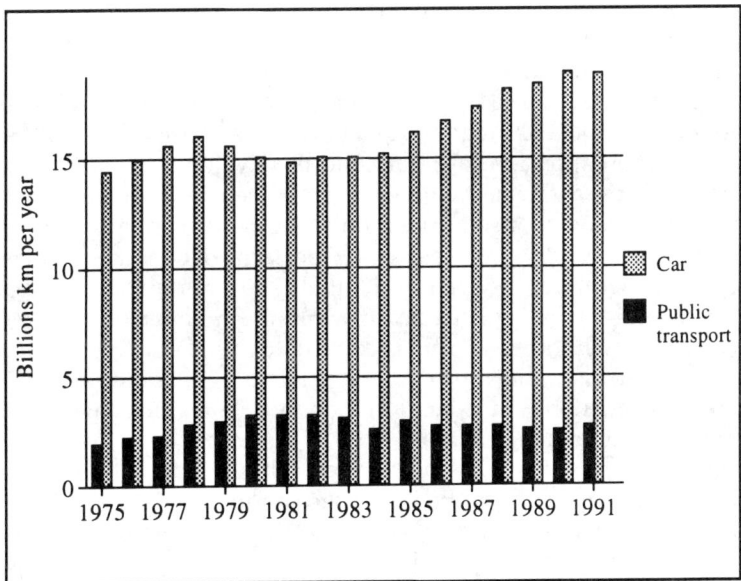

Figure 8.4   Modal split in traffic in Copenhagen, 1975–91

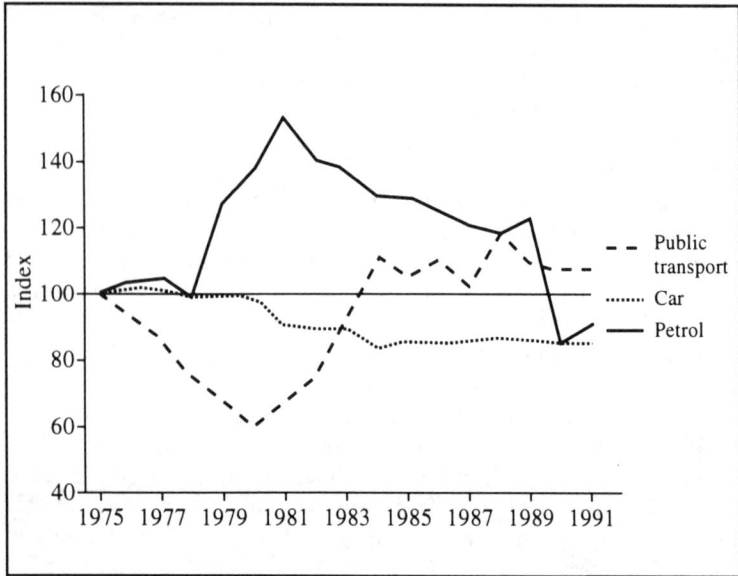

Figure 8.5   Development of relative cost of transport, 1975–91

car trips include the increasing cost of parking in the city centre and the construction of a southerly motorway diverting traffic from the west to the island of Amager out of the central city area.

A general traffic forecast for the period up to the year 2000 was provided in the 1989 regional plan. This was based upon three factors: population forecasts for cohorts, development of real income and cost associated with car travel. The plan concludes that there will be a slow rise in the number of passenger trips during the period (despite a forecast of a 3 per cent decline in population). Furthermore, the plan posits that the total number of trips by public transport will decrease while the number of trips by private car will increase. This is expected to be a major problem, not least because of its impact on the environment and on congestion. Policies should thus be formulated to change this balance in favour of public transport.

Future traffic policy in Copenhagen is based upon two principles: reduction of car traffic in densely populated areas and improvement of public transport. Interestingly, the main reasons for adopting these two principles are increased mobility and the environmental issues affecting urban environment, including pollution, safety and proper use of resources. Various measures are being considered with respect to the first principle. These include parking restrictions, reduction of road area for cars, changes in traffic control systems, development of park-and-ride facilities and, finally, improvement of conditions for cycles and mopeds (which are better already than in many European cities). With the exception of changes in traffic control systems, the other measures have been widely used in the region over the last few years. More dramatic measures, such as tolls for entering the inner city, have been under consideration by the Board of the Municipality of Copenhagen. The idea was scorned because it would create a barrier between various parts of the city. Road pricing was perceived as a more feasible means of control. This is particularly true if tolls can be collected electronically. The advantage of electronic monitoring is that pricing can be differentiated geographically and according to time of day in order to prevent congestion and protect environmentally sensitive areas. So far the most important means of limiting the traffic flow to the city centre have been raising parking fees, reducing the number of parking spaces and increasing the size of areas subject to parking restrictions.

The second principle is being pursued with a range of measures. When the Greater Copenhagen Council was dissolved, a reorganization took place of the regional transport authority. The already established joint ticketing and traffic zoning system between the regional transport authority, HT (*Hovedstadens Trafikselskab*) and DSB (*Danish State Railways*) makes it possible to buy tickets and season passes covering road as well as rail transport throughout the Copenhagen area. Also timetables and connections are given considerable attention, as is the possibility of combining bicycle travel with public transport. In the future the second principle will be pursued further by establishing new commuter train lines (*S-tog*). Furthermore, a new light rail will link the centre of Copenhagen to the island of Amager (see the section on the Ørestad development, later in this chapter). The increased demand for transport outside the centre of the city will be met by new bus lines, in particular circular routes. New equipment on bus routes and rail lines is considered an important inducement to passengers. The bus already has priority in the streets, and more bus lanes will be developed. Furthermore, according to the regional plan, most new workplaces should be located in the vicinity of the railway stations, especially where the radial railway system is crossed by major connecting roads. Owing to the intensive use in terms of number of workers per square metre, new office buildings should be concentrated at these points of intersection in the light of their high accessibility by public transport.

Paradoxically, other developments from the late 1980s, in particular the attempt to deregulate the regional transport authority, might very well make it difficult to fulfil the above-mentioned planning goals. One of the most striking effects of deregulation is that 45 per cent of all bus routes were slated for privatization by the spring of 1994. The argument is that privatization will lead to a more effective, thus cheaper, use of resources. But at the same time, deregulation suggests that transport subsidies are given a lower priority. As such, deregulation might very well contribute indirectly to the relative rise in the prices of public vis-à-vis private transport. That, of course, is in glaring contrast to conventional 'wisdom of deregulation'. However, the political establishment seems to have adopted the idea of collecting 'green' taxes, which might alter the price relations in favour of public transport. This measure will not necessarily divert a substantial amount of traffic away from heavily populated or ecologically sensitive areas. The aim to locate a major part of industrial activity in areas adjacent to regional railway stations may therefore prove to be a rather elusive planning goal, at least in the short run. In reality, one may fear that the introduction of 'green' taxes would not make it any easier to manage the development in a way that causes the least damage to the most sensitive parts of the environment.

Finally, the way the urban structure will develop over the next decades may help solve traffic problems. Basically, Copenhagen has a radial finger-like structure in its urban form (see Figure 8.1). At present, there is a net deficit of jobs in the outer areas of the fingers and a net surplus in the centre of Copenhagen. Urban expansion will occur in the fingers, but it is expected that jobs in the fingers will grow faster than the population. The fingers are basically served by the urban rail network. This provides for a more stable future public transport system, although 'cross-finger' public transport poses a problem.

Energy

It is generally recognized that there is an inherent contradiction between efficiency and negative externalities, in particular with respect to the environment. On the one hand, energy policies and savings have been of major concern to national policy, certainly since the oil crisis of 1972. On the other hand, energy production is one of the major factors affecting the environment. As both production and consumption are heavily concentrated in and around major urban areas, energy planning is of great and growing importance in urban planning.

The following is an overview of the sources of energy supply by type and production locality. Their distribution networks and their impact on the general urban environment will be considered. The reason for dwelling on energy is that this topic provides us with the best possible example of efficiency and control over negative externalities not necessarily proving to be incompatible goals. (For a more comprehensive examination of environmental problems in Copenhagen, see Engelstoft and Jensen-Butler, 1993).

Energy planning in the Copenhagen metropolitan region is complex. This is partly because many organizations and authorities are involved, and partly because several types of energy supply are used extensively. Furthermore, complicated interrelationships exist between the different types of energy. For example, there is an important relationship between warm water for district heating and electricity production in combined heat and power plants (CHP plants). An important basis for energy planning continues to be the regional plan for the Copenhagen Metropolitan Area (Hovedstadsrådet, 1988).

The Regional Heating Plan of 1988 was the first attempt at coordinated energy planning in the Copenhagen area. Although it deals specifically with heating, it is in fact the cornerstone of energy planning. The reason is that heating involves electricity production in CHP plants and the establishment of other supply networks, such as for natural gas. Energy planning in the Copenhagen metropolitan region is based upon six main objectives:

- increased use of local energy sources, including warm water from local power plants;
- increased coverage by district heating;
- consolidation of the natural gas supply;
- coordination between heat planning and other types of energy planning;
- energy savings, better coordination of supply and consumption;
- environmental considerations.

There are, however, a number of conflicts involved in attaining these goals. In an attempt to exercise them simultaneously, three types of heat supply districts have been defined (see Figure 8.6):

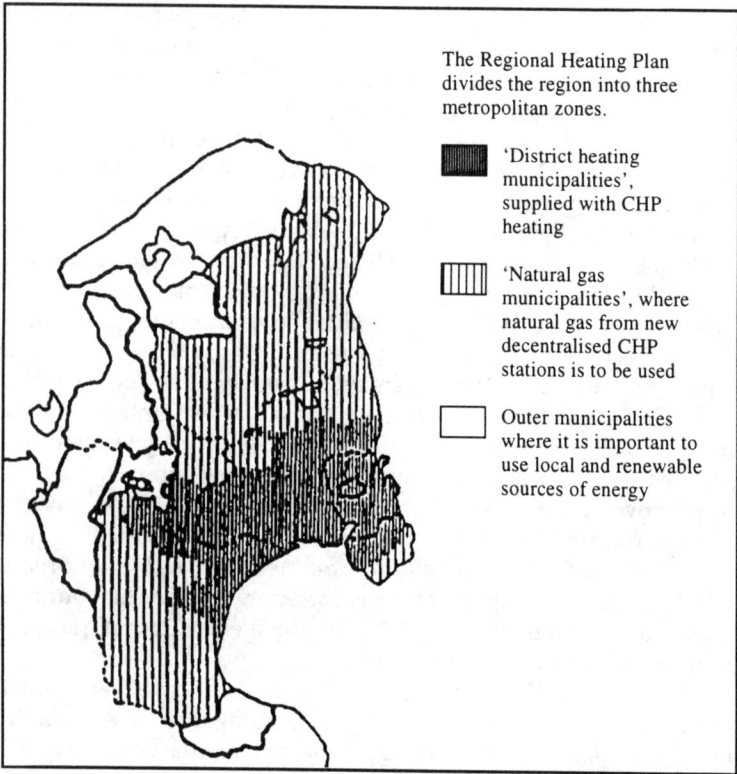

The Regional Heating Plan divides the region into three metropolitan zones.

▓ 'District heating municipalities', supplied with CHP heating

▥ 'Natural gas municipalities', where natural gas from new decentralised CHP stations is to be used

☐ Outer municipalities where it is important to use local and renewable sources of energy

Source: Lord Major's Office (1992, p.5).

Figure 8.6   Heating plan areas in the Copenhagen metropolitan region

- 'Heating districts', that is areas supplied from a number of different sources, including CHP plants, waste incineration and local oil-fired heat production;
- 'Natural gas districts', which are areas that are being supplied from the new national natural gas network;
- 'Other districts', namely areas with lower population densities and where local energy sources, including straw and biogas, may be viable. In these areas, individual oil-fired central heating units in each house or apartment block are common.

It is worthwhile to note the close relationship between the various 'heating plan districts' and the population density of the area in question (compare Figures 8.1 and 8.6). 'District heating municipalities' are thus constituted by the central municipalities plus the suburban municipalities to the southwest, that is the municipalities predominantly characterized by multi-storey housing. The 'natural gas municipalities' include those areas dominated by detached housing and the outer municipalities, which are not so densely populated and characterized by rural land use.

The following considerations refer to some important conflicts in energy supply for heating. First, expansion of combined heat and power produces great energy savings and low consumer prices per delivered gigajoule (GJ). On the other hand, growth of CHP plants implies increasing electricity consumption, as both electricity and hot water are produced simultaneously. CHP creates environmental pollution, the primary energy source being coal, as well as problems with solid waste. However, levels of pollution, particularly SO_2, are in fact reduced where CHP replaces individual oil-fired units. Furthermore, there are many conflicts between municipalities and suppliers. The reason is that major investments in transmission networks are extremely expensive. A typical conflict concerns the question of whether a municipality should pay marginal or average costs. Second, the semi-public national oil and gas distribution company DONG (*Dansk Olie og Naturgas a/s*) and its regional subsidiaries have a strong interest in ensuring as large a market for natural gas as possible. CHPs have the same interest. Large markets with a high population density are of immediate interest, which brings natural gas supply into conflict with CHP. Natural gas burns almost without pollution. Because of the nature of the supply contracts for natural gas in Denmark, however, it sells at high prices per delivered GJ. Finally, the 'other areas' have considerable interests in access to cheap network-based energy supply. Accordingly, they have an interest in extending networks into areas in which they are not commercially viable.

An important contribution to energy supply in the region is the concept of decentralized CHP production. This option involves a wide range of primary energy sources, including solid waste and straw. For instance, the excess straw production in the region can heat about 45 000 households (approximately 6 per cent of the total number of households in the entire region). Natural gas will be used in these decentralized plants. This type of production explicitly aims at reducing environmental pollution, through improved treatment of solid waste and increased use of natural gas. Furthermore, this type of plant generates electricity in an environmentally sustainable manner.

Location of energy production sites – electricity plants, CHP and windmills – coincides with the heating plan districts. Thus, district heating municipalities are supplied from the central CHP stations near the centre of Copenhagen, decentralized plants supply areas inside the natural gas supply area and in the outer area, and windmill parks are located on the coast, primarily in rural areas.

Reduction of pollution and of energy consumption are major considerations in the energy section of the regional plan. The plan proposes greater use of wind power, use of straw and widespread use of natural gas. Use of waste warm water from electricity generation in CHP is a major component of both pollution reduction and energy saving. This type of energy production lowers the level of wasted energy from 60 per cent to 20 per cent. An important component of the policy to reduce both pollution and energy consumption is the plans for decentralized CHP production. This gives great flexibility with respect to energy sources as well as in matching demand and supply. There are clear environmental, economic and planning advantages.

Energy consumption is also related to economic activity. In the more central parts of Copenhagen, the principal form of heating is warm water-based district heating, which is suitable for service and office activity. Natural gas is available in the outer suburbs of Copenhagen and parts of the more rural areas. Its presence reinforces the trend towards relocation of industry outside the more central urban areas and even in rural locations as it is more suitable as process energy. This movement clearly alleviates the environmental pressure on the centre of Copenhagen.

Environmental considerations are of major importance to Danish urban planning. When faced with the difficult choice between economic development and environmental protection, public opinion is increasingly in favour of the environment. This trend is clearly visible in the Copenhagen area (see the section on the Sound Link later in this chapter). The energy example provided here demonstrates that efficiency and negative externalities do not necessarily conflict. Since the oil crisis of 1973–4 (at a time when Danish domestic production of fossil energy was virtually non-existent), Danish energy policy has had energy saving as one of its primary goals. Several innovative solutions have emerged to the problem of supplying energy to urban areas. Today the metropolitan region has a supply system which is built on a fine balance between various sources of energy, each of which is adjusted to the local area. That balance is maintained by the extensive use of combined heat and power plants, the establishment of an extended pipeline network for heat distribution (steam) in dense urban areas and the use of alternative energy sources in more sparsely populated localities.

The differentiated use of energy resources is a result of strict planning policy, including taxes, rates and dues (almost a command-economy approach to planning). The result has been a fortunate combination of efficient use of resources, relatively cheap prices and environmental improvements. From a 'marketing' point of view, this ought to be considered an asset of the region.

Culture and tourism

It is no big surprise that many politicians in the city of the 'Little Mermaid' have suggested that the city should broaden its local economic base by stimulating international tourism and cultural events of European importance. A report prepared by the Danish Ministry of Industry suggests that tourism might become an important growth-initiating factor of the local regional economy (Industriministeriet, 1991). To realize the potential, greater hotel capacity and improved conference facilities are necessary. At present, the total number of hotel rooms in Copenhagen is just above 8300. This corresponds to 22 per cent of the national figure. In recent years, however, there has been a decline in the number of hotel rooms in Copenhagen compared with the country as a whole. Also, compared to other Nordic capitals, Copenhagen's growth in hotel capacity has been negligible. In fact, during the 1980s, the number of hotel rooms in central Copenhagen even decreased (by 7 per cent), in contrast to an increase in Stockholm and Helsinki (32 per cent) and in Gothenburg (60 per cent). Although the average occupancy rate is high, there are significant seasonal differences (see Figure 8.7) with the highest rates being from May to September. An increase in the number of overnight guests during the off season would therefore be an advantage. This goal might be achieved by improving Copenhagen's status as a conference city. Today roughly 60 per cent of all overnight guests come to Copenhagen for business purposes. Copenhagen ranks eleventh among the leading conference centres in Europe. This position can probably only be improved if the conference facilities are extended and modernized.

One of the most important ways to attract tourists is by promoting cultural activity. Like many other city councils, that of Copenhagen has adopted a culture-based urban revitalization programme. Central to this approach is the idea that the integration

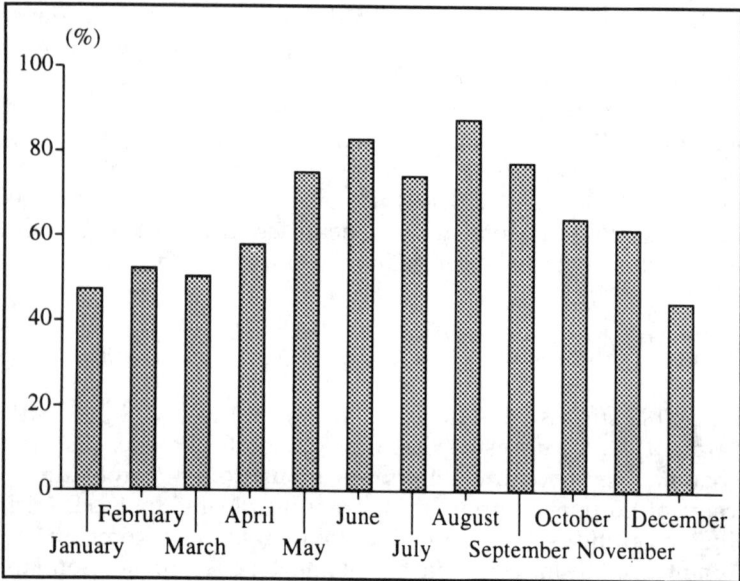

Figure 8.7   Average utilization of hotel rooms in Copenhagen

of cultural activities into a widely based revitalization project can work as a catalyst for physical and environmental renewal, attract tourists and capital investments, enhance a city's image and create new jobs (Lim, 1993). This notion of a culture-led approach to urban revitalization was emphatically endorsed by the organization that prepared Copenhagen for its designation as Cultural Capital of Europe in 1996 *(Kulturby 96)*: 'Copenhagen will avail itself of this opportunity to improve the artistic and cultural life of the Danish metropolis on a broad front and make every effort to enhance its position in the international art, culture and media scene.' The events in 1996 are described as 'a strategy for cultural revitalization of the entire area that would reach far into the 21st century. (...) to invigorate the city's innate qualities in the direction of an up-to-date and ideally balanced city culture that cares for the environment as well as for people' (Copenhagen 96's Secretariat, 1993).

The total activity budget for the '96 event' is a little more than D.Kr 750m. This amount is financed jointly by the Danish state, covering one-third of the costs, and the three metropolitan counties and most of the municipalities in the Greater Copenhagen Region. The remaining funding has been raised among private investors, sponsors and foundations. In addition, the Danish government has granted over D.Kr. 780m for expansion at national institutions of culture and at art schools in Copenhagen. For example, grants have been awarded to the Royal Danish Library and for plans to reuse the former naval station (see the next section). Some of the more noteworthy projects are initiated by nongovernmental organizations (NGOs) as with the building of a 'Museum of Modern Art' (located in the municipality of Ishøj) initiated and partly financed by the county of Copenhagen (Københavns Amt). Furthermore, there is funding for the construction of the municipal Concert Hall on the waterfront (expected cost D.Kr. 400m), the extension of the National Museum of Art and the enlargement of *Ny Carlsberg Glyptothek*, an art museum financed by the Carlsberg breweries (expected cost D.Kr. 200m).

Indirectly, cultural enterprise can create economic growth by attracting tourists who spend money on hotel rooms and so on. However, the economic outcome of Copenhagen 96 is closely related to a permanent increase in tourism. A substantial part of the money is being spent on lasting improvements and enlargements of museums. This might prove to be decisive, because museums and exhibitions are known to attract foreigners, including international conventions and similar events. Other activities in the course of 1996, such as theatre performances and concerts, would primarily attract local and regional citizens. To prevent the increased influx of tourists from being only temporary, Copenhagen 96 is collaborating with *Wonderful Copenhagen*, an organization promoting the city to tourists. With respect to attracting international corporations, there is some fear that Copenhagen 96 will not be of any significant importance. Indeed, studies indicate that culture certainly is not the first priority for firms considering potential locations (Hansen, 1993). Consequently, Copenhagen 96 is cooperating with a marketing organization *(Copenhagen Capacity)*, formed by the metropolitan counties in order to establish – and to market – a regional economic development policy.

Irrespective of the anticipated effects of a strategy promoting tourism and cultural activities, one of the advantages of this approach seems to be that local opposition to it is rather insignificant. This is probably because the inhabitants themselves have not seen the negative effects of tourism to the same extent as the residents of Venice, Florence, or Salzburg. As sketched in the beginning of this chapter, cultural revitalization strategies are conceived to be in line with the idea of a livable city.

The 'Grand Projects'

The above analysis illustrates that, although sectoral policies have been changing during the 1980s, they do not interfere with the basic traits of the redistributive city. Despite the economic constraints that were facing the (local) welfare state in the 1970s and the 1980s, urban renewal, energy and transport are still heavily subsidized and regulated by society. Although bus service has been privatized, it is still subject to public control. Decisions on fares, frequency and so on have not been turned over to the private bus companies.

In some ways, urban planning and policies were influenced more markedly by the adverse socioeconomic conditions. The neo-conservative critique of public-led institutions also had a greater impact at this level. The most notable effect was achieved by the replacement of regulative planning instruments by leverage planning practices (Brindley *et al.*, 1989): the 'Grand Projects'. In this section, we will focus on some of the changes in spatial planning and urban policy. This is done by discussing three large-scale projects for development in Copenhagen. These are plans that have caused a lot of debate: the development of Copenhagen's harbour front; the 'Ørestad' Development Corporation; and the fixed rail and road link to southern Sweden (the Sound Link).

All these projects were thrown into the limelight in the late 1980s. They were devised as instruments that should be used to strengthen the future role and potential of Copenhagen in a world of changing economic and political relations. All were introduced in Parliament by the conservative–liberal government (1981–93) in the early 1990s. At that time, it had become politically accepted that the future of Copenhagen was a question of 'national interest' rather than just a 'local' problem. In a condensed form, the main argument is that, in order to stay competitive, Denmark should not rely on local actions. Major initiatives and investments were needed to strengthen the national capital. Paradoxically, this argument was advanced by the very same government that – almost simultaneously – abolished the Greater Copenhagen Council without establishing an alternative body to coordinate planning in the area. An effort was made to coordinate in March 1990. Then a Metropolitan Development Board (*Hovedstadens Udviklingsråd*) was installed under the leadership of the Minister of Economic Affairs. In the same year, a Metropolitan Development Corporation (*Hovedstadens Udviklingsselskab*) was established. Both included members appointed by the government. The idea was inspired by the English Urban Development Corporations (UDC). Their tasks were to generate and supervise plans for the implementation of development and redevelopment projects, mainly on publicly owned land in the central parts of the city. The development corporation never really got off the ground. It had no power to supersede the general administrative and legislative planning framework. Furthermore, the lord mayor of Copenhagen, supported by a majority of the city council *(Borgerrepræsentationen)*, simply refused to participate. Requests to hand over vacant land, such as sites along the harbour front, to the development corporation were declined.

Harbour front development

Harbour front development has been on the political agenda in many cities. In the late 1980s, lessons from Baltimore, San Francisco, London and other places showed that it was possible to convert obsolete waterfront areas in or near the city centre with some success (Priebs, 1992). In Copenhagen, however, harbour front development was deadlocked. There are several reasons: the failure to form an active development corporation covering the metropolitan area; abortive efforts to create an overall plan for the harbour area; and four principal landowners with divergent opinions.

The plots of land adjoining the waterfront in the harbour of Copenhagen are owned by the Danish State, the municipality of Copenhagen, the port authority and a multitude of private landowners. The port authority and the private landowners in particular have (of course) tried to sell some of their land on the open market to get the highest possible price. This led to competing plans, including hotel and congress facilities, office buildings and high rent/high rise (at least by Danish standards) housing. In response, a committee was established to report on the harbour areas available for potential development. The report was delivered in mid-1989. Various development options were identified, mainly housing and assorted public uses. Commercial development was suggested only for the areas closest to the commuter train (*S-tog*) stations.

The municipal plan of Copenhagen has been adjusted according to the viewpoints of the committee. Nonetheless, partly owing to the impotence of the Metropolitan Development Corporation, none of the ideas presented in the report has been implemented. Furthermore, the market has prevented some projects from being completed, particularly because of the slack demand for new commercial space. The most notable example is the Scandinavian Trade

Centre just opposite some of the ministries in the very heart of the city. Old manufacturing buildings on the site were torn down, but the developer went bankrupt. Other developers hesitated to develop, because of the glut of office space in the early 1990s. Thus building cranes are few and far between along the 42 kilometres of quays and wharfs.

Some projects along the waterfront are in the process of being inplemented. For instance, an extension is being built to the Royal Danish Library directly adjoining the waterfront. Furthermore, the Danish Navy has left the historical Royal Dockyards (*Holmen*). The Ministry of Cultural Affairs will have roughly one-sixth of the area at its disposal. The lion's share of the area will be sold to private investors. As a start, private investors are developing the inner parts of the old free port area, but further activity is not expected until the economy has fully recovered and stabilized. On the whole, the fragmented ownership structure and the failure to form a dynamic development corporation have prevented the harbour front from being developed according to an overall plan. Along with the recession, these organizational factors have led to rather patchy development activities along the waterfront.

The prime goal of waterfront development has been to develop a high-class area by international standards. It should be able to attract European and other international investment capital. In this respect the goal is very similar to the ideas behind the 'Ørestad' project, which will be discussed next. It is clear that the municipality of Copenhagen counteracted the formation of a development corporation to cover the whole metropolitan area. In contrast, its actions were far from obstructionist when 'Ørestad' was proposed.

The 'Ørestad' development

The Danish Parliament passed legislation in June 1992 that paved the way for the Ørestad development. Based on the act, a development corporation (*Ørestadsselskabet I/S*), owned jointly by the municipality of Copenhagen and the Danish state, is going to plan and develop a plot of land. The parcel (almost 3 square kilometres, owned by the two bodies jointly) is situated a couple of kilometres from the very centre of the city. The Ørestad, which will be located on the island of Amager – between the city and Copenhagen Airport (*Kastrup*) – will be served by a light rail system. That system itself will be planned by the Ørestad Development Corporation, but its construction and operation will be subject to a public call for tenders. Funding will be derived from public loans, thus not encumbering the municipal budget. These loans will be repaid through the added value generated by the development of Ørestad, that is by selling off building sites, when the area is ripe for development.

Construction of the Ørestad will not be permitted until the overall plan is ready and the light rail system is completed. The planning process, which was initiated by an international competition of architects, will end with a supplement to the municipal plan as the basis for subsequent local plans. Allegedly, in the end, the area will contain attractive housing, cultural and educational institutions, research institutes and city-oriented commercial businesses. Indeed, it is the 'ultimate goal to improve Copenhagen's competitiveness in an open Europe' (City of Copenhagen, 1991).

Experience gained from other large urban developments has shown that proper timing of investments in public transport in relation to urban development schemes is crucial. One way to ensure good sequencing is to put one (private) development corporation in charge of all phases of the development. This idea is particularly appealing to the municipality of Copenhagen, since the development corporation (*Øresundsselskabet*) is underwritten by the state. From the point of view of the municipality, no budgetary constraints are to be taken into consideration. At the same time, the light rail system will improve mass transport to existing urban areas on Amager and it is expected to improve public transport even in central Copenhagen.

Like other large urban developments, the Ørestad has raised serious opposition. This is primarily because the appointed area will be adjacent to the large nature reserve of West Amager. The plan has caused an uproar, particularly among the citizens of Amager and the Danish Society for the Conservation of Nature (*Danmarks Naturfredningsforening*). One further factor has to be considered. At present there are in excess of 600 000 square metres of vacant office space in Copenhagen (Hartoft-Nielsen, 1992). Combined with the political uncertainty of this and other urban developments (for instance, the harbour front), investors have been very reluctant to show any interest in the Ørestad so far.

The Sound Link

Following a lengthy discussion, an agreement between the Danish and the Swedish governments was signed in 1991. The two countries thereby agreed to built the first physical link between northern Scandinavia and the rest of Europe. The Sound Link, *Øresundsforbindelsen*, foresees a combined tunnel and bridge, including the longest suspension bridge in the world. It is scheduled to open in the year 1999, but the path from plan to implementation has been a difficult one.

The idea of building a fixed link between the two countries across the Øresund (the narrow strait separating Denmark and Sweden) is not new. Earlier attempts have failed on technical and financial grounds. The reason why the plan passed through the political system at this particular time is undoubtedly connected to lobbying activities and recent shifts in EU policies on transport. For instance, delegates to the Roundtable of European Industrialists, including the former managing director of Volvo, strongly advocated investments that would integrate Europe economically and physically. In this vein, they identified a number of 'missing links' (to use their own terminology) where huge investments in infrastructure are needed. One of these is the link between Sweden and Denmark. These arguments have been supported by most liberal and conservative politicians in both countries. Within the Labour parties, the majority of the MPs of both parliaments are in favour of establishing a fixed link (Larsen and Sørensen, 1992). An 'alliance' between top industrialists and Labour politicians might seem peculiar. However, support from Labour is in accordance with their traditional demand-side policies emphasizing job creation.

The Sound Link has received strong support from politicians at the national level, but regionally also many politicians, along with the business communities, are in favour of the link. Indeed, one might identify an emerging pro-growth coalition supporting the idea of Copenhagen as a Nordic development pole. This emerging coalition tends to regard the link as a crucial growth-inducing factor. It will strengthen the position of Copenhagen as a competitor vis-à-vis Berlin, Hamburg, Gothenburg and Stockholm. Copenhagen can enhance its position by utilizing its geopolitical location as crossroads for maritime traffic to and from the Baltic region and for traffic between Scandinavia and continental Europe. Furthermore, the creation of a new conurbation of 2.5 million inhabitants (1.7 million in Greater Copenhagen and 800 000 in Greater Malmö) will produce a corresponding expansion of the commercial market, the labour market and the supply of cultural, educational and research facilities. The main argument of the coalition is that a fixed link will increase levels of contact between two information-rich regions. In theory, at least, that will increase creativity, thereby raising innovation potentials (Andersson and Matthiessen, 1993). Two events of 1995 might be seen as examples of the increasing competitiveness of Copenhagen: one is the decision of the airline companies of SAS and Lufthansa to use Copenhagen's airport (Kastrup) as one out of three hubs in their joint route planning (the other two being Munich and Frankfurt, not Berlin or Hamburg); the other is the announced intention of the US embassy in Copenhagen to more than double its staff, allegedly in order to expand diplomatic, commercial and other relations in the Baltic area and Eastern Europe.

According to the Danish–Swedish agreement, this huge investment of D.Kr. 19bn (1990 prices, according to the budget of November 1993) is to be paid for by future users (by the levying of tolls) and not out of public funds. Calculations made by the Danish Ministry of Transport are based on the assumption that the invested money will be paid back in 30 years on 'market terms' at an inflation-adjusted interest rate of 4 per cent. This is thought to be realistic, provided that the number of vehicles crossing the bridge grows by 1.7 per cent annually over a 20-year period after completion. The assumption indicates that the fixed link might cause the level of pollution to rise, unless, of course, emissions are kept at the current level by technical improvements. This implies that one of the prerequisites of the agreement – that the fixed link should prove to be a 'zero' solution in environmental terms – will be hard to fulfil, while financing is arranged on market terms. Thus the question is whether the Sound Link will be feasible while satisfying both of the requirements of the treaty: to be economically sound and yet have no major environmentally damaging effects.

On both sides of the Sound, the bridge has been opposed, primarily on environmental grounds. The debate has been particularly heated because of doubts concerning an unimpeded flow of salt water to the Baltic. The treaty between Denmark and Sweden stipulates that the construction of the link must have no environmental consequences. In fact, this has been a precondition for approving construction by some of the minor political parties (within the coalition governments in both countries). Opinion polls reveal that many are against the project. In 1992, more than 30 000 protests were lodged in Denmark. A recent opinion poll, however, shows that the opposition towards the link is decreasing. Within the metropolitan region, 51 per cent were against in January 1995, whereas in August the same year this figure was reduced to 41 per cent (Øresundskonsortiet, 1995). This has not prevented the demolition of 200 properties and 250 allotments that lay on the proposed site where the Danish rail and motorway connections are to be constructed. The construction work on the Danish side of the Sound started in August 1993, although the Swedish environmental assessments at that time were not yet completed.

Environmentalists in Copenhagen have gained support from grass-roots movements, planners and others. These parties all claim that the rail and road link to southern Sweden will just increase the flow of through traffic to northern Germany without much benefit to Copenhagen and the region. According to this argument, the benefits will not emerge if Norway, Sweden and Finland obtain full membership of the European Union. In that event, the number of Scandinavian companies that will invest in Copenhagen will most likely fall drastically. Consequently, Copenhagen will not be able to establish itself as a Nordic gateway to Europe in economic terms. The anti-link movement is thus questioning whether the link will cause anything but negative externalities – environmentally and economically.

Conclusions

This final section will evaluate urban policy issues as they have been pursued in Copenhagen. Possible contradictions between various goals will be highlighted. Furthermore, we will discuss whether Copenhagen has specific advantages over other European cities and whether these are being developed properly.

In the preceding sections, we have identified a range of activities and facilities. Some of these are related to the local welfare state, 'the redistributive city', that could be used as a marketable asset vis-à-vis other European cities. These include comparatively low crime and delinquency rates, combined with reasonable housing conditions (see the section on urban renewal); low levels of pollution as the result of efficient and integrated systems for heat and power production (see the section on energy); relatively few problems with traffic congestion thanks to a rather efficient public transport system (see the section on transport); and a culture-led revitalization strategy that would improve the livability of the city (see the section on culture and tourism). This suggests that the 'redistributive city' and a strengthening of the competitiveness of the metropolitan region do not necessarily exclude one another. Indeed, instead of promoting a part of Copenhagen as the sole contender on the European scene, the revitalization strategy should encompass the entire metropolitan region. By emphasizing economic equalization and overall political coordination, which are the main characteristics of the 'redistributive city', it is possible to avoid 'islands of renewal in seas of decay', which are often the result of growth-oriented policies (Berry, 1985).

In the wake of deregulation, privatization and more market-led planning styles, the focus on big city competition has resulted in a bias towards 'Grand Projects' in order to attract investors and developers. The developments in the 1980s have to a large degree led to the deterioration of coordinated, regulative planning practices. Such practices were at the heart of the planning systems that were created throughout western societies in the postwar period. Subsequently, it has become more and more difficult to prevent urban planning from losing touch with particular economic interests that might be connected with these single projects. Paradoxically, new urban problems have been piling up, whereas the capacity of the planning system has been reduced. Furthermore, in Copenhagen, the uncertainty as to whether development should be diverted to the Ørestad or to the harbour front (of course combined with the high vacancy rate for office space) have forced developers to postpone decisions on investments. So, in essence, the 'Grand Projects' strategy might leave the developers puzzled in a way they would not have been with the former coordinated, regulative planning practices. And uncertainty is not conductive to investment.

Although the political debate in the Danish Parliament has reached a level of consensus, national support for strengthening the international role of Copenhagen remains at the level of principle. It is not as yet backed by hard expenditure plans, although the state does participate in some of the public–private partnerships and is underwriting loans taken out by them.

The new approaches to urban revitalization will increase what has been called 'the challenge of distributional justice' (Dangschat and Ossenbrügge, 1990). The basic principles of the 'redistributive city' may not necessarily prevent growth-inducing strategies from being successfully introduced. However, the 'Grand Projects' are only partly aimed at these principles (the light rail system being one example). The question of distributional justice is exactly what the emerging no-growth movement, most notably the opponents of the Sound Link movement, is hinting at in questioning the ideas behind the 'Grand Projects'.

Thus a very complicated process has been initiated in Copenhagen. In this process, interests and actors representing both the public and private sectors are forming alliances on the basis of a common agenda for promoting economic growth. Opposing this, groups and organizations are defending the equity dimension of urban policies. At the same time, they propose plans and projects with the lowest level of negative externalities. So the formation of development policies is closely related to the debate on the equity/efficiency trade-off (Stone, 1987). The 'supply side' of the efficiency argument is sometimes presented as if business subsidies (for example by lowering development costs), combined with the avoidance of social welfare expenditures, are prerequisites for economic growth. Yet the issue is not that simple. Major concessions can be made to equity without harming efficiency. If not for other reasons, the political elite is still forced to balance economic accumulation and social legitimation policies. Furthermore, as the Copenhagen case has shown, even 'Grand Projects' have to be adjusted in order to minimize negative externalities – both economic and environmental ones.

References

Andersen, Hans Thor (1991) 'The political urbanization. Fringe development in Copenhagen', *Espace, Population, Sociétés*, 2, pp.367–79.
Andersson, Åke E. and Christian Wichmann Matthiessen (1993) *Øresundsregionen. Kreativitet, integration, vækst* [The sound region: creativity, integration, growth], Copenhagen: Munksgaard.
Berry, Brian J.L. (1985) 'Islands of Renewal in Seas of Decay', in P. Peterson (ed.), *The New Urban Reality*, Washington, DC: Brookings, pp.69–96.
Brindley, Tim, Yvonne Rudin and Gerry Stoker (1989) *Remaking Planning. The Politics of Urban Change in the Thatcher Years*, London: Unwin Hyman.
Bruun, F. (1991) *The Rise and Fall of the Greater Copenhagen Council*, Århus: Institute of Political Science, University of Århus.
City of Copenhagen (1991) *Municipal Plan for Copenhagen. Proposal for revision*, Copenhagen.
Copenhagen 96's Secretariat (1993) 'Copenhagen 96. Cultural Capital of Europe' (press release), Copenhagen.
Dangschat, Jens and Jürgen Ossenbrügge (1990) 'Hamburg: Crisis management, urban regeneration, and social democrats', in Dennis Judd and Michael Parkinson (eds), *Leadership and Urban Regeneration. Cities in North America and Europe*, Urban Affairs Annual Reviews 37, London: Sage, pp.86–105.
Engelstoft, Sten and Chris Jensen-Butler (1993) 'Copenhagen's overall project', *Sistema Terra* II, (1), pp.73–9.
Hansen, Trine Bille (1993) 'Kulturens Økonomiske betydning – "State of the Art"' [The economic importance of culture – 'state of the art'], AKF memo, Copenhagen.
Harding, Alan (1991) *Copenhagen: Comfortable capital or growing Eurocity?*, working paper, Liverpool: Centre for Urban Studies, University of Liverpool.
Hartoft-Nielsen, Peter (1992) 'Kontorbyggeri, ledige lokaler – og planlægning i hovedstadsområdet' [Office buildings, vacant floor-space and planning in the metropolitan area], *Byplan*, 44, (1), pp.26–30.
Hovedstadsrådet (1978) *Regionplanens 1.etape 1977–1992* [The first stage of the regional plan 1977–1992], Copenhagen.
Hovedstadsrådet (1988) *Regionplanredegørelse 1989/4 Energiforsyning og miljøbeskyttelse m.m.* [Account of the regional plan 1989/4. Energy supply and environmental protection, etc.], Copenhagen.
Industriministeriet (1991) *Turistens København* [Tourist's Copenhagen], Copenhagen.
Københavns Kommunes Plandirektorat (n.d.) *Fra sanering til byfornyelse i København* [From slum clearance to urban renewal in Copenhagen], Copenhagen.

Kommissionen om hovedstadsrådet (1983) *Betænkning afgivet af Kommissionen om hovedstadsrådet* [Report submitted by the Commission on the Greater Copenhagen Council], Betænkning nr.988, Copenhagen.

Larsen, Flemming and Claus Hedegaard Sørensen (1992) 'Socialdemokratiet og Øresundsbroen – Et sandt drama om magt, demokrati og miljø' [The Social Democratic Party and the sound bridge. A true drama about power, democracy and the environment], unpublished master's thesis, Aalborg.

Lim, Hoe (1993) 'Cultural strategies for revitalizing the city: A review and evaluation', *Regional Studies*, **27**, pp.589–95.

Lord Mayor's Office (1992) 'Energy and Environment in Copenhagen'. Department of Urban Planning, Copenhagen.

Ministry of the Interior (1993) *Municipalities and Counties in Denmark. Tasks and Finance*, Copenhagen.

Øresundskonsortiet (1995) 'Lille flertal imod Øresundsprojektet: både Sverge og Danmark' [A small majority against the sound project: both Sweden and Denmark], *Sund & Bro*, **11**.

Priebs, Axel (1992) 'Strukturwandel und Revitalisierung innenstadtnaher Hafenflächen – das Fallbeispiel Kopenhagen' [Restructuring and revitalization of inner city harbour areas in Copenhagen], *Erdkunde, Archiv für wissenschaftliche Geographie*, **46**, pp.91–104.

Stone, Clarence N. (1987) 'Summing up: urban regimes, development policy and political arrangements', in Clarence N. Stone and Aeywood T. Sanders (eds), *The Politics of Urban Development*, Lawrence: University Press of Kansas, pp.269–97.

Tonboe, Jens (1991) 'Centralized economic control in a decentralized welfare state: Danish central–local government relations 1970–86', in Chris Pickvance and Edmond Preteceille (eds), *State Restructuring and Local Power. A Comparative Perspective*, London: Pinter.

9 Athens: intersubjective facets of urban performance

Lila Leontidou

Introduction

It would be unfair to couch a description of Athens in the terms of economic discourse used in this volume and throughout the literature on urban performance, which usually either omits any mention of this city (for example, Hall and Hay, 1980; Van den Berg *et al.*, 1982; Cheshire and Hay, 1989) or distorts its characteristics (for example, Burtenshaw *et al.*, 1991, p.5; White, 1984, p.161). Athens has gone through many cycles of development and crisis in its recent history, as had its predecessors in antiquity and the Middle Ages. Now that the face of Europe has changed, and cities in all its corners draw attention with their success stories, Athens seems to be one of the most inert chapters in an economically driven comparative study. It is weak in all aspects of urban competition except 'equity' or, in the terminology we will use here, social equality and justice.

In a period of urban 'success' achieved on the basis of civic pride, but also by place marketing or 'selling places' (Kearns and Philo, 1993), Athens is still seeking its identity. Identifying its positive points is very difficult for a city that excavated for its metro recently, while congestion and pollution problems were at their peak. However, it is not only objective constraints reproducing the urban crisis; it is also caused by intersubjective assessments, which have clouded the image of Athens throughout the postwar period. There is a paradox here. Greeks share the urban-oriented traditions of the Mediterranean region, where the cultures of city-states, the *polis*, have shone through the centuries (Leontidou, 1990, pp.256–61), but are by no means proud about Athens. Urbanism is still a very important value, a strong orientation expressed in compact urban development and the presence of the affluent classes in the city centre, despite trickles of suburbanization caused by environmental pollution, congestion and emerging social problems. Paradoxically, urban-oriented traditions run parallel to preconceived ideas of an urban 'crisis', which are inherently anti-urban. Such intersubjective 'social constructions' of the city distort its objective image and spawn a cultural crisis. The vitality and competitive standing of Athens are threatened today by these stereotypes, no less than by the economic crisis itself.

Besides congestion and environmental pollution, the postwar period has been burdened by two negative stereotypes. Publications appearing up to the 1970s portrayed Athens of the 1960s (and implicitly later years) as a 'parasitic agglomeration', sapping the country's life with 'overurbanization'. This stereotype arose in a period when the efficiency dimension was strong; the planning misconceptions it bred are discussed in the final section of this chapter. Offshoots of the 'overurbanization' thesis still sprout up in the literature, culminating in the claim that Greater Athens contained no less than 57 per cent of the Greek population in 1980 (Burtenshaw *et al.*, 1991, p.5)! The actual figure was 31 per cent and is now in decline (Table 9.1).

Publications appearing in the 1990s now nurture a new intersubjective stereotype of 'deepening segregation' based on developments in the recent past. Authors thus misinterpret a period when social justice and cohesion were improving. In doing so, they impede the grounded comparison between older (inter-war) and new segregation trends in the 1990s. Actual desegregation trends in the agglomeration during the 1970s had entirely different causes from those of the 1980s, but were equally important. In both cases, inter-mixture of social classes within the urban fabric was achieved. Like earlier stereotypes, the current one also misinterprets the urban past, so that more recent trends cannot be seen in perspective, or be addressed by policy.

After discussing the structure of Athens and its development, dealing with externalities, economic efficiency, social equality and budgetary constraints, the final section deals with the lack of planning in Athens. Another intersubjective stereotype is at work here. Despite its solid objective basis, it does not consider alternatives to the market which do exist in Athens. In fact, the most important particularity in Greece, as in Mediterranean Europe in general, is the irrelevance of the public/private or the planning/laissez-faire dichotomy. It is the formal/informal dichotomy which is relevant for understanding urban development and performance in southern Europe. In fact, there is a triad involved if spatial regulation in the Mediterranean is taken into account: competition/redistribution/reciprocity. Therefore, instead of considering urban policy in Athens, a city without planning as defined in the north, we will stress urban performance.

Table 9.1   *Urbanization in Greece: population data, 1951–91*

	Greater Athens	Rest of Attica	Greece	Primacy indices Athens % of Greece	Salonika % of Athens
Population					
1951	1 378 586	177 443	7 632 801	18.06	21.56
1961	1 852 709	205 265	8 388 553	22.09	20.55
1971	2 540 241	257 608	8 768 641	28.97	21.94
1981	3 027 331	342 093	9 740 417	31.08	23.33
1991	3 096 775	425 994	10 256 464	30.19	24.94
Average annual growth rate					
1951–61	3.00	1.47	0.95		
1961–71	3.21	2.30	0.44		
1971–81	1.77	2.88	1.06		
1981–91	−0.23	2.22	0.52		
Economically active population					
1971	868 316		3 169 884		
1981	1 064 942		3 507 672		
1989	1 278 300		3 082 761*		
Activity ratio (%)					
1971	34.18		36.15		
1981	35.18		36.01		
1989	41.47		38.00*		

*1991.

Sources: Adapted from Leontidou (1990, p.104; 1993a, p.45); estimates for 1989–91 from ESYE census data.

Externalities: land use and environmental change

The bipolar agglomeration consisting of Athens and Piraeus, with their suburbs, was actually shaped during the inter-war period out of two separate cities that had been interlinked since antiquity by the 'long walls' running through Plato's Academy and Elaionas. This was the route of the first Greek railway line, built in 1869. Athens and Piraeus merged to form one agglomeration after the influx of refugees from Asia Minor in 1922. The agglomeration then urbanized rapidly, as shown in Table 9.1. Many of the city's housing and land use characteristics were established then, while some aspects have emerged more recently, especially since the

1970s. The creation of settlements and the official definition of administrative boundaries goes back to two peculiar types of gerrymandering during the 1930s (Leontidou, 1992). Later on, illegal building caused the built-up area to spill over the surrounding mountains.

Fragmented landownership and owner-occupation became especially widespread after two waves of state intervention, one in the inter-war period of refugee settlement and the other during the immediate postwar reconstruction period (Delladetsima and Leontidou, 1995). Urban development is unplanned and piecemeal. It is done by small entrepreneurs and self-building, rather than developers and the state. It takes the form of single buildings rather than overall neighbourhood redevelopment. It is also uncontrolled, in that illegal building precedes the inclusion of areas into the city plan. After the mid-1970s, spontaneous urban development by popular initiative gave way to speculation (Leontidou, 1990, pp.210–14). Illegal development is now spilling over to the coasts of Attica in the form of second homes, which are gradually becoming first ones. The built-up area is expanding beyond the metropolitan administrative boundaries and into the Attica region, as well as the distant metropolitan periphery (Beotia, Korinth, Euboea), where industrial zones and business sites are found. According to the 1991 general population census by the ESYE (see Appendix for list of acronyms), the population of the agglomeration is now stabilizing at 3.1 million, while the Attica region around Athens is growing fast, now approaching half a million inhabitants.

Environmental problems constitute the peak of the urban crisis on many levels: from the individual (Greece ranks first in smoking per capita in Europe) to the collective (congestion and pollution). Athens also suffers from the saturation of garbage disposal areas, without any recycling effort, and pollution from an airport virtually within the city. This urban crisis is partly objective and partly intersubjective. It is evidenced by the pro-verbial *nefos*: the smog blanket darkening the Athens sky, which in fact summarizes the environmental and social consequences of a long period of non-planning, can be found in other large cities, but Athens is the most self-reproaching one. City marketing is negative. Energy is channelled to short-term remedies for the *nefos*, as well as the economic crisis, rather than to long-term strategies of urban renewal, housing, production or the cultivation of culture, education, science, technology and excellence.

Ineffective policy combines with meteorological conditions to create a favourable environment for the *nefos*. The weather in

Athens is usually fair. The relative humidity is 50 per cent in July and the average maximum temperature is 31 degrees C in August. The yearly average rainfall is only 500mm, most of which falls in the December–March period (Lekakis, 1984, pp.75–6). These meteorological conditions have changed more recently towards drought. Pollution is related to the horizontal movement of the air mass (winds) from the south–southwest quadrant in the spring and from the north for the rest of the year, with stagnant air in the summer. Pollution is also related to the vertical motion (turbulent mixing) of air, which is often blocked by temperature inversions aloft. In addition, ground-based inversions influence the movement of polluted air masses above the sea and onto the land area. Since capping and inversions occur at altitudes below the crest of the surrounding mountains, pollutants concentrate in the limited mixing layer overlying the city. High-rise buildings and relatively narrow streets, especially in the urban core, then act as canyons trapping air pollutants. There are very few open spaces and forests within the dense urban fabric, and the built-up area is progressively climbing into the surrounding mountains and hills. Deforestation, by arson and other means, and the conversion of agricultural or grazing land to urban use are rapid.

Environmental policy, which is discussed below, clashes with the apathy of the population regarding environmental issues: residents pollute public spaces of the city, the coast and the sea; garbage collectors are frequently on strike; and political parties abuse public spaces, especially during election periods. Intellectuals speak of a half-finished city, of premature aging, and even consider the question of whether to move the capital elsewhere (a discussion was organized by *Eleftherotypia*, a daily paper, in December 1990). In outbursts of juvenile rioting, the city centre and its educational institutions have been devastated by fire. These incidents of vandalism, the frequent strikes and riots, arson in the forests and all around them, are indications of aggression against the city itself. They stress the intersubjective roots of the urban crisis.

Economic efficiency: against the 'parasitic city' stereotype

The following sections expand on the manifestations and the impact of a very interesting reversal of the urban development trends that had been prevalent in Greece until the mid-1970s. During the first postwar decades, rapid urbanization was paralleled by rising productivity, the opening up of jobs, culture and leisure activities.

Athens in the 1960s was the place of the Greek 'economic miracle', with rising productivity in the context of fast urbanization. Rural depopulation and rapid emigration, especially to West Germany, would have practically devastated the country if Athens, the main location of the Greek 'economic miracle' of the 1960s, had not exerted its stabilizing influence. Yet it was labelled 'parasitic', 'overurbanized' (for example, Burgel, 1981). Such views persisted among planners and citizens even after the population stabilized during the 1970s. Although the 'economic miracle' was then receding, Athens did not turn into a parasitic agglomeration. This is especially clear in comparison with other Mediterranean European cities (Leontidou, 1990, pp.106–9). Its vitality was still evident; but so was speculation, which brought about the problems of the next period. After the mid-1970s, Mediterranean Europe as a whole experienced a transition from polarization to depolarization at the regional, urban and local level, involving many sectors – population, employment, industry, tourism – in different countries. Athens was part of this trend, but the impact was different from that in other cities of southern Europe.

High-growth sectors and depolarization

Urban life cycles have been associated with population and industrial employment, commuting and productivity (Van den Berg *et al.*, 1982). Trends are negative or stabilizing in Athens in these respects, but not as negative as in certain northern European cities. Athens has not reached a 'counterurbanization' stage, as described by northerners (Champion, 1989). We should instead refer to a process of diffuse urbanization since the 1970s (Leontidou, 1990). If the concept of urban life cycles is broadened to include the role of the city, global contacts, cultural life and, especially, creativity and flexibility, however, then Greater Athens lags behind the rest of Europe's cities. After a transitional period of urban restructuring during the 1970s, together with other Mediterranean cities, it started to diverge from their pattern (Leontidou, 1994a).

Though this is only a recent trend, it is not recognized as such. Athens has always been analysed in the context of 'overurbanization' theories of rural–urban migration. Centralization at the national level is becoming less acute, though the city still concentrates over half of Greek administration, headquarters of large enterprises and businesses, universities and many other activities. Industry and education show evidence of a gradual decentralization. Population stabilization is even more recent. Dur-

ing the early 1990s, demographic stagnation and the announce-
ment of census figures have at last silenced the cries of
'overurbanization'. The city has stopped growing. Primacy is still
pronounced in the Greek urban system (Table 9.1), but the trends
have been reversed. At the regional level, rapid concentration has
given way to diffuse urbanization, while industrial polarization
has given way to decentralization processes. Living conditions
have improved in rural areas, especially in tourist resorts. In cities, by contrast, unemployment has risen; in rural areas, it has
declined (Leontidou, 1993a).

A great deal of the Greater Athens dynamism of the 1960s was
due to the building boom and industries related to it. The construction industry has been crucial, not only to the development
of the city, but also more generally as a motor in the manufacturing sector. The building boom has since ceased, and unemployment is closely related to this. The construction sector is still based
on short-term contracts, though labourers of the 1990s have a
different place of origin. In the 1960s, the central Athens cafes
were busy at sunrise with builders and craftsmen, migrants from
rural Greece waiting to be hired; now it is near the bakeries in
peripheral settlements that the new migrants (Albanians, Poles
and other eastern Europeans) congregate to be hired for casual
work. They assemble outside the agglomeration, for fear of the
police, hoping to find a job for a few days in construction, repair
services, agriculture or gardening.

Diffuse urbanization ran parallel to industrial decentralization.
Table 9.2 quantifies the sectoral composition of average annual
employment at place of work. These figures indicate that the most
important sectoral employment change is due to industrial decline (including manufacturing, energy and transport) and the
growth of the banking and service sectors. The relative concentration of employment in Greater Athens for each industry group is
shown in Table 9.3. The value of the location quotients fell for
textiles and machinery. Deconcentration trends did not seem very
important for other urban industries, especially printing and publishing, but also for miscellaneous industries of precision equipment and consumption goods.

Deindustrialization meant a drop in the share of the entire Attica region in Greek manufacturing employment, from 48.8 per
cent in 1978 to 42.8 per cent in 1984 and to 39.7 per cent in 1988
(adapted from provisional ESYE data). This is rather mild, compared with other European cities, but its impact has been devas-
tating in the inner city and the traditional industrial axis. In fact,
the estimated net loss of 52 000 jobs in the manufacturing industry

Table 9.2 Average annual employment in industrial establishments, Greater Athens, 1969–88 (at place of work)

Social economic sectors	Average annual employment			Average annual rates (%)	
	1969	1978	1988	1969–78	1978–88
1 Mining, quarrying	2 167	1 303	1 129	-5.50	-1.42
2–3 Manufacturing industry	233 779	281 821	246 880	2.10	-1.31
4 Electricity, gas, water	9 176	12 437	10 116	3.44	-2.04
6 Commerce					
Wholesale	47 976	58 748	67 942	2.28	1.46
Retail	82 927	104 026	88 640	2.55	-1.59
Restaurants, hotels	29 916	33 560	40 353	1.29	1.86
7 Transport, warehouses, communications	59 475	100 037	79 427	5.95	-2.28
8 Banks, insurance	27 909	43 957	55 117	5.18	2.29
9 Services	23 787	23 804	32 899	0.01	3.29
Total average annual employment	517 112	659 693	622 503	2.74	-0.58

Source: Adapted from ESYE (1969; 1978) and 1988 census data.

251

Table 9.3   Location quotient of manufacturing employment in Greater Athens; average annual employment as specified in ESYE censuses

		Location quotient, Athens versus Greece			
SIC products		1973	1978	1984	1988
20	Food products	0.52	0.57	0.63	0.66
21	Beverages	0.77	0.87	0.79	0.77
22	Tobacco products	0.75	0.66	0.68	0.47
23	Textile mill products	1.09	1.00	0.96	0.92
24	Fabric products, apparel	1.13	1.13	1.19	1.03
25	Lumber, wood products	0.63	0.65	0.66	0.58
26	Furniture and fixtures	1.14	1.13	1.12	1.11
27	Paper, allied products	1.26	1.26	1.22	1.20
28	Printing, publishing	1.76	1.89	2.07	4.12
29	Leather products	0.59	0.53	0.51	0.70
30	Rubber and plastics	1.40	1.41	1.23	1.11
31	Chemicals, allied products	1.38	1.37	1.46	1.44
32	Petroleum refining	0.74	0.41	0.36	0.65
33	Stone, clay, glass etc	0.68	0.65	0.59	0.58
34	Primary metals industry	0.27	0.29	0.17	0.27
35	Metal products	0.96	1.03	1.00	1.00
36	Machinery, non-electrical	1.16	0.96	0.99	0.91
37	Electrical machinery	1.48	1.36	1.35	1.33
38	Transport equipment	1.21	1.31	1.25	1.27
39	Miscellaneous	1.42	1.52	1.64	1.72

Source: Adapted from Leontidou (1990, p.190) and ESYE census of establishments (1988).

in the period 1973–84 in Greater Athens has been unequally distributed (Leontidou, 1994b). Industrial decline was moderate in absolute terms, but jobs lost to communities along the industrial axis constituted 98.2 per cent of the gross job loss in the whole agglomeration. The multiplier effects were considerable: unemployment affected not only those dismissed but also employees in industry, services and subcontracting: those dependent on the export base of the city (Leontidou, 1993a).

The other side of the coin was the growth of jobs in the metropolitan periphery. It started in the early 1970s, before inner-city deindustrialization and before any 'business land' had been provided in the form of industrial zones, parks or areas. It followed new legislation. In order to retain the agglomeration economies of Athens without losing benefits granted by new legislation for decentralization, many industries settled on the boundaries of the unassisted zone A and zone B: Attica, Beotia and Korinth. The new industrial axis expanding from Euboea via Attica to Korinth resembles metropolitan peripheries in other large Mediterranean capitals, which appear to be the most profitable locations (Hudson and Lewis, 1984, p.190, Leontidou, 1994b). Business land along national highways is visible in rural areas around Athens, but it is also seen around the cities of Lisbon and Oporto, in the eastern periphery of Rome and in the hinterlands of Barcelona and Madrid.

Dominant Greek industries are not high-tech but traditional. There are two components in the deindustrialization trend. The first comprises disinvestment, closures and decentralization. The second, found in modern sectors, is jobless growth. Most manufacturing jobs are still concentrated in the sectors of clothing, transport equipment (car repair and servicing rather than manufacturing) and food products. Small establishments predominated throughout the postwar period. Their average size tended to fluctuate in both Athens and Greece. Though Athens showed some substitution of capital for labour, this process was much faster in Greece as a whole. Industrial horsepower (HP) per person employed today in manufacturing is twice as high in Greece as in Athens (Table 9.4). The city concentrates traditional labour-inten-

Table 9.4   The size of manufacturing establishments in Greater Athens and Greece, 1969–88

	1969	1973	1978	1984	1988
Small manufacturing, 1–9 employees, Greater Athens					
% of total employment	39.82	36.00	37.81	44.65	44.65
% of total establishments	91.99	90.41	81.12	93.11	92.74
% of total HP	19.42	13.85	25.92	34.22	30.66
Persons per establishment	2.47	2.60	2.78	2.36	2.44
HP per person employed	1.22	2.02	2.37	3.36	3.66
Total manufacturing, average size, Greater Athens					
Persons per establishment	5.71	6.52	5.95	4.92	5.07
HP per person employed	2.50	5.24	3.46	4.38	5.33
Total manufacturing, average size, Greece total					
Persons per establishment	4.02	4.98	5.20	4.74	4.88
HP per person employed	4.02	6.24	6.73	8.98	9.74

Source: Adapted from Leontidou (1990, p.182) and ESYE census of industrial etc. establishments (1988).

sive small units and a large informal sector. Its competitive position within Europe is obviously weak in this respect.

High-growth sectors include banking and private-sector and government services. These dynamic activities are still concentrated in two centres. The nucleus of Piraeus, with foreign banks, producer services and shipping companies' headquarters, is often compared with the City of London, but the analogy should be kept in perspective. The public-service sector has been overstaffed, with low productivity (OECD, 1990). During the immediate postwar period, there was one state employee for every two productive workers; the ratio had swollen to 1:1 by 1983 (Tsoucalas, 1986, p.249). Although rates of growth appear moderate in the 1980s, absolute numbers are still growing enormously. One of the conditions imposed by Brussels for the approval of a loan to Greece in 1991 was rationalization in the government sector and dismissal of public-sector employees. Statism has created large monopolies in rail and air transport, telecommunications and electricity production. It has also fostered the concentration of credit in few state-controlled banks located mainly in the Athens and Piraeus cores. After 1990, however, privatization efforts began, creating vehement conflict and social upheaval. These efforts include large 'problem' state enterprises, as well as DEKO (public enterprises and organizations) and other large companies.

Tourism is not among the high-growth sectors. It is growing in the rest of Greece, but declining in Athens. Environmental problems predominate over cultural resources, curbing the role of Athens as a national and international centre of cultural tourism and recreation. Many visitors now bypass Athens, especially in the summer. The Greek islands are increasingly attractive thanks to tour operators' policy and direct charter flights (Leontidou, 1991). Land use factors are also important in explaining the decline of tourism in the capital. The concentration of hotels in the polluted centre of Athens discourages tourists. Some central Athens hotels have closed down or changed their use: the Grande Bretagne and Astir are recent and conspicuous examples. Tourist accommodation is concentrated on the seafront; a Sheraton hotel is among the latest projects.

The strong centralistic tendencies of economic activities have been undermined in the manufacturing and commerce sector. Retail sub-centres developed because of congestion in the central business district and traffic restrictions that were imposed for environmental reasons. The role of planning was negligible in the creation of sub-centres (Delladetsima and Leontidou, 1995). The plans of the 1980s proposed nine centres in the respective urban sub-sectors, but subsequent plans diffused the picture and made the policy ineffective. Planning has played a minor role in the crystallization of land use. Despite a mixed patchwork, however, the distribution of economic activities is not entirely haphazard. Some specialization in industry, commerce, services or tourism had spontaneously developed in the various regions of the Greater Athens area.

Knowledge base and education: barriers to creativity

Several new universities were established in the 1980s outside Athens, but the city remains the country's knowledge centre. It concentrates the major educational and research institutions, as well as facilities, libraries and laboratories for medical, nuclear and space development, and physical sciences. However, this concentration does not lead to creativity and innovation in a society offering a poor environment for scientific research; far from it. Besides underfinancing and mismanagement of research and education, bureaucratic obstacles to initiatives in universities and research centres are formidable. Social particularities also undervalue R&D and reproduce inertia in the academic community. Intersubjective negative stereotypes about the use of education in economic life affect intellectual workers. Expertise and technical and managerial skills are not appreciated in either the public or the private sector (Petmesidou and Tsoulouvis, 1990). Universities are not formally assessed and academic mobility is strongly discouraged. Long-established chairs often kill academic competition and excellence, obstructing the entrance of younger scientists. University graduates are 'penalized' by the broader socio-economic context. A university professor's salary today, at about $18 000 a year, is at the same level as that of a private-sector secretary or a self-employed technician, and induces people to look for a second job or find other sources of additional income.

Conditions in the industrial sector are largely responsible for this vicious circle. Statistics about R&D expenditures by private firms are non-existent, but it has been concluded indirectly that R&D is, at best, not export-oriented; at worst, industrialists do not demand any development of R&D. Meanwhile, the use of computer technology is spreading with the rapid diffusion of PCs (from 2600 computers in 1982 to 25 563 in 1986: Petmesidou and Tsoulouvis, 1990, p.224). Many of the installations in the public sector are left idle, for lack of expert staff to use them. In 1985, 47.7 per cent of all computers in Greece (1235, of which 76 large ones, representing a total value of US$128m) were concentrated in the public sector, but these were underutilized (Leontidou, 1990, p.208). The computers are all imported: Greece has not entered the globalization race in microelectronics. Wages are too high, compared with other peripheral countries, for the assembly of hardware. As for software production, R&D is too limited for there to be innovation. Nevertheless, market niches protected from international competition produce Greek tailor-made programmes and packages according to specifications of clients. These products cannot be standardized. The packages are usually for accounting purposes. They are used in keeping records and repeating familiar procedures that were once done manually. Firms use new technology for accounting rather than for production activities or innovation (Petmesidou and Tsoulouvis, 1990).

Social relations of production are important elements of this vicious circle. In both the public and the private sector, and even in electronics, managerial expertise is depressingly undervalued. The know-how in firms is monopolized by the owner–manager. Creating a highly skilled staff is risky, because qualified workers may soon aspire to open up their own business. Such crucial social considerations are totally obscured by the lack of social research. This has been undermined more than any other field of R&D; EIE and EKKE have been drained of funds since the early 1990s. Complex social, economic and technical questions necessitating research (and attracting it in other countries) are dealt with by public authorities by appointing short-term 'committees of experts'. These quickly find a 'solution', often an unsuitable one. Policy formulated after long research procedures is given the same standing as these rapid proposals. The formulation of the Athens Master Plan in 1979–80 and environmental policy in 1983–5 are relevant examples (Delladetsima and Leontidou, 1995). Policy formulation is also undermined by the reshuffling of expert staff in the public sector with every change of government (going back to the civil war traumas).

In theory, research and innovation are encouraged and financed by the GGET, but low budgets have adverse effects. In 1978–87, financial resources allotted to research in Greece almost doubled, yet they still constituted only 0.27 per cent of GDP in 1987 (Protonotarios, 1988, p.53). European Union programmes for R&D have few Greek applicants. A couple of companies created by the state to promote the production and application of new technology have been in the planning stage for several years now (Petmesidou and Tsoulouvis, 1990, pp.224, 253). Vocational training in the use of computer technology is encouraged by the European Union and is being adopted by local and central authorities. At the same time, however, a set of policies, such as support for artisans rather than small industrialists, overstaffing in the public sector and indifference towards managerial and technical skills, discourage modernization, technological development and the diffusion of innovations. In this way, the city's competitive standing is constantly undermined.

It is ironic that, while the population of Athens is extremely inventive in survival strategies – including the contravention of any kind of regulations – inventiveness with respect to R&D is extremely limited. Perhaps it is better to say it is poorly incorporated into Greek society, industry and academia. This can be contrasted with the inventiveness and the impact of the diaspora Greeks. Counteracting the continuing brain drain, Greek lobbies abroad do have a favourable impact at home. Many scientists known for their innovations in medical sciences, in sociocultural research, in computer technology and communications in Europe and the USA have roots in Greece. They maintain links among themselves and with their birthplaces. The diaspora is a longstanding particularity of Greek history. Now, however, in a period of competition among cities, the brain drain is acquiring a different dimension.

Social equality and cohesion: against the 'deepening segregation' stereotype

Greater Athens combines a concentric model of spatial development with an east–west sectoral model. It used to be split into two halves – the bourgeois and the proletarian city – by an axis running from the northeast to the southwest (Burgel, 1981; Pantazides and Kassimati, 1984; Leontidou, 1990). This axis is now weakening. In addition, despite the present urban crisis, there are positive trends, which make Athens rather exceptional in the EU context: low unemployment rates, social homogenization and desegregation. This constitutes the social equity dimension, as defined in this volume; we prefer to describe it as social equality, justice or cohesion. This dimension may be fragile, with the arrival of populations from eastern Europe and the Third World in poor urban enclaves, but it is something to nurture and reproduce. It is no coincidence that a recent survey on crime in urban Europe ranked Athens bottom (eleventh place).

The importance of family and the housing sector

In Athens, Salonica and all major Greek cities, poorer populations have traditionally colonized the urban periphery. Spontaneous urban development, combined with regionalism, has created agglomerations of migrants in particular places. Neighbourhood clusters by region of origin are still written in the street names recalling islands and provincial localities in Patissia, Peristeri and other communities of the western agglomeration. However, regional clustering has now weakened or disappeared. Athens is homogenized and mixed. At the same time, it is a palimpsest of migrant communities, a post-modern mosaic of regionally based settlements and neighbourhood associations (Leontidou, 1993a).

After a long history of illegal building, popular owner-occupation and self-help housing in peripheral areas, there is no homelessness as it is defined in northern Europe. Its absence must be largely attributed to self-built housing and the important role of the family in the wider distribution of wealth, owner-occupation and unemployment relief. The housing sector evidences certain particularities in comparison to the Anglo-American experience. The structure of housing production is dual, but not along the public–private dimension: it consists of a formal speculative and an informal self-built sector. The former produces the multi-storey apartment building (*polykatoikia*). The latter has housed popular strata, at the one extreme, and the bourgeoisie, at the other. It was hit hard by policies under the dictatorship (1967–74), which supported the speculative sector, especially in housing and tourism.

Public housing is negligible. It is interesting that public intervention during the inter-war period brought an informal sector into being (Leontidou, 1992). Housing is self-financed, mostly by a system of pre-selling and exchange arrangements called *antiparochi*, established in the 1930s (Marmaras, 1989) and by household savings in the self-built informal sector. Mortgage loans from banks started to infiltrate the speculative sector only in the 1970s (Delladetsima and Leontidou, 1995). The institution of leasehold does not exist. The high property transfer tax (13 per cent, compared with 1 per cent in the UK) discourages residential transactions and geographical mobility. Besides creating rigidities in the housing market, this taxation has contributed to desegregation: occupational mobility does not automatically lead to a change of neighbourhood. This is also due to family arrangements for property transfer. Parental donations have taken the place of dowry, which was institutionally abolished in 1984 by PASOK, but only formally. House property is transferred by this method, as is inheritance through generations. By 1986, 25 per cent of owner–occupiers in Athens had acquired their house through dowry, parental donation or inheritance. Most of these (41 per cent and 29 per cent, respectively) had bought or built on plots of which 35 per cent had been acquired by parental donation (adapted from Maloutas, 1990; pp.52, 166, 189, 241, 255). Construction used to be a booming sector; now it is in decline. Construction costs started to rise only in the 1970s. Meanwhile, there had been considerable improvement in housing conditions, especially with self-building practices and piecemeal urban redevelopment.

Emigrants and social classes in urban society

The period of rapid rural–urban migration now belongs to history. The population of Greater Athens has stabilized, growing at a mere 0.23 per cent average annual rate during the 1980s. For the first time in history, its growth rate is lower than that of Greece, reflecting outward movements that outnumber physical increase (see Table 9.1). Apparent migration of former residents to the rest of Attica or provincial Greece comprises many types of movements. These range from professionals moving to Europe and intellectuals moving to peripheral universities (but hoping to return to Athens) to construction workers escaping the Athens recession to join the provincial urban building boom.

Rapid emigration from Greece to West Germany also stopped two decades ago. Repatriation has begun, as it has in all southern European countries (King, 1993). Migrants have started arriving from Third World and eastern European countries, but the Greek population is not growing. Demographers and politicians are concerned about the nation's low fertility, though they do not press for any policy on child care, housing, single mothers or foreign immigrants. Greek population estimates by the ESYE for the 1980s indicate an average annual rate of physical increase of 0.6 per cent for the 1981–7 period, which lately has been falling to 0.3 per cent. The 1991 Greek population of 10 256 464 people found by the general census includes a certain number of immigrants. Unofficially, this number is estimated at 500 000, which may be an exaggeration. Though information is scarce regarding recent developments, there is documentation on 60 000 Pontos residents, who arrived from 1982 to 1990 (Voutira, 1992) and on about 13 000 foreigners arriving from the Balkans yearly to settle in the north and, in transit to other countries, pass through Athens.

The population is stable because of outmigration as well as negative demographic trends. One-person households are increasing, especially in the inner city, where the population is rapidly aging. Larger families still locate in western popular suburbs, but their average size is declining. The economically active population is very small in Greece compared with other European countries, for various reasons (Leontidou, 1990, pp.206–8). In Athens, the activity ratio kept falling, from 42.35 per cent in 1951 to 38.12 per cent in 1961 and 34.18 per cent in 1971, and then rose again (see Table 9.1). The sectoral composition of employment in 1981–91 changed rapidly. A fundamental socio-economic restructuring is evident. Manufacturing employment and the related working class have shown a tendency to stabilize since the 1970s. Employment in banks, social and public services is tending to increase rapidly, whereas employment in personal services is tending to shrink.

Class polarization that persisted until the 1970s has given way to depolarization more recently. At a superficial level, social homogenization can be studied through trends in earnings. The increase in minimum wages was coupled with the stabilization, or even deterioration, of higher salaries. It has been estimated that, in the public sector, the ratio of the highest to the lowest salary dropped from 4.2 in 1980 to 2.3 in 1988. Real wages rose by 20 per cent from 1981 to 1989 for low-wage labourers, but fell by 55 per cent for high-wage employees (*To Vima* weekly). This constitutes a disincentive to productivity. Conversely, some authors relate low postwar wages to the absence of any incentive for technological innovation by industries (for example, Vergopoulos, 1985, pp.113–20; Doukakis, 1985). We may ascribe this to a process of middle-class 'pauperization' which seems to be under way, while high incomes are concentrated in a narrower population group and among the diaspora Greeks, financiers and shipowners. Of course, income inequalities are difficult to measure because of the sizeable 'black economy', which is estimated at a minimum of 30 per cent of GDP (Pavlopoulos, 1987, pp.156–8).

The sizeable 'black economy' counteracts the pauperization process, as reflected in consumption patterns.These conditions interact with the reproduction of self-employment and the high incidence of unemployment among the young. Families choose to support their younger members by sharing income rather than by encouraging them to take up an unsuitable job. Subcontracting seems also to have expanded. It is regrettable that putting-out and irregular work are not recorded in censuses of industrial establishments. Such work is apparently concentrated in working-class and peasant–tourist regions (Leontidou, 1991). Social 'polyvalence', or holding a second job and moonlighting, also seems to have

spread among middle-class populations as well as peasants, public employees and other groups (Tsoucalas, 1986).

Intra-urban depolarization and desegregation trends

Class segregation was linked in the past with the 1922 refugee
inflow. The League of Nations and the Greek government established the RSC, which created settlements growing into 'red' enclaves on the west side. On the east, the 'inverse ghettoes' of
Psychico, Filothei and Ekali were created by upper- and middle-
class cooperatives (Leontidou, 1992). Class segregation deepened
during the civil war of the 1940s. As mutual fear grew among the
inhabitants, stigmas were attached to different neighbourhoods.
In the next generation, political passions changed their form and
yet later the popular urbanization waves of the 1960s subsided.
Today affluent populations are still concentrated in the inner city
and the eastern suburbs, and the working classes are mostly in
peripheral popular settlements. However, Athens is a city of increasingly mixed neighbourhoods and land uses. It is not segregated. Segregation is not a statistical index, but a sociocultural
process of stigmatization, exclusion and obstruction. Athens lost
this undercurrent as the civil war decades faded, and today in-
dexes also confirm that it is no longer a segregated city. It may
become one in the late 1990s, however, as it is flooded by migrants
from eastern Europe, the Balkans and the Third World.

Athens has been always a mixed city. In most of the urban
fabric, the informal economy, combined with the lack of planning
and coordination, has been evident in a patchwork of economic
activities, and only a few nuclei of exclusively business land. Mixed
land use, both horizontal and vertical (in the form of multi-storey
apartment buildings), brings residence, commerce, services and
noxious industries into close proximity. The strong work–residence relationship of the past has been broken by labour-market
constraints and the spatial fixity of the labour force. Long commuting movements in a congested city are increasing. Social area
analysis is inconclusive (see Maloutas, 1993, who, however, insists
on his 'segregation' idea), while an analysis of apparent migra-
tion/social mobility shows an important proportion of population
flows towards desegregation since the late 1970s.

At exactly the same time, however, a new negative stereotype
emerged in place of the 'overurbanized parasite': the 'deepening
segregation' stereotype. Arbitrary assessments always disregard
the sociocultural dimensions of segregation and misinterpret social differentiation. Their exercises range from general statements

about a widening 'gap between the east and the west of the basin' (Sklavounos, 1985, p.42), to exaggerated 'conclusions' on the basis of inconclusive positivist quantifications. The latter figures define segregation as a correlation coefficient among occupational categories (Maloutas, 1993). That analysis exaggerates dissimilarities at the municipality level in the 1970s, ignoring major shifts of social groups, which in fact undermine the east–west divide known in Athens since the turn of the century (Leontidou, 1990, p,234). Studies referring to the 1970s also tend to extend these 'observations' into the 1980s, that is the spatial homogenization period *par excellence*.

A brief reference to the dynamics of desegregation since the 1970s may be revealing here. This process started with concentrated efforts during the dictatorship on two fronts: to disperse the western 'red enclaves' of leftist politics and popular vote; and to promote the multi-storey apartment building. These policies had an effect upon the deep east–west divide of previous decades. Legislation enacted during the dictatorship boosted the speculative sector throughout the city. Consequently, vertical differentiation has tended to succeed neighbourhood segregation in many urban areas of apartment blocks *(polykatoikies)* (Leontidou, 1990, pp.233–5). Additional efforts in the 1980s enhanced sociospatial homogenization. In particular, the expansion of public investment in infrastructure to the western areas of the agglomeration during PASOK rule after Greece joined the European Community contributed much to the development of the western suburbs (Haremi, 1992). To these factors we should add several more: rigidities in the housing market (discussed below); the general social homogenization, through the 'pauperization' of the middle classes; and generational shifts within communities combined with the inheritance of family residences as working-class parents passed their property to their middle-class descendants.

Desegregation is especially evident in the weakening of the east–west divide. It does not eradicate spatial differentiation and dissimilarity among smaller spatial units. As suburbanization of affluent residents has been speeding up since the 1970s, filtering-down processes have emerged in the inner city (Leontidou, 1990, pp.235–6). These became especially visible in the 1990s with the arrival of migrants from eastern Europe. Before these moves speeded up, the central Athens municipality was already rapidly decentralizing: the growth rate dropped to –1.67 per cent annually. By 1991, the population of central Athens had fallen to 748 110, which was 140 000 less than the 1981 figure (ESYE general census data). The same is true of the centre of Piraeus, where the population had been declining continually since the early 1950s, although recent rates are not as high (a net loss of 27 000 people during 1981–91). Land use changes involved invasion of commerce, services and transport to replace residences. Meanwhile, the substitution of economic activities for population in the inner city is counterbalanced by a reurbanization process in certain pockets of gentrification, like Plaka. Poor newcomers, including foreigners, migrants and refugees, crowd into pockets of poverty in the inner city and the north of the city, creating nuclei of segregation and homelessness. There were already some poor communities of middle-eastern and Third World migrants around Piraeus, which were formed in the 1970s. Now there are destitute neighbourhoods around the centre of Athens and in some remote suburbs in Attica. Sociospatial homogenization has recently been undermined in the inner city by global restructuring and war.

Barriers to planning and problems in urban competition

Intersubjective stereotypes about Athens hamper the flowering of civic pride and diminish the prospects for place marketing in a period of urban boosterism. Greece is thus not able to compete with the Spanish success in 1992, when Madrid, Barcelona and Seville staged international events simultaneously (Leontidou, 1995). Athens continues to lag in urban competition, obstructed at three levels – global, national and local. Internationally, Athens lies outside the European development corridors, which are now improving with the TGV and the Channel Tunnel. Geopolitical strife is also very close at hand, though the Balkans also form a potential economic hinterland. At the national level, the allocation of funds, dispersal of authority in ministries and agencies, and intersubjective images of the city constitute barriers to urban development. Locally, the urban crisis, the underdevelopment of R&D, the discontinuity of local development and speculative rebuilding sap the vitality of the city.

The latter strategy consists of informal means of countering the crisis. This vitality can be understood in terms of a triple distinction: the notions of competition (market)/association (redistribution)/reciprocity. These notions, introduced by Polanyi (1977) and reconsidered by Mingione (1991), are particularly relevant here. The public–private dichotomy used in this book contrasts competition (market) with redistribution (planning). In essence, it neglects or even eradicates a third way to achieve spatial regulation and development, which is very widespread in southern Europe:

reciprocity, as reflected in the informal sector. Polanyi's triad high-lights the latter, thereby undermining the economic logic inherent in current urban analysis (Leontidou, 1995).

Market versus planning: spontaneity and speculation

Redistribution problems are illustrated by the post-1950 lack of planning, except in periods of disaster relief (Delladetsima and Leontidou, 1995). Piecemeal redevelopment and speculative atti-tudes among the population at large were evident from the mo-ment Athens became the capital of Greece (1834). Even industrial-ists preferred investment in land and housing to productive in-vestment (Leontidou, 1992). The speculative ethos of the popula-tion has never faded. Spontaneity is one of its aspects, whereby actions aim at use rather than exchange and economic exploita-tion (Leontidou, 1990).

Uncertainty about property rights has added discontinuities in urban development. The most recent period of reconstruction (1944–52) saw the implementation of a set of policies which go far in explaining this uncertainty: rent control, property transfer and annulment of property transactions that took place under German occupation (Delladetsima and Leontidou, 1995). These policies acted as barriers to the repair and refurbishment of buildings. Enhanced by rebuilding incentives of the *KH Psiphisma*, a legisla-tive decree supporting building activity, these policies speeded up the demolition of important neo-classical buildings and the erec-tion of faceless apartment blocks, *polykatoikies.*

The institutional milieu for metropolitan development has al-ways been polarized as central/local government, without any im-portant middle tiers (Wassenhoven, 1984). The former suffers from overstaffing and bureaucratic inertia, while the latter is underfunded and institutionally incapable of implementing plans. Only recently have local authorities acquired clearly circumscribed competencies (Delladetsima and Leontidou, 1995). The middle tier of metropoli-tan government does not consist of quangos such as DEPOS, which started ambitiously but has since declined, or the Organization for the Athens Master Plan, which was established a few years ago, but has remained quite inert. Rather, the middle tier basically consists of four prefectures in the Attica region, which implement central government's decisions and control those made by the local author-ity. Initiatives by some municipalities to form development corpo-rations such as ANDIP have been successful in planning and imple-menting development projects, whenever they were not undermined by professional associations like TEE.

Today, private capital predominates in the city-building process. The lack of planning and construction capital in housing (as opposed to infrastructure or business buildings), though interesting from a comparative perspective, can be quite disconcerting from an urban development viewpoint. Plans are drafted, but shelved. The Structure Plan of Athens has been published in the *Government Gazette* (LD. 1515/1985), but it is often violated or ignored by the government itself. Many interventions with a spatial impact remain uncoordinated: legislation on the building code, rent levels, land 'legalization', urban expansion and industrial decentralization (Delladetsima and Leontidou, 1995). Administrative and bureaucratic inertia, multi-authority interference, non-devolution of government, clientelist politics, pressures by landowners and the low ecological consciousness of the population are major barriers. There is no housing policy, but there do exist indirect interventions in the housing market through legislation, infrastructure provision and urban renewal, which mainly rests on land use control (Delladetsima and Leontidou, 1995). The activity of relevant institutions such as DEPOS and AOEK is very limited and rather marginal. This amounts to what is called disjointed incrementalism. It is based on an informal consensus, as will be discussed below.

Measures introduced in accordance with intersubjective myths discussed in previous sections are of special interest here. The 'parasitic overurbanization' myth plagued the city with planning efforts to control rather than channel population and economic activity. Infrastructure investment was blocked in order to curb population concentration, the decision makers believed (or pretended to believe), but legalizations of unauthorized settlements and permissive legislation for plot exploitation were habitual. This policy led to today's pollution and congestion. Other efforts resulted in unsuccessful regulations which were contravened, and only enhanced illegal practices. Those practices include building outside authorized city limits and operating in the informal economy, which has been estimated at the impressive level of 91 per cent in the housing sector and 71 per cent in the construction sector, the highest levels found for any economic activity (Pavlopoulos, 1987, pp.157–8).

The only policy which did have an impact – unfortunately to the detriment of efficiency and productivity – was anti-industrialization legislation. It came at a time when forces were driving the city toward deindustrialization anyway. Within the rhetoric of 'parasitic overurbanization' and environmental pollution, restrictions on industrial activity in Greek metropolitan areas were reviewed in the 1980s. Furthermore, decentralization policy at the national level was supplemented by legislation against environmental pollution. Direct restrictions on industrial development in Greater Athens were introduced from 1979 to 1985 (Leontidou, 1994b). LD 1262/1982 offered incentives to entrepreneurs moving into underdeveloped areas. In addition, the OAED developed a programme of special incentives in the form of unemployment relief for migrants from Athens and Salonica to peripheral regions (Karantinos, 1986, p.3; Leontidou, 1993a).

Without abandoning the stereotype of 'parasitic overurbanization' or the controversial policy emanating from it, the other stereotype, 'deepening segregation', is now gaining ground. Policies derived from it have not crystallized, because this is a new situation. However, this stereotype seems to affect policies with regard to immigrants and populations that are arriving at increasing rates, but research is still scarce, and this is not the place to take up this issue.

Reciprocity: informal consensus and clientelism

Reciprocity has both a negative and a positive impact, and the former is very pronounced in Athens. Personal contacts are necessary for even minimal transactions, from VAT and cheque payments to the circulation of information for appointments, research projects or statistical series. 'There is nothing easy, if you can make it difficult!' The centralistic and clientelist bureaucracy constitutes a barrier to many activities. Patronage and clientelism extend from labour recruitment in public service to local development processes. Development initiatives are often evaluated and financed on the basic of electoral support, where a system of patronage (involving individuals and corporate groups, but also local communities) secures votes for politicians. Like entrepreneurs cautiously keeping know-how to themselves for fear of losing expert staff to competitors or to self-employment (see above), so politicians keep their constituencies to themselves. An MP's votes could be lost to the local authority representative of a rival party if the latter were allowed more responsibility and power in local development. Decentralization is thus avoided. It is worth noting that PASOK was elected twice in the 1980s on a platform of devolution of government and a rhetoric of local self-government. Despite this fact, negligible steps were taken towards decentralization.

Clientelism clashes with civil rights; concessions are granted as personal favours, leaving recipients indebted and dependent. Local development support and funding is not a right, but a 'favour', a concession, within party politics and bureaucracies. No wonder this often breeds corruption, on the one hand, and dependence, on the other. A dialectical process is at work, whereby family networks protecting their members sustain and are reproduced by these structures. As for planning, an informal consensus between the state, landownership and the social and economic actors is formulated, in place of a planning consensus (Delladetsima and Leontidou, 1995). This produces unforeseen side-effects in urban development (Leontidou, 1993b). In fact, it is very difficult for policy makers to predict the impact of any legislation or reforms. These take on a new dimension in the hands of an eternally inventive population. The only strategy feasible in Athens at present seems to be to take small steps in organizing aspects of the economy, society and environment, and then to pause to look back at the unintended side-effects to each hesitant step.

On the positive side, forces of social cohesion are at work in Athens society. Living standards improved rapidly during the 1960s and more slowly later. The recent problem is a stabilization of conditions for the whole population coupled with the 'pauperization' of the middle classes, the black economy and the enrichment of top income categories, who often reside abroad. At the bottom of the earnings pyramid, the poor live in fringe municipalities of western Athens – especially in Perama, Acharnae, Elefsina and Lavrion – now surrounded by impoverished migrants from the Balkans. However, cases of demoralization, as found among the poor in other European cities, are quite rare among the Greek population. Social cohesion is sustained by informal means. Family bonds and strategies are central in Greek society, from political life (clientelism) to the relief of inequalities and homelessness. Family fills the gap left by the welfare state in many areas of social life. The recent arrival of poor foreigners and minorities is changing these conditions in some urban enclaves of the inner city and in the most remote northern and eastern outskirts.

Redistribution: current planning preoccupations

The EU is a novel factor in metropolitan and national planning. Its recent intervention has drawn planners towards more comprehensive policies. For the most part, these concern infrastructure provision, but they also deal with training, employment and spatial strategies. At the same time, however, the EU has entered the logic of disjointed incrementalism prevalent in Greek planning.

Its proposals, projects and strategies range from insistence on the dismissal of employees in the public sector to pilot projects like the one in the Queen's Castle area. Though proposed by the Organization of Athens, this EU pilot project (DG XVI) in the north of Athens has astonished many planners with its selection as a priority project for the city.

Current projects focus primarily on transport and the environment. Transport efforts involve major projects for roads, mass transport and parking. Communications projects include the modernization of the telecommunications network, which entails replanning and maintenance, as well as the installation of digital and mobile networks. The major current project is the Athens metro, which is now causing predictable confusion and traffic jams in the urban core as excavation work proceeds. After a long debate starting in the 1960s, and after delays which made it unmanageable in a dense city, the plan of the Legislative Decree for the creation of The Metro Co Ltd was at last submitted to Parliament in May 1991. This is a public–private partnership with 30 per cent financing by the EU (that amount rose to 50 per cent when the Delors package was approved) and 100 billion dr. contributed by the Greek government. Construction is proceeding slowly, but the most notorious vacillation involves another major transport decision: the relocation of the airport from Hellenico to Spata. The project has seen starts and stops for two decades now, and without a land policy it seems to be self-defeating.

In theory, the control of environmental pollution is a central task of both the Ministry of Physical Planning and the Environment and PERPA. Legislation against industrial pollution and in favour of regional development was passed in 1979, when restrictions on the use of private cars were also imposed. Today, only half of the cars are allowed to circulate daily within a 'ring' around the urban core. Ironically, that ring does not exist; ring roads have not been opened for this purpose. Industries earmarked for relocation by studies in 1983–4 (PERPA) have not moved. But new permits are not given to noxious industries, such as car repair shops. On days when the pollution exceeds certain limits, industrial production and car traffic are prohibited, but these measures are only temporary. Active environmental policy is restricted to the efforts of small ecology groups, one MP of the Ecologist-Alternatives, who had a seat in Parliament in the 1980s (none today) and the recent establishment of Greenpeace offices in Athens.

Rarely are there any important mobilizations, such as that of Elaionas, which unified radical groups and residents protesting against overbuilding in the industrial cavity at the heart of the agglomeration. The *Anti* fortnightly journal was involved in countering official plans. In July 1992, on the very day of heat, dense pollution and government emergency measures in Athens, ministry officials kept insisting in a Goethe Institute conference that Elaionas should be rebuilt rather than becoming an open space. This insistence is distressing. Athens can no longer afford such environment-assaulting government policies.

Conclusion: in search of a European identity

The urban crisis outlined in this chapter can, it is hoped, be considered as an ephemeral negative downturn, a stage in the cyclical process of urban growth and decline. Athens has survived, adapted and retained its vitality in more difficult times than these. No crisis or even disaster can take away the city's classical archaeological tradition, which is the core of its European identity. However, this identity cannot be eternally reaffirmed by historical reference alone, or by the recollection that Europe was named after a Greek goddess. Fortunately, the time has passed when PASOK and the left fought against European accession; but this is still a difficult challenge. Greece faces a crisis which complicates integration, and Greater Athens now diverges from other Mediterranean cities (Leontidou, 1994a). The Greek capital has certain comparative advantages in the European urban network and an inventive population, but it is constrained by a kind of inertia, which reaches from urban government to the difficulty of moving in a congested city and living in a polluted environment.

This urban milieu confronts us with an antithesis to the incubator hypothesis. Athens is the capital city and the knowledge centre of Greece, but it is neither a scientifically creative nor an economically flourishing city. Bureaucratic rigidities, remnants of clientelism and government centralization coexist with severe problems in education. As Isocrates would have put it, 'If democracy was defective, education was to blame. It is a consequence of defective education to regard undisciplined or ruthless behaviour as a democratic freedom.' Problems in civil society are reflected exactly in lack of discipline and negative attitudes towards planning. Planning could spur a learning process and constitute an incentive for the development of many sectors of activity and education. This cycle has not yet started in the case of Athens. Instead, we still encounter informality, spontaneous urban development, a speculative piecemeal real estate market which can by no means be disciplined, and a high property transfer tax, which creates rigidities. During a period of flexible organization of production and consumption, these rigidities reproduce inflexibility and inertia, thus blocking development and threatening even the comparative advantage of Athens in tourism, let alone creativity and revitalization.

These problems of economic efficiency and the lack of planning, however, are counterbalanced by considerable dynamism in the sphere of social equality. Athens in fact substantiates the hypothesis that economic efficiency is achieved at the expense of equality, and vice versa. Thus the city concentrates not only the negative characteristics of post-modernism but also many encouraging ones (Leontidou, 1993b). If there are several layers of problems in Greater Athens, acknowledged by both state and citizens, the classic urban problems like homelessness, sleeping on the streets, unemployment and crime are restricted and periodic. Reciprocity is a soft means of socioeconomic regulation compared with competition and redistribution in other cities; but it does help in building up a humane city. If the problems are not tackled in a rigorous manner, or if global conditions are further destabilized, however, development prospects may be damaged.

This is still a lively city, rooted in an urban-oriented culture that is now fading. Population stabilization does not create inner-city decay, despite filtering-down processes. Mixed land uses add to vitality day and night. Outdoor living and the interpenetration of public and private space enhance social cohesion. Recreation areas and retail commerce brighten up the city during all hours of the day. While suburbanization movements gain momentum, many well-off residents still cling to the centre. However, Athens does not seem close to a reurbanization phase in the near future, because the quality of life in the inner city is not improving and the environment is deteriorating. Urban segregation is not intensifying on the whole, but there are a few slum areas, and even fewer enclaves, stigmatized as 'dangerous districts'. Social depolarization, income sharing, owner-built housing and the family's material and moral support of its members create social cohesion and a low incidence of criminality. Exceptions do exist, unfortunately, as the economic crisis worsens: crime among minorities and the poor, but also the young; industrial strife, which has its fierce moments; incidents of juvenile delinquency; and political violence in the form of riots and terrorism. These acts of violence are always directed against the dominant social order, but they are often manifested as hatred against the city itself.

However, these are comparatively moderate problems in comparison with urban crime, homelessness and poverty in other countries. They do not in any way justify the negative stereotypes of 'overurbanization' and deepening segregation that have been attached to Athens. It has been the contention of this chapter that barriers to urban development are not only objective conditions but also intersubjective images. In a period of place marketing, the battle against the latter is perhaps as important as the battle against poverty in Athens.

Note

This article is based on research by the author for the EC FAST Programme in the context of the unfortunate URBINNO research network.

Appendix: list of acronyms

ANDIP   Development Corporation of the municipality of Piraeus
AOEK   Autonomous Organization for Working-class housing
DEKO   Public Enterprises and Organizations
DEPOS   Public Agency for Planning and Housing
EIE   Hellenic Research Foundation
EKKE   National Centre of Social Research
ESYE   National Statistical Service of Greece
GGET   Secretariat of Research and Technology of the Ministry of Industry
OAED   Organization for Labour Force Employment
PASOK   Panhellenic Socialist Movement
PERPA   Environmental Pollution Control Project
RSC   Refugee Settlement Commission
TEE   Technical Chamber of Greece

References

Burgel, G. (1981) *Croissance urbaine et développement capitaliste. Le 'miracle' Athénien*, [Urban growth and capitalist development. The 'miracle'], Paris: CNRS.

Burtenshaw, D., M. Bateman and G.J. Ashworth (1991) *The European City – A Western Perspective*, London: David Fulton.

Champion, A.G. (ed.) (1989) *Counterurbanization: The Changing Pace and Nature of Population Concentration*, London: Edward Arnold.

Cheshire, P. and D.G. Hay (1989) *Urban Problems in Western Europe: An Economic Analysis*, London: Unwin Hyman.

Delladetsima, P. and L. Leontidou (1995) 'Athens', in J. Berry and S. McGreal (eds), *Urban Planning and Property Markets in Europe*, London: E. & F.N. Spon, pp.258–86.

Doukakis, N.-L. (1985) 'Work relations and wage labour during the postwar industrialization and the present crisis', *The Greek Review of Social Research*, **59**, pp.3–40. (in Greek).

ESYE (National Statistical Service of Greece) (1940–94) published and unpublished data of the general population and employment censuses; annual labour force surveys; statistical yearbooks of Greece.

Hall, P. and D. Hay (1980) *Growth Centres in the European Urban System*, London: Heineman.

Haremi, V. (1992) 'The distribution of EC funding in the Attica region, 1984–1992', NTU diploma thesis, Athens: Department of Geography (in Greek).

Hudson, R. and J.R. Lewis (1984) 'Capital accumulation: the industrialization of Southern Europe?', in A.M. Williams (ed.), *Southern Europe Transformed: Political and Economic Change in Greece, Italy, Portugal and Spain*, London: Harper and Row, pp.179–207.

Karantinos, D. (1986) *Labour Market and the Filling of Vacancies by the Work Bureaus of OAED*, Athens: Ministry of Labour, OAED (in Greek).

Kearns, G. and C. Philo (eds) (1993) *Selling Places*, Oxford: Pergamon.

King, R. (ed.) (1993) *Mass Migrations in Europe: The Legacy and the Future*, London: Belhaven.

Lekakis, J.N. (1984) *Economics and Air Quality Management in the Greater Athens Area*, Athens: CPER.

Leontidou, L. (1990) *The Mediterranean City in Transition: Social Change and Urban Development*, Cambridge: Cambridge University Press.

Leontidou, L. (1991) 'Greece: prospects and contradictions of tourism in the 1980s', in A. Williams and G. Shaw (eds), *Tourism and Economic Development: Western European Experiences*, 2nd edn, London: Belhaven, Pinter, pp.84–106.

Leontidou, L. (1992) 'Greece', in C. Pooley (ed.), *Housing Strategies in Europe, 1880–1930*, London: Pinter (for the European Science Foundation), pp.297–324.

Leontidou, L. (1993a) 'Informal means of unemployment relief in Greek cities: the relevance of family, locality and housing', *European Planning Studies*, 1, pp.43–68.

Leontidou, L. (1993b) 'Postmodernism and the city: Mediterranean versions', *Urban Studies*, 30, pp.949–65.

Leontidou, L. (1994a) 'Mediterranean cities: divergent trends in a United Europe', in M. Blacksell and A.M. Williams (eds), *The European Challenge: Geography and Development in the European Community*, Oxford: Oxford University Press, pp.127–48.

Leontidou, L. (1994b) 'La periferia metropolitana frente al nucleo urbano: desarrollo irregular en las regiones urbanas mediterraneas' [The metropolitan fringe: irregular development in Mediterranean urban regions], in A. Alabart, S. Garcia and S. Giner (eds), *Clase, poder y ciudadania*, Madrid: Sigio Veintiuno Editores, pp.143–73.

Leontidou, L. (1995) 'Re-polarization of the Mediterranean: Spanish and Greek cities in Neo-liberal Europe', *European Planning Studies*, 3, pp.155–72.

Maloutas, T. (1990) *Athens, Housing, Family*, Athens: EKKE/Exandas (in Greek).

Maloutas, T. (1993) 'Social segregation in Athens', *Antipode*, 25, (3).

Marmaras, E. (1989) 'The privately-built multi-storey apartment building – the case of inter-war Athens', *Planning Perspectives*, 4, pp.45–78.

Mingione, E. (1991) *Fragmented Societies: a Sociology of Economic Life beyond the Market Paradigm*, Oxford: Blackwell.

OECD (1990) *OECD Economic Surveys: Greece*, Paris: OECD.

Pantazides, N. and K. Kassimati (1984) *Size and Structure of the Population of the Capital of Greece*, Athens: EKKE (in Greek).

Pavlopoulos, P.G. (1987) *The 'Black Economy' in Greece: a Preliminary Quantitative Approach*, Athens: IOVE (in Greek).

Petmesidou, M. and L. Tsoulouvis (1990) 'Planning technological change and economic development in Greece: high technology and the microelectronics industry', *Progress in Planning*, 33, pp.177–262.

Polanyi, K. (1977) *The Livelihood of Man*, New York: Academic Press.

Protonotarios, G. (1988) 'Technology research policy in Greece', *Scientific Thought*, 39, pp.49–64 (in Greek).

Sklavounos, G. (1985) 'Social division of urban space in Athens and the impact of transport on it', *The Greek Review of Social Research*, **57** (in Greek).

Tsoucalas, C. (1986) *State, Society, Work in Postwar Greece*, Athens: Themelio (in Greek).

Van den Berg, L., L. Drewett, L.H. Klaassen *et al.* (1982) *Urban Europe, Vol. 1: A Study of Growth and Decline*, Oxford: Pergamon.

Vergopoulos, Y. (1985) 'Economic crisis and modernization in Greece and other South European countries', *The Greek Review of Social Research*, **58**, pp.92–130 (in Greek).

Voutira, (1992) 'Pontic Greeks today: migrants or refugees?', *Journal of Refugee Studies*, **4**, pp.400–20.

White, P. (1984) *The West European City: A Social Geography*, London: Longman.

10 Budapest: return to European competition

György Enyedi

Introduction

In this book, ten cities represent the European metropolises. Eight of these are located within the European Union. They compete within a unified economic space, following common rules. Geneva and Budapest are the two 'outsiders'. Geneva, a middle-sized city, has metropolitan functions due to the presence of several international organizations, mostly members of the UN family. Budapest has only rejoined the fray by becoming reintegrated in the network of European metropolises. But it is not really a débutante on the European stage – the Hungarian capital has already played a macroregional (that is, international) metropolitan role. In the early twentieth century, the city was the eighth largest town in Europe (larger than Madrid or Rome). As the twin capital of the Austro-Hungarian monarchy, it had a strong influence within the Carpathian Basin and on the Balkans. This importance ended after the First World War. Over the last 45 years, the socialist system isolated the city from the European urban processes. Consequently, Budapest is different from other (western) European metropolises in many respects (Bernát and Viszkei, 1972; Lukács, 1988; Enyedi and Szirmai, 1992). The specificity of Budapest may be found in other central and eastern European metropolises as well. Accordingly, this chapter on Budapest may provide insight into the problems of metropolitan integration throughout Europe.

After the collapse of the state socialist system, there was a naive hope – mostly in central Europe – of rapid change. People realized that it would take time to equalize the standard of living between east and west, but they expected the process of institutional integration with the west to be fast. Moreover, they thought it will be helped to a great extent by the EU countries. The integration would be carried out once they accepted the rules and norms established in the European Union. This hope was fuelled by the

274

fact that the EU had admitted Greece and Portugal to help to integrate these countries. At the time of entrance, the economies of Greece and Portugal were no more advanced than those of the Czech Republic or Hungary today.

This chapter does not analyse why things have changed substantially during the first three years of the 1990s. A short list of major changes will suffice: the surfacing of internal tensions in the EU (which were artificially disguised for geostrategic reasons during the Cold War period); the effects of economic stagnation on the EU; and the slow and uneven transition to democracy and market economy in post-socialist countries. We may draw the conclusion that the European political and economic space is fragmented. Consequently, the competition between cities has different sets of rules across the continent. Budapest (and any other non-EU metropolis) has three fields of competition. The first field is related to the European urban core area. This is the centre of economic dynamism and power; metropolises located at the (geographical and social) peripheries of the continent have to try to link up with this core area. The rules of competition are more difficult for non-EU metropolises; the isolationism of the EU is growing, at least in the short run. The second field of competition for Budapest is eastern and central Europe. At present, Budapest, Prague and Warsaw are competing for a better opportunity to join the European core area. In the future, we can expect competition for special sub-centre roles within central Europe. There is a possibility that Berlin will grow into the nucleus of a central European dynamic urban zone. If that occurs, it will rearrange the competition field once again. Finally, Budapest can compete for transboundary influence in a more restricted region: the Carpathian Basin. The conditions of competition in the latter two fields are uncertain. First of all, there are no international norms (in some post-communist countries, there are not even national rules). Secondly, short-term predictions are impossible to make. Nevertheless, Budapest must compete. Budapest has to establish its influence in eastern and central Europe. It is hard to imagine that the city's international metropolitan functions could be based exclusively on western relations (Enyedi, 1992b).

The chapter is divided into three parts. The first part gives a short description of the Budapest metropolitan area, focusing on its special features. The second part is the main body of the analyses dealing with urban policy. In the third part, we discuss the options for a future role of Budapest within central Europe.

The Budapest metropolitan area

Specific features of the metropolitan area

The Budapest metropolitan area has 2.6 million inhabitants, out of a total of 10.3 million in Hungary. Suburbanization started early (in the 1870s) around the Hungarian capital, whereas much smaller provincial urban agglomerations developed only after the Second World War. Since 1867, population growth in the suburban zone has always been significantly higher than in the city of Budapest. The population of the inner suburban zone grew tenfold between 1869 and 1910, while the population of the urban core 'only' tripled. In addition to natural increase, population growth was fostered by three kinds of mobility.

The first of these was the outmigration of skilled workers from the expensive urban residential areas. The second was provoked by the transfer of industry to the northern (Újpest) and southeastern suburbs (Kispest, Pestszenterzsébet). The third was immigration from the overpopulated agricultural regions of eastern Hungary. By the end of the last century, suburban settlements were linked to the city by suburban trains and trams.

Several attempts have been made since 1901 to merge the capital city with the inner suburban zone. In 1950, the 'Greater Budapest' concept was put into practice. The city absorbed 23 neighbouring settlements (seven urban communes and 16 rural communes) into its enlarged administrative territory. The 1971 master plan delineated the outer suburban zone, which included 43 settlements, among them five towns outside Budapest, with about 400 000 inhabitants (Figure 10.1). Presumably, the actual (functional) agglomeration was larger than the territory delineated. In 1980, only 53 per cent of the daily commuters came from the 'official' agglomeration. The specific features of the metropolitan area reflect the development of the agglomeration, which was stranded in its first phase. The following are the most important features.

- 80 per cent of the metropolitan population still lives in the core city. The city is overbounded. People moving out of the central residential areas settled either in large housing estates (on the Pest side) or in a zone of villas and condominiums (on the Buda side) within the city's administrative territory. Middle-class, white-collar emigration outside the city is growing, but it is not yet extensive. Its main destinations include the villages and small towns in the hills along the right (Buda) side of the Danube.

- The socialist system preserved the character of the suburban zone as a blue-collar and part-time farmer area. The social structure shows a high proportion of poorly qualified, semi-skilled and unskilled labourers, especially in the southeast. In the blue-collar suburbs, immigrants came mainly from distant backward rural areas. The places where they took up residence have low social prestige; some of them show signs of social degradation.
- There is no administrative relationship between the agglomeration and Budapest. Nor is there any coordination among local governments. No joint authority exists to control development. The master plan for the agglomeration was prepared more than 20 years ago. Local authorities in the agglomeration jealously guard their autonomy and are reluctant to associate themselves with the capital.
- The general growth of the suburbs has been halted recently. The area has become highly differentiated. Between 1980

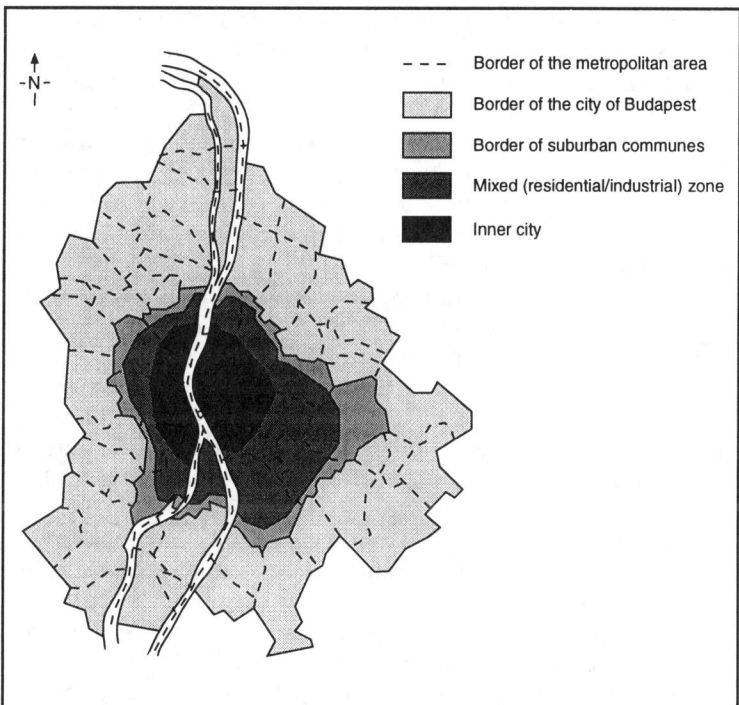

Figure 10.1   The Budapest metropolitan area

and 1990, out of the 38 settlements of the suburban zone, the population grew only in 15 and it fell in 23.[1] This decline occurred mainly in the blue-collar residential communities. The number of industrial workers commuting to Budapest dropped by 21 per cent between 1980 and 1990. The decline of the blue-collar population and the growth of white-collar suburbs reflect the way the Budapest agglomeration is adapting to the more advanced metropolitan development.

The role of Budapest within Hungary

The Hungarian capital plays an extraordinary role within Hungary. The main reason for this is that, since the 1860s, Budapest was for a long time the only Hungarian city to follow the path of European urbanization. The other cities' development was delayed for several decades. The Hungarian capital became an enclave of (western) European urbanization within the Hungarian urban network. For instance, in 1910, Budapest had one million inhabitants, making it the eighth largest city of Europe. At that time, the second-largest Hungarian city had 100 000 inhabitants; it was a rural market town with a large farming population. After the First World War, Hungary lost two-thirds of its earlier territory. Budapest then became the capital of a small country. Between the two world wars, Budapest was the only sizeable urban centre in the country. It was the only one that was able to increase its employment considerably. After the communist takeover, the excessive centralization of power and the central control of the nationalized economy made the role of the capital more dominant.

During the industrialization period, Budapest was an outstanding industrial centre. At present, it is an extraordinary centre for 'knowledge-based industries'. In 1990, 70 per cent of the R&D employees were concentrated in the capital city. Budapest accounted for 50 per cent of the teaching staff in higher education, 47 per cent of all employees holding degrees from institutions of higher education, 69 per cent of the country's architects and 79 per cent of leading business managers. Two-thirds of the patents for technical innovations have been registered by Budapest enterprises or individuals. This concentration was unhealthy from the point of view of the country's regional structure – but it made Budapest large and important. This situation has an ambiguous effect on the city's competitiveness. The presence of a great number of quaternary functions is advantageous. Nevertheless, the lack of a strong, highly developed national urban network makes the competitiveness too dependent upon external factors.

Urban policy and planning

Traditions in planned development: the Commission of Public Works

The need for regulated urban growth first arose in Budapest in the early eighteenth century, at the time of the first survey of Budapest. Parts of the city wall were pulled down and the streets were then paved and maintained. The first comprehensive master plan was completed in 1804. A so-called Improvement Commission was set up to execute the plan; this was the first professional planning body. The plan concentrated on the central part of Pest (the left bank). The main squares of the centre and the classical row of houses lining the Pest bank of the Danube were built at that time.

In 1870, the Commission of Public Works was established. This comprehensive planning authority directed urban development until 1949. The members of the Commission were delegated by both the government and the cities of Pest and Buda, on the basis of their expertise. The ex officio chairman of the Commission of Public Works was the prime minister. Thus the Hungarian government controlled and supervised the Commission. This fact expressed the centralizing effort of the government. It also indicated that the development of the capital city had become a national issue. The Hungarian government was in competition with Austria and, to rival Vienna, it decided to create a large European city which would be able to exercise its influence throughout southeastern Europe. Thus international urban competition was present from the beginning of modern urban planning in Budapest (Ságvári, 1973).

Rapid urban development transformed a medium-sized town into a modern metropolis within four decades (1870–1910). This urban 'explosion' (the size of the population tripled between 1870 and 1910) was carefully planned and the effect was delightful. Everything that marked the European standards of the age could be found in the rebuilt city; it had a system of ring roads and boulevards and a network of public transport. 'Catching up with Europe' was the general slogan. City planning was permeated by the idea of order. The principle of order determined where the roads and streets were traced; it dictated the height of buildings; and palaces and pairs of fountains were built in an identical style. Part of the mediaeval city was sacrified to this modern urban landscape. A number of valuable mediaeval buildings were destroyed: for example, all the city gates of Buda were removed, with the exception of Vienna gate (Lukács, 1988).

The First World War ended with the dismemberment of Austria–Hungary. The small state of Hungary sank into a long-lasting
crisis. Its spectacular period of modern urban planning had ended.
Nevertheless, some modernization continued in residential areas.
Housing conditions improved in the inner districts. The municipality – which became an equal partner to the Commission of
Public Works in urban planning – controlled real estate speculation in the inner city and permitted smaller plots and family housing construction in the outer zone.[2] Under these conditions, a lot
of subdivision was started, both in this outer zone and in the
suburbs.

It was characteristic of the whole period between 1870 and 1945
that the poorer social groups were left out of the integrative processes of urban policy and planning. City planners designed a
bourgeois and middle-class city. The poor social groups (such as
unskilled workers) were partly squeezed out, first to the outer
zone and then to the suburbs. Hence the blue-collar character still
to be found in the southeastern suburbs.

Immediately after the Second World War, young avant-garde
urban designers joined the Commission of Public Works. In 1945,
they presented a new master plan, entitled 'The uniform development of Greater Budapest and its environs'. This was the first
master plan for the whole metropolitan area. It formulated the
idea of the north–south development of the capital (along the
Danube). The centralized city, which had expanded around a single centre, was now envisaged as a decentralized one, broken up
into a number of sub-centres. It was at that time that the idea of
green areas of the city was advanced. Green belts were to surround the inhabited areas, and green strips were to penetrate the
inner parts of the city. These ideas were related to the most modern trends of international urban design, embracing, not only physical and technical planning, but also the handling of social tensions
in spatial terms. The avant-garde urbanism of western Europe
(and Soviet constructivism) saw collective housing and housing
estates as the solution to social and spatial tensions. They were
especially designed to address housing problems of the working
class. These ideas inspired some of the modern blocks of flats that
were built in Budapest in the late 1940s.

After the communist takeover in 1949, it became impossible to
carry out these earlier plans. The processes that had been set in
motion were abandoned and the Commission of Public Works
was abolished.

Urban planning under state socialism

In earlier publications we have explained our views on specific features of socialist urbanization (Enyedi, 1990; Enyedi, 1992a). Here a short summary will suffice, with special reference to Budapest. The following were characteristic of the whole socialist period.

- Planning could proceed unhampered by the restrictions of a property market or even by private real-property rights.
- Planning targets reflected expert opinions or political tendencies, but there was no opportunity to express group interests. There was no room – and no need – for social legitimation of planning (Compton, 1979).
- Urban planning was incorporated into the central planning system; urban development was financed by the national budget.
- Urban infrastructure as a whole was neglected, partly because the inefficient state industry absorbed a great number of budget subsidies. Emphasis was put on large-scale housing estates. Housing was the best tool for implementing government goals: to concentrate efficiently the labour force needed for rapid industrialization; to demonstrate spectacular urban development; to strengthen the political basis of communist power through the allocation of flats according to 'merits' (Szelényi, 1983).
- Urban policy was focused on the internal problems of the city: housing, physical planning, urban transport and the like, mostly within the administrative boundaries of the city. There was a master plan for the metropolitan area, but there was no authority to implement it. Budapest had no opportunity to develop international functions (except tourism). As far as the relations between Budapest and the countryside were concerned, there was only one clear urban policy: to limit population growth by controlling immigration to the city.

We can distinguish four periods within the socialist era. The first period (the 1950s) was characterized by extreme centralization and the strong presence of ideological–political goals in urban planning. There was no possibility of local planning. Urban development funds were designated and allocated by the Central Planning Office according to the interests and preferences of central authorities. The excessive centralization gave an advantage to Budapest; it became the site of all central authorities involved in the redistribution of development funds. The new master plan of Budapest was prepared by the municipality. It had to be confirmed by the National Planning Office and by the Ministry of Building and Public Works. Then it had to be endorsed by the government (1960). Until the late 1950s, it was the architects of the big design offices of the capital who directed the planning of provincial towns as well.

The other three periods were characterized by a continuing – though sometimes interrupted – tendency towards decentralization. In the second period (the 1960s), national urban planning used the growth pole model (the French '*métropoles d'équilibre*'). It developed regional centres in five provincial cities to counterbalance Budapest's weight. In this period, industrialization was the main tool for decentralized urbanization. The size of the industrial population has declined in Budapest since 1964. The capital has since been obliged to share its power with the strengthened regional centres.

The third period (the 1970s) was marked by the National Concept of the Development of the Settlement Network, an application of the central place theory that was passed into law in 1971. It ranked settlements according to size and function. Development funds were allocated along this hierarchical line. Besides Budapest, the 19 county seats also became centres for the redistribution of urban development funds. After planning directives were abolished by the economic reform of 1968, planning became a complicated bargaining process. This period made tertiary-sector development the focus of urban development, instead of industrialization. This situation again strengthened Budapest's position. The capital was the top of the settlement hierarchy; it had the strongest concentration of tertiary functions; and it had by far the strongest bargaining position among the cities.

The fourth period (the 1980s) marked the beginning of the desintegration of the state socialist system, as well as the beginning of its smooth transition to the market system. Privatization started in the early 1980s, both in housing and in the service industry. In 1986, the normative redistribution of urban funds diminished the importance of bargaining processes and created some opportunity for local planning. Budapest was affected by the same forces as other European cities; thus international metropolitan functions returned. Under the surface of official urbanization policy there was a significant 'parallel society' which tried to keep alive the traditional European urban values (Enyedi, 1992b). The state socialist system evaporated quite rapidly. The symbols of the socialist system have hardly affected the urban landscape (except for the presence of the large housing estates). There were a number of monuments dedicated to Soviet soldiers, some statues of Marxist revolutionaries, the parade road near the City Park, and there is the People's Stadium. By and large, their number is small and they are scattered throughout the city. (After 1990, the statues were moved to a special statue park on the outskirts of the city.)

For the past decade and a half, there has been growing interest in the historical Budapest of the late nineteenth and early twentieth centuries. The banks of the Danube and the Royal Palace have been rebuilt; the post-modern buildings could be easily attached to the buildings from the Art Nouveau period. The style of the shops in the inner city also follows these traditions. The present symbolism of the city passes on the message that this is an old city, a valuable city with a rich past, a central European city. This is not based on nostalgia or an idealization of the past. Rather, it represents a modern renewal of the historical roots that have been hacked at.

Urban policy in post-socialist transition

Changes in the political system introduced new approaches and a new mechanism for urban planning and urban policy in Budapest. The most important new elements brought by the political transition are the opening to the global market, the associate membership of Hungary in the European Community, the free travel across national borders, the privatization of urban land and the urban economy, the transformation of city government and the rebirth of a self-organized local society. These new elements gave Budapest the opportunity to develop international functions. The present urban policy again puts an emphasis on international competitiveness.

In this chapter we intend to analyse urban policy according to the principles and criteria formulated in Chapter 1 above. Our job is difficult, for various reasons. First of all, the new course in urban policy started only three years ago; thus its evaluation must remain partial. Secondly, not all the criteria that are widely used in western comparative urban studies (Keating, 1991) are available (for example, there are no GDP data at the regional or urban level). Furthermore, some of the urban processes which started during the socialist era are still continuing. Finally, the rapidly changing socio-economic transition makes it extremely difficult to prove the role of urban policy in urban performance.

There are no favourable conditions for working out a long-term strategic urban policy. The freely elected democratic Parliament passed the Local Government Act on 3 August 1990. Under the Act, Budapest has a two-tier public administration. The 22 districts represent as many local governments, which are not subordinated to the municipal general assembly. Representative bodies with 25 to 40 members are elected in the 22 districts, depending upon the number of inhabitants, and these bodies elect the district mayor. The municipal general assembly has 88 members: 66 are elected from party lists (voters elect both district and municipal representatives) and 22 members are delegated by the 22 districts. The municipal general assembly elects the chief mayor. This system was modified in 1994; for example, the mayor of Budapest was directly elected by the voters; the municipal general assembly gained more power vis-à-vis the districts.

The Local Government Act ruled that a separate act was to be passed for the capital by 30 November 1990, but the relevant bill was only submitted to Parliament in 1991. Comprehensive urban planning is difficult since districts have the same status in public administration as the municipality (and the Act for Budapest government makes no reference to cooperation within the metropolitan area). After 40 years of management from above, there is a burning desire for autonomy in every community and a lingering suspicion of any 'superior authority' or hierarchy. The desire for independence has been very strong in the districts. There is much discussion on how to share municipal property and budget subsidies between municipal government and district governments. Consequently, district development plans may be in conflict with the metropolitan development schemes.

Urban land has four types of owners: private parties, the state (for example, the land of state industrial enterprises), district governments (the whole municipal housing stock and basic public service institutions such as elementary schools) and the city of Budapest (infrastructure networks and specialized urban public service institutions). There are numerous conflicts between the municipal and the national governments. Budapest elected a (liberal) opposition local government. Thus (conservative) national government has no political interest in the success of Budapest. Nonetheless, the national government does not intend to seriously hamper the functioning of the capital city, because Budapest society carries exceptional political weight. Hence the endless discussions on budget subsidies and government responsibilities regarding the development of a national infrastructure.

Under the uncertain conditions, a number of improvisations have been necessary in urban management; short-run solutions have been provided for day-to-day problems. So far, the municipal government has produced three documents on urban policy. The first, issued in 1991, was entitled 'Mayor Gábor Demszky's programme for the capital city'. Although it formulated long-term goals and policy instruments, it was focused on the internal structural changes of the city. The second document contained only a two-year development programme (1993/94). Nevertheless, it formulated seven long-term strategic priorities as well: (1) the extension of the city centre along the Danube; (2) a new housing policy; (3) urban renewal through the reconstruction of the degraded inner-city residential zone; (4) the rearrangement of functional zones (new office and business areas); (5) a halt to environmental deterioration; (6) a new design for urban transport and communication; (7) development of Budapest as an international metropolis. In this list of priorities, policy goals are mixed with development projects. The third document was the programme of the new master plan (Budapest Föváros Altalános Rendezési Terve, 1993). Its introductory chapter presents the vision of Budapest's future functions. It also formulates three main goals of urban policy. The first goal is to create an attractive living space for the citizens by improving the environmental conditions, by improving the housing situation, ensuring space for leisure time, and by developing welfare services and institutions. The second goal is to foster cooperation among local (district and city) governments based on mutual interest for a better coordination of infrastructural development and environmental protection. The third is to allow Budapest to become an international metropolis. These are real policy goals. As such, they represent great progress since the 1991 technical–infrastructural development targets were formulated.

Budapest's city government has worked out an urban policy and has started its implementation. Because of the short time that policy has been in existence, urban success or failure depends only partly upon urban policy.

Policy evaluation

We intend to analyse urban policy along four dimensions: efficiency, equity, externalities and budgetary goals.

The efficiency dimension   Urban policy can contribute to the efficient use of local resources mostly by enhancing public services. Infrastructural development has been neglected under the state socialist system, hence the great need for development. Market solutions are efficient in certain sectors (such as telecommunication). In other sectors, policy intervention is desirable for market breakdowns. Budapest's government gives high priority to urban transport. This includes plans to modernize parking facilities, to extend the metro network, to build two new bridges over the Danube and to develop circular roads that would divert through traffic from the city centre.

The second element of the efficiency dimension is public finance. The success of urban policy depends on the extent to which the city can attract foreign capital. It also depends on the role of the capital in the formation of the Hungarian private economy. These two factors define the path of privatization.

Budapest has rapidly developed 'gateway' functions – not only for Hungary, but for southeastern and eastern Europe, too. Between 1989 and 1992, Budapest was the main target for western investors within east–central Europe. The city alone attracted 30 per cent of the sum invested by western capital in the 18 European post-socialist countries. In addition, Hungarian private enterprises are mushrooming in the city; 45 per cent of the country's limited companies and 60 per cent of the country's shareholders' companies and joint ventures are registered in Budapest (only 25–30 per cent are located East of the Danube). Urban policy contributes to the process of privatization in two ways. One is by privatizing a part of the operation of public services (for example, maintenance of social housing); the other is by beginning to create an entrepreneurial city (mostly on the real estate market).

Deep structural changes are occurring in the urban economy. The process of 'tertiarization' has speeded up. This sector has been able to enlarge its employment: the proportion of tertiary employment (61 per cent) is not high, but it is not very low either. Actually, it is higher than the share of tertiary employment in Barcelona or Lyons. The introduction of quality services, including high-level business services, had started during the last decade of the socialist system. There were two milestones in this process: the transformation of the banking system (establishment of commercial banks since 1986, the opening of a stock exchange in 1987); and the advancement of the private sector in services (private business investments rose sixfold in Budapest between 1980 and 1989). This process prepared the ground for the rapid changes that took place after 1989.

There has been a strong decline in the state industrial sector. On the one hand, diminishing industrial employment is a normal phenomenon on the path to a post-industrial economy. In Budapest, the number of industrial employees reached its peak in 1964; it has declined by more than 50 per cent since then. On the other hand, the consequences of the economic crisis, the sudden loss of the former COMECON market, the transformation and privatization of state industry seriously hit the modern sectors (the knowledge-based industries) as well. Even these sectors had over-employment and low efficiency under state ownership. Therefore industrial decline is very marked. After the stabilization of the economy, we could expect to see some growth in industry. Contrary to the decline of the state industry, the private and the tertiary sectors show dynamism. Consequently, Budapest has the lowest unemployment rate in the country (7 per cent, against 14 per cent for the national average and over 20 per cent in eastern Hungary) (Barta, 1993).

Urban policy has not had much influence on the structural changes of the economy. Nonetheless, there is an explicit urban policy to concentrate international institutions in the city and to make the Hungarian capital an international cultural centre. This policy has proved successful. A number of cultural, research and educational institutions have already been located there. These include the Collegium Budapest (a Princeton-type centre for advanced studies); the Central European University, established by George Soros; the Central European Centre for Environmental Protection; the International Management Training Centre; and many others.

In sum, the city has been successful in the efficiency dimension. Urban policy participated in this success, mostly in the sphere of culture and in the development of urban infrastructure. However, policy had little direct impact on economic change. Urban policy was purposeful; the liberal parties which dominate the city council are in favour of market regulation, especially after decades of a planned economy.

The equity dimension   Socialist urban policy formulated egalitarian goals. Although its implementation has never been fully successful, it did seriously damage the efficient functioning of the city. Post-socialist urban policy did not give much attention to the equity dimension, but local governments will have to change this standpoint soon. They will have to face two problems: (1) what will happen with social housing and (2) how to deal with rapidly growing social inequality.

In 1990, when the new urban government was elected, 53 per cent of the housing stock of Budapest was state-owned or owned by the municipality (Table 10.1). A limited amount of private housing construction started in the late 1960s. This thrust was mostly in the form of single-family homes on the outskirts and condominiums in the most prestigious areas. In the city centre, the share of state-owned flats reached 90 per cent; they were nationalized in 1952. The new state-owned flats were built in the form of large housing estates, using prefabricated elements. They look like social housing – like French HLM buildings. But in fact they were allocated to applicants only partly for social reasons; partly, people were awarded these units according to their 'merit' (political activity, being good workers and so on). The rents are low not even covering maintenance costs.

After the collapse of the socialist system, the state housing stock passed into the ownership of district governments. These bodies have various housing policies. Consequently, there is no comprehensive metropolitan housing policy. Housing construction has fallen enormously, while social housing has stopped entirely. There is confusion about rent regulation; generally, most people cannot pay higher rents because of the decline in real income. Earlier, rents were low because of enormous budget subsidies. The cost of renovating an apartment would amount to 90 years' rent; hence the long-term neglect of urban renewal. Most of the district governments rushed to sell off the apartments – on very favourable financial terms for the tenants.[3] (In Hungary, there was no reprivatization of flats. Previous owners received compensation in the form of state bonds.) In the most prestigious, hilly district, over 50 per cent of the state apartments were sold in three years. In the workers' districts, the figure is under 10 per cent. Since real estate prices are highly differentiated, privileged persons who had been allocated a state-owned apartment in the hilly districts will now

Table 10.1   Proportion of state housing in Budapest, 1950–90

Year	Total numbers of flats	Number of state-owned flats (000s)	Proportion of state-owned flats (%)
1950	410	140	29.9
1955	480	376	78.3
1960	536	384	71.6
1970	619	389	62.8
1980	709	408	57.5
1990	789	410	51.9

Source: Kovács (1992).

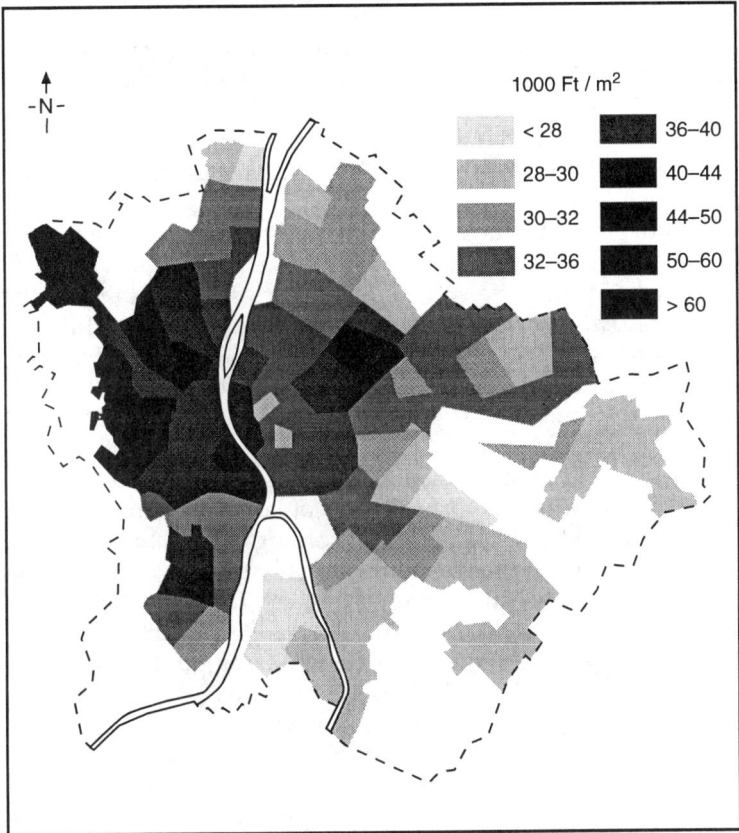

Source: Kovács (1992).

Figure 10.2 Apartment prices in Budapest, 1990

buy their valuable real estate at a very low price (Figure 10.2). Local governments got rid of the burden of maintenance and renewal costs of the (partly) old and neglected housing stock, and they had some financial resources. But it is evident that the new owners will not be able to renovate and keep up their units. Since the city's population is declining, the housing shortage is due to the poor quality of the housing stock and to the virtual cessation of social housing construction. Between 1980 and 1990, Budapest's population diminished by 2.1 per cent, whereas the housing stock grew by 8.8 per cent. In 1990, 10 per cent of the flats had only one room, and the proportion of large flats (over three bedrooms) was

14 per cent (the national average was 23 per cent). The municipal government intends to keep 30 per cent of the housing stock in municipal ownership. Urban renewal – especially in the inner-city residential zone – is one of the priorities of the 1993 master plan. The main conflict is that the market rent (which covers at least the interest rate of the invested capital) is twice the average net salary (Beluszky, 1992).

City governments have to deal with the growing impoverishment of the population. Evidently, income differences are much greater than during the socialist era. The lower one-third of the population earns 15 per cent of the national income, while the upper third earns more than 50 per cent (Csanádi and Ladányi, 1992). Budapest has again become a magnet for migration: its economic dynamism and its large black-market economy attract the rural unemployed and illegal immigrants (from post-socialist countries, mostly from Romania). This has led to an enlargement of marginal groups, the propagation of social deviance and the accumulation of homeless people (according to the estimates, there are 15–20 000 homeless, among them many illegal immigrants, in Budapest). These social ills are widespread in large cities in rich western countries as well, but the suddenness with which they broke out caught the city government unprepared. It has already recognized that market solutions are not adequate. The authorities have started to renew existing welfare institutions and to develop new forms of welfare, although budgetary constraints pose limits to their efforts. In sum, city government initially neglected the equity dimension; accordingly, their policies have not been very successful in this respect.

Negative externalities   The negative externalities dimension has played an important and continuously growing role in urban policy. Environmental problems, and air pollution in particular, are at the core of the policy. Traffic congestion and air pollution are strongly interrelated; all the urban traffic as well as the east–west through traffic cross the Danube in the central parts of the city. Several important measures have been taken already: a new bridge is being built in the southern part of the city; the first part of a circular motorway to divert the through traffic from the city has been opened; furthermore, a comprehensive plan to modernize the public transport system is being implemented. This entails the introduction of new city buses with less polluting engines ('green buses') and the enlargement of the underground system. The city council offered a subsidy and a low-interest loan to those owners of cars with a two-stroke engine (Trabant and Wartburg) who intended to buy a new, less polluting car (and turn in their two-stroke cars for demolition). Alternatively, they can choose a two-year free ticket for the public transport system.

Sewage treatment and waste diposal are also important externalities. Most of the sewage is only treated mechanically, and only 20 per cent is treated biologically. Budapest's waste water is discharged into the Danube, causing serious contamination of the river. One of the consequences is the accumulation of heavy metals in the river's sediments. Another is the high bacterial content, which makes the river unsuitable for recreation. Despite the high cost, two new sewage treatment plants are under construction, and the privatization of the Municipal Sewage Works has been prepared.

The city council has taken energetic steps to deal with negative externalities. In this respect, urban policy has been successful.

Budgetary goals   All cities face budgetary constraints on policy. In the case of Budapest, these constraints may be considered serious if we take into consideration the need for general change in the metropolitan transport system, the urban structure and environmental protection. Previously, the city's budget had to be balanced; budget constraints always led to the reduction of expenditures. In 1992, the city council decided to borrow for its capital expenditure. It obtained favourable loans (including loans from the World Bank and European Bank for Reconstruction and Development). The capital is used mostly for transport development.

The city budget contains a number of uncertainties. Local government subsidies are approved by Parliament within the national budget, but the rules have changed every year since the transition began. For instance, in 1991, all the income taxes paid by individuals remained in the budget of the local governments, but in 1992, only half, and in 1993, only 30 per cent (whereas 70 per cent was seized by the central budget). In the case of a large city, like Budapest, these measures have diminished the budget income by several billion forints. Local taxes are not important; since (national) income taxes are very high, local governments are reluctant to increase the burden on their own electorate. There is a business tax in Budapest. However, it should not be prohibitive, as business attraction is important. At the moment, privatization is also an (uncertain) income source. The inflation (23 per cent in 1992) makes it hard to predict the costs of long-term investments. Another difficulty arises from the poorly regulated relation between the city council and the district councils. One-third of the distribution of metropolitan and district resources requires political bargaining every year. In 1993, 86 per cent of the budget was needed to cover the running costs of the city; thus only 14 per cent remained for development. Hence the necessity to borrow.

In concluding the analysis of urban policy, we can state that it was successful within the budgetary constraints. The policy moved towards urban efficiency. It was perfectly capable of fighting negative externalities. And it was weak in the equity dimension. It seems that the lack of a comprehensive housing policy is the weakest point of the urban policy.

Budapest's position in the competition between cities

Budapest has been able to develop its metropolitan functions while competing with other cities for foreign capital, transnational companies and international institutions. In general, post-socialist cities are not well prepared for competition. Most of the capital cities, with the exception of Bratislava and Ljubljana, are large enough to be classified as metropolises. Presumably, Belgrade and Zagreb will have serious constraints for a long time to come because of the war in former Yugoslavia. As far as Bucharest and Sofia are concerned, neither their infrastructure nor their economic and social status will allow them to compete on the European stage in the immediate future. Owing to their poor communication system, the geographical distance from western Europe is a serious handicap. (Obviously, this situation could change in the future.) At present, Budapest, Prague and Warsaw may have an opportunity to enter the European urban competition. The transition towards political democracy and market economy is the most advanced; in the Czech Republic, Hungary and Poland these changes are irreversible. The final outcome of the transition is much more uncertain in the other post-socialist countries. Thus the competitiveness of Budapest should be related to that of Prague and Warsaw.

The competitiveness of Budapest

Budapest certainly has some advantages over the two other cities in its league. These advantages came from the historical situation. First of all, the international functions were prepared during the last two decades of the 'soft dictatorship' of the Kádár regime. Secondly, the conditions for metropolitan development are generally more favourable in Budapest than in other post-socialist cities. These advantages have been rewarded already by foreign direct investment and the location of transnational companies.

After the economic reform of 1968, more and more elements of European urbanization returned to Budapest. These included the following.

- The transition from industrial to tertiary city. In 1964, half of the industrial workforce of Hungary was concentrated in Budapest. This share dropped to 19 per cent by 1991. Half of these workers were employed in white-collar jobs in company headquarters.
- The growing share of high-quality and diversified services within the tertiary sector.
- Private-sector economy developing in Budapest from the end of the 1970s. Private business investments rose sixfold between 1980 and 1989 (still in the socialist period!). In 1986, two-thirds of the private enterprises of the country operated in Budapest.
- Openings to the west in various forms. The economy of Budapest had more foreign trade with the west than with COMECON countries; large state enterprises established direct links with western enterprises; during the 1980s, Budapest received the largest number of western visitors among the east-central European capitals, and every year approximately two million Hungarians travelled to the west.

As a consequence, the citizens of Budapest have some experience of the urban life of western cities. The rapid shift from state socialism to the market system did not cause a deep culture shock for the Budapest populace.

The geographical location of Budapest, Prague and Warsaw allows these cities to link up with the European metropolitan network. Budapest is larger and has a stronger metropolitan image than its competitors. It is close to Vienna; the very strong historical tradition of cooperation between these cities is favourable. On the other hand, the limited size of Hungary and the modest development of the national urban network is a disadvantage. The city has good possibilities to develop bridgehead functions towards eastern Europe and the Balkans. It has the most markedly metropolitan image in east-central Europe. Prague has the westernmost location; accordingly, the city could easily be connected to the German urban network. The Czech capital has highly esteemed cultural traditions and a valuable built environment. Its national territory is relatively small and relations with eastern Europe have been cut back. It will not be easy to develop macroregional (bridgehead) economic functions for Prague. Warsaw has an advantageous location half-way between two large economic spaces: German and post-Soviet. Poland has a common border with five post-Soviet republics and good access to the Baltic region. The city of Warsaw itself has a poor infrastructure. Moreover, the urban environment is less attractive than that of its competitors.

Budapest certainly has gateway functions. First of all, the city receives foreign capital, foreign firm headquarters and all sorts of foreign visitors. Between 1989 and 1993, Budapest was the main target for western investors, receiving 30 per cent of the total sum invested by western capital in *all* of the European post-socialist countries. The value of foreign direct investments has been over three and a half billion dollars during the last four years. Fifteen of the world's 20 largest transnational companies by sales have opened offices in the Hungarian capital (although only two – General Motors and General Electric – are among the largest investors). The great interest shown by TNCs cannot be explained by the Hungarian market – they are looking eastward. Budapest is able to challenge Vienna's gateway functions. Hungarian businessmen have a lot of experience in dealing with the Balkan and post-Soviet markets, where conditions are quite different from western European ones. At the same time, Budapest is the easternmost city, where the level of infrastructure is acceptable and all the modern business services (banking and insurance) are present. (In 1991, 10 large international insurance companies had headquarters in Budapest; there were none in Prague and four in Warsaw.)

Budapest is the outstanding intellectual centre of the country. It was the centre of social innovation under the state socialist system – not only for Hungary, but partly for other socialist countries, too. These innovations prepared the 'smooth transition' to the post-socialist era. The city is open enough to play the role of an international meeting place. It functions as a clearinghouse for east–west business information. (Some data about this openness: in Budapest, 10 per cent of the university students are foreigners; in Prague, the figure is 1.5 per cent, in Warsaw 1 per cent. Budapest organized 31 international fairs and exhibitions in 1991; Prague hosted 12, Warsaw 13. Nearly one per cent of Budapest's population consists of foreign citizens; Prague has 0.2 per cent, Warsaw 0.06 per cent.) (See Table 10.2.)

The analysis of metropolitan competitiveness pays too much attention to technical and economic aspects; social aspects have been frequently overlooked. We may assume that, in the case of post-socialist cities, European competitiveness will depend to a large extent on the mental (cultural and behavioural) capacities of

Table 10.2 Comparative data for selected European regional sub-centres, 1990

Data	F	A	Gl	Ge	M	Ba	Bu	P	W
Population (000s)	615	680	703	158	1 495	1 702	2 016	1 214	1 651
Population growth 1980/90 (%)	-2.58	-4.54	-9.18	4.64	-6.71	0.01	-2.10	2.69	3.45
Active pop. (%)	48.5	37.8	54.6	46.0	46.5	38.0	47.4	55.1	63.0
Unemployed (%)	8.0	10.7	14.8	2.0	6.1	24.0	5.7	3.4	9.8
Foreign pop. (%)	22	23	5.8	32.8	2.2	2.5	0.7	0.2	0.06
Number of trade exhibitions & fairs	22	31	9	13	57	26	31	12	13
Foreign insurance companies	37	66	6	6	27	20	10	0	4
Number of univ. students	37 820	41 000	11 000	11 500	135 000	146 438	42 441	43 453	67 500
Foreign students (%)	9.3	2.9	11.8	25.6	2.2	3.8	10.0	1.5	0.8
Visitors to museums (000s)	300	1 050	1 041	70	372	345	3 798	3 173	2 845
Number of foreign air companies	156	75	15	63	46	27	23	29	22
Air passengers (000s)	26 709	15 668	4 210	5 883	10 515	8 461	3 930	3 890	4 300

Notes:
F = Frankfurt; A = Amsterdam; Gl = Glasgow; Ge = Geneva; M = Milano; Ba = Barcelona; Bu = Budapest; P = Prague; W = Warsaw.

Source: Barta (1993).

the population. Generally, the level of education in these cities is good. But are the people well enough trained to run modern infrastructure and modern service institutions properly? Will the inhabitants of the cities accept such metropolitan values as cross-cultural (interethnic) intellectual life? Will they tolerate the presence of immigrants and foreign businessmen? Are they ready to run their city (public services, cultural life and so on) in ways similar to other European metropolises? Can they create an 'urban social climate' which could attract leading foreign businessmen (an important precondition for opening TNCs' regional headquarters)? In this respect, Prague has the strongest traditions in European urban life, but during the socialist period, Budapest and Warsaw were more willing to accept western influence.

Urban policy in Budapest stipulated the strengthening of the image and functions of an international metropolis among its strategic goals. The city administration subsidizes major cultural events, such as the Budapest Spring Festival, which can attract visitors from the neighbouring countries. In addition, a number of training centres have been opened up in the city where young experts from other post-socialist countries can receive specialized education (examples include the Central European University, the International Management Centre, the International Bankers' School and the Collegium Budapest Centre for Advanced Studies).

Budapest joins the fray: future scenarios

There are divers options for integrating Budapest into the European metropolitan network. These options delineate the different geopolitical areas within which Budapest has to compete. For sure, Budapest does not have the capability to become an all-continental centre. The Hungarian capital could be developed into a sub-regional centre, however. The city has to compete with other metropolises within eastern and central Europe.

The first option is to join the western European metropolitan network by the most direct route. In this case, Budapest would both compete and cooperate with Vienna. (Budapest has a more advantageous position than Prague or Warsaw; for the latter two, the nearest competing Western metropolis is Berlin.) Budapest can partly take over Vienna's gateway functions for western capital to southeastern and eastern Europe. At present, this first option is being implemented.

The second option is to develop a central European metropolitan network, and not necessarily to join the western European core area. In this scenario, Berlin would become a global city (as London and Paris are today) and would develop an urban system parallel to the present west European core area. This option presupposes the development of strong cohesion among central European cities. At present, this cohesion is weak; even communication is poorly developed.

The third and the fourth options are indicative of failures in western integration. According to the third option, Budapest would remain on the western edge of eastern Europe. It would develop transborder functions, mostly to eastern and southeastern Europe. In this scenario, political instability and economic uncertainty could hamper the development of important international functions in Budapest. The fourth option is that Budapest would remain the big centre of a small country. Its development would then be nourished by national sources. No important international functions would develop. These two pessimistic scenarios may come to pass as a consequence of the looming political instability and disintegration of the 'wider' Europe.

At present, the more optimistic first scenario is prevailing. Budapest is developing because it is a European metropolis. We can expect three functions of international significance to thrive here. The first is cultural–scientific; we mentioned earlier the cultural and scientific strength of the Hungarian capital. The second is the gateway function; this will grow further as Budapest businesses move to capture an increasing share of the eastern European market. The third possibility is to develop an international banking and business service centre. Hungarian financial services are the most advanced in post-socialist countries (although not sufficiently developed by western standards). Hungary's banks already receive deposits from and allocate capital to post-socialist countries. Presumably, Budapest will be able to fulfil the role of a subregional centre.

Notes

1 Population decline is general in Hungary. The country's population was 10.7 million in 1970, 10.5 million in 1980, and 10.3 million in 1990 (census data).
2 Before the First World War, only large plots were permitted in the outer zone. These were suitable either for the construction of tenement houses or for large villas with parks.
3 This type of privatization started in 1969, but it remained limited until 1982; 42 000 flats were sold to the tenants between 1982 and 1990, the last years of the socialist system (Kovács, 1992).

References

Barta, Gy. (1993) 'Budapest, Kelet-európai metropolisz 2005-ben' [Budapest, an Eastern European metropolis in 2005], Budapest: manuscript.
Beluszky, P. (1992) 'Budapest és a modernizáció kihívásai' [Budapest and the challenges of modernization], *Tér és Társadalom*, 6, (3–4), pp.15–54.
Bernát, T. and M. Viszkei (eds) (1972) *Budapest társadalmának és gazdaságának százéve* [One hundred years of society and economy of Budapest], Budapest: KJK.
'Budapest Fôváros Altalános Rendezési Terve' [Master Plan of the Capital City of Budapest] (1993), Budapest.
Compton, A.P. (1979) 'Planning and spatial change in Budapest', in R.A. French and F.E.I. Hamilton, *The Socialist City*, New York: Wiley, pp.461–92.
Csanádi, G. and J. Ladányi (1992) *Budapest térbeni-társadalmi szerkezetének változásai* [Changes in the sociospatial structure of Budapest], Budapest: Akadémiai Kiadó.
Enyedi, Gy. (1990) 'Specific urbanization in East Central Europe', *Geoforum*, 21, pp.163–72.
Enyedi, Gy. (1992a) 'Urbanisation in East-Central Europe: social processes and societal responses in the state socialist system', *Urban Studies*, 29, pp.869–80.
Enyedi, Gy. (ed.) (1992b) *Social Transition and Urban Restructuring in Central Europe*, Budapest: RURE.
Enyedi, Gy. and V. Szirmai (1992) *Budapest – A Central European Capital*, London: Belhaven.
Keating, M. (1991) *Comparative Urban Politics*, Aldershot: Edward Elgar.
Kovács, Z. (1992) 'A budapesti bérlakásszektor privatizációjának társadalmi- és városszerkezeti hatásai' [Spatial aspects of the privatization of state housing in Budapest], *Tér és Társadalom*, 6, (3–4), pp.55–73.
Lukács, J. (1988) *Budapest, 1900. A Historical Portrait of a City and its Culture*, New York: Weidenfeld & Nicolson.
Ságvári, A. (1973) *Budapest. The History of a Capital*, Budapest: Corvina.
Szelényi, I. (1983) *Urban Inequalities under State Socialism*, Oxford: Oxford University Press.

11 Milan: the failure of agency in the metropolis

Tomaso Pompili

Introduction: the main concepts

As an economic actor, each city has to compete with other cities for economic growth. Growth is thus a measure of success. In this context, goods and services are the city's output, and inter-city trade is an expression of functional relationships. At the same time, local private and public resources become the inputs and the basis for comparative advantage. Viewing a city in terms of inputs and outputs casts private and public decision making in the role of intermediate outputs. The focus on competition among cities for private and public resources highlights the role of markets. They constitute a mechanism that efficiently allocates scarce resources within and between cities, nationally and internationally.

Deviating somewhat from the above perspective, we do not view the city as a single economic actor. Instead, we prefer the principal–agent approach (Arrow, 1985; Hart and Holmstrom, 1987; Levinthal, 1988; Tirole, 1994). From this angle, the population can be seen as the principal in a model where the agents are private and public decision makers (employers, landowners, developers, local authority politicians and bureaucrats). The population leaves the decision making to the agents because of specialization advantages, which increase with city size. But at the same time, an information gap arises in the city: the population is not as fully informed as its decision makers. The problem is that the decision makers do not necessarily share the goals of the populace. This raises the question whether the incentives offered to the agents correspond to the interests of the principal.

The traditional way to resolve this problem depends on two assumptions. The first is that only public decision making is relevant to the city population. The second is that public decision makers can be held accountable, by imposing enforceable penalties or by appealing to their sense of public ethics. In Milan, however, a specific Italian mix of institutions has invalidated these assumptions. The purely proportional electoral system precludes the formation of clear-cut and stable majorities, which undermines accountability. Moreover, the lack of public resources invalidates the public-agent-only assumption, as contributions from private agents are necessary. And in practice, public ethics are low.

Decision makers depend on market mechanisms to reach the expected outcomes of their decisions. But the markets are not independent of their decisions. In fact, the outcomes are influenced by the market structure as well as by a variety of external factors. These include the objects being exchanged, the nature of the regulators, the actor composition of the demand and the supply sides, goals, strategies and instruments.

It is elucidating to study the city and metropolitan area of Milan using the conceptual framework of the principal–agent approach. Milan provides a distinctive case study because of the apparent 'private success and public failure' experienced in the 1980s. At present, the metropolitan area enjoys continental prominence although it is not a capital city and despite public policy. Indeed, public vice might have undermined private virtue, as manifested in the harsh effects of the 1990s recession.

After describing the policy context and the challenges faced by decision makers, we present and discuss policy responses. These, in turn, relate to planning policy, efficiency policies, equity policies, externality policies, and policy making itself.

Context and challenges

Restructuring the local economy

Milan traditionally plays a leading role in the Italian city system. This is reflected in its higher activity rates (hence higher level of affluence). Above all, this is demonstrated by its specialization in management jobs, service activities and large firms. That leading role is complemented by a high level of activity throughout the rest of Lombardy. One of the early manufacturing areas of Europe, the regional economy is rooted in diffused local entrepreneurship. However, the importance of manufacturing in the metropolitan ring and the general dominance of small firms is remarkable by continental standards. Milan has managed to retain its leadership in terms of its larger than proportionate share of all kinds of activities. Indeed, we observe a convergence between cities, but without change in the pecking order. This is a sign of the periphery's learning process rather than of metropolitan failure.

The rest of the country was clearly catching up with Milan in the 1970s. (Between 1971 and 1981, Milan's lead in per capita value-added declined from 52 to 33 per cent above the national average.) This was partly caused by development elsewhere, but it may also come from a loss of creativity (entrepreneurship and innovation) in Milan. In any case, the decline virtually halted in the 1980s; in 1991, Milan's per capita value-added was again the highest, rating 39 per cent above the national average. This suggests that creativity had not run out during the recession but had shifted from the quantitative to the qualitative side.

Deindustrialization is more a sign of changing intra-industrial specializations than of declining competitiveness. This is borne out by Milan's favourable export balance with the rest of Italy and the rest of the world. Indeed, until very recently, the northwest was virtually the only capital-exporting area of Italy and the main recipient of foreign direct investment. Historically, however, the strong entrepreneurial tradition in both manufacturing and services has limited the role of large corporations and the public sector more than elsewhere.

The province of Milan hosts 7 per cent of the national population but 8 per cent of the national active population. Milan's share of blue-collar workers reflects the country's average (7 per cent). But the overrepresentation of white-collar workers remains, despite some catching up by the rest of the country. It has declined only slightly, from over 12 per cent in 1971 to over 11 per cent in 1981 (Pompili, 1992, 1996). This dominance is reflected in the overrepresentation of jobs in services (around 8.5 per cent), with much higher levels in finance, insurance, real estate and business services (Table 11.1). The city dominates in manufacturing, where new and high-technology branches are especially prominent (Camagni and Pompili, 1990a, 1990b; Pompili, 1992). Milan's position suffered an absolute and relative loss throughout the 1970s, when its share declined from 13.5 per cent in 1971 to 12 per cent in 1981.

In terms of employment in non-agricultural firms, Milan's share of the national total remains disproportionately high. But again, there is evidence of a catching-up trend (12.5 per cent in 1971, 10 per cent in 1981, 9.6 per cent in 1991). These figures are influenced by the fact that the statistics for 1971 exclude the public sector and professionals. (Public employees account for a relatively low share of the occupational structure in Milan, although the city is a seat of government; the rates in the south are much higher because the market economy there remains weak.)

In terms of establishments and firms, the Milanese share is lower than its overall position would warrant (Table 11.2). But again, a

Table 11.1   Development of the active population (thousands) by economic sector (workers as percentage of active population) 1971–91

	Census year	Milan city	Milan province	Italy
Active	1971	711	1 599	19 805
population	1981	695	1 791	22 551
(000s)	1991	612	1 819	n.a.
Workers in	1971	41.00	52.26	31.12
manufacturing	1981	27.57	39.40	26.23
(%)	1991	20.37	32.28	n.a.
Workers in	1971	11.74	11.49	16.05
infrastructure	1981	11.47	11.43	14.82
(%)	1991	12.25	12.31	n.a.
Workers in	1971	45.64	33.17	31.54
services	1981	54.67	42.11	38.80
(%)	1991	62.69	50.87	n.a.

Table 11.2   Development of the number of firms and number of establishments (thousands) 1971–91

	Census year	Milan city	Milan province	Italy
Firms	1971	87	165	2 236
(000s)	1981	86	190	2 847
	1991	94	228	3 281
Establishments	1971	95	180	2 425
(000s)	1981	108	234	3 514
	1991	102	254	3 784

converging tendency can be discerned, due mostly to counting criteria (7.4 per cent in 1971, 6.7 per cent in 1981 and 1991). The average establishment size converged markedly in the 1970s and (more slowly) the 1980s. Highly integrated multi-establishment firms characterize neither the Italian nor the Milanese economy. This is also reflected in the distribution by size. Milan's share of employment by establishment is above average for all size classes above 20 employees and even higher among the larger firms. The same is true, but with increasingly wide differentials, for the number of establishments and the number of firms. However, over time, the trend is one of declining divergences. This is due to two continuing processes: the periphery is catching up and the tertiary sector is expanding. The shares of large and medium-sized businesses are much higher in Milan, yet even in this city almost all firms and establishments still employ fewer than 20 people. These firms account for 40 per cent (1981) of total employment, compared to 50 per cent in the rest of the country.

The social structure in flux

The economic leadership of Milan is also borne out by the large size of the working age cohorts and particularly of their most educated segments. Another characteristic is the relatively small size of households. However, the last two traits are still quite different than on the rest of the continent.

The population of the metropolitan area has remained stable since 1971, while the central city of Milan has declined. However, the number of families has remained stable in Milan and has increased in the metropolitan area. Population dynamics respond to several demographic trends. The period 1975–84 witnessed a nationwide 'baby bust'. In 1975, mass migration to Milan from the rest of the country came to an abrupt halt. The provincial influx was replaced by a significant inflow from developing countries in the late 1980s. Since the 1970s, the city started to lose increasing numbers of people to its surrounding hinterland, rather than to the rest of the country. In other words, there was little evidence of return migration.

In contrast with the province's share of 7 per cent of the national population and 8 per cent of the nation's active population, Milan's shares of both the young (0–19 years) and the elderly (60+ years) are small (each around 6.5 per cent of the national share). The share of the young experienced a slight absolute and relative decline during the 1970s, which speeded up during the 1980s (Table 11.3). Overrepresented are people with a high-school diploma and with a university degree (each around 9 per cent of the national share). With respect to the share of the elderly, there are clear signs of convergence. Changes in educational attainment parallel the relative dynamics of blue- and white-collar labour. Nevertheless, people with less than a high school diploma still accounted for five people out of six in 1981 (three out of four, when the cohort younger than 20 years old is excluded – Table 11.4).

The number of families remains relatively high, although they are dwindling in size. Singles tend to be elderly widows rather

Table 11.3   Development of the population (thousands) and population
structure, 1971–91

	Census year	Milan city	Milan province	Italy
Population	1971	1 732	3 904	54 137
(000s)	1981	1 604	4 018	56 557
	1991	1 369	3 922	56 411
Population	1971	24.90	28.73	31.54
0–19 years	1981	23.83	27.61	29.73
(per cent)	1991	17.37	20.28	n.a.
Population	1971	18.10	15.19	16.65
60 years and over	1981	19.71	15.73	17.42
(per cent)	1991	25.33	19.82	n.a.

Table 11.4   Development of the adult population (thousands) by
educational attainment (percentages) 1971–91

	Census year	Milan city	Milan province	Italy
Population	1971	1 300	2 782	37 059
20 years and over	1981	1 222	2 908	39 740
(000s)	1991	1 131	3 127	n.a.
Adults with	1971	15.97	10.88	9.08
high school	1981	22.86	18.45	15.15
(per cent of adults)	1991	32.32	27.97	n.a.
Adults with	1971	5.44	3.15	2.38
university degree	1981	7.73	4.64	3.72
(per cent of adults)	1991	10.82	6.23	n.a.

than yuppies. Even a cursory inspection of the population data for the central city and the province suggests a continuing suburbanization process. The city's population dwindled from 44 per cent to 35 per cent of the metropolitan figure in 20 years, impelled by the sudden halt of immigration early in the 1970s. This development, driven in part by high costs in the urban core, has made the suburban population more, rather than less, similar to that of the central city.

The metropolitan area, like the entire region, is among the wealthiest areas in Europe. Such affluence has allowed a massive expansion of home and car ownership. The income distribution became more equitable throughout the 1970s and early 1980s. A slight subsequent reversal of the trend coincided with generally rising incomes up to 1991. Substance abuse, petty crime and organized crime tend to be much more prevalent in Milan than in non-metropolitan areas. Indeed, these problems have become increasingly visible since the early 1970s. Nevertheless, the rates are still lower than those in major world cities. The incidence of social stress, including dissatisfaction with one's own neighbourhood, is distributed equally on the edge of the central city and in the first ring of municipalities. These are the areas that have borne the brunt, socially and physically, of the postwar economic boom. The rates of stress here are higher than in the core of the city or in the outer metropolitan ring. However, being a polycentric city (unlike Turin, Genoa or Rome) Milan has not experienced the excesses of social marginality and segregation that occur elsewhere. Even in the 1980s, the core–ring dichotomy did not worsen.

Neighbourhood and family networks have declined as sources of help for people in need, but this has been matched by a higher propensity to use public services. This is especially true in the metropolitan area, where needs are most diversified. As a matter of fact, informal networks persist, but workmates have been substituted for neighbours. Even the family can no longer offer sufficient assistance. Especially the unemployed and people evicted from their housing need support from institutional services.

However, not all traditional institutions have been sidelined. The Milan metropolitan area still takes pride in its strong civic tradition. This is apparent in the strength of the voluntary sector (especially springing from Catholic roots), of grassroots movements (labour and subsequently middle-class) and in the centuries-old tradition of municipal activism.

The physical consequences of restructuring

The metropolitan character of Milan is demonstrated by a high population density as well as by a low home-ownership rate. Both the age of the housing stock and its composition show that the heyday of development is past.

The population decline does not imply a less inhabited or less utilized city. In a sense, the city merely extends its area to include the previous hinterland. In fact, the declining household size increases the number of households and, consequently, the demand for housing. The rise of household income boosts the demand for larger dwellings. Meanwhile, the supply of housing remains severely constrained by the rigidity of the structures and the developed areas, and by the limited availability of vacant land. Outmigration from central and nearby areas is dictated by housing market conditions more than by consumer preferences regarding quality of life. These processes continue to exert pressure for increased land consumption and the expansion of the built-up area. It has a strong negative effect on the quality of the environment. Milan lies in a region well endowed with surface and underground water, but urbanization and industrialization have gradually deepened the underground aquifers, polluting them at the same time.

The form of the metropolitan area is monocentric. The central city of Celtic origins is clearly dominant. However, the presence of strong medium-sized centres with intense interrelations makes the metropolitan area more and more polycentric. During the postwar period, the historical settlements have grown, though few were destroyed in the process. Only those near the central city succumbed to the mass migrations of the 1950s and 1960s. Commuting is intense and still increasing.

Fully one-third of the region was urbanized in 1990/91. A further 8.8 per cent was already slated for urbanization. Another 18.7 per cent lacks zoning protection from the onslaught of urbanization. Urban development is barred in only 38.9 per cent of the region. The metropolitan core and the northern section of the suburban ring are clearly the most urbanized, but there is widely scattered development throughout the region, especially in the north. Only small parcels of undeveloped land remain, and their size prevents adequate conservation.

Since the 1970s, manufacturing plants have moved outward from central locations to the urban periphery and beyond into non-metropolitan areas. This has vastly increased the consumption of land, while areas in the central city and older industrial zones have been turned into wastelands. Industrial wasteland increased by 50 per cent in a brief period (1983–6), now covering an area equal to 7.5 per cent of the industrially zoned area. In 1990, 9.7 million square metres of wasteland (7.8 per cent of industrial land) remained unutilized. Of that unused land, 4.37 million square metres (31.3 per cent of the city's total area) is located in the central city and 5.35 million square metres (4.8 per cent) outside it. However, small plots (the average size of a piece of wasteland property is rarely greater than 5000 square metres) are reutilized quickly in a lively market. Lots in the central city are put back onto the market by rezoning from manufacturing to office, commercial or residential use. Elsewhere, manufacturing use persists, albeit on a much smaller scale.

Change of land use is an important issue. As tertiary functions expand, large manufacturing parcels and small residential plots alike are slated for rezoning. Corporate office buildings and other commercial land use take over the large lots abandoned by manufacturing. Professional and producer services set up on former residential plots. Although large-scale developments attract most public attention, the encroachment of office space on housing already involved 0.75 million square metres back in the 1970s. In the 1980s, office floor space increased by 38 per cent, of which half by piecemeal land use changes. The conversion process only slowed because of the massive increase in office building on former manufacturing land. This caused a glut on the office market just as the 1990s recession started.

Housing construction slowed in the 1970s and 1980s to around 15 000 dwellings a year. This represents just over half the output of the 1950s and 1960s. Most of the latest new construction is found outside the central city, which accounted for not more than a quarter of new housing. In fact, very little housing has been built in the central city since 1975. The housing stock in the rest of the metropolitan area increased, by one-quarter in the 1970s and by one-fifth in the 1980s (ignoring the loss through conversion). Also the expansion of the metropolitan stock slowed considerably in the 1970s and 1980s (above 120 000 and 80 000 respectively – Table 11.5).

Since 1971, the Milanese housing market has grown tighter. Milan's share of the national housing stock used to be greater than its share of the population, but these figures were reversed in 1981 and again in 1991. This is due to the decline of family households in Milan but also to housing developments elsewhere. One such factor is the boom in vacation homes in other parts of the country. Another is the tendency among migrants to retain their original homes in the south. The rate of home ownership in Milan is much lower than the average rate for the country. It was below 60 per cent in 1991, when the nationwide share was above 70 per cent. Rental stock is much more prevalent in the central city than outside, where the share resembles the national average. In the areas in the metropolitan ring, rental housing has dwindled.

Ownership in the private rental sector is very fragmented. Access to housing, especially for the middle class, is provided through market mechanisms. Less formal arrangements, such as housing included in a dowry, obtained through inheritance or self-built,

Table 11.5   Development of housing characteristics: numbers of
dwellings (thousands), occupancy, tenure and age (percentages)
1971–91

	Census year	Milan city	Milan province	Italy
Number of	1971	643	1 323	17 433
dwellings	1981	658	1 496	21 937
(000s)	1991	640	1 606	24 802
Occupied dwellings	1971	94.47	95.11	87.77
(%)	1981	93.16	93.32	79.96
	1991	90.03	92.21	78.66
Rental dwellings	1971	78.35	68.33	49.24
(%)	1981	64.49	53.32	41.09
	1991	48.86	37.92	n.a.
Pre-war dwellings	1971	77.85	67.60	68.96
(%)	1981	68.79	52.02	50.22
	1991	64.25	44.81	n.a.

are prevalent elsewhere in the country but scarce in Milan. Within
the region, such diverse arrangements are most prevalent in the
non-metropolitan areas. But informal networks (family, friends,
workmates) do play an important role in the dissemination of
information on housing vacancies.

Housing deprivation is now a typically metropolitan phenomenon, reflecting social marginality and the problem of affordability.
In particular the tens of thousands of immigrants from developing countries – and some local homeless people – either depend
on the voluntary sector for accommodation or rent sub-standard
private units. Social housing remains a good intention but ineffective. Young people in general and young families in particular
suffer from the affordability crisis. A relatively new group with
severe housing problems are the 'deprived owners' of low-value
housing. They are unable to sell out and move up, given the
increasing quality of new housing.

Real estate values tended to increase rapidly in the prosperous
years (especially in 1985–91), especially in the central city. The
values are very high, even by continental standards, and do not
seem to fall – at least in nominal terms – during recessions. Prices
did drop after 1992, when value assessments were made for the
introduction of a real estate tax. Poor-quality housing is not re-

flected in falling prices but rather in the depopulation of a neighbourhood and its subsequent rehabilitation. Price increases are more common, denoting an increase in home ownership, the potential for conversion to professional offices, the strong international demand in the central city since the 1980s and the drop in new supply. In fact, a sharp decline in new supply occurred in the 1980s, when many big developers shifted to more lucrative commercial projects.

The polity facing restructuring: overall goals and strategies

For 45 years, the Italian local political system has been based on proportional representation and on a balance of power tilted towards the councils (versus the mayors). In Milan, this system has been tinged by the hegemony of a strong and reformist Socialist Party, increasingly given to pure power brokering. Since 1975, left-wing majorities have dominated in first-ring municipalities and in Milan, while centrist ones have dominated the national and regional governments. The regions became important policy makers in the 1970s. For Milan, this meant a permanent state of central–local conflict. The influence of the national government in urban policy making has been negligible, with the exception of the period in which the Socialist Party dominated all the tiers of government. The characteristic conflicts translated into political instability, reducing institutional decisions to personal commitments. The conflicts also slowed the implementation of decisions and made local government unreliable.

The administrative systems, dating from 1915, are based on the French Napoleonic model and focused on ex ante legitimacy of decisions. They do not reflect the increasing complexity of policy issues. Nor do these systems take intergovernmental relations into account. Even the massive redistribution of powers in the round of administrative reform of 1977 did not improve the situation. The local authority areas have expanded greatly, generating stricter operational and financial constraints in the process. Local decision making had been curtailed by the public finance reform of 1971, which stripped local governments of their fiscal autonomy. The municipalities retained spending autonomy but were required to maintain a balanced budget. Meanwhile, the main source of local finance, transfers from the national government, dwindled. As the money ran out, the opportunities to implement new policies disappeared. The void could not be filled by turning to municipal enterprise, the alternative traditionally favoured by local government, because these companies were in trouble themselves.

After the crisis of the mid-1970s, Milan promoted itself anew in the early 1980s as a national leader. It also took on the new role of international gateway and tried to fit the profile of a continental node. Milan sought to become, in a word, a winner. Milan's role in Italy is historically curtailed. Italy has always been a polycentric country. Only in the mid-nineteenth century did it become a single state. Milan itself was the capital city of a regionwide government for five centuries. No metropolitan area, not even the capital city, dominates the urban system. In fact, Milan, the economic capital of the country, is on a par with Rome (Camagni and Pompili, 1990a, 1990b). However, metropolitan areas in Italy do not dominate the non-metropolitan ones, as witnessed in their socioeconomic performance. Twenty years of Italian debate on local competitiveness have emphasized the comparative advantages of districts and metropolitan areas, milieux and networks alike (Pompili, 1992, 1996).

Nevertheless, the position and role of Milan in Europe as one of continental primacy (London and Paris excluded) emerged clearly from data on the early 1980s (Camagni and Pio, 1988). This situation persists, although more recent data indicate a decline in dynamics during the 1980s (Mutti, 1993).

We have sketched above the challenge to Milan. We turn now to its response. The strategy apparently adopted to achieve the envisioned continental role is to be competitive. Local policies are viewed and designed as instruments to that end. The 1980s were years of debate and proposals, reflected in a multiplication of research, monitoring and policy-advising agencies. These were the successors of an intermunicipal planning centre (founded in the 1960s by the city of Milan and a hundred surrounding municipalities) and the regional research institute (founded in the 1970s by Region Lombardy). Among these efforts and agencies we encounter an applied research project, a joint city–province economic and planning monitoring unit, a consortium of advanced research institutes operated jointly by the private sector and the universities, and a mutually operated think-tank. Each of these undertakings involved academic and corporate participants, to carry out the analysis and to formulate policy proposals. Surprisingly, no new permanent initiative on public finance was created. Despite this wealth of expertise, few policies were formulated. Those that were put forward were never implemented. The early 1990s are years of involution.

Part of the problem can be formulated in theoretical terms. The principal's goal is a persistently high quality of life in terms of health, social integration, job opportunities, job security, income level and so on. But the agents' goals (hence strategies) may differ. Private decision makers (landowners, developers and, especially, employers/producers) tend to pursue maximum profits, and the main goal of public decision makers (state, region, province, but above all city politicians and bureaucrats) is to stay in power. The diverse aims of the agents tend to prevail, as some of these agents (state and region) also function as regulators.

Policy responses

Urban planning and metropolitan policy

Planning is the most important power of local government. This is the field where the goals of public and private agents are most likely to conflict. And conflict will occur unless maximum profits from physical development are equated a priori with maximum city efficiency and equity considerations are discounted.

Italian planning law (codified in 1942) assumes the existence of a rational public decision maker with the same interests as the community. This assumption is also encountered in the regional planning laws of the 1970s (for Lombardy codified in 1975 and 1984). Consequently, the planning authority sets its own standards of behaviour and defines the correct (hierarchical) relationships between planning levels. This concept of planning also excludes ex ante (bargaining/agreement) relationships with private interests and citizens. Instead, only as-of-right permits are allowed and the intervention is evaluated by observation after the fact.

Such an unrealistic framework is sure to cause problems, exacerbated by the paucity of the planning authorities' expertise in design and control and by the short terms of office for political personnel. There are four types of problems. First, the top-down hierarchy of plans tends to ignore the issue of implementation. The plans are based on abstract analyses and set unrealistic goals. Furthermore, decisions are open to legal challenges and the coordination between technical and financial decisions is poor. Secondly, the plans are based on prior consultations with interested actors, but these are not closely regulated. The consultations are indirect. They take place through bureaucratic or political channels, which creates opportunities for bribery. There is little transparency in the procedures. This is inevitable when alternatives are conceptualized as an opposition of rigidity and discretionalism (in favour of the former). Flexibility is not considered to be a merit. Thirdly, major projects require planning by agreement between public and private agents to achieve a real step forward for the city. This improves the chances of implementation, given the need for financial and other private resources. Fourthly, large-scale planning also requires contact between tiers of government. Otherwise, the legality of the public monopoly of supply may be challenged unless there is high demand.

Attempts to address these problems in the 1980s leaned heavily on business experience. The planning approach became a goal-oriented, problem-solving, decision making process (strategic planning). In this context, the various public and private interests are recognized as potentially conflictual but share a desired outcome. Planning ceases to be a zero-sum game. Nevertheless, attempts aimed at resolving the last two problems, in particular, have apparently failed (see below) (Centro Studi PIM, 1993).

Up to the latest general regulatory plan (city approval 1976, regional ratification 1980), the abundance of resources led people to believe that efficiency and equity issues might be reconciled through planning. Since then, however, conditions have changed. The lack of resources and the presence of a left-wing political option led the authorities to give the primacy to the goal of equity. That could only be pursued through strong planning control. Planning was considered to be the sole instrument to reach the many goals of overall development. It was supposed to accommodate the constraints and hierarchical decision making resulting from the inherently conflictual relationship between public and private agents and between levels of government. It also had to cater to the pro-manufacturing ideology bent on commercial development. The ability to control development was vastly overrated, and the power of the market mechanisms was never given due credit. Despite these expectations, the reality proved to be different. Expropriation and utopianism of planning-led development in a pluralistic social context allowed only piecemeal implementation. Control over the myriad land use changes in the central city was never achieved. In practice, the authorities bent to the pressure to rezone industrial wasteland outside the central city and to redevelop it into commercial centres.

The *Documento Direttore* (which was given city approval in 1984), was allowed by a new regional law. It was inspired by the logic of French 'schémas directeurs'. These are essentially strategic programme agreements among public agents, incorporating major private agents when necessary. They dispense with the requirement to make detailed plans and specify constraints. Since their introduction, the efficiency considerations have predominated. Public–private as well as public–public cooperation replaced the ambition for strategic planning starting at the drawing-board stage. However, the intellectual left and the university planners voiced their opposition to this approach. They opposed it on methodological grounds (being against the involvement of private and localist interests in the definition of the general public good). And they also opposed it because it would weaken social and spatial equity principles.

Metropolitan-scale planning, primarily involving relationships between government tiers, dealt with the coordination of plans. While its ambition was to be prescriptive, it did not bind the municipalities. Planning only had effects when the plans were rewritten in strategic terms and linked to proposals for major infrastructure. These plans never became operational, in contrast to city planning. Nor did they prevent the proliferation of spontaneous local committees, usually the personification of the NIMBY syndrome, which were often supported by the local authorities.

Major projects primarily involved public–private agent relationships. More precisely, they entailed the restructuring of industrial areas by private landowners, after securing local government approval. Such integrated projects brought together for the first time various private agents (manufacturing companies, development companies, banks, industrial associations). Even so, an open discussion among conflicting interests was avoided, which eventually caused implementation to fail. In some cases, the formal decisions upon which they were based were even retracted by court order.

Industrial wasteland was regulated by the region in 1981 and again in 1990. However, the regulation never addressed city planning issues. A plan is only required when the size of a redevelopment project could affect long-term urban prospects. The presence of wasteland lay at the roots of most major projects, such as the international fair (city and regional agreement 1994) and two technology centres (agreement protocols 1985, regional ratification 1989 and 1993, respectively) inside and outside the central city. Only the transport projects such as the underground regional railway (agreement protocols 1985) and the intercontinental airport (projects in 1979 and 1986) were not inspired by the availability of wasteland. These transport projects also involved different private actors (namely, the state and regional railways, the national air carrier and the municipal airport corporation). Apparently, the fact that these were publicly (state) owned made it difficult for them to take financial responsibility. In general, progress was a serious problem. The timing was badly miscalculated. The public decision-making process involves multiple steps. And there was a political yearning for unanimity. These plans are still not fully implemented, having suffered from the 1990s economic recession.

The power of big developers became a central issue in the political debate. The opposing positions were to stop all speculation or to give free rein to developers. Yet the fact that developers continue to start projects in the city shows that it is alive and viable. The key issue is how to harness private resources and to stimulate competition. For lack of a demand-led local economic policy, decisions are made by a supply-led private land value policy. The general regulatory plans barely regulate. They simply register major land use changes, ex post. Thereby, they have forgone the opportunity to take a strategic approach. In reality, however, bargaining over planning did take place. It led to a culture of bribe taking, to the extent that it has been said that major projects were 'invented just to reap bribes'. Currently, both public opinion and the polity seem to have given up hope of reconciliation among public and private interests. Some advocate rigid planning constraints, environmental conservationism and the zero-development philosophy. Others propose equating sectoral private interests with the public good.

Another issue of planning failure has been debated only among specialists because of its minor electoral impact. This issue concerns small-scale land use change. In the past, the economic, social and cultural change of the city resulted in the development of new parts of the city. Yet, nowadays, attempts are made to limit the urbanization process. Thus functional symbiosis may become functional conflict. Two contrasting consequences arise. On the one hand, there is greater need to control land use change within the built-up city. On the other, widely dispersed spontaneous development is taking place, which may fundamentally modify the city itself. Yet it cannot be controlled because of its functional (rather than morphological) nature.

The impact of land use change (micro and macro) bears little relationship to the volume of construction. In a clear case of overestimating the effectiveness of regulation, the volume of construction was cited as a reason to defend vulnerable and mixed land use. Actually, regulations were gradually weakened for lack of a general regulatory link between land use change and planning (as opposed to architectural) criteria. This hollowing out was aggravated by allowing major changes. Some were made by applying the 50 per cent rule for tertiary development in industrial areas. Others were facilitated by the 1982 national judicial deregulation of small land use changes where no building permit is needed (in such cases, only notification is required). Indeed, building rehabilitation has often coincided with planning blight, leading to degradation of quality of social life both inside and outside the central city. The issue can be recast in terms of planning procedures. Since control is not feasible, policy should utilize incentives (participation in local planning) rather than prescriptions.

City planning has been by far the most actively pursued policy option in Milan. This is the area where public agents became most involved. Therefore the consequences of its failure – brought about by excessive time lags in decision making and implementation – are particularly serious. However, excluding periodic voting choices, the principal's interest was clearly focused on the one issue of immediate concern: small-scale land use change.

Policies to promote metropolitan efficiency

These policies are the least contentious, since the goals of private and public agents generally do not conflict. The main agents on the supply side are not the municipalities but the region or even the state. This strengthens the public role, as the region subscribes to the principle of competitive demand.

The Italian Constitution restricts the regional role in overall economic development of a territorial community. The regional authorities do wield powers in specific economic sectors 'with local content' (agriculture, crafts, fairs, tourism and vocational training). However, the experience gained through restructuring of the 1970s and 1980s proved this interpretation to be both inadequate and impracticable. The regions (of which Lombardy has always been one of the most active) were directly elected for the first time in 1970. Initially (up to 1977) the regions claimed a role in economic planning and set out to create the necessary instruments (statistical and financial). However, since 1978, the regions have opted for a gradual widening and functional integration of their role in economic development initiatives (IReR, 1993). They moved to make their influence felt in not yet legislated issues (disadvantaged groups of the labour force, small and starting firms, research and innovation, export promotion). Initially, this was tolerated by the state but, eventually, the national law makers endorsed neo-centralization. Only in 1991 was a national law passed that defined small-business industrial districts as a policy area for or by the regions.

Future constitutional reform will enshrine the region as the appropriate governmental tier for issues of the economic environment (but not for the economy). Developmental powers will be designated by field and no longer by activity. The metropolitan area, and a fortiori its central city, is widely assumed to have the appropriate expertise and the necessary efficiency, at least by Italian standards. Therefore, so far there has not been a real public debate, let alone initiatives, in metropolitan economic policy, except when mediated by planning. As law-making and policy-making powers were vested in the region (apart from those reserved by the state), policies were not designed for the metropolitan area. Such initiatives have remained limited to declining old industrial areas. This void has, however, been partially filled by private actors (industrial associations, chambers of commerce and universities) and by regional and municipal enterprises.

Other important policy initiatives concern long-term transport plans. The national and local expressway network, including ring roads, was completed by 1973, but rail transport has remained seriously inadequate for years. The expectations for goods transport are not optimistic (road transport will continue to account for over four-fifths of the total). Improvements in passenger service, including high-speed railways and a regional railway, have been planned since the mid-1980s. The full impact will not be clear before the late 1990s. Finally, the air transport system in Milan, managed by a municipally owned company, has increased its facilities from one to three airports since the early 1970s, yet supply cannot meet demand. Investment has remained sluggish, as the national air carrier concentrated all its efforts on Rome's airports.

City-marketing remained subdued as a competitive strategy to attract outside investors. Its absence in Milan is clear – or rather, an explicit and coherent city-marketing policy that is linked to actual developments in the city is absent. Several indicators confirm this. There is little or no private or public interest in high costs and low quality/price ratios for business and cultural tourism. The issue of inadequate international (airport) accessibility has met with a minimal response. The forgone opportunity for learning and marketing provided by city twinning and city networks raises no protest. The attitude towards the foreign press remains passive. The only initiatives have involved image-building campaigns. These have been linked to (often foiled) bids to attract big international events or institutions. Such prizes were coveted less for their intrinsic value than as an excuse to improve the city's infrastructure by building public works while applying emergency procedures. (An added benefit would be that simplified procedures 'to cut red tape' would facilitate bribe taking.)

Implicitly, the general consensus was that the city did not really need an active promotion policy. The strong private sector was seen as a guarantee of success. The problems of some of Milan's industries of national prominence (for instance, the Stock Exchange) could supposedly only be resolved by new national legislation. Even the principal did not seem to expect much from its local agents, except possibly during the trough of the recession. At that time, the populace expected its agents to advocate the preservation of local jobs.

Policies to safeguard metropolitan equity

The promotion of equity includes safeguarding access to local transport, housing, welfare and social services. This task is still principally the domain of the state. The state acts as the regulator (except in the field of social services) and as the source of finance for the public agent, that is, the municipalities. In the past, finance for capital expenditures (infrastructure) could be secured without planning for future management. The municipalities now pay the price for this omission, and this constrains future policy options. One area where this is abundantly clear is on the issue of institutionalized care for the elderly, but across the board, the decision to switch tracks brings about a high-cost transitional period. At the same time, the principals' demand is increasing and diversifying more rapidly than public supply is able to accommodate. Private agents cannot usually step in, because they tend to have limited financial autonomy. This entices private agents to comply with the municipal service standard. But, above all, they are enticed to comply by replacing the maximum profit goal with one of minimum uncertainty. This has maximized the supply to the public at below-market prices.

The main provision for local private transport, the ring roads, was completed by 1973, although widening has been undertaken subsequently. Dedicated infrastructure for public transport (rail) is less complete. Within the central city, the underground network comprises two lines dating back to the 1960s (1964 and 1968). Over the last 20 years, the expansion of the system has been slow. The third line was opened only in 1990, and the plans for the fourth line were shelved in late 1993. Thus, although the Milan network is the most developed of Italian underground rail systems, it remains insufficient by European standards. Since the late 1980s, the construction of 'light metro' surface lines has been discussed, but this interest basically reflects marketing initiatives by potential producers. Another public initiative has been the provision of an underground connection between the state railway stations in Milan. This project could eventually be a building-block in a regional railway service like the one in Paris. While the decision to go ahead was made in 1984, the link is still under construction. The project ran into serious trouble when the state reduced its support for the national railways. It has also suffered a serious setback from a scandal over illegal contributions to political parties.

Public transport in Italy is heavily subsidized, for equity reasons especially. This reduces the effective fares substantially. Milan's public transport (run by a municipal enterprise) comprises the underground railway, tramways, trolley bus routes, and regular bus lines. The system provides extensive coverage of the city of Milan, also at off-peak hours and at night, and is extremely popular. However, despite their low cost, there are few dedicated lanes. Consequently, the average speed is low and the service cannot run on schedule in peak hours. The public transport network still provides good coverage of the nearby part of the metropolitan area, with good connections to the central city. Service further out is provided by subsidized private bus companies and by state or regional railways. Ring links in the network remain uncommon, however, possibly capping the growth of demand for them.

Housing (IReR, 1991) is largely subject to national regulation. Since the mid-1970s, owner occupancy has been promoted by widely available bank mortgages. Other policy instruments comprise subsidies to self-building cooperatives and municipal price-control agreements with private developers. However, the sale of publicly owned real property has remained limited, as the first enabling legislation dates from only 1991 and 1992. Rent controls were lifted only in 1978. They have been replaced by 'fair rent' acts, which set objective criteria for the rent level, but since these do not adequately take inflation into account, the effect has been increasing scarcity of supply on the legal market. Since 1993, controlled rents have been phased out in favour of free market rents. This also provides some compensation to owners for the introduction of a new real-estate tax.

Since 1962, public housing construction has benefited from a national law. In Milan, that legislation was embedded in a deeply rooted tradition of both provincial housing boards (since the First World War) and municipal activity (also via inter-municipal consortia, established in 1972 in Milan). Public housing has accounted for 30 per cent of all new housing. But even the Milan housing board controlled only 12 per cent of the local housing stock in the 1970s. During the postwar period, public housing construction provided recent immigrant working-class families with better housing in the periphery than elsewhere in Europe, in terms of architectural quality, servicing and accessibility. Social and age-based segregation has subsequently emerged. In 1978, ten-year housing plans were introduced (such as the Milan consortium's 1979–87 plan).

During the 1970s, full services were being provided to older public estates, while new ones were built fully serviced. But public housing construction declined, especially in the 1980s, remaining relatively important only in the central city. Its prominence here is mostly due to the weak performance of private construction. However, private building has changed in nature. Most recent private building, especially by large private construction firms, has been largely publicly agreed and publicly constrained, in terms of mixture and prices. In contrast, in pure private building for the market, local authorities and institutional investors tend to intervene only as a buyer/renter of last resort. A Milan housing plan proposed in 1982 (and decided upon in 1986) was apparently a successful public–private agreement. It was born of a lack of public resources and the private sector's need to put an end to the standardization of supply as a way to reflect more closely the variations in demand. However, one developer exploited an information advantage derived from links to the political elite, thus acquiring a pre-emptive land monopoly.

Until recently there has not been much concern about the depletion of the potential supply of land, but two regional laws, passed in 1986 and 1990 signalled the official end of major city expansion planning which started with the first general regulatory plan in 1889. This demonstrates the general shift in focus from quantitative growth to qualitative improvements, which had started to become visible in the late 1970s. Residential rehabilitation plans, now automatically part of general regulatory plans, specifically aim at upgrading historical peripheries through both restructuring and rebuilding.

Welfare issues remain regulated by the state: old-age and disability pensions are not a matter for local policy. However, since pensioners tend not to make their needs explicit in the form of demand, private-sector involvement remains limited. Therefore, in addition to the institutional solution provided by nursing home care, facilities to link demand and supply are being set up, and self-help is encouraged. Municipal enterprises also play a role (for example, pharmacies and the milk board).

Social services cover education (including pre-school and kindergarten, compulsory education being the norm in this metropolitan area), health, social aid and cultural–recreational services. The last two categories of service tend to reinforce social stratification, along lines of age, education and birthplace. Exclusion from all but the most basic services (general health and compulsory education) reinforces social marginality. The bottleneck in social services provision remains the lack of a single access point, such as is provided by the general practitioner in the field of health services. Social aid services are by their very nature selective and specific but therefore also ill-equipped to deal with multiple deprivation.

Education and health are regulated and financed at the national level, while social services fall under the jurisdiction of the regions (Ciorli and Tosi, 1986; Ranci, 1989). Lombardy's 1986 law (which has been fully implemented since 1991) is based on the principles of unitary, universal, free and equal provision. It operates according to a method of three-year needs and resources planning with an annual census of resources. And it sets management and structural standards enforced through inspections. The 1986 law caused a change in the private agents' identity. This accelerated the replacement of free voluntary (religious) bodies by contractual public–private (and also private–private) arrangements. Private providers of services have to meet minimum standards, but the limited financial resources of private agents constrains organizational autonomy. Another safeguard of quality is that families in Italy cover part of the cost of services (unlike the situation in other countries). Consequently, they demand a high quality of service.

The public–private distinction in provision is fading, although the public sector still provides the norm for quality–price ratios. Furthermore, the public agent retains its regulating role, collects information and distributes it to users. The role of the public sector has thus clearly shifted from the provision of services to planning and control, while cutting its expenditures. Most private agents are currently still largely publicly financed, but the entry of insurance-type private agents is foreseen. They can offer low costs because of the large volume of their product. Also others may join the fray, offering turnkey investments and management for the affluent segment of the market.

In the 1970s, an income-based logic for social aid prevailed. This monetized needs and institutionalized the weakest groups. Entitlement-based programmes were also supported by active grass-roots movements. Budget constraints were not a priority, and management practices did not distinguish between efficiency and effectiveness. In those years, programmes proliferated, decentralization to municipal authorities took effect, prevention was emphasized instead of care and quality standards were widely

adopted (on the UK example). Political conflicts emerged as the
family-centred views of the 1950s and 1960s were superseded by
public-centred ones. The most contentious issue was the provision
of municipal childcare centres. However, even in Milan, social
service provision throughout the metropolitan area was achieved
only in the late 1980s.

In the early 1980s, tight resources provoked a backlash. Top
priority was then given to decision making and efficiency, which
meant a limited implementation of previous laws. The backlash
underlined the decline of grass-roots movements and the emergence of lobbies (including charities, social cooperatives and associations). This process also signalled a shift from pressure on public services to self-organization. In the early 1990s, a logic based
on entitlement to social security prevailed. The aim was to integrate people in their own social context (family, neighbourhood).
Although effectiveness remained as important as it was in the
1970s, this goal became embedded in the context of privatization
of the 1980s. Even non-profit organizations view services as a
business, competing in terms of quality. As in other organizations,
management is their most important resource.

The shift in policy towards a competitive strategy has not been
very deliberate, possibly because it was non-partisan. The shift
has been most evident at management level rather than at the
political or operational level. In a social sense, equity policies are
still not considered to be part of a competitive strategy of the city.
The equity policies are treated differently because of the culture of
the service providers and the decision makers. An additional factor is the efficiency–equity trade-off. It is difficult to define the
profit that goes to the producers, when these are private individuals, except in terms of the reduction of the visibility of social
problems. The approach of the public agent is to manage equity
issues efficiently and this provides three ways to meet current
challenges. The first option is to reduce the total budget of social
services by cutting all benefits. At best, this could coincide with a
choice for quality improvement by making innovations, but not
by economizing on labour inputs.

The second option is to renounce the entitlement principle in
favour of affirmative action. Entitlement is derived from general
citizenship rights and an assumed equitable endowment. This
implies an equally distributed supply, limited only by site availability, need intensity and supply–take-up mismatches. It results
in inertia of expenditure over time. In contrast, positive discrimination (affirmative action) is linked to the individual's right of
self-determination. This approach implies a distinction between

basic universal rights and priority-based access in a dual service network. In such a network, the non-basic services are allocated on the basis of social characteristics defined as relevant by the supplier (for instance, income or profession). The price of services plays no role in this allocation.

The third option is to shift from public provision to private provision of services. The providers may be informal groups (social networks), non-profit associations (which are undergoing a genetic mutation from religious boards to social coops) or even for-profit organizations. This would lead to a new role for the public service providers (safeguarding price competition, innovation and quality).

Spatial equity concerns equality of opportunities across the metropolitan territory. In this respect, Milan is increasingly a polycentric metropolis, but not by a conscious policy of the central city or the region. The city is rarely given to a truly metropolitan vision. The region remains more interested in reinstating equilibrium in favour of non-metropolitan areas. Polycentrism (functional diversification) results from the success that local communities have had in attracting Milanese functions. These communities are thus becoming more like the central city. Their governments have been more effective in providing infrastructure and services and in preserving visibility than the historical centre.

The spatial distribution of the supply of services is a disputed issue. It is possible to choose equity (through the preservation of minimum standards) without ensuring equal access or take-up. Otherwise the choice would be to match the supply to spatial inequities in demand (ranging from observed need to actual use). The latter option ascribes a redistributive role to services. In practice, the former option is generally chosen. One reason is that for many services this situation has been achieved only recently, as problems of site availability persist. The central city was better endowed and its population less needy. But the residents of the core are no longer the least needy nor the best supplied.

With respect to these policies, the principals were least content to express their preferences only at election time. Some measure of success has been achieved in terms of improved urban equity of services provision. At least there has been some improvement relative to the country as a whole, though probably not compared to Europe. Another noted outcome is the ability to adopt more management-based (if not market-based) approaches under pressure of financial constraints.

Policies to control metropolitan externalities

The concern over the quality of the environment, focused on the issues of pollution and congestion, was highly visible throughout the 1980s. This has encouraged national rather than règional legislation. In this field, the conflict between individual and collective goals is perhaps most compelling. In fact, it is often difficult to see policy frameworks as defining some sort of market context. The reason is that private individuals do not really compete. However, an externality–efficiency trade-off emerges during periods of recession. Under economically more prosperous conditions, the NIMBY syndrome is more likely to prevail.

Environmental policies focus on green spaces, waste and energy. The importance of green areas was recognized during the 1970s. Consequently, the region established natural parks in the mountains and in river valleys, some of which were located on the fringes of the metropolis. In 1985, a major step was taken to restrict development by regional law. Yet conservation planning has still not been integrated with urban development. This jeopardizes the nature preserves on their fringes. Moreover, the creation and maintenance of green spaces within urban areas proves to be increasingly difficult, except for municipal parks.

In the city of Milan, the collection of waste is managed by a municipal agency. It started the trend of separating waste (glass, paper, batteries, medicine). Since then, several other municipalities have followed suit, with some success. However, an increasingly serious intraregional conflict has emerged regarding disposal methods: incineration versus dumping. This led to a permanent disposal crisis in the central city. So far, the municipality has refused to build sufficient capacity for incineration to process its own waste. Consequently, NIMBY objections to metropolitan incineration plants now compete with NIMBY objections to non-metropolitan dumping sites.

Energy in Milan is the responsibility of a municipal agency, rather than the nationalized board. It also serves several of the nearby municipalities. There has been a gradual move towards less polluting generating plants (located away from the city). In the late-1970s, the municipalization of the city gasworks allowed for widespread use of natural gas. But no action was taken on proposals for (energy-saving) district heating.

Pollution controls deal with air, water, noise and the cityscape. The level of air pollution was serious enough to mobilize public opinion early. Conditions were also worsened by the unfavourable characteristics of the local atmospheric system. Consequently, industrially generated pollution has been reduced by the strict application of a 1976 law. The conversion of collective heating plants to natural gas (1984–94) has also led to significant improvement. The emissions from car traffic have been largely unregulated. The exception is the introduction of monitoring in the central city (the first and still the best system in Italy) and parts of the metropolitan area. Only occasionally since the late 1980s, when pollution limits were exceeded, has private car traffic in the central city been banned.

The regulation of water resources is difficult because the jurisdiction is fragmented. Most water resources fall under municipal control. This unfavourable situation should be redressed by reforms that have been instigated by the adoption of a new national law, passed in 1993. The provisions spelled out in the clean water act of 1976 have been applied throughout the metropolitan area. There is one major exception: faced with local opposition, the central city did not build a sewage treatment plant. Finally, river purification plans were also an issue raised in the 1980s at the regional level, but private–public collusion and corruption prevented the implementation of such plans.

Awareness levels about noise and cityscape pollution are still fairly low among the general public. Therefore no policy initiatives have been discussed.

Congestion is always a serious concern in a monocentric city that is two thousand years old. The policies have focused on diverting truck traffic from the central city. This is to be accomplished by the outward relocation of manufacturing plants and building a new customs office on the periphery. However, progress on this facility has been exceedingly slow. After years of discussion and work, it is still not open for business. Furthermore, policies have also focused on public transport. Its use is encouraged through the construction of municipal underground railway lines. However, the demand for mobility has increased more rapidly than the supply of travel modes that offer an alternative to private cars. Eventually, the authorities decided to prohibit car access to the city centre during office hours. This decision was taken after a referendum in 1985. Recently, there have been lively debates on a road-pricing system, but no concrete steps have been taken yet.

Is success feasible in this field of policy? Certainly both principal and agents are much more aware of the problem and have gone further towards resolving it than elsewhere in the country. There is even some awareness that the issues may affect the competitive position of the city. But with respect to concrete measures, Milan clearly lags behind the rest of Europe.

Policies for metropolitan government

The principal–agent approach is most appropriate in this context. The principal demands collective decisions from public decision makers. With elections always in the background as a threat, the citizens use their votes as leverage to maximize their own well-being. At the same time, bureaucrats and (competing) politicians demand resources from private decision makers. The authorities use legally binding decisions as leverage to maximize their own power and its durability.

The main problem in the government of the metropolitan area of Milan, and especially of its central city, is the increasing ineffectiveness of decision making (IReR, 1992). Attempts have been made to bypass the bottleneck through national urban policies. This is evident in the creation of a Ministry of Urban Areas in the late 1980s, a post first held by a former mayor of Milan. The adjustment of political systems started in earnest with the passing of national reform laws in 1990 and 1993. That legislation gave more autonomy to local governments and, within them, more power to the executive branch, that is, the mayors. However, the main agent for change was not the political elite. The reforms followed the ongoing uncovering since 1992 of 'Tangentopoli' (Bribesville) by the judiciary. The new structure must replace the all-party decision-making cartel that controls planning, public works and procurement, and municipal enterprises. The reforms were also stimulated by the action of the electorate, which voted overwhelmingly for the Lega (Lega Lombarda) after 1990. The suspicion, however, is that the cartel broke down because the economic recession made its costs too high for the private sector, while the lack of implementation made its cost-effectiveness too low for citizens. Its breakdown resulted in the local election reform of 1993. One of its key provisions, the direct election of mayors, led to the disappearance of the old political elites. The process of electoral reform was expected to continue through the 1994 national and European elections as well as the 1995 local and regional elections. Possibly, the energies would then turn towards constitutional reform, restructuring national–regional relations in a federal or quasi-federal way. This process remains inconclusive due to the new political stalemate that emerged after the election. The danger is that the victory of 'common sense' will simply mean that the authorities will be unable or unwilling to see the 'big picture.' Instead of trying to meet challenges, they may narrow their focus to limited public and private interests.

The second major problem of government is the inefficiency of implementation. The overhaul of administrative systems was de-

layed until after the 1990 reform of local government. This reform
consolidated the autonomy of local governments. At the same
time, it enhanced the autonomy of technocrats rather than politicians (the judiciary having failed to eradicate petty corruption
among bureaucrats). The proposal to create a metropolitan province seems to have been dropped. The issue of taxation and
finance has become increasingly important, especially after the
financial and budget constraints were tightened under the Fiscal
Reform Acts (1971). The response to the growing managerial and
financial difficulties has been a call for more public–private cooperation. However, many good intentions have been given lip-
service only. This is especially clear if one ignores the illegal side-
effects of the delegitimization of collective control over sectoral
interests. New interest in local taxation powers and the resulting
efficiency–equity trade-off did not emerge until the late 1980s. It
was boosted by the introduction of municipal rates in 1992 and
the concomitant cuts in social benefits. That interest became increasingly visible in the early 1990s, as the concern with constitutional reform came to a head. The ensuing debate revolved around
regionalism versus federalism. These issues found a tangible expression in proposals for fiscal federalism, a formula for redistributing powers between the state and the regions.

Conclusion

Milan's performance in the 1970s and 1980s is characterized by an
increasing potential of human resources and other urban inputs.
This was offset by a stagnant infrastructure and a deterioration of
intermediate inputs (decision making). Production and exports,
both already at high levels, increased further, strengthening the
role that Milan had traditionally filled. The city was able to resist
competition from non-metropolitan areas. Rising competition was
even countered in the 1980s, when a European challenge was
taken up. Its profitability was expanded in the 1980s with respect
to most indicators (such as value added, built-up area and real
estate values). Population size was the only indicator that did not
increase. Growth continued until 1990–91. During the subsequent
economic downturn, the city experienced an extremely serious
crisis in its political performance.

In spite of the recession of the 1970s, Milan successfully defended its traditional role as a national leader. The city went on to
consolidate its more recent position of international gateway thanks
to the prosperity of the 1980s. This success reflects its own abso-

lute advantage, which is based on the ineffectiveness of the competitors rather than the merits of its own competitive policies.

In some situations, Milan could not build on existing advantages: for instance, in its quest for a nodal role on the continental scale. Apparently, the city was then unable to harness its potential. From following close on the heels of London and Paris, it has slipped to the level of the cities that had been behind it. And now even its leadership in south-central Europe is subject to more intense competition. Thus the question arises whether Milan simply experienced success by default. If so, that success would have subsequently turned into failure when global conditions were no longer favourable. The city's apparent inability to design effective policies requires an examination of public decision making.

Planning policy, was the locus of the city's competitive effort. The fact that the effort failed for lack of implementation is a serious flaw. Moreover, it remains unclear to what extent planning policy was supported by the principals other than the intellectual elites. However, the argument that the quest for metropolitan competitiveness must be based on planning has been won. And since planning will remain the prime power of city government in the foreseeable future, the city's strength should not decline.

Policies to boost efficiency have been missing so far. The agents have been waiting for national legislation or have been counting on the private sector. In this respect, the agents were not corrected by the principals. This situation may not last. Competition on the continental scale will require a more effective form of public–private interdependence. However, as regional legislative powers become strengthened by the impending creation of a metropolitan province, they must address this issue.

Equity policy was actively pursued for its own sake. At the same time, it was taken up because the public could easily be mobilized to play a direct role. Equity policy was not propagated as furthering the city's competitiveness. Nevertheless, the pursuit of equity did not diminish Milan's leadership, or undermine its role as gateway to the rest of Italy. Equity policy will continue to coalesce.

Policy to correct externalities was designed to deal with increasingly obvious problems. Partly, such policy was formulated in response to pressure by the principals. The connection with competition was perceived. However, it is not easy to reconcile the long-term advantages and the adverse short-term effects of these policies on competitiveness. As the pressure from the principal grows to regulate more stringently, this difficulty will increase.

Government policy, and politics in particular, remain a liability in the region. They have weakened the crucial link between decision making and implementation. This situation is further aggravated by corruption. In fact, the failure of other policies was not really brought about by disagreement. Rather, the cause was poor implementation and sometimes flawed design. Despite a wealth of analyses and proposals, there was no follow-up in the form of operational decisions. Implementation often ignored time constraints. This weakened the possible contribution of infrastructure to metropolitan competitiveness. Even though management has a lower symbolic value to the principals, management remains more crucial than infrastructure. The former is a precondition for solving problems with respect to the latter. In sum, the major bottleneck remained the production of intermediate inputs, that is urban decision making.

The concept of intermetropolitan competition provided a perspective for restructuring processes that were already under way. In this respect, it was a successful strategy. However, the value of this concept changed when the period of prosperity ended. The old ways of decision making had been adequate to retain national leadership, but it became clear that these procedures were grossly inadequate to achieve a continental advantage, or even to maintain existing leads.

Why did the agents in Milan (the decision makers) fail to supply their principals (the population) with living conditions of the same standards as in the rest of the continent? The failure to reach that goal curtailed the growth of the city, as measured by any indicator. And how can the decision making be improved, allowing Milan to realize its full potential in the future? A technical explanation is that failure resulted from the lack of a global strategy. Specifically, it was caused by the interdependence of diverse policies, all of which were related to urban planning, but not based on real metropolitan needs. The appropriate response would be to reorganize the command structure of local government. One official (acting as mayor and secretary-general) 'endowed with vision' and his office would be elevated high above the others. This actually happened in the early 1990s. Indeed, inasmuch as vision depends on expert advice, the area has a long, rich tradition of think-tanks and academic consultants. However, in this particular case, this response missed the point. In Milan, failure did not emanate from content or from a particular policy mix. Rather, it was due to poor timing and sheer lack of implementation.

A more charitable explanation is that there were real limits to what could be achieved by local decision makers. They had to act in accordance with their role in the regulatory system. This would support the drive for a constitutional reallocation of power towards a federal state and largely autonomous local governments. The latter was already partially arranged by reform laws in the early 1990s, while the former is still under discussion. However, this response is partial at best and may prove to be a delusion. In a state with multiple tiers of government – that is, a proliferation of public decision makers – the issue of intergovernmental conflict is bound to arise. The real issue then becomes how to identify conflict-solving procedures.

The most widespread explanation is that failure was caused by an ethical problem. The problem is said to be one of excessive corruption, of biased goals and strategies on the actors' side and/ or of ineffective control by the city's principals. If this is the case, the appropriate response would be to replace the old political elite with a new, supposedly honest one. At the same time, bureaucrats should be subjected to private labour market discipline. An alternative, perhaps complementary, response would be to change the institutions. This would entail a move from a feudal to an absolutist decision-making system. Such a shift could be accomplished by strengthening the legitimacy and powers of mayors vis-à-vis councils and political parties. Another means to this end is to separate the powers of top bureaucrats from those of top politicians. Since mid-1993, both these remedies have been tried in Milan, and in Italy generally. However, once more this response is partial. It requires a leap of faith to assume that the new elites will forever stay honest under the new rules. That notwithstanding, this does not tackle the issue of the relationship between private and public agents.

Overall, these responses to the decision-making crisis clarify the rewards to political and bureaucratic decision makers. The political decision makers are identified, which makes them accountable to the electorate. The responsibilities of the bureaucrats are distinguished from those of the politicians. This strengthens the incentives for politicians to monitor the bureaucracy. However, rational principals realize that it is efficient to delegate decisions and to exercise control only in the medium term at election time. This does not apply to cases where interests are immediately affected. Short-term reactions are only likely when the cause–effect link is apparent in the short run. Apart from this, recent experience shows that the responses have focused on the agents rather than on the more important relationships between them. In particular, the responses missed the crucial point of metropolitan competitiveness. A competitive position is served by interdependence of public and private decision making. Post-Bribesville consensus seems to prefer the easy way out by returning to the traditional rule of independence and separation, a rule that has been invalid for two decades. The current solutions will therefore invite new violations of the rule in the future.

Acknowledgements

The author acknowledges the cooperation of dr. Z. Moscheni (Comune di Milano), dr. C. Boesi (Regione Lombardia), dr. A. Carvelli and dr. A. Ciorli (Istituto Regionale di Ricerca della Lombardia), arch. L. Minotti and arch. S. D'Agostini (Centro Studi Piano Inter-comunale Milanese). They provided invaluable information. However, the author remains solely responsible for this text.

References

Arrow, K. (1985) 'The economics of agency', in J. Pratt and R. Zeckhauser (eds), *Principals and Agents: the Structure of Business*, Boston: Harvard Business School Press, pp.37–51.

Camagni, R. and A. Pio (1988) 'Funzioni urbane e gerarchia metropolitana europea' [Urban functions and the European metropolitan hierarchy], in Dip. Economia Politica Un. Bocconi (ed.), *La trasformazione economica della città*, Milano: Angeli, pp.59–84.

Camagni, R. and T. Pompili (1990a) 'Inter-regional and inter-urban economic power relations as command over local resources', in S. Oberg and A. Shachar (eds), *The World Economy and the Spatial Organisation of Power*, Aldershot: Avebury, pp.187–218.

Camagni, R. and T. Pompili (1990b) 'Competence, power and waves of urban development', in P. Nijkamp (ed.), *Sustainability of Urban Systems: a Cross-national Evolutionary Analysis of Urban Innovation*, Aldershot: Avebury, pp.37–86.

Centro, Studi PIM (1993) *Governo delle aree metropolitane e pianificazione strategica* [Governing the metropolitan area and strategic planning], Milan: Comune di Milano (Settore Studi).

Ciorli, A. and A. Tosi (1986) *L'uso dei servizi sociali e sanitari in Lombardia* [The use of social and health services in Lombardy], Milan: IReR.

Hart, O. and B. Holmstrom (1987) 'The theory of contracts', in T. Bewley (ed.), *Advances in Economic Theory*, Cambridge: Cambridge University Press, pp.71–155.

IReR (1991) *Social Survey in Lombardia*, Milan: Angeli.

IReR (1992) *Il governo locale possibile: poteri e operativita'* [Options for local government: potential and practices], Milan: Angeli.

IReR (1993) *La legislazione lombarda in campo economico nei vent'anni dell'esperienza regionale* [Twenty years of experience with Lombardy's economic regulation], Milan: Angeli.

Levinthal, D. (1988) 'A survey of agency modes of organizations', *Journal of Economic Behaviour and Organization*, pp.153–86.

Mutti, M. (1993) 'Funzioni urbane e gerarchia metropolitana' [Urban functions and metropolitan hierarchy], in C. Morandi (ed.), *Ivantaggi competitivi delle città: un confronto in ambito europeo*, Milan: Angeli, pp.233–60.

Pompili, T. (1992) 'The role of human capital in urban system structure and development', *Urban Studies*, **29**, pp.907–34.

Pompili, T. (1996) 'Labour occupations and urban performance', in Y. Hayuth and G. Tornqvist (eds), *Towards a new Europe*, London: Belhaven.
Ranci, C. (1989) *Accesso ai servizi e disuguaglianze sociali a Milano* [Access of social services and facilities in Milan], Milan: I.R.S.
Tirole, J. (1994) 'The internal organization of government', *Oxford Economic Papers*, **46**, pp.1–29.

12 Stockholm: welfare and well-being

Bo Wijkmark

Introduction

From welfare state to market orientation

There are broad similarities between Stockholm and other middle-sized metropolitan areas in Scandinavia and Europe. Traces of the 'roaring sixties' as well as the international architectural modes and ideals are clearly visible in the modern and modernized parts of the region, but under the surface there are differences.

The first two or three postwar decades were in many respects the formative years of today's Stockholm and the capital city's region. Those were the days of indisputable economic progress and optimism, increasing dependence on motorized transport, and growing private consumption, comprehensive planning and expansion of the built-up area. It was also a period of almost unquestioned social-democratic hegemony and paternalistic social engineering.

The planning doctrines were widely accepted and implemented, both in the city and in the region of Stockholm. As with any other metropolitan region, there is socioeconomic segregation in and around Stockholm, but this has never been accepted by planners and politicians, and they have gone to great lengths to counteract spatial segregation. Social equity, improved housing standards, attractive public transport and a wholesome environment were the guiding principles. Formally, regional planning has a rather weak position – advisory instead of decisive – but in reality it has been more influential. Consequently, there are fewer socio-economic differences between Stockholm and its neighbouring municipalities than exist in many other metropolitan regions.

During the most recent decades, many of the former doctrines – and in fact, the entire 'Swedish model' – have been questioned. At the same time, Swedish society has become more amenable to market solutions and European integration. That development is discussed in this chapter with special reference to its implications for planning and regional and local politics (for example, Petersson, 1990; Johansson, 1993; Törnquist, 1993).

From competition within Sweden to international competition

The number of inhabitants of both Sweden and its capital region has grown very slowly for a long time. For decades, the county of Stockholm accounted for a little less than a fifth of the whole country's population. The relative growth of Stockholm was stronger in the 1950s and 1960s than afterwards. Nevertheless, many still claim that Stockholm is growing too fast, and that this causes problems and backwardness in the more remote parts of Sweden.

Thus politicians and planners in Stockholm have long tried to make people see the capital as a national asset, and to regard the growth and prosperity of Stockholm as a means to further development in Sweden as a whole. Another line of defence has been to point out that Stockholm does not grow primarily because of migration from other parts of Sweden, but mostly because of a natural population increase, in combination with immigration from Finland and other countries. This is as true today as it was earlier in the postwar years.

Until recently, international competition has not been very much on the minds of politicians and planners in Stockholm. A shorthand and somewhat simplified version of the predominant opinion among them could be phrased like this: We are responsible to the people and voters in Stockholm, and we have to develop our city and region into a socially, economically and physically attractive environment for our present and future inhabitants without a side glance to other regions and other countries. Stockholm is a threat to nobody and should be treated as any Swedish region. It is not the nation's milch cow which can be milked over and over again to support other parts of the country.

For some time, however, there has been a growing awareness that Stockholm has to compete in an international arena, and that the qualities of the region have to be mobilized to attract investors, entrepreneurs, businesses, opinion makers, researchers and so on. But which are its most competitive qualities?

Stockholm in the postwar years: a brief history

The welfare state era

Stockholm's land acquisition policy began 90 years ago in response to the lack of space in the inner city. The shortage was acute because of the then rapidly growing number of industrial workers arriving from poorer parts of Sweden to find jobs in Stockholm. It was also intended to counter the risks that proletarian workers would cause unrest and threaten the governing classes. The politically conservative rulers intended to create new garden cities on municipally-owned land outside the old city boundaries. These were mainly intended for workers, who could lease the lots cheaply for their self-built cottages and small gardens. 'Homeowners do not make revolutions' was the idea. The policy was successful, and these attractive parts of Stockholm have been popular ever since – although no longer inexpensive (Johansson, 1974, 1987).

These areas of single-family houses built along the roads, railways and tramway lines were not, of course, an economical way of using municipal land. Moreover, this development led to long and expensive transport and utility lines. In the period between the two world wars, public opinion tended to favour more efficient land use, and multi-storey districts were built here and there in the suburban area. The region was not comprehensively planned, and politicians and planners in Stockholm looked abroad for new ideas. They found them in the Abercrombie Plan of Greater London, which became the model for postwar Swedish planning. In 1952, a new and rather schematic master plan (*Generalplan för Stockholm*, 1952) envisaged the structure of Stockholm's new suburbs outside the old ones. The tramway lines were modernized and connected to underground lines in the inner city. New districts were built along them like pearls on a string. Each had a local centre close to the station, surrounded by multi-family houses and another ring of single-family houses. For each line and for each group of districts there was a larger centre with offices, department stores and more exclusive shops. Each district was surrounded by a green belt; these, in turn, were interconnected to form long green wedges between the lines pointing towards the inner city. As Stockholm is built on islands, there is much open space between the built-up districts; the metropolitan area is characterized by these blue and green wedges (Lanesjö, 1989).

The largest expansion of modern Stockholm took place in the first two decades after the Second World War, as happened in many other countries and regions; this shaped the Stockholm metropolitan area. This expansion was based on the same reasons as lead to urban growth elsewhere: an expanding economy with new possibilities of satisfying the demand for good homes and wholesome living, mass motorism and, in the case of Stockholm, large immigration from northern Sweden, Finland and other European countries.

The central city was under heavy pressure from expanding commercial offices, banks, newspaper offices and public services. Stockholm embarked upon a radical reconstruction of its central business district to meet the new demands without allowing the city functions to disperse. A great number of historic buildings were torn down, streets were widened, subway lines were built and the utility systems were modernized. Today most people regret this radical restructuring and the loss of many historic buildings and neighbourhoods. But Stockholm managed to keep its core functions in the city centre.

The building of new suburbs and underground lines was coordinated in place and time. The fares were heavily subsidized in order to make public transport accessible for all income groups, ages and for both sexes. Public transport was used to promote economic equity and to safeguard air quality. The city authorities underwrote the state housing policy which favoured municipal housing companies. Their policy was to rent flats to all types of households, and to keep the rents controlled and rather low. The agencies decided what proportion of small, medium-sized and large flats they should build, on the basis of registered demand and the composition of the existing housing stock. The aim was to attain a local mixture of families and small households, both in the inner city and in the suburbs. The accumulated effect of this policy quite naturally led to a large and expensive housing sector with high-quality, spacious dwellings for almost everybody – and it created a black or grey market for flats in the most attractive areas. Another negative side-effect of the costly and rather rigid housing policy was that the number of housing completions fluctuated strongly with varying economic conditions.

However, the regional and metropolitan expansion could not take place within Stockholm (Figure 12.1). The city's future lay outside its own boundaries, and the authorities took a number of initiatives to overcome the problems: regional planning; land acquisition in neighbouring municipalities; the founding of new housing companies, jointly owned by Stockholm and the host municipality; and formal cooperation with suburban municipalities. Moreover, a major constitutional reform was carried out. A new county council was made responsible for public transport in the entire region, for broadened regional planning and for a regional health care system (Anton, 1975; Hägglund, 1987). Many of the leading politicians, planners and managers in Stockholm shifted to positions in the new county administration, and others obtained positions at both levels. It is often said that this was a period of complete social-democratic hegemony and a firm belief

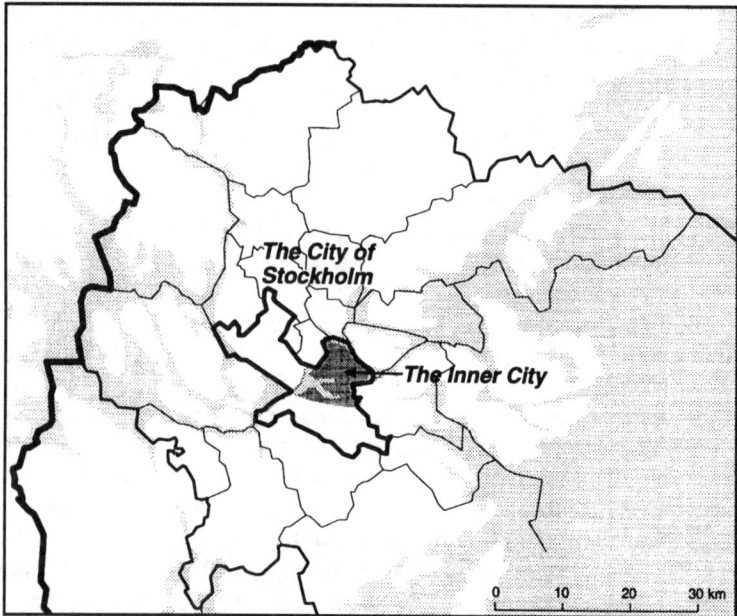

Figure 12.1   The Stockholm metropolitan area

both in economies of scale and in the welfare state doctrine. Eventually, much of the policy was accepted by the other political parties and implemented under shifting political majorities (Lanesjö, 1989).

The first regional plan was published in 1958. Two years later came the city's traffic circulation plan. This was supplemented in 1962 by the land use plan for the urban core, and in 1964 by the regional subway plan. All these plans were coordinated and in part even prepared by the same planners and adopted by the same politicians. These actors really held a strong grip on both planning and implementation in the capital region. In many respects, this concentration of power was deemed necessary to meet the challenges of the postwar boom. At the same time, the effective managing of the regional expansion and urban renewal gave room only to the ideas of a limited number of influential people, and subsequently there has been much criticism of this situation.

The plans were prepared mostly by architects and planners in the service of municipal and regional authorities, and they were adopted and implemented by their political masters. Goals and strategies were formulated by these authorities, and they knew very well which means they controlled: for example, the public transport system, municipally owned land and the power to adopt and change building codes. They used these means effectively to create a wholesome and prosperous city and metropolitan area. The leading social democrat in Stockholm in the 1940s phrased it like this: 'A city of labour, health and beauty'. His main opponent in the city council used almost the same words to describe the vision of the liberal party. 'Equity and justice' became the favourite words among the political leaders in city government during the 1960s and 1970s.

One of the main ideas, which almost no one would oppose today, was to defend at any cost the green wedges between the built-up areas along the railways and subway lines. This structure provides the inhabitants with close access to green areas, almost irrespective of where they live in the region. This wedge structure remained the central element in planning for Stockholm. It featured in the master plan of 1952, the regional plans adopted since 1958, and the traffic circulation and underground plans. Still, the structure was threatened many times by road planners and developers, who coveted this undeveloped and easily accessible land. Given its situation, it would be relatively cheap to develop. As a rule, the inhabitants and the local authorities of Stockholm and the nearby municipalities were united in defending the green backbone of the region, although they have often criticized other elements of the regional plans. And in the latest plan of 1991, the green wedges were augmented by a popular green belt around Greater Stockholm.

These planning principles were easily defended as a consequence of the city and regional authorities' environmental consciousness, or intentions to maintain the green structure of Greater Stockholm. But those who were mainly interested in and responsible for the municipal economy often considered them to be extravagant and a waste of resources. The conflict was easily resolved throughout the early 1960s, when the economy grew rapidly and a rather naive optimism about the future was predominant among planners and decision makers. But during the following decade, economic arguments became more important again. In the mid-1960s, a national 'million programme' was launched to boost residential construction (one million flats in ten years). Since Greater Stockholm was charged with the construction of a fifth of the national programme, the region had to triple its residential construction efforts quickly. This required intensified planning, new methods of production and financing, and so on. One new suburb was built every year in Stockholm, near the extended underground. Another one would be completed in another municipality, but less well connected to public transport. The main principles were not abandoned, but new areas were more intensively used, with higher buildings, smaller open areas and narrower streets than the older ones.

Towards the end of the era of social engineering

In order to establish good planning principles and better conditions for the inhabitants of the whole county, an 'outline regional plan' for a very expansive future of Greater Stockholm and the surrounding regions was published late in 1966. This proved to be barely a year and a half before May 1968, when the strong leftist student movement vehemently opposed what were seen as manipulated, inflated growth forecasts and plans, and the establishment's positive attitude towards motorized vehicles. The movement protested against the willingness to demolish the city's history in the united interests of business and public institutions, against the interests of the people.

Stockholm was in no way an exception to the international movement that had started with riots at the Sorbonne in Paris, and subsequently spread all over the world, but politicians and planners felt slighted, since their intentions had been the improvement of living conditions, housing standards and commuting possibilities, mainly for lower- and middle-income classes. In a way, this was the first attack from the left upon the social-democratic hegemony and its ideals of paternalistic social engineering: the 'Swedish model'. The effects were not immediately visible, but a few years later the city council gave completely new directives to the planners, with a marked orientation towards conservation of historic environments and restrictions on motorized traffic.

In the 1950s and early 1960s, when for the first time in history almost everyone could afford a car, increasing the capacity for both private and public transport had been an important policy goal. Soon it was discovered that this could not be done, for economic and environmental reasons. The city council had to choose and, in the early 1970s, they opted for public transport. Fewer and narrower motorways were built, residential districts were divided into traffic zones, parking regulations were introduced and streets were reserved for buses, delivery vehicles, cyclists and pedestrians. The oil crisis and the growing ecological movement with its antagonism towards consumerism and waste of natural resources of course played a role in this change.

The 1970s gave birth to larger variations in society, between left and right, between ecology and economy. At the same time, there occurred a gradual transition from planning ideals to market orientation and growing differences between the political practices of the various municipalities in Greater Stockholm. This signalled the beginning of the dissolution of regional solidarity. Another important change in the prerequisites for Stockholm's planning in the early 1970s was the rapid 'collectivization' of nursing and caring, leading to the creation of numerous new jobs in public service for women. The activity rate for women grew close to that of men. Women had their own incomes and felt more equal and independent than before. This trend was so strong in Swedish cities that migration and the housing demand from new households diminished, as many of the new jobs were taken by women in already established households. The need for new housing and new suburbs declined and, for the first time since the 1930s, there were many empty flats in less attractive areas. This caused economic difficulties for many suburban municipalities and led to the creation of a system of subsidies from the county to those municipalities.

In those days, Sweden still maintained a generous immigration policy, and many immigrants were housed in the less attractive new multi-storey suburbs. Soon some suburbs were virtually dominated by immigrants from other countries and cultures. In the same period, other suburban municipalities took advantage of the growing purchasing power and tax-paying capacity of families with two instead of one income earner. They started to build wasteful, new areas for single-family houses in pleasant surroundings, where families could buy their own house instead of being tenants in multiethnic, multi-storey districts. The housing market became more varied, and there were signs of a growing spatial segregation. There was also an increased dependency on private cars for commuting; the extensive single-family housing districts could not be optimally served by public transport.

The 1980s: change of policies and strategies

The late 1970s and the 1980s witnessed a gradual shift in mentality in Sweden. People turned away from social engineering and the belief in a strong society and in economies of scale. They turned towards the more market-oriented and individualized views that had become accepted everywhere. The former way of planning and policy making had proved to be rather expensive and, at least in some respects, not very effective. Inflation was high and the development of GNP, though positive, was laggardly. Sweden fell from a position close to the top among OECD's richest nations to a place in the middle ranks. Manufacturing was undergoing a structural crisis, and many traditional sectors and companies collapsed. Still, Sweden was able to keep its very low unemployment figures during the recession in the early 1980s.

At the national level, the social democrats lost power in 1976, for the first time in 40 years. But in the city of Stockholm, in its neighbouring municipalities, and in the county council, there had been occasional shifts during the entire postwar period. The 'Swedish model' had not, however, been really questioned during the changes of political majorities. The mentality shift was a product of the 1980s, under social-democratic rule and during a prospering economy. It had many roots, both internal and external. Many ordinary Swedes travelled abroad, where they became familiar with other cultures; they became used to international television channels and other information media; young people studied and worked abroad. More than before, Sweden became a mixed country because of the large immigration that began in the 1950s. Swedish manufacturing went multinational, Swedish firms were sold abroad and Swedish capital was invested in London, Brussels and other cities.

Another popular explanation in those days was that young and middle-aged Swedes had no first-hand experience of unemployment and poverty; they took social security for granted. At the same time, they became more and more aware of the fact that taxes and the fraction of national income in the public sector for transfer payments and public expenditure were high compared to almost any other country.

The social democrats regained control of Parliament in 1982 and proceeded to form a new government. This happened also in the city and region of Stockholm, as well as in many other Swedish municipalities. Their return coincided with the beginning of the long international economic boom. This proved to be fortuitous for the whole Swedish economy. It made the capital region a real winner; demand for new office and dwelling space was so strong that the authorities had to take action to slow it down. Economic activity was stimulated in Stockholm during the second half of the 1980s; production and consumption boomed, unemployment was almost erased and inflation accelerated.

Under the new social-democratic government, national policy gradually became more similar to the policy of other European countries. It reflected the younger generation's desire to decide more for themselves; in other words, it became more liberal and non-interventionist. Sweden applied for membership of the EU, and even the old doctrine of neutrality was questioned (Eklund,

1993). Many of the traditional supporters of the social-democratic party no longer 'recognized their old party', and the social democrats lost power almost all over Sweden in the 1991 elections. For the first time since the 1920s, Sweden had a conservative prime minister heading a coalition government. His party became the largest one in the county council of Stockholm, and it took over the leadership of 22 out of the 25 municipalities in the capital region. National, regional and municipal policy in Sweden and the Stockholm region shifted even more in the direction of the mainstream of European policy. Swedes were confronted by new political attitudes towards unemployment, taxes and user fees, markets and non-intervention, privatization and so on.

More recently, there has been a strong shift back to the left. The social democrats regained power in Parliament, almost every council and most municipal councils in 1994. In Stockholm and Stockholm County they formed a coalition with the leftist party and the greens. The fact that the new regime came to power when the economy was hit by a severe recession intensified the shift in attitudes. Unemployment and deficits in the public budgets rose to a much higher level than ever before during the postwar years.

Environment, equity and efficiency

Compromises and conflicting goals

As can be seen from this short history of planning in the postwar period, great changes have taken place in the ideological setting. But what real effects have they had on the attitude towards fundamental planning goals such as better environment, social equity and economic efficiency? The answer is not simple; in the same period, there has been a tremendous increase in knowledge about environmental threats and the necessity to pay attention to ecology. Economic efficiency is always needed, but it has become much more important since the oil crisis, which marked the end of an era in which sustained economic expansion looked plausible. The promotion of equity has come closer to the core of politics and it signifies the difference between left and right. Although these goals are no longer front-page news, they are still important to most planners and policy makers.

Planning is always a matter of compromise: one cannot accomplish everything one wants. Therefore planners have to choose, to set priorities. The thesis of this chapter is that efficiency goals have never been important in regional and municipal plans until the stage of their implementation. During periods of economic strain, plans were postponed rather than rewritten. There are many examples of this, but of course one can always find plans or parts of plans which have been completely rejected, often for lack of economic realism. The prognoses of the 1960s for the development of the economy and population growth have lost their relevance. Many physical details of the old plans – such as the selection of the areas to be developed or the choice of a transport link – have also been discarded. But in general, the current plans have preserved the physical structure of their predecessors. To transform the Stockholm region from a monocentric one to a structure with numerous centres remains one of the most important goals. Today, however, politicians and urban planners have a larger region in mind than before. The former focus on Greater Stockholm and the administrative area of the county of Stockholm has been enlarged to include the whole Stockholm–Mälar region (see below).

Conflicts between environmental and equity goals have changed along with changing views on environment and ecology in planning. During the early postwar decades, most environmental questions at the regional level were about the green structure: the green wedges between the monocentric region's tentacles, green areas around every new suburb, the undeveloped archipelago and nature reserves. At the local level, environment has always been a question of open areas and green space, as well as a question of sanitary conditions and health. At the regional level, the attention also shifted gradually to pollution and health. As long as environment was only an issue of extensive land use, the increased need for long-distance transport could be dealt with by building more railroads and expressway lanes. Low-income groups could be compensated by the provision of better and cheaper public transport. But when environment became an issue of clean air, traffic took on added significance. Emissions from motor vehicles and even their circulation had to be reduced. Traditional physical planning goals to retain green areas had to be supplemented by new legal and economic instruments for the city's and region's management. No doubt these have a greater impact on low-income groups than on the better off.

From green wedges to greenhouse effects

Swedes are in general nature-loving. The worldwide shock caused by Rachel Carson's book, *Silent Spring*, was very strongly felt in Sweden. Swedes were used to having undeveloped and healthy forests, fields and islands very near their built-up areas. These provide much room for recreation, sports and other outdoor activities. Now, suddenly, signs of threatened and damaged nature were seen everywhere. Until the 1950s, one could swim in Lake Mälaren and other outdoor bathing areas in Stockholm, but in the 1960s, some swimming places had to be roped off for sanitary reasons, and a number of lakes were closed to fishing.

During the 1960s and 1970s, the state introduced subsidies for various environmental protection measures, as well as penalties for pollution. The municipal and regional authorities in the metropolitan area of Stockholm adopted a big investment programme to clean the lakes and coastal waters, and later also the air and soil. The water and sewage systems in Stockholm and its suburbs were regionalized and modernized, which has had a very rapid effect. Once again, people can swim and catch salmon right in the centre of Stockholm. District heating systems have been built on a large scale to eliminate many local emission sources.

Environmental protection has been on the agenda of every Swedish administration ever since, at the national, regional and local level. There are few political differences in these matters. All parties are in favour of a healthy natural environment and good living conditions for everyone. But some parties are more inclined to regulate the behaviour of industry and households than others. Although much has been achieved, there remains much to be done. This is obviously difficult; pollution is partly caused by emissions from other countries and partly by a large number of diffuse domestic emissions. Persuading ordinary people to change their lifestyle is much more difficult than adopting laws and regulations against the production of industrial emissions and the dumping of toxic waste.

The economic boom and its planning effects

Transport plays an important role in environmental policy. There is good reason to believe that mobility will keep growing as a consequence of and prerequisite for economic progress (Karlsson, 1989–90; Produktivitetsdelegationen, 1991). During the economic boom of the 1980s, the urgent need for better communications became evident. This was not least an effect of the internationalization of the Swedish economy and the increased awareness of the long distance to the European mainland. Infrastructure investment had been lagging during the 1970s and early 1980s. Economic and political reasons were at the root of this, as the ruling social democrats were more in favour of equity and transfer payments than of public investment. But it was also the result of the widespread negative attitude towards motorized vehicles for environmental reasons. Suddenly, almost everyone argued for more railways, more expressways, more telecommunication. The national telecom company was authorized to use its profits for investment, and it increased its capacity dramatically in a short period. But it took many years to get from words to deeds in railway and highway construction. This type of investment was a matter for government and parliamentary decision making, and it had to compete with other expenditures in the state budget.

The need for an expansion of infrastructure investment in the three Swedish metropolitan regions led the government to appoint an official negotiator for each. For Stockholm, the manager of the Bank of Sweden, Bengt Dennis, was appointed to negotiate with the regional and local authorities on a balanced investment programme and to find ways of financing it. The proposals would have to be acceptable to the local and regional as well as the national authorities. The programme had to provide for an expanded capacity of the transport system and for improved environmental quality and safety. The starting-point for the negotiations was the regional plan. The three largest political parties agreed to halve the period for the implementation of the plan by investing 30–40 billion Swedish crowns in public transport and roads over a period of 15 years. For environmental reasons, this infrastructure was largely to be built in tunnels. A main element of the agreement was the introduction of a toll system for motorized traffic to the inner city of Stockholm and on the ring road around the city. It was soon accepted by the councils of the city and region and the affected municipalities, and detailed planning for the implementation of the proposals started. Government and Parliament have recently made the necessary decisions on the financial appropriations and the underwriting of the programme. This signalled the start of the largest coherent investment programme for infrastructure in Sweden this century.

There is, of course, opposition to the 'Dennis package' from the political parties which were kept outside the agreement. There is also opposition from environmentalists, who claim that it is the fruit of out-of-date thinking. According to their views, the package will increase motorized traffic and the environmental load, instead of preparing for new sustainable ways of life. On the other hand, few infrastructure plans have been accompanied by so many analyses of environmental impact as the Dennis package. These were carried out to show that this programme is the only realistic way of matching the ambition for better accessibility and less congestion with the desire to improve the quality of air and security while providing for noise abatement.

Others say that there are contradictions in the agreement, as the car tolls have two purposes: to reduce car traffic in the inner city and to attract car traffic to the ring road in order to generate the necessary funds. The present solution – a toll cordon outside the ring road – is the reason for this scepticism; there is an old adage that you cannot accomplish two goals with one instrument. Anyhow, it is quite possible that such a big programme will not be totally completed, as there will always be unforeseen facts and changes of opinion. Only the future will show the effects.

Stockholm in the international market-place

From introvert to extrovert politics

Undoubtedly, these changes have had an effect on the attitude among politicians and planners in the city and region concerning Stockholm's role in the international arena. But the reorientation has come gradually, over the last two decades.

Nowadays, it is widely accepted that Stockholm has to compete with similar cities. Until the end of the 1960s, very few leading politicians were ready to admit this. The official policy was to resist any desire for urban growth and the attraction of more inhabitants and businesses. In the mid-1940s, officials even launched a campaign to discourage migration to Stockholm. They papered Sweden with big posters showing a homeless man sitting on his suitcase in a snowstorm outside the Central Station with the appeal, 'Don't move to Stockholm'. But few showed such a negative attitude. In fact, the Chamber of Commerce started a promotion agency. It made a major effort to beautify the central park in Stockholm and turned it into the arena for the celebration of the 700th anniversary in 1953. But the city's authorities had a more introvert attitude. It was, therefore, a new official approach when the city founded the Stockholm Site and Development Company in 1973. Its mission was to promote trade and industry, fairs, exhibitions, congresses and conferences. Five years later, in cooperation with the county council, the city founded the Stockholm Information Service, with even more explicit promotion goals: 'to put Stockholm on the map', as it was often stated.

During the boom of the 1980s, there was again some hesitation about whether Stockholm should try to attract new businesses, and the budgets of the promotion agencies were cut. The national level intervened in the region's affairs with restrictions and penalties on investments in building for commercial purposes in Stockholm and the most attractive neighbouring areas. The city and county of Stockholm began to look around for help outside the region's borders to divert some of the pressure. The concept of a larger, multinuclear region was born. This was welcomed by the neighbouring regions which had experienced difficulties in retaining their businesses and inhabitants.

The Stockholm-Mälar region

This region (Figure 12.2) was, in fact, an expansion of the ideas underlying Stockholm's regional plans during the last decades. Those plans strongly advocated a transition from a monocentric structure to a region with a number of sub-centres. The plans had not been too successful; the traditional pattern was very resistent to change, both in its physical expression and as a concept in the

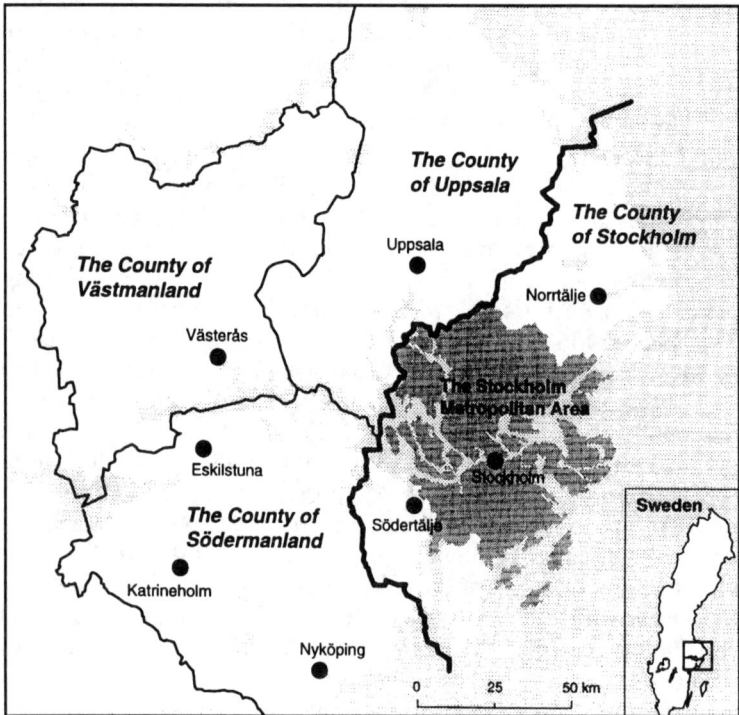

Figure 12.2   The Stockholm–Mälar region

potential investors' minds. New centres would have to attain a certain size to be attractive, and they had to be easily accessible from different parts of the region. This could lead to increased consumption of land, and to a less competitive public transport system than the traditional monocentric structure provided for.

The enlargement of scale led to a qualitatively new situation. The alternative cores under discussion were no longer newly-built, relatively small centres inside the metropolitan area of Stockholm. Instead, they were independent, medium-sized cities with a history as long as that of Stockholm. They had their own traditions, as well as their own structures and economic bases. Stockholm is much larger than any of them; still, it is now more a question of a cooperation between peers. Therefore, the initiative has better prospects for success.

Five years ago, the city and county of Stockholm, together with the three neighbouring counties and their main cities, began to cooperate informally on matters of strategic importance for the common future: regional planning, infrastructure, environment, trade and industry, universities and research. The two main goals were to improve the intraregional distribution and to strengthen the competitiveness. The Stockholm–Mälar Region – with almost one-third of Sweden's population and an even larger proportion of the country's economic activity, research and higher education – was to develop into a prospering 'European Region of the Future' (Linzie and Boman, 1991).

The cooperation was formalized in 1992, when the Stockholm–Mälar Regional Council was founded. In 1993, the vast majority of the municipalities in the region became members of the council. At the same time, culture and tourism were added to its agenda. The format of the council is that of a voluntary association without any legal status. Its importance and strength lie in the members' belief in concerted action and their resolve to position the region in a European context. There can be no doubt, however, that the founding of the council is rooted partly in the worldwide trend towards regionalism. Sweden has been a country with strong central institutions and a hierarchical political and mental structure. But over the last decades, municipal and regional desires for more independence have grown throughout Sweden. The nation's uniformity is being questioned by a growing number of opinion makers and analysts. They foresee that the relative strength of the national level will diminish in favour of EU authorities as well as regional and local agencies.

The regions around Gothenburg and Malmö have applied for a new legal and administrative regional structure. In that structure some powers of the state and provincial authorities would be taken over by elected regional councils. Recently, a royal commission published a proposal for a limited experiment in these two regions. The Stockholm–Mälar Council has opted for another way; it handles only matters that lie unquestionably in the jurisdiction of the regional and local councils. The state has nothing to fear from it and has nothing to do with its affairs.

The founding of the Stockholm–Mälar Regional Council raised several questions: With whom do we compete? In which arena? And by which means?

Stockholm in Scandinavian competition

If there is a traditional rivalry between Stockholm and anyone else, it is in relation to the second-largest city and region of Sweden, Gothenburg and the west coast. Both regions claim to be the main Swedish centre for sports, culture and exhibitions. But the competition is really very good-natured; the two cities have much in common and cooperate in many fields (*Nordiska storstadsregioner*, 1992).

The politicians of Stockholm are well aware that Malmö, at present the third city of Sweden and the one nearest to the European continent, has a very impressive potential because of its close cooperation with Scandinavia's largest city, Copenhagen. This will be borne out particularly when the two regions are united by a combined rail and road bridge and tunnel. At that time, the corridor will become the outstanding Scandinavian region for university education, research and future-oriented industry. Its advantage lies in its location 600 kilometres closer to Europe's mainland than Stockholm. However, very few people seem to have taken the consequences for Stockholm seriously. In a way, it is reminiscent of the way people ignored the new city of St Petersburg in the early eighteenth century. St Petersburg was founded by the czar in the marshes around the Neva on captured Swedish land in 1704. For centuries, Copenhagen and Stockholm had competed for the position of the capital of northern Europe. But only 20 years after its birth, St Petersburg had become the unrivalled capital. Indeed, that capital remained unrivalled until the Soviet Union lowered the iron curtain and isolated itself behind it.

The Copenhagen–Malmö region may well surpass the Stockholm–Mälar region in two decades or so, but once more they can both be eclipsed by a new and democratic St Petersburg (Andersson and Wichmann Mathiessen, 1993). Stockholm's relations with Oslo and Helsinki remain somewhat ambiguous. These two capital cities are much smaller than Stockholm. Nevertheless, they are strong enough to be taken into consideration as potential competitors in certain niches.

There is, however, a strong sense of Nordic solidarity and cooperation in Sweden. Therefore competition inside Sweden and Scandinavia is not really acceptable as an official policy of a city or region. To compete with regions in Europe's mainland is, on the other hand, entirely respectable.

Stockholm in European competition

Does Stockholm compete with cities and regions on the continent? Of course it does. But the city administration has not, until very recently, formulated any strategies to bolster its position. Nor has it selected potential partners for a strategy that may be necessary or mutually advantageous. London, Paris, Berlin and Rome are too big to be taken on. It would not be unrealistic for Stockholm to devise a strategy to compete with other capital cities of about the same size. The location on the border between east and west may be one of Stockholm's potential advantages when more links are being forged. Accordingly, competition with cities and city regions in the borderlands of former West Germany may emerge in the future. This scenario is more probable than entering into competition with Vienna and Prague, as Stockholm is very much oriented towards northern Europe. In this respect, Stockholm's main airport, Arlanda, may be counted as an important asset. It has recently been modernized, it has sufficient capacity, it is located outside the congested airspace of central Europe and it lies within reach of Japan. Arlanda could possibly become one of the European hubs for long-distance flights (Andersson and Strömquist, 1988).

The foundation of the Stockholm–Mälar Regional Council has marked a new way of thinking on long-term development in an international perspective. In the long run, every person and every business is a potential mover. What, then, would be the reason for moving to – or staying in – the Stockholm region?

Regional quality as an asset in competition

In this book, the emphasis lies on policies to promote efficiency, equity and environmental quality. The traditional policy of Stockholm has stressed the two latter types of policy but has not until recently, given much consideration to efficiency. Now, however, the city points to Stockholm's qualities as a business arena and localization spot for international companies in information technology, pharmaceutics, transportation and so on. All three goals are taken into consideration in the Stockholm–Mälar region's visions of its future. Railway connections of a high standard, improved road connections and an electronic highway are seen as important means to create a genuinely multi-core region out of the four present smaller regions. This merger would promote its efficiency. New university institutions to educate the youth and raise the competence level of those who are already in the labour market would also contribute to efficiency. Furthermore, the equity dimension would also be served by locating such institutions in areas currently lacking them but containing knowledge-oriented industries (for example, ABB in the western part of the region). The environmental quality would be enhanced by new regional actions to improve the water and sewage systems, to improve the safety of transport on Lake Mälaren and to maintain air quality control and management. This goal would also be served by the protection of the traditional agricultural landscape. These are just three examples of proposals for concerted action by the members of the council. They are combined in the next step in the planning process (Mälardalsrådet, 1993). The council is not the only organization that takes environmental quality to heart: research and education in new university institutions is to be directed towards environmental matters in order to stimulate the creation of an internationally competitive industry with expertise in environmental protection and improvement techniques (Andersson, 1988).

Marketing of the Stockholm–Mälar region in an international context should emphasize regional qualities that are attractive to foreign businesses and organizations. One of the points advanced in the discussions concerns the mentality of the Swedish population. Swedes are known as peace-loving and open-minded people. Sweden is a country where negotiation and agreement are embedded in the national culture, which avoids open conflict. Another asset is the relatively high standard of manufacturing and the willingness to renew it to keep up with changing conditions. New techniques are readily accepted in production and consumption (as befits 'a country and region of engineers'). A third important characteristic is the high standard of housing and public transport. And a final factor that counts in the international context is the green and wholesome character of the countryside and the cities. There is a widespread, genuine interest in ecological qualities. The Dennis package is an example of the efforts to unite environmental considerations and good transport facilities (Lundqvist, 1993).

Environment as a means to stimulate growth and competitiveness

The basic idea underlying the Dennis package is to ensure good access to the central parts of the city for necessary transport, while creating a pleasing environment for inhabitants and visitors. Clean air and traffic-sheltered streets for pedestrians, cyclists, buses and trams are essential ingredients of the package. Such an environment is presumed to be more attractive to modern, knowledge-oriented businesses than to traditional manufacturing industry. Therefore it could contribute to the modernization and economic growth of the city. The policy makers and planners of Stockholm count the environment as one of the city's prime assets in the future competition among European city regions.

Much has already been done to improve the quality of the water. The inhabitants of the city and visitors alike are reminded of these efforts every August, when the city centre is kept car-free for a great 'Water Festival' with numerous attractions and festivities. On this occasion, an international Water Prize is awarded for achievements in water treatment, water-quality research and so on. Air quality has been improved by district heating, low-emission buses and similar measures. The Dennis package will be the next political attack on bad air in the city.

Looking at the brochures, films and other marketing materials produced by the city of Stockholm, the county and the other agencies in the Stockholm–Mälar region, the qualities most frequently used to describe the city and the region are 'green and blue'. They offer innumerable pictures of green forests, flowering fields and clean water. Pictures of the archipelago show people walking in the forests, gathering mushrooms or canoeing in the rivers. The materials depict an active lifestyle: fishing, swimming, sailing or skating in the centre of Stockholm. Of course, Nobel Prize ceremonies, the Wasa Warship, Stockholm's City Hall, old castles, beautiful buildings, charming neighbourhoods, sporting events, cultural activities, modern products of the manufacturing industry and so on are shown in the marketing media.

Stockholm has been designated as the cultural capital of Europe for 1998. The city has decided to apply to host the Olympic Games in the Summer of 2004. Alongside more factual argumentation, the beautiful nature and wholesome environment of Stockholm play an important role in the marketing of these activities to the target groups by decision makers (SML, 1993).

The Stockholm–Mälar region as a tool for growth and competitiveness

In summary, the protection and enhancement of the environment is one of the main elements in the presentation of Stockholm as an attractive and prospering place. Another one is the intensified regional cooperation. Two-thirds of the inhabitants of the Stockholm–Mälar region live in the county of Stockholm. Within its borders one finds an even larger proportion of the region's companies, public agencies, business headquarters and so on. Therefore the competiveness of the enlarged region is completely dependent on what happens in Stockholm and its metropolitan area. The Stockholm–Mälar Regional Council would be much weaker without the collaboration of Stockholm.

The city and county of Stockholm have found that a strong and prosperous Stockholm–Mälar region is in their own interest. Former misunderstandings, and even conflicting interests, between the city of Stockholm and its neighbours have taught all parties some historic lessons. The ways of solving them lie at the root of this positive cooperation between the city's and county's politicians, planners and managers. Only cooperation and mutual trust between the members can create a strong and competitive region of the future.

References

Andersson, Åke E. (1988) *Universitet – Regioners Framtid* [Universities and the Future of Regions], Stockholm: Regionplanekontoret.
Andersson, Åke E. and Ulf Strömquist (1988) *K-Samhällets Framtid* [The Future of the K-Society], Stockholm: Prisma.
Andersson, Åke E and Christian Wichmann Mathiessen (1993) *Öresundsregionen. Kreativitet, integration, vaekst* [The Sound region. Creativity, integration, growth], Copenhagen: Munksgaard.
Anton, Thomas (1975) *Governing Greater Stockholm*, Berkeley: University of California Press.
Eklund, Niklas (1993) 'Svensk demokrati i förhandling', [Swedish democracy under negotiation], in Janerik Gidlund (ed.), *Den nya politiska konserten*, Malmö: Liber Hermods.
Generalplan för Stockholm [Master Plan for Stockholm], (1952) Stockholm: Stockholms stad.
Hägglund, Sam (1987) *Storstockholmsproblemet* [Problems of Greater Stockholm], Stockholm: KTH.
Johansson, Börje (1993) *Ekonomisk dynamik i Europa* [European Change in Europe], Malmö: Liber Hermods.
Johansson, Ingemar (1974) *Den stadslösa storstaden* [The Metropolis without Cities], Stockholm: Byggforskningen.
Johansson, Ingemar (1987) *Stor-Stockholms bebyggelsehistoria* [The History of Urban Development in Greater Stockholm], Stockholm: Byggforskningen.

Karlsson, Jan O. (ed.) (1989–90) *Storstadsutredningen* [Green Paper on Large Cities], Stockholm: SOU.

Lanesjö, Bo (ed.) (1989) *The Development of Stockholm*, Stockholm: City of Stockholm.

Linzie, Jan and Dag Boman (1991) *Mälarregionen i ett gränslöst Europa* [The Mälar Region in a Europe without Frontiers], Stockholm: Regionplane- och Trafikkontoret.

Lundqvist, Lars (1993) 'Traffic and Environment in Northern Capitals', in Lars Lundqvist and Lars Olof Persson, *Strategies in European Integration*, Berlin: Springer Verlag.

Mälardalsrådet (Stockholm–Mälar Regional Council) (1993) *Utskottens visioner* [The Committee's Vision], Stockholm: Mälardalsrådet.

Nordiska storstadsregioner i text och siffror [Nordic Metropolitan Areas in Text and Figures] (1992) Helsinki: Helsingfors stads faktacentral.

Petersson, Olof (ed.) (1990) *Maktutredningen* [Green Paper on Power Sharing], Stockholm: SOU.

Produktivitetsdelegationen (1991) *Drivkrafter för produktivitet och välstånd* [Forces for Productivity and Wealth], Stockholm: SOU.

SML (Stockholm Site and Development Co) (1993) *För näringsliv och sysselsättning i Stockholm* [For Industry and Employment in Stockholm], Stockholm: Stockholms stad.

Törnquist, Gunnar (1993) *Sverige i nätverkens Europa* [Sweden in European Networks], Malmö: Liber Hermods.

PART III
POLICY FIELDS

13 Policies to improve the efficiency of urban areas

William F. Lever

Introduction

In some senses it may seem paradoxical to suggest that public-sector intervention, by local or by central government, is required to increase the efficiency of an urban economy. Surely, it might be argued, if the private sector is in some way inefficient then there are neo-classical economic mechanisms which will lead to the eradication of the inefficiency. If there are shortages of capital then interest rates will rise to enhance the supply: if there are labour shortages then either there will be migration of workers to the area of shortage in pursuit of higher wages, or participation rates will rise in response to higher wages, or retraining will take place, or there will be capital–labour substitution: if there are shortages of land or premises then rents will rise and more space will be provided; lastly, if there is a shortage of information on products or processes then companies will invest in research and development to increase their knowledge base. Thus within the production function shifts are possible to enhance corporate efficiency without intervention.

Secondly, there have historically been objections on political grounds to the creation of private-sector efficiency. Why, it has been argued, should public money be used to increase the profitability of private-sector businesses? The broadly socialist view has been that people who invest in business for profit should accept the risk of loss or low profits as part of the process and should not expect the public sector to intervene in ways which increase competitiveness or efficiency so that profits are raised above 'natural' market levels. Thus, in the early years of British regional policy, intervention by government took the form of public works such as road building, the provision of infrastructure services such as water supply and the creation of factories and sites rather than direct subsidies to individual enterprises (McCrone, 1969). More recently, as city governments have become more involved in local economic development, the same tendency has manifested itself. Thus, in the city of Glasgow, the socialist administration has chosen predominantly to spend its local economic development budget on infrastructure which is of use to the economy as a whole rather than on incentives (grants, loans, tax relief and so on) to individual establishments (Moore and Booth, 1988).

Such arguments, however, overlook the wider economic effects of a profitable and efficient private sector, such as the reinvestment of profits in the local economy, the creation of additional employment with subsequent rounds of employment through income expenditure multiplier effects, and the overall cumulative causation model of local economic growth which stresses how agglomeration advantages lead to successive growth rounds for a long period before agglomeration diseconomies begin to choke off that growth (Pred, 1977).

In this chapter we examine four elements of local economic policy for efficiency in a Europe which comprises a network of competing cities. First, we examine the extent to which there is a need for such policies by examining the extent to which cities, or rather their private sectors, appear to operate inefficiently. In this section we also examine the need for efficiency policy by looking at the way local, urban or regional economies in Europe behave relatively, in terms of growth or unemployment, at different stages of the macrobusiness cycle. Secondly, we look at the way cities develop policies to assist private sector efficiency at the establishment level by adjusting the supply of production functions such as labour, capital and space, where there is evidence that these markets are, at the local level, operating inefficiently. Local authorities also seek to improve efficiencies at this level by adjusting demand levels with procurement contracts in order to even out volatility in some product markets and to support local business through import substitution. In the third section we look at urban efficiency, treating the city as an economic entity in its own right which has a production function through which output may be maximized. The local authority of the city may increase its efficiency through the provision of public goods such as transport systems and information systems and by removing internal diseconomies such as pollution or congestion. At the city level the product, the city itself, may be marketed like any other product and this is an important part of competition between cities. To an extent all cities are unique, in their location for example, but with the increased mobility of capital, of labour, of employment opportunities and of permanent or temporary institutions, cities compete and city governments are important players within these competitions.

Fourthly, cities experience the impacts of wider-scale policies for efficiency in several ways, and the more successful cities are those which respond to these external pressures most effectively by taking advantage of the opportunities which are generated. In this chapter we use two examples of such policies. The first is the implementation of the single European market which is designed to increase efficiency within the member states by reducing or removing tariff barriers, by standardizing products and services, by removing constraints on flows of capital and labour and by removing restrictions on trade such as those, for example, which prevent a limited public-sector tendering. While the effects of such regional trade liberalization have been studied at the national economy level, the changes embodied in the implementation of the single European market do affect urban economies and city authorities have framed responses to such changes. Secondly, the concept of sustainability has led to some European cities developing policies which seek to ensure that economic growth is not achieved at the expense of the future environment. While not strictly a policy of greater efficiency, the adoption of the idea of sustainable growth incorporates the idea that temporal negative externalities or spillovers are as important as spatial negative externalities currently dealt with by land use planning. The inference is that to permit or indeed to foster current economic growth in ways that are prejudicial to long-term economic growth must therefore be regarded as inefficient, and policies to eradicate unsustainability must be regarded as policies for efficiency.

Laissez-faire as a policy for efficiency

The measurement of inefficiency

The simplest way of measuring the extent to which inefficiency in the private sector occurs in European cities is by some form of standardization technique which compares the performance of establishments in a particular city with equivalent establishments in the nation as a whole or in Europe as a whole. Performance may be measured in either output or in employment terms. Were the whole of Europe, or all European cities, equally efficient, differences between cities in terms of employment change would solely reflect the structural composition of employment. Lagging cities would, in this situation, lag because they had a disproportionate share of the nation's (or Europe's) growing or declining sectors. The fact that problem cities perform, in employment terms, even more poorly than their sectoral structure suggests should happen indicates that some form of inefficiency exists in those cities. Thus, in an analysis of the British inner city problem, Danson *et al.* (1980) used shift-share analysis to divide the problem of declining employment between structural and competitive effects. In the period 1952–76 in the six largest British cities, the inner cities, given their employment structure, should have increased employment by 700 000 jobs, but actually they lost a total of 1.1 million jobs, a differential loss of 1.8 million jobs from a total of 6.9 million. By contrast, the outer areas of the same six cities were expected to lose 80 000 jobs, but in fact grew by 600 000, a differential gain of 680 000 jobs on a base of 1.6 million jobs. The clear inference therefore was that there were spatially focused problems in the inner areas of the largest cities which were reflected in low new firm formation rates, high closure rates, poorer in situ growth performance of continuing establishments and a net outward movement of firms. Inner city firms, therefore, could be deemed inefficient.

On the European scale we may wish to estimate the relative performance of cities or city-regions by comparison, not with national rates of change, sector by sector, but with European rates of employment change. Thus, in the study of Flanders and Wallonia by Vanhove and Klaassen (1987) for the period 1950–70, the reference is the EEC growth rate rather than the national growth rate. Over the 20-year period, employment in Flanders grew by 166 000 and that in Wallonia declined by 136 000. By comparing these actual changes with expected totals generated by applying EEC growth rates at sectoral levels, it is possible to conclude that the Flanders economy slightly outperformed the economy of the EEC as a whole, by about 3000 jobs, whereas Wallonia 'lost' about 270 000 jobs relative to its expected 1970 total. Thus the poor economic performance of Wallonia in 1950–70 would appear to be due, not to the often-stressed poor economic structure, but to local factors which diminish the efficiency and competitiveness of local enterprises.

It should be stressed that shift-share analysis is merely a standardization technique which does not offer any guidance as to the source of inefficiencies and competitive disadvantage. But it can be used to set a baseline against which the set of European cities, or individual cities, can be measured (Camagni and Cappellin, 1985). Accordingly, data on 31 European cities over the period 1978–91 were subjected to analysis to determine the relative contributions of the European macroeconomy, the structural mix and the residual comparative effect to employment change. Table 13.1

shows that overall employment in the 31 cities rose from 48.0 million in 1978 to 51.6 million in 1991. Over the whole of western Europe (the 12 members of the European Community plus Austria), employment grew by 8.02 per cent, so *ceteris paribus* we would expect total employment in the 31 cities to rise by 3.85 million jobs. Above that, the favourable sectoral composition of the 31 cities which have above-average shares of the expanding sectors – market services and non-market services – and below-average shares of the declining sectors – agriculture, energy, manufacturing and construction – should provide a further 1.43 million additional jobs. Thus the expected job growth of 5.28 million jobs can be compared with the actual job growth of 3.57 million jobs, a residual or comparative 'loss' of 1.71 million jobs. This figure can be interpreted as a decline in the competitive advantage of western Europe's largest cities, relative to smaller urban areas and rural regions. There must be some factors in the large cities which reduce their efficiency as locations for market and non-market establishments.

Table 13.1   Shift-share components, 31 major European cities, 1978–91

European cities[a], 1978: total employment	48 027 000
European component, change 1978–91	+3 852 000
Structural component	+1 426 000
Residual component	–1 707 000
European cities, 1991: total employment	51 598 000

Note: [a]31 cities = Berlin, Hamburg, Munich, Frankfurt, Stuttgart, Cologne, Düsseldorf, Vienna, Paris, Lyons, Lille, Marseilles, Rome, Milan, Turin, Bologna, Athens, Amsterdam, Rotterdam, Utrecht, Brussels, Copenhagen, London, Birmingham, Manchester, Glasgow, Edinburgh, Cardiff, Madrid, Barcelona, Lisbon.

Source: Eurostat data yearbooks.

Table 13.2 lists the shift-share components for the 31 major cities over the time period 1978-91. As the whole of Europe was expanding, the European component for each city shows an expected positive employment change of just over eight per cent. The majority of cities have positive structural components because, as the largest urban centres, they are likely to have employment shares in the two service sectors above the European average share. The exceptions are cities in which manufacturing has survived longer into the 1980s and which thus reduces the contri-

Table 13.2 Shift-share analysis of European cities

	1978 Total empl. (000s)	Structural component 1978–91	Residual component 1978–91	Total empl. component	Residual 1991	%
Berlin	864	+69	+56	+10	999	+1.2
Hamburg	885	+71	+77	−68	965	−7.7
Munich	1 621	+130	+8	+172	1 931	+10.6
Frankfurt	1 491	+119	+41	+97	1 748	+6.5
Stuttgart	1 598	+128	−33	+162	1 855	+10.1
Cologne	1 566	+126	+28	+75	1 795	+4.8
Düsseldorf	2 084	+167	+23	+13	2 287	+0.6
Vienna	756	+61	+132	−176	773	−23.3
Paris	4 817	+386	+346	−567	4 982	−11.8
Lyons	1 990	+160	+9	−20	2 139	−1.0
Lille	1 383	+111	+2	−211	1 285	−15.3
Marseilles	1 458	+117	+81	−147	1 509	−10.1
Rome	1 601	+128	+76	+169	1 974	+10.5
Milan	3 477	+279	−61	+165	3 860	+4.7
Turin	1 822	+146	−67	−97	1 804	−5.3
Bologna	1 646	+132	−45	+10	1 743	+0.6
Athens	1 108	+89	+48	+54	1 299	+4.9
Amsterdam	805	+65	+56	+169	1 095	+21.0
Rotterdam	1 065	+85	+68	+189	1 407	+17.7

Utrecht	396	+32	+26	+27	481	+6.8
Brussels	699	+56	+83	−145	693	−22.1
Copenhagen	864	+69	+43	−61	915	−7.1
London	4 004	+321	+393	−1 030	3 688	−25.7
Birmingham	1 351	+108	−5	−251	1 203	−18.6
Manchester	1 213	+97	+35	−199	1 146	−16.4
Glasgow	1 061	+85	+35	−166	1 015	−15.6
Edinburgh	827	+66	+25	−109	809	−13.2
Cardiff	729	+58	+15	−99	703	−13.6
Madrid	1 417	+113	+93	+84	1 707	+5.9
Barcelona	2 019	+162	−5	+32	2 208	+1.6
Lisbon	1 410	+113	−2	+59	1 580	+4.2

bution of the sectoral component to employment growth because of Europe's 10 per cent decline in manufacturing employment between 1978 and 1991. Examples of such cities include Stuttgart, Barcelona, Turin and Birmingham. Some cities, such as Bologna, are further handicapped by a relatively large agricultural sector, given that western Europe's agriculture workforce fell by 30 per cent between 1978 and 1991.

From the perspective of efficiency and competitiveness, the most interesting column is the residual component, especially when expressed as a percentage of the 1978 employment base. The most successful cities, once structure is taken into account, have been Amsterdam, Rotterdam, Rome, Munich and Stuttgart. The least successful cities have been London, Brussels, Birmingham, Vienna, Manchester, Glasgow and Lille. In terms of efficiency or growth, the most effective cities seem to have been located in the European growth zone or *dorsal* and to have good connections, and only Rome seems to presage the growth of southern European cities. Cities close to the east-central European frontier (Vienna and Hamburg) have done poorly, and so have British cities. The 'World Cities' – London, Paris and Berlin – have proved relatively unsuccessful.

Convergence or divergence

The shift-share analysis establishes the fact that different European cities have experienced different growth rates even when their economic structure is taken into account. Whether there should be intervention to assist the slow-growing or declining cities, and if so through what agency, will in part depend on what we believe will happen in the absence of such intervention (Hinkel, 1990). We have two sets of spatial economic theory which suggest different development strategies. On the one hand there are 'spread' theories which argue that markets are self-equilibrating and growth disperses from the fastest growing areas to slower growing ones (Temple, 1994, p.166). In its most extreme form such a theory argues that growth and investment are crowded out of the areas of fastest growth by rising labour and space costs and by negative externalities, or inefficiencies, such as traffic congestion. On the urban scale this is the point at which urban agglomeration diseconomies more than outweigh the advantage of urban size. Not all such disadvantages, however, are a function of urban size alone, for fast-growing medium-sized cities may be even more prone to such crowding-out effects as, given their size, they may have more constraints on the supply of labour and the supply of space. Therefore the price of these factors will rise even more sharply. The other side of this argument is that lagging regions or cities will in time begin to attract investment and growth simply because earlier demand deficiency has led to an excess supply of labour and space which in consequence have lower prices. Thus, in a study of the contribution which different factor prices make to profits and losses, Tyler *et al.* (1984) demonstrated that, not only were profits in two manufacturing sectors – engineering and clothing – inversely correlated with urban size, but the lower profits experienced in the largest cities were attributable to the high costs of labour and space. Moreover, they were disadvantaged by higher rates of local taxes which might be regarded as congestion or scarcity charges levied by the local authorities in the largest cities. Conversely, profits in establishments in small urban centres were higher than elsewhere and this was attributed to lower space and labour costs, partly because establishments had greater control over labour supply in smaller labour markets which manifested itself in lower labour turnover and few industrial relations problems (Lever, 1984a).

On the other hand, 'backwash' theories suggest that growth is cumulative and that rapidly growing regions and cities derive further benefits from their growth. These benefits include the income expenditure effects of the existing high-wage labour force generating a second round of demand for goods and services. In addition, there are in the fastest growing locations labour force advantages of a large and diversified labour supply able to fill all vacancies with appropriately qualified workers, scale and agglomeration economies which ensure that a diverse range of support services are available, and the concentration of investment in new technologies as the return on investment is likely to be maximized. The installation of new telecommunication technologies such as fibre optics and cellnet telephone systems in the largest and fastest growing cities is a good example of this last process. This tendency towards cumulative growth has been described by Myrdal (1956) and Friedmann (1972) and has the effect of polarizing economic growth between fast-growing and slow-growing or declining regions or cities.

In terms of urban economic policy for efficiency, if the spread effects predominate then policy is merely required to expedite the processes by which growth is disseminated. This can be achieved by conferring upon less efficient regions and cities those attributes which generate efficiency in the most successful location. If backwash effects predominate then the need for policy is substantially greater and policy has to run counter to market trends, seeking to offset, perhaps on a near permanent basis, the disadvantages and inefficiencies of some cities and regions, and relieving bottlenecks in successful areas.

In order to determine whether spread or backwash effects predominate, there are a number of studies which seek, at the urban or urban–regional level, to measure, in terms of an economic variable such as GDP per inhabitant, whether the spatial units are becoming more or less alike: convergence or divergence, respectively. Perrons (1992) used GDP per inhabitant controlled for purchasing power for the 171 regions which comprise the European Community to argue that, over the period 1980–88, divergence was occurring because the average value for the poorest ten regions fell from 47 per cent of the community average to 45 per cent of the community average, whilst the average value for the most affluent ten rose from 45 per cent above the average to 51 per cent above the average. However, analyses over a longer time period indicated that inequalities diminish over time when there is general economic expansion. But they widen when there is economic recession. Thus there was a period of convergence during the early years of the Community until the mid-1970s, followed by a period of recession and stagnation (the crisis of Fordism) in the early 1980s when divergence occurred, followed by further convergence. In policy terms, it therefore looks as though policy is most needed when there is least growth to be reallocated.

In a second study, Cheshire (1993) over the period 1971–88, using data only for urban centres exceeding a population of 200 000, found a trend of divergence. There were several reasons for this. Overall, larger centres were growing faster, and improving their economies faster, than smaller urban centres, thus entrenching their position. The lagging cities in 1971 were of two types: the old industrial centres of northern Britain, the Nord–Pas de Calais–Belgian coalfield and industrial north Germany, and the underdeveloped cities of southern Italy, Spain and Portugal. With a few exceptions, these cities failed to match even average rates of improvement within the European Community and thus were further marginalized, economically, by the end of the 1980s, largely because of difficulties in the early 1980s' recession. A further study, based on Cheshire's data (Lever, 1993) also indicated the tendency for lagging cities to fail to catch up the European average despite regional policy within the European Community. Nevertheless, there is now some evidence that the cities of the south are beginning to attract disproportionately more investment, although not the cities of the furthest south, such as in Andalusia and Sicily.

The balance of evidence thus suggests that divergence is happening between European cities and that policy intervention is necessary and is likely to continue to be necessary. Clearly, the theory of self-sustaining growth, used as a justification for intervention in the 1960s, has not been borne out in the longer term. When we look at the theoretical justification for spatially discriminant policies for local economies in Europe, there is an interesting shift. In the period of most rapid economic growth in Europe, namely the 1960s, local economic policy and regional policy were justified on the grounds that aggregate, national, economic output was thereby enhanced. The logic behind this statement was that, at the level of local labour markets, there were bottlenecks and capacity shortages which inhibited output. Demand for factors of production was so high that prices were pushed up unnecessarily, particularly wages. The use of government subsidies to divert investment and new employment creation to locations which would not have been the companies' first choice could be justified on the grounds that aggregate output would be higher as a consequence. It was in these terms that Moore and Rhodes (1976) were able to justify British government expenditure on regional policy incentives in the 1960s forcing manufacturing investment to areas of high unemployment such as Scotland and the north of England. With the onset of global recession in the early 1980s, it was not possible to continue using the 'national aggregate efficiency' argument to justify spatially selective interventions. By then, few if any local economies were without excess labour, and wage rates were, in relative terms, falling. The justification for spatial intervention then switched to equity: if there were areas with high levels of unemployment and areas with significantly lower levels then it was only fair that the government intervene to shift labour demand to equalize employment opportunity. If the cost of this intervention was both public subsidy and lower production, because enterprises were being moved to locations which were not their first choice, then this was a price which was justifiable. In a study for OECD, Lever (1984b) argued that, in their most extreme form, equity policies could be justified on the grounds that, if unemployment differentials were allowed to increase without intervention, then civil unrest, often along lines of ethnic segregation might well result (cf. Chapter 14, below).

It is significant that the transition from efficiency-based policies to equity-based policies occurred at the time when the spatial scale of intervention was changed from regional to urban. Prior to the mid-1970s, there was little by way of true local urban economic policy. It was not a specific aim of demand management and, even though spatial and sectoral policies of national governments had profound effects on the economies of urban areas, these effects were by-products rather than explicit targets of policy (Fox-Przeworski, 1991). Governments such as that of the UK transferred the focus of economic policy to the inner areas of the largest cities because it was recognized that, without economic stimulus, policies on housing, social matters, the environment, health and education would not suffice. The 'inner area' studies of London, Birmingham and Liverpool, for example, traced how a moribund economy in an inner city area led to poor housing which, because it was spatially concentrated into poor neighbourhoods, led to poor levels of public services in health and education. These in turn generated a labour force which was even less able to compete for such employment as was available (Lawless, 1989). In many countries, what appears to have happened is that regional policy incentives have been applied at the urban level; in many other countries, distinctive and specifically urban policies to enhance economic efficiency have been developed.

Urban policies to enhance private-sector efficiency

Classical location theory initially stressed the view that the most efficient or profitable locations for private-sector establishments, especially in the manufacturing sector, could be identified in terms of transport costs. The location which minimized the costs of assembling inputs at the factory and distributing products to markets was by definition the most efficient. This view was supplanted by one which allowed for a trade-off between market access and revenue, on the one hand, and the minimization of transport costs, on the other. By the 1960s, however, this transport cost model had largely been supplanted in turn by one which stressed production functions and the costs and substitution between land, labour and capital (Chapman and Walker, 1990, p.44). The production function approach has, implicitly or explicitly, been adopted by local authorities and development agencies in framing their intervention to enhance urban efficiency. In the introduction to his study of Milan, Pompili (Chapter 11, above) explicitly relates the city's output for its own and other cities' consumption to the manner in which it utilizes private and public resources, including capital, human capital within the labour force, information, and land and infrastructure. The accumulated stocks of these inputs are seen as the basis of comparative advantage (Camagni and Pompili, 1990) and urban policies designed to reduce their cost or increase their supply are likely to enhance the efficiency of establishments operating in their areas.

Land policy

Of the three basic factors, land, labour and capital, local government and development agencies have most frequently focused on land. This is not because it is the most important but because they are most likely to have powers to manage land through the land use or physical planning system. Intervention in the land market by local authorities can take several forms. These range from anticipatory land use zoning to seek to guarantee an adequate supply (and therefore at reasonable cost) of land for industry, commerce and distributional use, through land preparation, especially where this is likely to be expensive, as in the case of waste 'brownfield' sites with high levels of pollution, to the actual ownership and management of sites and premises, sometimes with subsidized rentals. The importance of an adequate supply of land, particularly for manufacturing in the inner city, has been stressed by Fothergill and Gudgin (1982) and by Fothergill *et al.* (1987) who point out the extent to which the reduction in space for industry in London (–17.2 per cent in 1967–82) and in the English conurbations (–4.1 per cent) caused by aggressive demand for space by commercial office activities correlates with employment loss in manufacturing. This compares with a growth in factory floorspace and manufacturing employment in rural areas and small towns and is believed to be a strong factor in the urban–rural shift.

Western Europe offers a large number of examples of local authorities who have focused on land as a primary factor in economic development policies. In Dortmund, for example, the economic efficiency of new industry was constrained by the restrictive landholding policies of the declining coal and steel industries. Surveys in the early 1980s indicated that only 25 per cent of the land zoned for industry was actually available because of these constraints. But the creation of the Real Estate Fund Ruhr by the Nordrhein–Westphalia government permitted the utilization of almost the whole of the remainder. Local government was able to offer finance for the reclamation of particularly difficult sites by drawing together grants derived from a wide range of public-sector programmes often with quite different objectives (Hennings *et al.*, 1991). In Barcelona, cooperation between a large number of local authorities has facilitated the rational planning of land for economic activity, particularly land abandoned by the older industries, under the aegis of the Metropolitan Corporation of Barcelona (Vegara-Carrio, 1989). This more integrated perspective on land management has permitted not only the creation of open spaces to enhance the quality of life in the city, but the provision of space for new sectors such as services and the opening up of industrial spaces to a newly revitalized port facility through the district of Poblenou.

In the case of Salonika, rapid urban growth took place without the benefit of a programme of land management, thus generating high land prices, traffic problems and problems of negative externalities, particularly within residential areas. Consequently, central government has sought to regulate land supply through the creation of a Land Reserve Bank to manage industrial buildings, and laws to zone land and to update the fiscal treatment of land ownership (Chiotis and Cocossis, 1989). At the more local (city) level, the state programme of creating industrial estates through the Hellenic Bank for Industrial Development (ETVA) is passing into the management of local authorities who are able to utilize land in their ownership to reduce costs in the creation of industrial estates.

In Milan, Pompili (Chapter 11, above) describes how, since the early 1980s, industrial wasteland has been regulated and brought back into productive use, firstly for manufacturing and more recently for major projects such as international fair sites, transport infrastructure and technopoles. He stresses, however, that, where these major developments are based on public–private partnerships occupying a common site, the timing of projects and the levels of bureaucratic intervention have proved difficult.

The general view is that effectively managed land policies in cities help economic efficiency by guaranteeing the supply of land, by reducing externalities and by reducing costs. Yet some cities and national governments are concerned that too much intervention in the land market can lead to inefficiencies which deter development. The British Enterprise Zone programme typifies this belief, in that it designated a number of large sites in which there would be little planning regulation through the use of 'accelerated procedures', leaving developers to undertake the speedy reclamation of land and the provision of premises. From 1981 to 1986, the national government spent £400m. on land acquisition, tax relief and infrastructural programmes in 23 such zones, which attracted 2800 businesses and 65 000 jobs (Moore, 1989; Downs, 1993). Once displacement and deadweight were allowed for, the cost of job creation in the Enterprise Zones was quite high. And surveys of the establishments involved showed that their major attraction was not the ease of planning permission applications, but the absence of local property taxes for periods of up to ten years.

Policies for labour

Local policies for land have the attraction for local authorities that they create permanent assets in the form of serviced sites and premises. If the businesses fail then the assets remain, either for reletting or for sell-off. Neither of these conditions necessarily holds for the two other factors of production – labour and capital. Where the local authority chooses to intervene in the labour market, through retraining for example, they may create a stock of human capital which remains an enduring asset to help attract investment and increase the efficiency of local establishments. But the asset, being mobile, may move away. The earliest forms of labour market intervention in pursuit of enhanced efficiency have depended upon this mobility. Where national and local labour markets have been tight, the movement of unemployed workers from regions of surplus labour has proved cost-effective, reducing wages and welfare payments and proving cheaper than moving 'work to the workers' (Vanhove and Klaassen, 1987, pp.380–81). However, such labour mobility policies are not open to local authorities whose boundaries are coterminous with local labour markets.

Local authorities have become involved in labour market policy either as a result of concern for equity, using labour retraining as a means of enhancing the re-employment prospects of the unemployed, or in an attempt to upgrade the skills of workers to overcome labour shortages for particular types of labour. The transition from manufacturing to services in the economies of most west European cities has had the effect of excluding many former manual workers from the workforce, thus permitting the simultaneous existence of both fairly buoyant national economies and stubborn pockets of high urban unemployment (Kasarda and Friedrichs, 1986). Some commentators (Boddy *et al.*, 1986, pp.207–12) have argued that, even in dynamic local labour markets, newly created jobs are not occupied by formerly redundant workers who have undergone retraining. Instead, employers prefer to recruit from other sectors of the labour market such as school leavers and housewives returning to work. But others have stressed the importance of retraining workers to guarantee a well-supplied local labour market where labour costs are kept down (Hall, 1993, pp.67–8).

The study by Bosch (1990) describes how, in the context of the threat of major redundancies in the manufacturing sector in France and Germany in the 1980s, initiatives were developed by employment planning in Germany and reconversion in France to restructure the local labour market. Employees threatened with dismissal were offered the opportunity of retraining and ways were found of financing this by merging private and public programmes. These plans were specifically aimed at preventing redundancies by creating new, more competitive employment where the redundancy was to have occurred. These policies to create a more efficient local labour market succeeded in stemming the threat of mass dismissal, especially amongst the unskilled and semi-skilled workforce with long service with the firms concerned. These programmes, usually designed in partnership with the works councils, increased the quality of the workforce and thereby increased their chances of re-employment. Moreover, they made it more possible to attract inward investment by enhancing the stock of human capital in the locality.

Lastly, some local urban authorities have intervened in local labour markets by offering labour market subsidies. In Glasgow, for example, the regional authority has operated a scale of labour subsidies utilizing European Social Fund money to induce employers to take on long-term unemployed workers using a scale from 30 to 60 per cent of the wage cost, depending on the degree of disadvantage experienced by the worker in the labour market in terms of duration of unemployment, age, lack of skill and level of any disability. While such programmes are not strictly 'efficiency' policies and may in fact lead to the inefficient use of labour, they may improve the firm's competitive efficiency by reducing overall wage costs per unit of output.

Policies for capital

As the most mobile of the three factors, capital has been least attractive to local authorities seeking to develop policies to increase land efficiency. There has always been a concern that, where public funds are used to assist private enterprise, either the enterprise will close and thus lose public funds or the enterprise will move and take the locally generated funds with it. Nevertheless, economic restructuring and the breaking up of vertically integrated plants has created demands for inputs and services which small enterprises can supply, and for subcontracting. It is these small enterprises which have most need of venture capital and which are least able to offer security against start-up loans or working capital. Keeble and Wever (1986) offer other explanations for the growth in the number of European small firms, including redundancies in the recession of the early 1980s, technological changes and income growth. Studies of new firm formation in cities such as Copenhagen (Illeris, 1986) and Amsterdam and Breda (Wever, 1986) have shown that about one-third of all new start-ups have difficulty in raising the necessary capital. Most of the programmes of financial assistance to new businesses are operated at the national level (Allen and Yuill, 1990) but many have a regional dimension which advantages areas such as the Mezzogiorno in Italy and Wallonia in Belgium. With the increasing emphasis on urban policy rather than regional policy, programmes of venture capital assistance have taken on an increasingly urban perspective. Thus Mason and Harrison (1991), in a study of the venture capital industry in the UK, point to two urban trends, the increasing concentration of venture capital in London, which by the late 1980s had between 55 and 60 per cent of all venture capital, and the emergence of 'second tier' urban centres of venture capital often associated with high-tech development in cities such as Cambridge and Bristol.

Procurement

While the local policies described above have sought to increase the competitive efficiency of enterprises by subsidizing or in other ways reducing the costs of factor inputs, which might be termed supply-side intervention, some local authorities have also sought to intervene on the demand side. Policies of this type are usually focused on the use by local authorities of their purchasing power to support local suppliers of goods and services. While this in itself may not increase efficiency, where local authorities' purchasing programmes are able to guarantee longer contracts, to smooth out peaks and troughs in non-local authority demand and to increase overall production levels, thus achieving scale economies, efficiency may be enhanced. These types of policy are particularly associated with the so-called 'radical' large city authorities in Britain led by the new urban left in the early 1980s (Mawson and Miller, 1986). These policies were administered by bodies such as the Greater London Enterprise Board and the West Midlands Enterprise Board who, in exchange for allocating supply contracts for goods and services with local producers, often required that they meet conditions pertaining to employment conditions, equality of opportunity and racial policies (Atkinson and Moon, 1994). However, by the late 1980s, the ethos of many of these bodies had changed, conditions of social responsibility were dropped and the enterprise boards, where they survived the dissolution of the metropolitan authorities, had become more entrepreneurially focused (Lawless and Ramsden, 1990).

Urban efficiency

The policies described above are concerned with local authority intervention to assist the efficiency of individual establishments. However, the city as a whole can be treated as a unit of production of greater or lesser efficiency than competing cities, and intervention and policy may occur to enhance this collective efficiency. Most urban economic theory which seeks to measure economic efficiency highlights urban size, measured in terms of total population, as the key explanatory variable. Cities which are too small lack the full range of external economies such as public goods and agglomeration economies: cities which are too large find their scale economies overwhelmed by agglomeration diseconomies such as traffic congestion and by high factor prices such as high rents. While there is some evidence to link private-sector efficiency (and profitability) inversely with city size, there is unlikely to be a policy movement towards an urban system comprised of nothing but small urban places. More likely, the policy intervention will take the form of a set of physical and economic planning policies (population overspill, the creation of new towns, the creation of green belts, urban motorways to reduce congestion, and industrial relocation and decentralization policies) to reduce the growth of the largest cities in the urban hierarchy (Henderson, 1977). Short of policies which seek to act on urban efficiency by influencing city size, we can identify two policy elements in the field of public goods which affect efficiency: transport and information.

Urban transport

Vanhove and Klaassen (1987, p.23) describe the inefficiencies inflicted upon urban economies by traffic congestion. They argue that regional planning has been adopted in Great Britain, the Netherlands, France and Italy to encourage decentralization. Large daily flows of commuters impose high infrastructural investment costs, socioeconomic costs and increasing environmental costs on cities. Klaassen earlier (1965) had argued that urban growth should be restricted once the rate of congestion and agglomeration diseconomies began to grow more quickly than per capita income. More recently, however, the transport argument has focused on the public–private modal split, emphasizing the need to encourage the former and control the latter (Hart, 1993). Whereas in the period 1960–84 policy had been directed at accommodating the private car by the construction of urban motorways and providing additional parking, the concern after the early 1980s was the improvement of public transport and restriction on the use of private cars through systems such as road pricing. In a policy sense, planners have had to tread a thin line between restricting private vehicle usage in order to increase average travel speeds for those vehicles which continue to use city streets, such as freight vehicles, and being excessively restrictive for both lorries and cars and thereby deflecting investment to urban centres with less draconian policies for private vehicles. For example, Priemus (1994) describes how the heavily interventionist planning policies in the cities of the Randstad, such as Rotterdam and Amsterdam, intended to force new investment to sites which are highly accessible by public transport, have in some instances deflected investment and development to Dutch cities outside the Randstad, such as Groningen, which have much less restrictive policies towards the private car. Nevertheless, concerns about environmental degradation including acid rain and global warming have forced a reduction in investment in roads, such as the cancellation of urban motorways in cities such as Paris and London. Concerns are even more heightened where the city under threat is of particular historical or cultural importance: Nanetti (1991) describes, for example, how the city of Florence has subsidized the creation of a light rapid transit system, implemented a system of road pricing within a set of concentric zones and used vacant land on the city edge with good access to the motorway system and the airport as the preferred location for new industrial and commercial developments away from the historic core. Perhaps the best indication that restructured transport policies can make to urban efficiency is to be found in the European Commission's *Green Paper on the Urban Environment* (1990). It sees the redesigning of cities in a denser, more compact form as the way to introduce more 'user-friendly' movement systems with an enhanced role for pedestrians and cyclists and a marked reduction of private car transport (down by two-thirds in the proposed model of the Netherlands, between 1984 and 2010). At the same time, it allows for a much more effective freight transport by both public transport and private road transport where there is no economically viable alternative.

Information

With the globalization of the world's economy and the shift in western urban economies from manufacturing to information-processing activities, the success of individual cities is increasingly likely to be based on their ability to create environments in which knowledge is available and valued (Knight, 1995). Knight argues that, with the removal of European economic frontiers, cities will need to develop policies to foster specialized knowledge bases if they are to remain efficient: cities which lack information or knowledge are likely to become more inefficient. Some types of knowledge, such as research and development, international finance, administrative headquarters of higher-level organizations and multinational corporations are tending to become increasingly concentrated. Other types of knowledge of a sociocultural nature are less formalized and more widely dispersed (Lever, 1995). Studies by the European Community show how the geography and structures of information and knowledge enhance the efficiency of cities and urban regions. A study of four technologies (biotechnology, aeronautics and space, artificial intelligence and textiles and clothing) found that 80 per cent of all innovative research and development in these fields is in firms based in ten 'islands of innovation'. Moreover, these ten were all major city-based nodes in the European core (London, Randstad, Paris, Ruhrgebiet, Frankfurt, Stuttgart, Munich, Lyons–Grenoble, Turin and Milan: Hinkel, 1990). In a study commissioned by the European Community, cities were asked specific questions concerning knowledge resources (European Community, 1992). The cities involved rated six types of information as being important in determining their efficiency and their comparative advantage. In rank order the types of knowledge resources were (1) science and technology, including universities and private-sector R&D, (2) commerce and financial services, (3) industry and production technology, (4) administration and coordination, (5) arts and culture, and (6) creativity. About half the cities in the study acknowledged the importance of universities, libraries, research facilities and cultural facilities, but science and technology and production technology were seen as the most important elements in the knowledge base. Asked about constraints on the development of the knowledge base, cities most often cited institutional inadequacies and the lack of financial resources. Lack of cooperation and synergy amongst the elements was cited by two-thirds of the cities and a lack of efficient knowledge transfer mechanisms and cooperation between supply and demand was cited by more than half.

In terms of policies to enhance the knowledge base, Leontidou (Chapter 9, above) stresses how Athens dominates the university, library and laboratory provision within Greece, but also points out that lack of finance and the existence of bureaucratic obstacles means that this concentration of knowledge is not translated into scientific creativity or into economic growth. While some impediments, such as the failure of the land market to provide space in Athens for new knowledge-based development, are potentially amenable to policy intervention, others, such as Greek society's low regard for knowledge workers, is less easy to counteract. In contrast, Budapest (Chapter 10, above) is seen to capitalize on its high concentration of information sources with 70 per cent of the nation's R&D employees, 50 per cent of the higher education places, 47 per cent of the graduate population and almost 80 per cent of business management and administration. Even during the state socialist era, Budapest was able not only to take the lead in Hungarian economic development, but also to act as an informational and cultural gateway to the west and within the bloc of socialist countries.

Hepworth (1991) takes the argument that city administrations should assist in the creation of the information city somewhat further. He identifies the more comprehensive approaches such as those of Manchester, the 'wired city', Amsterdam, the 'information city' and Barcelona, the 'telematics city'. Assistance generally takes the form of financial aid, usually through a public–private partnership. This may lead to the creation of a comprehensively planned facility such as Amsterdam's teleport-fibre optic cable network aimed at enhancing the city's status as a global business centre, particularly for corporate head offices and financial services. Other planning initiatives include the creation of an 'information belt' in the waterfront area where urban renewal is to be based on the promotion of audiovisual industries, conference centres and mixed land uses, the implementation of a city-wide broadband system and the Cargonaut network which links the airport, import–export firms and a local economic development growth pole. In other cities, such as Oslo, the development of an 'information city' not only increases the efficiency of existing businesses but acts as a showcase for national computer manufacturers and telecommunications carriers (Dragland *et al.*,1985).

In its most extreme form, public intervention to create information-based urban economies is to be seen in technopoles, such as Montpellier, France's fastest growing regional capital between 1975 and 1987 (Donzel, 1994). The technopole is a public–private partnership, initially set up to manage industrial science parks in the town, but it now offers entrepreneurial advice, research facilities and links to the universities. It specializes in five areas of research: health care, computing and robotics, agriculture, communications, and tourism and leisure industries.

Urban marketing

If it is possible to treat cities as entities, the production of which can be rendered more efficient by improving their transport systems and their information flows, they can be marketed as such. The idea of selling places as if they were marketable commodities received growing attention by public authorities in the 1980s and is now an accepted part of urban management (cf. Chapter 17, below). It is usually conducted by means of promotion and the shaping of a favourable place image and/or the removal of an unfavourable image. This is seen as a vital element of taking part in intra-urban competition for visitor income and for inward investment in all sectors. Ashworth (1994) describes the contrasting processes of urban marketing in the cases of Groningen in the Netherlands and Debrecen in Hungary which stress good quality of life, recreational quality and low property prices, but with peripheral location in the case of the former and position as a trade gateway in the latter.

Sánchez (Chapter 7, above) describes how Barcelona was successful in overcoming its old industrial image in order to secure the 1992 Olympic Games on the basis of earlier major events such as the World Exhibitions of 1888 and 1929. Dawson (1994) similarly described how Seville was able to circumvent the backward image of Andalucia in order to attract Expo 1992 to the city. In both cases, the successful bid not only brought a major boost to tourism spending in the relevant year but also led to the creation of substantial infrastructure and to the expectation of continuing inward investment in subsequent years.

City marketing, however, is not always successful. Pompili (Chapter 11, above) points out that Milan has not been successful in this respect, largely because attempts to promote the city have not been linked to actual changes and improvements in the city. Examples of this failure include the inability to stimulate private-sector interest, especially in cultural tourism, the minimal response to the improved accessibility of Linate airport, the failure to utilize twinning and city networks as a vehicle for marketing and an inability to cultivate the foreign press.

Cities, transnational efficiency policies and sustainability

The 1990s have seen the emergence of transnational groupings such as the single European market and the North American Free Trade Area which, through the removal of internal barriers to trade, hope to increase competitive efficiency within world trading patterns. While these are policies designed to respond to the globalization of the world economy and the increasing mobility of capital and labour, they do have local effects (Thompson, 1993, pp.200–201). Similarly, increased concern for sustainability in both economic and urban growth may yield policies which will have local effects.

Trade liberalization

Trade liberalization within the European Community is intended to create an internal market within which there is free movement of goods, people, services and capital. Much greater efficiency will be achieved by the eradication of frontier delays and customs controls, by the removal of technical barriers relating to differing national product standards, business laws and public procurement practices and by the removal of fiscal barriers relating to different national indirect taxation systems. The Cecchini Report (1988) anticipated that the aggregate benefit of implementing the single European market would be a stimulus of 200 billion ECU; it would achieve a price deflation equivalent to 6.1 per cent; and there was the prospect of creating two million new jobs. If all the financial benefits were reinvested, additional employment might rise to five million (Williams, 1991, p.91).

Kresl (1992) has argued that individual cities will need to adjust their economic development policies to take advantage of the great macroefficiencies offered by the single European market. His hypothesis is that the cities located in the urban core of Europe, the 'blue banana', are sufficiently well placed to take advantage of any European developments. But cities of the north and south, being more peripheral, even after allowing for enlargement of the Community, will find development more difficult. In a study of ten cities he finds that only four – Amsterdam, Copenhagen, Lyons and Turin – have attempted a qualitative restructuring of their economies in response to 1992. The remaining six have merely chosen to expand their existing activities. Amsterdam and Copenhagen are seeking to establish themselves as point-of-access cities, Lyons is moving into high-technology industries such as medicine, biotechnology and energy, and Turin is seeking to lose its car industry image and replace it with a high-technology image based on electronics, aerospace, food and materials. Barcelona and Stuttgart are using the greater trade freedom to expand their export base from existing industry and Hamburg is becoming a bridge city, not only into the former GDR, but into the countries of east-central Europe that have been liberalizing their economies. Seville and Munich are developing their roles as the regional capitals of Andalucia and Bavaria. Manchester is thought to have the greatest problems in capitalizing on the unified and enlarged market because of its peripheral location and the impact of transport costs (Chisholm, 1995).

Sustainability

There has been increasing concern, on an international scale, that economic development, particularly in the west, has been achieved at a substantial ecological cost. The raw materials and fossil energy sources have been utilized in a way which discounts future discoveries of stocks. Moreover, the waste and toxic emissions of the processes of production and consumption have been dumped in many cases without adequate thought to their treatment. The European Commission is now giving thought to setting standards for problems of air pollution and waterborne waste disposal, and is seeking to bring the legislation of the member states into unison (CEC, 1991).

At the urban level, much of the policy effort has focused upon the limitation of private transport to reduce pollution and on reducing energy consumption for domestic heating and other uses. Knight (1994) has argued that the shifts in urban economies from manufacturing to knowledge and information-based industries should mean that there will be less utilization of energy and materials and less generation of waste for disposal. The emergence of post-industrial cities in western Europe may well mean fewer rather than more ecological problems, although this will depend on patterns of consumption as much as on patterns of production.

Conclusion

We have demonstrated that market forces alone will not lead to the highest levels of economic efficiency in western European cities. The neo-classical mechanisms of price adjustment and factor substitution do not act swiftly enough to guarantee optimal production functions. At the local level, local government and other bodies have intervened to facilitate the supply of land, labour and capital and sought to adjust local demand levels through procurement policies. Local agencies have been and are responsible for the supply of local public goods such as transport infrastructure to support the local economy and a favourable urban image. Cities are also overtaken by macropolicies for economic efficiency such as the creation of the single European market and policies for environmental efficiency which seek to eradicate temporal negative externalities.

In the next chapter, equity issues are debated, examining how different groups are included within, or excluded from, the enjoyment of the urban and private goods which this process of economic growth generates. Important as those issues and the policies developed by local authorities to adjust distributional patterns are, local authorities in western Europe in the 1990s appear increasingly to conform to the maxim, 'Growth first, then distribution'.

References

Allen, K. and D. Yuill (1990) 'Financial instruments for the promotion of regional development', in H-J. Ewers and J. Allesch (eds), *Innovation and Regional Development*, Berlin: de Gruyter, pp.169–80.

Ashworth, G. (1994) 'The transition to market economies and marketing cities', in Z. Hajdu and G. Horvath (eds), *European Challenges and Hungarian Responses in Regional Policy*, Pecs: Centre for Regional Studies, Hungarian Academy of Sciences, pp.334–47.

Atkinson, R. and G. Moon (1994) *Urban Policy in Britain: the City, the State and the Market*, London: Macmillan.

Boddy, M., J. Lovering and K. Bassett (1986) *Sunbelt City: a Study of Economic Change in Britain's M4 Growth Corridor*, Oxford: Oxford University Press.

Bosch, G. (1990) *Retraining – not Redundancy: Innovatory Approaches to Industrial Restructuring in Germany and France*, Geneva: International Institute for Labour Studies.

Camagni, R. and R. Cappellin (1985) *Sectoral Productivity and Regional Policy*, Document 92-825-5535-6, Brussels: Commission of the European Communities.

Camagni, R. and T. Pompili (1990) 'Competence, power and waves of urban development', in P. Nijkamp (ed.), *Sustainability of Urban Systems: a Cross-national Evolutionary Analysis of Urban Innovation*, Aldershot: Avebury, pp.37–86.

CEC (1990) *Green Paper on the Urban Environment*, Brussels: Commission of the European Communities.

CEC (1991) *Europe 2000: Outlook for the Development of the Community's Territory*, Brussels: Commission of the European Communities.

Cecchini, P. (1988) *The European Challenge: 1992: The Benefits of a Single Market*, Aldershot: Wildwood.

Chapman, K. and D.F. Walker (1990) *Industrial Location*, 2nd edn, Oxford: Blackwell.

Cheshire, P.C. (1993) 'Some causes of western European patterns of urban change, 1971–88', in A.A. Summers, P.C. Cheshire and L. Senn (eds), *Urban Change in the*

United States and Western Europe: Comparative Analysis and Policy, Washington, DC: Urban Institute, pp.145–90.

Chiotis, G.P. and H.N. Cocossis (1989) 'Thessalonika', in L.M. Klaassen, L. van den Berg and J. van der Meer (eds), *The City: Engine Behind Economic Recovery*, Aldershot: Avebury, pp.211–30.

Chisholm, M. (1995) *Britain on the Edge of Europe*, London: Routledge.

Danson, M., W.F. Lever and J.F. Malcolm (1980) 'The inner city employment problem in Great Britain, 1952–1976: a shift-share approach', *Urban Studies*, **17**, pp.193–210.

Dawson, J. (1994) 'Seville', in A. Harding, J. Dawson, R. Evans and M. Parkinson (eds), *European Cities Towards 2000: Profiles, Policies and Prospects*, Manchester: Manchester University Press, pp.179–93.

Donzel, A. (1994) 'Montpellier', in A. Harding, J. Dawson, R. Evans and M. Parkinson (eds), *European Cities Towards 2000: Profiles, Policies and Prospects*, Manchester: Manchester University Press, pp.144–60.

Downs, A. (1993) 'Contrasting strategies for the economic development of metropolitan areas in the United States and western Europe', in A.A. Summers, P.C. Cheshire and L. Senn (eds), *Urban Change in the United States and Western Europe: Comparative Analysis and Policy*, Washington, DC: Urban Institute, pp.15–54.

Dragland, T, K.-O. Mathisen and K. Sinkerud (1985) *The Telematic Sandbox: a Field Trial with Cable Television*, Oslo: Norwegian Telecommunications Administration Research Establishment, Report 17/85.

European Community (1992) *The Future of European Cities*, Brussels: FAST EC/DG12.

Fothergill, S. and G. Gudgin (1982) *Unequal Growth: Urban and Regional Change in the UK*, London: Heinemann.

Fothergill, S., M. Kitson and S. Monk (1987) 'Industrial buildings and economic development', in W.F. Lever (ed.), *Industrial Change in the United Kingdom*, Harlow: Longman, pp.86–107.

Fox-Przeworski, J. (1991) 'New roles for local government: mobilization for action', in J. Fox-Przeworski, J.B. Goddard and M. de Jong (eds), *Urban Regeneration in a Changing Economy: an International Perspective*, Oxford: Clarendon, pp.116–37.

Friedmann, J. (1972) *Regional Development Policy*, Cambridge, Mass.: MIT Press.

Hall, P. (1993) 'Priorities in urban and economic development', in A.A. Summers, P.C. Cheshire and L. Senn (eds), *Urban Change in the United States and Western Europe: Comparative Analysis and Policy*, Washington: Urban Institute, pp.55–85.

Hart, T. (1993) 'Transport, the urban pattern and regional change, 1960–2010', in R. Paddison, W.F. Lever and J. Money (eds), *International Perspectives in Urban Studies*, **1**, London: Kingsley, pp.160–81.

Henderson, J.V. (1977) *Economic Theory and the Cities*, New York: Academic Press.

Hennings, G., R. Kahnert and K.R. Kunzmann (1991) 'Restructuring an industrial economy: breaking up traditional structures in Dortmund', in J. Fox-Przeworski, J.B. Goddard and M. de Jong (eds), *Urban Regeneration in a Changing Economy: an International Perspective*, Oxford: Clarendon, pp.141–63.

Hepworth, M. (1991) 'Planning for the information city: the challenge and response', in J. Fox-Przeworski, J.B. Goddard and M. de Jong (eds), *Urban Regeneration in a Changing Economy: an International Perspective*, Oxford: Clarendon, pp.24–52.

Hinkel, A. (1990) *Diversity, Equality and Community Cohesion*, Brussels: FAST EC/DG12.

Illeris, S. (1986) 'New firm creation in Denmark', in D. Keeble and E. Wever (eds), *New Firms and Regional Development in Europe*, London: Croom Helm, pp.141–50.

Kasarda, J. and J. Friedrichs (1986) 'Comparative demographic-employment mismatches in U.S. and west German cities', in H-J. Ewers, H. Matzerath and J.B.

Goddard (eds), *The Future of the Metropolis: Economic Aspects*, Berlin: de Gruyter, pp.221–49.

Keeble, D. and E. Wever (1986) 'Introduction', in D. Keeble and E. Wever (eds), *New Firms and Regional Development in Europe*, London: Croom Helm, pp.1–34.

Klaassen, L. (1965) 'Regional policy in the Benelux countries', in F. Meyers (ed.), *Area Development Policies in Britain and the Countries of the Common Market*, Washington, DC: Urban Institute, pp.124–37.

Knight, R. (1995) 'Knowledge-based development: policy and planning implications for cities', *Urban Studies*, **32**, pp.225–60.

Knight, R.V. (1994) 'Sustainable development imperative', in Z. Hajdu and G. Horvath (eds), *European Challenges and Hungarian Responses in Regional Policy*, Pecs: Centre for Regional Studies, Hungarian Academy of Sciences, pp.255–71.

Kresl, P.K. (1992) *The Urban Economy and Regional Trade Liberalisation*, New York: Praeger.

Lawless, P. (1989) *Britain's Inner Cities*, London: Chapman.

Lawless, P. and P. Ramsden (1990) 'Sheffield in the 1980s', *Cities*, **7**, pp.202–10.

Lever, W.F. (1984a) 'Industrial change and urban size: a risk theory approach', in B.M. Barr and N.M. Waters (eds), *Regional Diversification and Structural Change*, Vancouver: Tantalus, pp.153–61.

Lever, W.F. (1984b) *The Relationship Between National Economic Policy and Urban Growth*, Paris: OECD.

Lever, W.F. (1993) 'Competition within the European urban system', *Urban Studies*, **30**, pp.935–48.

Lever, W.F. (1995) 'Economic globalisation and urban dynamics', in A.J. Scott (ed.), *Cities, Enterprises and Society on the Eve of the XXIst Century*, Newbury Park, CA: Sage.

Mason, C.M. and R.T. Harrison (1991) 'Venture capital, the equity gap and the north–south divide in the United Kingdom', in M.B. Green (ed.), *Venture Capital: International Comparisons*, London: Routledge, pp.202–47.

Mawson, J. and D. Miller (1986) 'Interventionist approaches in local employment and economic development: the experience of labour local authorities', in V. Hausner (ed.), *Critical Issues in Local Economic Development*, **1**, Oxford: Clarendon, pp.145–99.

McCrone, G. (1969) *Regional Policy in Britain*, London: Allen & Unwin.

Moore B. (1989) 'Enterprise Zones: an evaluation of the experiment in the UK', in OECD (ed.), *Policy Innovation and Urban Land Markets*, Paris: OECD Urban Affairs Programme, pp.30–46.

Moore, B. and J. Rhodes (1976) 'Regional economic policy and the movement of manufacturing firms', *Economica*, **43**, pp.17–31.

Moore, C. and S. Booth (1986) 'The pragmatic approach: local political models of regeneration', in W.F. Lever and C. Moore (eds), *The City in Transition: Policies and Agencies for the Economic Regeneration of Clydeside*, Oxford: Oxford University Press, pp.92–107.

Myrdal, G. (1956) *Economic Theory and Underdeveloped Regions*, London: Duckworth.

Nanetti, R.Y. (1991) 'Conserving and innovating a Renaissance city: economic development policies in Florence', in J. Fox-Przeworski, J.B. Goddard and M. de Jong (eds), *Urban Regeneration in a Changing Economy: An International Perspective*, Oxford: Clarendon, pp.199–216.

Perrons, D. (1992) 'The regions and the Single Market', in M. Dunford and G. Kafkalis (eds), *Cities and Regions in the New Europe: the Global–Local Interplay and Spatial Development Strategies*, London: Belhaven, pp.170–94.

Pred, A.R. (1977) *City-Systems in Advanced Societies*, London: Hutchinson.

Priemus, H. (1994) 'Sustainable urban planning in Europe: challenges and limitations', paper presented at the Conference on 'Cities, Enterprises and Society at the eve of the XXIst century', Lille, France: Institut Fédératif de Recherche sur les Economies et les Sociétés Industrielles.

Temple, M. (1994) *Regional Economies*, London: Macmillan.

Thompson, G.F. (1993) *The Economic Emergence of a New Europe: the Political Economy of Cooperation and Competition in the 1990s*, Aldershot: Edward Elgar.

Tyler, P., B. Moore and J. Rhodes (1984) *Geographical Variations in Industrial Costs*, Discussion Paper 12, Cambridge: University of Cambridge, Department of Land Economy.

Vanhove, N. and L.M. Klaassen (1987) *Regional Policy, a European Perspective*, Aldershot: Gower.

Vegara-Carrio, J.M. (1989) 'Barcelona', in L.H. Klaassen, L. van den Berg and J. van der Meer (eds), *The City: Engine behind Economic Recovery*, Aldershot: Avebury, pp.171–9.

Wever, E. (1986) 'New firm formation in the Netherlands', in D. Keeble and E. Wever (eds), *New Firms and Regional Development in Europe*, London: Croom Helm, pp.54–74.

Williams, A.M. (1991) *The European Community*, Oxford: Blackwell.

14 Urban policies to promote equity

Jan van Weesep

Introduction

Development creates paradoxes. A particularly compelling one for today's cities results from their reaction to the continuing economic transformation. As we have seen in the previous chapter, the cities themselves attempt to adapt to the changing economic reality by promoting development. Such policies to boost the efficiency of the urban area are meant to create benefits for the local population. The paradox is that, the harder the cities push to transform their economy, the more social problems they create.

Some segments of the population profit significantly from the professionalization of the economy, which is the core of the economic transformation, whereas others are being victimized. Their participation in the new economy is marginal, while some are even excluded outright. In this light, increased efficiency seems to coincide with diminished equity, and economic growth seems to spawn social injustice. A *dual society* (Castells, 1989) is the result when the benefits of economic growth do not reach the people who have been relegated to the fringes of the new economy. A *dual city* emerges where, through the working of the housing system, social inequity corresponds to spatial inequity, where the losers are spatially segregated from the winners. The successful city is characterized not only by the shining edifices of the private sector and the wealth flaunted by the newly affluent but also by decaying neighbourhoods, concentrations of disadvantaged ethnic groups and the abject poverty of the homeless in the street. In terms of the ideology of the welfare state, this paradox cries out for redistribution of the benefits of the economic transformation. But the model of the redistributive welfare state is losing its once wide appeal. The liberal notion of 'betting on the strong' is rapidly replacing it.

However, ignoring the equity dimension may in the long run frustrate the economic transformation itself. The flow of new investment may falter where the social fabric becomes threadbare, signifying inequities between population segments or between neighbourhoods within the city, between the city and its suburbs, or showing up as urban criminality and riots. The increasing heterogeneity of people and businesses in the city makes it difficult to define common interests and shared policy goals. Social contrasts may prevent the creation of broad coalitions of government, private sector and the populace, and such coalitions are needed to design the equitable strategies for growth and renewal on which success is built. The promotion of equity is not only a convenient way to pay off the laggards and the outcasts and thus to maintain the peace: it may be a necessary condition for long-term success in the competition for growth.

Equity policies cover many fields. They are intended to promote fair access to jobs, housing, education, social services and health care. Improvements in public transport can be described in terms of promoting social justice when they provide everyone with ease of mobility and access to services, to places of work, to recreation facilities, and the option to maintain their social contacts. Job training programmes may be inspired by the need to upgrade the local workforce and thereby to increase the efficiency of an area. But when job training is aimed specifically at helping the unemployed and the unemployable, such programmes contain a strong equity dimension. Environmental controls designed to foster clean air and water can be seen primarily as means to control negative externalities. At the same time, they contribute to greater equality in standard of living, since the externalities are generally unevenly distributed. Many urban policies have an equity dimension, even though their primary purpose may lie elsewhere.

This chapter focuses on a specific set of urban equity policies, namely housing policies. The social equity dimension is exemplified by the differences in housing and living conditions among various population groups. Fair housing policies include programmes to provide the disadvantaged population with affordable homes. The dimension of social justice is illuminated by discussing the issue of spatial equity, that is, the segregation of the increasingly heterogeneous urban population. To provide the proper backdrop, the increasing heterogeneity of the urban population will be discussed. But first, urban development and the forces that affect it are briefly reviewed.

Throughout this chapter, reference will be made to situations and policy developments in cities across Europe, although the policy trends in the Netherlands will be accentuated as a case in point. Although Dutch policy is a specific variant, its development closely resembles the evolution of urban policy elsewhere, particularly in northern Europe. The discussion focuses on the winners and the losers of urban restructuring in the 1990s, but places this process in the historic evolution of equity policies of the past 50 years.

Urban development and public policy

Urban development trends

The development of cities reflects processes at work in society at large. At certain points in time, rapid, fundamental change takes place in both contexts. These transitions alternate with longer periods in which the changes seem to work themselves out gradually. Western societies are now living through one of those transitional periods when many trends seem to have reached a breaking point; consequently, the cities are also changing. The previous transition gave rise to the industrial city and industrial society. Once again, changes are being linked to technological developments. Castells (1989) saw the proliferation of new information technologies as the seedbed of the current transition. Their introduction has been directly linked to economic restructuring and social change and, by implication, to the sociospatial patterns emerging in society.

The informational economy, thrust forward by developments in transport and information technology, embodies the comparative advantage principle. The transition set off a spiral of deindustrialization in many European cities with concentrations of older, less competitive manufacturing industries. The decline of industry decimated the goods-handling sector. These developments went hand-in-hand with the growth of managerial functions, especially in a few select cities – the Eurocities – which are assuming ascendency. Hall (1993) argues that Brussels stands to gain because of its prominence as the 'capital' of the European Union. Bonn is another likely winner; it has a strong incentive to claim a new role when many of its current government functions move to Berlin. Bonn might very well succeed, because it offers excellent facilities and a prime location in the heart of urban Europe. Some of the existing financial centres will host new European organizations, adding to their prominence. Berlin and Vienna seem destined to recapture some of the important functions they lost when the Iron Curtain was lowered almost 50 years ago. And, as Enyedi argues in his study of Budapest, the capitals and major regional centres of the countries of east-central Europe stand to gain as well, especially if they can become junctions in the new transport systems of airlinks and high-speed trains.

Although cities everywhere seem to be moving in the same general direction, their trajectories are idiosyncratic. Each built environment reflects the period during which it evolved, as well as the culture of the region. The functions of a city remain intricately linked to the society of which it forms a part. Likewise, a city's development is preconditioned by the specific role it plays within wider society. But each city is also influenced by its geographical location and its ability to adapt. The numerous trajectories of change are determined less by their geographical and historical contexts than by specific selections from and responses to sets of local conditions, both physical and organizational (Van Weesep and Dieleman, 1993).

Ultimately, as in the past, much development of cities is the result of decisions made by the private sector. Individuals and businesses make investment decisions; in the aggregate, these decisions determine the economic functions of cities. There are many examples of cities that flourished with the growth of a single industry, as the cities of the Industrial Revolution vividly remind us. There are still cities whose fortune is determined by a single corporation or by the development of a single industry. The typology of cities in Chapter 2 of this book reflects this pattern, especially where it concerns specialized cities (cf. Brunet, 1989).

The public sector has also become deeply involved in the dynamics of cities. It creates the general economic conditions in which the private sector thrives or falters. The state either provides the major infrastructure that may determine the future role of a city or sets the stage for its construction. The vignette of Copenhagen in Part II of this volume provides a prime example in its analysis of the future impact of the anticipated road connection across the Sound. The state may also promote major events that act as a catalyst for redevelopment, such as the Olympic Games in Barcelona. National governments attempt to capture European institutions as prizes from Brussels, with which to boost the development of individual cities. But all such public works carry the risk of promoting uneven development; where one city grows at the expense of others, urban development becomes inequitable. It is precisely this risk that has enticed national governments to apply corrective measures in the past.

Regional (urban) development policies

The reduction of disparity in living conditions through income redistribution and general welfare policies has been a key target of the welfare state. Urban and regional development policies were added to increase equity between places. In the 1960s and 1970s, such regional development initiatives spearheaded public policy. In some European countries, this was formulated in general terms such as 'prevention of regional imbalances' (Britain) or the need for 'balanced development' (France). French regional development was designed to counter the dominance of Paris by creating *pôles d'équilibre*. Other countries, including Germany and Sweden, have been more explicit, specifying minimum standards and requirements of accessibility for all places (Stöhr and Tödtling, 1979).

As elsewhere, the Netherlands pursued the elusive goal of spatial equity by applying alternating policy instruments for decades from the early 1950s (Van Weesep, 1988). If the post-1945 transition to an industrial society had been left to the private sector, investment would have been concentrated in the urbanized western part of the country. This would have exacerbated existing regional disparities, prompting considerable migration to the cities in the west. In the political climate of the time, this propensity had to be rectified through planning and government initiative (Bartels and Van Duijn, 1984). Policy was needed to deal with two related problems. One was the lack of economic opportunities and the resulting social deprivation in the periphery. The other was fear of serious congestion – and, consequently, economic slowdown – in the urban agglomerations in the west. Thus regional policy to promote economic development was complemented by urban policy to bring about a balanced development of the urbanized part of the country.

The record of the first 30 years of Dutch regional policy shows a gradual expansion of programmes and target areas, but it also shows sudden reversals in response to changes in the nature of the problem and the ability of government to steer social development. Initially, regional policy aimed to make rural regions more attractive to industry by carrying out public works there. In addition, the policy promoted migration by implementing a workers-to-jobs strategy. Of course, that strategy would not only compound congestion in the urban regions but would also have a negative impact on the socioeconomic structure of the periphery. This realization led policy makers to emphasize the decentralization of employment and adopt a jobs-to-workers strategy (Wever,

1986). Decades of regional policy helped change the economic structure of peripheral rural regions but did not cure their economic weakness. This temporary respite was probably due to the relatively meagre funding of the programmes. The allowance was set at 0.07 per cent of gross domestic product, about the same level as in Germany and France. But this amounted to no more than half the Swedish rate and to only a fraction of the 0.50 per cent spent in the UK (Weaver, 1984).

The major shift in Dutch regional development programmes, however, resulted from the need to promote restructuring in traditional mining and manufacturing regions around 1970. Industrialization incentives were then extended to urbanized areas in the country's periphery. Subsidy programmes were also made available to the service sector. Besides public works and subsidies on investment in the designated regions, the instruments included relocation subsidies, wage supplements, relocation subsidies for employees moving with firms relocated from the west and the stimulation of tourism. Government-financed development corporations were set up to provide venture capital to private firms, to recruit new (foreign) businesses and provide know-how. This was the first concrete step towards giving local authorities a task in economic development. The purpose was to create an equitable distribution of income. The government also decentralized several of its own agencies in an effort to create regional growth poles and alleviate the pressure on the cities in the west. At the same time, the spectre of congestion in the west was to be avoided by urban decentralization within the region to new towns and 'growth centres'.

The next turnabout of policy was inspired by the observation that the anticipated growth of the big cities did not materialize because of changing demographics. Instead of growing at a rapid rate, the cities lost a substantial number of their inhabitants. A second factor was that traditional industries closed down in the cities. Their economic basis was further undercut when the growing service sector started to relocate to the suburbs. Consequently, the cities themselves exhibited unexpected symptoms of decline. The planners then turned their attention from promoting and regulating the 'overspill' of people and businesses to the task of revitalizing the cities themselves (Ottens, 1984). Eventually, regional policy adopted the view that spatial equity is best served by letting each region develop its own potential (Clement, 1991). This evaluation of the policy experience is consistent with the experience of other European countries. In general, spatial equity policies have a poor record on improvements in objective and subjective indicators of living standards. In most market and mixed economies, spatial inequities have not decreased. Where they have been reduced, for instance at the interregional level, they have usually increased within urban regions (Stöhr and Tödtling, 1979).

Cities in competition

For a long time, local authorities in the Netherlands had limited jurisdiction and few powers to devise their own development strategies. Although localities have formal autonomy, national policy making takes precedence over local and regional initiatives when these conflict with national development schemes. As in other countries, local authorities are supposed to implement national programmes and provide public services. But unlike other countries, Dutch municipalities are kept from becoming proactive in development policies by their greater dependence on the national government for their finances. Much more funding is channelled through general contributions and special-purpose grants than is the case for cities elsewhere in Europe (Table 14.1). This dependence also meant that the local effects of the fiscal retrenchment at the national level in the early 1980s were severe, further limiting their room to manoeuvre. When faced with reductions in the contributions from the national government, many cities had to cut expenditure and raise additional revenue from local sources. However, such measures to balance the budget, while practised widely, could only partly resolve their problems. Therefore innovations in policy making, entailing a shift to future-oriented in-

Table 14.1   Sources of local government income in various European countries, 1980

	Local taxes	Other local sources	Grants from higher authorities
The Netherlands	5.5	0.5	94.5
Denmark	39.4	3.7	56.9
Italy	59.7	32.3	8.0
Norway	54.0	31.1	14.9
Sweden	45.8	29.1	25.1
United Kingdom	33.8	20.2	46.0
West Germany	34.3	36.1	29.6

Source: Kreukels and Spit (1989, Table 6.4).

vestments, became the preferred option, especially in the big cities with their greater capacity for policy development and their potential attractiveness to the private sector (Kreukels and Spit, 1989). This reorientation reveals a new climate of entrepreneurial politics in Dutch local administration.

In most European countries, the national government realized that local authorities were in the best position to analyse local problems and find appropriate solutions. Therefore responsibilities were decentralized and this set the stage for the popularity of the concept of the entrepreneurial city. Increasingly, local governments turned to partnerships with the private sector to resolve their problems. Once again, the private sector played an important role in urban development, through cooperation with local administrations, as the dependence of local authorities on the national governments diminished. Major redevelopment schemes now have a much larger private-sector component than before, as well as an emphasis on the efficiency dimension. And the cities have become active players in economic development, wooing private investors and attracting major corporations.

The capacity to attract new economic activities no longer depends exclusively on the resources the city offers to entrepreneurs for their production processes. Nor does it depend solely on good infrastructure. The cities have to be watchful to retain existing firms, because so many firms have become footloose. They or their mother companies are targets of competing cities seeking to entice them to relocate. Likewise, major events and other non-commercial activities must be courted. Sometimes this draws the cities into a game of competitive bidding. Alternatively, political decision making involves enlisting the cooperation of the national government.

The assets that matter in the competition are increasingly beyond the range of the traditional, primary economic location factors. These have been reproduced in all major cities. Of course, new transport networks may introduce new disparities when they bypass places that used to be well integrated (Bruinsma and Rietveld, 1993). Cities now succeed for reasons other than their primary location factors. Indeed, success is largely due to the appeal of their level of general services, to their social, commercial and cultural amenities, and to their reputation as places where things get done, where conflicting interests do not stand in the way of progress. Contrary to the general impression, many of the older metropolitan cores have been surprisingly successful in attracting corporate headquarters, producer services, research and development organizations, the arts, cultural facilities and high-level public administration. Many of the newer suburbs of older industrial centres have developed substantial concentrations of high-tech industries, modern distribution centres and important producer services. They are attractive to such businesses because of secondary yet important assets such as better communication infrastructure, cleaner environments, cheaper land and housing, accessibility of technical and research institutions, and proximity to leisure opportunities (Parkinson *et al.*, 1992). The appeal of successful cities also includes an adequate level of social and spatial equity and its concomitant lack of social strife.

Urban problems still determine the image of the central cities of the large agglomerations. These have become concentration areas of social problems. Of course, problems are not limited to big cities, but the large concentrations of disadvantaged population groups gives them the critical mass for social strife. Hence the people concerned run a greater risk of becoming socially isolated from mainstream society. This trend towards 'separate and un-equal' may – in extreme situations – turn the disadvantaged mem-bers of society into a separate underclass.

Urban restructuring and the urban population

The evolving social structure of the urban population

The social structure of the city has been deeply affected by eco-nomic restructuring through the mediating role of the labour mar-ket. Most authors agree that the segmentation of society has changed fundamentally, even to the point of polarization. Yet there is still a lively debate on the emerging shape of urban society in Europe and on the nature of the dividing lines between its popu-lation segments (Pahl, 1988; Marcuse, 1989; Hamnett, 1994). The shifts are strongly related to the dramatic changes in the sectoral composition of the (urban) economy.

Manufacturing activities in the major cities of northern Europe have contracted at an ever-increasing rate since the 1970s. The process was initiated by the move of manufacturing plants to peripheral regions of these countries themselves, often with the support of regional development programmes. But, as part of the globalization of the economy, many firms have moved their pro-duction facilities further afield in search of ever cheaper locations. Many of the remaining plants were eventually closed down. This trend is clearly reflected in the changing composition of the na-tional economy (Table 14.2). In the big cities these changes tend to

Table 14.2 Employment change by industrial sector, UK, 1980–90

Industry	Share of employment 1990 (per cent)	Level of employment 1990 (000s)	Net change 1980–90 (000s)	Average growth 1980–90 (per cent p.a.)
Primary & utilities	3.8	1 007	−334	−2.8
Manufacturing	20.5	5 432	−1 654	−2.6
Construction	6.9	1 832	213	1.3
Distribution, transport	27.2	7 199	598	0.9
Business & misc. services	21.8	5 780	2 058	4.5
Non-marketed services	19.7	5 217	249	0.5
Whole economy	100.0	26 458	1 130	0.4

Source: Owen and Green (1992, Table 1).

be even more extreme. Southern European cities profited at first from this search for cheaper locations because of their skilled labour force. But as we have seen in the vignettes of Part II, even here deindustrialization is now proceeding. The manufacturing activities that remain in the cities tend to be either those that require highly skilled labour or those that are so closely entwined in the local market that they are trapped. They have to look for other strategies to cope with the global competition by cutting costs. One way to achieve this is to tap into the vast reservoir of cheap, unskilled immigrant labour. Another way is to ignore the regulations on working conditions. The typical forms of urban manufacturing are plants with high-tech applications in their production processes – demanding specific skills from the labour force – and the sweatshops of the informal sector.

The process of deindustrialization was accompanied by the rapid expansion of the service sector. Financial and business services have grown rapidly, along with personal services. Together their growth more than makes up for the loss of jobs in manufacturing. Another significant change took place within the manufacturing sector. There was a clear movement away from the factory floor to the front office. Both trends have boosted the share of managers and specialists in the workforce (Table 14.3). This has had major repercussions on the social structure of urban society. Several authors have emphasized the demise of intermediate-level functions and the vigorous growth of low-paying positions in the service sector (Gordon and Sassen, 1992).

Table 14.3 The Netherlands occupational structure, 1981–91

	1981 (per cent)	1990 (per cent)	Absolute change (000s)	Percentage change
Managers	2.6	4.3	+139	+103
Specialists	19.6	23.9	+509	+51
Administrative	18.7	17.8	+169	+18
Commercial	10.3	11.0	+176	+32
Service	11.2	12.3	+206	+36
Manual labour	29.3	24.3	+38	+2
Others	8.3	6.3	−26	−6
Total	100	100	+1 202	+23.5

Source: Hamnett (1994, Table 1).

As a result of the economic transformation, two types of jobs tend to be concentrated in the big cities: those at the higher end and those at the lower end of the scale. But the implied polarization of the labour market is disputed by Hamnett (1994), who argues that, while a continuing professionalization can easily be demonstrated, the official sources do not document a vigorous growth of low-skilled and low-paid service jobs in the big cities of Europe. But it should be kept in mind that statistics may not reveal the full extent of employment in personal services, tourism, hotels and restaurants and so on. Many of these jobs are filled by unregistered part-time, casual or undocumented workers. Labour market dynamics contribute to polarization in yet another way: by the high rate of unemployment and its longer duration. For instance, as recently as 1975, 70 per cent of the unemployed males (and 75 per cent of the females) in the Netherlands had been out of work for less than six months. Only 12 per cent and 10 per cent, respectively had been unemployed for longer than 12 months. A decade later, however, the situation had almost reversed itself. By 1985 only 29 per cent of unemployed men and 32 per cent of unemployed women had been out of work for less than six months, while over half of these men and women had been looking for a job for more than 12 months. At the same time, a large number of unemployed had been removed from the files of the labour exchange because it would be virtually impossible to find a suitable job for them (Van Weesep and Van Kempen, 1992).

These trends are most painful in the cities, where the expansion of the service sector provided little solace to the redundant industrial workforce. Throughout the western world, the same categories of workers are being bypassed by the growth of the service sector. But the welfare state, for as long as it lasts, masks the social inequity resulting from the economic transition. The trends are therefore much more clearly visible in those transforming European cities where the welfare provisions have traditionally been much less comprehensive than in northern Europe, or where they have already been curtailed.

The new urbanites

The population of European cities has become increasingly diversified demographically over the past three decades. Everywhere the rate of population increase slowed considerably after the mid-1960s, in what has become known as the second demographic transition (Van de Kaa, 1987). The term applies to the demographic consequences of important social and cultural changes that in-

duce people to avoid marriage and parenthood. Longevity, affluence, women's emancipation and a number of other sociocultural
developments have led to a rapid increase in the number of the
elderly, a precipitous drop in birth rates, a steep rise in divorce
rates, a (relative) decline in the number of families with children
and a concomitant increase in the number of single persons and
two-person households. In addition to the growing number of
households, there has been more variety in living arrangements
within specific age groups and types of households. Singles may
be of all ages, two-person households may consist of adults only
or an adult plus a child. While these changes have affected the
structure of the national populations in general, urban populations
have been affected to an extreme degree.

Champion (1994) points out that demographic change has two
implications for urban change: it alters the sociodemographic profile of the sitting population, and it affects the patterns of population distribution and migration. Because of the almost universal
incidence of these trends, few places will escape their consequences.
Urban populations everywhere exhibit an increasing variation in
household size, composition and lifestyle (Table 14.4). These
changes are related to development of the labour market, but they
appear to be rather insensitive to economic ups and downs. Even
during the economic recessions of the 1980s, the demographic
transition continued unabated.

Cities have long accommodated a heterogeneous population
with respect to lifestyle, ranging from 'urban villagers' to 'cosmo-
politans'. During the 1960s and 1970s, high-income households
tended to prefer suburban lifestyles. In contrast, Bell's urban-
oriented 'careerists' and 'consumers' (Bell, 1968) were back on the
urban housing market in the 1980s and 1990s. Single working
persons and dual-career households prefer to live close to their
place of work in an environment with a wide variety of facilities
and services. Living in an urban setting, they can combine several
activities in a single trip and minimize the time spent on house-
keeping chores. People with a high income can also afford to pay
someone to perform household tasks. Households with more than
one adult can share the responsibilities. Thus they become less
dependent on proximity to concentrations of employment opportunities and the facilities found in the urban environment. This
allows them to live in the suburbs, especially if their contributions
to the household tasks are asymmetrical. The most telling example of this is the traditional household with a single wage-earner.
They can live in a distant suburb only because of their extreme
time–space division of responsibilities. The woman takes care of

Table 14.4 Composition of the population of the Dutch Randstad by household type and by residential environment, 1985–6

	Four big cities		Entire Randstad	
	Percentage of all households	Index (1981=100)	Percentage of all households	Index (1981=100)
Singles and two-person households	70.1	107	54.0	111
Head aged 35 or younger	28.5	105	25.8	93
Head aged 55 or older	40.0	91	34.4	100
Households without children	66.5	105	51.7	111
Singles and cohabitating couples with children	46.4	114	29.1	124
Cohabitating couples without children	27.7	91	28.4	99
Single-parent families	7.8	134	5.6	108
Head unemployed	8.3	193	3.4	170
Head retired	27.4	97	21.5	104
Dual-income households	15.1	90	23.1	99

Source: Kruythoff (1993, Table 4.3).

all the domestic chores within the home and its surroundings, allowing the husband to concentrate on his career (Van Engelsdorp Gastelaars and Vijgen, 1991).

In spite of the effects of the demographic development and change of lifestyle, migration has the most pervasive effect on the geography of the population. There have been population flows back and forth between different parts of the metropolitan areas, as urbanization gave way to suburbanization, which subsequently evolved into reurbanization, but international migration has been at least as important for the increasing diversity of the urban population. It has made the cities the stage for a wide range of lifestyles and is turning them into colourful multicultural societies.

Increasing ethnic diversity

Most European countries now host large communities of international migrants. Many of these migrants have become concentrated in the cities because of job opportunities, access to housing or the presence of others from the same country of origin. In the late 1980s, the share of immigrants in the total population of major German cities ranged from 6 to 25 per cent. In the Netherlands, this share ranged from 13 to 21 per cent. In France a few years earlier, their share averaged some 12 per cent, while in Belgium it ranged from 8 to 24 per cent (White, 1993).

Two processes underlie the increasing ethnic diversity of societies that were once relatively homogeneous. The decolonization process in the 1950s and 1960s enticed many people to move to the 'mother' country. Organized labour migration of the 1960s added many new migrants from other countries. These guest workers were eventually followed by their dependants, as they settled permanently in their host countries. These two processes explain the specific composition of the foreign population in the big cities of Europe. The foreign population reflects a country's colonial history and the geography of its treaties. The relatively uneasy population balance that resulted was tipped in the 1980s, when new waves of migrants arrived. A large proportion of these new international migrants were refugees and political asylum seekers, fleeing famine, war or persecution. The migration patterns then came to reflect variations in the immigration laws of the destination countries, the presence of culturally related groups and the countries' location with respect to regions in upheaval and international transport links. Consequently, the diversity of the migrant population in the cities has increased dramatically.

Today's international migration from virtually the entire Third World has destinations in all European countries. This has changed the position of most southern European countries. Many of them were emigration countries until the mid-1970s but have since become net receivers of international migration flows (Pugliese, 1995). However, this does not mean that immigrants are more easily assimilated there. Immigration of diverse ethnic groups has caused more tensions in certain cities than in others, bordering on xenophobia in some. Virtually everywhere, clashes in lifestyles between the indigenous population and the newcomers have kept the newcomers from integrating. The differences in lifestyle have led to significant social unrest in most places. By and large, any big city in Europe now consists of two nations, separate and unequal. Socially and economically, low-income migrant groups form a marginal population, contributing to the formation of a dual society. Spatially, their concentration in the older and less desirable neigbourhoods suggests the development of dual cities.

The social status of the migrants is mainly determined by the niche they occupy in the labour market. As manual labourers, the guest workers have had to bear the brunt of the current economic restructuring. The jobs they came to fill in the past have now largely disappeared, while their qualifications do not generally fit the employment opportunities of the new economy. Owing to the recurrent economic crises in the 1980s, the refugees have also had a hard time finding an equitable place in the host societies. Among migrants, unemployment rates are much higher than among corresponding categories in the indigenous population. Their lack of assimilation into the host society is related to their poor language skills and low levels of formal education. These factors have hampered attempts to improve their position. Even in Britain, where many immigrant groups have been settled longer and have a good command of English, there are distinct differences in economic performance between the indigenous British people and the various ethnic groups (as well as within the ethnic population).

During the 1980s, the ethnic population of the UK kept on growing. Overall, the creation of jobs kept pace with population growth. There was a slight decline in the number of people unemployed and on government training schemes (but also the inactive population increased, suggesting the removal of long-term unemployed from the files of the labour exchange). The number of people who were employed grew most slowly among the West Indians and most rapidly among smaller ethnic groups. However, these groups also showed the greatest rise in unemployment and economic inactivity. And where unemployment declined, this decrease occurred at the same time as an above-average rise in economic inactivity (Table 14.5).

As the ethnic populations are generally economically deprived, they may be expected to occupy marginal positions in other respects as well. Overall, their housing conditions are below average. They are usually relegated to the older, low-quality stock, where they live in overcrowded conditions because of their relatively large households. In spite of substantial improvements during the 1980s, they are hardly catching up with the indigenous population (Van Weesep, 1995). Many live in the older parts of the central cities, or in the least desirable parts of newer neighbourhoods. Even where they have dispersed to newer areas of the cities, their segregation has generally not diminished.

Table 14.5   *Changing economic activity by ethnic group in the United Kingdom, 1981–1987/1989*

Ethnic group	Population of working age 1981 (000s)	Change employed 1981–1987/89 (per cent)	Change unemployed 1981–1987/89 (per cent)	Change inactive 1981–1987/89 (per cent)
White	39 770.5	5.4	–2.7	1.2
West Indian	356.3	0.2	–8.0	10.6
Indian	485.0	20.7	–17.8	8.0
Pakistani	156.0	24.5	81.2	67.3
Bangladeshi	27.0	79.4	121.2	145.5
Chinese	60.9	84.1	20.1	31.0
African	47.2	115.4	232.2	40.9
Arab	28.1	79.8	86.0	95.2
Mixed	98.1	43.8	–20.2	38.2
Other	132.7	0.8	–29.8	–39.1
All	41 162.5	5.9	–2.3	1.8

Source: Owen and Green (1992, Table 5).

Spatial inequities on the metropolitan scale

Suburbanization has fundamentally altered the residential structure of urban areas. With the growth of affluence, the range of housing options has increased. Greater prosperity also allowed people to purchase a private car, which they need for commuting and other daily activities in a more dispersed setting. The suburban alternative proved to be especially appealing to families with children, who want the suburban lifestyle and a house with a garden. In most cities, many of those who could afford it left the crowded inner neighbourhoods for new homes in the more spacious new suburbs that were springing up everywhere. This migration has involved a wide range of social status categories. It embraces people from the growing category of managers and professionals seeking to reconstruct the lifestyle of the early railroad commuters; it spans middle-class employees and blue-collar workers. In southern European cities like Athens, Barcelona, Lisbon and Milan, high-income groups have long clung to their traditional apartment, living in the central city. Yet even there, the dream of a single-family home in a suburb is rapidly gaining in popularity. Until recently, the poor and the working class had been relegated to high-rise complexes in the towns of the first suburban ring. But now the cities of southern Europe are being turned inside-out. They increasingly resemble cities of the north. Many of the older neighbourhoods of cities throughout Europe have become the domain of the elderly and the recent immigrants, as well as of the 'new urbanites', underlining the heterogeneity of the urban population.

Because of the great variation in quality of the towns on the urban periphery, mass suburbanization has not eliminated the spatial inequities in living conditions. Rather, these inequities have been reproduced in a wider region. High-income groups have moved to attractive estates in choice parts of the suburban ring. Their private cars provide them with access to all the facilities corresponding to their lifestyles. Low-income groups have moved to planned suburbs and new towns. Compared to the old neighbourhoods they left behind, they may have improved their housing quality. But the lack of accessible facilities and services may nevertheless make them feel deprived. Two vived examples are the vast social housing estates near Glasgow and the *grandes ensembles* in the vicinity of Paris. This spatial inequity has a gender dimension. In the Netherlands, the term 'green widows' denotes the plight of housewives trapped in their terraced houses in new towns and commuter villages.

The other spatial inequity brought about by suburbanization is widely known as spatial mismatch. This term refers predominantly to the suburbanization of jobs. Large numbers of the remaining firms offering low-skilled employment opportunities have left the central cities and moved to the suburban ring, while the population dependent on those jobs stayed behind. At the same time, the high-level employment opportunities in the financial and business services are still largely concentrated in the central cities, even though decentralization to new office parks on the periphery of the cities is increasing (for example, La Défense in Paris). Thus spatial mismatch creates the inconvenience of long commuting trips on congested highways or in crowded trains for the suburban higher-income groups. At the same time it contributes significantly to the high rates of unemployment among the ethnic, low-skilled central city population (Holzer, 1991).

The effects of the changing urban space economy and the concomitant changes in the labour market are hard to disentangle from the concurrent demographic and sociocultural changes. Yet their impact on the population structure, and thereby on the functioning of cities, is evident. The simultaneous increase of the poor and the affluent does not necessarily lead to a dual city in the sense of a socially and spatially segregated city, where the rich and the poor live in isolation from each other. There are still many urban households with intermediate incomes; most people are neither very rich nor very poor (Marcuse, 1989). Furthermore, income position and prospects are not the only criteria that stratify the urban population. Variations in lifestyle and culture can help people to cut across socioeconomic divisions. Conversely, these factors can underscore social isolation.

In fact, European cities show signs of impending social polarization. The spatial effects of polarization can only be controlled as long as the equity policies of the diminishing welfare states remain on the books. Many governments still give priority to the ideal of equal access to education, social services and health care. In northern Europe, housing has also been identified as a critical element in the well-being of people. Consequently, the provision of affordable housing of good quality has enjoyed a high priority on the policy agenda. The extent to which that agenda has been implemented is witnessed in the construction of social housing and the availability of housing subsidies. Housing market regulations have been applied to safeguard fair access for low-income households. But such programmes have not been equitable in all respects. They are now also under fire, even in the most stalwart of welfare states.

Housing policies and urban social development

The urban response to changes in the economy is mediated by the housing system. Housing policy affects the way social and spatial inequality emerges and is modified. Through housing, the economic restructuring of the cities has a localized impact. Depending on their nature, housing policies may either alleviate the social injustices brought about by economic restructuring or underscore them.

Government intervention in housing

Many governments, particularly in northern European welfare states, have become deeply involved in the provision of housing. The purpose of intervention is to guarantee decent housing for everyone at a reasonable price. National housing policies of the past have set the stage for current housing issues. At present, those policies largely define how equitable the housing system is.

In many countries, the hand of the public sector in construction can be seen in the composition and the use of the current housing stock. After 1950, social housing accounted for over 50 per cent of new construction in Sweden and the Netherlands. In these two countries and elsewhere, much residential construction also benefited from subsidies, making new housing more affordable. Table 14.6 shows the magnitude of intervention in construction after 1950 and the variations among countries. Table 14.7 further illustrates this point by specifying the 1985 share of the gross national product that was committed to direct and indirect housing subsidies in that year. Big cities have been particularly affected by the accent on social housing in construction programmes. An extreme example is Glasgow where, in the mid-1970s, an astonishing 70 per cent of the housing stock was publicly owned.

The accessibility of the new stock for low-income groups differs vastly, depending on the mix of social and subsidized housing

Table 14.6   Share of construction in the public and subsidized sector in various countries, 1950–85

	Social housing	All subsidized housing
Belgium	17	50
Denmark	31	31
France	26	72
Germany	24	55
United Kingdom	53	53
Netherlands	55	82
Sweden	54	90

Source: Feddes (1995, Table 5.7).

Table 14.7   Housing subsidies as percentage of GNP in various countries, 1985

| | Direct subsidies | | |
	Construction	Housing costs	Fiscal subsidies
Belgium	0.31	0.02	—
Denmark	0.51	0.49	—
France	0.59	0.30	0.52
Germany	0.33	0.13	0.44
United Kingdom	0.40	1.42	1.38
Netherlands	1.77	0.35	1.24
Sweden	1.42	0.82	1.50

Source: Feddes (1995, Table 5.7).

and the proportion of owner–occupier and rental housing constructed with government aid. In Sweden, some 40 per cent of social housing was built as cooperative property, which requires an investment by the occupant; this shows the extent to which middle-income groups have been included in the social housing programmes. The social rental sector in the United Kingdom grew rapidly at first, but was eroded by the massive sale of such dwellings to the tenants, who were given the right to buy in the early 1980s. The large-scale public intervention in France was mostly in the form of subsidies to landlords and homeowners. This contrasts sharply with the situation in the Netherlands, where the social sector consists almost exclusively of rental housing. As the result of rent controls, the older complexes now offer inexpensive housing. In principle, this should make for a more equitable housing provision, if the lowest-income groups can gain access to the low-rent units. In the next part of this section, we elaborate on the housing situation in the Netherlands, highlighting the potential contribution of housing to social equity, and subsequently to spatial equity.

Differences in housing situations in Dutch cities

In the context of social equity, the relevant aspect of housing development in the Netherlands is the housing situation of low-income households in the four largest Dutch cities: Amsterdam, Rotterdam, The Hague and Utrecht. These cities have many low-income households, who struggle to gain access to adequate housing.

The social housing stock expanded from 10 per cent of the stock in 1945 to 25 per cent by 1960. In addition, an extensive system of price controls, tenure security and housing allocation was put in place to guarantee the equitable distribution of the dwellings. Social rental housing accounted for 50 to 65 per cent of the annual housing production, and direct housing subsidies increased from 0.8 per cent to 3.8 per cent of the total government expenditure (Van Weesep and Van Kempen, 1993).

Deregulation set in during the 1960s. Non-subsidized housing became more prevalent, though it still did not account for more than one-third of new construction in any given year. By the end of the decade, housing controls were being abolished wherever the housing shortage seemed to have been eradicated (Van Weesep, 1984). Deregulation has continued since the early 1970s. Decentralization of powers from central government agencies to local authorities was added to the array of measures to release the government from its housing responsibilities in the late 1980s. Still, the social rental sector kept expanding: by 1986, it accounted for 42 per cent of the stock. And while bricks-and-mortar subsidies were severely curtailed, the budget for rent subsidies skyrocketed. Only recently has the government succeeded in decreasing its housing expenditures in real terms, cutting direct and indirect subsidies to 7.7 per cent of its budget in 1990.

An essential ingredient of post-1945 housing policy was the controlled allocation of new homes and vacant dwellings to households that met certain criteria. Allocation was meant to ensure the equitable use of available housing, bolstering the chances of low-income people. It was supposed to balance the size of the dwelling with the household composition, income and the price of housing. Inexpensive dwellings were reserved for low-income households. Nevertheless, owing to the composition of the stock (much low-cost housing) and tenure protection, the tenants of low-cost rental housing are mixed with respect to their income positions. The trend of the 1980s shows a gradual increase in the share of the lowest income groups (Table 14.8). But low-income households have not been restricted to the cheapest dwellings; a quarter of the tenants in the more expensive housing belong to the lowest income quartile, which is largely made possible by the rent subsidies. Increasingly, low-income households became underrepresented in the owner–occupier sector in the 1980s. Overall, as far as the distribution by tenure is concerned, the figures indicate that a fairly even distribution has been maintained. This situation

Table 14.8   The distribution of income groups in the housing stock in the four big cities of the Netherlands, 1981 and 1989

	Inexpensive rental dwellings		Expensive rental dwellings		Owner–occupier dwellings	
	1981	1989	1981	1989	1981	1989
1st income quartile (low)	39.6	43.8	24.5	25.6	18.3	12.3
2nd income quartile	28.2	31.0	24.1	29.2	18.9	18.8
3rd income quartile	19.4	16.5	25.4	24.1	25.2	27.6
4th income quartile (high)	12.8	8.7	26.0	21.1	37.6	41.3
Total (%)	100	100	100	100	100	100
Total (000s)	445	478	251	138	138	166

Source: Housing Need Surveys (1981, 1989/90).

may be considered equitable as long as the least expensive dwellings offer decent housing.

As far as housing costs are concerned, the equity dimension is much less prevalent. In spite of a rent subsidy programme on an entitlement basis – in 1989, just over half of all the households with a minimum income received the benefit – low-income households still carry a heavier burden than higher-income groups. On average, the net rent amounts to a rent ratio (share of taxable income devoted to rent) of 20.2 per cent at the minimum income level. This compares to 14.2 per cent among renters at the upper end of the income distribution. The inequity also shows up when rent burdens are calculated differently. Only 17 per cent of the minimum income renters have a rent ratio of less than 15 per cent, while 77 per cent of households earning two or three times the modal income have a rent ratio of this low level. Conversely, 51 per cent of the minimum income households in rental housing spend over 20 per cent of their income on rent, against 3 per cent of the higher-income group (Van Weesep and Van Kempen, 1993). This is partly the result of the presence of many households with higher incomes in low-cost rental housing. Too few tenants move out when their incomes increase. This bias in housing tenure has now become a major issue in housing policy. It leads to inequities through the misappropriation of subsidies and by blocking access to inexpensive housing by low-income households. Adaptations of the rent-subsidy programme have not resolved the issue.

Housing allocation rules and statutory tenure protection modify the relationship between income and housing situation. Considering the housing situations of the various household types, the 'iron law' of the housing market ('the lowest-income households live in the poorest housing, and high-income groups occupy the best') obviously does not apply strictly to Dutch cities. This serves the equity principle, but at the same time it may imply direct competition between the affluent and the poor for the same housing. And this may not be in the best interest of those low-income households that still need to attain a place in the housing system.

Recently, the allocation rules have been tightened to reduce the need for individual rent subsidies. Low-income households are now virtually barred from new, more expensive rental housing. This poses a dilemma for the authorities, since the mixed population of low-cost housing has helped to avoid stigmatization of social housing and has promoted relatively mixed neighbourhoods (Murie, 1990).

Spatial inequity in the housing stock

Each of the big cities in the Netherlands has a relatively high share of immigrants. In 1990, people born outside the country accounted for 7.8 per cent of the national population; in the cities with over 200 000 inhabitants, the figure was 20.4 per cent. More than 40 per cent of the total immigrant population lived in the four biggest cities, while only 11.5 per cent of the Dutch population resided there (Dieleman, 1993). Within those cities, the residential patterns of the immigrant groups are fairly similar to those of Dutch households with a comparable income and household structure. This reflects the improvements in their housing situation since the early 1980s. Thus, even though the immigrants live in the cheaper parts of the housing stock, they are no worse off than similar Dutch (large) family households that remain in the cities.

Family reunification became common during the latter part of the 1970s. By that time, the guest workers from Morocco and Turkey – the dominant groups among the immigrants – had gradually improved their housing conditions. Initially barred from social rental housing by regulations that discriminated against newcomers, they moved out of lodgings into other poor-quality dwellings in the late nineteenth-century working-class neighbourhoods. These were mostly private rental dwellings. In Utrecht (and in the medium-sized cities), however, these areas contained numerous cheap owner-occupied dwellings. Although cheap rental housing was formally regulated and indigenous low-income households had priority, in reality few would accept this housing because of its poor quality, allowing the immigrants to enter.

By the early 1980s, changes in the allocation rules gave immigrants access to social rental housing. Gradually, they became more prevalent in neighbourhoods with inexpensive social housing, especially in districts built between 1906 and 1930 and directly after the Second World War. However, this may not have improved their housing conditions greatly (Blauw, 1991). First, immigrants moved into post-1945 areas following their rejection of better but more expensive renovated housing in urban renewal areas. Secondly, they became concentrated in the neighbourhoods built in the 1950s. There, large and inexpensive flats abound, but many of them no longer meet current standards.

On occasion, the emergence of new concentrations of immigrants has provoked hostile reactions from the indigenous population. In an effort to pre-empt violence and promote social integration, an effort was made to disperse the immigrants throughout the social housing stock. Officially or informally, several towns set a quota per building or complex (Mik, 1991). This restricted the immigrants' housing opportunities. When challenged, these policies were ruled discriminatory by the courts and were subsequently abandoned. However, in one form or another, both the policies and the debate resurface from time to time.

The Amsterdam metropolitan area provides a clear picture of the dynamics of immigrant housing. Amsterdam's policies demonstrate that the desire to promote integration of immigrants and provide equitable housing opportunities is inherently incompatible with the reality of the persistent concentration of ethnic minorities. Within the city, there is some dispersal of the Turkish and Moroccan population, but in many areas these groups remain strongly overrepresented (Table 14.9). They have become less predominant in some of the older neighbourhoods, while their share has risen in districts built in the 1950s. At the regional level, the rapid growth of the Moroccan and Turkish population in Amsterdam has led to an increasing contrast between the central city and the surrounding municipalities, although several of the latter accommodate numerous ethnic households.

In 1983, there were only four areas in Amsterdam where immigrants (Moroccan, Turkish and Surinamese) accounted for more than 25 per cent of the population; by 1990, there were ten such areas. The striking drop in the share of immigrants living in the older neighbourhoods and their growing presence in postwar areas does not imply a dispersal. Rather, it indicates a shift in the concentration areas. The shifts in the pattern are strongly related

Table 14.9 Distribution of Turkish and Moroccan population of Amsterdam by neighbourhood type, percentages

Neighbourhood types	Turkish 1983	Turkish 1990	Moroccan 1983	Moroccan 1990	Total population 1983	Total population 1990
Inner city	2.4	2.2	3.5	3.5	8.4	10.9
Prewar high status	2.5	0.8	2.0	1.2	8.9	7.9
19th c. working class	21.7	16.2	25.8	18.7	16.6	13.9
1906–30	45.7	43.1	42.3	37.5	24.0	21.0
1931–45	10.0	13.5	8.3	11.5	6.6	7.0
1945–60	10.9	14.9	10.9	17.7	13.2	12.5
1960s	4.8	5.7	4.6	6.3	13.1	10.1
New neighbourhoods	1.5	3.3	2.2	3.2	7.9	15.5
Mixed neighbourhoods	0.5	0.3	0.4	0.4	1.3	1.2
Total (= 100%)	15 900	21 800	23 700	31 600	678 700	689 300

Source: Adapted from Van Kempen and De Klerk (1993).

410

to the greying of the Dutch population and its mobility. In the post-1945 areas, many dwellings are vacated by the aging Dutch population. The largest of these dwellings are particularly suited to the large families of low-income immigrants. Young Dutch households do move into these areas, but they depart again quickly, as they pursue their housing career. The immigrants comprise the stable population groups in the neighbourhoods.

Eventually, the immigrants came to dominate the dwellings in the older post-1945 neighbourhoods which had lost favour with many of the more affluent indigenous family households. Taking up the rejects does not necessarily imply that immigrants have a weaker housing market position than members of the indigenous population with a corresponding socioeconomic status. This step in their housing career has more to do with their household characteristics and the high mobility rates in this part of the social housing stock, as elderly households are dissolved and families move from the cities to the suburbs. The immigrants were simply allocated housing where the most (suitable) dwellings became available. Large numbers have thus vastly improved their housing conditions. Yet, in some ways, they remained one step behind the indigenous population, even though the broad patterns suggest similarities. They occupy the least attractive parts of the stock. The future is not promising for low-income households. Dutch housing will depend increasingly on market principles, and the social rental sector will continue to grow, but at a diminished rate. This policy shift can jeopardize the slow but steady progress that the immigrants have made.

Even though immigrants entered other neighbourhoods as vacancies became available, the overall pattern of concentration within the cities remains intact. The indices of segregation between the population groups are still low. Nonetheless, the pattern reveals some segregation. This may have some benefits for the immigrants as long as they have not become fully integrated in the host societies. But it may also complicate attempts to rectify inequities in their housing situation.

As new categories of disadvantaged foreigners are emerging and the housing system is under increasing stress, the housing perspectives for ethnic minorities are becoming much bleaker than they seemed only a few years ago. As the immigrant groups increase in size, the competition for the shrinking resources and disappearing jobs intensifies. There is little hope for a turnaround in the economy that will boost their position. If anything, the present migration tendencies will relegate the older guest workers to increasingly marginal positions. Many newcomers have rapidly bypassed the previous groups of migrants. In contrast to the 1960s and 1970s, the major flows of labour migrants in Europe no longer consist of manual labourers. The guest workers of yesterday have largely been replaced by highly educated professionals, moving within internal networks.

As the new groups of migrants leave the older ones behind, and as the guest workers remain marginal, their only hope of catching up is long-term. It may be a slim hope at that; they may gradually improve their situation if the economy picks up again and the welfare state retains its basic programmes. But will they catch up with the indigenous population?

The underclass: convergence of social and spatial inequity

For decades, northern European countries have put the ideal of promoting equity into practice by providing social benefits, health care and housing and by intervening in the labour market. Each country has built a system of its own, rooted in its historical development and its institutions. Consequently, a variety of welfare state models has emerged. Admittedly, the unemployed, the disabled, the elderly and the unskilled fare better in one system than in another. The models range from the liberal welfare state of the United Kingdom, to the conservative corporatist states of Germany and France, to Sweden's social-democratic welfare state (Musterd, 1994; see also Hansen and Jensen-Butler, 1996). The liberal welfare state relies largely on the market mechanisms and provides modest benefits only after means testing. The corporatist state ties its benefits to social status and class in an attempt to preserve social differentiation. In contrast, the social-democratic welfare state is bent on the eradication of such differences through universalism in the redistribution of resources. It aims to achieve equality at the highest standards, not at the minimal needs level. Other countries, such as Belgium and the Netherlands, have developed their own particular mix of the elements of these models.

The housing systems of the respective countries do not accurately reflect these principles. As we have pointed out above, some welfare states place more confidence in influencing the market. Others have intervened to a much greater extent to shape the housing stock into an instrument of greater equity. Yet even the Netherlands, with its large social rental sector and extensive allocation controls, has not achieved an equitable housing market. Nonetheless, where large social housing sectors exist, there tends to be more social mixing of people and less spatial segregation of social categories.

The overall trend of privatization, however, is leading the countries away from their strong emphasis on equity. The reforms of the welfare system were initiated because of its presumably stifling effect on private initiative and its high costs. But the reforms aggravate the negative effects of the economic transformation on equity. They may have resulted in the growth of the number of jobs – at the top and at the bottom of the scale – but they have also increased social deprivation. It may be expected that the current privatization trend, especially in housing, will widen existing gaps in society.

The cities are expected to exhibit increased segregation as a result of the changes to the welfare state models. This could disrupt the equity that has been achieved. Where large numbers of socially deprived people converge, there is the danger that the concentration itself aggravates the plight of the poor. Spatial separation of people diminishes their ability to build and maintain social contacts with inhabitants of different areas and members of different groups. The negative effects on the unemployed, for instance, are well known. Separation deprives them of one of the most effective sources of information on available jobs. Lack of social contacts with working people largely prevents them from getting back into the labour market (Morris, 1987). Segregation can extend the negative effects to society as a whole, as segregated housing leads to segregated schools, shopping areas and recreational facilities. Such comprehensive segregation has been linked to the hostility, mistrust and discord that characterize the divided city (Saltman, 1991).

Segregation in itself does not preclude equity. Voluntary segregation among migrants helps them to maintain social contacts because of proximity. A specific culture can thereby survive, whereby the norms and values of a particular group can be retained and needed facilities supported. Segregated and tightly clustered ethnic neighbourhoods support cultural and social cohesion within the group, providing them with a protected space (Aldrich *et al.*, 1981). Indeed, some researchers have emphasized the positive social roles of ghettoes, which may marginalize the people with respect to mainstream society, though not with respect to their own group. The tight social bonds bring the group together in one place, but this place may result from a minimum choice in the housing market, determined by pre-emptive choices of others. Yet more typical is segregation brought about by the conditions imposed by society. Housing allocation rules applied by local housing authorities steer people to a particular segment of the stock, which may be concentrated in a particular type of neighbourhood. The residential construction policies of a central government can also lead to unintended segregation.

The mixing of dissimilar population groups is no panacea for social problems either. In many cases, it has led to the perception that the other group is competing for the same scarce resources. It might even be felt that the other group has a head start when positive discrimination is invoked to help them surmount a historical handicap. This can easily evolve into blaming the others for the problems, a development which may have grave consequences: 'A large proportion of racist beliefs stem from a perceived conflict with black people over the allocation of scarce resources, particularly housing' (Phizacklea and Miles, 1979). In the aggregate, it can lead to xenophobia and serious disturbances. There is no general model of causes and effects of segregation and mixing. The outcome depends very much upon the social relations fostered at the local level and the way local institutions mediate in these relations. Community building is possible among dissimilar people but, where the competition between the groups is strong or is perceived as such, the chances of discord increase.

Large concentrations of socially deprived people, along with their inadequate integration in mainstream society, can perpetuate a marginal situation, even from one generation to the next. This is readily apparent in the problems of second-generation migrants. They often lack the qualifications to participate fully in the labour market above the most basic level of casual work. In the event that spatial mismatch occurs because routine unskilled or semi-skilled jobs have moved out of the city, beyond their reach, their chances of integrating are severely curtailed. The concentration of similar people may also deprive them of positive role models, to nurture their aspirations. This convergence of social and spatial inequity foments what has been called in the USA the *underclass*. Its basic precondition is a large concentration of socially excluded people. They have very low incomes and lack the ability to earn more. The underclass is spawned from a culture of poverty. Unemployment runs rampant, dependence on social benefits is ubiquitous, deviant or illicit behaviour is the norm. Wilson (1987) especially has emphasized the close relationship between the severity of the problems and the degree of spatial concentration; he speaks of a ghetto underclass. Their problems differ vastly in nature and intensity from those of the poor living in smaller concentrations of socially and economically deprived people.

The warning that an underclass may be about to emerge has been sounded by several researchers who have studied the dynamics of cities such as Amsterdam, Berlin, Brussels, Paris or Stockholm. In Brussels, several social contrasts have been charted. There exists a strong polarization tendency between the affluent suburbs and the empoverished inner-city areas of this aspiring European capital. But within the older neighbourhoods there is also polarization, closely tied to the residual private rental housing available to the immigrants. In fact, some blocks have been called social disaster areas (Kesteloot, 1994). Even in Stockholm, long the shining example of the welfare state, the underclass is emerging in response to the economic crisis and the reassessment of the expensive welfare institutions. Deep cuts in employment in the public sector, tax reform and changes in the subsidies for housing have contributed to the growth of income inequality. In particular, the differences between the Swedes and the immigrants have increased (Borgegard and Murdie, 1994).

Conclusions: equity policy and competition between cities

The landscape of the urban societies in Europe is becoming increasingly diversified. The economic transformation spreads its benefits unevenly; some population groups reap significant advantages from the growth of professionalism, others are being relegated to the fringes of the economy and society. Inasmuch as those people keep playing a part in the new urban economy, they move at a slower speed. The trend towards social polarization is even more visible in the increasing numbers of people who have been cut off from mainstream society. Of course, most people in cities are neither very rich nor destitute, but the point is that the groups at the top and at the bottom of the social hierarchy are growing in size, and are increasingly disconnected from each other. The rapidly growing, diverse groups of ethnic minorities and other immigrants especially risk social exclusion. This polarization tendency is underlined by wholesale changes in policy.

The welfare state is under siege, and everywhere deep cuts are being made in once generous programmes meant to maintain equity. Policies to promote social justice were the hallmark of the welfare state. Cities have a long experience in this policy field. In the past, many programmes have been implemented to improve the conditions of the poor, to promote more equality in living conditions and to give the socially and economically disadvantaged a decent livelihood. Some of these programmes were circumscribed by allocated budgets, while others were defined as open-ended entitlement programmes. Some aimed to help the disadvantaged catch up, whereas others were meant to give them a head start. Almost invariably, such equity policies expanded in times of growing affluence. The pie was readily shared as long as prosperity lasted. But social justice is often seen as non-productive, a luxury that must be cut back when budgets have to be balanced. Equity policies are rarely defined in relation to the competitive strategies of cities. Nevertheless, equity is an important element of the *good city*, the city where the most vulnerable members of society are less disadvantaged and victimized than elsewhere (Donnison and Soto, 1980). Such cities of the new economy are more prosperous and egalitarian than others. For any given social group, opportunity and standards of living tend to be greater there than in cities with a traditional economy (Knox, 1989). But do these good cities attract investment because of their relatively high quality of life and their lack of inequity? The fact is that equity-promoting policies are rarely implemented on the grounds of their contribution to overall income growth and, in the current climate of cost cutting, this aspect has little chance of gaining prominence.

In most cities, social inequity translates readily into spatial inequality. Housing has been shown to play a major role in the creation and sustenance of deprivation (Lee, 1994). Across European cities, segregation of immigrant groups has been remarkably persistent. The values of segregation indices are as high today as in the time when new immigrants were largely excluded from social housing on the basis of their status as temporary workers or their position as newcomers. On the macro scale, concentrations result from the pattern of job opportunities. The distribution of minorities within cities has more to do with the spatial variations of sociocultural facilities, variations in the housing stock and the mechanisms of housing allocation. The areas where minorities concentrate may expand at their fringes, but typically they still include the neighbourhoods where the immigrants first settled. And even where new ethnic concentrations emerge in areas of older social housing, dispersal is rare.

Especially when segregation does not emanate from choice, from the desire to maintain social networks within the group and a particular cultural identity, its effects can be severe. It leads to segregated schools, recreational facilities and commercial services and eventually to a disconnected society in which disadvantaged groups can become an underclass. Local housing and economic conditions, together with patterns and modes of welfare delivery, interact to produce new regions of social exclusion (Lee, 1994). Segregation as the ultimate form of social exclusion can have severe repercussions for the functioning of cities and for their ability to shape their future. Yet enforced integration, the mixing of diverse population groups, may yield similar problems. It may pit one group against another in competition over scarce resources, whereby the others are blamed for the deficiencies in one's own situation. This turns social conflicts into local conflicts, leads to antagonism between groups, and may ultimately result in xenophobia.

Given the dilemmas the pursuit of equity poses to policy makers, it is not surprising that, in most countries, the results of equity policies have been disappointing. They have yielded poor results with respect to objective and subjective indicators of standard of living. This has led to growing discontent among diverse social groups about the economic and political developments and their own diminished ability to influence their direction (Stöhr and Tödtling, 1979). One symptom of this is the violent eruption of xenophobia in many cities across Europe. Another is the rise of local resistance to the construction of urban freeways or airports, the organization of major international events, massive urban revitalization schemes, political consolidation of metropolitan areas and other initiatives to restructure the cities in order to boost their competitive power. Such examples show how difficult it has become to generate broad support for development strategies, to forge long-lasting coalitions to rebuild the cities and urban societies.

A frequently heard argument for cutting back on equity-promoting programmes is that cities can no longer afford the luxury of programmes of transfer payments in their many shapes and forms. However, this is putting the proverbial horse behind the cart. The question should be whether cities can afford *not* to pursue equity policies if they intend to play a major role in shaping their own destinies. The case for equity policies is not solely based on moral considerations, but also has rational economic grounds.

By becoming entrepreneurial in their attempt to improve their own performance, European cities have entered into competition with each other. As Jensen Butler argues in Chapter 1 above, success is measured above all in terms of increased income, resulting from the creation or attraction of economic activities. Some cities have indeed developed innovative policies to boost their economic well-being (Parkinson *et al.*, 1992), but others still seem to be focused on balancing the books by cutting expenses. As a consequence of the variations in strategies, the economic fortunes of the cities differ significantly. Success, however, does not result automatically from an innovative idea, a novel application or a well-

defined objective. Successful strategies have to be broadly supported by a long-lasting coalition of actors on the local scene and
at least the tacit support of the principal, the local population (cf.
the vignette on Milan in Chapter 11 above). Agreement between
the local administration and major players from the business community is insufficient to bring a growth strategy to fruition. The
local electorate must broadly support major initiatives, which implies that they must be able to identify long-term benefits. The
development of human resources is insufficient if the newly em-
powered disadvantaged population is not offered opportunities
to participate in the new economy. If they do not support such
schemes, the city can make no headway in the long run. When the
simple fact of equity of opportunities and outcomes is ignored by
the policy makers, they take the initiatives at their peril.

References

Aldrich, H.E., J.C. Cater, T.P. Jones and D. McEvoy (1981) 'Business development
    and self-segregation; Asian enterprise in three British cities', in C. Peach, V.
    Robinson and S. Smith (eds), *Ethnic Segregation in Cities*, London: Croom Helm,
    pp.170–90.
Bartels, C.P.A. and J.J. van Duijn (1984) 'Implementing regional economic policy:
    an analysis of economic and political influences in the Netherlands', *Regional
    Studies*, **18**, pp.1–11.
Bell, W. (1968) 'The city, the suburb, and a theory of social choice', in S. Greer
    (ed.), *The New Urbanization*, New York: St.Martin's Press, pp.132–68.
Blauw, W. (1991) 'Housing segregation of different population groups in the Neth-
    erlands', in E.D. Huttman, W. Blauw and J. Saltman (eds), *Urban Housing Segre-
    gation of Minorities in Western Europe and the United States*, Durham, NC: Duke
    University Press, pp.43–62.
Borgegard, L.E. and R. Murdie (1994) 'Social polarization and the crisis of the
    welfare state: the case of Stockholm', *Built Environment*, **20**, pp.254–68.
Bruinsma, F. and P. Rietveld (1993) 'Urban agglomerations in European infra-
    structure networks', *Urban Studies*, **30**, pp.919–34.
Brunet, R. (ed.) (1989) *Les Villes Européennes* [The cities of Europe], Montpellier–
    Paris: RECLUS-DATAR, La Documentation Française.
Castells, M. (1989) *The Informational City: Information Technology, Economic Restruc-
    turing and the Urban–Regional Process*, Oxford: Basil Blackwell.
Champion, A.G. (1994) 'International migration and demographic change', *Urban
    Studies*, **31**, pp.653–77.
Clement, C. (1991) 'Regional economic policy for the next few years', *Tijdschrift
    voor Economische en Sociale Geografie*, **82**, pp.227–31.
Dieleman, F.M. (1993) 'Multi-cultural Holland: Myth or reality?', in R. King (ed.),
    Mass Migration in Europe: The Legacy and the Future, London: Belhaven, pp.118–
    35.
Donnison, D. and P. Soto (1980) *The Good City. A Study of Urban Development and
    Policy in Britain*, London: Heinemann.
Feddes, A. (1995) *Woningmarkt, Regulering en Inflatie: Het Na-oorlogse
    Volkshuisvestingsbeleid van Tien Noordwest-Europese Landen Vergeleken* [Housing
    markets, regulation and inflation: a comparison of post-war housing policies of

ten northwestern European countries], Netherlands Geographical Studies 194, Utrecht: KNAG/Faculteit Ruimtelijke Wetenschappen.

Gordon, I. and S. Sassen (1992) 'Restructuring the urban labour market', in S.S. Fainstein, I. Gordon and M. Harloe (eds), *Divided Cities*, Oxford: Blackwell, pp.105–28.

Hall, P. (1993) 'Forces shaping urban Europe', *Urban Studies*, **30**, pp.883–98.

Hamnett, C. (1994) 'Social polarization in global cities: Theory and evidence', *Urban Studies*, **31**, pp.401–24.

Hansen, F. and C. Jensen-Butler (1996) 'Economic crisis and the regional and local effects of the welfare state', *Regional Studies*, **30**, pp.167–87.

Holzer, H. (1991) 'The spatial mismatch hypothesis: What has the evidence shown?', *Urban Studies*, **28**, pp.105–22.

Kesteloot, C. (1994) 'Three levels of socio-spatial polarization in Brussels', *Built Environment*, **20**, pp.204–17.

Knox, P.L. (1989) 'The vulnerable, the disadvantaged and the victimized: Who they are and where they live', in D.T. Herbert and D.M. Smith, (eds), *Social Problems and the City; New Perspectives*, Oxford: Oxford University Press, pp.32–47.

Kreukels, A. and T. Spit (1989) 'Fiscal retrenchment and the relationship between national government and local administration in the Netherlands', in Susan E. Clarke (ed.), *Urban Innovation and Autonomy; Political Implications of Policy Change*, London: Sage, pp.153–81.

Kruythoff, H. (1993) *Residential Environments and Households in the Randstad*, Housing and Urban Policy Studies 8, Delft: Delft University Press.

Lee, P. (1994) 'Housing and social deprivation; relocating the underclass and the new urban poor', *Urban Studies*, **31**, pp.1191–1209.

Marcuse, P. (1989) '"Dual City": A muddy metaphor for a quartered city', *International Journal of Urban and Regional Research*, **13**, pp.697–708.

Mik, G. (1991) 'Housing segregation and policy in the Dutch metropolitan environment', in E.D. Huttman, W. Blauw and J. Saltman (eds), *Urban Housing Segregation of Minorities in Western Europe and the United States*, Durham, NC: Duke University Press, pp.179–98.

Morris, L.D. (1987) 'Local social polarization: a case study of Hartlepool', *International Journal of Urban and Regional Research*, **11**, pp.331–50.

Murie, A. (1990) 'Housing market developments in Britain; implications for research and policy in the Netherlands', *Stedebouw en Volkshuisvesting*, **71**, pp.11–16.

Musterd, S. (1994) 'A rising European underclass? Social polarization and spatial segregation in European cities', *Built Environment*, **20**, pp.185–91.

Ottens, H.F.L. (1984) 'A new urban policy report for the Netherlands', *Tijdschrift voor Economische en Sociale Geografie*, **75**, pp.232–4.

Owen, D. and A. Green (1992) 'Labour market experience and occupational change amongst ethnic groups in Great Britain', *New Community*, **19**, pp.7–29.

Pahl, R. (1988) 'Informal work, social polarisation and the social structure', *International Journal of Urban and Regional Studies*, **12**, pp.247–67.

Parkinson, M., F. Bianchini, J. Dawson, R. Evans and A. Harding (1992) *Urbanisation and the Functions of Cities in the European Community. A Report to the Commission of the European Communities*, Liverpool: European Institute of Urban Affairs.

Phizacklea, A. and R. Miles (1979) 'Working class racist beliefs in the inner city', in R. Miles and A. Phizacklea (eds), *Racism and Political Action in Britain*, London: Routledge & Kegan Paul, pp.93–123.

Pugliese, E. (1995) 'New international migrations and the "European Fortress"', in C. Hadjimichalis and D. Sadler (eds), *Europe at the Margins; New Mosaics of Inequality*, Chichester: Wiley, pp.51–68.

Saltman, J. (1991) 'Theoretical orientation: residential segregation', in E.D. Huttman, W. Blauw and J. Saltman (eds), *Urban Housing Segregation of Minorities in Western Europe and the United States*, Durham, NC: Duke University Press, pp.1–17.

Stöhr, W. and F. Tödtling (1979) 'Spatial equity: Some anti-theses to current regional development doctrine', in H. Folmer and J. Oosterhaven (eds), *Spatial Inequalities and Regional Development*, The Hague: Martinus Nijhoff, pp.133–83.

Van de Kaa, D.J. (1987) 'Europe's second demographic transition', *Population Bulletin*, 42, pp.1–57.

Van Engelsdorp Gastelaars, R. and J. Vijgen (1991) 'Stadsbuurten en woonkernen in de jaren negentig; hun veranderende betekenis als lokaal woonmilieu' [Urban neighbourhoods and towns in the 1990s: their changing roles as residential areas], in R. van Kempen, S. Musterd and W. Ostendorf (eds), *Maatschappelijke Verandering en Stedelijke Dynamiek*, Delft: Delft University Press, pp.107–20.

Van Kempen, R. and L. De Klerk (1993) 'Randgemeenten open voor allochtonen?' [Opening up the suburbs for migrants?], *Rooilijn*, 93/5, pp.222–7.

Van Weesep, J. (1984), 'Intervention in the Netherlands: Urban housing policy and market response', *Urban Affairs Quarterly*, 19, pp.329–53.

Van Weesep, J. (1988) 'Regional and urban development in the Netherlands: the retreat of government', *Geography*, 73, pp.97–104.

Van Weesep, J. (1995) 'Housing the "guestworkers"', in C. Hadjimichalis and D. Sadler (eds), *Europe at the Margins; New Mosaics of Inequality*, Chichester: Wiley, pp.167–94.

Van Weesep, J. and F.M. Dieleman (1993) 'Evolving urban Europe: Editors' introduction to the special issue', *Urban Studies*, 30, pp.877–82.

Van Weesep, J. and R. van Kempen (1992) 'Economic change, income differentiation and housing: Urban response in the Netherlands', *Urban Studies*, 29, pp.979–90.

Van Weesep, J. and R. van Kempen (1993) 'Low income and housing in the Dutch welfare state', in G. Hallett (ed.), *The New Housing Shortage: Housing Affordability in Europe and the USA*, London: Routledge, pp.179–206.

Weaver, C. (1984) *Regional Development and the Local Community: Planning Politics and Social Context*, Chichester: Wiley.

Wever, E. (1986) 'Dutch regional policy', *Tijdschrift voor Economische en Sociale Geografie*, 77, pp.149–53.

White, P. (1993) 'Immigrants and the social geography of European cities', in R. King (ed.), *Mass Migration in Europe: The Legacy and the Future*, London: Belhaven, pp.65–82.

Wilson, W.J. (1987) *The Truly Disadvantaged: The Inner City, the Underclass and Public Policy*, Chicago: University of Chicago Press.

15 Alternatives to the polluting city

Gert de Roo

Introduction

The European answer to the evil known as urban sprawl takes the form of multifunctional, high-density urban cores. Undoubtedly, the so-called 'compact city policy' has many advantages, but it has also some negative side-effects. A multifunctional area is prone to conflicts between environmental pressure and the quality of urban life. These conflicts may very well affect political choices, economic investments and the competition between urban areas.

Strangely enough, the quality of an area, particularly its environmental quality, was not fully acknowledged as a political issue in the western world until the 1980s. In 1972, the Club of Rome wrote their world-renowned report, *The Limits to Growth* (Meadows, 1972). It was published at the crest of the first environmental wave. The report is based on the assumption that human beings are part of a universal ecosystem and cannot survive without it. However, the same worldwide ecosystem is under heavy attack by the human species. Only one year later, in 1973, the oil crisis drew attention away from the survival of the ecosystem toward the viability of the economy. Still, ecology had found its place in society, and the public retained a general interest in the topic. Efforts to save or protect the ecosystem were focused on animals and plants; the policies dealt with soil, water and air quality and more or less excluded humans. This could very well explain why efforts to protect the ecosystem mainly concerned the countryside instead of the environmental quality in the urban areas.

Humans are dependent on the ecosystem and the ecosystem needs to be protected. This is now generally accepted. It is also recognized that humans have to be protected from their own activities, although the seriousness of this threat is not yet fully understood. Environmental danger is only acknowledged when people almost literally die in their own dirt. And most of this dirt is hidden in the soil. During the 1960s and 1970s, water and air were reasonably well protected against pollution, probably because pollution of these elements is easy to detect. For a long time, the soil has been the most ideal place to deposit wastes. But there, chemical waste became an ecological time bomb. In the early 1980s, most western countries faced huge environmental, economic and social problems because of soil pollution. Since then, people have realized that they were players in the game. This marked the beginning of the second environmental wave in the western world. Soil pollution can be found mostly in or near urban areas. People living in cities became very interested in the quality of their daily living environment. Policy makers acknowledged the environment as a topic of political concern. Also industrialists discovered the importance of a clean and healthy environment. They realized they should protect it if they want to keep industrial activities as an urban function. The physical environment, its quality and the urban area became interrelated topics.

Issues such as social safety and crime are very important urban topics, but the discussion in this chapter will focus on problems of the physical environment in the city. The physical environment can be defined as 'the whole of living and non-living elements, apart and in their mutual cohesion, namely water, soil, air, humans, animals, plants, goods and relations among them'. This means that the physical environment consists of an abiotic, a biotic and an artificial environment; in fact it comprises the material environment.

Since the early 1980s, the quality of life is no longer determined exclusively by our health, a good job and a nice house. Aspects like a good and safe physical environment play an important part in discussions of how an urban area should look. These discussions are reminiscent of the ideas of Ebenezer Howard, who introduced the 'garden city' in the 1920s (Howard, 1970). Although the early and the recent designs may look the same, the functions of the urban area have changed dramatically over the years. Howard wanted to create a place for people to live, away from intrusive activities. Nowadays the functions found in an urban area are highly interrelated. Environmentally intrusive activities are spread throughout the urban area. Many of these activities take place near environmentally sensitive areas, such as parks and residential areas. The compact city policy will create even more of these situations in the near future.

Today, this policy is a popular means of reducing urban pressure on the countryside. The result is the 'paradox of the compact city'. The concentration of activities in the city as a multifunctional, densely developed area concentrates environmental pollution in the urban area. The compact city policy has a positive environmental effect on the region but negative effects on a local scale.

This brings us to the major questions which have to be answered in this chapter. What environmental problems does the modern western city have to face? What solutions can be found? And where will this all lead to?

Modern urban catastrophes

On 16 July 1976, an explosion at the ICMEA plant in Seveso near Milan, Italy, released TCDD (dioxin) into the air. Besides the human toll, the accident had a severe impact on the local ecosystem. In December 1984, a container of methyl isocyanate started leaking at the Union Carbide plant in the city of Bhopal, India. The result was a cloud of poisonous gas which killed more than 2500 people. In 1992, a chemical accident near the second-largest city in Mexico, Guadalajara, shocked the world. Every decade has well-known disasters in urban areas. These examples (Cutter, 1993) are the most infamous ones; a wide range of smaller accidents mostly take place in or near urban areas. Other occurrences are more insidious. For instance, exposure over a long time to toxic and carcinogenic substances also poses a real threat. In the long term, it may claim many victims, yet these substances are too often ignored. One wonders if cities are safe and healthy places to live in. Chemical emissions are not the only environmental issues in urban areas. Soil pollution has become a major environmental problem too. Over the years, our waste has been buried in the soil; we have built our new residential areas on top of it. Other less dramatic nuisances are noise, odour and smog, yet these are problems for almost every urban inhabitant. One might wonder if cities are still a pleasant place to live in, although it seems to have hardly any effect on where people choose to live. Dog excrement and graffiti pollute in another way, giving the city a bad reputation. Safety, nuisance and health are important topics, because they have an impact on the quality of life in the city.

A major source of environmental pressure in a densely developed society has been recognized only recently: transporting and redistributing matter from one place to another. In our modern society, complex industrial processes are needed to produce high-quality products, but we do not always realize that progress can have negative effects. Our society is highly dependent on materials, despite the digital evolution. Since the beginning of the industrial age, the transport of raw material and energy has expanded enormously. Removing matter from a place where it has been for a very long time will disturb the ecological balance at that particular place. When this matter is used as a raw material in the production process, emissions are an almost ubiquitous by-product. These emissions may negatively affect the area around the industrial site where production takes place. The effect is particularly dangerous when emissions consist of carcinogenic and toxic substances (see the section on integrated environmental zoning below). A product ready for consumption will eventually wear out and end up as waste. Part of that waste can be recycled, and part of it will remain unusable (see Figure 15.1). Emissions and waste will have a negative effect on the ecological balance too. Where emissions take place, the environment will change; the situation will never be the same again. In many cases, the environmental change has negative results and is therefore unwanted. Especially when emissions lead to uncontrolled negative effects, the flow of matter should be reduced.

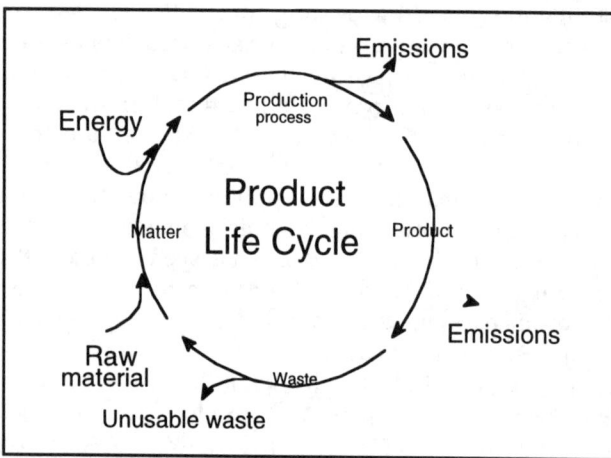

Figure 15.1 Product life cycle

These environmental effects can be classified as pollution, exhaustion, disturbance and adverse effects. Pollution can be defined as the negative result of a high concentration of substances in the environment. An adverse effect is an irreversible change of the environment, like the transformation of the landscape through human interference. The continuous need for raw materials leads to the exhaustion of resources, which will have a negative effect on sustainability. Disturbance or disruption is caused by calamities and nuisance such as noise, smell or the emission of harmful substances. Pollution and disturbance have local effects and are therefore closely related to the development of the compact city.

A high-quality urban area in a modern society is only feasible when there is enough knowledge about the processes influencing its environment. Only then can policies be developed to reduce the negative effects of environmental intrusion and to improve the livability of the city.

The consuming city

Most of the production of goods takes place in or near an urban area. Furthermore, the use of goods, and therefore the waste production, is concentrated largely in urban areas. Thus the negative effects of waste and emissions are concentrated at the local level and must be dealt with there.

A city can only produce waste and emissions if there is an input of matter and energy. Using matter and energy implies that negative effects occur somewhere else because of the city's need for input. The use of matter and energy impedes the effort to achieve sustainability. We are removing resources (for instance, oil and tropical hardwoods); these can no longer be used by future generations. On the one hand, urban 'consumption' affects sustainability worldwide.

On the other hand, the urban output has negative effects on the urban area itself. Therefore urban output has a negative effect on the livability of a city. This observation has some interesting implications. From it, we can derive a model of the quality of the city or the urban area (Figure 15.2). This model has quantitative as well as qualitative aspects. Matter, energy, emissions and waste can all be quantified. These quantitative variables affect sustainability and livability in a negative but unspecified way. Many scholars have tried to develop a strategy to deal with sustainability (for example, Opschoor and Van der Ploeg, 1990; Siebert, 1992) but have failed to come up with a workable solution. Livability is a qualitative measure that is of great importance, not only for the coming generations, but for the viability of the city itself.

During the past two decades, we have become aware of the ways environmental problems could be classified. Climatic change is currently ranked as the biggest global problem. Acidification is seen as a problem of continental scale, as it is caused by emissions from agriculture, transport and traffic. Eutrophication is an envi-

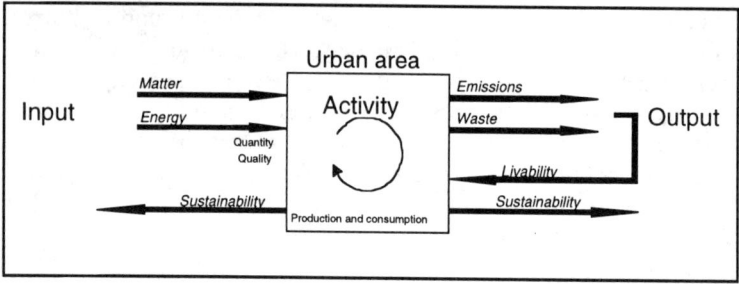

Figure 15.2   Input–output model for the urban environment

ronmental issue with a regional effect. It increases the amount of nutrients in the environment and thereby disrupts ecological processes. (Soil) pollution and disturbance are environmental issues on a local and urban scale, particular prevalent in urban areas. To maintain or to achieve a good quality of life in a densély populated urban area, environmental policy should be developed with respect to noise, odours, dust and other forms of local environmental disturbance. Disturbance of the living and working environment has a major impact on the livability in cities and on areas designated for nature and recreation (NEPP, 1989).

Livability

Livability can be seen as the combination of three criteria: spatial, environmental and social quality. In this chapter, we take a closer look at the spatial and environmental quality of urban areas. Spatial quality is highly dependent on the urban functions located in the city and the way these functions can be used, now and in the future. Today, the multifunctional city, full of spatial and functional variation, is seen as the model for the modern European city (CEC, 1990). In addition to the use of functions, perception of space also determines spatial quality. Urban residential areas in the formerly socialist countries of eastern European countries are monotonous in design, which hardly contributes to a positive perception. Variation in urban functions influences perception positively. Also, people would rather have parks instead of heavy industry next to their residential areas. The translation of spatial quality into operational and quantified measures is still very difficult. However, this is not the case with environmental quality. Environmental quality can be quantified easily by using environmental standards or general objectives, which are the political translation of environmental quality (see Figure 15.3).

Figure 15.3 shows how policy makers could react to negative environmental impacts. When it becomes clear that the environmental quality is in danger, environmental laws will be made. These are laws which will initiate a planning procedure with the aim of affecting environmental quality in a positive way. Economic and consumer action cause a political reaction. Generally speaking, objectives in one country (for example, the USA) and strict standards in others (such as The Netherlands) are used as a bridge between action and reaction. Standards are used especially when there is a political desire to protect every individual from an excessive environmental load. Most of these standards are therefore highly anthropocentric. In itself, this is not unusual, because the city is a human-oriented area, despite all kinds of ecological phenomena.

Environmental standards are mostly expressed in terms of the concentration of matter or (chemical) substances. With the exception of a few negative environmental effects such as noise and vibration, almost all environmental problems arise from the presence of (chemical) substances. The magnitude of the effect depends on the concentration and the nature of the substance. The environmental standard results from political decision making with

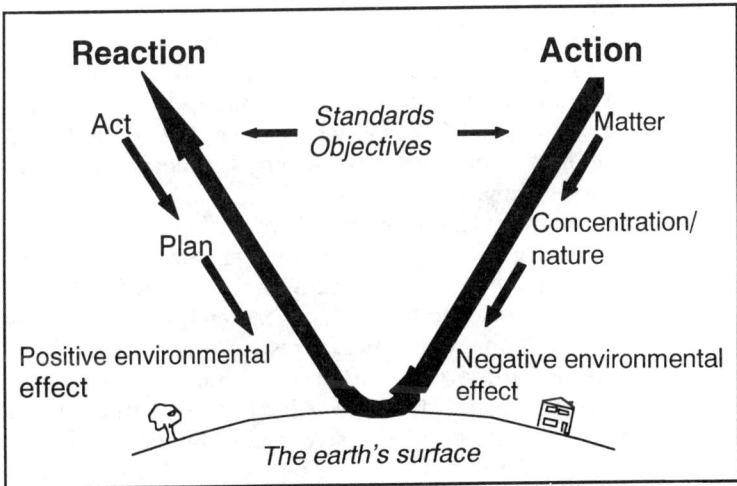

Figure 15.3   Relation between negative environmental activities and environmental policy

respect to the amount of unwanted negative effects that is considered acceptable.

Together, spatial and environmental quality determine the physical quality of the area. Although the physical quality of urban areas is the central topic of this chapter, it is obvious that social quality will affect the livability of an urban area as well. It is well known that a social reaction may arise against plans that favour the region but negatively affect local quality. A good example is the planning of a railroad line or an airport (see also Chapter 9 on Athens). The region as a whole may benefit from such initiatives, but people who see railroad tracks running through their back yard will not be very happy with this decision. Spatial and environmental decisions which lower social quality will lead to the so-called 'NIMBY' effect (not in my back yard) (see also Chapter 11 on Milan). The NIMBY effect can be defined as a local reaction against locally undesirable land uses (LULUs), as expressed by people who are not hindered by difference in social background (Vesilind *et al.*, 1990; Blowers, 1990). Individuals do not want to shoulder the burden for the benefit of society without compensation or a chance to move. Governments have the responsibility to find the balance between individuals, groups and society when making choices that have different effects at different levels.

Environmental issues and urban functions

The model presented in Figure 15.2 can be applied at almost any level. To make it an urban model, the box should be filled with urban functions such as housing, employment, recreation and transport (see Figure 15.4). This model expresses the possibility of influencing the input and output of the city by reorganizing the spatial functions in the urban area.

In many countries, policy makers and researchers are developing ways of reducing the output (emissions and waste) of urban activities, yet they have given hardly any thought to reducing the input. Methods or policies to lower the urban environmental output are mostly based on environmental restrictions. Most of these methods or policies are formulated on an ad hoc basis, although they are increasingly being structured. But this takes time; it is a long-term goal to design a policy based on coordination and integration of spatial and environmental policies. But only such a policy could optimize livability. Integration is also necessary to create the flexibility that can ensure economic activity in the urban area. At present environmental restrictions may turn a dy-

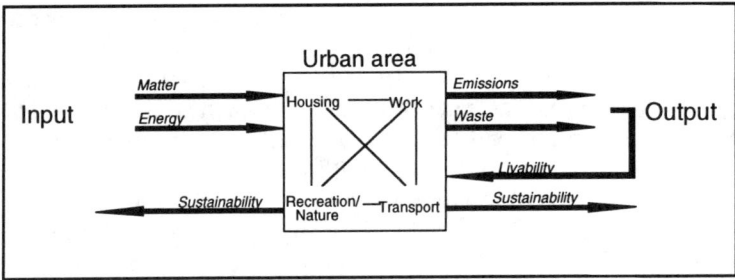

Figure 15.4 Urban functions in relation to environmental input and output of the urban area

namic area into a passive one. In the long term, those restrictions will influence the quality of the urban area negatively.

Housing

One of the urban functions is housing. It can make a positive contribution to sustainability and livability when houses are built in an ecologically sound manner. When an ecologically sound house reaches the end of its life, the materials of which it was constructed can be reused relatively easily.

Initiatives to construct environmentally friendly houses abound in Europe, largely limited to the insulation of houses and offices, the provision of (still too expensive) solar boilers and the reduction of CO_2 emissions. But some more advanced projects have also been put in place. In Germany (Berlin) and The Netherlands (Alphen aan den Rijn, Drachten) whole neighbourhoods have been built of environmentally friendly material. For instance, there are roofs made of sod. Houses are designed and positioned to receive the full benefit of climatic conditions, such as sunlight. Unfortunately, this type of construction is still not fully accepted. The main reason is that this type of construction is more expensive in the short turn than conventional building methods. (This is probably not the case in the long run.) As yet, this new type of construction still has some problems.

Although ecologically sound houses have become more and more popular, the link with an ecologically oriented spatial plan has not been made. The ecological neighbourhoods that can be seen today lack an environmentally friendly design. The traditional layout does not ban cars, nor does it favour alternative (and more environmentally friendly) forms of transport. For an example of an ecological neighbourhood, we have to look for projects specially designed for this purpose. A very good example is the Dutch town of Houten. This town is built in concentric circles around a shopping centre (see Figure 15.5) which is intersected by a railway line and a road for cars. Residential areas surround the shopping centre. The only way to get into the residential areas by car is to enter from the edge of town. Driving to the shopping centre is only possible by using the ring road outside the town. The centre is directly accessible from the residential areas only by bicycle paths. In this way, an environmentally friendly infrastructure has been created. The bicycle is favoured above the car for short distances.

The best way to attain environmental quality in residential areas is by giving attention to both infrastructure and construction methods. Until now, environmental quality has been largely based on only one of these aspects.

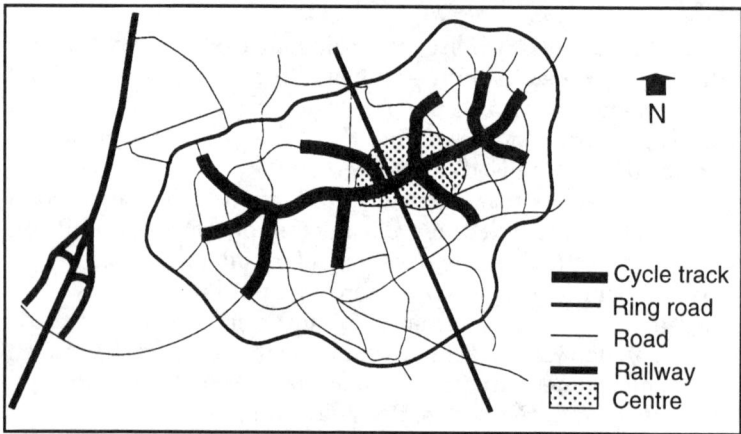

Source: De Jong and Bosch (1992).

Figure 15.5   The town of Houten, with a 'car-unfriendly' and 'bicycle-friendly' infrastructure

Employment

Another urban function is work. Employment is a major contributor to livability and sustainability, not only of the urban area but also on a much larger scale. Manufacturing is still one of the major causes of negative externalities in the urban area. Industry is responsible for the material production process of which emissions are a side-effect. These may be carcinogenic and toxic substances, but noise, odours and dust may also be generated. Reduction of these emissions at source is the most effective way to prevent negative effects on the environment. This means that reduction of emissions will affect livability in a positive way (see the section on integrated solutions). Manufacturing can also influence the environment through the quality of its products. For example, improving the quality of products may lighten the bulk of waste that is generated each year. Not only will the amount of waste be lower, but the need for raw materials – the input in the model – will be less. Thus improving the quality of products will influence sustainability in a positive way too! Special attention should be given to products that consume low levels of energy. In brief, industry has a major responsibility in closing the cycle of matter. Policies that urge industry to take certain measures are based on one of two options: the ALARA principle (as low as reasonably achievable) or the best technical means approach. The choice depends on how important the economic system is relative to livability and sustainability.

Industries might pollute their surroundings and thus affect the area in a negative way. This could give the area a bad image, which is likely to be a factor in urban competition. On the other hand, there is not yet enough evidence to accept the hypothesis that the decision on where to start new economic activities is influenced by livability and sustainability arguments. The local political climate, subsidies, accessibility by road, rail, air and information networks, agglomeration factors, and the costs and availability of labour seem to be far more important factors in the location decision for new economic activities (Cheshire and Gordon, 1993; Ashworth and Voogd, 1990).

Traffic

Cars are responsible for the emission of NO_x, which causes acidification. They also produce noise. The number of cars is already large and still growing. Most traffic movements are confined to the urban area, which leads to congestion in almost every city. Congestion increases traffic nuisance, which will influence the quality of the environment, but it also affects the spatial quality of the urban area negatively. It becomes hard to get from A to B without delay. This decline of spatial quality will also have a negative effect on economic growth.

Various policies have been developed to reduce the number of cars and the amount of pollution they create (see also Chapter 6 on Lisbon; Chapter 8 on Copenhagen; and Chapter 11 on Milan). In Europe, the policy is mainly focused on reduction of the number of cars, a measure that is hardly discussed in the USA, which has adopted another strategy. There environmental groups forced the powerful American Automobile Manufacturers Association to accept the consequences of the Clean Air Act, which led to an emission return system that is built into cars (*Washington Post*, 25 February 1994). The American approach will have a far better result on pollution control than the European approach. In Europe, traffic policy will only reduce the future growth of the number of cars. And continued growth means that Europeans must accept more pollution and congestion in the near future.

In Europe, most of the traffic reduction policies are based on the strategy to discourage car use. On the one hand, the strategies are based on getting people out of the car. This is done by building speed bumps or barriers in built-up neighbourhoods 'or at the entrance to the city centre, by constructing car-free zones and by reducing the number of parking spaces. Some local governments even try to raise the price of fuel, but this has proved to have little effect. The car is one of the 'holy cows' of our society. On the other hand, there are strategies to entice people to take other forms of transport. Good and inexpensive public transport may be a pull factor, although it may attract people who used to bike. Cycle paths can also be a factor, but a bicycle is only a feasible alternative when the travel distance is less than ten kilometres. The decision to take the bike is also highly dependent on the weather and the relief of the landscape.

Companies demand the best accessibility possible. They perceive accessibility as a major factor of their success. Almost every city in Europe is trying to create the best possible locations to attract economic activity, such as locations near highways. Unfortunately, high accessibility often leads to congestion, especially during rush hour. In The Netherlands, the national government is trying to control locations where the private sector can build offices, shops, warehouses, stores and manufacturing plants. The purpose is to reduce congestion, to improve accessibility, to shift the means of transport away from the car towards public transport, and to relieve traffic pressure on the city centre. The idea behind this is that much congestion and pollution caused by car traffic is generated by commuters travelling to and from work during the rush hour.

The policy is based on accessibility and mobility profiles. A city can use three types of accessibility profile. A location which can be reached easily by public transport is classified as a type-A location. Most type-A locations are right around the main railway stations of the big cities. These type-A locations should attract economic activities with a mobility profile based on a large number of individual trips. This is mostly the case with offices. Type-B locations are also reasonably accessible by public transport as well as by car. Type-C locations are found at the edge of the city, where accessibility by car is superior. The type-C location has a mobility profile based on the need for bulk transport. Here heavy industry can be found, as well as goods distribution.

The type-A locations are often in or near the city centres. The restricted parking is an important push factor to reduce the number of cars in the centre. Municipalities are responsible for the parking policy in the city, but competition between municipalities to attract economic activities has turned the parking policy into a failure in The Netherlands. Along with other forms of traffic reduction policies, this ABC traffic policy (Ministry of Housing, 1992) might influence the structure of the city. That, in turn, should lead to spatial and environmental relations between the urban functions of traffic, employment and housing. Also it should foster a better urban environment, although it is too early to expect clear results. An interesting aspect of this Dutch example is that spatial planning is used to reach environmental goals. On the other hand, local governments see the ABC policy and parking restrictions as impediments to their efforts to attract economic activities.

Nature and recreation

One of the reasons to promote the multifunctional, high-density city is to relieve the environmental pressure on rural areas. There is rising concern over the shrinking basis for the survival of flora and fauna. Natural environments are scarce and scattered. At the European level, a policy has been developed to concentrate the scattered natural environments (Institute for European Environmental Policy, 1991). The purpose is to extend the genetic basis for flora and fauna by interconnecting these concentrated natural areas. The question is: should urban areas be included in this Eeconet structure (European Ecological Network, also called Natura 2000)? If urban areas are barriers in the Eeconet structure, then urban green zones can be useful. This means that green areas in and around the city not only have recreational functions but perform a biological function too. Therefore green zones within the urban area can have a positive effect on biological and environmental quality and at the same time they can boost the spatial quality of the area (see also Chapter 12 on Stockholm).

The urban functions themselves are important, but the relation-ships between the different functions are important too. They can influence the quality of life in the city as well as its sustainability. The opportunities to influence these relations and thereby en-hance livability and sustainability are of special interest. Planners have to find the best possible locations for all urban functions. Traditionally, planners were only interested in the spatial quality of the area, but this narrow focus is changing rapidly. Increasingly, planners are taking the environmental quality of the area into account when locational choices are being made. Planners are becoming aware of the fact that functions have an effect on local environmental problems, such as disturbance and waste. When we look at the model that was introduced above (see Figure 15.4), the output in particular has a major effect on the livability of the local area. This is why cities or municipalities are keen on reduc-ing emission and waste – the output of the model – rather than reducing the input. But it is a mathematical law that lowering the output will affect the input, a fact local officials and urban plan-ners should become more aware of. It is therefore very important that policies deal with both inputs and outputs of the model. It is not always possible for governments to reduce the urban input – they have no control over most of it – but when, for example, developing social housing, governments can use their influence. City planners can also locate new neighbourhoods to minimize commuting distances. The decision on where to locate an indus-trial site should be made in relation to other functions in that area.

We may conclude that the model described here (Figure 15.4) can be used to elucidate the spatial relations between functions and the inputs and outputs of the urban area. Knowing that there are spatial relations, we can expect to make spatial choices to influence livability and sustainability. If we take this conclusion seriously, we may very well embark on a new era in urban plan-ning.

Separation and interlacing

Environmental spillovers affect only some aspects of an area's quality. Spatial factors must also be considered. To create good urban quality, environmental policy and physical planning should go hand in hand. In The Netherlands, for example, there is a strong tendency to integrate these two policy fields. The rationale is that both environmental policy and physical planning aim at the same target: a good and healthy area to live in. Only the method of reaching that target is different. Sometimes the methods are so different that the policies oppose each other instead of working hand in hand. Although integration is very much needed, this opposition makes it a difficult task to achieve.

Sustainability and livability are concepts closely related to environmental issues. Unfortunately, this is only true in a very abstract sense. Operational environmental policy needs quantitative standards and quantified general objectives. Therefore the local, more operational part of the contribution of environmental policy manifests itself in a highly quantitative form. Physical planners are expected to create an area in which society can function optimally. Such an area should be flexible and dynamic. Since society is constantly changing, it necessarily leads to a changing physical structure as well. To create a multifunctional and dynamic area, planners try to interweave all kinds of functions within the same area (see Figure 15.6). This means that in a residential area people can go shopping, visit a library, send their children to school, see a doctor and, if possible, go to work. This same neighbourhood would benefit from a location very near the highway, while being easily accessible by public transport. Such a multifunctional area will have a high quality of life, at least from a functional point of view. Planners will try to locate spatial functions by relating them to other functions or interests.

Functions which should be located in close proximity from a physical planning point of view could conflict with each other, according to environmental rules. A very clear example is the spatial conflict between environmentally intrusive activities, such as heavy industry, and environmentally sensitive land uses, for example housing. Environmental policy can be very strict, especially when the rules are enforced in terms of standards. On the basis of environmental standards, spatial functions sometimes have to be separated from each other (see Figure 15.6). For instance, dwellings very near the runway of an airport should be located somewhere else: the environmental load from activities which are going on around and above the airport is unacceptable. Furthermore, housing too near the airport will restrict the functioning of that airport.

Soil pollution is another example of environmental conflicts that can occur within the urban area. In all European countries, soil pollution is seen as a major environmental problem. In most cases, the cost of sanitizing the soil is very high. Many contaminated sites can be found in those parts of the urban area that are

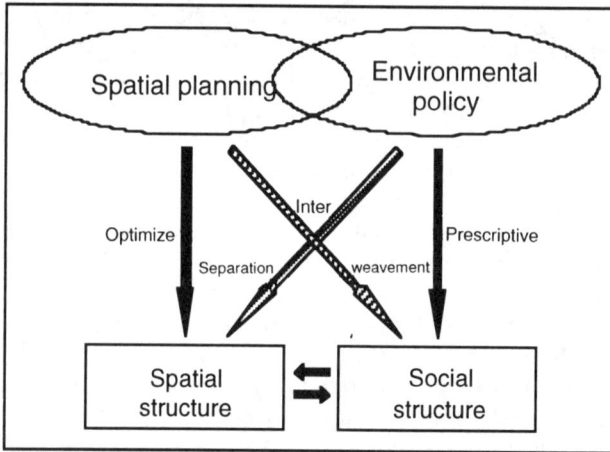

Source: De Roo (1993a).

Figure 15.6   Interlacing and separation, a conflict between environmental and physical policy

economically most dynamic. In many countries, such as The Netherlands, new activities are not allowed on sites where soil sanitation is needed. Because so many of these sites lie in urban areas, the soil pollution may turn a dynamic area into an economically and socially passive one. Many cities fear that soil pollution will cause economically attractive areas to slip into backwardness, as they become unattractive for new economic activities.

The need for standards to create a bridge between environmental problems and environmental solutions can be shown by comparing The Netherlands with the USA. Environmental policy in The Netherlands has a top–down structure. This means that strategies made at the national level should be followed up and carried out by regional and local authorities. The national government takes the primary responsibility for environmental issues. Accordingly, it establishes environmental standards. These should be used by the regional and local authorities when issuing permits and drafting physical plans. This procedure is based on the premise that the maximum allowed environmental load has to be the same everywhere in the country. In theory, everyone gets the same protection.

This is absolutely not the case in the USA, where many environmental issues with a spatial impact fall under the responsibility of local authorities. Thus there cannot be a unified policy regarding environmental loads in the USA and, consequently, environmental quality depends largely on the local political setting. This situation is not always favourable, as we can see in the case of Brooklyn, New York. One neigbourhood there, Greenpoint/Williamsburg,

> is home to many industries, large and small, that use a wide array of hazardous substances. ... Greenpoint/Williamsburg also houses the only operating facility in New York City permitted to store low level radioactive and hazardous waste, separated from each other by only a steel door. This facility also shares a common wall with a residential structure and is located down the block from a public school and a playground. ... Some residents would like to protect the local environment by having all manufacturing move out regardless of the impact on jobs and the local economic base. The majority of the residents who also depend on those manufacturing jobs for their livelihoods, would prefer to find mutually agreeable solutions to the problem. (Anderson *et al.*, 1994)

Environmental policy and physical planning have the same target, yet these policies can be opposed to each other because of the strategy needed to reach their target. Environmental policy uses environmental standards or general objectives to create a framework in which physical planning can take place. Thus environmental policy can be very restrictive to physical planning. There is a danger that the most dynamic locations in the urban area, which are mostly locations with an economic function, can turn into passive areas if the environmental load is too high. When such a situation occurs, environmental policy dominates physical planning. The result will be good environmental quality, although the quality of an area as a whole may deteriorate. The best possible quality of the area should be achieved in terms of both environmental and spatial quality.

We may draw the conclusion that a top–down structure is advisable. That is because solutions to environmental issues mainly call for a protective policy. A top–down structure to deal with environmental issues is fine, especially when the system allows some flexibility. But a top–down structure that leads to stifling rules should be avoided. Flexibility can be created in many ways, one of which is the introduction of area-differentiated standards. Environmental policy in the urban area should provide a flexible framework, allowing physical planners to create a dynamic area. The plan should take both spatial quality and environmental quality into account in an attempt to reach the best quality that area can possibly attain.

The compact city

The quality of life in the city depends on the variety and the 'efficient, time and energy-saving combination of social and economic functions' (CEC, 1990). The result is an urban area where pressure on the land is high. Because of high density and pressure, the city tends to expand into what can be called urban decentralization or sprawl. But decentralization and concentrated decentralization cannot solve conflicts, such as urban congestion and rural negligence. The economy, which has been under pressure since the mid-1970s, needed a strong urban basis with all economic, spatial and social functions. Another important argument for a strong and concentrated urban area is the negative effect of urban sprawl. Too many parts of the rural area have come under urban influence. A proposed solution to the problems of the past is the so-called 'compact city'.

Although the compact city has been welcomed by many authorities, it poses some contradictions that should be taken into account:

- high density versus environmentally clean areas,
- high density versus congestion-free urban areas,
- high density versus suburban quality of life,*
- high density versus access to green areas,*
- high density versus vigorous rural economy.*
  (* Based on Breheny, 1992.)

Together, these contradictions are known as 'the paradox of the compact city'. The compact city turns the conflict between interlacing and separation of functions into an acute problem. Not only are social and economic functions concentrated in the compact city; environmentally intrusive activities can also be found within the same dense area. Unfortunately, most authorities are still hardly aware of the spatial consequences of the conflict between environmentally intrusive activities and environmentally sensitive land uses in the urban area.

Integrated solutions in the compact city

The Netherlands is known for the rigorous application of standards. The restrictions, or perhaps we should say the impossibilities, encountered in the application of standards are well known in this country. Nevertheless, standards are considered to be an important bridge between negative environmental effects and political solutions to them (see Figure 15.3). The use of standards and their restrictions may lead to a spatial and environmental paradox. While these standards do not really create competition between cities, they do create conflicts between each city and its economic activities.

Two proposed methods of planning will be discussed. One is Integrated Environmental Zoning (IEZ). This type of zoning is based on standards and is mainly used to separate environmentally intrusive activities (such as manufacturing) from environmentally sensitive land uses in the urban area (for example, residential areas). IEZ is an excellent example of how to deal with environmental pollution in an urban area. The other method is no more than a reaction to IEZ. It is still in a very abstract and theoretical phase, but it is nevertheless a basis on which to discuss the usefulness of environmental standards. This method is called Dome. It is based on the idea that the total environmental quality of an area, conceived as being overarched by a single dome, should be the focus of the discussion. We should no longer talk about the conflict between intrusive overspill into residential areas. The main difference between IEZ and Dome is the difference between a standard and a comprehensive approach. The latter is only concerned with the rise in livability as environmental pollution declines in a given area. These two approaches prove to be the Yin and the Yang of the Dutch progressive environmental planning discussion about the urban area. This discussion highlights the difficulty that urban environmental planners face today. In their attempts to create a good and healthy environment, they are trying to develop a high-quality urban area.

Integrated Environmental Zoning

The method known as Integrated Environmental Zoning was developed by the Dutch Ministry of Housing, Physical Planning and Environment (Ministry of Housing, 1990). Environmental zoning, in this sense, has hardly anything to do with land use zoning or performance zoning, both of which characterize the traditional spatial planning. Environmental zoning is a reactive form of zoning. In this procedure, a zone is determined by the confrontation between overspill from industry or traffic and the location of environmentally sensitive areas. In cases dealing with nuisance and safety, environmental zoning is based on standards that set criteria for what is acceptable and what is not. Standards can be applied to zones; these zones make clear which part of an area is being

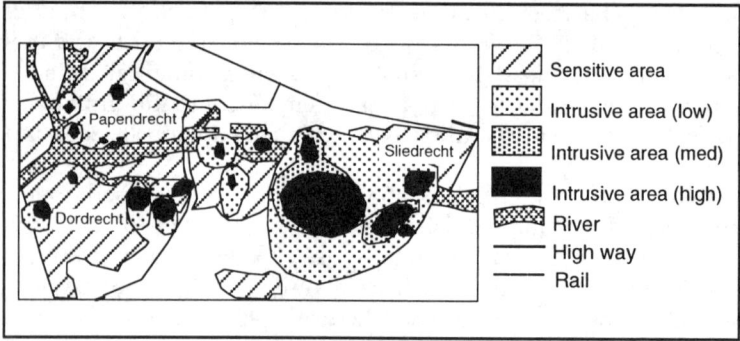

Source: Stuurgroep IMZS-Drechtsteden (1991).

Figure 15.7   *Environmentally sensitive areas and environmentally intrusive externalities in the Drechtsteden urban region*

intruded upon and which part is not. When the environmentally intrusive zone overlays the environmentally sensitive areas, we have a problem: an unacceptable situation arises (see Figure 15.7). Zones can thus be interpreted in terms of their spatial consequences. When the presence of an intrusive zone is acceptable – which in some cases is only possible after taking some necessary measures – the zone can be included in a local land use plan. This is a way to prevent spatial and environmental conflicts in the future.

The concept of environmental zoning is not new. In fact, the zoning of activities that create noise nuisance is old and one of the best examples of environmental zoning. But the combination of different forms of intrusions into one overall environmental zone has not been done before. Also the method takes real environmental loads into account, instead of using standardized tables, which was the usual approach. The method also takes cumulative effects into account. This means that, when someone lives in an area that is afflicted by a large amount of noise and is also affected by objectionable smells, more than one portion of intrusive load determines the spatial consequences. In this way, the environmental quality can be quantified more precisely.

Integrated Environmental Zoning proved to be very effective in determining the environmental quality of an area. So far, the Dutch results are shocking. IEZ revealed how much of the environmentally sensitive area is covered by an excessive environmental load. In some cases, intrusive activities are causing such a great load that the spatial consequences are drastic. Whole neighbourhoods have to be demolished and factories have to close. This illuminates the extent of the social and economic conflict. But the awareness that something is very wrong in a particular area is very important. It helps the authorities to develop a policy that is realistic enough to improve the environmental quality, while allowing economic activities to survive.

At present, IEZ is being tested in 11 pilot projects in The Netherlands. Pending the outcome, the system does not yet have a legal basis. The pilot projects will result in an accumulation of experience, upon which a workable system can be built. One of the pilot projects is located in the city of Arnhem, a middle-sized city of about 200 000 inhabitants. At first sight, the city seems to be a very pleasant place, but industries in the industrial estate, Arnhem-Noord, are polluting so much that an area of eight by eight kilometres has become a so-called 'black area', an area with an unacceptable environmentally intrusive overspill. This overspill is mainly caused by two substances. One is H_2S, which is a malodorous substance; the other is CS_2, which is toxic. The IEZ pilot project being conducted in Arnhem has produced a map of an area at least five by five kilometres in size which is completely black. The system also tells us what to do in this situation. First, we should try to reduce the environmental load at source. If this is not effective enough, houses have to be demolished or industries have to close. In this case, it is impossible to reduce the environmental load enough, at least over the next few years. The goal would be to limit the area that receives an unacceptable load to the boundaries of the industrial estate. As a result, either a major part of Arnhem would be demolished or the factories would close. However, these factories employ hundreds or even thousands of people. So what should be done? (See De Roo, 1993b.)

IEZ is largely based on standards which clarify the difference between good and bad environmental quality. The system proved to be very successful in depicting environmental quality, but the spatial consequences it suggests can be unacceptable. Polluting economic activities are not yet tending to move away. The cost of moving is still higher than that of taking sanitation measures. In many instances, the industry started its activity a long time before environmentally sensitive functions were located around it. Who, then, is liable for the sanitation costs? At the moment, research is under way to see if flexibility in time is a solution to the very rigid bottlenecks of IEZ. Flexibility in time means the acceptance of the (long) period needed to reduce the environmental load to an acceptable level.

The quality of an area is not solely based on the quality of the environment; spatial quality also has to be taken into account. The Integrated Environmental Zoning system is not yet flexible enough to include spatial quality as well. Although researchers are working hard to make the system more adaptable, another system is being developed. This is known as the Dome approach.

The Dome concept

The dome concept is not only an improvement upon Integrated Environmental Zoning; it also supplements that system by proposing solutions to the paradox of the compact city. The concept was developed under the auspices of the city of Amsterdam. The aim of the municipal authorities was to reduce the total environmental load on the city, instead of having to meet environmental standards at every single location (the usual approach). Only in the long run would the city dome, which is in fact the total amount of environmental load produced in a city, have to meet environmental standards. To reduce the city dome, it is not necessary for every part of the city to achieve the same degree of reduction. The amount of the reduction needed is related to the characteristics, functions and spatial opportunities of the area. Every area within the city can have its own dome (see Figure 15.8). If it is not possible to reduce the environmental load within one dome, this concept should be replaced by other measures to improve the quality of the area in question. Alternatively, a trade-off can take place with another dome which is also defined within the city dome. The method is flexible; it permits an exchange of different

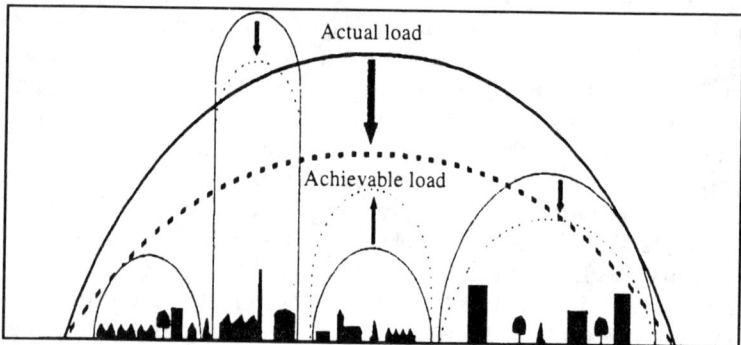

Source: Department of Physical Planning and Environmental Affairs (1994).

Figure 15.8   The city dome and secondary domes

environmental loads. Also substitution and compensation of measures are facilitated by using this concept.

The height of the dome is calculated by bringing the different environmental loads together in one index. That figure represents the total environmental load. It is found by using sub-indices based on individual environmental loads. The environmental index makes it possible to appreciate the area differentiation. In an area that is not very sensitive, a higher environmental load may be acceptable. That same load may not be acceptable in an environmentally sensitive area, where the environmental load will reach the maximum value on the index sooner than in less sensitive areas.

The Dome concept seems very promising, because it facilitates area differentiation. Also substitution and compensation of measures are made possible by applying this concept, which will thereby improve environmental control. Consequently, using the concept has the potential to resolve conflicts between environmental policy and physical planning. Although the dome concept is promising, many difficulties still have to be overcome. For example, the concept does not concern the protection of the individual; it only applies to the macro level: it does not apply to the micro level because it is not based on standards. Environmental standards are designed to protect individuals as well as society as a whole. Another drawback is that applying the dome concept ignores some crucial questions. How much environmental load will be acceptable as a maximum? How far will the environmental dome have to be lowered, and over what length of time? Furthermore, the desire to include qualitative variables in order to express the livability of an area more precisely should also be subjected to critical discussion. Another important factor has been neglected during the discussions so far: the choice of scale. The use of variables to express the livability, the environmental quality or the environmental load underneath the dome will depend on the spatial scale of the dome or secondary domes.

The Integrated Environmental Zoning system is a procedure which should become part of daily practice at the local urban level in The Netherlands. In contrast, the dome concept is above all indicative in nature, therefore it should only be used as a guideline to support spatial and environmental decisions.

We have reviewed two completely new methods that offer an inside view of the environmental externalities or load in the urban area. These methods are by no means perfect, but they tell a great deal about the environmental quality of the area. Both methods are also spatially oriented. Therefore they can both form a useful bridge between environmental policy and spatial planning. It is hoped that more countries will develop methods like the ones presented here. European cities will profit from such initiatives. Further refinement of these methods could point the way to developing good and healthy urban areas where intrusive activities and environmentally sensitive land uses are separated in a sustainable way.

Conclusions

The modern European city is a compact city. It is a multifunctional and dense area with much spatial and functional variety, but it also has many environmental bottlenecks. The compact city calls for careful spatial planning, with flexible environmental rules to create a sustainable and livable urban area. European environmental policy is basically top–down policy. This procedure largely prevents competition between cities on issues such as environmental pollution and sustainability. In this way, environmental issues will not be traded off for economic issues, which is beneficial as it safeguards health and livability. Economic activities will only move away if cities do not meet the environmental standards or objectives, or if they cannot reduce their congestion. Top–down environmental policy has some positive aspects, yet flexibility is needed in practice, because environmental rules should support the local situation as much as possible.

At present we are only beginning to understand the complexity of including environmental issues in urban planning. But we are advancing in the direction of a good and healthy urban area. As each new development appears, initiatives are undertaken on an ad hoc basis. This is also the case with urban environmental planning. Here and there, cities are trying to experiment with ecologically beneficial dwellings. Experiments are also being carried out concerning traffic and transport issues. Most of these experiments are isolated efforts, having no relation to other urban environmental issues. Relatively recent experiments have been started in The Netherlands to integrate environmental policy with spatial planning. This is to be achieved by separating, in a sustainable way, environmentally intrusive activities from environmentally sensitive land uses. These initiatives are a step towards a more sophisticated form of environmental planning. At the same time, they may mark the beginning of a new era in urban planning.

References

Anderson, N., E. Hanhardt and I. Pasher, (1994) 'From measurement to measure: land use and environmental protection in Brooklyn, New York', paper presented at the International Symposium on Urban Planning and Environment, University of Washington, Seattle.

Ashworth, G.J. and H. Voogd (1990) *Selling the City: Marketing Approaches in Public Sector Urban Planning*, London and New York: Belhaven.

Blowers, A. (1990) 'Narrowing the options: political conflicts and locational decision making', in Milieu en Ruimte, verslag van het 13e ASYS lustrum congres. Amsterdam: Amsterdamse Studievereniging voor Sociaal-geografen, pp.94–102.

Breheny, M.J. (1992) 'Towards sustainable urban development', in S.R. Bowlby and A.M. Mannion (eds), *Environmental Issues in the 1990s*, Chichester: Wiley.

Cheshire, P.C. and I.R. Gordon (1993) *European Integration: Territorial Competition in Theory and Practice*, Reading: Centre for the Study of Advanced European Regions, University of Reading.

CEC (1990) *Green Paper on the Urban Environment*, Brussels: Commission of the European Communities.

Cutter, S.L. (1993) *Living with Risk*, London: Edward Arnold.

Department of Physical Spatial Planning and Environmental Affairs (1994) *Beleidsnota Ruimtelijke Ordening en Milieu* [Policy paper on spatial planning and environment], Amsterdam.

Howard, E. (1970) *Garden Cities of Tomorrow*, London: Faber & Faber.

Institute for European Environmental Policy (1991) *Towards a European Ecological Network*, Arnhem: Institute for European Environment Policy.

Jong, H. de and T. Bosch (1992) 'Houten, model voor de toekomst', *Verkeerskunde*, [Houten, an example for the future], 2, pp.16–19.

Meadows, D.L. (1972) *The Limits to Growth, A Report of the Club of Rome on the Predicament of Mankind*, New York: Universe.

Ministry of Housing, Physical Planning and Environment (1990) *Ministerial Manual for a Provisional System of Integral Environmental Zoning*, Leidschendam: MVROM.

Ministry of Housing, Physical Planning and Environment, Ministry of Transport and Public Works, Ministry of Economic Affairs (1992) *The Right Business in the Right Place*, The Hague: SDU.

National Environmental Policy Plan (NEPP) (1989) *To Choose or to Lose*, Ministry of Housing, Physical Planning and Environment, The Hague: SDU.

Opschoor, J.B. and S.W.F. van der Ploeg (1990) 'Duurzaamheid en Kwaliteit' [Sustainability and quality], in *Het Milieu: Denkbeelden voor de 21ste eeuw*, Commissie Lange Termijn Milieubeleid, Zeist: Kerckebosch.

Roo, G. de (1993a) 'Integrale milieuzonering, patstelling of synthese' [Integrated environmental zoning, dilemma or synthesis], in *Kwaliteit van Norm en Zone*, Groningen: Geo Pers.

Roo, G. de (1993b) 'Environmental zoning: the Dutch struggle towards integration', *European Planning Studies*, 3, pp.367–77.

Siebert, H. (1992) *Economics of the Environment*, Berlin: Springer.

Stuurgroep IMZS-Drechtsteden (1991) *Inventarisatie Milieubelasting, Rapportage Eerste Fase* [Inventory of environmental load, report of the first stage], The Hague: SDU.

Vesilind, P.A., J.J. Peirce and R.F. Weiner (1990) *Environmental Pollution and Control*, Boston: Butterworth-Heinemann.

16 Competitive political and administrative systems

Joan-Eugeni Sánchez

Territorial organization and political agents

Political action takes place within a delimited territory, and political management must start with a territorial organization suited to its objectives. To this end, jurisdictions are carved out and ranked hierarchically. Such a political organization of space can provide the conditions to derive maximum benefits from the production process. In this respect, political intervention pertains first to the development of business locations, the provision of transport and communication infrastructure, the regulation of labour markets and so on. Secondly, political action also relates to the distribution of the benefits of economic activity. It intervenes to develop human resources by influencing the settlement pattern of the population and by providing appropriate collective services, housing, education facilities and so on. In short, political action is meant to enhance the quality of life.

The social structure and social developments, on the one hand, should correspond to the territorial structure and spatial developments, on the other. If the administrative–territorial organization does not coincide with the functional organization of an urban region, it will be very difficult to reach specified social goals. The most concrete form of intervention is found at the local level. It is there that policies and agents can be clearly linked. Like every individual, every political group with an interest in exercising territorial interventions will attempt to establish a power base at the local level. This allows them to induce the spatial changes that facilitate the attainment of their political, economic and social targets. Personal interest and concerted action with political aims combine in the political arena at the local level. Private and public agents, and those with a stake in both realms, are the participants in social life and spatial developments at the local level.

Timing is crucial to political action, as it is to social and spatial developments. Indeed, policy can be defined as expectations for the future based on current decisions. In other words, political action is intended to shape the future. To succeed, policy must specify both the aims and the means to attain the desired situation. This does not always imply a need for direct intervention. The choice to take no action also represents a strategy of the respective agents. Therefore the analysis of political action should not be limited to plans and projects; it must include the political agents as well.

Territorial policies have two inherent dangers. One is that territorial interventions are virtually irreversible. The other is that problems and solutions are perceived differently when studied on different scales. The element of scale harbours conflicts of interest. For instance, decisions relating to the siting of facilities which exert negative externalities, such as refuse dumps or prisons, may satisfy regional needs but sow discontent among the neighbours. All political decisions are made by agents who have interests in their intervention. Therefore policies must be understood in relation to the agents. They design and implement such measures. Meanwhile, other agents may oppose these efforts and try to modify policies, on the grounds of partisan or personal interests.

The close link between decision making and the characteristics of a specific territory leads one to define the problems in terms of acute personal relations and interests (Pompili, 1992). In this vein, it is fruitful to investigate the institutions of the political power structure. Even more importantly, it must be determined which individuals wield political power. They, not the institutions, constitute the real locus of power. Indeed, urban policies are intimately linked to the characteristics of these actors. They choose to implement measures which they consider to be the most appropriate, thus determining the eventual outcome of policy (Sánchez, 1992a).

Agents and institutions in metropolitan policy making

To be effective, policies must suit the basic institutions of a given territory (Gaspar, 1992). These institutions vary widely among the states and the regions of Europe, depending on each country's political organization. At present, the division of territorial power in Europe is highly complex. It is the outcome of two types of dynamics; one is functionally determined, whereas the other results from a historical process. From the functional perspective, each of the states has introduced a territorial organization geared to the needs of its economy, its social life and its political realities.

But these organizational forms are modified by concrete historical developments, making every administrative structure unique. Accordingly, the policies of regionalization as applied in France or Italy reflect the perceived need for administrative decentralization. The regions in these countries are not autonomous in policy making. They were delineated to meet the needs of local administrations that implement major decisions made by the central power as they apply to smaller territorial units. In fact, these lower-tier administrations are meant to improve the functioning of the state as a whole by allowing state policies to be implemented in the regions.

National policy initiatives, whatever their own virtues, may run counter to the historical–political realities of individual regions. Each specific situation is the product of the differences in culture, ethnic composition and other regional characteristics. If policies are to be effective, these differences must be taken into account. Measures have to accommodate the local psychosocial attitudes, both of the majority of the population and of regional minorities. The current political–administrative complexion of Europe has a very long history. Historical developments have shaped the current geopolitical organization of each state. Most European countries are highly centralistic, but each has established administrative sub-divisions in order make the political management of its territory more efficient. The centralist tendencies are rooted in a desire to create nation-states out of fragmented territories as a way to defend territorial integrity against incursions by neighbouring states.

In general, three tiers of political–territorial units are found in European countries. Irrespective of local labels, they can be classified as state, region and municipality. In some countries, the administrative–territorial division is more complex, designating more intermediate levels with specific jurisdictions. In France, Spain and Belgium, for instance, there are intermediate-level administrations between the region and the municipality (departments, provinces or similar divisions). The regional entity is the largest subdivision in each of the countries. It takes on various forms relative to its jurisdiction (depending on whether the state is a federation, confederation or a unitary state). And the regions are known by different names: the Länder of Germany, Swiss cantons, regions of France, Belgium or Portugal, counties of the UK, autonomous regions ('autonomías') of Spain. The differences reflect distinct historical–political processes, representing the nationalist, ethnic or religious make-up of the respective countries. By distinguishing regions and empowering these with specific responsibilities, long-running conflicts within the nations are meant to be neutralized.

It makes a difference whether the regions were created by the state as a means to establish effective control over its territory, or reflect a long historical process. In the latter case, the regions are more than administrative divisions. They express the regional identities that preceded the formation of the nineteenth-century nation-states. The regions of the UK, Spain and Belgium, for instance, provide clear examples of the latter type of entities.

The basic territorial unit is the municipality, which occupies the position between the household and the region. As an administrative unit, it circumscribes individual behaviour while at the same time allowing for interaction between agents. Above all, it is at this level that racial, ethnic, religious, linguistic and ideological differences between people are expressed in social relations. This local scale is the most significant level for social relations. These reflect the mechanisms of political intervention in space through planning, land use regulations and the allocation of functions to specific areas. At the same time, they show how the different levels interact, since local and regional authorities cannot act independent of the state. They are essentially subordinate to the state as they were meant to facilitate effective control by the state. The local level best expresses the dialectic of the state as the ultimate regulator, but whose actions can only be effective through the interpretation and implementation of the regulations by local agents (Goodwin *et al.*, 1993).

The metropolitan area: a new jurisdiction

As we have noticed throughout this book, the metropolitan area has emerged over the last few decades as a new territorial configuration associated with the rapid pace of 'metropolization'. This new configuration is particularly important with regard to the competition among European cities. The fiercest competition takes place precisely among cities that have attained the status of metropolitan areas. Recognizing the metropolitan area as a territorial entity introduces some distortion into the classical view of jurisdictions. It opens new fields of territorial competition on two scales. On the one hand, it leads to competition between the central city and the surrounding municipalities within the metropolitan area. On the other hand, it encourages competition – and conflicts of interest – between the metropolitan area and their regions or even with the national entities.

In the course of analysing metropolitan areas, two problematic issues arise at the political–administrative level. On the one hand, their municipalities are increasingly less functional. They are usually small areas and they are often poorly equipped to resolve the new challenges posed by the technological society. The problem is that technological innovation prompts a relative contraction of the territory. Technological development has enhanced the concentration of human activities, but it has also facilitated long-distance commuting, allowing people to cover greater distances in the same amount of time. And it raises the level of consumption in terms of the array of goods and services. In the process, social needs are increasing. But neither the facilities nor the services required to meet this rising demand can be found within the old municipal boundaries and certainly not in the municipalities that make up the metropolitan area.

A second outcome of the same process of expanding social relations across municipal boundaries is that the negative effects upon the environment are becoming more and more tangible. Moreover, economic relations – forward and backward linkages, multiplier effects – affect increasingly wide areas. This means that the dependency of a local area, even of metropolitan areas, upon the outside world is increasing steadily. In terms both of procuring resources and of serving expanding markets, the necessity to control a territory is more and more acute. We are referring to the interurban, regional, national or international systems of communication and transport. This need of control is particularly manifest in the area of utilities: water, gas or other energy sources, sewer and drainage systems, rubbish dumps and pollution effects. Furthermore, we must consider the effects of leisure activities and tourism, second homes and so on on areas reaching far beyond the metropolitan area itself. In addition, there are the consequences of the internationalization of the production process to be taken into account. Plants have grown increasingly dependent on decisions made far beyond the local area.

When the increasing dependency is plotted on a time–space continuum, two basic models emerge. These models depict the role of the municipality and the direction of its transformation as it evolved into a metropolitan area. The classic municipality was a 'self-contained' unit in the sense that several functional scales coincided with municipal boundaries. These also largely circumscribed the spatial extent of the activities of people's everyday life. Moreover, the municipality functioned as a closed labour market, as agriculture, services and even manufacturing industry were found within its boundaries.

The newly emerged metropolitan areas are different in many respects. As the greater part of everyday activities – living, working, shopping and entertainment – are conducted outside the municipal boundaries, serious administrative contradictions result. New kinds of territorial conflicts emerge with respect to the provision of services as social needs evolve. New problems result from the concentration of large numbers of people. They reveal the limitations of the democratic management of conflicts, weighing the demands of effective control against the need for citizen participation.

Finally, the metropolis wields a vastly increased power, as it becomes the node through which the expanded contacts between its region and the world are channelled. If the network in which it operates contains a number of 'international cities', it is all the more powerful.

Because of these fundamental changes, there is a need for new territorial management. A single metropolitan area contains new functional entities and new social–territorial problems. Its vastly increased size, as compared to the old city, alienates the citizens, now classified as the 'masses', from the new administration. The conflicts become very complicated when the traditional local authorities are opposed to merging into the new metropolitan area by handing over their responsibilities. Existing interests often favour maintaining the traditional structures.

The cases analysed throughout this book demonstrate above all lack of courage or political will to redesign the administration of the new territorial unit. There are precious few examples of recent attempts to create new metropolitan governments. The difficulties encountered in reorganizing the municipal structures of the large cities in The Netherlands are a case in point. The metropolitan region of Rotterdam – 'Rijnmond' – was dissolved after only a few years of operation. New attempts to create metropolitan governments in The Netherlands have focused on selected tasks for these units. The proposals entail the simultaneous merger of suburban municipalities into the 'super-city' and the dissolution of the central cities into smaller 'new-style' municipalities. Thus the basic units of the metropolitan area would be more balanced to alleviate the fear of smaller suburban municipalities of the overwhelming domination by the powerful central city. But the all-out effort finally to implement concrete reform proposals ran afoul of the sentiments – and the votes – of the inhabitants who identify strongly with the city, not with its districts. It also proved to be difficult to cultivate real cooperation among the local authorities within the metropolitan regions, in spite of the efforts of the authorities at a higher tier in the administrative hierarchy (Van den Berg *et al.*, 1993).

In the opposite direction, this increasing weight of the metropolis normally provokes conflict at the state and/or regional level. More and more, the new territorial configuration creates the feeling of menace to the state and to the regions, especially from an economic and political perspective. The metropolis appears to be a countervailing power. One single metropolitan area may have more than half of the population of the wider region, and, furthermore, the metropolitan area tends to control the most important part of its economic base.

Studies of national urban systems have shown that cities are the premier places of concentration because of their centrality. This tends to perpetuate their central position. Centrality confers upon cities a clear advantage of accessibility, which promotes the development of innovations (Rozenblat, 1991). For this reason, metropolises exude an aura of power. They form privileged links with interests abroad, which reinforces their role of connecting a region with the rest of the world. As nodes in a network, metropolises are increasingly expanding the role of the network of cities to a worldwide scale. Faced with all these new circumstances, analysts (such as Van den Berg *et al.*, 1993) have identified five critical areas on which to judge the performance of a metropolitan government. They call for scale adequacy, competence, comprehensiveness, democracy and efficiency–effectiveness. We may add a sixth factor: personal leadership.

The new metropolitan configuration is formed by grouping municipalities, but this approach does not always yield an entity of adequate scale. One of the most thorny questions concerns the appropriate dimensions for the new metropolitan functions. The right size will have to be established in each particular case. The decision must be based on the diversity of functions that have to be managed. It will have to take into account the specific territorial dimension related to every political problem. And the difficulty of merging municipalities must not be underestimated.

A more controversial issue concerns the competence of these new entities. In this regard, we may consider several possibilities. A first distinction is based on leadership: who takes the initiative to establish the metropolitan area? Frequently, this step is the outcome of a decision made by the municipalities themselves. They usually see this option as a way to deal with the new problems of scale of operation, but in other cases (for example, some French metropolises such as Lille or Strasbourg) the initiative was taken by the central government (Van den Berg *et al.*, 1993). The political and economic power that was created along with these new jurisdictions has ushered in a new source of contention. A struggle ensued for the control of these new entities, pitting the political powers of the central city of the metropolitan area against the regional and national authorities. Such conflicts have led to the demise of regional bodies, especially where opposing political parties controlled each of the tiers of government. Authorities have returned to governing by fragmentation tactics in some of the oldest metropolitan areas of Europe. London, Birmingham, Copenhagen, Barcelona and Valencia are clear examples of excessive political competition. At first glance, this process appears to be a weak point in the power plays in each of these cities; this point is elucidated in several of the city vignettes in the second part of this book (see also Van den Berg *et al.*, 1993).

Another aspect to consider is the role of central government in these power relations. This is pertinent to some national capitals such as Paris or Copenhagen, where 'Grand Projects' are undertaken at the instigation of central government (Burgel, Chapter 4, Engelstoft and Jørgensen, Chapter 8 in this book). Intervention by higher authorities is one of the main exogenous forces shaping metropolitan development.

Efforts have been made to develop an integral policy vision encompassing several areas. Such comprehensive reviews have been highly diverse for each metropolitan administration. For instance, in Paris, Lisbon and Rotterdam there is a tendency to turn to integral policy, yet in most cases the metropolitan authorities only deal with individual policy facets. In particular, they tend to retain control over infrastructure. In Frankfurt, for instance, a voluntary partnership of municipalities has been formed. The partners perform a number of tasks in the areas of spatial planning, the supply of drinking water and the disposal of solid waste and waste water. Their mandate is limited to the designation of land uses in the region. It does not include the coordination and control of the region's spatial–economic development (Van den Berg *et al.*, 1993). Similar situations prevail in Valencia and Barcelona (Sánchez, 1992b). In an ideological sense, the period of urban politics came to an end in the late 1980s when planning gave way to a managerial role for government in the great cities (Gottdiener, 1987; Wilson, 1989).

The way in which a metropolitan government is elected is crucial to its democratic functioning. As long as old municipalities persist within metropolitan areas, the officials of the metropolitan government will generally represent the constituent municipalities, rather than be elected directly. This procedure moves the administration further away from the citizens. It also moves any conflict into the field of intermunicipal controversy. This may not expedite finding a solution to such problems. And as Van den Berg *et al.* (1993) remarks, 'If the local governments involved do not recognize the need to form a regional administration, they will be unwilling to help establish such an administration and to give substance and implementation to the policy such as an administration wants to pursue.' But even with the consent of existing political structures, success of restructuring is not guaranteed.

Where municipal restructuring has been attempted to avoid such conflicts, as in the case of Rotterdam cited above, a different problem emerged when the issue was put to a referendum. The overwhelmingly negative verdict of the electorate on the proposed abolition of the central city showed how difficult it is to introduce intramunicipal decentralization.

In order to attain efficiency–effectiveness, the administration must be able to act promptly and decisively. Conditions that we have seen up to now do not warrant great expectations about how a European metropolis can reach a high level of efficiency. There are two main obstacles to decisive action: one is the absence of a unitary government; the other is the safeguarding of municipal power. For instance, it is very difficult, if not impossible, for municipalities to collaborate on general economic development and planning. This may be because of the overwhelming power of the central city vis-à-vis the suburban municipalities (as in Barcelona and Valencia) or because of the absence of leadership (as in Lisbon).

We can add a few more obstacles to this list: the prevailing scarcity of financial resources; the problem of fiscal redistribution in the process of territorial restructuring; and the relation between movements of people and of firms, on the one hand, to the financing of supramunicipal services, on the other (Van den Berg *et al.*, 1993). Finally, as Stoker (1991) notes in regard to Britain (and his conclusion applies to every case reviewed in this book) local authorities are pivotal elements in a complex system of government, inside which personal leadership marks the differences.

In summary, there is great variety of political institutions among the European metropolitan areas. Also within these areas, there are differences in management capacity and conflicts of interest. These lead to inefficiency and inconsistency in policy making. Furthermore, the key position of the local government constitutes a weak element in the process of decision making. It impedes the implementation of tasks that have an impact far outside the local area. It is clear that the contradiction among scales – specifically those of political decision making and socioeconomic functioning – makes the resolution of these problems hard. This drawback pertains especially to the provision of facilities and services such as airports, drinking water supply and waste disposal, to the creation of an adequate transport network, the training of the labour supply, the control of commuter flows and so on.

The individual municipality is by no means always the appropriate level at which to study, monitor, control or finance development in urbanized regions. This is especially true for aspects of the spatial–economic transformation. Where the main reason for devising policies and programmes is the development of the labour market, the appropriate unit is where local labour market policy shows its limits and its potential (Foley, 1992; Heinelt, 1992).

We might conclude that policies tend to follow the spontaneous trends of the national economy rather than initiating them or preceding them. After years of promoting decentralization as the ideological target, long-term trends reveal a process in the opposite direction. As Burgel notes in Chapter 4 of this book for France, and for Paris in particular, the current period shows a revival of urban centrality, benefiting the large cities. Although urban centrality was widely criticized in the early 1980s, great cities continue to be privileged places. This is largely due to their capacity to create agglomeration economies (Rozenblat, 1991). But it is hard to know how these dynamics of growth, expansion and power concentration in the great cities will affect the peripheral regions of the European Union (Vázquez Barquero, 1990).

Qualities that make a city internationally competitive

The focus of our work is on cities that are struggling to maintain or improve their place in the European system of cities. In order to reach that goal, they have to perform at least a minimum number of international functions. These are concentrated in a relatively small number of cities, especially those with high connectivity in an international network. Some cities perform a wide range of these functions, others only a few (Rozenblat, 1991). All policies must presume at least minimum levels of competitiveness in all or some of these international functions. These are the assets that make a city international. According to several authors (Labasse, 1981; Rozenblat, 1991; Brunet, 1989; Meier and Friedman, cited in Junyent and Gimenez Capdevila, 1989), it is feasible to build a model of the internationally competitive city. This entails a set of functions that must reach a critical level in terms of several criteria.

- Population over one million; a diverse, qualified labour force; the presence of great universities (by enrolment numbers and reputation), of high-level research and of a complete infrastructure.
- International activities that earn the city a place in networks of economic, scientific and cultural exchange and make it a financial centre; a high volume of air traffic; being well-served by advanced telecommunications facilities.
- A high level of specialization and the availability of services at an international level (above all, business services for multinational corporations); the ambition to serve as a location for headquarters of international corporations.
- Facilities that allow the organization of international events such as congresses, trade shows and festivals.
- Resident communities of foreign officials and business leaders with their associations or clubs.
- A cultural infrastructure, including press agencies and book publishers, museums, monuments to be visited, cultural events of international renown; artistic manifestations that project it as a centre for business, culture, leisure and tourism far beyond the national borders.
- To boost its competitive position, it should strive to remain distinct among the set of competitors in a global context, spanning the cultural, political and economic fields.

The city's challenge: to revitalize its metropolitan policy

The target of urban policy for this kind of city has been to provide as many amenities as possible at the international level. At the European level, London and Paris rank highest (Rozenblat, 1991). The analysis of several European cities (Van den Berg *et al.*, 1993) allows some conclusions about the conditions for success. In order to achieve these aims, a regional administration should meet certain spatial–economic criteria, which are formulated as specific opportunities and threats impinging upon the regional economy and its spatial organization. One of these criteria, for instance, would be the degree of dominance of the central city. In addition, there are administrative–political circumstances (government organization, attitudes of officials and political objectives). And the authorities should pay heed to the inherent qualities of the population (such as the entrepreneurialism of its 'key figures'). Such conditions apply to four important dimensions of urban policy: economic efficiency, social and spatial equity, control of negative externalities and budgetary constraints. These conditions have been conducive to change in the nature of local power. Increasingly, local authorities employ a managerial approach. Local government is no longer confined to territorial administration. More and more, the city and its metropolitan area act as an enterprise. It needs to manage its territory as a resource base and as a generator of resources.

From the perspective of competition among cities, defined by the three Es: efficiency, equity and externalities/environment, efficiency is the goal most vigorously pursued for political, administrative and management reasons. A high level of efficiency is crucial to be effective in the arena of international competition among cities. The efficiency must be related to the city's own objectives and its organization. It has to emanate from the political and administrative structure. And it must be generated by the people who participate. We emphasize that, in a competitive situation, efficiency is the main target.

Cities participate in a world with an increasing tendency to interact through nodal networks. Great metropolitan areas are the nodes in telecommunications and telematics. There is also a tendency for multinational corporations to occupy a position of hegemony. This structure corresponds closely to the model of management of the economic empires of multinational firms. In general, a city constitutes a territorial locus of power. On the one hand, that centre of power represents the needs of the city's entire metropolitan area. On the other hand, the city represents each of the business headquarters within its territory in its varied relationships within the country, and with the rest of the world. All this demands the creation of new institutions of metropolitan organization and political control. These must extend beyond the central city. Only on a larger scale can such an institution respond to the needs of the new functional space.

A city cannot escape the stamp of the 'trademark' of the nation of which it is a part. The prestige or drawbacks of such an image in the rest of the world will induce effects on a particular territory (Sánchez, 1994). An essential component of a city's potential competitiveness is the prestige of its country. For instance, it means one thing to be located in an investor country such as the USA, Switzerland, Japan, Germany or, to a lesser extent, Sweden. Yet it is quite something else to be part of a recipient country, such as Spain, Australia, Norway, Austria, Belgium, Denmark or Italy. Then again, a city is in a different situation as part of an 'investment crossroads', countries both investing and receiving investments, such as the UK, Finland, The Netherlands, France or Canada

(Rozenblat, 1991). At the same time, less tangible characteristics can put a virtually inescapable label on a city; it makes a difference whether a city is associated with such psychosocial qualities as 'artistic', 'hard-working' or 'undisciplined'. It is for this reason that many serious efforts made by a city remain fruitless. The city may be unable to neutralize a negative image of its country.

Metropolitan policy for economic and social revitalization

The greatest policy challenge to European cities over the last few years has been how to improve their image in order to revitalize their economy. Such policy had to support existing economic activities and firms, and to attract new ones. Across Europe, cities have used similar instruments in their competition for the same (transactional) businesses.

As we have noted above, it has been necessary for public agents to take charge of their city's economic development. Their performance as economic entities has been boosted by the implementation of a range of policies: building infrastructure to support production and consumption; deregulation; reversing declines in consumption and the deterioration of public facilities and services; or devising instruments to change the economic structure, for instance by stimulating the development of a high-technology sector in the city (Shachar and Felsenstein, 1992). This explains the great push to modernize in particular the transport and telecommunication infrastructure of recent years. But the policies must move beyond this, and address all aspects of the processes of production, circulation, consumption, distribution and movement of capital and surplus.

The policies introduced by several metropolitan agents have had direct and indirect effects. The agents have attempted to develop the potential strengths of their cities and to correct drawbacks that might weaken the city's position relative to other cities within the country or abroad. While they must fit their microeconomic policy initiatives to the major economic developments and structures, there are many options. In this context, it is relevant to note that local authorities in various parts of the world increasingly take on the role of entrepreneur in pursuit of economic growth for the city (Cox and Mair, 1989; Leitner, 1990). As European cities are strengthening their positions in international networks, they have taken their cue from cities elsewhere and adopted similar policies to improve their competitive position.

In summary, various major policy avenues may be distinguished. Several deal with the economy of cities. As current industrial development has shifted from the central cities to their metropolitan surroundings, the cities either try to revitalize their traditional industrial base (Lever, 1992; Perrin, 1993) or they attempt to create a new one (Engelstoft and Jørgensen, in Chapter 8 of this book). In a similar vein, it may be noted that one of the most important historical roles of the city has been to serve as a centre of innovation. A current direction in regional policy in the process of modernization is to enhance this role (Hilpert, 1991).

Considering the availability of capital resources, one of the most important targets of metropolitan policies has been, and will remain, to attract international investment. This may take the form of productive or speculative investment. In this respect, the role of cities as nodes in capital flows appears to be very important. Europe is the biggest pole of attraction for multinational firms (Rozenblat, 1991). These may represent global moves (related to the USA or Japan) as well as movements inside Europe, among EU countries, or with others. This potential 'market' is one of the bigger fields of competition for cities, and especially for metropolitan areas. All metropolitan regions appear to fight to attract corporation headquarters to their central city and production units to their surroundings. Whatever the function (distribution, production or research), metropolitan areas where the conditions allow for a quick restructuring of firms at the end of one product cycle and the onset of a new one appear to have been particularly successful. But it should be noted that the city is more than a mere spatial framework. Therefore those cities with a track record of innovation have been particularly successful competitors for functions (Rozenblat, 1991).

Some cities may actually have selected policies to attract firms in specific industries. Every economic sector requires a different type of location and different facilities. A range of strategies have been applied to permit urban specialization. For instance, two recent examples are related to the build-up of pharmaceutical services in London and financial services in Frankfurt. These examples show that, if a city is interested in promoting manufacturing activities, it is necessary to offer tailor-made production sites, up-to-date logistic support systems and state-of-the-art transport infrastructure. Such amenities must be well located in relation to the wider transport network. If, on the other hand, the city wants to attract insurance companies or other financial institutions, it should try to boost its stock market. Similar reasoning can be applied to build the appropriate infrastructure to attract R&D institutions, which would have a preference for proximity to research centres or high-quality universities. In other words, every activity requires a specific milieu. The spatial patterns will also be diverse. As we reiterated at the beginning of this chapter, every function is related to an appropriate scale of operation, which coincides with a specific functional territorial organization.

At this point, it is interesting to return to the differences between cities that offer a wide range of functions (London and Paris) on the one hand, and those that exhibit a certain degree of functional specialization. It would be interesting to determine whether those different types of cities compete for the same activities. Such efforts would only lead to the relocation of activities. What is needed, instead, is the creation of a new base to develop new products, which may necessitate the restructuring and retraining of the labour force and the provision of new infrastructure.

Services have become the undisputed leaders of the metropolitan economy. This is especially true of producer services (Daniels, 1985; Coffey and Bailly, 1992). They form the basis for all development schemes of international cities and for every regional development policy (Philippe, 1984). In the services sector, one of the most coveted goals for cities that aspire to global stature is to become a major financial centre. In the framework of interurban competition, however, only some cities can participate in the global economy as major financial centres and generators of venture capital (Lee and Schmidt-Marwede, 1993). Among the top 25 investment management centres in the global economy, there are 12 European cities that play an important role: London (in third place), Geneva (4), Zurich (5), Paris (7), Frankfurt (8), Edinburgh (13), Basle (15), Milan (17), Stockholm (18), Munich (19), Amsterdam (21) and Brussels (22).

In order to become a major centre for corporate head offices, it is essential that cities resolve existing bottlenecks in infrastructure and services provision. All of the cities studied have made major strides towards offering good services. These efforts were focused primarily on access to transport and telecommunication networks. These allow for efficient communication between the headquarters and their subsidiaries anywhere in the world. Communication is the lifeblood of companies, be it within the organization or with purchasers and suppliers within the metropolitan area, or elsewhere. More and more, firms depend on subcontracting, as 'just-in-time' systems are being applied in industrial production. Rapid feedback from the market is essential where batch production dominates. At the same time, such organizational innovations require an adequate social–territorial infrastructure to tap the full potential of the regional labour market.

In many instances, the city itself is promoted as a commodity. Paris, where the national government still exerts a major influence on local development, offers a paradigmatic model in this sense. In his discussion of this city, Burgel (Chapter 4 in this book) equates La Défense with the central business district of Paris and considers its facilities as an important asset in the international competition to attract economic functions. At the same time, its appeal is felt wider as it has become an integral part of the city's image. Burgel even ranks the Spreckelsen Arch – a 'must' for the average tourist – at the same level as the Pompidou Centre and the Orsay Museum. The city tries to make the most of the possibilities its cultural landscape offers, whereby it can also offer attractions to its own inhabitants.

Many politicians suggest that any city should broaden its local economic base. The idea is to depend more on international tourism and cultural events of European importance (Engelstoft and Jørgensen, in Chapter 8 of this book). The promotion of culture and tourism in general have become important aims. City councils (such as Copenhagen, Glasgow, Madrid, Lisbon and, of course, Paris and London) have adopted a culture-based urban revitalization programme. Central to this approach is the perception that the integration of cultural activities into a widely-based revitalization project can provide the catalyst for physical and environmental renewal. It serves to attract tourists and capital investment alike, while enhancing the city's image and creating new jobs.

Beyond the stimulation of the economy, sharing the wealth generated has become a major goal in urban policy. In recent years, housing policy in competitive cities has been provided for the middle classes rather than for workers (for instance, the new towns in the Paris region, or the Olympic village in Barcelona). At the same time, the renewal of housing and the improvement of existing residential environments have been achieved through the gentrification of the historical urban centres (Van Weesep and Musterd, 1991; Van Weesep and Van Kempen, 1992). Be that as it may, one trend is clearly emerging: the capitalist process of hierarchization and polarization in housing distribution is now taking place on the metropolitan scale. Development decisions are being made across municipal boundaries. This situation has two implications. On the one hand, it means an expansion of the labour market area; in effect, the metropolitan area has become a single integrated labour market. On the other hand, the present housing problems have a metropolitan dimension. It is impossible to resolve the social problems emanating from an inadequate housing supply if housing policy is maintained as a closed system inside each municipality. Indeed, any problem of the entire metropolitan area needs a solution on the same scale.

These are the targets for the economic and social development of the city in the context of European and worldwide inter-city competition. At present, traditional economic urban plans have lost much of their stature as neo-liberal attitudes gain ground. In this framework, the solution found by many local governments has been to apply strategic planning. This model is used not only by the central cities of metropolitan areas, but also by towns in their regions.

To be successful in all these aims, big cities have defined more concrete targets. In order to realize large-scale revitalization programmes, cities have on several occasions organized major international events. Such events draw in a huge amount of money. The large budgets permit the local authorities to finance major urban renewal projects. This has been the fundamental reasoning behind the organization of several of the world exhibitions of the past. Brussels pioneered this strategy. Its efforts created the urban amenities that allowed it to become the capital of the EU. Similar great projects have been promoted by city councils (as in Glasgow and Barcelona) or by central governments in the cities (as in Brussels, Madrid, Paris and Copenhagen). But this strategy is fraught with danger if the authorities are unable to generate sufficient local political support for the undertaking. Several aborted attempts have shown that gaining this support from the national government and the financial backing from the private sector is not enough to see the project through.

In any case, it is necessary for a city to maintain its present economic and productive capacity to be successful in an internationally competitive context. Cities must aggressively pursue the renewal of their territorial and functional infrastructure, their capacity for organization, their technological base and the quality of life. That is to say, the short-term targets should make it possible to renovate the city and to create adequate conditions to face the future with positive expectations.

In order to be successful in the long term, certain conditions are considered to be important (Van den Berg *et al.*, 1993). These include the control over spatial–economic conditions (opportunities for and threats to the metropolitan economy and its spatial organization; for instance, controlling the degree of dominance of the central city). Cities are well advised to make a critical assessment also of the administrative–political circumstances they offer, such as an efficient administrative organization, a favourable administrative culture and consistent political objectives. A key aspect of this is to make certain that the cities enlist the best individuals for the jobs. They should do all they can to boost the entrepreneurial quality of their 'key players'.

Common denominators of attempts to boost competitive positions

In the present context of internationalization, the historical competition between cities has acquired special importance. Every large European city tries to find the right mode to compete with others in an increasingly competitive framework. That competition is played out at two levels: the global and the European.

It is possible to distinguish several broad strategies used by competing cities. Each city devises a strategy that corresponds to its particular historical, political and territorial position. In developing a strategy, each city takes advantage of its inherent qualities or of its position in an administrative–political context. Existing strengths may be coupled to its historical role as a great capital (like London, Paris and, currently, Berlin) or its role as a state or regional capital. Advantages may also be derived from its position at a crossroads location (as in the case of Milan, or as Budapest may be in the foreseeable future). Another tangible factor is the city's position within a nation-state. This plays a role against the background of state competition in Europe, especially in the further development of the EU. In recent years, cities such as Brussels, Frankfurt or London have been able to profit from this position. The corresponding strategies are to foster good relations with the national government, which can champion the city's cause.

Cities can also bank on an existing high degree of specialization (as is the case of Munich, Zurich or Geneva). Because of their profile, they may be able to expand this function by attracting new firms or other organizations that could profit from its synergistic milieu. Their geographic location with respect to other centres with a similar, or supplementary, function profile can boost their attempts to expand on it. A location within the European urban heartland (the 'European blue banana') or a strategic position in multiple worldwide contacts, such as applies to the large central European cities, or Amsterdam, can also be enlisted to achieve this goal. The common strategies are directly related to providing for the location demands of the particular activities – be they provision of infrastructure or facilities – and in general to being receptive to the signals emitted by potential newcomers. Fostering a good business climate is particularly important.

We must not forget that the city within its administrative boundaries is not an independent entity. In many respects, it is subordinate to decision making elsewhere, or suffers from the effects of external processes or actions. The influence of the strategies and actions of transnational corporations upon countries and cities provides a clear example; and in spite of a general tendency towards the decentralization of political initiative, there are many examples of the direct involvement of national governments in local affairs. Such external conditions are very important: they either further the local policies or restrict a city's efforts to promote itself; the prestige or a negative image of the nation as a whole clearly induces effects upon specific locations within that country.

This point is especially significant in the context of the EU in view of its internal territorial pressures. The organization of the EU on the basis of nations can hold the cities' dynamics hostage. In many policy initiatives, the central governments are the major players, while the cities are their territorial pawns. Recently, we have seen living proof of this relationship, as cities were poised in apparent competition with each other as locations for European agencies. We should stress this role of the city as a political instrument – a bargaining chip – in the process of building the EU in the competition between states.

From another perspective, the city is faced with the increasing need to adapt to changing administrative contexts. This is particularly clear with regard to the aspirations of the regions in the continuing effort to construct a new Europe. Increasingly, there is a tendency to view the region as a substitute for the state. The aim of the regions is to draw the new map of Europe along the lines of 'regional' states where 'local' interests can be reinforced. On that map, the city exists as a territorial manifestation of local power relationships. It is a centre of decision making and forms a tangible expression of the regional territory in its material and ideological conditions. Many cities have a long experience of dealing with the regions of which they form a part; they have often learned to dominate regional decision making. At the same time, the regions are being redefined. Their shapes and jurisdictions are increasingly fluid. Not only will the nature of the international boundaries of the states change, but the regions themselves will be redefined within the changing context of the EU. For those who are aware of the historical realities of the regions, it is not too far-fetched to imagine major changes in the territorial make-up of the regions of Europe, ignoring current national boundaries. In several places the process of transborder cooperation is already visible.

But at the same time, large cities will be loath to give up their position as the locus of their regions; they aspire to becoming the real centres of the regional organization, not subordinates to regional power. Against this background, it must be expected that urban policies will attempt to reinforce their role in the process of European unification. This may imply that the spirit that informs the process of European restructuring will be one of more competition, rather than of collaboration. Consequently, the field of social relations will also be increasingly dominated by concepts like winners and losers, with respect both to people and to places.

This phenomenon is reinforced by the current neo-liberal, conservative tendencies. Competitiveness will be the background of the ideological blueprint from which the new Europe is being constructed. In this context, we may well ask if the rivalry will be profitable or damaging, and for whom. With respect to strategies and instruments, the corresponding question is whether it is advisable directly to confront obstacles and delays in projects and actions. Or is it preferable to work with incentives to produce more and better, as a means to prevail over the opponent?

Both these trajectories require new and imaginative forms of territorial management. Appropriate measures are needed in order to overcome historical tensions and suspicions. People must be ready to move in a new direction to resolve society's new social challenges. At the same time, the selection of the optimal scale of management for every one of these new intermediate territories is a delicate issue. The choice is between the established local power base and the new regional or state powers. New needs compel new solutions. The new challenges may require the introduction of new territorial policies and new administrative forms. The agents invested with authority will need to rethink the entrenched dichotomies: concepts such as territorial equilibrium versus disequilibrium, and homogenization of the territory versus uneven development. Essentially, they will have to redefine the concept of social and spatial equity.

References

Brunet, R. (ed.) (1989) *Les Villes Européennes* [The cities of Europe], Montpellier–Paris: RECLUS-DATAR, La Documentation Française.

Coffey, W.J. and A.S. Bailly (1992) 'Producer services and systems and flexible production', *Urban Studies*, **29**, pp.857–68.

Cox, K.R. and A. Mair (1989) 'Urban growth machines and the politics of local economic development', *International Journal of Urban and Regional Research*, **13**, pp.137–46.

Daniels, P.W. (1985) *Service Industries. A Geographical Appraisal*, London: Methuen.
Foley, P. (1992) 'Local economic policy and job creation; a review of evaluation studies', *Urban Studies*, 29, pp.557–98.
Gaspar, J. (1992) 'Societal response to changes in the production system', *Urban Studies*, 29, pp.827–37.
Goodwin, M., S. Duncan and S. Halford (1993) 'Regulation theory, the local state and the transition of urban politics', *Environment and Planning D, Society and Space*, 11, pp.67–88.
Gottdiener, M. (1987) *The Decline of Urban Politics; Political Theory and the Crisis of the Local State*, Newbury Park: Sage.
Heinelt, H. (1992) 'Local labour market policy – limits and potentials', *International Journal of Urban and Regional Research*, 16, pp.522–8.
Hilpert, U. (1991) 'The optimization of political approaches to innovation; Some comparative conclusions on trends for regionalization', in U. Hilpert, (ed.), *Regional Innovation and Decentralization. High-tech Industry and Government Policy*, London: Routledge, pp.291–302.
Junyent, R. and R. Gimenez Capdevila (1989) 'Societat i transport a les agglomeracions de Barcelona, París i Milà' [Society and transport in the agglomerations of Barcelona, Paris and Milan], *Revista Catalana de Geografia*, 9, pp.43–51.
Labasse, J. (1981) 'Profils de villes européennes à vocation internationale' [Profiles of European cities in international competition], *Cahiers de Géographie du Québec*, 66, pp.403–11.
Lee, R. and U. Schmidt-Marwede (1993) 'Interurban competition? Financial centres and the geography of financial production', *International Journal of Urban and Regional Research*, 17, pp.492–515.
Leitner, H. (1990) 'Cities in pursuit of economic growth. The local states as entrepreneur', *Political Geography Quarterly*, 9, pp.146–70.
Lever, W.F. (1992) 'Local authority responses to economic change in West Central Scotland', *Urban Studies*, 29, pp.935–48.
Perrin, E. (1993) 'Traditional industrial cities in Europe and the urban policy challenge conference – Lille, May 1992', *International Journal of Urban and Regional Research*, 17, pp.129–31.
Philippe, J. (1984) *Les services aux entreprises et la politique de développement régional* [Business services and the politics of regional development], Lugano Association de Science Régionale de Langue Française.
Pompili, T. (1992) 'The role of human capital in urban system structure and development. The case of Italy', *Urban Studies*, 29, pp.905–34.
Rozenblat, C. (1991) 'Mesurer l'attractivité des villes européennes pour les multinationales' [Measuring the attractiveness of European cities for multinational corporations], *L'Espace Géographique*, 19/20, pp.343–8.
Sánchez, J.-E. (1992a) *Geografía Política* [Political geography], Madrid: Síntesis.
Sánchez, J.-E. (1992b) 'Societal responses to changes in the production system; the case of the metropolitan region of Barcelona', *Urban Studies*, 29, pp.949–64.
Sánchez, J.-E. (1996) 'The administrative structure of the delivery mechanisms', in F.W. Lever and A.S. Bailly (eds), *The Spatial Impact of Economic Changes in Europe*, Aldershot: Avebury pp.294–322.
Shachar, A. and D. Felsenstein (1992) 'Urban economic development and high-technology industry', *Urban Studies*, 29, pp.839–55.
Stoker, G. (1991) *The Politics of Local Government*, London: Macmillan.
Van den Berg, L., H.A. Klink and J. Van der Meer (1993) *Governing Metropolitan Regions*, Aldershot: Avebury.
Van Weesep, J. and S. Musterd (eds) (1991) *Urban Housing for the Better-Off; Gentrification in Europe*, Utrecht: Stedelijke Netwerken.
Van Weesep, J. and R. Van Kempen (1992) 'Economic change, income differentiation and housing: Urban response in the Netherlands', *Urban Studies*, 29, pp.979–90.

Vázquez Barquero, A. (1990) 'Las regiones periféricas de la Comunidad ante el desafío del mercado único' [Peripheral regions of the Community before the establishment of the unified market], *Estudios Territoriales*, **32**, pp.49–64.

Wilson, D. (1989) 'Toward a revised urban managerialism; Local managers and community development block grants', *Political Geography Quarterly*, **8**, pp.21–41.

17 Marketing the city

Michael Krantz and Ludwig Schätzl

Introduction

Competition between European cities is likely to increase in the future. At the same time, economic and social conflict within those cities will probably grow too. The local authorities will have to respond to these structural changes in interurban and intra-urban relations by making fundamental alterations in their development policy.

Interurban competition will only be aggravated by European integration. This process entails, for example, the unimpeded movement of goods and production factors within the European Union and the gradual merger of western and eastern European economies. This competition between cities and city regions will produce winners and losers. The outcome will depend on each individual city's readiness and capacity (for example as regards endogenous development potential and fiscal constraints) to accommodate structural change.

The range of urban functions is expanding, (for example in the spheres of social welfare, social housing and care of the old). In part, these tasks are imposed by European or national legislation, yet these mandates are insufficiently funded. When cities are unable to fulfil these obligations, their fiscal competence may be compromised. Failure to perform can lead to intra-urban conflicts. Up to now, most cities have reacted to these challenges with isolated policy measures. For instance, to improve interurban competitive ability, they have used selected instruments to attract investment or to mobilize endogenous research and development potential (local technology centres, research parks and so on). Another approach is to stabilize the fiscal position. To accomplish this, they have transferred some public activities to the private sector (selective privatization). Alternatively, to lessen intra-urban conflicts, they have introduced new forms of citizen participation.

Various attempts have been made to cope with the challenges of the future. A growing number of scholars and policy makers are calling for a new approach to urban management. They demand a more comprehensive, integrated urban policy; an entrepreneurial management-oriented policy; and an urban development policy based on a modern city-marketing concept. The implementation of city marketing should help improve the interurban competitive position of a city or a city region. At the same time, city marketing should make management of intra-urban conflict more efficient.

The theoretical concept of city marketing

In order to discuss marketing for the city region, we first have to clarify the term 'marketing'. The marketing discipline has much more to offer than just a new name for what has always been known as urban development policy. As a first step, we will consider applicability of marketing theory to the problems encountered by the municipalities. In commercial organizations, marketing has undergone a change in meaning. No longer exclusively applied to sales, it is a comprehensive concept referring to strategic leadership. Nowadays, marketing denotes a type of operation that directs all its activities towards the current and potential needs of customers in order to achieve its business goals (Meffert, 1991). Marketing decisions represent the efforts of an organization to intensify or to alter the processes of exchange with its target groups.

The adoption of marketing by the public sector was prompted by two developments. On the one hand, scanty resources have reinforced the trend to accommodate the needs of the recipients of public support. On the other hand, competition has become stiffer as the target group gains access to more opportunities for substitution (Töpfer, 1990). The question considered here is whether traditional marketing principles can be used to manage recent urban changes. The application of the marketing approach to noncommercial organizations is based on the assumption that the exchange processes are very similar (analogy thesis). In addition, it is assumed that non-commercial organizations also pursue goals of market penetration and persuasion with regard to their exchange partners. These goals can be realized much more efficiently by marketing (efficiency thesis) (Raffée and Wiedmann, 1983).

The rest of this section provides a theoretical basis for marketing transfer. To that end, the analogy and efficiency theses are analysed in relation to the exchange relationships of the public sector.

The analogy thesis

It is frequently implied that the problems in the private sector are completely different from those in the public sector. Furthermore, some say that the two sectors have no comparable exchange relationships. Exchange processes can be classified according to the principles of gratification, interaction and sovereignty. These three principles take a specific form in a system of relationships (Schneider, 1993). By analysing these forms, we may gain insight into the applicability of the marketing concept to city management.

The gratification principle   The gratification principle classifies exchange processes according to their goals and their exchange equivalents. The question concerning the goals within the field of local politics implies the next question concerning differentiation between this sector and the private sector. Guaranteeing competitiveness, which is becoming more and more important even for local authorities, can be said to be the primary and most important goal. The goals of private enterprises, which are predominantly profit-oriented, contrast with a dual set of profit and non-profit goals in urban development policy (Töpfer, 1990). The concretization of goals is rather weakly developed within the local government sphere. The goals of urban development policy, such as achieving income, security of employment and security of services provision, and the goals of environmental policy are not only difficult to operationalize but also partly conflicting.

The second feature is that gratification is directly tied to exchange equivalents. The possible services in return can be of very different kinds. In addition to tangible monetary yields (for example, trade tax), non-monetary services may also be given in return. It is characteristic of the exchange system of cities that it is not clear how taxes, dues and charges paid are connected to the facilities and measures financed by them (indirect gratification).

The interaction principle   Exchange relationships can also be characterized according to the number, size, structure and position of the parties involved. Schneider (1993) distinguishes five potential interaction partners for the urban system: supplier, clients, trustees, active publics and general publics. As territorial authorities, cities and regions are bound by democratic principles. Therefore, in urban development policy, more importance has to be attached to the active and passive publics than in the policy of a business. On the one hand, the urban exchange relationships prove to be more complex than in the private sector. On the other hand, interactions in the local authority sphere are more predictable because of the legal framework and the high degree of formalization.

The sovereignty principle   The last statement reveals that sovereignty is more restricted in the shaping of urban exchange relationships than it is in the private sector. Market transactions can be formed freely in the business community. In the case of cities, the scope for action is restricted by legal and standardized conditions. However, the integration of local authority tasks into superordinate political goals does not invalidate the application of marketing. But it is necessary to focus on those forms of marketing that are sensitive to restrictions (Wagner, 1984).

By analogy with the expansion to the non-profit field, the application of marketing to the problems of cities appears to be sensible. There is a wide range of exchange relationships and a high level of complexity. In this framework, city marketing has to take the specific features of the local authorities explicitly into account. This leads us on to consider the basic principles of marketing that permit an efficient application of marketing to cities.

The efficiency thesis

Does 'city marketing' only mean 'old wine in new bottles', as is often suggested? Of course, marketing instruments have always been employed in local authorities in an uncoordinated way. However, the planned application of the whole range of marketing technology, using detailed market information, signifies a new attitude in local government policy. Van der Meer (1990) describes city marketing as a set of activities intended to attune the supply of urban functions to the demand for them by the inhabitants, businesses, tourists and other visitors. Consequently, city marketing is not an especially intensive type of advertising strategy. Instead, it is a method of matching the demand for and supply of local authority provision with a particular goal.

According to Meffert (1989), the general principles of classical marketing must be taken into account if city marketing is to be applied efficiently.

- The services provided by the local authority must be oriented towards the potential target groups (philosophy aspect).
- Systematic market research and expectation analyses are an essential prerequisite for successful city marketing (information aspect).

- Long-term strategic orientation and the systematic employment of marketing instruments must be aimed at the desired market reaction (strategy and action aspect).
- City marketing demands an approach that is specific to the target group both inside and outside the city (segmentational aspect).
- In addition to the differentiated treatment of the market, the effectiveness of marketing is increased by coordinated planning (planning and coordination aspect).

At the municipal level, too, consistent application of these guiding principles would bring about an increase in efficiency. In the rest of this discussion, the term 'city marketing' refers to the city as a whole. We agree with Van den Berg *et al.* (1990, p.3) that 'the term "city marketing" refers specifically to marketing and to urban and metropolitan development', while we also realize that there is an implicit demand for the regional application of marketing concepts.

Marketing strategies for urban policy

Urban development has historically been identified with growth. Accordingly, processes of stagnation and shrinkage represent an entirely new problem at the municipal level. The central strategy is to try to achieve medium-term to long-term goals for the 'product city' by means of measures that optimize the use of the product (Meffert, 1989). Here a distinction can be made between two strategic plans of attack. One is directed outwards, in order to participate in the increasing intermunicipal competition for growth potential. The other is directed inwards, in order to stimulate the endogenous potential (Häussermann and Siebel, 1994).

From the point of view of economic geography, city marketing aims at attracting external growth determinants (such as purchasing power, investments and public support funds) and at mobilizing internal growth determinants (for example, production potential and innovations: Schätzl, 1992). This goal of local government policy does not, in fact, represent any new development. However, the more difficult competitive and budgetary situation requires cities to be flexible. They must continuously adapt their socioeconomic and administrative structures to the dynamic events in the market. For this reason, we devote special attention to the following strategic components within the framework of marketing planning: the strategic basis concept, strategic positioning and differentiated treatment of the market.

The strategic basis concept

Technology is the decisive determinant of the economic transformation process. Thus technical progress has far-reaching effects on spatial differentiation (Schätzl, 1993a). From the point of view of microeconomics, the regional product life cycle hypothesis tries to explain phase-specific demands on locations through their dynamics. The optimum location from the economic point of view changes during the course of a product life cycle because of the different production and marketing conditions (Schätzl, 1992). In the end, the competitiveness of each of the locations is also determined by the age of the products manufactured by its firms or industrial sectors. A distinction is made between phases of growth, maturity and decline in the dynamic development of agglomerations. During the growth phase of certain branches of industry, cities and regions take in large private and public profits. During the saturation and shrinkage phases, they are faced with social burdens and the resulting costs (Göb, 1987). Within the framework of a municipal marketing concept, this has several consequences. Potentials specific to the location have to be investigated. Furthermore, three strategic options have to be considered. Which one will be pursued depends on the position of a city in the regional life cycle. These options are the expansion or diversification strategy, the consolidation strategy and the reduction strategy (Schneider, 1993).

The expansion or diversification strategy   A number of alternatives for action can be subsumed under the expansion or diversification strategy (Schneider, 1993). According to one approach, comprehensive acquisition is accompanied by simultaneous expansion of the entire range of services provided by the local authority. Alternatively, selective acquisition is supported by innovative activities. This approach aims at 'unité motrice' as sectoral growth poles, as described by Perroux. The cities and regions with a high proportion of 'growth sectors' at the start of their product life cycle have the most favourable development possibilities. This is the reason why support for the high-tech field currently takes priority in regional–economic policy. Yet another approach seeks to develop endogenous potential and intensify the utilization of urban provision. During their attempts to mobilize their own forces, the cities must initiate, develop and put their stamp on the economic development. In the end, the crux of the matter is to organize innovation (Häussermann and Siebel, 1994).

The consolidation strategy   Within the framework of the consolidation strategy, the measures taken so far have to be continued efficiently. In addition, the environment of municipal policy has to be analysed with regard to developments that endanger stability. An extension of the provision of services by the cities would be to the disadvantage of the regular clientele. For example, when local authorities undertook economic promotion, they would have to guarantee and look after the existing firms. As with the theoretical concept of the regional growth cycle, however, for a high concentration of branches in the maturing phase it would be possible to predict a development that could endanger the status quo. A municipal policy aimed at stability would have to counteract this danger by means of the diversification strategy.

The reduction strategy   The reduction strategy entails the restriction of the range of services. This strategy is being discussed at the local government level in connection with the theoretical concept of optimum city size. If the progressively rising per capita costs exceed the per capita benefit, urban functions can no longer be performed efficiently. Agglomeration effects (localization and urbanization economies) have a positive effect during an early phase of urbanization. After a certain conurbation density has been reached, negative agglomeration effects predominate. These may include increasing factor costs or increasing environmental pollution (Maly, 1990). The optimum size of cities has not been empirically determined. Furthermore, many structural changes in cities are irreversible. 'Lean management' within the local authority may relieve the budget, but it can permanently damage the quality of the location. In addition, during a phase of stagnation and/or regression, agglomerations also run the risk of no longer being able to revise a cumulative socioeconomic shrinkage process, as described by Myrdal.

Strategic positioning

In many municipal authorities, marketing activities are reduced exclusively to advertising the city. Differences between the services offered are not made clear because of the general and stereotyped statements made in the advertising. City marketing ought to make it possible for the city to have a profile when compared with other locations. The marketing term 'unique selling proposition' (USP) denotes a set of unique advantages in the provision of services. This strategy of special emphasis follows the goal of activating demand by drawing distinctions between the essential features of one's own product and the products offered by the competition (Wagner, 1984).

As a result of the increasing intensity of competition, it can be regarded as a strategic task to develop systematically the foundations of a 'corporate identity' within the framework of city marketing concepts. The general goal is to construct a 'corporate image' with the aid of a well-balanced system of behaviour patterns and communicative measures.

Differentiated treatment of the market

The shaping of the provision of services by a city ought to be geared to the needs specific to each of the target groups. It should be possible to adapt those services to suit changing needs (Jacobs, 1990). So far, however, cities have used an undifferentiated approach. The efficiency in realizing their goals could be raised considerably by concentrating on segments of the market. Ashworth and Voogd (1988, p.70) consider a segmentation approach based solely on functional criteria ('such as shoppers, workers, tourists, residents') to be methodologically dubious. The demand side of the 'multifaceted city' including a wide range of 'products' is extremely heterogeneous and complex. This makes differentiation between homogeneous target groups more difficult. In the end, the segmentation criteria in city marketing depend on the context in each situation.

The instruments of city marketing

The components of marketing can be classified under the headings of product, price, distribution and communication. Decisions regarding these traditional areas tend to be disjointed. In contrast, a systematic approach to the marketing mix produces a wider view of the problem, crossing the borders between the different areas. The systematic deployment of all the instruments of marketing must be based on marketing information and guided by general marketing strategies. Only then is it feasible to achieve the goals of urban policy (Raffée and Wiedmann, 1983). Public administration is a matter of shaping the provision of services to suit the target groups. Besides this, it is a matter of optimizing the infrastructure. The result of a product and/or service policy of this kind must be broadcast in an inward and outward direction by means of the instruments of communication policy (Jacobs, 1990).

Product and service policy

The increasing competition between the individual locations is leading people in the cities and regions to think about improving the quality of the locations. Locations must create assets and differentiate their service provision in order to avoid price competition. According to Ashworth and Voogd (1988), the 'product city' is more than the location with its characteristics. It is also a cluster of benefits in kind and services to be provided there. As far as product policy is concerned, differentiation between products is therefore recommended. These products should be defined according to the specific needs of the target group and the provision of comprehensive solutions to problems.

In the sphere of economic support in the cities, competitive advantages can arise. For example, continuous accompaniment of development processes within a business may create competitive advantage. Or it may be generated by the arrangement of opportunities for financing, by modern location information systems or through efficient organization of the administration. Bunching of solutions to problems would lead to the upgrading of the location and justify the term 'service enterprise city' (Göb, 1987). This is not only a matter of doing justice to the new framework conditions of economic development by adapting the 'hard' location factors. In the future, it will also be a matter of including the improvement of the 'soft' location factors in the local authorities' calculations concerning urban development. Advantages in establishing an image in the competition between the different local authorities could be achieved under the title 'new urbanity'. This involves taking 'gentrification, cultural innovation and physical upgrading of the urban environment' into account (Albrechts, 1991, p.127). When all is said and done, it is therefore a matter of improvements to develop a city 'geared to market requirements' (Heinz, 1990, p.345). At the same time, there is a danger that the improvements reflect simple copying behaviour, without any real positive effects.

But what problems emerge in shaping a local authorities' service programme that is geared to market requirements? Meffert (1989) draws attention to the decisions of product policy in the local authority field. He points out many characteristics and components of the city that are not subject to consistent goal-oriented intervention. The restructuring process takes place very slowly and in a spatially selective manner (Heinz, 1990). Its pace and locus are a result of the 'persistence' of urban structures as well as the great diversity of financial, legal and political restrictions.

The strong pressure to adapt causes cities to overcome their limited opportunities for action by means of strategic partnerships. In this regard, Heinz (1992, p.210) mentions the increasing importance of public–private partnerships (PPPs), both in a qualitative and a quantitative sense. Their ascendancy can be traced to the liquidity problems of the local authorities. PPPs are often seen as the only way to achieve the development goals that are deemed necessary for competition reasons. Public–private cooperation is perceived as a means to attain the goals of flexibility, effective management, a better flow of information and the mobilization of private capital. The merits of this form of organization are clear. However, criticism is aimed at the lack of accountability and short-term project orientation (Häussermann and Siebel, 1994; Heinz, 1992).

Public–private partnership is becoming considerably more important in Germany. Nonetheless, there is a lack of institutionalized points where cities, businesses and special interests can establish a dialogue. This drawback could be compensated by organizing city marketing within the local administration (Helbrecht, 1992).

Communication policy

Communication policy plays a special role in city marketing. Many services provided by the local authority involve immovable and immaterial goods. The strategic purpose of communication policy is to trigger reactions on the demand side that are appropriate to the goal (Meffert, 1991).

A strategic fundamental decision in communication policy is whether the focus should be outward or inward. In the case of goals directed outwards, the intention is for a city to stand out against competing cities as a result of its distinctive positive image. In order to achieve this, it is imperative to highlight those strengths that the target groups deem essential for a positive image on the basis of an empirical survey. On the other hand, those weaknesses must be removed which, because of their negative image, run counter to the identity to be presented (Töpfer, 1990).

The goal of communication policy directed inwards is reconciliation of interests and reinforcement of the identification of citizens with their city. Inwardly directed communication has to fulfil three basic functions in order to achieve an (affective) attachment of the citizens to their city (Schneider, 1993):

- The informational function (the task of elucidation, explanation and instruction).

- The exploratory function to reveal the suggestions of the citizens.
- The function of mediation to bind the interests of the citizens to the urban development policy.

In communication policy, one can thus distinguish between the internal and the external effect of communication. A city's own image characterizes the ideas and attitudes of the city's inhabitants. The 'foreign' image associates the orientation patterns of external groups of people with the city (Tietz and Rothaar, 1991; Meffert, 1989).

Within the framework of a 'corporate identity' there is great demand to harmonize all the measures of communication policy formally, geographically and in terms of content in order to avoid inconsistent impressions. The following discussion is restricted to the instruments of communication policy. These are advertising the city and the public relations work of the local authorities.

Advertising the city   Advertising the city is to be regarded as the instrument to promote the outward-directed interests of the city's policy. Its goal primarily concerns growth policy. Hamburg presents itself as the 'high point in the north' Frankfurt as 'the city that likes its people' and the Ruhr district as 'a strong part of Germany'. It is not uncommon to find advertisements for cities or regions side by side with advertisements for consumer goods. In addition, hardly any opportunity is missed for a city to put itself in the limelight in order to make its mark or brighten up its image: Hanover's 750th Anniversary, The Port of Hamburg's 800th Anniversary, Bonn's 2000th Anniversary, and so on.

One can distinguish four main targets: businesses (as taxpayers and employers), the population (as taxpayers and as the constituency), purchasing power and tourism, with its multiplier effects (Singer, 1988). In a competitive situation it is inefficient to make the 'product city' known to an anonymous clientele by using undifferentiated advertising. Advertising the city is only sensible if the information content is directed towards the strategic positioning of the city and if the selection of the target group is attuned to it. In the case of the business acquisition oriented towards target groups, it is necessary to identify the economic sectors that form the potential target in accordance with an analysis of the city's strong and weak points. With regard to the current and future chances of growth, the next step involves the selection of those businesses that correspond to the positioning of the city in each case. In this way, the funds for communication policy are concentrated in areas where the chances of success are greatest and the needs of the local authority are best fulfilled (Institut für Kommunalwissenschaften, 1992).

The public relations work of the local authorities   Meffert (1991) defines public relations work as the planned and systematic attempt to build up mutual understanding and trust between an institution and the public. We may add the demand for participation of the citizens in the system of urban democracy. With this addition, the information, consultation and participation policy can also be subsumed under public relations work.

At the local authority level, various forms are available for a continuous dialogue (Schneider, 1993). These include citizens' advice bureaus and citizens' question time, advisory committees with citizen participation, working groups and round-table discussions. City marketing explicitly creates an opportunity to get local authority projects accepted at an early stage. This is accomplished by means of measures designed to build trust and to determine where a consensus can be achieved. Here the concrete discussion with diverging private and public interests must replace top–down conduct. Systematic public relations work aimed at the target groups is the basis for the necessary reconciliation of conflicting interests.

The role of 'major events' in city marketing

The more intense competition between the cities also manifests itself in competition for large-scale events, such as the Olympic Games, trade fairs, conferences and world expositions. These prestige-laden events have led to a kind of 'festivalization of urban development policy'. The goal is to reconstruct the city, mobilize endogenous potential, improve the city's image in the world outside and identify the inhabitants with their city. However, conceptual weaknesses and the neglect of existing internal conflicts of interest pose a danger. Not only the event itself but also the goals of urban development policy may fail. The decision by Budapest not to stage the world exposition in 1996 is the most recent reflection of this.

According to what has been stated so far, as an instrument of coordination city marketing has a difficult task. It has to harmonize the positive functions of a large-scale event with the development strategy of the local authority. At the same time, it has to make conflict management within cities possible. In this section, we will discuss the chances and risks of large-scale events with respect to urban development. We will then assess the possibility of providing instruments that are consistent with the marketing concepts used by the local authorities.

Large-scale events comprise cultural, political, sports, economic and scientific activities. Since the events are so diverse in their content, they cannot be classified under a few headings. Therefore the features of 'setting a time limit', 'rarity/uniqueness' and 'size' are used here as characteristics. Large-scale events take place over a limited period of time. They require a long planning and preparation process. As far as rarity and uniqueness of large-scale events are concerned, regularly recurring, sporadically recurring and events that are held only once can be distinguished. 'Size' can be indicated in various ways. It can be measured in volume (number of participants and visitors, space required), monetary value (capital budget, profit) and psychological effects (image). (See Witt and Martin, 1988.)

In addition to these characteristic features, large-scale events may be classified as tourist resources, media events or as regional development programmes. It remains difficult to make a sharp distinction between kinds of large-scale events, therefore Table 17.1 serves to classify selected types of large-scale events in accordance with the criteria mentioned above (Kramer, 1993).

The organization and staging of a large-scale event has a lasting influence on the host city and region. With the aid of cost–benefit analyses, an attempt is made to identify and quantify effects resulting from the event. Direct economic effects, indirect economic effects and non-pecuniary benefit and cost can be distinguished as the levels of activity (Kramer, 1993; Schneider, 1993).

Analytical deficits make a complete accounting of the effects of large-scale events impossible. Thus the question arises, what are the medium-term to long-term effects on urban development policy? In general, there are four forms of utility. First, the city profits fiscally from direct surplus revenues and increased income from taxes. Second, the city enjoys multiplier effects in the employment field. Third, the city derives benefit from improvements to the infrastructure. Fourth, there is an improved image and an increased identification of the inhabitants with their city.

The strategically significant effects on the quality of the location depend on the intensity with which capital, space and innovations were employed in the large-scale event. However, the need for political consensus grows with innovative planning. A slight change in the status quo makes it possible to take a wide range of organized interests into account. In contrast, a radical change is

Table 17.1   Characteristics of selected types of large-scale events

Characteristics	Olympic Games Barcelona	Expositions Seville	CeBIT Trade Fair Hanover	Live-Aid Festivals London
Uniqueness	yes	yes	no	yes
Limited period of the provision of services	yes	yes	yes	yes
Long planning and preparation phase	yes	yes	no	no
Number of participants	large	large	large	large
Number of visitors	large	large	large	large
Area required	large	large	large	fairly small
Employment of funds	large	large	medium	fairly small
Media interest	very large	large	large	very large
Boost for the location relevant to its welfare	large	large	fairly large	fairly small
Main focus of content	sport	culture, science	commerce, industry	culture, politics

Source: Kramer (1993, p.164).

associated with redistribution and resistance (Häussermann and Siebel, 1994).

On the one hand, then, these events make a positive contribution towards urban development. But on the other hand, there are a number of risks. The planning and acquisition costs incurred before the city is finally awarded the event could prove to be a bad investment. Furthermore, there is a considerable expenditure risk that results from incorrect estimates of costs and mistakes in the implementation of the work as well as from the peculiarities of the political and administrative system. A lack of appropriate use after the end of the event means there is a danger that surplus capacity will be established in the infrastructure. And there is further planning risk and possible delay if the population affected by the planning object to it.

In the light of what has been stated so far, an investigation should be conducted to clarify some issues. One is whether or not the running of large-scale events permits the possibility of strategic positioning. Another is whether conflict management within the cities is supported or made more difficult by these events. It may be desirable to change the location factors in a way that is appropriate to the goals within the framework of marketing concepts in the municipalities. If so, the location, the period and the type of large-scale event should be oriented towards the existing potential and desired profile of a city. This should occur during the conception phase. Basically expansive effects extend from large-scale events to the services provided by the local authority. Therefore these events would support a growth-oriented urban development policy but would counteract strategies of reduction. However, large-scale events also offer the opportunity to approach existing or new target groups.

Active participation of the public in planning the event is necessary in order to make use of development potential. The acceptance of the measures by the majority of the local population must be guaranteed for the inward-oriented goals of urban development planning; these goals are the reconciliation of conflicting interests and the identification of the citizens with the event. Of course, the population is more intensively aware of the planning of large-scale events than of individual measures. For that reason, a larger number of inquiries and protests by those affected by planning must be reckoned with.

In order to guarantee a strategic consensus, the state of information in local politics ought to be improved. This can be done by means of written/oral surveys, various forms of dialogue (such as public debates) and by the management of complaints. In addition, the active participation of the local population can be guaranteed by far-reaching instruments of participation, even including referenda. A communication policy directed towards dialogue would permit permanent self-regulation of the urban development policy by means of feedback effects. It would thus fulfil a demand of marketing: it should orient itself consistently towards the needs of the target groups.

To summarize, integration of the event into local and regional marketing strategies is absolutely essential. This is the best way to avoid 'muddling through' at the level of local policy when large-scale events are being planned and presented. Gains in efficiency through the acceleration of urban development projects and through the goal-oriented mobilization of endogenous potential can only be achieved if the event matches the long-term strategy of cities. For that reason, the project must be widely supported.

The problem has been described theoretically in the above sections. It will be illustrated in the next section using the example of EXPO 2000 in Hanover.

Case study of EXPO 2000 in Hanover

The economic position of Hanover at the end of the 1980s

The idea of applying for the honour of organizing a world exposition was born in Hanover during the late 1980s. The economic situation of the Hanover region at that time is described in the following (Schätzl, 1993b).

First of all, it should be kept in mind that the interregional competitiveness of the Hanover region had worsened in the course of the 1980s. As far as employment dynamics are concerned, almost all economic sectors in the region showed less favourable development than the average in the Federal Republic of Germany. This applies particularly to the most important branches of manufacturing in Hanover (plastics and rubber processing, steel, machinery and vehicle construction, electrical engineering, chemicals and foodstuffs). Most of the service sector, primarily the business services, also developed more slowly in the Hanover region than in the Federal Republic as a whole. In view of this unfavourable economic situation, it is not surprising that the unemployment rate was also distinctly higher than the national average. In addition, increasing debts restricted the city of Hanover's scope for action as far as economic and social policy was concerned.

484 European Cities in Competition

At the end of the 1980s, one fundamental reason for the weakness of the Hanover economic region (and this still applies today) lay in the structural problems of part of the manufacturing industry. The proportion of enterprises producing 'older' products was considerably higher than in the rest of the country. Such standardized mass products are subject to serious price competition. There is thus a danger that their production will be relocated to countries with lower wages. The Hanover economic region had few head offices but an above-average proportion of branch plants. The region had deficits with respect to high-tech industries. Besides receiving large amounts of state support, these firms are characterized by high research and development intensity. Above all, the large manufacturing enterprises located in the region were relatively weak when it came to innovation.

These weaknesses dominated the overall development, but the Hanover economic region did, of course, have strengths as well, among them some internationally competitive large firms in the service sector (trade fairs, tourism and insurance). There are efficient universities and large-scale research institutions. A number of small and medium-sized manufacturing firms carry out intensive research and development (among other things, on products for environmental protection).

The economic and social problems in the Hanover region at the end of the 1980s were clear to decision makers in the public and the private sector. They saw the need for far-reaching structural change. In order to prevent the inhabitants of Hanover from having to put up with stagnation to the bitter end, fundamental technological and economic modernization had to be carried out. The growing pressure of economic problems and the increasing readiness of the actors to bring about a structural change formed a breeding-ground for the development of new ideas. The dire state of affairs also created the preconditions for pushing through new solutions.

Let us now examine the issue of the universal world exposition (EXPO 2000), which is planned for Hanover in the year 2000. In the sense of a city-marketing concept oriented inwards and outwards, can EXPO reduce the intra-urban potential for conflict? Specifically, can the inhabitants of the region be convinced that it is necessary to hold the large-scale event? And at another level, would EXPO improve the position of the Hanover economic region within the interregional competition in Europe?

The decision-making process and citizen participation

After preliminary 'fireside' talks, the plan to hold a world exposition with the theme 'Man, Nature, Technology' in Hanover at the turn of the millennium was introduced for the first time at a meeting of the supervisory board of the Deutsche Messe AG. The protagonists of the world exposition were members of the management board and the supervisory board of the Deutsche Messe AG (including the minister of finance of the state of Lower Saxony and the mayor of the city of Hanover). In the spring of 1988, the Federal minister of economics submitted an official application to the Bureau International des Expositions (B.I.E.) in Paris on behalf of the Federal Republic of Germany to hold a world exposition in Hanover. At the General Meeting of the B.I.E. on 14 June 1990, Hanover was given preference over the other applicant, Toronto, by one vote.

While the protagonists celebrated, the population of Hanover was somewhat uncertain. The application and the decision had taken place largely with the public excluded. Opinion polls carried out in Hanover during the second half of 1990 revealed that only about half of those questioned were in favour of holding EXPO 2000 in Hanover. As a result, in 1991 (that is, only after the official decision by the B.I.E.) the city council and the city administration informed the public in Hanover about the world exposition through a number of different measures. Among these were the founding of an EXPO forum, the opening of an EXPO shop and information and discussion meetings. Only then did a lively public discussion take place. In the course of this debate, discussion became polarized and emotionally charged. Even the ruling 'red–green' coalition of the city council disagreed amongst themselves. While the majority of the Social Democratic Party (SPD) supported the world exposition, the Green Alternative Citizens' List (GABL) emphatically rejected it. The issue was not so much the realization that the population should participate. Rather, it was the lack of political consensus within the ruling coalition that led to the city council's decision (by a small majority) to hold a local referendum. When the referendum was held in June 1992, the turnout was 61.7 per cent; 51.5 per cent were in favour and 48.4 per cent were against holding a world exposition in Hanover in the year 2000.

An effort was made to obtain detailed information about the profile of the supporters and opponents of EXPO 2000. The Department of Economic Geography of the University of Hanover carried out a survey among the population of the city in May 1992 (Kramer, 1993). Selected results are summarized in Table 17.2.

Table 17.2   Selected results of a written stratified sample survey concerning EXPO 2000 among the inhabitants of the city of Hanover (size of the sample = 1962, n = 747)

	In favour of EXPO (%)	Against EXPO (%)
Party preference		
SPD	58.1	41.9
CDU	73.5	26.5
FDP	58.7	41.3
GABL	10.1	89.9
Rep.	30.6	69.4
Others	27.3	72.7
Non-voters	40.0	60.0
Total	49.1	50.9
Age group		
18–29	37.7	62.3
30–39	38.6	61.4
40–49	56.0	44.0
50–59	58.4	41.6
60–69	58.7	41.3
70 and older	60.0	40.0
Total	49.1	50.9
Occupation		
Manual workers	64.7	35.3
Skilled workers	51.4	48.6
Employees/civil servants in low-level positions	38.3	61.7
Employees/civil servants in mid-level positions	43.4	56.6
Employees/civil servants in managerial positions	51.3	48.7
In private practice	52.2	47.8
Other self-employed	61.6	38.9
Not employed, military service/ community service	46.2	53.8
Training, studying, at school	37.2	62.8
Retired	61.6	38.4
Unemployed	75.0	25.0
Total	49.1	50.9

As far as party preferences are concerned, three-quarters of the Christian Democratic Party (CDU) voters support the world exposition; the majority of supporters of the SPD and the Liberal Democratic Party (FDP) are also in favour of EXPO. The Green Alternative Citizens' List and the right-wing Republicans have the largest proportion of people who oppose EXPO. It is apparent that the voters of the groups on the margins of the political spectrum reject the world exposition most decisively.

With regard to the age structure of those surveyed, we see that the acceptance of EXPO rises with increasing age. Neither the initiators of the world exposition nor the city of Hanover succeeded in convincing younger voters of the attractiveness of the theme 'Man, Nature, Technology'. Differentiation of those questioned according to their occupation is revealing. In addition to the unemployed, manual workers and the self-employed have the highest proportions of EXPO supporters. These occupational groups expect the world exposition to bring them economic advantages. The highest proportion of EXPO opponents is found among students and among employees and civil servants from the low and middle wage groups. Above all, these groups fear that they will have to bear the social burden of the large-scale event.

To summarize, no attempt was made to involve the public during the preparatory phase of EXPO 2000. Even after the B.I.E. decided to hold the world exposition in Hanover in the year 2000, the participation of the inhabitants was not oriented towards a well-thought-out city marketing concept conceived for the long term. Rather, they were asked to rubber-stamp a decision that had been reached by local politicians in their absence. So far, the decision in favour of EXPO 2000 has not contributed to a more efficient management of intra-urban conflict in the Hanover region. On the contrary, it has led to the polarization of public opinion.

Economic effects and interregional competitiveness

Whether or not EXPO 2000 can strengthen the position of the Hanover region in interregional competition depends largely on the positive effects of the world exposition for Hanover as a business location. Immediately after the decision by the B.I.E. in 1990 (at a time when little had been decided about the concept and the extent of the world exposition) the spectrum of 'expert' opinion ranged from a 'horror scenario' to a 'euphoria scenario'. The advocates of the horror scenario argued that EXPO 2000 would lead to a dramatic rise in the cost of living, an increasing housing shortage, segmentation of the population into a few rich people and many poor people, and destruction of the environment; in brief, it was forecast to provoke a collapse in the quality of life and the environment in the city of Hanover. The supporters of the euphoria scenario expected that merely because of EXPO 2000 – and, if possible, without any effort of its own – Hanover could enter into competition, if not with world cities like London, New York or Tokyo, then at least with the German metropolises of Berlin, Hamburg, Frankfurt or Munich.

Reliable information about the design of the event and about the size and structure of the planned investments is necessary. Only then is it possible to make a realistic estimate of the effects of this large-scale event; after all, it will not take place until the year 2000. Initially, it was the size of the investment and the distribution of the financial burden among the city of Hanover, the state of Lower Saxony, the Federal government and private enterprise that was highly controversial. Only in the middle of 1994, with the signing of a general agreement, was it possible to reach a compromise and to create a certain level of planning security. Article 2 of this general agreement provides for the founding of a 'Company for the Preparation and Implementation of the World Exposition EXPO 2000 in Hanover' (Expo Company). The following are providing the authorized capital for the Expo Company, which amounts to DM100 m: the Federal Republic of Germany (40 per cent), the state of Lower Saxony (30 per cent), German business (20 per cent), the state capital, Hanover (6 per cent), the district of Hanover (2 per cent) and the association of municipalities, 'Großraum Hannover' (2 per cent).

When estimating the economic effects of EXPO 2000, it is usual to make a distinction between the effects during the preparatory phase, the implementation phase and the possible long-term effects that extend beyond the year 2000.

Preparatory phase (construction phase)   The world exposition project EXPO 2000 consists of four basic elements. First of all, it comprises the actual world exposition on a central EXPO site. The existing Trade Fair Site (90 ha.) would be used. In addition, an adjoining site of 70 ha. would be developed for this purpose. Besides the exhibitions by the participating nations, a 'Theme Park EXPO 2000' is proposed which would form the central attraction of the world exposition. The theme park has the function of conveying the theme of the world exposition, 'Man, Nature, Technology', to the public. After the world exposition is over, the theme park would be used as a 'Museum of the Future'.

The second basic element is the 'EXPO Settlement'. Construction of 2500 dwellings is planned in the immediate vicinity of the world exposition site. This housing estate has two functions. First, it is an exhibit of the world exposition. As a demonstration of urban and landscape planning, it takes economic, ecological, social and cultural aspects into account. Secondly, it provides housing to reduce the pressure on the local housing market resulting from the world exposition.

The third basic element comprises complementary projects outside the EXPO site. These are to be found in the Hanover region ('The City and the Region as an Exhibit') and also at other locations (for example, in the eastern part of Germany). The projects at 'correspondence locations' are designed to demonstrate solutions concerning various aspects of the theme 'Man, Nature, Technology' that have been realized in practical applications.

The fourth element is traffic infrastructure. EXPO 2000 is expected to attract up to 300 000 visitors a day. There are plans to establish a traffic infrastructure that makes it possible to overcome the problem of mobility in a conurbation in a way that does not harm the environment and is 'user-friendly'.

According to calculations by the Department of Economic Geography of the University of Hanover and The Norddeutsche Landesbank (Bredemeier and Schätzl, 1995), investments amounting to DM10.8 bn are necessary during the construction phase until the year 2000. The funds would be used, for instance, for the development of the EXPO site, the construction of the pavilions of the national and international exhibitors, the EXPO housing estate, the project 'The City and the Region as an Exhibit', and for the improvement of the traffic infrastructure. As a result of multiplier effects, these investments lead to a value-added effect amounting to approximately DM11.1 bn. Of the 10.8 billion of investments, 70 per cent consist of building investment and 30 per cent of investment in equipment. Input–output analyses show where the benefits will accrue. It is primarily the building sector and, induced by the multiplier effects, mainly commerce and the other private services that profit from the building investment. The effects deriving from the investment in equipment are distributed, above all, over machinery construction, the electrical industry and, as a result of multiplier effects, commerce.

Implementation phase EXPO 2000 will be held in Hanover between June and October 2000. The organizers of the world exposition expect that a daily average of 290 000 people will visit the exhibition on the 150 days when it is open. With 43 million visits and an average entrance price of DM40 per person, the sale of admission tickets alone will produce an income of DM1.7 bn. The total tourism expenditure by visitors to the world exposition from home and abroad is estimated at DM4.6 bn. This tourism expenditure will lead to a value-added effect amounting to DM4.5 bn. When this is considered sector by sector, it is the restaurant and hotel trade, the foodstuffs sector, commerce and the remaining services that will profit from expenditure by tourists.

It is certain that the investment necessary until the year 2000 and the demand by tourists during the world exposition will have considerable positive effects on the local economy. In particular, the building trade, the sector supplying the construction industry and the private services will benefit. According to estimates currently available, the proportion of the effects of investments received by the Hanover economic region ought to be around a maximum of 40 per cent and that of expenditure on tourism up to about 60 per cent.

After the end of EXPO in the year 2000, however, these positive economic effects will evaporate. For the Hanover region, EXPO 2000 represents an important but, unfortunately, temporary 'economic recovery programme' that shows certain similarities to the increase in demand in Hanover at the beginning of the 1990s as a result of German unification.

Long-term effects   Statements about the possible long-term economic effects of EXPO 2000 for the Hanover region are full of imponderables. There is no doubt that, in the long term, EXPO 2000 will strengthen the situation of Hanover as a trade fair location. This is also absolutely essential. Competing cities with trade fairs in other European countries (Paris, Milan, Madrid, Birmingham, London) as well as in Germany (Berlin, Leipzig, Düsseldorf, Cologne, Frankfurt, Munich) are continually improving the infrastructure that is oriented towards their trade fairs. The strengthening of the national and international competitiveness of the trade fair has considerable economic significance for the economic region of Hanover. The direct and indirect turnover induced by the trade fair amounts to DM1.6 bn. The employment effect directly accompanying it is around 11 000 people per year (Schätzl *et al.*, 1993).

Input–output analyses prove that a broad spectrum of economic sectors profit from the activities connected with the trade fair. With EXPO 2000, a world exposition is being organized in a classic trade fair city for the first time. The world exposition is being held on the trade fair site and in its immediate vicinity. This means that the additional investments in the infrastructure necessary for holding a world exposition are comparatively small. It also means that the difficult problem of how the site is to be used subsequently can also be solved more easily.

The slogan 'Man, Nature, Technology' offers German business the opportunity to prove to a broad public all over the world that it has a high level of competence in solving environmental problems. Unlike the fields of microelectronics, biotechnology and genetic engineering, the environmental protection industry has not yet shown a clear regional specialization, either globally or in Europe, and certainly not in Germany. Germany might be able to seize the opportunity to become the spatial core of concentration for this basic innovation. The beginnings of an environmental industry are already present in the Hanover region. EXPO 2000 will improve the location conditions in the Hanover region for developing the technology of the future into an interregionally and internationally competitive growth industry.

EXPO 2000 improves the competitive position of the Hanover trade fair and opens up promising development perspectives for the environmental industry. It is less certain whether or not EXPO 2000 can accelerate the economic development of the region. The preconditions are not unfavourable. In the past, the weakness in Hanover's growth was also explained by its peripheral position within the European Community. The first extension of the EC to the north and to the south occurred in the 1970s and 1980s, respectively. That shift increased Hanover's peripheral position even further.

In the 1990s, the geographical position of the Hanover region has undergone a lasting improvement. Starting with the unification of Germany, which took place in 1990, a second extension of the Community to the north appeared on the horizon and economic relations were intensified with the countries of eastern Europe. Hanover is moving from a peripheral location to assume a central position within Germany and Europe. The large west–east and north–south European traffic axes intersect in the Hanover region. In addition to the 'new geographical position', the new investments to be made in connection with EXPO 2000 also improve the position of Hanover in the competition between European regions. In particular, strides have been made to improve the intraregional traffic infrastructure and to enhance the ecological quality of the city. Empirical studies show that the environmental quality of a city or region is receiving increasing attention in decisions concerning investments.

Whether or not EXPO 2000 will be the motor for the technological and ecological modernization of commerce and industry depends on several factors; decisive is the constructive cooperation of the competent actors from politics, the administration, commerce and industry, and science in the city and region of Hanover.

Efforts to reach consensus by means of 'regional conferences' have not been very impressive so far. One important element of cooperation is the development of a modern marketing concept: a marketing plan oriented both inwards and outwards that is for the city and region of Hanover, reaching beyond the year 2000. The economic success of EXPO 2000 depends to a large extent on the quality of the marketing concept. However, it also hinges on the contribution that the world exposition is able to make towards the long-term development of the city and the region.

References

Albrechts, L. (1991) 'Changing roles and positions of planners', *Urban Studies*, **28**, pp.123–37.

Ashworth, G.J. and H. Voogd (1988) 'Marketing the City. Concepts, processes and Dutch applications', *Town Planning Review*, **59**, pp.65–79.

Bredemeier, S. and L. Schätzl (1995) 'Regionalökonomische Wirkungen der Weltausstellung' [Regional economic effects of the world exhibition], *EXPO 2000 in Hannover*, report, Landeshaubtstadt Hannover.

Göb, R. (1987) 'Kommunale Wirtschaftspolitik' [Communal economic policy], *Archiv für Kommunalwissenschaften*, **26**, pp.66–89.

Häussermann, H. and W. Siebel (1994) 'Neue Formen der Stadt- und Regionalpolitik' [New forms of city and regional policy], *Archiv für Kommunalwissenschaften*, **I**, pp.32–44.

Heinz, W. (1990) 'Die marktgerechte Stadt' [The market conform city], *Der Städtetag*, **43**(5), pp.344–45.

Heinz, W. (1992) 'Partnerschaftsprojekte für die Stadtentwicklung – Lehren und Thesen' [Partnership projects for city development – experiences and theses], *Der Städtetag*, **45**(3), pp.210–13.

Helbrecht, I. (1992) *Limitierende Faktoren im Stadtmarketing. City-Management Gesellschaft für kommunales und gewerbliches Marketing* [Limiting factors in city marketing], Munich: CIMA.

Institut für Kommunalwissenschaften (ed.) (1992) *Wirtschaftsförderung in der Diskussion Bausteine zur Gestaltung einer Entwicklungsagentur* [Business promotion in discussion. Principles for establishing a development agency], St. Augustin: Konrad-Adenauer-Stiftung.

Jacobs, S. (1990) *City-Marketing. Möglichkeiten und Probleme der Attraktivitätserhöhung von Innenstädten durch Anwendung der Marketing-Technologie* [City-marketing. Possibilities and problems of raising the attraction of cities by the application of marketing-technology], Mannheim: Institut für Marketing, University of Mannheim.

Kramer, J. (1993) 'Mikroökonomische Verfahren der Präferenzermittlung für öffentliche Güter und ihre Einsatzmöglichkeiten im Rahmen erweiterter Nutzen-Kosten Analysen von Großveranstaltungen' [Valuing public goods in cost-benefit analysis for big events], unpublished dissertation, University of Hanover.

Maly, U. (1990) *Wirtschaft und Umwelt in der Stadtentwicklungspolitik* [Economy and environment in city development policy], Wiesbaden: Deutscher Universitätsverlag.

Meffert, H. (1989) 'Städtemarketing – Pflicht oder Kür?' [City-marketing – duty or free exercise?], paper delivered at the Symposium, 'Stadtvisionen, Stadtstrategien und Städtemarketing in der Zukunft', March, Münster.

Meffert, H. (1991) *Marketing*, 7th edn, Wiesbaden: Gabler.

Raffée, H. and K. Wiedmann (1983) 'Nicht-kommerzielles Marketing – ein Grenzbereich des Marketing?' [Non-commercial marketing – a fringe subject of marketing?], *Betriebliche Forschung und Praxis*, 3, pp.185–207.

Schätzl, L. (1992) *Wirtschaftsgeographie 1 – Theorie* [Economic geography – theory], 4th edn, Paderborn: Schöningh.

Schätzl, L. (1993a) 'International, national, regional and local implications of economic restructuring', in B. Blanke and R. Smith (eds), *The Future of the Medium-sized City in Britain and Germany*, London: Anglo-German Foundation, pp.29–46.

Schätzl, L. (ed.) (1993b) *Wirtschaftsregion Hannover. Ausgewählte Untersuchungsergebnisse des NIW* [The economic region of Hanover. Selected research results of NIW], NIW-Vortragsreihe 8, Hanover: Niedersächsisches Institut für Wirtschaftsforschung E.V.

Schätzl, L., J. Kramer and R. Sternberg (1993) 'Regionalökonomische Wirkungen der 1991 in Hannover veranstalteten Messen und Ausstellungen' [Regional economic effects of trade fairs and exhibitions held at Hanover in 1991], in K.E. Goehrmann (ed.), *Politik-Marketing auf Messen*, Düsseldorf: Wirtschaft und Finanzen, pp.97–112.

Schneider, U. (1993) *Stadtmarketing und Großveranstaltungen* [City marketing and large-scale events], Berlin: Duncker and Humblot.

Singer, C. (1988) 'Kommunale Imageplanung' [Communal image planning], *Archiv für Kommunalwissenschaften*, **27**, pp.271–80.

Tietz, B. and P. Rothaar (1991) *City Studie. Marktbearbeitung und Management für die Stadt* [City study. Market research and management for the city], Landsberg am Lech: Moderne Industrie.

Töpfer, A. (1990) 'Marketing im öffentlichen Sektor' [Marketing in the public sector], *Die Verwaltung*, **23**, pp.409–24.

Van den Berg, L., L.H. Klaasen and J. Van der Meer (1990) *Marketing Metropolitan Regions*, Rotterdam: Erasmus University, EURICUR.

Van der Meer, J. (1990) *The Role of City-marketing in Urban Management*, Rotterdam: European Institute for Comparative Urban Research (EURICUR – Erasmus University).

Wagner, G.R. (1984) 'Kommunales Marketing' [Municipal marketing], *Verwaltungsrundschau*, **30**, pp.225–32.

Witt, S.F. and C.A. Martin (1987) 'Measuring the impacts of mega-events on tourism flows', *AIEST*, pp.213–21.

18 Perspective: competition, urban planning and urban policy

Chris Jensen-Butler and Jan van Weesep

Globalization and competition between cities

The phenomenon of competition between cities is ancient, but has recently taken a new twist. Historically, cities have been the locus of political power and, as such, a spatial expression of centralized control. The successful cities of previous epochs – Rome, Lisbon, Madrid, London and Paris – were those whose action radius had the widest span, both geographically and economically. These cities were the pivots of competing global empires, rivals in the political, ideological and military arenas. Each of the empires centred on these cities had economic sub-systems that served the needs of the centre. Worldwide, their subsidiary centres of control were arranged hierarchically. The international relations of these lower-order cities were complementary and mostly confined to relationships with the centre of their own sub-system.

In recent times, this limited form of global competition between the centres of empires has been replaced by another form of competition between major cities everywhere, based largely upon the market. Regional and national economies have become increasingly tied to the global economy, where they do not feel the restrictions imposed by belonging to a single state. Giddens refers in this respect to high modernity where 'the influence of distant happenings on proximate events, and on intimacies of self becomes more and more commonplace' (Giddens, 1991, p.4).

Because of the proliferation of international contacts, it is clear that, with respect to their functioning, cities are no longer place-bound. People everywhere are bombarded by images of distant events which impinge on their lives. Jolts to the urban land market in Tokyo affect economic activities in the cities in Europe; at the same time, European cities react to decisions taken in the financial markets of New York and to the vagaries of worldwide commodity exchange. The disembeddedness of social institutions is reflected in multiplying interactions between cities in different countries and continents, and the increasing dislocation of the urban economy from both its hinterland and its national economy. Transactions between people who never meet have become commonplace, often mediated by the Internet. Decision support systems and expert systems are becoming more and more international, fostered by networked cooperation between cities. Traditional goals for urban administrators and politicians are also changing from the management of a spatially delimited territory to promoting the city as a player in the international arena: the entrepreneurial city has burst upon the scene.

From physical planning to strategic action

Technical solutions to urban problems

The first true urban policy initiatives were devoted exclusively to enhancing the quality of urban life in the face of the negative externalities generated by the late nineteenth-century industrial city. They were prompted by efficiency demands and manifestations of market breakdown. These early instances of urban policy focused intently on the improvement of local conditions. Intervention was a response to the two pressing urban problems of the time. First, spontaneous urban development was producing negative externalities in the form of pollution and disease, reflected in declining standards of public health. And secondly, rapid development led to the congestion of the centres of the industrial cities, which lowered their economic efficiency. These problems, in turn, led to huge increases in public expenditure and labour costs. The solutions called for housing improvement and land-use planning, for which national legislation was needed. Consequently, housing acts were adopted in many countries shortly after the turn of the century. That first generation of housing legislation laid the foundation for modern physical planning.

Poor housing conditions were addressed by enforcing strict building standards and, especially in northern and western European cities, by establishing social housing programmes. Such programmes were based on the experience gained from model housing projects undertaken by philanthropic and mutual building societies in the second half of the nineteenth century. This formed the social context for the garden city concept, propagated in Britain by Howard (1898). Originally intended as a tool for social reform, it eventually became the most successfully emulated housing programme of all time. The model was reinterpreted across Europe and beyond. Its success was largely determined by its combination of improved housing conditions and new urban development principles.

The second problem addressed by the newly introduced physical planning was congestion. There was a major effort to improve intra-urban transport systems, which facilitated the separation of nuisance-generating production facilities and residential functions, as well as mass-suburbanization and social segregation on a large scale. Concretely, the programmes entailed the construction of underground mass transit systems and electrified light rail systems, as well as road improvement programmes.

Thus local land use planning was brought about by national legislation. Within that constraining context, planners initially aimed at improving both efficiency and equity in urban areas. The applicability of planning to these goals remained the rationale for local government involvement in the functioning of cities for many decades. The urban policy maker of that era was both engineer and architect; planning was above all a technical vocation. Its mission was to pave the way for private investment and to resolve the problems of market breakdown. However, even at an early stage, dissenting voices could be heard. Patrick Geddes, for example, advocated a social and economic approach to town planning in the early twentieth century; his motto, 'survey before the plan', became commonsense practice in later decades (Hall, 1988).

Urban renewal as a strategy to improve local conditions

Notwithstanding the differences among the European countries, notably in the regulation regimes practised in their urban areas, everywhere urban policy evolved along broadly similar trajectories. Around 1970, urban policy shifted its accent from city forming and peripheral urban expansion to urban renewal. Earlier interventions to renew the built environment had accentuated slum clearance. Urban policy makers had utilized this type of intervention to attain various goals: besides removing unsightly slums and eradicating their appalling housing conditions – in the hope that the social problems would be eliminated along with the dilapidated structures, and that the displaced population would find better housing conditions elsewhere – the large-scale demolition programmes made room for the expansion of the city centre and for the construction of new traffic infrastructure to improve its accessibility. These schemes brought to light an inherent conflict between economic investment, which is part and parcel of the efficiency-based approach, and the welfare of the population. In the 1960s, this conflict was brought forcefully into the political realm, as local resident groups took to the streets and the demands of grass-roots movements eventually came to dominate local politics; the movements increased their stature at the expense of developers and the business community. Consequently, urban policy makers changed their tune in the subsequent decade of urban renewal. Then programmes strongly emphasized equity principles; they were predominantly concerned with the improvement of the housing conditions of low-income residents.

This form of urban renewal was widely embraced in the 1970s, especially in the cities of western and northern Europe. By then their populations had stopped growing and the expansion of the housing stock became a less urgent goal. Urban renewal became the preferred way to redress the serious shortcomings in living conditions in the older parts of the cities, as well as a way to control deviant behaviour. Rather than wholesale demolition of neighbourhoods, practised during the preceding period to facilitate urban restructuring, the strategy of rehabilitation of the older housing stock gained the upper hand. Heeding Geddes' earlier recommendations, large-scale surveys were held to identify the nature of the problems in the older areas before renewal plans to benefit the local population were drawn up. Coalitions of city administrations and local resident groups successfully canvassed national governments for funding. As the urban renewal machine rolled on, large areas of the older cities were transformed; many of their once run-down working-class neighbourhoods now offer decent housing, one of the goals of the earliest housing legislation. Nevertheless, many other social problems – poor-quality education, unemployment, poverty, crime and lack of services and facilities – were not adequately addressed. Neighbourhoods did not turn out to be the safe and decent places they were hoped to be. Because of the changing structure of the urban population, various groups were pitted against each other in fierce competition for a dwelling in the city. This competition exacerbated the social problems in the cities.

The policy shift from urban expansion to urban renewal was initially much less pervasive in the cities of southern Europe, which still needed to accommodate a growing population, but eventually urban renewal consisting of housing improvement and neighbourhood rehabilitation also made headway there, as has been alluded to in the vignettes of Athens, Barcelona, Lisbon and Milan in Part II of this book.

The drawback of the 'social urban renewal model' was that, apart from strengthening the social fabric, it hastened the removal of productive activities. Manufacturing had been mixed with residential use in these older neighbourhoods as the hallmark of the industrial city. Its forced removal led to a vast improvement in local living conditions, but also to a dramatic loss of jobs. Many businesses were not able to bear the high costs of a move to the newly opened peripheral industrial estates, and many workers could not follow their departing jobs. Many of the firms that made the move could not sustain the higher operating costs at the new site or function in the vastly different setting without the old networks of contacts. Small businesses became fully exposed to international competition; many larger ones took advantage of their new-found freedom of location and moved beyond the city limits or even across international boundaries to low-wage countries. Consequently, urban renewal deepened the economic crisis of the cities. It revealed the many drawbacks of the new competitive environment and of the urban strategies that had been pursued.

Focusing on the activities of planners and policy makers in her discourse on the 'death of the inner city', Coleman (1980) argued that their deliberate attempts to remove industrial activities caused irreparable damage. She showed how, in London's East End, local decision makers in league with the local population had systematically reduced all land uses that generate income and employment, while land uses that lived off public financing had been systematically increased. The dispersal of population, commerce and manufacturing reduced the local capacity for sustenance, leading to ever heavier burdens on those remaining and setting a vicious circle of decline into motion. She concluded that the disastrous financial state of the local authority was brought about by the deliberate application of land use policies. In the end, she accepted that the economic death of the area was due to an accident: 'Death came at the hands of local politicians and planners, who were applying established policies which proved to be counter-productive. Death was due to the pursuit of good intentions, combined with the inability to understand their implications' (Coleman, 1980, p.21).

The same sequence of events as Coleman described for East London is encountered in cities across northern and western Europe. Many traditional jobs disappeared forever as the joint effect of economic restructuring and official attempts to clean up the cities. Obviously, equity policies combined with those stressing the efficiency principle can lead to adverse effects if they go unchecked. To resolve this problem, the urban policy maker had to change his role. Rather than remain the technician called upon to allocate land use in the most optimal fashion, he had to become an urban manager, resolving conflicts and distributing numerous resources in an equitable manner. Eventually, the manager had to become an entrepreneur and adopt a proactive strategy. The previous stages of development had determined the structure of the cities, the background against which their competitive strategies must be understood, and the policy goals to be achieved. The structure also defines the latitude for action in the attempts to revitalize the cities.

Urban revitalization schemes

By the 1980s, the negative effects of the exclusion of the private sector from policy making for urban renewal had become fully apparent, and urban policy shifted again. As the vignettes of Part II show, policy initiatives have since paved the way for new economic activities by promoting the development of office complexes and commercial centres in the central cities and in their suburban areas. Subsequently, residential development shifted away from its accent on housing provision for the poor to facilitating the construction of luxury apartment complexes and the gentrification of older, potentially attractive neighbourhoods. Once more, the main thrust of policy was aimed at increasing the efficiency of the urban area. And once more, policy makers were expected to spread its benefits throughout the urban population since, without guidance, economic restructuring can easily lead to social exclusion. At the same time, they had to address the increasingly serious negative externalities and the recurrent budget crisis.

As is alluded to in the case studies of Part II, the urban policy makers and the population at large gradually realized that without a healthy urban economy, the welfare of the people was in jeopardy. Urban revitalization became the new catchphrase among local authorities. Once more, the strategies became remarkably similar among the European countries. One reason was that large-scale funding by national governments was no longer forthcoming. Budget cuts became the order of the day during the deep economic recession that tethered European cities after the second oil crisis. Another reason was that, everywhere, high unemployment rates demanded a rethinking of urban policy. The persistent concentration of unemployment in the older residential areas led to a reconsideration of the urban renewal policies. This development was accentuated by the serious repercussions of the failure to achieve a 'social urban renewal'. With the shift from new residential construction to rehabilitation, the expansion of the housing stock had slowed significantly. While many poor-quality dwellings were improved, their costs also increased. In the climate of diminishing subsidies, this moved them out of reach of the lowest income groups. The 1980s revealed a 'new housing shortage' in the largest cities throughout northern and western Europe (Hallett, 1993) and uncovered serious social problems associated with deep urban poverty.

The second problem that emerged was the neglect of planning at the level of the city, as attention had focused on the eradication of the disadvantages at the neighbourhood level. In most countries, the bulk of urban development plans were abolished during the 1970s. Those incidental plans that were adopted during that period were mainly administrative versions of initiatives that took place in the neighbourhoods. As a result of this bottom-up approach, adaptation of the basic infrastructure in metropolitan areas was neglected. Where upgrading was still pursued, the process became slow and cumbersome. A striking example is the tedious progress made on the so-called 'Dennis package' in Stockholm, described by Wijkmark in Chapter 12 of this book. This seriously undermined the competitive strength of many of the big cities in their quest for income growth.

In the light of the persistent social problems and the decentralization of responsibilities from the national to the local level, the cities themselves needed to devise strategies to create a new economic impetus. Urban development policy thus veered away from its narrow focus on the equity approach. The cities were aided by the general improvement of the economic climate in the 1980s. Italy and Spain caught up rapidly with northern and western Europe, and their cities benefited accordingly. The other European countries also profited from the favourable trend in the global economy. The new economic activities demonstrated a strong preference for urban locations and this induced massive commercial development. Many older manufacturing areas and sites that had been abandoned by goods-handling activities – notably the old port areas – were transformed by flows of new investment. In most of these areas, the redevelopment was mixed in character. Living on the waterfront became fashionable, and new cultural and tourism facilities (museums) were established in the same areas. Many cities demonstrated a sudden, unexpected capacity for economic growth.

The reorientation of urban policy had a major impact on the nature of urban renewal (Rosemann and Kroes, 1991). In the 1980s, all western European countries showed a tendency to abandon the traditional area approach to urban renewal through which dilapidated neighbourhoods were renovated. On the one hand, this led to a more comprehensive urban renewal strategy. Apart from housing problems, attention was increasingly given to bottlenecks for businesses, employment issues, circulation problems and the deteriorating quality of the environment. This meant a broadening of the scope of urban renewal to include the entire city and the whole urban society. The narrow focus on older neighbourhoods in the inner cities gave way to a diversity of initiatives to improve areas throughout the metropolitan area, including the post-1945 residential neighbourhoods and former concentration areas of economic activities. On the other hand, the aim of renewal shifted from the improvement of housing and living conditions of the poor to the revitalization of the city at large. More and more, the mission of urban policy was to buttress the competitive position of the city. Urban renewal was no longer exclusively concerned with the amelioration of disadvantages. It became a tool to boost the potential of each of the discrete areas of the cities and of the urban area as a whole. As entrepreneur, the urban policy maker had to change course. The vignettes of Part II illustrate the profound effect this proactive approach has had on the development of most European cities. It heralded a major shift away from measures to improve equity towards the promotion of urban efficiency. The direction was new and posed a challenge; but fortunately, the urban entrepreneurs could draw upon the lessons of tried policies with a regional scope.

Entrepreneurial urban policy

The Great Depression had provoked the development of regional economic policy in a number of European countries. This type of regional policy was initially based upon equity considerations and relied heavily on subsidies for both capital and labour. At first, there was no explicit urban dimension to this policy. Urban areas in the regions received assistance by virtue of their location in a development area. Lever (1987) noted that regional economic policy even discriminated against cities. However, some economic initiatives were partially directed toward the cities. For example, advance factories were built in or near urban areas, and trading and wholesaling estates often had an urban component, as with the model Team Valley Estate south of Gateshead in the UK.

Gradually, however, regional economic policy acquired a specific urban component. The concept of the growth pole pioneered in France did much to promote this aspect. It demonstrated the need for agglomeration economies and high-quality urban services to sustain decentralized manufacturing industries. It also addressed the diseconomies brought about by congestion in the main urban areas and exacerbated by the overspill of population and economic activities to nearby new towns and more distant growth centres. The urban context was most forcefully expressed in the concept of *poles d'équilibre*, the large regional centres on which the French development policy pinned its hopes. The policy was designed to counteract the overwhelming role of Paris in the French national space economy, as Burgel argues in his vignette on Paris (Chapter 4). In the post-1945 period, decentralization became the most important element of regional policy throughout Europe. Before the era of urban renewal, policy makers preferred to design regional development schemes rather than attempt to resolve the housing problems in the old industrial cities. Growth centres were supposed to help restructure the economy of backward, peripheral regions. The new town of Washington in the UK is an example of such a growth centre, but others can be found throughout northern and western Europe. At the same time, they were supposed to help alleviate the pressure on the older urban neighbourhoods in the major cities and cause gradual, spontaneous improvement there.

The equity approach underlying the policy of decentralization for regional development meant that policy was not explicitly directed towards supporting the most dynamic, forward-looking and productive firms in the economy. Indeed, some firms and sectors used regional development aid as a cushion rather than as a mechanism to restructure. However, those elements of urban policy directed towards solving congestion problems in cities were grounded in an overall efficiency policy goal with respect to the national urban system.

The application of regional economic policy accentuated a number of serious problems in urban areas. As Lever (1987) has pointed out for the British case, the major problem was that some urban labour markets in prosperous regions had higher unemployment rates than some labour markets in development areas. Thus transfers of businesses from cities in the richer regions to poorer regions – also fitting the objective of urban renewal to remove nuisance industries from residential areas – and the allocation of funds for their development became a source of urban problems, as we argued above, citing Coleman.

The same observation applies in countries other than the United Kingdom; Copenhagen and the major Dutch cities are cases in

point. The crippling effect of (social) urban renewal on the livelihood of the urban population gave rise to the push for a specifically urban economic policy. As depicted in the vignettes of Part
II, the policy came in various guises. These variations of urban
policy have been classified by Wolman and Goldsmith (1992) in
the following policy categories:

- promotion or advertising,
- subsidies for inward investment,
- improving local competitive advantage,
- encouraging business creation from within,
- assistance to make existing firms more competitive.

This typology clearly shows that urban policy had become oriented more towards efficiency aims than previously, eclipsing
latent goals relating to equity. It is possible to distinguish between
urban economic policy in richer and poorer cities. Poorer cities
still tend to base their economic policy more on equity than efficiency considerations, partly because they are at a disadvantage
in the competition for inward investment from the private sector.
Richer cities tend to leave economic development largely to the
market, supplemented by measures to deal with market breakdown. Among those measures, the prevailing philosophy is trickle-
down theory, which assumes that eventually the beneficial effects
of economic growth will improve the situation for all, including
the poor. Some of these measures are characteristic of the entrepreneurial city, while others are more conventional equity-based
measures. In the British case, an example of the development of
this type of policy was the 1978 Inner Urban Areas Act. This Act
was designed to assist local authorities experiencing severe urban
problems; accordingly, the basic underlying principles are related
to equity. But the strategy emphasizes economic development by
aiming to improve the efficiency of urban areas. The Urban Development Grant Programme introduced in the 1980s in Britain was
designed to attract private funds into inner-city areas by providing partial public finance as leverage for development projects.
Such projects often involved the conversion or reconstruction of
older buildings. Again, this indicates a basic equity goal, but with
a much wider-ranging ambition. Similar examples can be witnessed throughout urban Europe; the development in peripheral
areas in the city of Milan and its inner suburbs described by
Pompili (in Chapter 11 of this book) is a case in point.

The transition from urban management to an entrepreneurial
form of urban economic policy implies a gradual move away from

equity considerations in urban policy. Instead, there is a conscious effort to invest in and promote selected activities. Such investment may be concentrated upon sectors and firms in the city which will, in the long term, be economically successful. Enterprise is expected to contribute to the restructuring of the urban economy and society, and not least to its image. A preferred vehicle for such policy initiatives is the staging of a major event. Several of the vignettes in Part II of the present volume outline how local governments have embraced this strategy for change. Being chosen as the year-long Cultural Capital of Europe, the host of a World Exposition, the site of an international soccer tournament or other major sporting event, and so on can serve to enhance the image of the city in question. Nowhere has this strategy been used to greater effect than in Barcelona, the Olympic city, yet, while the city has been fundamentally altered into a place for international business activities in the wake of the games, Sánchez has shown in Chapter 7 that the strategy was no panacea for all the urban problems of his city. New contrasts and conflicts emerged during the preparation for the event and following upon the conclusion of the games. As in Barcelona, other places gearing up for large-scale events may find that the massive investments required to make the events possible can create a basis for new, local, long-term comparative advantage and for increases in place productivity. Yet the temporary disruptions and the long-term restructuring effects associated with the huge amount of capital investment required may be such a frightening prospect that the ambition to be the organizer becomes hotly disputed in the local political realm, as in Hanover (see Chapter 17) or evaporates, like Budapest's intention to host a World Exposition (see Chapter 10).

The entrepreneurial approach is more total than partial. It involves the development of infrastructure, services, cultural facilities and housing. At the same time, it presupposes that initiatives will be directed towards the private sector. This is an option open to all cities, both rich and poor. Yet it is clear that the abandonment of an equity-based policy may be more difficult for poor cities than richer ones. Nevertheless, as Lever demonstrates in his description of Glasgow (Chapter 3), this city has an exceptionally successful record of entrepreneurial policies, despite its political tradition steeped in equity goals. Likewise, Engelstoft and Jørgensen (Chapter 8) show how Copenhagen has embarked on a similar course against all political odds, while Gaspar (Chapter 6) indicates that Lisbon is beginning to move in the direction of forceful policy intervention. Using the competitive policy format, the urban policy maker becomes a true entrepreneur rather than a technician or manager, as in earlier policy models. But as in the world of private enterprise, to stay this course, cities must make strategic alliances.

Future urban policy: competition through cooperation

As a result of all the changes that they have undergone in recent decades, cities have become more reflexive. Their social activity and relations with nature are revised and constituted by their knowledge about them. As Giddens (1991) argues, the breakdown of traditional (and more place-bound) society confounds the certainty of knowledge. The world has become more insecure, and so has the place of the city.

Curiously, globalization enhances the role of the local in societal development. At the same time, the national and even the regional declines in importance. It is the interaction between processes occurring at great distance and the characteristics of the local that constitutes the new great arena of development – economic, social, ideological and political. Small differences between localities can become crucial for their role in global processes and for their fortunes. The prophets of the end of geography (O'Brien, 1992) thus seem to be in error. Geography understood as regions or even continents may well be moving towards its end, but a new geography is emerging, that of the global and the local. The processes which form this geography are what Giddens terms the dialectic between the global and the local.

The city is a type of locality of vital importance in this period of high modernity. It is a true locality with its intense internal relations, high density of activity and people, clear external image and a local sense of identity. Furthermore, the city possesses a number of key qualities which make it a dynamic locality: variety, instability, high levels of internal interaction and ease of access to other localities. Cities are the nodes of many types of networks. These are also key features of creative localities (Törnqvist, 1990).

Competition in the market-based sense concerns fundamentally the ability to promote income creation in the city locality, through either endogenous investment or the attraction of inward investment (Lever, 1993). This in turn is related to the ability of the locality to generate income. It is this ability which gives rise to the capacity for control of part of the global system while, earlier, control was a precondition for development of an economic system. The new global economy is based upon the worldwide integration of trade, production and finance, to which must be added

the globalization of high modern values, culture and social practice. Thus, while the globalization of the economy is no new phenomenon, it is becoming more intense with the increasing need for
technological progress. The control of technological development,
and the increasing need of capital for R&D activities in particular,
force firms into cooperation agreements, into strategic alliances,
indeed into merging with the more and more elitist firms that
exist only at the worldwide level.

Cities are not outside this movement. On the contrary, because
of all the services, knowledge, equipment and infrastructure (education, research and specific services) that they concentrate and
enhance by their functions in information creation and communication, they constitute the melting pot of innovation. They frequently promote actively the firms located in the city and engage
in searches for partners for them. They have to create enticing
conditions to attract these partners. When such exchange and cooperation develops, the cities also participate in the processes of
globalization of the economy. And they themselves are in need of
cooperation with similar and with contrasting places, forging strategic alliances to reach their goals. Competition is thus connected
to cooperation. Cities need to learn from each other by exchange
of information. They must also undertake joint activities, if only to
capture the prizes from the many programmes that 'Brussels' uses
to make its influence felt in areas that have been reserved as the
domain of the member states. The various urban networks programmes (see Chapter 2) are a clear case in point, where the EU
has resolved to stimulate the building of networks of cities to
promote its own goals.

Another clear example of the need for cooperation is the difficulty cities face in overcoming the negative externalities associated
with current development. Many environmental problems, such as
acid rain, nuclear accidents, maritime disasters and deforestation,
become evident around the world, affect large areas and can only
be solved satisfactorily on this global scale. But others, more typical
of the most developed countries, intensify specific urban environment problems, as de Roo argues above (Chapter 15), and these add
to urban diseconomies. They include increasing atmospheric pollution, disposal of industrial and domestic waste, and intensive and
polluting forms of peri-urban agriculture, in addition to congestion
of cities, housing degradation, crime and other social anomalies. It
is especially with respect to attempts to overcome such drawbacks
of development that local policy can learn from the experience of
other places and apply this knowledge to the purpose of making its
influence felt in the global realm.

At present, cities are setting their course by two beacons, following two different development trajectories. Traditionally, cities have been embedded in regional or national economic, social and political systems. Their size, location, spacing, internal functions and external relations have been strongly determined by this fact. With the rapid globalization of the economy and of society, the forces determining growth, decline and character are changing dramatically and rapidly. It is the ability to navigate these two cross-currents – the regional/national and the global – which will eventually determine the success of the city on its voyage. If cities do not build upon the experience of other places, do not heed the warning signs these provide, but set out individually on a policy course through uncharted waters, they sail at their peril.

References

Coleman, A. (1980) 'The death of the inner city: Cause and cure', *The London Journal*, 6, pp.3–22.

Giddens, A. (1991) *Modernity and Self-Identity*, Cambridge: Polity Press.

Hall, P. (1988) *Cities of Tomorrow. An Intellectual History of Urban Planning and Design in the Twentieth Century*, Oxford: Blackwell.

Hallett, G. (ed.) (1993) *The New Housing Shortage; Housing Affordability in Europe and the USA*, London: Routledge.

Howard, E. (1898) *To-Morrow: A Peaceful Path to Real Reform*, London: Schwan-Sonnenschein.

Lever, W.F. (1987) 'Urban Policy', in W.F. Lever (ed.), *Industrial Change in the United Kingdom*, Harlow: Longman, pp.240–57.

Lever, W.F. (1993) 'Competition within the European urban system', *Urban Studies*, 30, pp.935–48.

O'Brien, R. (1992) *Global Financial Integration: The End of Geography*, London: Pinter.

Rosemann, J. and H. Kroes (eds) (1991) *Wonen in een Veranderende Context. 10 Jaar Stadsvernieuwing - Stedelijke Vernieuwing in Europa* [Housing in a changing context. 10 years of urban renewal – urban revitalization in Europe], Delft: Research Instituut voor Woningbouw, Volkshuisvesting en Stadsvernieuwing.

Törnqvist, G. (1990) 'Towards a geography of creativity', in A. Shachar and S. Öberg (eds), *The World Economy and the Spatial Organisation of Power*, Aldershot: Avebury, pp.103–27.

Wolman, H. and M. Goldsmith (1992) *Urban Politics and Policy. A Comparative Approach*, Oxford: Blackwell.

Name index

Adorno 36
Albrechts 476
Aldrich 413
Allen 373
Amin 4, 9, 11
Anastassiadis 122
Andersen 29, 216
Anderson 437
Andersson 5, 12, 25, 238, 348, 349, 350
Anguera 191
Anton 335
Area d' Economia i Empreses 180
Arees 200
Arrow 299
Asheim 6
Ashworth 35, 378, 431, 475, 476
Atkinson 373

Badcock 10, 12, 19, 31
Bailly 10, 11, 132, 132–146, 136, 137, 138, 140, 460
Baptista 155, 157
Barcelona 200, 201, 202
Barta 287, 295
Bartels 389
Bastié 113
Beaucire 117
Beckouche 124
Bell 84, 397
Beluszky 290
Benko 9
Berger 16
Bernát 274
Berry 47, 240
Bertrand 56
Bish 21, 22
Blauw 409
Blowers 428
Boddy 371
Boman 347
Bonneville 55, 63, 134
Booth 96, 358

Borgegard 415
Borja 179, 195
Bosch 371, 430
Bosch i Jou 190
Boulianne 136, 137, 138, 140
Boyle 98
Bradbury 33, 51
Bramanti 25
Bredemeier 489
Breheny 438
Brindley 234
Bruhat 45
Bruinsma 52, 392
Brunet 44, 47, 51, 55, 57, 59, 62, 133, 134, 135, 388, 455
Bruun 213
Burgel 103–131, 113, 116, 117, 122, 123, 124, 125, 127, 249, 257, 453, 461
Burtenshaw 244, 245
Busquets 184, 200

Camagni 7, 25, 44, 49, 72, 301, 310, 360, 368
Cambridge Econometrics 53
Cameron 26, 89
Camhis 50
Canals Ramon 187
Cappellin 21, 360
Carcel Ferrer 187
Carmona 113
Carson 342
Casas 191
Castells 17, 385
Cawson 17
CCRLVT 155, 159, 161, 163, 165
CEC 3, 5, 9, 10, 20, 51, 58, 161, 375, 376, 380, 426, 438
Cecchini 379
Centro Studi PIM 312
Champion 89, 249, 397
Chapman 368
Chaslin 115

Subject index